The Mālavikāgnimitram of Kālidāsa

THE

MĀLAVIKĀGNIMITRAM

OF

KĀLIDĀSA

With the Commentary of Kāṭayavema, *various Readings, Introduction, Translation into English and Critical and Explanatory Notes by*

M. R. KALE

Revised by

JAYANAND L. DAVE

S. A. UPADHYAYA

MOTILAL BANARSIDASS PUBLISHERS
PRIVATE LIMITED • DELHI

4th Reprint : Delhi, 2018
Revised Edition : Bombay, 1960

ISBN : 978-81-208-1685-5

MOTILAL BANARSIDASS
41 U.A. Bungalow Road, Jawahar Nagar, Delhi 110 007
1 B, Jyoti Studio Compound, Kennedy Bridge, Nana Chowk, Mumbai 400 007
203 Royapettah High Road, Mylapore, Chennai 600 004
236, 9th Main III Block, Jayanagar, Bengaluru 560 011
8 Camac Street, Kolkata 700 017
Ashok Rajpath, Patna 800 004
Chowk, Varanasi 221 001

Printed in India

by RP Jain at NAB Printing Unit,
A-44, Naraina Industrial Area, Phase I, New Delhi–110028
and published by JP Jain for Motilal Banarsidass Publishers (P) Ltd,
41 U.A. Bungalow Road, Jawahar Nagar, Delhi-110007

PREFACE

It is a matter of great pleasure and a proud privilege for us to revise the edition of Mālavikāgnimitram by late M. R. Kale, so as to suit the needs of present day students. Kale's edition, with its scholastic and comprehensive contents has been very useful to students as well as to scholars and teachers and hence the same, in its revised form, is made available, to-day, by us.

The English translation, in the present edition, is printed opposite to the corresponding Sanskrit text for immediate and ready reference. The topics viz. 'The Sanskrit Drama', 'Kālidāsa and Bhavabhūti', 'Technical Remarks', and the 'Time analysis of the Play' from the Introduction to the last edition are not included in this edition, as, we feel, they are not required to be studied by the F. Y. Arts students, for whom the present edition is mainly intended.

The Prākṛta text, the Sanskrit commentary of Kāṭayavema and the variant readings will, no doubt, help and enlighten the study of the play. At the end, an alphabetical Index of verses, an index of the Subhāṣitas occurring in the play and a detailed note on the metres, are retained in this edition to facilitate the needs of readers.

We hope, that the present edition will be a useful and an enlightening one to the students and scholars alike.

We take this opportunity to thank Shri Harkishandas A. Sheth of M/s A. R. Sheth & Co. for his willing cooperation.

J. L. Dave

S. A. Upadhyaya

PREFACE TO THE SECOND EDITION

The prose order of the verses and the critical appreciation of each act are added in this edition for the benefit of the students.

We take this oppourtunity to express our thanks to our professor-friends and students whose encouragement has made it possible for us to bring out a new edition of the play

J. L. D.

S. A. U.

CONTENTS

INTRODUCTION

THE POET

HIS LIFE, WORKS AND POETRY

His Life

At the outset, it must be admitted that we have absolutely no trustworthy information regarding the personal history of Kālidāsa, by universal consent the greatest of Indian poets.. The curiosity of the querist who would ask—'Where and when was he born?', 'Who were his parents?', 'When did he die?' must ever remain unsatisfied. The poet has studiously observed complete silence about himself in his works. Read them however we may, we find no allusion, no incident mentioned, that may directly shed any light on any remarkable event of his life. His poetical productions alone stand as an immortal monument of his surpassing poetic excellence. And we must content ourselves with gathering what little information we can about a poet of such world-wide repute from external sources and a few incidents found here and there in his works which may be supposed to have a distant bearing upon the history of his life. Reserving for another Section the question of the date of the poet, we proceed here to state the few facts that can thus be known about him. A time-honoured tradition supported by internal and external evidence, associates the name of Kālidāsa with that of the epoch-making king, Vikramāditya of Ujjayinī. The keen interest and admiration with which the poet describes the Mahākāla, the Śiprā, and other beauties of Ujjayinī, unmistakably point to the conclusion that he must have been a native of that city. And the various covert references to the name of Vikrama in fully eulogistic terms which are doubtless meant to immortalize king Vikramâditya are inexplicable, if that monarch be not regarded as the poet's patron. Kālidāsa also betrays considerable acquaintance with court-life in his works. This circumstance, coupled with the fact that there is no allusion in his writings to the Goddess of Wealth having ever frowned upon him, shows that he was in affluent circumstances and had not the misfortune ever to drink the bitter cup of poverty. He was a Brâhmaṇa by caste and was a devout worshipper of Śiva, though by no means a sectarian. He seems to have travelled a good deal, at least in Northern India. For, as Dr. Bhâu Daji remarks, he is the only poet who describes a living saffron flower, the plant of which grows in Kāśmir. His graphic description of the Himālayan scenes looks very much like that of one who was an eye-witness. Unlike Bhavabhūti and many other brother-poets, he appears to have enjoyed great popularity during his life-time. He was an admirer of field-sports and describes their beneficial effects with the exactness of a true sportsman. Though fond of pleasures, he was not the unscrupulous voluptuary he is supposed to be by some critics, as is clear from the many noble sentiments expressed in the Sākuntala (*cf.* अनिर्वर्णनीयं परकलत्रं &c. Śāk. V. and our note *ad loc.*). It also appears from the same play that he was against love-marriages though always actuated with the most generous sentiments towards the fair sex. His works bear further testimony to his considerable acquaintance with the Vedas, the philosophy taught by the Upaniṣads, the Bhagavadgītā, the systems of Sāṃkhya, Yoga, and Vedānta as propounded by Bādarāyaṇa, Medicine, and the rudiments of Astronomy. Beyond these few facts, nothing is known for certain about our poet at present. A few conjectures have been advanced as to some other particulars, but to test their correctness or otherwise falls within the province of the antiquary.

His Works

The poet's silence about himself in his works gave an opportunity to many unscrupulous inferior poets to father their own works upon him. The following is a list of the works generally attributed to him :—(1) शाकुन्तल (2) विक्रमोर्वशीय (3) मालविकाग्निमित्र (4) रघुवंश (5) कुमारसंभव (6) मेघदूत (7) कुन्तेश्वरदौत्य (8) ऋतुसंहार (9) अम्बास्तव (10) कल्याणस्तव (11) कालीस्तोत्र (12) काव्यनाटकालंकाराः (?) (13) गङ्गाष्टक (14) गङ्गाष्टक (another) (15) घटकर्पर (16) चण्डिकादण्डकस्तोत्र (17) चर्चास्तव (18) ज्योतिर्विदाभरण (19) दुर्घटकाव्य (20) नलोदय (21) नवरत्नमाला (22) पुष्पबाणविलास (23) मकरन्दस्तव (24) मङ्गलाष्टक (?) (25) महापद्यषट्क (26) रत्नकोश (27) राक्षसकाव्य (28) लक्ष्मीस्तव (29) लघुस्तव (30) विद्वद्विनोदकाव्य (31) वृन्दावनकाव्य (32) वैद्यमनोरमा (33) शृङ्गारचन्द्रिका

(34) शृङ्गारतिलक (35) शृङ्गाररसाष्टक (36) शृङ्गारसारकाव्य (37) श्यामला-दण्डक (38) श्रुतबोध and (39) सेतुबन्ध. Of these, the first six are acknowledged by all critics to be his. (7) is not yet discovered but is known only in a quotation by the Kāśmirian scholar Kṣemendra in his Aucityavicāracarcā. The authorship of (8) is somewhat doubtful; while the remaining ones are certainly to be dismissed as the productions of other poets. In Sanskrit literary history there have been many poets who bore the name Kālidāsa, and at least three were known to Rājaśekhara who wrote एकोऽपि जीयते हन्त कालिदासो न केनचित्। शृङ्गारे ललितोद्गारे कालिदासत्रयी किमु॥ It is possible, therefore, that other Kālidāsas than the author of the Raghuvamś'a are responsible for the trifling pieces mentioned just now. Here, therefore, we are concerned with the first six alone. The most convenient and reliable method of studying the development of the poet's mind and its relation to his productions would be to read his works in their chronological order. But we have no external evidence whatsoever to ascertain the chronology of Kālidasa's works. It must, therefore, be based wholly on internal evidence. Judged as such, the works would stand in this order: Poems—कुमार०, मेघदूत and रघुवंश: Plays—माल०, विक्रमो० and शाकुन्तल; or both indiscriminately as—कुमार०, मालविका०, विक्रमो०, मेघदूत, शाकुन्तल and रघुवंश. Space will not permit us even to refer to these briefly. We shall only remark in passing that the last three are the outcome of the poet's matured poetic faculties and riper years. Of these, we shall deal fully with the मालविकाग्निमित्रम् in a separate section.

His Poetry

Kālidāsa is indisputably the greatest master-mind in Sanskrit poetry. His genius has been recognized in India from very early times. He has been and will ever be enshrined in the hearts of his contrymen as the prince of Indian poets. That his countrymen place him at the head of all Sanskrit poets, unparalleled and unsurpassed by those who have preceded or followed him, is natural enough; but he has evoked spontaneous outpourings of praise and manifestations of admiration from the foreign scholars and poets who had access to his works either directly or through translations. Goethe has voluntarily bestowed the highest meed of praise on him—so much was he enraptured by the charms of Kālidāsa's Muse and struck with his poetic genius. This is what he says[1] about the S'ākuntala—

" Would'st thou the young year's blossoms and the fruits of its decline,

And all by which the soul is charmed, enraptured, feasted, fed,

Would'st thou the earth and heaven itself in one sole name combine ?

I name thee, O Śakuntalā, and all at once is said ! "

When we remember that Goethe himself was the greatest poet of Germany and one of the greatest of the world, we realize the importance of his estimate of our poet. The well-known philosopher and traveller Humboldt pronounces the following judgment—" Kālidāsa, the celebrated author of the Śākuntala, is a masterly describer of the influence which nature exercises upon the minds of lovers......Tenderness in the expression of feeling and richness of creative fancy have assigned to him his lofty place among the poets of all nations" The celebrated critic Schlegel has also assigned him a very high position amongst the glorious company of the 'Sons of Song.'

Several eminent Orientalists have also offered their tributes of praise to our 'Indian Shakespeare,' as Sir William Jones was the first to call him—the very comparison of Kālidāsa to Shakespeare is the highest form of eulogy that could be bestowed upon him by foreign critics. Sir M. Monier-Williams while writing about the Śākuntala thus expresses himself–'No composition of Kālidāsa displays more the richness of his poetical genius, the exuberance of his imagination, the warmth and play of his fancy, his profound knowledge of the human heart, his delicate appreciation of its most refined and tender emotions, his familiarity with the workings and counter–workings of its conflicting feelings,—in short, mere

1 As translated from the German by Mr. E. B. Eastwick.

S'ākuntala entitles him to rank as the "Shakespeare of India". Prof. Lassen calls him 'the brightest star in the firmament of Indian poetry'. We thus find that Kālidāsa has established his sovereignty in the hearts of all alike. Now it may be asked, 'What is that in Kālidāsa which establishes his undisputed claim to the highest honour which is thus bestowed upon him ?' Unless this question is answered satisfactorily, Kālidāsa's merits as a poet cannot be said to be determined. (We have discussed this question in the last Section of our introduction to the Śākuntala to which the student is referred.)

We shall now briefly consider Kālidāsa s poetry, his style and diction in general. His poetic genius has brought Sanskrit poetry to the highest elegance and refinement. His style is peculiarly pure and chaste. It has 'neither the laxity of the Purāṇas nor the extravagant colouring of later poems'. It is unartificial and characterized by brevity consistent with perspicuity. An unaffected simplicity of expression and an easy-flowing language mark his writings which are embellished with similes unparalled for their beauty and appropriateness, and pithy general sayings. His diction is marked by the absence of long compounds, involved constructions overwrought rhetoric, and artificial puns. Kālidāsa excels other poets in his description of the sublime and the beautiful. It is a principle recognized by all modern critics that 'Nature must be the life and essence of poetry'; and in respect of this Kālidāsa may be said to be essentially a poet of Nature (of course, in the limited sense of the term, which it is possible to attach to it in those times of gay luxury and general prosperity). He describes with most effective touches the gorgeous scenery of the mountain Himālaya—its snow-clad and mineral-covered summits, the peaks where sunshine ever reigns, the fragrant and cool breezes blowing there, the wilds with the hunters, the musk-deer, the potent herbs shedding lustre at night, the *cāmara*-deer, the Mānasa lake &c.; and his description of the Ganges and the peaceful hermitage-life is very striking and lifelike. His descriptive powers are great and some of the scenes in the Śāk., the Megh. and the Ragh. are so enchanting as to hold his readers spell-bound.

KĀLIDĀSA'S DATE

The problem of the date of Kālidāsa is a vexed one and it has yet to be finally settled. The earliest mention of Kālidāsa by name is in the Aihole Inscription dated 634 A. D., and it furnishes the 7th century A. D. as the downward limit of the poet's date. Traditions mention Kālidāsa as a contemporary and a court-poet of King Vikramāditya. One king of that name founded the Era known after him, which is accepted as commencing with 57 B. C. Some antiquarians once did not accept this date as the correct one, but brought Vikramāditya down to A. D. 544, propounding what was known as the Korur theory. The battle of Korur marked a turning-point in Indian history, Vikramāditya having defeated the Mlechchhas in it. Mr. Fergusson held that to commemorate that battle, an era was invented, and that its beginning was placed back 600 years. So he put the true date of Vikramāditya at 544 A. D.; and this theory for a time held sway, since no inscription was discovered bearing a date prior to 600 of the Vikrama era. But the discovery of the Mandasor Inscription which is dated Saṃvat 494, made this theory untenable, and the traditionary date remained unshaken. Then there is the theory of the *Nine Gems.* Nine eminent men called the 'nine gems' adorned the court of Vikramāditya—

धन्वन्तरिक्षपणकामरसिंहशङ्कुवेतालभट्टघटकर्परकालिदासाः ।

ख्यातो वराहमिहिरो नृपतेः सभायां रत्नानि वै वररुचिर्नव विक्रमस्य ॥

Of these, अमरसिंह is said to have lived between 414 A. D. and 642 A. D. Varāhamihira is believed to have died in 587 A. D. On the strength of these dates of Kālidasa's supposed contemporaries, Dr. Kern placed him in the latter half of the sixth Century. But in this there are many *a priori* conclusions and speculations as to probabilities. If the tradition proves anything definitely, it proves the connection of Kālidāsa with king Vikramāditya; but as regards the contemporaneity of the nine authors, the tradition cannot be true. Next, there is the theory of Renaissance propounded by Prof. Max Müller. He divided the whole Sanskrit literary period into two parts The first began with the Vedas and ended with the First Century A. D. Then came an *interregnum*, a period during which foreigners invaded India and so literary activity was dormant. The Professor placed the Renaissance of Sanskrit learning in the sixth Century A. D. with the reign of Vikramāditya. But, as has been shown by Drs. Peterson and Buhler, the period called *interregnum* was really not destitute of literary productivity, and therefore if Kālidāsa is to be considered as the first poet of the new school, he must be placed considerably earlier than Prof. Max Muller did.

There are some minor things which have been pushed into the controversy. These are (1) the alleged covert references to Dinnāga and Nicula in the Meghadūta, the former a foe and the latter a friend of Kālidāsa, (2) the identity of Mātṛgupta, a king of Kas mir and Kālidāsa ; (for, names in Sanskrit are often titles and Mātṛgupta *lit.* 'protected by the mother' may also be taken as Kāligupta or Kālidāsa); (3) and the supposed astronomical reference in the works of Kālidāsa to the astronomical theories of Āryabhata who lived in 476 A. D. Prof. R. N. Apte has examined all these at some length and on the first point he comes to the conclusion that Dinnāga and Nicula were not contemporaries of the great Kālidāsa, but must have been contemporaries of some other Kālidāsa, On the second point, he observes that Mātṛgupta and Kālidāsa were two different persons, since they are differently quoted by Kṣemedra and other writers and commentators. The supposed astronomical references have really no astronomical significance at all and it cannot be said that Kālidāsa was acquainted with the astronomical works oi Āryabhaṭa. Mr. K. B. Pathak, the latest exponent of the 6th century theory, repeats the arguments given above, but principally grounds his conclusion on his theory about the Hūṇa kings, allusion to whom is made by the poet in the Raghuvaṃśa. He argues that since there is no mention made of the Hūṇas in the Rāmāyaṇa, the conclusion follows that Kālidāsa unconsciously refers to the Hūṇa kings of his own time who held sway over the Punjāb and Kāśmir, in the second quarter of the sixth century. But this rests merely on assumption ; for, there are references to the Hūṇas even in the Mah.-Bhā. Prof. Apte has also shown that just beyond Bactria or the threshold of ancient India, the Hūṇas had constituted a powerful empire from the middle of the 3rd century B. C. to the end of the 1st or the 2nd century A. D.

Vatsabhūti, the author of the Mandasor Inscription, copies several ideas from Kālidāsa; the latter must, therefore, have lived prior to 472 A. D. Again, Aśvaghoṣa, the author of a life of the great Buddha in Sanskrit, has numerous passages similar to those occuring in the works of Kālidāsa. Now Kālidāsa was an orginal poet borrowing his subjects from Vālmīki and other ancient authors. Aśvaghoṣa was more of a philosopher than a poet and may with greater probability be supposed to have borrowed his ideas from Kālidāsa. The date of Aśvaghoṣa is given as 78 A. D., and; if we suppose him to have borrowed from Kalidāsa, the latter will have to be placed earlier than 78 A. D. And in this view, Dr. Peterson also concurs when he says, 'Kālidāsa stands near the beginning of the Christian era, if, indeed, he does not overtop it.'

There is also internal evidence pointing to the same conclusion. We have first the evidence obtained from the state of the law of inheritance and the penalty for theft as they are indicated in passages in the Śākuntala. The passage in the sixth Act of the drama, announcing the death of the merchant Dhanamitra who is dying heirless, seems to Prof. Apte to refer to a period when the widow of a deceased person could not inherit his estate. Such a period is to be found only before the Christian era, when Manu, Āpastamba and Vasiṣṭha held sway, and Bṛhaspati, Śaṅkha, Likhita and Yājnavalkya had not yet written their Codes. The penalty for theft as indicated in the prologue to the sixth Act seems to have been the extreme one, it being the theft of a jewel. There is also a passage of similar import in the Vikramorvaśīya (आत्मनो वधमाहर्त &c. V. 1). The penalty for theft has been from time to time mitigated with the progress of civilization. Manu and Āpastamba lay down the extreme penalty, the option of fine being introduced later on, as we find it in the Smṛti of Bṛhaspati. These two circumstances tend to show that Kālidāsa flourished at a period which is anterior to

Bṛhaspati, the latter being generally placed in the first century A. D.

Prof. Apte further calls attention to the fact that there is no reference to the Nyāya philosophy in the works of Kālidāsa [except perhaps Ragh. XIII. 1. in which the word शब्दगुण (आकाश) occurs, but which the poet might have borrowed from the Sāṃkhyas] and concludes that he must have lived before the development of that philosophy. Then, again, we have the evidence of style. The artificiality of diction and the fondness for long compounds and double-meaning words which mark the writings of Daṇḍin (who in his Kāvyādars'a says that an abundance of compounds forms the very strength of poetry), Bāṇa, Bhavabhūti (7th century A. D.) and other mediæval writers, are entirely absent in Kālidāsa's writings, a fact which shows that he must be placed some six or seven centuries before them—a period necessary to cause such a revolution in the art of literary composition, considering the scanty means of the propagation of learning in those times. It thus becomes clear that Kālidāsa lived in the Ist century B. C. at the latest.

Some modern scholars, however, yet hold that Kālidāsa must have flourished under one or more of the Gupta Kings. The Gupta period (about 300-650 A. D.) was noted in ancient Indian history for a revival of Sanskrit learning and arts. Mr. Vincent A. Smith in his *Early History of India* (3rd ed., 1914) believes that Kālidāsa must have flourished in the reigns of one or more of these Gupta-Kings—

Candragupta II (c. 357-413)

Kumāragupta I (413-455)

Skandagupta (455-480)

Both Candragupta II and Skandagupta had adopted the title of *Vikramāditya*. Mr. Smith says :—"It is not unlikely that the earliest works of Kālidāsa......may have been composed before A D. 413, that is to say, while Candragupta II was on the throne ; but I am inclined to regard the reign of Kumāragupta I (413-455) as the time during which the poet's later works were composed, and it seems possible, or even probable, that the whole of his literary career fell within the limits of that reign. It is also possible that he may have continued writing after the accession of Skandagupta". Mr. Smith thus makes Kālidāsa's literary career extend over a period of less than thirty years. There is thus nothing wrong in the tradition about a *Vikramāditya* having been our poet's patron ; only, we must arrive at an understanding as to which Vikramāditya is meant, because various kings in the history of ancient India called themselves by that title.

THE PLAY

(1) THE PLOT

The *Mālāvikāgnimitra* is a drama in five Acts based on a love-intrigue set on foot by King Agnimitra of Vidiśā who is the Hero of the play, Mālavikā, a princess in the service of Dhāriṇī, the chief Queen, being the Heroine. The scene is laid in Vidiśā and in its vicinity. The following detailed analysis of the story will be found useful for ready reference and for the better understanding of the various topics to be discussed in the subsequent Sections :—

Act I. After an invocation of the Deity (Śiva) as an auspicious act, the stage-manager enters, followed by his Assistant. In their conversation they state that the play shortly to be performed is Kālidāsa's *Mālavikāgnimitra.* This is the Prelude (*prastāvanā*). In the course of the next scene, two maid-servants of Agnimitra's palace, whose names are Bakulāvalikā and Kaumudikā, are introduced. Bakulāvalikā is sent by Queen Dhāriṇī to inquire about the progress of her maid, Mālavikā, in the art of dancing in which she was being instructed by the dancing-master Ganadāsa ; while Kaumudikā is carrying a certain ring with the figure of a snake on its seal, sent to the Queen by her jeweller (this ring will play an important part in the subsequent incidents). The two relate how Mālavikā was accidentally seen by the King in a group-portrait of the Queen and her attendants, how the King was struck by her charms, and how, therefore, the girl was being sedulously kept away from the King's sight, so as to prevent any access to her, by the Queen whose jealousy has been roused. Then Gaṇadāsa is introduced, who praises the intelligence and skill of Mālavikā, and questions Bakulāvalikā about her, when she tells him that she came from the Queen's brother Vīrasena, who sent her to his sister to serve as an attendant maid. In the next Scene, the King enters with his minister. Agnimitra had imprisoned the brother-in-law of Yajñasena, the King of Vidarbha; Mādhavasena, Agnimitra's cousin, who with his sister was coming to Agnimitra's kingdom with a view to negotiating a marriage between the two, was attacked and taken prisoner by a vassal of Yajñasena. The sister was lost in the confusion of the skirmish. Agnimitra demanded the release of Mādhavasena, but the Vidarbha king offered to *exchange* the prisoners. The offer did not suit Agnimitra's dignity, and an expedition against him was forthwith ordered, under the command of Vīrasena, the Queen's brother. When this business is finished, the King's friend, companion and the court-wit, Vidūṣaka Gautama, enters. The King had told him about Mālavikā, and asked him to discover some means of seeing her again. The Vidūṣaka, therefore, by means of some sarcastic remarks and comments, brings about a quarrel between the two dancing-masters, Gaṇadāsa and Haradatta, about their respective superiority and efficiency as teachers. The quarrel comes to the King for decision, who, in consultation with the Queen and her own saintly female attendant (*Parivrājikā*), arranges that the two Professors should hold an exhibition of their teaching art, where the pupil of each would perform, and thus a decision could properly be given. The Queen is suspicious and disapproves of the whole affair, but in the end reluctantly consents.

Act II. The exhibition of Gaṇadāsa's pupil, Mālavikā, is first held, and the King has thus an opportunity of feasting his eyes with the sight of Mālavikā as she sings and dances. His passion is now developed, when he exclaims, 'आत्तसारश्चक्षुषा मे स्वविषयः।' (p. 54). The sole purpose of arranging the exhibition having been achieved, further examination of the instructors' claims is postponed for the time being, and the King leaves the stage with the declaration 'सा वामलोचना म स्नेहस्यैकायनीभूता ।' (p. 62).

Act III. In an Interlude (*Praveśaka*), during the course of conversation between two maid-servants, it is stated that Gaṇadāsa won in the contest; the king is quite love-sick and Mālavikā is now the more carefully guarded from him. In the next Scene, the King enters with the Vidūṣaka. The Vidūṣaka has found an ally in Bakulāvalikā. She has promised to help in furthering the King's suit. In the meantime, the King and the Vidūṣaka go to the pleasure-garden, where Irāvatī, the second Queen of Agnimitra, had invited the King to come, so that they might together enjoy the sport of swing-riding (दोलाधिरोहण). As it happens, Mālavikā is deputed by Queen Dhāriṇī to touch the Aśoka tree with her foot, a recipe which was supposed to make it blossom early. (The Vidūṣaka had contrived to injure the Queen's leg, and she was therefore unable to do this herself). Mālavikā was promised a substantial reward अभिलाषपूरयितृकं प्रसादं (p. 76) if the Aśoka blossomed within five days. Mālavikā comes to the garden at the very time the King and the Vidūṣaka go there. She soliloquizes about her own deep passion for the King. Then enters Bakulāvalikā, who decorates Mālavikā's foot with dyes, anklets, etc. Then comes the king's second wife, Irāvatī, in a state of mild intoxication. She and the King, unseen by each other, stand as unobserved witnesses to the conversation between Mālavikā and Bakulāvalikā wherein the latter, in accordance with her promise to the Vidūṣaka, speaks to her about the King's passion. The King then shows himself, but the love-scene is promptly marred by Irāvatī who breaks in upon them, sends off Mālavikā, and herself departs in high anger after an altercation.

Act IV. The King had sent the Vidūṣaka to obtain news of Mālavikā. He returns and relates how Irāvatī called upon Dhāriṇī and informed her of what had happened. Thereupon Dhāriṇī at her suggestion had Mālavikā and Bakulāvalikā put into a cellar as prisoners, and orders were issued to their guard that they were not to be releassed, unless the Queen's own snake-seal ring was produced by the messenger as guarantee of good faith. The Vidūṣaka devises an ingenious scheme to procure their release, and he proceeds to put it into execution. The scene is now shifted to where Dhāriṇī is nursing her injured leg and is attended upon by the Parivrājikā. The Vidūṣaka enters, wailing and fainting, pretending that he is bitten by a serpent as he was plucking flowers for the Queen. He is removed for being treated by the famous Physician Dhruvasiddhi, and a message, purporting to come trom the latter, is brought in, asking for that very snake-seal ring of the Queen, which, it is alleged, is necessary for certain operations connected with the healing treatment. The unsuspecting Queen hands it over to the attendant who takes it to the Vidūṣaka being in his secret. The party then breaks up as the King is called away on urgent business by the minister—another false message. The next Scene discovers the jubilant Vidūṣaka relating the success of his *ruse* to the King. By showing the signet-ring to the guard, Mālavikā and Bakulāvalikā were set at liberty. The King now goes to the place where they are staying, and the Vidūṣaka mounts guard outside. But the bungling schemer falls asleep, in which condition he is seen by a passing servant, and the news is immediately taken to Irāvatī. She thereupon goes to the place, in the hope of finding the King there, from the fact of the Vidūṣaka's presence; but instead she finds Mālavikā, Bakulāvalikā and the King—and the whole story of the Vidūṣaka's trick is presently made clear to her. While the King is in a fix as to what to do and say next, a welcome diversion is created by the door-keeper bringing in news of an accident to Princess Vasulakṣmī, which makes every one hurry off. Mālavikā and Bakulāvalikā also depart, their only hope being in the kindness of the Queen, who had promised a reward to Mālavikā, if the *Aśoka* blossomed within five days—which it did, as they just learn.

Act V. In an Interlude (*praveśaka*) the success of Vīrasena's expedition against the Vidarbha king is announced. In the next Scene, in the presence of the King, the Queen, Mālavikā, and others, two captive maid-servants brought from the Vidarbha expedition are introduced, who at once recognize Mālavikā. She, it turns out, was none other than the missing sister of Mādhavasena. The minister of Mādhavasena, one Sumati by name, in the confusion of Mādhavasena's capture, took flight with Mālavikā and his own sister. But Sumati was attacked by highwaymen while on his way to Agnimitra's capital, and Mālavikā and Sumati's sister were separated. Mālavikā in the meanwhile was secured from some foresters by Vīrasena who sent her as a present to Dhārinī, where she was seen and recognized by Sumati's sister, who had turned a Parivrājikā and had also happened to attach herself to Dhārinī's court. But she could not give out the identity of Mālavikā, as she knew of a prophecy that Mālavikā would remain for a year as a servant and then be married to a suitable husband.It is now proposed to bestow one-half of the kingdom of Yajnasena (the King of the Vidarbhas) on Mādhavsena. News is also brought of the victory of Agnimitra's son Vasumitra who was employed by Agnimitra's father Puṣpamita to guard his sacrificial horse. The Queen, amid general rejoicings, and mindful also of her promise to reward Mālavikā, gives her to the King, and gladly consents to their union. After this happy termination of the course of the royal love, the play ends with the customary *Bharatavākya* [see our note on V. 20] which here takes the form of an expression of general peace and happiness among the King's subjects.

The principal points, it will be noted, in the development of the plot of the play are—(1) the quarrel between the two teachers; (2) the exhibition; (3) the visit of Mālavikā to the Aśoka tree; (4) Bakulāvalikā's revelation to Mālavikā of the King's love; (5) Irāvatī's interference and the consequent imprisonment of Mālavikā; (6) the feigned snake-bite; (7) Mālavikā's release by the trick; (8) the love-scene in the fourth Act; (9) the victory of Vīrasena; (10) the discovery of Mālavikā's identity; and (11) the final union of the lovers with the consent of the two Queens.

(2) THE AUTHORSHIP OF THE PLAY

In the early years of the history of Sanskrit literary research, some Western scholars, led by Prof. Wilson in his well-known *Select Specimens of the Theatre of the Hindus* (1826–1827), did not accept Kālidāsa's authorship of the *Mālavikāgnimitra*. The late Prof. Weber also in his *History of Indian Literature* (1882) first inclined to the same view, but saw reason later to change his opinion, and in the Introduction to his German translation of the *Mālāvikāgnimitra*, published in 1856, he refuted Wilson's theory. He was followed by the late Mr. Śankar Paṇdurang Paṇdit, the learned editor of the play in the Bombay Sanskrit Series [1], who fully re-examined the question with some additional proofs, and conclusively established that the author of the *Mālavikāgnimitra* was identical with the poet Kālidāsa, who wrote the Śākuntala, the Meghadūta and other works, and that he was not *some other* Kālidāsa as assumed by Wilson. The controversy practically ended with Mr. Pandit's reply and has now become obsolete, being merely of interest to the student of Sanskrit antiquarian research. Briefly, it may be re-stated as follows. Although the name of Kālidāsa is distinctly mentioned in the Prastāvanā (see p 4), it was held that he was not *the* Kālidāsa, the famous author of the Śākuntala, but a Kālidāsa, some later and inferior writer of that name. Three main reasons were adduced in favour of this view, (1) that there is not the "same melody" in the verse of the *Mālavikāgnimitra*. as is found in the *S'ākuntala* and the *Vikramorvaśīya*, (2) that there is not the "same fancy" in the thoughts, and (3) that the manners depicted in the play seem to belong to a "degenerate" state of Hindu society.

Now, as regards (1), the appreciation of melody depends upon the musical ear of the reciter, and perhaps it may be a matter of taste. But Hindu readers (and who are better judges in this respect) have failed to discover this alleged want of melody in the *Mālavikāgnimitra*, whose verses are as smooth-flowing and melodious as any of Kālidāsa. "The verse in the Māla.," remarks Mr. Paṇdit, "is as regular and model-like as that in the two sister-dramas of the poet. The metres too are nearly the same in all the three dramas; so that if

1. First ed. 1869, 2nd ed. 1889. The arguments are set forth in the Pre ace, which is the same in both the editions.

they are melodious in the Śāk. and the Vik., they are not less so in the Mālavikāgnimitra." As regards (2), while it is true that the subject chosen for the drama—the life in the court of a historic prince, with its bare actuality and comparatively scanty concerns—afforded less ground for the play of fancy, it cannot be maintained that there is no fancy in the occasional descriptions met with in the play (*cf.* सलिलनिधिरिव प्रतिक्षणं मे । I. 11, and others); the fancy is not as high-soaring as in the other two plays, but this can be easily explained by the fact that the *Mālavikāgnimitra* is apparently an early and therefore immature production of the poet, when his genius had yet to find its highest level, as is indeed evident from the tone of the Prastāvanā itself. While the (3) third objection about the "depravity" of the manners depicted is, as Mr. Paṇḍt puts it, "little deserved" by the *Malavikāgnimitra.* The manners, in fact, do not differ from those portrayed in the two other plays. Agnimitra is as pure and chivalrous in his principles as Duṣyanta or Purūravas. Polygamy is even to this day the privilege of a Hindu, especially of a Prince. And there is nothing illicit in Agnimitra's passion for Mālavikā, who was a maid-of-honour in attendance on the Queen, and whom he honestly desired to formally install as one of his wedded Queens. Again, there is nothing in the character of Mālavikā herself or of Queen Dhāriṇī, that can truly be called degenerate.

Independently of these objections, it may be stated that Indian literary tradition has never questioned Kālidāsa's title to the *Mālvikāgnimitra*, but has universally accepted him as the author of the three plays now so well known. So far as external evidence goes, there is nothing to show that the play belongs to another Kālidāsa and internal evidence also abundantly proves that all the three plays are written by the same hand. Every great writer has a settled, distinct style of composition, and the same simplicity and the peculiar Kālidāsian grace of style is observable in all the three plays. Moreover, the same words, phrases, expressions, images and ideas occur so repeatedly and frequently in each, that they unmistakably point to the conclusion of one authorship. Mr. Pandit has collected some of these analogies, and many have been pointed out in the Notes to this Edition as they occur. The Student can easily bring together many more. Some of the commoner ones are, the use of words like उपचार, पुरोभागिन्, परिच्छेद, अत्याहित, पर्युत्सुक, दुर्जात, विभावय, लब्धक्षण, अनात्मज्ञ, स्वरयोग; of phrases like स्वनियोगं अशून्यं कुरु, अस्ति विशेषः, प्रथमः कल्पः, एतावान्मे विभवः; of the word विशेष *in fine composition*. as in the expressions आकृतिविशेष, शिलाविशेष ; of the double negative in sentences like न वो न विदितम्, संपत्स्यते न गोप्तरि नाग्निमित्रे. Some of the commoner conceits are, the trustworthiness-*cum*-cheating of Cupid,; the withdrawing of characters off the stage under the feint of driving away young deer ; the pigeons sitting on the roofs of houses ; the comparison of foliage to fingers ; the comparison with the thief caught in the act. Other features, such as the predominance of the *Āryā* metre over others, a modest Introduction, and the shortness and simplicity of the Nāndi, will also strike the student. It should be added, in the end, that no European or Indian *savant* now holds the view once propounded by Prof. Wilson, and the controversy is not likely to be revived again, Kālidāsa's authorship of the three plays being generally accepted without dispute.

(3) THE SOURCES OF THE PLAY AND ITS HISTORICAL BACKGROUND

While Kālidāsa in his Vikramorvaśīya and Śākuntala based his stories on mythological and epic sources, in the Mālavikāgnimitra he has followed a different course. The actual story of the play is of the poet's own invention and is not borrowed from any Paurāṇic or legendary work.[1]. At the same time, however, he has given it a substantially correct historical setting The Hero Agnimitra and his father Puṣpamitra (mentioned in the fifth Act) are real historical personages and some incidents (*e. g.* the sacrifice performed by Puṣpamitra) are parts of authentic history, which can be corroborated by independent evidence. It seems that while he invented the plot round which the interest of the piece is centred, Kālidāsa preferred to relate it with Agnimitra and

---

1. The, resemblance with the Kathāsaritsāgara is striking, but we do not think it is the source ; we have discussed this point in the next Section.

his conquests, the memory of which must have been current and fresh in his day among his audience. It is an interesting point of coincidence that his illustrious successor, Bhavabhūti, also worte two of his plays—the Uttararāmacarita and the Mahāvīracarita—on mythological themes, but invented a subject of his own for his Mālatī-Mādhava, which, however, is more original than the Mālavikā., inasmuch as it does not borrow its characters from history.

Before we proceed to consider the details of historical information that are to be gathered from the play, it is necessary to summarize briefly the actual history of that period as ascertained from inscriptional and other reliable records.[1] In 185 B. C. one Puṣyamitra,[2] who was the general of the Maurya kings, slew his master Bṛhadratha, usurped his throne, and founded what is known as the S'uṅga dynasty which lasted till *circa* 73 B. C. The kingdom of Puṣyamitra corresponded roughly to the modern provinces of Bihar, Tirhut and the United Provinces of Agra and Oudh. During the latter years of his reign, he came into collision with the Greeks under Menander,[3] whose invasion was finally repelled after a severe struggle. During the progress of this war the outlying southern districts extending to the Narmadā river were governed by his son Agnimitra, who had his capital at Vidiśā[4] (the modern Bhilsā in Scindia's territory). Agnimitra engaged in a struggle with the king of the Vidarbhas (the modern Berars) whom he succeeded in defeating. Puṣyamitra now determined upon performing the

1. What follows is a *resume* of the account given by Mr. Vincent A. Smith in his excellent *Early History of India* (3rd ed. 1914), chapter VIII.

2. Kālidāsa's spelling is *Puṣpamitra*, but °*ya*° is the correct form accoding to Mr. Fleet and Dr. Bühler. As found in old MSS. the two letters य and प may easily be confounded.

3. A relative of the Bectrian King Eukradites, and then the King of Kabul and Punjab, who, desirous of emulating the exploits of Alexander, advanced with a formidable force into the interior of India (B. C, 155-153).

4. Pandit questions the correctness of the statement that Vidiśā was Agnimitra's capital, but it is accepted by Mr. Smith. Vidiśā is mentioned as the capital in Act IV. (P. 120 line 2 of this Ed.), but Mr. Pandit ignores the reading विदिशेश्वर : there, although itis supported by the occurrence of विदिशा again further on.

famous horse-sacrifice (As'vamedha)[1] which according to sacred tradition could only be performed by a paramount sovereign. The duty of guarding the horse was entrusted to Agnimitra's son, Vasumitra, who discharged it successfully and well, having defeated certain *Yavana* troops who ventured to challenge him. Mr. Smith adds—"The performance of the solemn rite [राजयज्ञ] probably was witnessed by the celebrated grammarian Patañjali, who alludes to the event in terms which imply that it occurred in his time". According to the semi-mythological stories of Buddhistic writers, Puṣyamitra was a determined oppressor of the Buddhists and is said to have savagely persecuted them, and there is some evidence to support these allegations. Puṣyamitra died about 149 B. C. and was formally succeded by his son Agnimitra, who was already ruling as the Viceroy of the Southern provinces. He died after a few years and was succeeded by Vasujyeṣṭha, probably his brother, who was followed by Vasumitra, presumably that son who valiantly guarded the horse of his grandfather when a young prince. Little is known of the remaining six kings of the dynasty, which lasted for a hundred and twelve years in all.

Coming to the play itself, in addition to the names of Puṣya-(pa)-mitra, Agnimitra, and Vasumitra, which are indisputably historical, Kālidāsa also mentions Vāhataka, the minister of Agnimitra; Vīrasena, Agnimitra's brother-in-law; Yajñasena, the Vidarbha King; Mādhavasena, the cousin of Yajñasena; and Sumati, the minister of Mādhavasena. These are also probably historical, though not mentioned in available records. A *Maurya-Sachiva* is mentioned at I. 7, who was probably a minister of King Bṛhadratha Maurya, slain by Puṣyamitra. Vasulakṣmī and Dhāriṇī are also probably historical; and the name Mālavikā seems to suggest that she was a princess of the Mālava country. The rest of the characters appear to be invented by the poet. The drama was probably written, as Mr. Paṇḍit conjectures, while the story of Agnimitra's conquests was yet fresh in men's minds and not invested with the hazy mist of

1. See our Notes Act V for a detailed description of this sacrifice and its significance.

legendary obscurity.[1] At the same time it was not quite so fresh as to make it too recent to be made the subject of a drama. Kālidāsa must have had before him some tradition[2] of Agnimitra's romantic marriage with a Malava princess, round which he has built a slender edifice of palace-intrigues, finally succeeding into a happy conclusion. The only fact in the drama which appears to be historically untrue and therefore somewhat puzzling, is that Puṣpamitra is referred to in the play as the General (सेनापति),—of Agnimitra as it may appear, though he was the king. But Mr. Paṇḍit has correctly pointed out that Puṣpamitra, who was the सेनापति of the Mauryas, must be understood to have retained his title even after he founded a kingdom of his own. The *Yavana* band which met Vasumitra on the bank of the *Sindhu* river was, no doubt, part of the army of Menander. Beyond this, the play has no reference to the Greek invasion, but there is a more detailed account of the Vidarbha expedition which starts in Act I and whose success is announced in Act V. According to Mr. Smith the capital of the Śunga dynasty "presumably" continued to be Pāṭaliputra, as it was the capital of the Mauryas. But Agnimitra's Capital is here stated to be Vidiśā and whether it was originally or afterwards Pāṭaliputra is not known.

From the play we also get some information about the extent of Agnimitra's dominion. The Narmadā river is mentioned as the Southern limit, as Vīrasena, the brother-in-law of Agnimitra, is stated to have been in charge of a border fortress on this river. In the war with Yajñasena the latter was compelled to cede half his territory to Mādhavasena (who became the King's brother-in-law), and the Varadā (modern *Wardhā*) river was fixed as the boundary of the kingdoms of

1. This fits in with the date 56 B. C. often assigned to Kālidāsa, and the efforts of H. H. Wilson to drag down the composition of the play to the tenth or eleventh (!) century must now be placed in the category of long-exploded theories of early Orientalists.

2. This tradition was most probably oral. Mr. Paṇḍit believes that there must have been extant in the days of Kālidāsa some regular composition (like Bāṇa's *Harṣacarita* or Bilhaṇa's *Vikramāṅkadevacarita*) in which the victory of Agnimitra was celebrated. This is merely a supposition and has nothing to support it.

the two princes. The Northern limit was probably the river *Sindhu* near the bank of which Vasumitra beat of the Yavana bands. This Sindhu, as Mr. Smith points out, is not to be confounded with the Indus, but it is the river which now forms the boundary between Bundelkhand and the Rajputānā States.

While other accounts have related Puṣyamitra's persecution of the Buddhists, there is no direct mention of that fact in the drama. The introduction of the *Parivrājikā* (a female wandering-mendicant of the Buddhistic faith) goes to show that the play was composed at a time when Buddhism was looked upon with reverence and not with disfavour, since the Parivrājikā could so easily attach herself to the Queen's court in a position of dignity and trust. The spirit of the play is thus apparently inconsistent with the alleged persecution. Mr. C. H. Tawney conjectures that whatever might have been the attitude or deeds of Puṣyamitra, Agnimitra must have been a friend of the Buddhists, and he ingeniously suggests that Agnimitra might have quarrelled[1] with his father upon this very ground. The truth seems to us to be that in any case the strong prejudice against Buddhists must have died down in the days, when Kālidāsa wrote, who, even if he was aware of Puṣyamitra's suppression of the Buddhists, must not have thought it advisable to revive the memories of unpleasant persecutions.

The only other important piece of information afforded by the play about ancient Indian history is the mention in the Prologue[2] of three older playwrights भास, सौमिल्लक and कविपुत्र. Of Bhāsa, thirteen plays have been recently discovered and published from MSS., but of the other two writers nothing is hitherto known beyond their names. Students of literary parallels will be interested to note that Śri Harṣa, a famous writer who came after Kālidāsa, very closely follows the Mālavikāgnimitra in his play the *Priyadarśikā*, which is a great tribute to the genius ot the premier Sanskrit dramatist

1 *Cf.* the expression विगतरोषचेतसा Act V. which Mr. Paṇḍit has tried to explain in a different and not very satisfactory way.

2 See our Notes on p. 2.

of ancient India. Śrī Harṣa must have honoured Kālidāsa as much as the latter honoured Bhāsa, Saumillaka and Kaviputra, who no doubt first served as literary models to the young artist, whose mature talent was to give the *S'ākuntala* to the world.

(4) THE RESEMBLANCE TO THE STORY IN THE BṚHATKATHĀ

We have said in the preceding Section that the story of the play is of the poet's invention. That is not disputed as regards the main incidents—the quarrel between the Nāṭyācāryas, the exhibition that follows, the Aśoka tree's *dohada* and its fulfilment, and the pretended snake-bite. But it has been pointed out that the story of Mālavikā *in its main outline* bears some resemblance to that of Bandhumatī *alias* Manjulikā in the ancient collection of fables called the *Bṛhatkathā.* This Bṛhatkathā was originally written in the Paiśacī language by one Guṇāḍhya, and is stated to have been equal in extent to our present Mahābhārata. It is now no longer extant and has probably perished along with so many other ancient works. But faithful summaries of it are available in the Bṛhatkathāmanjarī of Kṣemendra and in the Kathāsaritsāgara of Somadeva Bhaṭṭa. From the latter work we extract the passage[1] that relates to Bandhumatī—

किं च बन्धुमतीं नाम राजपुत्रीं भुजार्जिताम् ।
गोपालकेन प्रहितां कन्यां देव्या उदयनम् ॥
तया मञ्जुलिकेत्येव नाम्नान्येनैव गोपिताम् ।
अपरामिव लावण्यजलधेरुद्गतां श्रियम् ॥
वसन्तकसहायः सन्दृष्ट्वोद्यानलतागृहे ।
गान्धर्वविधिना गुप्तमुपयेमे स भूपतिः ॥
तच्च वासवदत्तास्य ददर्श निभृतास्थता ।
प्रचुकोप च बद्ध्वा च सा निनाय वसन्तकम् ॥
ततः प्रव्राजिकां तस्याः सखीं पितृकुलागताम् ।
स सांकृत्यायनीं नाम शरणं शिश्रिये नृपः ॥
सा तां प्रसाद्य महिषीं तया सैव कृताज्ञया ।
ददौ बन्धुमतीं राज्ञ पेशलं हि सतीमनः ॥

(Kathāsaritsāgar, II. 6. 67–72)

---

1 The King in the passage is Udayana, the sovereign of the Vatsas; the Queen is his consort Vāsavadattā; Gopālaka is her brother; and Vasantaka is the King's merry companion, like the Vidūṣaka in plays.

The *Bṛhatkathā* served as a store-house of plots to many later writers, including Bāṇa, Śrī Harsa, Bhavabhūti, and Viśākhadatta as Holinshed's Chronicles did to Shakespeare and other dramatists. It is not originality of the plot that determines genius, but rather the original way of presenting the same. We think, however, Kālidāsa could not have connected an *imaginary* love-story with a *historical* character like Agnimitra. His story must have had some basis of fact, some romantic tale of a princess living in disguise at his Court, as we have said in the previous Section. It is hardly likely that the poet would invent a Queen—as Mālavikā becomes one at the end of the play—for Agnimitra, though he could without impropriety invent the details of their *gāndharva* marriage. That the story resembles that of Bandhumatī is probably an accident; or perhaps both had a common source. The Bandhumtī-plot is the source of S'ri Harṣa's *Priyadars'ikā* which, as we have said before, is largely modelled upon our play.

(5) GENERAL CRITICISM

The *Mālavikāgnimitra* is essentially a love-play; it is not only the shortest, but also the earliest of Kālidāsa's dramas; probably the earliest of all his works, as the rest of them show a technical skill, a poetical power, and a general command over smooth and brilliant expressions which must belong to a maturer period of development. As we have shown elsewhere, this play presents all the graces and special peculiarities of Kālidāsa's style of composition, though everywhere in a cruder form than are to be found, for instance, in the *S'ākuntala* or the *Meghadūta*, showing the young writer cautiously feeling his way along the path of poetic composition. Kālidāsa especially excelled in his similes, which he mostly draws from his keen observation of Nature and natural phenomena (*cf.* in this play सलिलनिधिरिव प्रतिक्षणं मे। &c. I.11; मधुरस्वरा परभृता भ्रमरी च विबुद्धचूतसङ्गिन्यौ। कोटरमकालवृष्ट्या प्रबलपुरोवातया गमिते ॥ IV. 2; धाराभिरातप इवाभिहतं सरोजं दुःखायते मम मनः सुखमश्नुते च। V. 3; and others which the student should notice). Whether in prose or in poetry, his language is perfectly free from all the unnaturalness, the bad taste, and the extravagance and the artificiality of latter-day Sanskrit. The stanzas of poetry interspersed in his plays are often lyrical gems of the highest beauty. The *Mālavikāgnimitra,* however, compares unfavourably with the other two plays of Kálidāsa in respect of style; for the two plays are throughout more finished, more polished, and more smooth-flowing; in other respects also the *Mālavikāgnimitra* will be found to be on a lower level, though the reasons for the inferiority are part of the very design of the play. Thus the *Śākuntala* and the *Vikram.* are in some parts set in a background of beautiful natural scenery, and the whole of the fourth Act of the latter play is a long description of Nature's splendour; this element is practically absent in the *Mālavikāgnimitram.* The mythological hero is almost always more charming and more interesting in the eyes of the Hindu audience steeped in spiritual traditions; and the semi-divine passions of the *Vikram.* will be proportionately more attractive than the humdrum court-intrigues of the *Mālavikāgnimitra.* In truth, it is the conventional plot of a royal love that has spoiled the play—we are speaking comparatively—and failed to gain for it appreciative plaudits from a large circle of readers. We make no apology for quoting Prof. Rider[1] on this point, with whom we are in complete agreement :—

"Criticism of the large outlines of this plot would be quite unjust, for it is completely conventional. In dozens of plays we have the same story : the king who falls in love with a maid-servant, the jealousy of his harem, the eventual discovery that the maid is of royal birth, and the addition of another wife to a number already sufficiently large. In writing a play of this kind, the poet frankly accepts the conventions; his ingenuity is shown in the minor incidents : in stanzas of poetical description, and in giving abundant opportuntity for graceful music and dancing. When the play is approached in this way, it is easy to see the *griffe du lion* in this, the earliest work of the greatest poet who ever sang repeatedly of love between man and woman, troubled for a time but eventually happy." (P.·114).

---

1. "Kālidāsa: Translation of S'ākuntala and Other Works" (Dent's *Everyman's Library*). In this book, which the student will find suggestive and useful, the learned author has given full translations of the S'ākuntala and the Meghadūta, and summaries and criticisms of other works.

There is one more point of importance which we must deal with, before we bring this detailed survey of the *Mālavikāgnimitra* to a close. Treating as it does of human intrigues of a world not far removed in time from that of its composition, it gives us glimpses of the state of society as it existed in Kālidāsa's day. Much has heen said of the polygamy of his heroes, which seems strange and shocking to Western critics ; but the practice is a part of the social structure of the Hindus, and still continues to some extent in the households of Indian princes. Not only that it was never considered a sin, but there was no trace of immoral and impure tendencies even in polygamous couples ; compare the fine sentiment expressed by Agnimitra in अनातुरोत्कण्ठितयोः प्रसिध्यता समागमेनापि रतिर्न मां प्रति। परस्परप्राप्तिनिराशयोर्वरं शरीरनाशोऽपि समानुरागयोः॥ (III. 15). The highest sense of chivalry and courtesy prevailed towards the fair sex, who in turn considered their husbands as their all-in-all (see V. 19). Kālidāsa was a court-poet and he has made us familiar with the atmosphere of royal *Darbārs* of his age. India was a rich, prosperous and well-governed land, in spite of its being occasionally infested by robbers (V. 10) ; extensive commerce was carried on by merchants travelling in caravans. Literature and fine arts flourished under royal patronage. The play abounds in references to dancing, music, painting and general *Śilpa*. Teaching was not a mercenary profession but was considered as a sacred duty (I. 16, 17). There are references to the वेदत्रयी, अध्यात्मविद्या (I. 15.), कामतन्त्र (p. 156); *cf.* also Bakulāvalikā's दौत्य in Act III. The King shows great respect to his ministers who have studied treatises on Politics and are consummate politicians (I. 8). Medicine was practised in all its branches ; Dhruvasiddhi was a court-physician and a poison-specialist ; physicians laid down times for meals, which the poet is careful to impress upon his audience through the Vidūṣaka (उचितवेलातिक्रमे चिकित्सका दोषमुदाहरन्ति । p. 60) ; and the cures for a snake-bite given in Act IV have not been superseded by better ones even in these days of Western Medical discoveries. As in the twentieth century, so in the days of Kālidāsa, astrology seems to have been largely in popular favour ; the references to that science are rather numerous (दैवचिन्तकैर्विज्ञापितो राजा सोपसर्गं वो नक्षत्रम् etc. p. 130 ; यावदङ्गारको राशिमित्रानुवक्रं प्रतिगमनं न करोति। p. 110 ; आयुर्निमित्तं दक्षिणां

देवी दक्षिणीयैः परिग्राहयति। p. 162) ; and even the Parivrājikā holds fast to her belief in a *Sādhu's* prophecy (Act V.). The introduction of the Buddhist[1] nun Kaus'ikī, who is honoured by such titles as पण्डिता and भगवती, shows that the Buddhistic persuasion was held in reverence, and in this connection the comment of Agnimitra who calls it a सज्जनस्य पन्था : (p. 184) is very significant.

(6) THE PRINCIPAL CHARACTERS

Agnimitra

King Agnimitra, the hero of the Play, is of the type technically called *Dhīrodātta*—brave and noble-minded. Some critics call him an unheroic hero, a reckless voluptuary and a hypocrite. But we do not think his character deserves to be painted in such bad colours. The play is set in an atmosphere of courtly life favourable to love-intrigues (we should rather say love-matters), and therefore it offers no opening for the display of king-like qualities, such as undaunted courage or high political wisdom. We see Agnimitra, however, twice in his political capacity ; once when he orders the Vidarbha expedition in Act I., which he does with the approval of his ministers and in accordance with standard treatises on policy—an act which bears clear testimony to his high sense of self-respect and kingly dignity ; and again in the last Act, where his generosity towards the conquered foe is displayed when he restores Yajñasena to half of his kingdom ; while the fact that he had a body of good ministers who respected him and whom he consulted on all important matters (see p. 188 : कल्याणी देवस्य बुद्धिः। मन्त्रिपरिषदोऽप्येवमेव दर्शनम्।) shows that he was an adept in state policy.

The principal trait of his character, however, as depicted in the play, is दाक्षिण्य or 'equal and impartial behaviour towards all his queens.[2]' He himself states that

---

1. There is little room for doubt that the Parivrājikā was a Buddhist nun, although no word corresponding to Buddha or Buddhism is to be found in the play. A widow, who puts on red garments, and takes to the life of a wandering mendicant after the death of her husband, is not and was never acknowledged as following the Brāhmanical religion.

2. अनेकासु नायिकासु अवैषम्येण स्नेहानुवर्ती दक्षिणो नायकः। (Pratāparudrīya).

it is almost a sacred family-tradition with kings of his line to be दक्षिण, and this is amply borne out by his acts. He is afraid to wound the feelings of his Queen, even where his own passion is concerned and which he could have done with impunity. (*Cf.* केवलं देव्या धारिण्याश्चित्तं रक्षन्नात्मनः प्रभुत्वं न दर्शयति। p. 66.); the Vidūṣaka, too, compliments him on his *dākṣiṇya* 'so well-known in the palace' (अन्तःपुरप्रतिष्ठितं दाक्षिण्यं p. 72). And if we find him telling small lies to keep up appearances (*cf.* सुन्दरि न मे मालविकया कश्चिदर्थः। etc. p. 106, नार्हति कृतापराधो.... इति मोचिते मयैते। IV.17 &c.), we can excuse him; for it is due to this *Dākṣiṇya*. Although he loved Māl., he did not like to marry her without making sure that she too loved him as well, and even then he accepted her only when she was presented to him by the senior Queen herself. It is, therefore, sheer hazard to call him a reckless voluptuary. Beyond his gallantry, however, there is very little in his character which impresses us; and in this respect he compares unfavourably with the other two heroes of the poet, Duṣyanta and Purūravas. We might explain it on the score of the smallness of the play and the want of variety in the sequence and character of the incidents. Moreover, Agnimitra was a mortal, while Duṣyanta and Purūravas had more picturesqueness about them because of their semi-divine powers. Both Duṣyanta and Purūravas had access to Indra's court and distinguished themselves by assisting the King of gods; Agnimitra's conquests are gained for him by his generals, and again they do not form part of the actual action of the play, as Purūravā's encounter with the demon in Vikr.I does. The characters of Duṣyanta and Purūravas are set in further relief by the beautiful portraits of their sons; while, although there was an excellent opportunity for introducing Vasumitra in Act V, the poet seems somehow to have neglected it. In fact, it seems, it was the poet's object to portray in Agnimitra the character of a King, purely mortal, who being left free from the cares of state, could turn his attention to luxury and domestic happiness.

The Vidūṣaka

Next to the King, the Vidūṣaka is the most important person in the drama. If the play is put on the stage, we think the audience will take the greatest interest in him and his doings, not merely because of the fun provided but also because all the more exciting incidents of the drama are designed and executed by him with singular skill and foresight. He it is, who starts the ball rolling by bringing Gaṇadāsa and Haradatta together at loggerheads. He takes the Parivrājikā in his confidence and secures also Bakulāvalikā's help in the matter. When Mālavikā's examination is over, he contrives to detain her on the stage, so that the King may look at her for a longer time. He manages that the Queen has a fall, so that the As'oka's *dohada*-fulfilment comes to be entrusted to Mālavikā; and the snake-bite trick is an invention of his own fertile brain. It is thus, and not without reason, that the King considers him his कार्यान्तरसचिव (p. 20), and also pays him the respect due to a Brāhmaṇa (सिद्धिदर्शिनः ब्राह्मणस्य वचः। p. 86), though very likely he was a *Brahmabandhu* as Irāvatī calls him in her wrath (p. 102). He is represented as being especially in terror of snakes (भुजंगभीरु p. 150), and, like all other Vidūṣakas in plays, exceedingly fond of eating (पानभोजनं त्वरय p. 60), drinking (सीधुपानोद्वेजितस्य मत्स्यण्डिका p. 76). and sleeping (p. 142). He is supposed to be dull-witted (*cf.* मन्दोऽप्यमन्दतामेति etc. p. 52), and in common with court-fools, he does not hesitate to call himself a want-wit (मन्दस्य मे p. 130; मूढा जातिः p. 56), evidently for the sake of fun; for we know that he is not such a fool as he is supposed or as he calls himself to be. He is a successful schemer, His witticisms are never indelicate or coarse, and will always produce smiles and titters in the audience; the following are some of these :—

P. (32) भवति पश्याम उरभ्रसंपातम्।

(32) अन्योन्यकलहितयोर्मत्तहस्तिनोरेकतरस्मिन्ननिर्जिते कुत उपशमः।

(46) उपस्थितं नयनमधु संनिहितमक्षिकं च।

(54) प्रथमं ब्राह्मणस्य पूजा कर्तव्या। सा ननु वो विस्मृता।

(56) "किमिति त्वमाभरणं ददासि"—परकीयमिति कृत्वा।

(104) "वयस्य का प्रतिपत्तिरत्र"—किमन्यत्। जङ्घाबलमेव।

(106) कर्मगृहीतेन कुम्भीलकेन संधिच्छेदे शिक्षितोऽस्मीति वक्तव्यं भवति।

(110) यावदङ्गारको राशिमिवानुवक्रं प्रतिगमनं न करोति।

The Vidūṣaka in the Mālavikāgnimitra thus compares, more favourably with the Vidūṣaka in the other two plays, where he occupies a minor place. In the Vikramorvaśīya, the Vidūṣaka does little to help the King's suit; on the contrary, he dissuades Purūravas from what he calls 'the pursuit of a mirage'; and when he is forced to help the King in dispelling, his longing, he does it unwillingly. While in the Śākuntala, he does not even see the Heroine, much less does he assist Duṣyanta in obtaining her. In the Mālavikāgnimitra, the Vidūṣaka proves himself a resourceful and most practical person and he comes on the stage in every one of the five Acts, so indispensable he is to the development of the story. In the Vikramorvaśīya, the Vidūṣaka is absent from the stage during two out of the five Acts, and in the Śākuntala, during four out of the seven; as a matter of fact, he appears in these two plays more as a conventional appendage than as a necessary person of the drama.

MĀLAVIKĀ

Of the female characters, the three ladies, Mālavikā, Dhāriṇī and Irāvatī, present three different types of Heroines. The poet has given us in Mālavikā the model of a lovely, pure-minded, and accomplished girl. Her uncommon beauty not only makes conquest of the King's heart at once, but rouses the admiration even of the jealous Irāvatī (स्थाने शङ्कितं मम हृदयं p. 96). She is nobly-born, and though only from 14 to 16 years old (for she is called दारिका and बाला in the play), she displays great self-command, as we never hear her complaining of her position as a servant; she respects and fears Dhāriṇī as befits the age and position of the latter (*cf.* देवीं चिन्तयित्वा वेपते मे हृदयम्। p. 158). Being young, she is naturally timid; for she betrays fear even at the recital (p. 182 तूणीरपट्ट० etc.) of the description of the robbers' attack. She is highly endowed with natural gifts, and Gaṇadāsa compliments her as परमनिपुणा मेधाविनी च। (p. 12). She has a tender heart; her affection for the King is shown when, as soon as the alarm is given of the supposed presence of a snake, she follows him with भर्तः मा तावत्सहसा निष्काम। सर्प इति भण्यते। (p. 150); at the same time she is very modest (p. 142; ससाध्वसं तिष्ठति; p. 144. संश्लेषं परिहरति). Her *naive* simplicity is best seen when she becomes angry with the King in his portrait (p. 136). There can be no comparison between her and उर्वशी or शकुन्तला, since Mālavikā was a princess grown up in the tender, educative atmosphere of a royal home, while उर्वशी was a heavenly courtesan and शकुन्तला a hermit-girl living in rural surroundings.

DHĀRINĪ

Dhārinī, the crowned Queen, is an elderly lady of about thirty-five or so, as she has a son, Vasumitra, who is old enough to command an expedition. She is represented as an ideal Āryan wife who regards her husband as her all-in-all, and who subordinates all personal comforts to his happiness. As befits her age, she is sober and steady in her affection, and is entirely free from violent spasms of jealousy such as visit the younger and more irascible Irāvatī. Her jealousy is mild and temporary, and no severer taunt escapes her lips than the remark अहो अविनय आर्यपुत्रस्य। (p. 42) which, it may be noted, is not uttered aloud, but to herself. The language she uses in finding fault with the King is also more becoming (यदि राजकार्येष्वपीदृश्युपायनिपुणता आर्यपुत्रस्य ततः शोभनं भवेत्। p. 42). Her love for the King is too deep-rooted and long-established to be ruffled by the slight tempest of a new passion; the King also knows this when he says मदपेक्षानुवृत्त्या धारिण्याः पूर्वचरितैः संमान्यत एतत् (p. 161), and the Parivrājikā's description of her (p. 200) as a भर्तृवत्सला साध्वी is no empty compliment. Her sense of courtesy and propriety is shown on p. 120, when the King goes to see her and she tries to get up even when her foot is paining. Her nature is unsuspicious and she quite readily parts with the snake-seal ring without thinking twice. Last of all, she is very kind and forgiving at heart. She shows more concern than any one else, when Vidūṣaka's life was supposed to be in danger. It is true that she imprisoned Mālav. and Bakulāv., but it was at the instigation of and out of deference to the wishes of Irāvatī ; she relents almost immediately afterwards (cf., न मे एष मत्सरस्य कालः p. 148) and voluntarily offers Mālavikā to the king. There is no Queen in the Śākuntala ; but Auiśinarī in the Vikramorvaśīya is her prototype. Auśīnarī too, of her own accord, gives her sanction to the union of Purūravas and Urvaśī with the words अद्यप्रभृति

यां ब्रियमार्यपुत्रः प्रार्थयते या चार्यपुत्रस्य समागमप्रणयिनी तया सह मया प्रीतिबन्धेन वर्तितव्यम् (Vik. III. p. 82). But Dhāriṇī's picture as drawn here is better finished and more dignified and impressive than Auśīnarī's.

Irāvatī

Irāvatī offers a great contrast to Dhāriṇī. She is more jealous, more hot-tempered and less disposed to overlook the faults of the King. Being youthful and the King's favourite, she is very quick at scenting an intrigue, and the King's remark निसर्गनिपुणाः स्त्रियः fits her perfectly (p. 72). The poet has represented some of her unseemly acts as being due to the influence of drink, *e. g.* her sudden and somewhat un-ladylike interruption with the words पूरय पूरय (p. 104) and her being ready to strike her husband when exasperated by the words of Vidūṣaka (p. 108); her unforgiving temper, which the King very properly characterize as दीर्घरोषता (p. 116), is shown throughout her treatment of Mālavikā. She induces Dhāriṇī to put her in chains. She is dissatisfied when Dhāriṇī proposes to liberate Mālavikā and indirectly indicates her disapproval of it (p. 148) and even when Mālavikā's high descent is known and the Queen formally gives her to the King, she declines to be reconciled with her; for, instead of coming herself, she is content with sending a half-hearted, halting message of lukewarm congratulations.

Parivrājikā

Coming to the two remaining female characters of importance, we might say that they—the Parivrājikā and Bakulāvalikā—between them accomplish pretty much the same that is done by Kāmandakī with the help of Avalokitā and Lavaṅgikā in Bhavabhūti's Mālatī-Mādhava, though of course Kāmandakī's bussiness was more intricate and a heavier responsibility rested on her. The Parivrājikā is a woman of remarkable fortitude and patience. When she loses her brother Sumati, instead of despairing, she does what was necessary, and chalking out her future course goes in the habiliments of a Saṃnyasini and attaches herself to the court of Agnimitra, where by her learning she gets the title of पण्डितकौशिकी (see p. 30). Her prudence and foresight are well brought out by the fact that after she sees Mālavikā at the palace, she does not make the disclosure at once, but knowlng that Mālavikā was loved by the King, patiently awaits the course of events, doing what she could to lead them to a happy termination. With this object in view she assists a good deal in an indirect way towards the furtherance of the scheme formulated by Vidū aka in Act I. Her skill in the practical arts is demonstrated by her various remarks in Act I. (*e. g.* शिष्टा क्रिया कस्यचिदात्मसंस्था etc. śl. 16), by her judgment on Mālavikā's performance (II. 8) and by the Queen's words यत् त्वं प्रसाधनगर्वं वहासि etc. (p. 168). Her knowledge of the science of medicine is well indicated by the remedy she suggests for the cure of snake-bite. (see p. 122.) She is called पीठमर्दिका on p. 28 and we have fully discussed the significance of the title in our Notes, to which the student may refer.

Bakulāvalikā

Bakulāvalikā being struck with Mālavikā's superior charms and accomplishments (*cf.* अतिक्रामन्तीमिवेरावतीं पश्यामि। p. 14), takes interest in her well-being and readily enters into Vidūṣaka's plot to accomplish the King's object and promises her full help to him. She is pleased when Mālavikā is praised (see p. 16 यावदस्या आर्यस्य परितोष० &c.) She fosters her love for the King, and acquits herself creditably of the task entrusted to her, for which see pp. 92, 94, 96. The success of her artful measures elicits the King's remark स्थाने प्राणाः कामिनां दूत्यधीनाः (p. 96), and she is a good though not a perfect type of the class of निसृष्टार्था दूती referred to by Sanskrit writers (*cf.* बकुलावलिके, दिष्टया दूत्याधिकारविषया संपूर्णा ते प्रतिज्ञा। p. 152).

Important Abbreviations.

:o:

अ० रा०—Appāśāstrī Rashivdekar (commentator).
Amara. or *Ak.*—Amarakos'a.
Amaru.—Amarus'ataka.
Bg.—Bhagavadgītā.
Bh.—Bhartṛhari's Śatakas*.
Bhatti.—Bhaṭṭikāvya*.
Brih.-S.—Bṛhatsaṃhitā of Varāhamihira.
Brih.—Up.—Bṛhadāraṇyakopaniṣad.
Cf.—Compare.
Chap.—Chapter.
Com.—Commentary; Com.—Commentator.
D.-K.—Das'akumāracarita*
D.-R.—Daśarūpaka.
Gīt.—Gītagovinda.
H.-Ch.—Harṣacarita.
Hitop.—Hitopadeśa. *
Kād.—Kādambarī.*
Kāt.—Kātayavema (Commentator).
Kathā.—Kathāsaritsāgara.
Kāv.—Kāvyādarśa of Daṇḍin.
Kir.—Kirātārjunīya. (I-III)*
K.P.—Kāvyaprakāśa.
Kum.—Kumārasaṃbhava.*
Madhyam.—Bhāsa's Madhyamavyāyoga.*
Mah.-Bh.—Mahābhārata.
Mālav.—Mālavikāgnimitra.*
Mall.—Mallinātha.
Māl.-M.—Mālatimādhava.*
M. S.—Manusmṛti.
Megh.—Meghadūta. *
Mk.—Mṛchchhakaṭika.
Mudrā.—Mudrārākṣasa. *
M.-W.—Sir M. Moiner—Williams.
N.-Ch.—Naiṣadhīyacarita.
Pān—Pāṇini's Aṣhṭādhyāyī.
Pānchar.—Bhāsa's Pancarātra.*
Pt.—Pancatantra.*
Ragh.—Raghuvaṃśa.*
Rām.—Rāmāyaṇa.
Ratn.—Ratnavalī.*
Ṛig.-V.—Ṛgveda.
Ṛitus.—Ṛtusamhāra.*
S.—Sūtra.
Śāk.—Śākuntala. (Of Kālidāsa).*
Sāmkhya-K.—Saṃkhyakārikas of Iśvarakṛṣṇa.
Sāh.-D.—Sāhityadarpaṇa.
S.-K.—Siddhānta-Kaumudī.
S'is'.—S'is'upālavadha.
S.P.P.-S.P. Paṇḍit (Editor of the Mālav.)
Sub.—Subhāṣita.
Svap.—Bhāsa's Svapnavāsavadatta.
S'vet.-Up.—S'vetās'vatara Upaniṣad.
Up.—Upaniṣad.
Uttar.—Uttararāmacarita.*
Var.—Varāhamihira.
Vārt.—Vārttika.
Veṇi—Veṇī-saṃhāra.*
Vid.—Viddhaśālabhañjikā.
Vikr.—Vikramorvaśīya.*

* **Annotated by the Editor.**

Dramatis Personae

MALES

सूत्रधारः—The stage-manager.

पारिपार्श्विकः—The assistant of the Sūtradhāra.

राजा (अग्निमित्रः)—The Hero, the King of Vidis'ā.

विदूषकः (गौतमः)—A Brāhmaṇa, the King's personal friend and court-wit.

अमात्यः (वाहतकः)—The chief minister of Agnimitra.

हरदत्तः (आचार्यः)—A dancing-master attached to the Court.

गणदासः (आचार्यः)—Another dancing-master attached to the Court, and a rival of Haradatta.

कञ्चुकी (मौद्गल्यः)—The Chamberlain.

सारसिकः—A servant of Queen Dhāriṇī.

वैतालिकः (०कौ)—A bard (or bards) attached to the Court.

Attendants.

FEMALES

मालविका—The Heroine, sister of Mādhavasena.

धारिणी (देवी)—The principal wife of Agnimitra, and the Queen.

इरावती—Another wife of Agnimitra, junior to Dhāriṇī.

परिव्राजिका (कौशिकी)—A female ascetic, attached to Dhāriṇī's court.

प्रतीहारी (जयसेना)—The door-keeper of the palace.

बकुलावलिका—A maid-servant of Queen Dhāriṇī and a friend of Mālavikā.

कौमुदिका, नागरिका—Maid-servants of Dhāriṇī.

निपुणिका—A maid-servant of Irāvatī.

समाहितिका—A servant of the Parivrājikā.

उद्यानपालिका (मधुकरिका)—Gardener of the *Pramadavana*.

ज्योत्स्निका— } Artisans from Yajñasena's Court;
मदनिका— } Orginally the maid servants of Mādhavasena.

Attendants.

OTHER PERSONS MENTIONED

यज्ञसेन—The King of the Vidarbhas.

माधवसेन—A cousin of Yajñasena, and the brother of Mālavikā.

सुमति—Mādhavasena's minister.

पुष्पमित्र—Agnimitra's father.

वसुमित्र—Agnimitra's son.

वीरसेन—Agnimitra's brother-in-law, the brother of Queen Dhāriṇī.

मौर्यसचिव—'the minister of the Mauryas'-the brother-in-law of Yajñasena

ध्रुवसिद्धि—A Court physician, specialist in toxicology.

वसुलक्ष्मी—A princess in the palace.

माधविका—A maid-servant, keeper of the underground cellar.

चन्द्रिका—A maid-servant of Irāvatī.

Scene

Vidis'ā and the adjoining gardens.

भूमिका ।

निर्गतासु न वा कस्य कालिदासस्य सूक्तिषु ।
प्रीतिर्मधुरसार्द्रासु मञ्जरीष्विव जायते ॥

—बाणस्य ।

साकूतमधुरकोमलविलासिनीकण्ठकूजितप्राये ।
शिक्षासमयेऽपि मुदे रतलीलाकालिदासोक्ती ॥

—आचार्यगोवर्धनस्य ।

इह खलु सकलविद्याकलापदिपीठेऽस्मिन्भारते वर्षे निजयशःसुरभीकृत-दिगन्तरालाः प्रतिभाशालिनः परःशता महाकविपदमारूढः कवीश्वराः स्वकृतिमण्डनै-र्वाग्वधूं मण्डयन्ति स्म । तेषामपि कीर्तिशालिनां सुधांशुरिवोडुपुञ्जमध्यगतः कालिदासोऽग्र्यपदमारोहतीति सर्वेषां प्राचीनार्वाक्तनानां पण्डितानामभ्युपगमः । "पुरा कवीनां गणनाप्रसङ्गे कनिष्ठिकाधिष्ठितकालिदासा । अद्यापि तत्तुल्यकवेरभावादनामिका साऽर्थवती बभूव ॥" इति सुविश्रुतं सुभाषितमेवात्र निदर्शनम् अयं च कविचक्र चूडामणिः मालविकाग्निमित्र-विक्रमोर्वशीय-शाकुन्तलाख्यानि परस्परापेक्षयावरमध्यमो-त्तमगुणानि त्रीणि रूपकाणि, मेघदूत—कुमारसंभव—रघुवंशाभिधानि च त्रीणि सुललितपदविन्यासानि काव्यानि निबबन्ध । ऋतुसंहाराख्यं खण्डकाव्यमप्येतदीयमेवेति प्रायो वादः । नलोदय—श्रुतबोध—शृङ्गारतिलकादयश्च बहवोऽन्ये प्रबन्धाः कालिदास-कृतितया प्रसिद्धा अपि न कालिदासीयकाव्यगुणविशेषकक्षामवगाहन्त इति परकर्तृत्वमेवै तेषां पण्डितैः प्रस्थापितम् । कालिदासीया अन्येऽपि केचित्प्रबन्धाः कालवशमित्वाधुना विनष्टाः स्युरित्येतदपि कल्पयितुं शक्यम् ।

एवं सत्यप्ययं महाकविः कं देशं स्वजन्मनालंचकार, कौ वास्य धन्यौ पितरौ, कस्मात्क वाऽसौ विद्याधिगमं कृतवानित्यादि याथातथ्येन नैवैतर्हि ज्ञातुं शक्यते । केवलमयं कृतविद्यो लब्धमहाकवियशाः श्रीमतो विक्रमादित्यस्य राज्ञः सदसमलंचकारेति किंवदन्त्योपलब्धम् । उक्तं च केनापि—"धन्वन्तरिक्षपणकामरसिंहशङ्कुवेतालभट्टघटकर्पर-कालिदासाः । ख्यातो वराहमिहिरो नृपतेः सभायां रत्नानि वै वररुचिर्नव विक्रमस्य ॥" इति । विक्रमादित्यश्च शालिवाहनशकात्प्राक् १३५ मितेऽब्दे राज्य-पदमारूढ इति तद्विदुषां निर्णयः । अयमेवास्य कवेः कालः इति मन्यामहे । केचित्तु यूरोपीया ऊरीकृतसंशोधनकर्माणः संख्यावन्तः कविरयं खिस्तीयशकस्य प्रथमशतकादूर्ध्व-मित्यपरे चतुर्थपञ्चमशतकयोरन्तरालेऽभवदिति तर्कयन्ति तदहो संशयगहनविनष्टः कविकालाभ्यूहः ।

श्रीमता कालिदासेन सर्वत्रापि वैदर्भी रीतिरेवावलम्बितात्मकृतिषु। तामिमां रीतिं श्रीबिह्लण इत्थं वर्णयति–"अनभ्रवृष्टिः श्रवणमृतस्य सरस्वतीविभ्रमजन्मभूमिः। वैदर्भरीतिः कृतिनामुदेति सौभाग्यलाभप्रतिभूः पदानाम्।॥" इति। ईदृश्यस्य कवेर्वश्या वाक् यत्–"श्लेषः प्रसादः समता माधुर्यं सुकुमारता। अर्थव्यक्तिरुदारत्वमोजःकान्तिसमाधयः॥" इति दण्डयुक्ताः सर्वेपि काव्यगुणाः समुसल्लसन्त्यस्य निबन्धेषु तत्रापि प्रसादः शेखरीभूतः। रसश्च शृङ्गारो मूर्धन्यत्वेन कालिदासीयग्रन्थेषु समुपनिबद्धः। उपमाचातुर्येण कल्पनाविशालात्वेन पदमाधुर्येणासमासभूयस्त्वादिगुणैः सर्वाङ्गीणमनोज्ञतयास्य प्रबन्धानामयमितरकविभ्यः सुतरां श्लाघ्य इति जानन्त्येव सुधियः। आहुश्च रसिकाः—"उपमा कालिदासस्य" इति।

एतन्मालविकाग्निमित्रं नाटकं शाकुन्तल-विक्रमोर्वशीयापेक्षया हीनगुणमित्युक्तं प्राक्। अस्य पञ्चाङ्काः। अस्मिन्नपि पदघटना तथा मधुरवर्णोपेता यथा सर्वत्र द्राक्षापाक एवोपलभ्यते। न क्वचिदपि 'नारिकेलफलसंमितत्वं' वचसाम्। तथा चेदं तत्र तत्रानुप्रासैः क्वचित् श्लेषादिभिः कुत्रचनोचितैरलंकारैरार्थैश्चोद्भासितम्। अत्र नायकोऽग्निमित्रो धीरोदात्तः। नायिका मालविका बाला मुग्धा च। संभोगशृङ्गारः प्रधानो रसः। इतिवृत्तं चास्य प्राय ऐतिहासिकमंशतः कविकल्पनोत्पादितं च। अस्मिन्नाटके वर्णितं कथावस्त्वङ्कविभक्तं सारांशतः सुलभावगमार्थमत्रोपनिबध्यते—

प्रथमाङ्के तावदादौ नान्दीपठनम्। ततः प्रस्तावनायां सूत्रधारपारिपार्श्विकौ कालिदासकृतिर्मालविकाग्निमित्रं नाम नाटकं वसन्तोत्सवसमये प्रयुज्यत इति कथयतः। ततश्च नाटकारम्भः। तत्र चेटीद्वयसंकथायाः "अथैकदा विदिशाधीशो राजाऽग्निमित्रो देव्या धारिण्याः परिजनमध्यगतां चित्र आलिखितां कामपि समुपारूढनवयौवनां कन्यकां प्रेक्ष्य तद्रूपमोहितः संस्तस्या नामधेयादिकं राज्ञीं पप्रच्छ। सा तु साशङ्का राज्ञस्तां निगूहितुमात्तप्रयत्ना न किमप्युत्तरं ददौ। किं तु कुमार्या वसुलक्ष्म्या बालभावसुलभेन चापल्येन मालविकेत्यस्या नामेति राज्ञे कथितम्" इत्यंशो विष्कम्भकादवगम्यते। अथ च मालविकागतैकमना राजा तां द्रष्टुकामो विदूषकेण सह मन्त्रयित्वा धारिण्या देव्या आसन्नचरीं परिव्राजिकां पण्डितकौशिकीं च स्वपक्ष आकार्य प्रयोगं कृतवान्। तद्यथा–विदूषको जनितपरस्परविज्ञानसंघर्षयोर्नाट्याचार्ययोर्हरदत्तगणदासयोः कलहमुत्पाद्य तन्निर्णयाय तौ नृपसमीपं प्रापयामास। तत्र च पण्डितकौशिक्या 'प्रयोगप्रधानं नाट्यशास्त्रम्। उपदेशदर्शनान्निर्णयः। अतो द्वाभ्यामपि युवाभ्यां प्रेक्षागृहे संगीतरचनां कृत्वा शिष्यासंक्रान्त उपदेशो दर्शयितव्यः' इति निश्चितम्। राज्ञा देव्या च धारिण्या यथाकथंचित्तदनुमतं च।

द्वितीयाङ्के गणदासशिष्या मालविका नाट्यशालायां नृत्ताभिनयपूर्वकं शर्मिष्ठायाः कृतेरङ्ग चतुष्पदं वस्तु गायति—"दुर्लभः प्रियस्तस्मिन्भव हृदय निराशमहो अपाङ्गको मे प्रस्फुरति किमपि वामः। एष स चिरदृष्टः कथमुपनेतव्यो नाथ मां पराधीनां

त्वयि गणय सतृष्णाम् ॥ " इत्येवंरूपम् । तत्र ' जनमिममनुरक्तं विद्धि ' इति अहमेव प्रार्थनाव्याजमुक्त इति राजा मन्यते स्म । एवं तस्यापि तस्यामनुरागातिशयः समजनीति स एवाङ्कान्ते स्पष्टयति " सर्वान्तःपुरवनिताव्यापारप्रतिनिवृत्तहृदयस्य । सा वामलोचना मे स्नेहस्यैकायनीभूता ॥ " इत्यनेन पद्येन ।

तृतीयाङ्के तावत् अन्योन्यसंघर्षितयोर्नाट्याचार्ययोः समानागमित्वेऽपि शिष्यागुणविशेषेण गणदासः प्रशंसितः इति, दृढं च मालविकायां साभिलाषो राजा राजन्यपि मालविकेति कौलीनं सर्वत्र राजकुले प्रसृतम्, इति च प्रवेशकादुपलभ्यते । अत्रान्तरे विदूषकेण राज्ञो मनोगतं मालविकायाः सख्यै बकुलावलिकायै ज्ञापयित्वा तस्याः साहाय्यं प्रार्थितं तयापि चास्यै प्रतिश्रुतम् । अथ च प्रमदवनपालिका मधुकरिका चिरायमाणमुकुलोद्गमस्य तपनीयाशोकतरोर्दोहदं पादताडनरूपं धारिण्यै निवेदयामास । किं तु सरुजचरणत्वात्स्वयं तन्निर्वर्तयितुमशक्नुवती सा तत्र मालविकां न्ययोजयत् । यदि चासौ पञ्चरात्राभ्यन्तरे कुसुमं दर्शयति तदाहमभिलाषपूरयितृकं प्रसादं दास्यामीत्यपि देव्या तस्यै प्रतिज्ञातम् । अथ मालविकागतचित्तो राजा सविदूषकः प्रमदवनं प्रविष्टः । तत्र च मालविका बकुलावलिका चाशोकदोहदपूरणार्थमुपागते । अमुं प्रस्तावमुपलभ्य बकुलावलिकया मालविकाया राजन्यनुरागः सुदूरमारोपितः । लतान्तरितः सविदूषको राजा सर्वमेतदालोक्य यावदात्मानं दर्शयति तावत्प्रमदवने दोलाधिरोहणार्थं कृतसंकेता राज्ञो भोगिनी नायिकेरावत्यपि तत्रस्थैतदवलोकयन्ती तत्कालमात्मानमदर्शयत् । तां दृष्ट्वा संभ्रान्तं राजानं च भृशं निर्भर्त्स्यानुनीयमानापि प्रसादमगृहीत्वा सा कुपितैवापससार ।

चतुर्थाङ्के देवीं धारिणीं विज्ञाप्येरावत्या मालविकाबकुलावलिके बन्धनं कारिते भूगृहे निक्षिप्ते च । भूगृहव्यापृता माधविका च देव्या संदिष्टा—मम नागमुद्रिताङ्गुलीयकमदृष्ट्वा न मोक्तव्ये एते इति । वृत्तान्तमिमं विदूषकमुखेन श्रुत्वा परं खिन्नतामापन्नो राजा ' अप्यत्र कश्चिदुपक्रमः स्यात् ' इति विदूषकं पृष्टवान् । अस्ति परं कर्णे कथयामीत्युक्त्वा तथा कृतवन्तं तं ' प्रयुज्यतां सिद्धये ' इति सपरितोषं राजा विसर्जयामास । स्वयं च प्रवातशयननिषण्णां देवीं धारिणीं द्रष्टुमगात् । ततो विदूषकः केतकीकण्टकैर्दंशपदसदृशमात्माङ्गुष्ठे छिद्रयित्वा ' सर्परूपेण कालेन दष्टोऽस्मि ' इत्याक्रोशन् राज्ञोऽन्तिके विषवेगमलीकमेव रूपयामास । तं च राजा ध्रुवसिद्धेर्विषवैद्यस्य विज्ञापनानुरोधेन तत्सकाशं नीयतामयमिति निष्क्रामयामास । ततश्च ' ध्रुवसिद्धिर्विज्ञापयति उदकुम्भविधाने सर्पमुद्रितं किमपि कल्पयितव्यम् । तदन्विष्यताम् ' इति तस्मादागतं संदेशं श्रुत्वा ब्राह्मणजीवितस्य संशयदोलारूढ्या जातकातर्या देवी स्वयमेवात्मनो नागमुद्राङ्गुलीयकं संभ्रमाद्दत्तवती । तच्च लब्ध्वा विदूषकेण मालविकाबकुलावलिके बन्धनान्मोचिते । मालविकां च समुद्रगृहं नीत्वा तत्र राज्ञा । तां संगमयांचकार । अत्रान्तरे भूयोऽपीरावती उपचारातिक्रमस्य प्रमार्जनार्थं चित्रगतमार्यपुत्रं प्रसादयामीति कृत्वा

तदेव समुद्रगृहं प्राप्ता राजानं मालविकया सह कृतप्रणयं निर्भर्त्सयितुमारेभे। किं तु पिङ्गलवानरेण त्रासिताया वसुलक्ष्म्याः प्रकृत्यनवस्थानमस्मिन्नेव समये प्रतीहार्या निवेदितं ज्ञात्वा सर्वे सत्वरं निष्क्रान्ताः। कातरहृदया शङ्किता च मालविकापि तदैवाशोकमुकुलोद्भमवार्तां श्रुत्वा प्रतिश्रुतप्रसादाया राज्ञ्याः सत्यप्रतिज्ञतां प्रति जातप्रत्यया किंचिदाश्वस्तचित्ता सख्या सह निरगात्।

पञ्चमाङ्के तावत् 'राज्ञोऽग्निमित्रस्य दण्डचक्रेण वशीकृतस्तास्यमित्रो विदर्भराजो यज्ञसेनः' इति प्रवेशकाज्ज्ञातम्। पश्चात् देवी धारिणी प्रतिज्ञातार्थसंपादनाय मालविकां परिव्राजिकया विवाहनेपथ्येन मण्डयित्वा ताभ्यां सह प्रमदवनं जगाम नृपं च तत्राशोकप्रसूनलक्ष्मीसमवलोकनव्यपदेशत आनीतवती। अस्मिंश्च समये विजितविदर्भनाथविषयादुपायनत्वेनानीते द्वे शिल्पकारिके तत्र कञ्चुकिना प्रवेशं कारिते। ते च मालविकां परिव्राजिकावेषामार्यां कौशिकीं च प्रत्यभिजज्ञाते। ततः कौशिक्या ताभ्यां चाशेषो वृत्तान्तः श्रावितो यस्मान्मालविका राजदारिका माधवसेनस्य कनीयसी भगिनी चेति ज्ञातम्। अत्रान्तरे च राज्ञः पित्रा पुष्पमित्रेण प्रेषिताल्लेखादात्मजं वसुमित्रं सर्वत्र विजयिनं निशम्योभावपि देवो देवी च प्रहृष्टौ। धारिणी च पारितोषिकव्याजेन राज्ञे मालविकां प्रादाद्राजापि तां सव्रीडं ससंमानं च परिजग्राहेतिसर्वं शुभोदर्कत्वेन समाप्य कविरग्रे भरतवाक्यमुपन्यबध्नात् "आशास्यमीतिविगमप्रभृति प्रजानां संपद्यते न खलु गोप्तरि नाग्निमित्रे" इति॥

महाकविकालिदासविरचितम्

मालविकाग्निमित्रम् ।

नानाभावोपसंपन्नं नानावस्थान्तरात्मकम् ।
लोकवृत्तानुकरणं नाट्यमेतन्मया कृतम् ॥

दुःखार्तानां श्रमार्तानां शोकार्तानां तपस्विनाम् ।
विश्रान्तिजननं काले नाट्यमेतद् भविष्यति ॥

न तज्ज्ञानं न तच्छिल्पं न सा विद्या न सा कला ।
नासौ योगो न तत्कर्म नाट्येऽस्मिन् यन्न दृश्यते ॥

—नाट्यशास्त्र I–112, 114, 116.

अथ

मालविकाग्निमित्रम् ।

प्रथमोऽङ्कः ।

एकैश्वर्ये[1] स्थितोऽपि प्रणतबहुफले यः स्वयं कृत्तिवासाः
कान्तासंमिश्रदेहोऽप्यविषयमनसां यः [2]परस्ताद्यतीनाम् ।
अष्टाभिर्यस्य [3]कृत्स्नं जगदपि तनुभिर्बिभ्रतो नाभिमानः
सन्मार्गालोकनाय व्यपनयतु स [4]वस्तामसीं वृत्तिमीशः ॥ १ ॥

(नान्द्यन्ते ।)

सूत्रधारः—(नेपथ्याभिमुखमवलोक्य ।) मारिषे[5] इतस्तावत् ।

(प्रविश्य ।)

पारिपार्श्विकः—भाव अयमस्मि ।

वेदादीनां विशुद्धानां विद्यानां जन्महेतवे ।
पार्वतीपरतन्त्राय परस्मै वस्तुने नमः ॥

भाग्यं नाम समग्रमीदृशमतिस्त्रेहैकपात्रं यतो
वीरं काटयवेम उद्धतरिपुध्वंसे नियुज्य स्वयम् ।
नित्यं नन्दति नर्तनैरभिनवैः कान्तैर्वसन्तोत्सवैः
संतानाभ्युदयैः कुमारगिरिभूपालो नृपालोत्तमः ॥

अत्र कविः कालिदासः प्रारिप्सितस्य ग्रन्थस्याविघ्नेन परिसमाप्त्यर्थमिष्टदेवतास्मरणपूर्वकमाशिषं प्रयुङ्क्ते—**एकैश्वर्य इत्यादि** । स ईशः परमेश्वरः सन्मार्गालोकनाय सन् प्रशस्तो मार्गः पन्था मोक्षमार्गस्तस्यालोकनाय दर्शनाय वो युष्माकं तामसीं तमःसंबन्धिनीं वृत्तिं प्रवृत्तिं व्यपनयतु अपाकरोत्विति संबन्धः । कथंभूत ईशः । यः प्रणतबहुफले । बहूनि फलानि यस्मात्तत्तथोक्तम् । प्रणतानां प्रणामं कृतवताम् । भक्तानामित्यर्थः । बहुफलं तस्मिन् । एकैश्वर्ये । ईश्वरस्य भाव ऐश्वर्यम् । एकं

---

१ श्वर्यस्थितोपि॰ फलो. २ पुरस्तात्. ३ सर्वं. ४ नः ५ अस्मात्प्राक्—अलमतिविस्तरेण इति एकस्मिन् पु॰.

MALAVIKĀGNIMITRA

ACT I

May that Lord (Īs′ a—God Śiva), who, though abiding in sole supremacy which yields manifold blessings to his devotees, is himself clad in skin (*i. e.,* elephant-hide) ; who, though his body is united with that of his beloved, stands above ascetics whose minds are not affected by objects of sense ; in whom there is no arrogance, though he supports the whole world with his eight forms :—(may he) remove your state of darkness (ignorance) that you may behold the path of good ! (1)

(At the end of the Benediction)

Manager :—(*Looking towards the tiring-room*) Actor, come here for a moment.

(Entering)

Actor :—Sir, here I am.

मुख्यम्। अनन्यसाधारणमित्यर्थः। तच्च तदैश्वर्यं च। तस्मिन् स्थितोऽपि अणिमाद्यैश्वर्ययुक्तोऽपीत्यर्थः स्वयम् आत्मना कृत्तिवासाः कृत्तिश्चर्म वासो वसनं यस्य स तथोक्तः। यः कान्तासंमिश्रदेहोऽपि कान्तया स्त्रिया संमिश्रः संमिलितो देहः शरीरं यस्य स तथोक्तः तादृशोपि सन्। अविषयमनसाम् न विद्यन्ते विषयाः शब्दादयो येषां तान्यविषयाणि तानि मनांसि येषां ते तथोक्ताः तेषाम्। यतीनां संयमिनां परस्तात् परः श्रेष्ठः। 'दिक्शब्देभ्यः सप्तमीपञ्चमीप्रथमाभ्यो दिग्देशकालेष्वस्तातिः' इत्यस्तातिप्रत्ययः। अष्टाभिस्तनुभिः पृथिव्यादिमूर्तिभिः पृथिवी सलिलं तेजो वायुराकाश एव च। सूर्याचन्द्रमसौ सोमयाजी चेत्यष्टमूर्तयः॥ इति यादवः। कृत्स्नं सर्वं जगत् लोकं बिभ्रतोऽपि धारयतोऽपि यस्य अभिमानः प्रणयो ममत्वं न भवति। एषु विशेषणेषु विरोधालंकारेणास्य लोकातिशायित्वमुक्तं भवति। स्रग्धरा वृत्तम्। १॥ अत्र प्रणतबहुफलत्वैकैश्वर्यस्थित्या कान्तासंमिश्रणेन जगद्धरणेन ईश इत्यनेन च लोकोत्तरः कश्चिद्राजास्मिन्नाटके वर्ण्यत इति सूच्यते। सन्मार्गालोकनायेत्यनेनात्र कश्चिन्मार्गाभिनयः प्रतिपाद्यत इति सूच्यते। मार्गो नाम नाट्यविशेषः। यथोक्तम्—

सूत्रधारः—अभिहितोऽस्मि विद्वत्[1]परिषदा कालिदासग्रथितवस्तु [2]मालविकाग्निमित्रं नाम नाटकमस्मिन्वसन्तोत्सवे प्रयोक्तव्यमिति । तदारभ्यतां संगीतम् ।

पारिपार्श्विकः—[3]मा तावत् । प्रथितयशसां [4]भासकविपुत्र-सौमिल्लकादीनां प्रबन्धानतिक्रम्य वर्तमानकवेः कालिदासस्य क्रिया[5]यां कथं परिषदो बहुमानः ।

सूत्रधारः—[6]अयि विवेक[7]विश्रान्तमभिहितम् । पश्य ।

पुराणमित्येव न साधु सर्वं न चापि काव्यं नवमित्यवद्यम् ।
सन्तः परीक्ष्यान्यतरद्भजन्ते मूढः परप्रत्ययनेयबुद्धिः ॥ २ ॥

पारिपार्श्विकः—आर्यमिश्राः प्रमाणम् ।

'मार्गोऽपि देशी तद्भेदः कथितो नाट्यवेदिभिः । अत्र मार्गो भवेन्नाट्यं नाट्य-वेदोक्तलक्षणम् ॥' इति । एष नान्दीश्लोकः । नान्द्यादिलक्षणं तु शाकुन्तल-व्याख्यान एवाभिहितम् । अत्र 'पदादिनियमोऽपि वा' इति विकल्पात्पदादिनिय-माभावः ॥ अथ प्रस्तावनां विवक्षुस्तदङ्गयोः प्ररोचनामुखयोः प्ररोचनां प्रस्तौति—**नान्द्यन्ते सूत्रधार इत्यादिना** । मारिष इतस्तावत् । आगम्यतामिति शेषः । नटः सूत्रधारेण मारिष इति वाच्यः । 'सूत्री नटेन भावेति तेनासौ मारिषेति च ।' इत्युक्तत्वात् । परिपार्श्वं यथा भवति तथा वर्तते इति पारिपार्श्विकः । नट इत्यर्थः । 'परिमुखं च' इत्यत्र चकाराट्ठक् । **अभिहितोऽस्मीत्यादि** । विद्वत्परिषदा विदुषां विपश्चितां परिषत्सभा तया । अनेन सभाप्रशंसा कृता । कालिदासग्रथित-वस्तु कालिदासेन ग्रथितं वस्तु कथा यस्मिंस्तत्तथोक्तम् । मालविकया सहितः अग्नि-मित्रः मालविकाग्निमित्रः तमधिकृत्य कृतं नाटकं मालविकाग्निमित्रम् । 'अधिकृत्य कृते ग्रन्थे' इत्यण् । यथा मालतीमाधवम् । वसन्तोत्सव इत्यनेन कालनिर्देशः कृतः । संगीतं तौर्यत्रिकम् । तथा चोक्तं संगीतरत्नाकरे—'नृत्तं गीतं तथा वाद्यं त्रयं संगीतमुच्यते ।' इति । आरभ्यतां प्रयोक्तुं यत्नः क्रियताम् ॥ मा तावत् । मा इति निवारणे । भास–कविपुत्र–सौमिल्लकाः प्राक्तनाः कवयः । प्रबन्धान् रूपकाणि । अतिक्रम्योल्लङ्घ्य । परिहृत्येत्यर्थः । कालिदासस्य कालिदासनामधेयस्य कवेः ।

---

१ विद्वत् इति नास्ति क्वचित्. २ ०मित्रीयम्. ३ भाव. ४ भासकविसौमिल्लकविमिश्रा० धावकसौ० कवि०; भास सौमिल्लकवि० ५ कृतौ; कृतौ किं कृतौ बहुमानः; क्रियामिमां द्रष्टुं कथं. ६ अये. ७ विवकश्रान्तं.

Manager :—I have been told by the assembly of learned men that I should act at this spring-festival the play, named Mālavikāgnimitra, the plot of which is arranged by Kālidāsa; therefore let the music be begun.

Actor :—This should not be (I pray). How should the assembly have respect for the work of Kālidāsa, a modern poet setting aside the compositions of poets of established fame like Bhāsa, Saumillaka, Kaviputra and others ?

Manager :—Ah! You have spoken without giving thought to it. Observe—

Every thing (poem) is not good, because it is old; nor is a poem to be condemned, because it is new; wise men (sound critics) accept one or the other after due examination: the blockhead has his judgment guided by the opinion of others. (2)

Actor :—Your honour is an authority (for me) in this matter.

क्रियायां कृतौ रूपके। कथं बहुमान आदरातिशयः। कथमित्याक्षेपे। विवेकविश्रान्तं विवेकदुर्बलम् विवेकशून्यमित्यर्थः। क्रियाविशेषणं चैतत्। **पुराणमिति**। सर्वं काव्यं कवेः कर्म। कृतिरित्यर्थः। पुराणमित्येव पुराणत्वादेव साधु रम्यं न भवति। नवमिति च नवत्वादेव अवद्यं गर्ह्यं न भवति। [अवद्यपण्य इति निपातनात्साधु।] किं तु सन्तो विद्वांसः [प्रेक्षावन्त इत्यर्थः] परीक्ष्य पुराणं नवं च काव्यं गुणतो दोषतश्च परामृश्य अन्ततस्तयोरेकं पुराणं नवं वा। गुणयुक्तमित्यर्थः। भजन्ते स्वीकुर्वन्तीत्यर्थः। मूढः अज्ञस्तु परप्रत्ययनेयबुद्धिः परस्यान्यस्य प्रत्ययेन ज्ञानेन नेया प्राप्या बुद्धिर्यस्य स तथोक्तः। अनेन कविकाव्यप्रशंसा कृता। उपजातिः छन्दः ॥ २ ॥ **शिरसेत्यादि**। शिरसा मूर्ध्ना प्रथमगृहीतां पूर्वस्वीकृताम्। शिरसो ग्रहणेन भक्त्यतिशयो गम्यते। परिषदः सभाया आज्ञां शासनं कर्तुं निर्वर्तयितुमिच्छाम्यभिलषामि। अत्रोपमामाह—धारिण्या देव्याः। धारिणी नाम कथानायकस्य पत्नी। तस्या आज्ञां सेवादक्षः परिचर्यानिपुणः अयं पुरोवर्ती परिजन इव। परिचारको जनः परिजनः। अनेन पात्राक्षेपहेतुः प्रयोगातिशयो नाम मुखाङ्गमुक्तं भवति। तदुक्तं दशरूपके—एषोयमित्युपक्षेपात्सूत्रधारप्रयोगतः। पात्रप्रवेशो यत्रैष प्रयोगातिशयो मतः ॥ इति ॥ आर्याच्छन्दः ॥ ३ ॥ **प्रस्तावना** ॥ तल्लक्षणम्—नटी विदूषको वापि पारिपार्श्विक एव वा। सूत्रधारेण सहिताः संलापं यत्र कुर्वते ॥ चित्रैर्वाक्यैः स्वकार्योत्थैः प्रस्तुताक्षेपिभिर्मिथः। आमुखं तत्तु विज्ञेयं

सूत्रधारः—तेन हि त्वरतां भवान् ।

शिरसा प्रथमगृहीतामाज्ञामिच्छामि परिषदः कर्तुम् ।
देव्या इव धारिण्याः सेवादक्षः परिजनोऽयम् ॥ २ ॥

(इति निष्क्रान्तौ ।)

प्रस्तावना ।

(ततः प्रविशति चेटी ।)

चेटी—आज्ञप्तास्मि देव्या धारिण्या । अचिरप्रवृत्तोपदेशं चलितं नाम नाट्यमन्तरेण कीदृशी मालविकेति नाट्याचार्यमार्यगणदासं प्रष्टुम् । तत्तावत्संगीतशालां गच्छामि । (इति परिक्रामति ।) (क)

(ततः प्रविशत्याभरणहस्ता द्वितीया चेटी ।)

प्रथमा—(द्वितीयां दृष्ट्वा ।) सखि कौमुदिके कुतस्त इयं धीरता यत्समीपेनाप्यतिक्रामन्तीतो दृष्टिं न ददासि । (ख)

द्वितीया—अहो बकुलावलिका । सखि इदं देव्याः शिल्पिसकाशादानीतं नागमुद्रासनाथमङ्गुलीयकं स्निग्धं निध्यायन्ती तवोपालम्भे पतितास्मि । (ग)

(क) आणत्तह्मि देवीए धारिणीए । अइरप्पउत्तोवदेसं चलिअं णाम णट्टअं अन्तरेण कीरिसी मालविअत्ति णट्टाअरिअं अज्जगणदासं पुच्छिदुं । ता दावे संगीतसालं गच्छह्मि । (ख) हला कोमुदीए कुदो दे इअं धीरदा जं समीवेण वि अदिक्कामन्ती इदो दिट्ठिं ण देसि । (ग) अम्हो बउलावलिआ । सहि इदं देवीए सिप्पिसआसादो आणीदं णाअमुद्दासणाहं अङ्गुलीअअं सिणिद्धं णिज्झाअन्ती तुह उवालम्भे पडिदह्मि ।

नाम्ना प्रस्तावनापि सा ॥ इति ॥ कविरिदानीमङ्कमारभमाणः कथोपयोगितया प्रथमं मिश्रविष्कम्भं नामार्थोपक्षेपकं प्रस्तौति—ततः प्रविशतीत्यादिना । अचिरं प्रवृत्त उपदेशो यस्य । नाट्यमन्तरेण अवस्थानुकृतिर्नाट्यं तदुद्दिश्य । अन्तरेणेत्ययं निपात उद्देशार्थे वर्तते । चलितं नाम नृत्यविशेषः । तदुक्तम् 'तदेवतच्च-(च्छ) लितं नाम साक्षाद्यदभिनीयते । व्यपदिश्य पुरावृत्तं स्वाभिप्रायप्रकाशकम् ॥'

---

१ बकुलावलिका. २ अपरा चेटी आभर०. ३ अइरोवणीदा छलिअणा०. ४ छलिअं छलिकं); सुच०. ५ जाव (यावत्). ६ समीवे वि. ७ सप्प.

Manager:—Then you should make haste.

I wish to carry out the order of the audience already received (by me) with bowed head, like the attendants of the Queen Dhāriṇī, here, diligent in the execution of their duty. (3)

***(Exeunt* Both).**

(*End of the Introductory Dialogue or the* Prelude.)

(*Enter* Bakulāvalikā, *a female servant.*)

Bakulāvalikā :—I am ordered by Queen Dhāriṇī to ask the teacher of dancing, the noble Gaṇadāsa, what progress Mālavikā has made in the dance called *Chalita*, instruction in which has been recently (lit. not long ago) begun. To the music-hall then I will go. (*With these words she walks about*).

(*Then enter another female-servant, with* an *ornament in her hand.*)

First Female-Servant :—(*Having seen the second*) Halloo ! Kaumudikā ! Whence this gravity in you (why are you in such a brown study) that, though passing close to me, you do not cast a glance in this direction ?

Second Female-Servant:—Ah, here is Bakulāvalikā ! My Friend, engaged in contemplating (looking intently at) this beautiful ring of the Queen's with its seal (furnished) with a snake-impression, brought from the artist, I came to merit (to be an object of) your reproof.

इति ॥ चतुर्विधाभिनयवद्यज्जातिस्वरसंभृतम् । शृंगाररसभूयिष्ठं सलयं चलितं विदुः ॥ इति व्याख्यान्तरम् । हला—हलेति सख्या आह्वाने ‘हण्डे हञ्जे हलाह्वाने नीचां चेटीं सखीं प्रति ।’ इत्यमरः । शिल्पी सुवर्णकारविशेषः । नागमुद्रया नागविषहारिमणिरचनाविशेषेण सनाथं युक्तम् । स्निग्धं सप्रेम । निध्यायन्ती पश्यन्ती । उद्भिन्नाः किरणा एव केसराः किञ्जल्का यस्य तेन । कुसुमितः जातकुसुमः । कुसुमान्यस्य संजातानि । ‘तदस्य संजातं तारकादिभ्य इतच्’ इति इतच् । अग्रहस्तः अग्रश्चासौ हस्तश्चेति समानाधिकरणः समासः । हस्ताग्राग्रहस्तयोर्गुणगुणिनोर्भेदाभेदादिति वामनः । ईदृशेन नाट्योपदेशग्रहणरूपेण । असंनिहिता परोक्षे स्थितेत्यर्थः । भर्त्रा राज्ञा । नीचै राजा एवं वक्तव्यः । तदुक्तं–भट्टेति चाधमैः इति । आमित्यङ्गीकारे । प्रत्यग्रः

बकुलावलिका—स्थाने खलु सज्जति दृष्टिः। अनेनाङ्गुलीयकेन उद्भिन्नकिरणकेसरेण कुसुमित इव तेऽग्रहस्तः प्रतिभाति। (क)

कौमुदिका—सखि कुत्र प्रस्थितासि। (ख)

बकुलावलिका—देव्या वचनेन नाट्याचार्यमार्यगणदासमुपदेशग्रहणे कीदृशी मालविकेति प्रष्टुम्। (ग)

कौमुदिका—सखि ईदृशेन व्यापारेणासंनिहितापि दृष्टा किल सा भर्त्रा। (घ)

बकुलावलिका—आम्। देव्याः पार्श्वगतः स जनश्चित्रे दृष्टः। (ङ)

कौमुदिका—कथमिव। (च)

बकुलावलिका—शृणु। चित्रशालां गता देवी प्रत्यग्रवर्णरागां चित्रलेखामाचार्यस्यावलोकयन्ती तिष्ठति। तस्मिन्नन्तरे भर्तोपस्थितः। (छ)

कौमुदिका—ततस्ततः। (ज)

बकुलावलिका—ततश्चोपचारानन्तरमेकासनोपविष्टेन भर्त्रा चित्रगताया देव्याः परिजनमध्यगतामासन्नतरां (—चरां) तां प्रेक्ष्य देवी पृष्टा। (झ)

(क) ठांणे खु सज्जदि दिट्ठी। इमिणा अङ्गुलीअएण उब्भिण्णकिरणकेसरेण कुसुमिदो विअ दे अग्गहत्थो पडिभादि (ख) हला कहिं पत्थिदा सि। (ग) देवीए वअणेण णट्टाअरिअं अज्जगणदासं उवदेशगहणे कीरिसी मालविअत्ति पुच्छिदुं। (घ) सहि ईरिसेण वावारेण असंणिहिदा वि दिट्ठा किल सा भट्टिणा। (ङ) आम्। देवीए पास्सगदो सो जणो चित्ते दिट्ठो। (च) कहं विअ। (छ) सुणाहि। चित्तसालं गदा देवी पच्चग्गवण्णराअं चित्तलेहं आअरिअस्स ओलोअन्ती चिट्ठदि। तस्सिं अन्तरे भट्टा उवट्ठिदो। (ज) तदो तदो। (झ) तदो अ उवआराणन्तरं एक्कासणोवविट्ठेण भट्टिणा चित्तगदाए देवीए परिअणमज्झगदं आसण्णअरं तं पेक्खिअ देवी पुच्छिदा।

---

१ ठाणे सज्जते दे. २ तुमं कहिं. ३ सुणाहि दे०; देवीए एव्व. ४ नाडआ. ५ दासं देखिदुं...मालविअत्ति. ६ ईदिसव्वा०: दिट्ठा कहं एसा. ७ बि सा कंह भट्टिणा. ८ एतन्नास्ति क्वचित्. ९ अन्ती चिरं; आलोअन्ती जाव चिट्ठदि तहिं दाव भट्टा. १० आसण्णदारिअं; आसण्णपरिचारिणी देक्खिअ.

Bakulāvalikā :—(*Observing it*) Your gaze was riveted on a thing worth-looking at. By means of this ring, with filaments of (streams) of rays breaking forth from it, the forepart of your hand appears, as it were, adorned with flowers.

Kaumudikā :—Friend, where are you going ?

Bakulāvalikā :—I am going, by the order of the Queen herself, to ask the noble Gaṇadāsa, the teacher of dancing, what sort of a pupil Mālavikā has shown herself to be (or how she is progressing) in the matter of receiving instruction.

Kaumudikā :—Friend, though kept out of the way of the King (*lit.* though not near him) by such an employment, she was, I hear, seen by the King.

Bakulāvalikā :—Oh yes, the girl was seen by the Queen's side in a picture.

Kaumuldkā :—How possibly ?

Bakulāvalikā :—Listen. The Queen had gone to the hall of painting and was looking at a painting of the drawing-master's, the hues of the colouring of which were still fresh ; at that time came the King.

Kaumudikā :—What happened then ?

Bakulāvalikā :—Then, after the usual formalities, the King, who sat down on the same seat with the Queen, beholding her (Mālavikā) in the midst of the Queen's attendants and very near to her, asked the Queen.—

वर्णरागः रञ्जनद्रव्यरागो यस्याः । चित्रलेखां चित्रनिर्मितिं देव्या इति शेषः । उपचारानन्तरं भर्त्रागमने उचितादरदर्शनानन्तरम् । नाम एव नामधेयं किं नामधेयं यस्याः सा किंनामधेया । आकृतीनां विशेषा आकृतिविशेषाः । तेषु पदं करोति उत्पद्यते । अवधीरितं प्रत्युत्तरादानेनावगणितं वचनं यस्य । अनुबद्धं निर्बन्धेन प्रष्टुम् । आवुत्तेति । 'भगिनीपतिरावुत्तः' इत्यमरः । बालभावस्य बालबुद्धेः । सदृशं

कौमुदिका—किमिव। (क)

बकुलावलिका—अपूर्वेयं दारिका आसन्ना च देव्या आलिखिता किंनामधेयेति। (ख)

कौमुदिका—आकृतिविशेषेष्वादरः पदं करोति। ततस्ततः। (ग)

बकुलावलिका—ततोऽवधीरितवचनो भर्ता शङ्कितो देवीं पुनः पुनरप्यनुबन्द्धुं प्रवृत्तः। ततो यावद्देवी न कथयति तावत्कुमार्या वसुलक्ष्म्याख्यातम्। आवुत्त एषा मालविकेति। (घ)

कौमुदिका—(सस्मितम्।) सदृशं खलु बालभावस्य। अतः परं कथय। (ङ)

बकुलावलिका—किमन्यत्। सांप्रतं मालविका सविशेषं भर्तुर्दर्शनपथाद्रक्ष्यते। (च)

कौमुदिका—सखि अनुतिष्ठ आत्मनो नियोगम्। अहमप्येतदङ्गुलीयकं देव्या उपनेष्यामि। (इति निष्क्रान्ता।) (छ)

बकुलावलिका—(परिक्रम्यावलोक्य च।) एष नाट्याचार्य आर्यगणदासः संगीतशालातो निष्क्रामति। यावदस्मायात्मानं दर्शयामि। (ज)

(क) किं विअ। (ख) अपुव्वा इअं दारिआ आसण्णा अ देवीए आलिहिदा किंणामहेअत्ति। (ग) आकिदिविसेसेसु आअरो पदं करेदि। तदो तदो। (घ) तदो अवहीरिअवअणो भट्टा सङ्किदो देवीं पुणो पुणो वि अणुबन्धिदुं पवुत्तो। तदो जाव देवी ण कहेदि दाव कुमारीए वसुलच्छीए आचक्खिदं। आवुत्त एसा मालविअत्ति। (ङ) सरिसं खु बालभावस्स। अदो वरं कहेहि। (च) किं अण्णं। संपदं मालविआ सविसेसं भट्टिणो दंसणपहादो रक्खीअदि। (छ) हला अणुचिट्ठ अत्तणो णिओअं। अहं वि एदं अङ्गुलीअअं देवीए उवणइस्सम्। (ज) एसो णट्टाअरिओ अज्जगणदासो संगीदसालादो णिक्कम्मदि। जाव से अत्ताणं दंसेमि।

---

१ किंति. २ अपुव्वरूवा. ३ तुह आसण्णा आलि°; आसण्णलि°. ४ णं आ°. ५ भट्टा देवीं सङ्किदो. ६ णिब्बं°. ७ एतन्नास्ति क्वचित्. ८ अज्ज. ९ दाणिं णि*, णिग्गच्छदि.

Kaumudikā :—What, I pray ?

Bakulāvalikā :—"This is a strange (hitherto unseen—extraordinary) girl and drawn very close to you : what is her name ?"

Kaumudikā :—Extraordinary forms (forms of surpassing loveliness) command respect. What followed then ?

Bakulāvalikā :—Then the King, whose words were disregarded, becoming suspicious, began to importune the Queen again and again. Then, when the Queen did not tell, Princess Vasulakṣmi said, "Sire, she is Mālavikā."

Kaumudikā :—(*with a smile*) That is, indeed, quite in keeping with child-nature. Tell me, what happened next ?

Bakulāvalikā :—What else than this ? Mālavikā is now kept with especial care out of the range of the King's sight.

Kaumudikā :—Friend, go about your errand. I too will take the ring to the Queen.

(*Exit* Kaumudikā.)

Bakulāvalikā :—(*Walking round and looking about*) Here is the noble Gaṇadāsa, the dancing-master, issuing out of the music-hall ; let me show myself (before him).

योग्यम् । दर्शनस्य पन्थाः दर्शनपथः तस्मात् 'अपुव्वा इअं दारिआ' इत्यारभ्य 'दंसणपहादो रक्खीअदि' इत्यन्तेन वाक्यकदम्बकेन गम्यमानो मालविकागोचरो राज्ञोऽभिलाषोऽत्र नाटके बीजमित्यनुसन्धेयम् ॥ अकामानुमतौ कामम् इत्यमरः । कुलविद्या कुलक्रमागता विद्या । मिथ्या अवास्तवं गौरवमादरः । न केवलं कुलविद्येति नाट्ये आदरः किं तु तस्य महत्त्वातिशयादेव । तदेव प्रतिपादयति ॥ **देवानामिति** । मुनयो भरतमतङ्गादय इदं नाट्यं देवानामिन्द्रादीनां क्रतुं यज्ञमामनन्ति । कीदृशम् । कान्तं मनोहरम् । शान्तं सौम्यम् । पशुविशसनादिरहितमित्यर्थः । पुनः कीदृशम् । चाक्षुषं चक्षुरनुभाव्यम् । नयनतृप्तिकरमित्यर्थः । अस्य नाट्यस्य क्रतुत्वनिरूपणं चतुर्वेदसारनाट्यवेदविहितकर्मत्वादिति मन्तव्यम् । तथा च कुमारसंभवे (२-२२)—'कर्म यज्ञः फलं स्वर्गः' इति । अस्य चतु-

(इति परिक्रामति।)

(प्रविश्य।)

गणदासः—कामं खलु सर्वस्यापि कुलविद्या बहुमता। न पुनरस्माकं नाट्यं प्रति मिथ्यागौरवम्। कुतः[1]।

देवानामिदमामनन्ति मुनयः कान्तं[2] क्रतुं चाक्षुषं[3]
रुद्रेणेदमुमाकृतव्यतिकरे स्वाङ्गे[4] विभक्तं द्विधा।
त्रैगुण्योद्भवमत्र लोकचरितं नानारसं दृश्यते
नाट्यं भिन्नरुचेर्जनस्य बहुधाप्येकं समाराधनम्[5]॥ ५॥

बकुलावलिका—(उपेत्य[6]।) आर्य वन्दे। (क)

गणदासः—भद्रे चिरं जीव।

बकुलावलिका—आर्य देवी पृच्छति। अप्युपदेशग्रहणे नातिक्लेशयति वः शिष्या मालविकेति। (ख)

गणदासः—भद्रे विज्ञाप्यतां[7] देवी परमनिपुणा[8] मेधाविनी चेति। किं बहुना।

यद्यत्प्रयोगविषये भाविकमुपदिश्यते[9] मया तस्यै।
तत्तद्विशेषकरणात्प्रत्युपदिशतीव मे बाला॥ ५॥

(क) अज्ज वन्दामि। (ख) अज्जं[10] देवी पुच्छदि। अवि उवदेसग्गहणे णादिकिलेसेदि[11] वो सिस्सा मालविअत्ति।

वेदसारत्वं भारतीये प्रतिपादितम्—'सर्वशास्त्रार्थसंपन्नं सर्वशिल्पप्रदर्शनम्। नाट्यसंज्ञमिमं वेदं सेतिहासं करोम्यहम्॥ एवं संकल्प्य भगवान्सर्वान्वेदाननुस्मरन्। नाट्यवेदं ततश्चक्रे चतुर्वेदाङ्गसंभवम्॥ जग्राह पाठ्यमृग्वेदात्सामभ्यो गीतमेव च। यजुर्वेदादभिनयान्रसानाथर्वणादपि॥ वेदोपवेदसंबद्धो नाट्यवेदो महात्मना॥ एवं भगवता सृष्टो ब्रह्मणा ललितात्मना॥ उत्पाद्य नाट्यवेदं तु ब्रह्मोवाच सुरेश्वरम्' इति। प्रकारान्तरेणाप्यस्य क्रतुत्वं प्रतिपादितम्—'प्रयोगं यश्च कुर्वीत प्रेक्षते चावधानवान्॥ या

---

१ तथा हि. २ शान्तं. ३ चाक्षतम्. ४ स्वाङ्गैः, ५ राधकम्. ६ उपगम्य, उपसृत्य. ७ विभाव्यताम्. ८ परं नि०. ९ उद्दि०. १० अज्जं. ११ किलिस्सदि (क्लिश्यति).

(*Enter* Gaṇadāsa)

Gaṇadāsa :—Granted that every one, of course, thinks highly of his own hereditary lore; but the great regard I have for the dramatic art is not without reason. For,

Sages regard this as an agreeable sacrificial feast to the eyes of the gods; it has been divided in two different ways by Śiva in his body which is blended with that of Umā; herein is seen the behaviour (life) of men arising from the three prime qualities and distinguished (chequered) by various sentiments; Nāṭya (scenic art, or dancing) is mostly the one (chief) amusement of the people (though) of varied tastes. (4)

Bakulāvalikā:—(*Advancing*) Revered sir, I salute you.

Gaṇadāsa :—My good girl, may you live long!

Bakulāvalikā :—Noble Sir, the Queen wishes to know (lit. asks) whether your pupil Mālavikā does not trouble you much in receiving instruction.

Gaṇadasā:—Let the Queen be informed that Mālavikā is exceedingly clever and intelligent; or, in short,

Whatever movement expressive of sentiment is taught by me to her in the way of acting (or dramatic representation), the girl, as it were, teaches me the same in return, by her superior performance of it (*i. e.* by improving upon it). (5)

गतिर्वेदविदुषां या गतिर्यज्ञयाजिनाम् । या गतिर्दानशीलानां तां गतिं प्राप्नुयान्नरः ॥' इति । पुनः कीदृशमिदं नाट्यम् । रुद्रेणेश्वरेणोमाकृतव्यतिकरे उमया पार्वत्या कृतो व्यतिकरः संबन्धो यस्य स तथोक्तस्तस्मिन्स्वाङ्गे आत्मदेहे द्विधा द्विप्रकारेण लास्यताण्डवरूपेण विभक्तं पृथक् कृतम् । तथा चोक्तं संगीतविद्याविनोदे—'उद्दण्डताण्डवमुदञ्चितलास्यलीलां कर्तुं स्वयं युगपदेव समुत्सुकात्मा । यः कामिनीकलितकम्रतरार्धकायः सोऽयं विभाति विभुरादिनटः सुराणाम् ॥' अत्र नाट्ये । त्रैगुण्योद्भवम् त्रयो गुणाः सत्त्वरजस्तमांस्येव त्रैगुण्यम् । चतुर्वर्णादित्वात्स्वार्थे ष्यञ् । तस्मादुद्भवमुद्भूतं लोकचरितं लोकानां लोकस्थानां रामाद्यनुकार्याणां चरितं सुखदुःखमिश्रात्मकं चरितं नानारसं नाना बहुविधा रसाः प्रियतमोपभोग्या यस्मिंस्तत्तथोक्तं दृश्यते ज्ञायते । सामाजिकैरनुभूयते इत्यर्थः । लोकेऽनुकार्यस्य चरितं सुखदुःखमिश्रात्मकमपि नाट्यं

बकुलावलिका—(आत्मगतम्।) अतिक्रामन्तीमिवेरावतीं पश्यामि। (प्रकाशम्।) कृतार्थेदानीं वः शिष्या यस्यां गुरुजन एवं तुष्यति। (क)

गणदासः—भद्रे तद्विधानामसुलभत्वात्पृच्छामि। कुतो देव्याँ तत्पात्रमानीतम्।

बकुलावलिका—अस्ति देव्या वर्णावरो भ्राता वीरसेनो नाम। स भर्त्रा नर्मदातीरेऽन्तपालदुर्गे स्थापितः। तेन शिल्पाधिकारे योग्येयं दारिकेति भगिन्या उपायनं प्रेषिता। (ख)

गणदासः—(स्वगतम्।) आकृतिविशेषप्रत्ययादेनामनूनवस्तुकां संभावयामि। (प्रकाशम्।) भद्रे मयाँ यशस्विना भवितव्यम्। यतः।

पात्रविशेषे न्यस्तं गुणान्तरं व्रजति शिल्पमाधातुः।
जलमिव समुद्रशुक्तौ मुक्ताफलतां पयोदस्य॥ ६॥

(क) अदिक्कँमन्तिं विअ इरावदिं पेक्खामि। किदत्था दाणिं वो सिस्सा जँस्सिं गुरुअणो एव्वं तुस्सदि। (ख) अत्थि देवीए वण्णावरो भादा वीरसेणो णाम। सो भट्टिणा णम्मँदातीरे अन्तवालदुग्गे ट्ठाविदो। तेण सिप्पाहिआरे जोग्गा इअं दारिअत्ति भईणीए उवाअणं पेसिदा।

नटेनाभिनीयमानं सत्सुखरूपेणैव प्रतीयत इति भावः। पुनः कीदृशम्। नाट्यं नटप्रयोगः। एकमप्येकैकमपि भिन्नरुचेर्भिन्ना बहुविधा रुचयः प्रीतयो यस्य स तथोक्तः तस्य जनस्य बहुधा बहुप्रकारेण शृंगारहास्यादिरूपेण समाराधनं संतर्पकम्। तथा चोक्तं भारतीये—'त्रैलोक्यस्यास्य सर्वस्य नाट्यं भावानुकीर्तनम्॥ धर्मो धर्मप्रवृत्तानां कामः कामोपसेविनाम्। अर्थोपजीविनामर्थो धृतिरुद्विग्नचेतसाम्॥ नानाभावोपसंपन्नं नानावस्थान्तरात्मकम्। लोकवृत्तानुकरणं नाट्यमेतन्मया कृतम्॥ एतद्रसेषु भावेषु सर्वकर्मक्रियासु च सर्वोपदेशजननं नाट्यमेतद्भविष्यति॥ न तज्ज्ञानं न तच्छिल्पं नासौ विद्या न सा कला। नासौ योगो न तत्कर्म नाट्येऽस्मिन्यन्न दृश्यते॥' इति। शार्दूलविक्रीडितं वृत्तम्।॥ ४॥ **यद्यदित्यादि**। प्रयोगविषयेऽभिनयार्थे मया तस्यै मालविकायै यद्यद्भाविकं भाववत्। 'अत इनिठनौ' इति ठन्। नृत्यमित्यर्थः।

---

१ देव्याः २ आत्म०. ३ तिविनयप्र०, आकृतिप्र०; इमाम०. ४ मयापि. ५ पश्य. ६ शेषन्य०. ७ इरा० विअ अदि०. ८ जाए. ९ कूले, मन्दाकिनी०. १० भणिअ (भणित्वा) भइ० देवीए; भट्टिणै.

Bakulāvalikā :—(*To herself*) I regard her as if outstripping Irāvatī. (*Aloud*) Blessed is your pupil now with whom her instructor is so well satisfied.

Gaṇadāsa :—My good girl, persons like her are hard to find ; and so I ask you,–whence has the Queen brought such a worthy person ?

Bakulāvalikā :—The Queen has a brother of inferior caste, Vīrasena by name; he has been placed by His Majesty (the King) in command of a frontier fortress on the banks of the Narmadā. He sent this girl as a present to his sister, thinking her to be fit for learning accomplishments (or being initiated in arts).

Gaṇadāsa :—(To *himself*) From the conviction brought to me by the special excellence of her form, I conjecture that she is of good birth (lit. not of inferior descent). (*Aloud*) My good girl, I am sure to become successful (in her case). For,

The skill of the teacher, when imparted to a worthy object (an essentially fit pupil), attains greater excellence, as the water of a cloud when dropping into a sea-shell, acquires the state of (is converted into) a pearl. (6)

यथोक्तम्—‘ आङ्गिकाभिनयप्रायमल्पवाचिकसात्त्विकम् । भावानामास्पदं नृत्यं पदार्थ-व्यञ्जनात्मकम् ॥ ’ इति । उपदिश्यते बोध्यते । तत्तद्विशेषकरणात्तस्य तस्य भाविकस्य विशेषेणातिशयेन करणात् निर्वर्तनात्सा बाला मे प्रत्युपदिशतीव प्रतिबोधयतीव । अनेन तस्या नृत्ये प्रावीण्यातिशयो गम्यते । वाच्या क्रियोत्प्रेक्षालंकारः । आर्या छन्दः । ॥ ५ ॥ अतिक्रामन्तीं शिक्षाग्रहणपाटवेनातिशयानाम् । वर्णेनावरः वर्णावरः । तस्याः पितुर्हीनवर्णभार्यायाः वैश्यकुलोत्पन्नाया जातत्वात् । तेन शिल्पाधिकारे कलाविद्याधिगमे इयं योग्या इति मनसि कृत्वा भगिन्यै देव्या उपायनमुपदा इति प्रेषिता । अनूनवस्तुकामनूनमनल्पं विशिष्टं वस्तु वृत्तं यस्याः सा तथोक्ता तां संभावयामि मन्ये । **पात्रविशेष इति** । आधातुः उपदेष्टुः शिल्पं कुशल [कला] विद्यां पात्रविशेषे विशिष्टपात्रे न्यस्तं [निहितं] सत् गुणान्तरं गुणविशेषं व्रजति प्राप्नोति । अत्रोपमामाह—पयोदस्य मेघस्य जलं समुद्रशुक्तौ न्यस्तं सत् मुक्ताफलतां मौक्तिकत्वमिव । आर्या छन्दः ॥ ६ ॥ **इदानीमित्यादि** । पञ्चाङ्गाभिनयं पञ्च अङ्गानि यस्य तत्तथोक्तम् । प्रेरणमित्यर्थः । तस्याभिनयः प्रयोगः [तम्] इदानीमद्यैवोपदिश्य शिक्षयित्वा । प्रवातं प्रकृष्टो वातो यस्मिन्देशे [स तथोक्तस्तम्] प्रेरणस्याङ्गपञ्चकमुक्तं

बकुलावलिका—अथ कुत्र वः शिष्या। (क)

गणदासः—इदानीमेव पञ्चाङ्गाभिनयमुपदिश्य मया विश्रम्यतामित्यभिहिता दीर्घिकावलोकनगवाक्षगता प्रवातमासेवमाना तिष्ठति।

बकुलावलिका—तेन ह्यनुजानातु मामार्यः। यावदस्या आर्यस्य परितोषनिवेदनेनोत्साहं वर्धयामि। (ख)

गणदासः—दृश्यतां सखी। अहमपि लब्धक्षणः स्वगृहं गच्छामि।

(इति निष्क्रान्तौ।)

मिश्रविष्कम्भः।

(ततः प्रविशत्येकान्तस्थपरिजनो मन्त्रिणा लेखहस्तेनान्वास्यमानो राजा।)

राजा—(अनुवाचितलेखममात्यं विलोक्य।) वाहतर्कं किं प्रतिपद्यते वैदर्भः।

अमात्यः—देव आत्मविनाशम्।

(क) अह कहिं वो सिस्सा। (ख) तेण हिं अणुजाणादु मं अज्जो। जाव से अज्जस्स परितोसणिवेदणेण उच्छाहं वड्ढेमि।

[संगीत] नृत्तरत्नाकरे—'नृत्तं तथा च कैवारो घ[म]मेरो जागरं [बागडं] तथा। गीतं चेति समाख्यातं प्रेरणस्याङ्गपञ्चकम्॥ त्रिभिस्त्वेतत्प्रयोज्यं स्यात्कैवारं [बागडं] जागरं विना॥' इति। चित्ताक्षिभ्रूहस्तपादैरङ्गैश्चेष्टादिसाम्यतः पात्राद्यवस्थाकरणं पञ्चाङ्गोभिनयो मतः॥ इति केचित्। अत्रादिपदेन 'आङ्गिको वाचिकश्चैवमाहार्यः सात्त्विकस्तथा।' इति चतुरङ्गकोपि ग्राह्य इति वाचस्पतिः। अत्र पञ्चाङ्गरूपनृत्तान्तरोपक्रमकथनेन चलितकनृत्तं साकल्येन परिचितं परिशीलितमिति सूच्यते॥ दीर्घिकाया अवलोकनं यस्मात्तथाभूतं गवाक्षं गता। प्रकृष्टो वातः प्रवातः तम्। लब्धक्षणो लब्धः प्राप्तः क्षणो निर्व्यापारस्थितिर्विश्रमो येन स तथोक्तः। स्वगृहमात्मगृहम्॥ मिश्रविष्कम्भः॥ तल्लक्षणम्-वृत्तवर्तिष्यमाणानां कथांशानां निदर्शकः। संक्षिप्तार्थस्तु विष्कम्भ आदावङ्कस्य दर्शितः॥ मध्येन मध्यमाभ्यां वा पात्राभ्यां संप्रयोजितः। शुद्धः स्यात्स

---

१ पञ्चाङ्गमभि०; ०गादिकम०. २ अग्र—पुरो—वार्त. ३ स्थिति. ४ ०तव. ५ अज्ज; आस्मात्प्राक्-अह इं (अथ किम्) इति पुस्तकान्तरे, कहिं दाणिं. ६ हि पुणो. ७ आआरिओ (आचार्यः) ८ अज्जपरि०

Bakulāvalikā :—Well, where is your pupil ?

Gaṇadāsa :—Having just now taught her the five-limb-dance (or acting consisting of five parts), I asked her to rest, and so she has gone to the window which commands a view of the garden-tank, and is enjoying the plentiful breeze.

Bakulāvalikā :—Then your reverence should give me permission (to go), so that I may stimulate her zeal by informing her that your reverence is quite satisfied with her.

Gaṇadāsa :—See your friend. I, too, having got an interval of leisure, will go to my house.

[*Exeunt* Gaṇadāsa *and* Bakulāvalikā.]

(*Here ends the* VIṢKAMBHAKA.)

(*Then enters the* King *with his retinue standing apart and attended by the* Minister, *seated behind with a letter in his hand.*)

King :—(*Looking at the Minister who had read the letter to himself*) :—Vāhataka, what does the King of Vidarbha propose to do ?

Minister :—To destory himself.

तु संकीर्णो नीचमध्यप्रयोजितः ॥ इति ॥ **ततः प्रविशतीत्यादि** । वाहतकेति तस्यामात्यस्य नाम । वैदर्भो विदर्भराजः किं प्रतिपद्यते किं कार्यं मन्यते । संदेशं संदिष्टार्थं श्रोतुमिच्छामि । अनेन वैदर्भेणेदं प्रतिलिखितं प्रत्युत्तरत्वेनाभिलिखितम् । पूज्येन पूज्यार्हेण त्वया अग्निमित्रेणेत्यर्थः । अहं वैदर्भ आदिष्टः आज्ञप्तः । तमेवादेशं विवृणोति—**भवत इत्यादिना** । भवतस्तव पितृव्यपुत्रः पितृभ्रातृसुतो माधवसेनो नाम प्रतिश्रुतसंबन्धः प्रतिश्रुतोऽङ्गीकृतः संबन्धः कन्यका [भगिनी] प्रदानरूपो येन स तथोक्तो ममोपान्तिकं मत्समीपमुपासर्पन् [उपगच्छन्] अन्तरा मध्ये त्वदीयेन त्वत्संबन्धिना । अन्तपालेन सीमादुर्गरक्षकेणावस्कन्द्य पथि प्रहृत्य गृहीतो निरुद्धः । बन्दीकृत इत्यर्थः । स माधवसेनस्त्वया भवता मदपेक्षया मय्यपेक्षा इच्छा । स्नेह इत्यर्थः । तया हेतुना । सकलत्रसोदर्यो भार्याभगिनीसहितः । 'वोपसर्जनस्य' इति सहशब्दस्य सादेशः । मोक्तव्यो विसर्जनीयः । इति समासौ । एतावता वैदर्भेणाग्निमित्रप्रेषितपत्रिकार्थानुवादः कृत इत्यनुसंधेयम् । इतः परं प्रत्युत्तररूपं वैदर्भवचनमुच्यते **तन्न वो विदितमित्यादि** । तद्वक्ष्यमाणं वो युष्माकं विदितं न इत्यत्र काकुरनुसंधेया । तुल्याभिजनेषु समानवंशेषु । भूमिहरेषु ज्ञातिष्वित्यर्थः । राज्ञां वृत्तिर्वर्तनमीदृश्येवंविधेति यत्तन्ननु वो विदितमिति संबन्धः । अतोऽस्मात्कारणादत्रा-

राजा—संदेशं[1]मिदानीं श्रोतुमिच्छामि।

अमात्यः—इदमिदानीमनेन प्रतिलिखितम्। पूज्येनाहमादिष्टः—पितृव्यपुत्रो भवतः कुमारो माधवसेनः प्रतिश्रुतसंबन्धो ममोपान्तिकमु[2]पगच्छन्नन्तरा त्वदीयेनान्तपालेनावस्कद्य गृहीतः। स त्वया मदपेक्षया सकलत्रसोदर्यो मोक्तव्य इति। तन्न[3] वो न विदितं यत्तुल्याभिजनेषु भूमिहरेषु[4] राज्ञां वृत्तिरीदृशी। अतोऽत्र मध्यस्थः। पूज्यो भवितुमर्हति। सोदर्या पुनरस्य ग्रहणविप्लवे विनष्टा। तदन्वेषणाय प्रयतिष्ये। अथो[5]-वश्यमेव माधवसेनो मया पूज्येन मोचयितव्यः श्रूयतामभिसन्धिः।

> **मौर्यसचिवं[6] विमुञ्चति यदि पूज्यः संयतं मम श्यालम्।**
> **मोक्ता माधवसेनं[7] ततोऽहमपि बन्धनात्सद्यः॥ ७॥**

इति।

राजा—(सरोषम्।) कथं कार्यविनिमयेन मयि व्यवहरत्यनात्मज्ञः। वाइर्तक प्रकृत्यमित्रः प्रतिकूलकारी च मे वैदर्भः। तद्यातव्यपक्षे स्थितस्य पूर्व[9]संकल्पितसमुन्मूलनाय वीरसेनप्रमुखं दण्डचक्रमाज्ञापय।

अमात्यः—यदाज्ञापयति देवः।

राजा—अथ वा किं भवान्मन्यते।

स्मिन्नर्थे पूज्यो भवान्मध्यस्थः समो भवितुमर्हति। अस्य माधवसेनस्य सोदर्या पुनः स्वसा पुनर्ग्रहणविप्लवे [ग्रहणसंमर्दे] विनष्टा तिरोहिता। तदन्वेषणाय तस्य अन्वेषणाय गवेषणाय प्रयतिष्ये। अथ वेति पक्षान्तरे। माध्यस्थ्यत्यागे इत्यर्थः। मोचयितव्यस्त्याजयितव्यः। अभिसंधिर्निश्चयः। **मौर्यसचिवमित्यादि।** पूज्यो भवान्संयतं त्वया निगडितं मम श्यालं पत्नीभ्रातरं मौर्यसचिवं मौर्यसचिवनामानं विमुञ्चति यदि त्यजति चेत् ततस्तस्मात्कारणान्मया सद्यः सपदि माधवसेनो बन्धनान्निगडान्मोक्ता मुक्तो भविता। मुञ्चतेः कर्मणि लुट्॥ ७॥ इति लिखितार्थसमाप्तौ। प्रकृत्यमित्रः स्वभावतः शत्रुः। अत्र प्रकृत्यमित्रत्वं च विषयानन्तरत्वा-

---

१ लिखितं सं., निर्देशं, निदे०. २ उपसर्पन्; आगच्छन्. ३ तन्न वो विदितं यत्तुल्याभिजनेषु भूमेरिव राज्ञां प्रवृत्तिः; एतन्ननु वो विदितं...जनेषु राज्ञाः प्रवृत्तिरीदृक्; तत्र बो न विदितं. ४ भूमिधरेषु. ५ अथ वा. ६ आर्यस०; मौद्गल० मुञ्चति. ७ सेनस्ततो मया (टी०) ८ ०तव ९ पूर्वं; ०ल्पितमुन्मू०.

King:—I want to hear his despatch now.

Minister:—He has, on the present occasion, sent the following reply: "The illustrious one (i. e. Agnimitra) wrote to me, 'Your cousin, Prince Mādhavasena, who had promised to enter into a matrimonial alliance with me, was, while coming to me, on the way attacked by your frontier guard and taken prisoner. He, with his wife and sister, should be ordered to be set free by you out of regard for me.' Now, you know full well that such is the course of action of kings with respect to relatives of equal descent; therefore, the honoured one (i. e. Agnimitra) should assume a neutral position in this matter; as for the prince's sister, she disappeared in the confusion of the capture; I will do my utmost to find her. Now if your Majesty wishes that Mādhavasena should necessarily be caused to be set at liberty, please mark the terms:—

If the revered one will set my brother-in-law, the Maurya-minister free, whom he has imprisoned, then I will immediately release Mādhavasena from confinement." (7)

These are the contents of the letter.

King:—(*In rage*) How, does the foolish fellow deal with me by (proposing) an exchange of services? Vāhataka! the king of Vidharba is my natural enemy, and has acted adversely towards me; therefore, give orders to the army-corps under the command of Virasena, for the extermination as already determined upon, of him who is regarded on the side of my foes (*lit.* those who deserve to be marched against or attacked.)

Minister:—As your Majesty commands.

King:—Or what do you think about it yourself?

दिति मन्तव्यम् ॥ **अचिराधिष्ठितेत्यादि** । अचिरात् अधिष्ठितं प्राप्तं राज्यं येन स तथोक्तः। नवो राजेत्यर्थः। प्रकृतिषु प्रजासु अरूढमूलत्वात्। रूढं मूलं यस्य स रूढमूलः। लब्धप्रजानुराग इत्यर्थः। तथा न भवतीति अरूढमूलः। तस्य भावः तत्त्वं तस्मात्। समुद्धर्तुमुन्मूलयितुं सुकरः सुलभः। क इव। नवं यत्संरोहणं तेन शिथिलः श्लथः तरुः इव। पूर्णोपमालंकारः। आर्या वृत्तम् ॥ ८॥ तेनारूढमूलत्वेन हेतुना तन्त्रकारवचनमर्थशास्त्रकारवचनमवितथं हि सत्यमेव। भविष्यतीति शेषः।

अमात्यः—शास्त्रदृष्टमाह देवः। कुतः[१]—

अचिराधिष्ठितराज्यः शत्रुः प्रकृतिष्वरूढमूलत्वात्।
नवसंरोहे[२]णशिथिलस्तरुरिव सुकरः समुद्धर्तुम्॥ ८॥

राजा—तेन ह्यवितथं तन्त्रकारवचनम्। इदमेव[३] निमित्त[४]मादाय समुद्योज्यतां[५] सेनापतिः[६]।

अमात्यः—तथा। (इति निष्क्रान्तः।)

(परिजनश्च यथाव्यापारं राजानमभितः स्थितः।)

(प्रविश्य।)

विदूषकः—आज्ञप्तोऽस्मि तत्रभवता राज्ञा। गौतम चिन्तय तावदुपायं यथा मे यदृच्छादृष्टप्रतिकृतिर्मालविका प्रत्यक्षदर्शना भवतीति। मयापि तत्तथा कृतम्। यावदस्मै निवेदयामि (इति परिक्रामति।) (क)

राजा—(विदूषकं दृष्ट्वा।) अयमपरः कार्यान्तरसचिवोऽस्मानुपस्थितः।

विदूषकः—(उपसृत्य[७]।) वर्धतां भवान्। (ख)

राजा—(सशिरःकम्पम्।) इत आस्यताम्।

(विदूषक उपविष्टः।)

वयस्य कच्चि[८]दुपेयोपायदर्शने व्यापृतं ते प्रज्ञाचक्षुः।

विदूषकः—प्रयोगसिद्धिं पृच्छ। (ग)

राजा—कथमिव।

विदूषकः—(कर्णे।) एवमिव। (घ)

(क) आणत्तो ह्मि तत्तहोदा रण्णा। गोदम चिन्तेहि दाव उवाअं जहा मे जदिच्छादिठ्ठप्पदिकिदी मालविआ पच्चक्खंदसणा होदित्ति। मए[९] वि तत्तहा किदं। दाव[१०] से णिवेदेमि (ख) वड्ढदु भवं। (ग) प[११]ओअसिद्धिं पुच्छ। (घ) एव्वमिव[१२]।

---

१ एतन्नास्ति क्वचित्. २ रोपण. ३ एव वचनम्. ४ मुपादाय. ५ समुद्यज्युतां. ६ सेनाधिपतिः. ७ उपगम्य. ८ कच्चिदपाय०; अपि किंचित् उपायोपेय. ९ मए अ १० जाव. ११ आः पओ०. १२ इत्यावेदयति–इत्यधिक क्वचित्.

Minister :—Your Majesty says (just) what is prescribed in the Sāstras. For,

An enemy, that has but recently occupied a kingdom, is very easy to extirpate, owing to his not having taken root in (the hearts of) his subjects, like a tree infirm on account of its being lately planted. (8)

King :—Then the words of the writer of the treatise on politics must prove true ! Let the General be ordered to start on the campaign, setting this forth as an excuse,

Minister :—So it will be done. [*Exit* Minister].

(The retinue remain standing round the King according to their respeciive duties).

(Enter the VIDŪṢAKA. *)*

Vidūṣaka :—I was ordered by His Majesty : "Gautama, devise some expedient by which I shall obtain the actual sight of Mālavikā whose picture was seen by me by accident". I too have done that accordingly and will now inform him of the fact.

(He walks about.)

King :— *(Seeing the* VIDŪṢAKA). Here is another minister coming to me having charge of another department of my affairs.

Vidūṣaka :—*(Approaching)* May your Honour prosper !

King :—*(With a nod of his head)* Sit down here.

(The Vidūṣaka *sits down.)*

Friend, has the eye of your talent been employed in devising a means of attaining our desired object ?

Vidūṣaka :—(Rather) ask about the success of the device.

King :—How do you mean ?

Vidūṣaka :—(*Whispers in his ear*) Thus, it is.

हिशब्दोऽवधारणे । ' हि हेताववधारणे ' इत्यमरः । इदमेव वैदर्भस्य कार्यविनिमयरूपमेव वचनं वाक्यं निमित्तं हेतुमुपादायावलम्ब्य समुद्योज्यतां प्रवर्त्यताम् ॥ आज्ञप्त इति । यदृच्छया अकस्माद् दृष्टा प्रतिकृतिर्यस्याः । अत्र गम्यमानं राज्ञो मालविकादर्शनौत्सुक्यमारम्भो नाम प्रथमावस्थेति मन्तव्यम् । अत्र बीजारम्भयोः समन्वयान्मुखसंधिरित्यनुसंधेयम् ॥ अन्यत्कार्यं कार्यान्तरं तत्र सचिवः उपेयोपायदर्शने

राजा—साधु वयस्य निपुणमुपक्रान्ता । इदानीं दुरधिगमसिद्धावप्यस्मिन्नारम्भे वयं[1]माशंसामहे । कुतः ।

अर्थं[2] सप्रतिबन्धं प्रभुरधिगन्तुं सहायवानेव ।
दृश्यं तमसि न पश्यति दीपेन विना सचक्षुरपि ॥ ९ ॥

(नेपथ्ये ।)

अलमलं बहु विकत्थ्य । राज्ञः समक्षमेवा[3]वयोरधरोत्तरव्यक्तिर्भविष्यति ।

राजा—(आकर्ण्य ।) सखे त्वत्सुनीतिपादपस्य पुष्प[4]मुद्भिन्नम् ।

विदूषकः—फलमप्यचिरेण द्रक्ष्य[5]सि । (क)

(ततः प्रविशति कञ्चुकी ।)

कञ्चुकी—देव अमात्यो विज्ञापयति । अनुष्ठिता प्रभोरा[6]ज्ञेति । एतौ पुनर्हरदत्तगणदासौ—

उभावभिनयाचार्यौ परस्परजयो[7][8]द्यतौ ।
त्वां द्रष्टुमिच्छतः साक्षाद्भावाविव शरीरिणौ[9] ॥ १० ॥

राजा—प्रवेशय तौ ।

कञ्चुकी—यदाज्ञापयति देवः । (इति निष्क्रम्य पुनस्ताभ्यां सह प्रविश्य ।) इत इतो भवन्तौ ।

हरदत्तः—(राजानमवलोक्य[10]) अहो दुरासदो राजमहिमा । तथा हि ।

(क) फलं वि अइरेण[11] देक्खिस्ससि ।

उपेयस्य साध्यस्य मालविकासाक्षाद्दर्शनस्योपायदर्शने साधनज्ञाने ते प्रज्ञाचक्षुः प्रतिभादृष्टिः किंचिदीषदपि व्यापृतं प्रसृतम् । अपिः प्रश्ने । अत्र गम्यमानस्य मालविकारूपस्य [–काभिलाषस्य] बीजस्य विन्यासादुपक्षेपो नाम संध्यङ्गमुक्तं भवति । **कर्णे**–एतद्वचनं नियतश्राव्यावान्तरभेदस्य गुह्यतरार्थस्य प्रयोगे कविना प्रयुक्तम् । तथोक्तम्–'कर्णे एवमिवेत्युक्त्वा ज्ञाप्यः पश्चात्प्रसङ्गतः ।' इति ॥ **इदानीमित्यादि** । अस्मि–

---

१ आशास्महे. २ सप्रतिबन्धं कार्यं. ३ मेवाधरोत्तमतोः, अधरोत्तरयोः, ४ कुसुमं ५. द्रक्ष्यते ६ राजा. ७ जयैषिणौ. ८ मुद्यतौ. ९ विवादिनौ. १० विलोक्य. ११ एतन्नास्ति बहुषु पुस्तकेषु

King :—Excellent, my friend ! You have made a clever start ! Now we entertain hopes in this enterprise, though success in it is difficult to be attained. For,

It is only the man having an assistant that is able to gain an object hampered by obstacles ; even one having eyes, cannot, without a light, perceive an object in the darkness. (9)

(*A voice behind the scenes*) Enough, enough of your excessive boasting. In the presence of the King himself will be manifest (decided) which of us is superior and which inferior.

King :—(*Having heard*) Friend, a flower has shot forth on your tree of intrigue.

Vidūṣaka :—Very soon you shall see its fruit also.

(*Then Enter the* Chamberlain.)

Chamberlain :—Your Majesty, the Minister begs to inform you that your orders have been executed. But here are Haradatta and Gaṇadāsa,—

The two preceptors of acting, each eager for victory over the other, (who) wish to see you like two (dramatic) sentiments in bodily form. (10)

King :—Introduce them.

Chamberlain :—As your Majesty commands. (*Going out and returning with them*) This way, this way, gentlemen.

Haradatta :—(*Looking at the* King) Awful (lit. unapproachable) is the majesty (splendour) of the king. For,

---

न्नारम्भे मालविकासाक्षाद्दर्शनोद्योगे दुरधिगमसिद्धौ दुर्लभसिद्धावपि इदानीं त्वद्वचनश्रवणानन्तरं वयमाशंसामहे सिद्धिमपेक्षामहे ॥ **अर्थमित्यादि** । प्रतिबन्धेन सहितं सप्रतिबन्धं सप्रतिरोधमर्थं प्रयोजनमधिगन्तुं लब्धुं सहायवानेव जनः प्रभुः समर्थो भवति । सचक्षुरपि जनः तमसि दृश्यमर्थं दीपेन विना अलब्धदीपसहायो न पश्यति । 'इदानीम्' इत्यादिना 'सहायवानेव' इत्यन्तेन तस्य बीजस्य बहुलीकरणात्परिकर इति संध्यङ्गमुक्तं भवति ॥ ९ ॥ **नेपथ्य इत्यादि** । बहु विकत्थ्यात्मश्लाघां कृत्वालम् । अलमिति प्रतिषेधे । 'अलंखल्वोः प्रतिषेधयोः प्राचां क्त्वा' इति क्त्वाप्रत्ययः ॥ फलमप्यचिरेण द्रक्ष्यसि । अत्र बीजस्य दृढीकरणात्परिन्यासो नाम

न च न परिचितो न चाप्यगम्यं-
श्चकितमुपैमि तथापि पार्श्वमस्य।
सलिलनिधिरिव प्रतिक्षणं मे
भवति स एव नवो नवोऽयमक्ष्णोः ॥ ११ ॥

गणदासः—महत्खलु पुरुषोकारमिदं ज्योतिः। तथा हि।

द्वारे नियुक्तपुरुषानुमतप्रवेशः
सिंहासनान्तिकचरेण सहोपसर्पन्।
तेजोभिरस्य विनिवर्तितदृष्टिपातै-
र्वाक्याद्दते पुनरिव प्रतिवारितोऽस्मि ॥ १२ ॥

कञ्चुकी—एष देवः। उपसर्पतां भवन्तौ।

उभौ—(उपेत्य।) विजयतां देवः।

राजा—स्वागतं भवद्भ्याम्। (परिजनं विलोक्य।) आसने तावदत्रभवतोः।

(उभौ परिजनोपनीतयोरासनयोरुपविष्टौ।)

राजा—किमिदं शिष्योपदेशकाले युगपदाचार्ययोरुपस्थानम्।

गणदासः—देव श्रूयताम्। मया तीर्थादभिनयविद्या शिक्षिता। दत्तप्रयोगश्चास्मि। देवेन देव्या च परिगृहीतः।

संध्यङ्गमुक्तं भवति ॥ उभावित्यादि। परस्परस्य जयः तत्रोद्यतौ। उभौ अभिनयाचार्यौ शरीरिणौ मूर्तौ साक्षाद्भावौ प्रत्यक्षभावाविव नृत्याभिनयार्थाविव ॥ स्थितौ त्वां द्रष्टुमिच्छतः ॥ १० ॥ न च नेत्यादि। अयं राजा परिचितः संस्तुतश्च न भवतीति न। किं तु परिचित एव। अगम्यः अनाश्रयणीयः अरम्योऽसौम्यश्च न। किं तु [गम्यः] रम्य एव। तथापि चकितं सभयं यथा भवति तथास्य पार्श्वं समीपमुपैमि। स एवायं सलिलनिधिः समुद्र इव परिचितोपि प्रतिक्षणं अक्ष्णोः नवो नवः अपूर्वो भवति ॥ ११ ॥ द्वारे इत्यादि। द्वारे नियुक्तः पुरुषः दौवारिकः तेन अनुमतः प्रवेशः यस्य। सिंहासनस्यान्तिके चरतीति तेन कञ्चुकिना। विनिवर्तितः दृष्टिपातः यैः तैः विनिवर्तितदृष्टिपातैर्विनिवारितदृष्टिप्रसरैरस्य राज्ञस्तेजोभिः पुनः प्रभाविशेषैस्तु वाक्याद्दते प्रतिषेधवाक्यं विना प्रतिवारित इव निरुद्ध इवास्मि ॥ १२ ॥

---

१ प्यरम्यः. २ षाधिकार. ३ भिमत. ४ आचार्याभ्यामत्र. ५ स्रुतौ०. ६ दृष्टप्रयोगोऽस्मि देव्या। देवेन च परिगृहीतः, दत्तप्रयोगो दत्तानुयोगश्चास्मि।

He is neither unfamiliar to me, nor is he difficult to be approached; and yet I approach his side with trembling; though the same, he appears every moment new to my eyes, even like the mighty ocean. (11)

Gaṇadāsa :—Powerful, indeed, is this lustre in the form of man. For,

I, with my entrance permitted by the man appointed to keep guard at the door, and advancing with the person in close attendance upon the throne, am again prohibited, as it were (from entering), without words, by his effulgence which repels my glance. (12)

Chamberlain :—Here is His Lordship. Your honours may approach.

Both :—(*Advancing*) May the king be victorious (prosper) !

King :—Welcome, gentlemen. (*Looking at the attendants*) Just two seats for the gentlemen.

(*Both sit down on seats brought by the attendants*).

King :—What means this simultaneous coming of preceptors, when it is the time to give instruction to the pupils?

Gaṇadāsa :—May you listen, my Lord; I learned the art of acting from a competent teacher. I have given practical lessons in the art (of dramatic representation). I have been favoured (patronized) by Your Majesty and the Queen, as well.

तीर्थादित्यादि । तीर्थाद्विशिष्टाद्गुरोरभिनयविद्या नाट्यविद्या शिक्षिता अभ्यस्ता । दत्तप्रयोगश्चास्मि । दत्तः शिष्येभ्यः प्रतिपादितः प्रयोगो विनियोगो येन स तथोक्तः ॥ न केवलमागमं किं तु तस्य क्रियासंक्रान्तिमपि जानामीत्यर्थः । अधिक्षिप्तः भर्त्सितः । परिवादो निन्दा । विमृशतु तारतम्यभावेन पर्यालोचयतु । अधरोत्तरतया निश्चिनोतु इत्यर्थः प्रथमः कल्पो मुख्यः पक्षः ॥ न्यायादनपेतः न्याय्यो युक्तः । व्यवहारो विवादः निर्णय इति यावत् । संरम्भे संघर्षे । कथं पश्यसि कथं मन्यसे । अनयोः कतरस्य पराजयं विचारयसीत्यर्थः । **अलं स्वपक्षेत्यादि** । अत्र परिव्राजिकायाः स्त्रीत्वात्प्राकृते प्राप्ते संस्कृताश्रयणं लिङ्गित्वादिति मन्तव्यम् । तथा चोक्तम्— 'देवद्विजनरेन्द्राणां लिङ्गिनां संस्कृतं वचः' इति ॥ स्वपक्षस्य गणदासस्य अवसादः पराजय इत्यर्थः । तस्य शङ्का तया ।

राजा—इदं[1] जाने। ततः किम्।

गणदासः—सोऽहममुना हरदत्तेन प्रधानपुरुषसमक्षं[2] नायं मे पादरजसाऽपि[3] तुल्य इत्यधिक्षिप्तः।

हरदत्तः—देव अयमेव मयि प्रथमं परिवादकरः[4]। अत्रभवतः किल मम च समुद्रपल्वलयोरिवान्तरमिति[5]। तदत्रभवानिमं मां च शास्त्रे प्रयोगे च विमृशतु। देव एव नौ विशेषज्ञः प्राश्निकः[6]।

विदूषकः—समर्थं प्रतिज्ञातम्। (क)

गणदासः—प्रथमः कल्पः। अवहितो देवः श्रोतुमर्हति।

राजा—तिष्ठतु[7] तावत्। पक्षपातमत्र देवी मन्यते। तत्तस्याः[8] पण्डितकौशिक्या[9] सहितायाः समक्षमेव न्याय्यो व्यवहारः।

विदूषकः—सुष्ठु भवान्भणति। (ख)

आचार्यौ—यद्देवाय रोचते।

राजा—मौद्गल्य अमुं प्रस्तावं निवेद्य पण्डितकौशिक्या सार्धमाहूयतां देवी।

(क) समत्थं पइण्णादं। (ख) सुठ्ठ भवं भणादि।

राजपरिग्रहोऽस्य हरदत्तस्य प्रधानत्वमुपहरति। **अयीति**—अत्रभवत्या राज्ञीपदभाक्त्वादुभयोस्तुल्यत्वमित्यर्थः। **अतिमात्रेत्यादि**। अनलः अग्निः भानोः सूर्यस्य परिग्रहात् निशि स्वस्मिन् तेजः संक्रमात् अतिमात्रमत्यन्तं भासुरत्वं दिवातनवह्न्यपेक्षया तेजस्वितां पुष्यति धारयतीत्यर्थः। तथा च श्रुतिः–'आदित्यो वा अस्तं यन्नग्निं प्रविशति' इत्यादि। महिमानं तेजःप्रकर्षम्॥ १२॥ पी०मर्दो नाम कामपुरुषार्थसहायो नायकसमीपवर्ती पुरुषः कथ्यते। तथा चोक्तम्–'पीठमर्दः समीपस्थः कार्यालोचनकोविदः' इति। अत्र विदूषकः परिहासेन परिव्राजिकायां पण्डितकौशिक्यां तद्धर्ममारोपयतीति मन्तव्यम्। **मङ्गलेत्यादि**। मङ्गलालंकृता मङ्गलं शोभनं यथा भवति तथालंकृता भूषितैषा धारिणी यतिवेषया यतेः परिव्राजकस्य वेष इव वेषः

---

१ बाढम्. २ क्षमयं मे ०रजसा तुल्यः, अयं न मम. ३ रजसा. ४ रतः ५ मस्तीति. ६ ०कश्च. ७ तिष्ठ यावत्. ८ तदस्याः. ९ शिकीस०.

King :—I know it well. What, then ?

Ganadāsa:—I, a man with such antecedents, was insulted by this Haradatta in the presence of the chief men of the court, saying: "This man is not equal even to the dust on my feet".

Haradatta :—My Lord, he himself was the first to indulge in abuse of me thus : "In truth, there is the same difference between your honour and myself that there is between the ocean and a puddle." Let Your Majesty, therefore, be pleased to examine him and me in theoretical knowledge and in practical skill (in theory and practice). Your Majesty alone is a critical judge (connoisseur) of us both.

Vidūṣaka :—A fair proposal.

Gaṇadāsa :—An excellent idea (alternative). Your Majesty will be pleased to listen to us with all attention.

King :—Stop a while ; the Queen may suspect (consider it) partiality in this matter ; therefore, the case had better be tried in the presence of the Queen accompanied by the learned Kaus′ikī.

Vidūṣaka :—Your Majesty says what is right.

The two Professors :—Just as Your Majesty pleases.

King :—Maudgalya, call the Queen, together with the revered Kaus′ikī, having informed them of this occasion (turn of events).

काषायादिधारणं यस्याः सा तथोक्ता तया कौशिक्या समं सार्धं भाति प्रकाशते । अत्रोपमामाह–विग्रहवत्या शरीरिण्याध्यात्मविद्यया समं त्रयीव वेदत्रयीव । विग्रहवती-त्यत्रापि विभक्तिविपरिणामेन योजनीयम् ॥ १४ ॥ **महासारेति** । महासारप्रसवयोः । महान् सारो वरः प्रसवः संतानो ययोस्ते तयोः । यद्वा महान् सारो बलं यस्य तथा-भूतः प्रसवः अपत्यं यस्याः । पक्षे महता आसारेण धारासंपातेन सह प्रसवः धान्या-द्युत्पत्तिर्यस्याः तयोः । सदृशक्षमयोः सदृशी समाना क्षमा सहिष्णुत्वं ययोस्ते तयोः । शरदां शतं शरच्छतम् । 'कालाध्वनोरत्यन्तसंयोगे' इति द्वितीया । श्लेषालंकारः । आशीरलंकारश्च ॥ १५ ॥ आर्यपुत्रः–आर्यपुत्रेति संबोध्यः पतिः पत्नीजनेन वा । इति भरतः । संघर्षः स्पर्धा अस्त्यनयोस्तौ संघर्षिणौ । अत इनिठनौ इति मत्वर्थे इनिः ।

कञ्चुकी—यदाज्ञापयति देवः। (इति निष्क्रम्य सपरिव्राजिकया देव्या[1] सह प्रविष्टः।) इत इतो देवी[2]।

देवी—(परिव्राजिकां विलोक्य।) भगवति हरदत्तस्य गणदासस्य च संरम्भे[3] कथं पश्यसि। (क)

परिव्राजिका—अलं स्वपक्षावसादशङ्कया[4]। न परिहीयते प्रतिद्वन्द्विनो[5] गणदासः।

देवी—यद्यप्येवं तथापि राजपरिग्रहोऽस्य प्रधानत्वमुपहरति। (ख)

परिव्राजिका—अयि राज्ञीशब्दभाजनमात्मानमपि[6] तावच्चिन्तयतु भवती। पश्य।

> **अतिमात्रभासुरत्वं[7] पुष्यति भानोः परिग्रहादनलः[8]।**
> **अधिगच्छति महिमानं चन्द्रोऽपि निशापरिगृहीतः॥ १३॥**

विदूषकः—अपिहा[9] अपिहा। उपस्थिता पीठमर्दिकां पण्डितकौशिकीं पुरस्कृत्य देवी धारिणी। (ग)

राजा—पश्याम्येनाम्। यैषा

> **मङ्गलालंकृता भाति कौशिक्या यतिवेषया।**
> **त्रयी विग्रहवत्येव सममध्यात्मविद्यया॥ १४॥**

(क) भअवदि हरदत्तस्य गणदासस्य अ संरम्भे कहं पेक्खसि। (ख) जइवि एव्वं तह वि राअपरिग्गहो से पहाणत्तणं उवहरइ। (ग) अविह अविहं[10]। उवट्ठिदा पीठमद्दिअं पण्डिअकोसिइं पुरोकरिअ देवी धारिणी।

विज्ञाने शिल्पज्ञाने संघर्षिणौ तयोः। 'विज्ञानं शिल्पशास्त्रयोः' इत्यमरः। प्राश्निकपदं सभ्यस्थानम्। उपालम्भेन परिहासेन। ग्रामे अनभिज्ञजनवासे इत्यर्थः। पण्डा सूक्ष्मा बुद्धिः संजाता अस्याः असौ पण्डिता। पण्डिता चासौ कौशिकी च। मध्यस्था समानोभयपक्षा। अपक्षपातिनीति यावत्। प्रयोगप्रधानं प्रयोगः अभिनयः प्रधानः पटुत्वनिश्चये यत्र तत्। वाग्व्यवहारेण विवादेन। नाट्यशास्त्रप्रावीण्यं केव-

---

१ परि० देव्या च २ भवती; देवी धारिणी. ३ ०म्भं. ४ पक्षपातश० ५ प्रतिवादिनः—ना; न च पराजीयते केनचिद् गण० ६ त्मानं नानुचिन्तयति. ७ भास्व०; भानुः परिग्रह्याहद: ८ दहनः. ९ अयि भो— १० अह्हि भो उव०

Chamberlain :—Just as Your Majesty commands. (*With these words he goes out, and returns with the* Queen *accompanied by the* Parivrājikā). This way, this way, Your Majesty.

Queen :—(*Looking at the* Parivrājikā) Revered lady, what do you think of this contest between Gaṇadāsa and Haradatta ?

Parivrājikā :—Enough of (do not) fear about your *prote'ge'* (*lit.* side) being defeated ; Gaṇadāsa is in no way inferior to his antagonist.

Queen:—Even though it is so, still the favour of the King gives his rival the advantage (or superiority).

Parivrājikā :—Ah ! Consider at the same time that you too are the holder of the title of Queen.

While the fire attains extreme brilliancy by its being assisted by the sun, the moon, too, acquires greatness when favoured by the night. (13)

Vidūṣaka :—Look ! Look ! Here comes the Queen preceded by the learned Kaus'ikī, her companion (**पीठमर्दिका**).

King :—I see her, who, indeed,—

Decorated with auspicious ornaments, and accompanied by Kaus'ikī in the dress of an ascetic, appears like the triad of the Vedas incarnate, accompanied by metaphysical lore (the knowledge of the Supreme Soul). (14)

लेन विवादेन निर्णेतुं न शक्यते इत्यर्थः । समाना विद्या यस्य स समानविद्यः तस्मात् । हरदत्तादित्यर्थः । परिभवनीयं पराभवक्षमम् । उरभ्रसंपातं मेषयुद्धमिति नर्मोक्तिः । 'मेढ्रोरभ्रोरणोर्णायुर्मेषवृष्णय एडके' इत्यमरः । उदरंभरिसंवादमिति पाठे उदरम्भर्योः स्वोदरभरणपरयोः संवादम् । कलहितयोराचरितकलहयोः । सुष्ठु इत्यस्य भावः सौष्ठवं सौष्ठवेनाभिनयः । स्वांगे सौष्ठवाभिनयः तम् । प्रत्याययितव्यं प्रतीतिविषयीकर्तव्यम् । **शिष्टेत्यादि** । कस्यचित्कस्यापि पुरुषस्य क्रिया शिक्षा । विद्याभ्यास इत्यर्थः । आत्मसंस्था आत्मनिष्ठा सती शिष्टा प्रकृष्टा श्लिष्टा संगता । रम्या भवतीत्यर्थः अन्यस्य पुरुषस्य संक्रान्तिः शिष्येषु क्रियासंक्रमणम् । संक्रान्तिशब्दोऽत्रान्तर्भावितण्यर्थः । विशेषयुक्ता अतिशयवती । यस्य पुरुषस्योभयं आत्मसिद्धिः परसंक्रमणं च साधु रम्यं स पुरुष एव शिक्षकाणामुपदेशकानां धुर्यग्रे प्रतिष्ठापयितव्यः प्रतिष्ठां प्रापयितव्यः ।

परिव्राजिका—(उपेत्य।) विजयतां देवः।

राजा—भगवति अभिवादये।

परिव्राजिका—

महासारप्रसवयोः सदृशक्षमयोर्द्वयोः।
धारिणीभूतधारिण्योर्भव भर्ता शरच्छतम्॥ १५॥

धारिणी—जयत्वार्यपुत्रः। (क)

राजा—स्वागतं देव्यै। (परिव्राजिकां विलोक्य।) भगवति क्रियतामासनपरिग्रहः।

(सर्वे यथोचितमुपविशन्ति।)

राजा—भगवति अत्रभवतोर्हरदत्तगणदासयोः परस्परं विज्ञानसंघर्षो जातः। तदत्र भगवत्या प्राश्निकपदमध्यासितव्यम्।

परिव्राजिका—(सस्मितम्।) अलमुपालम्भेन। पत्तने विद्यमानेऽपि ग्रामे रत्नपरीक्षा।

राजा—मा मैवम्। पण्डितकौशिकी खलु भगवती। पक्षपातिनावनयोरहं देवी च।

आचार्यौ—सम्यगाह देवः। मध्यस्था भगवती गुणदोषौ नः परिच्छेत्तुमर्हति।

राजा—तेन हि प्रस्तूयतां विवादः।

परिव्राजिका—देव प्रयोगप्रधानं हि नाट्यशास्त्रम्। किमत्र वाग्व्यवहारेण। कथं वा देवी मन्यते।

देवी—यदि मां पृच्छसि एतयोर्विवाद एव न मे रोचते। (ख)

(क) जेदु अज्जउत्तो। (ख) जइ मं पुच्छसि एदाणं विवादो एव्व ण मे रोअदि।

---

१ यथार्हमु० २ परस्परेण, रेण ज्ञान०, परस्परवि०; विज्ञानसंघर्षिणोर्भगवत्या; तदत्रभवत्या. ३ सति. ४ क्षकाः. ५ नैतदेवम्. ६ गुणदोषतः, ७ प्रक्रियताम्. ८ विवादवस्तु. ९ राजा—कथं वेत्या०

Parivrājikā :—(*Advancing*) May the King be victorious !

King :—Revered lady, I salute thee.

Parivrājikā :—

Mayest thou be for a hundred years the lord of Dhāriṇī and of the Earth, the support of living creatures ; the two, whose progeny is of great vigour aad whose (power of) forbearance is worthy of themselves. (15)

Queen :—May my Lord prosper !

King :—Welcome to the queen ! (*Looking towards the* Parivrājikā) Revered lady, you will be pleased to take a seat.

(*They all sit down in due order.*)

King :—Revered lady, a dispute about superiority in knowledge has arisen between Gaṇadāsa and Haradatta ; your reverence, therefore, must occupy the position of judge in this matter.

Parivrājikā :—(*With a smile*) Spare your taunt. When a town is accessible, should a jewel be tested in a village ?

King :—Not so, not so. You are indeed the "Learned Kaus'ikī," whereas the Queen and I are interested parties with respect to these two (Haradatta and Gaṇadāsa).

The Two Professors:—His Majesty has spoken truly. Your reverence being in a neutral position should be pleased to decide (as to) our merits or deficiencies.

King :—Then let the discussion begin (be opened).

Parivrājikā:—My Lord, the art of dancing consists chiefly in practical demonstration (representation) ; what is the use of a verbal controversy ? Or, what does her Ladyship think of this ?

Queen :—If you ask me, I do not at all like the very dispute between these two.

एवमाभ्यामात्मसंस्था क्रिया शिष्यसंक्रान्तिश्च प्रत्याययितव्ये । तत्र आत्मसंस्था क्रिया प्रतीतपूर्वैव । अतः शिष्यसंक्रान्तिरेव केवलाधुना प्रत्याययितव्येति स्थितमिति तात्पर्यार्थः । उपजातिश्छंदः ॥ १६ ॥ एष पिण्डितार्थः निष्कर्षः । उपदेशदर्शनेन इति । अत्र मालविकादर्शनसंदेहनिर्णयाद्युक्तिर्नाम संध्यङ्गमुक्तं भवति ॥ यदेति । मन्दा मेधा यस्याः सा । 'धीर्धारणावती मेधा' इत्यमरः । मलिनयति दूषयति । नुः प्रश्ने । दोष इत्यर्थः । आपद्यते प्रकृते प्राप्नोति । आपठ्यते इति पाठे जनैरुच्यते इत्यर्थः ।

गणदासः—देवी न मां समानविद्यतः[1] परिभवनीयमवगन्तुमर्हसि।

विदूषकः—भवति पश्याम उरभ्रसंपातम्। किं मुधा वेतनदानेन। (क)

देवी—ननु कलहप्रियोऽसि। (ख)

विदूषकः—मैवम्। अन्योन्यकलहितयोर्मत्तहस्तिनोरेकतरस्मिन्ननिर्जिते कुत उपशमः। (ग)

राजा—ननु स्वाङ्गसौष्ठवाभिनेयमुभयोर्दृष्टवती[2] भगवती।

परिव्राजिका—अथ किम्।

राजा—तदिदानीमतः[3] परं किमाभ्यां प्रत्याययितव्यम्।

परिव्राजिका—तदेव वक्तुकामास्मि।

शिष्टा[4] क्रिया कस्यचिदात्मसंस्था
संक्रान्तिरन्यस्य विशेषयुक्ता।
यस्योभयं साधु स शिक्षकाणां
धुरि प्रतिष्ठापयितव्य एव॥ १६॥

(क) भोदि[5] पेक्खामो उरब्भसंवादं[6]। किं मुहा वेअणदाणेण। (ख) णं कलहप्पिओसि। (ग) मा[7] एवं। अण्णोण्णकलहिदाणं[8] मत्तहत्थीणं एक्कदरस्सिं अणिज्जिदे कुदो उवसमो।

अप्रशस्तं द्रव्यमद्रव्यम्। कुशिष्येति यावत्। तस्य परिग्रहः शिक्षणीयतया स्वीकारः। लाघवं मान्द्यम्। ०परिग्रह एव इति पाठे बुद्धेः लाघवं सूक्ष्मत्वं पटीयस्त्वमित्यर्थः। पूरयित्वा। अलंखल्वोः इति क्त्वा। विरम। जुगुप्साविराम-इत्यादिना अपादानत्वम्। सुलभ०—मुखनिग्रहेणेति पाठे मुखस्य निग्रहः खादनप्रतिबंधो यस्मात्तेन इत्यर्थः। अत्र निन्दाया गम्यमानत्वात् व्याजस्तुतिरलंकारः। **लब्धास्पदोऽस्मीत्यादि।** लब्धमास्पदं प्रतिष्ठा येन स लब्धास्पदः तथाभूतोस्मीति कृत्वा विवादात्

---

१ विद्यातः, विद्यया; अभिनयविद्यातः परि० मन्तु०: न मां देवी...मनुमन्तुमर्हति; समानविद्यतया परिहीनमवः० २ सौष्ठवं, वातिशयम्. ३ अतः किम्; किमतः परं द्वाभ्याम्. ४ श्लिष्टा. ५ देवि. ६ उअरंभरिसं० ७ मा चण्डि, मा दाव. ८ कलहप्पिआणं.

Gaṇadāsa:—O Queen, you should not consider me likely to be beaten by one who is only my equal in knowledge.

Vidūṣaka :—Queen, let us see the contest of the two rams. What is the good of giving them salary for nothing ?

Queen :—Certainly, you are a lover of quarrels.

Vidūṣaka:—No, not so. But when two infuriated elephants are quarrelling, how can there be peace (an end of strife), until one of them is vanquished?

King:—Surely, your Reverence has seen the acting with graceful limbs exhibited by these two in person.

Parivrājikā:—Yes, I have.

King:—Then, what more have they now to show by way of a further convincing proof ?

Parivrājikā:—That is the very thing I wish to speak about.

One man is at his best, when exhibiting his art in person; another has as his special qualification, the power of communicating his skill; he who possesses both (these excellences), should be placed at the head of teachers. (16)

भीरु भयशीलः तस्य । भियः क्रुक्लुकनौ इति क्रुः । विवादे कदाचित्पराभूतिः स्यादिति शङ्कया भीतस्य । तथा च परेण कृतां निन्दां तितिक्षमाणस्य सहमानस्य । तिजेः क्षमायामिति सनि लटः शानच् । यस्य शिक्षकस्य आगमशास्त्रज्ञानं केवला जीविका तस्यै वृत्त्यर्थमेव केवलं भवति । तं ज्ञानमेव पण्यं विक्रेयं वस्तु यस्य तं ज्ञानपण्यं ज्ञानविक्रयकारिणं वणिजं वदन्ति । पण्डिता इति शेषः । अतः यशःकामेन विवादान्न भेतव्यं इति भावः । अत्र वणिजः पण्यस्य चारोपणात् साङ्गं समस्त-वस्तुविषयं रूपकमलङ्कारः । उपजातिश्छंदः ॥ १७ ॥ अचिरोपनीता अचिरेण उपनीता उपदेशग्रहणार्थं समीपं प्रापिता । न दीर्घकालं गृहीतोपदेशेत्यर्थः । अपरि-निष्ठितस्य अचिरोपनीतत्वेन अलब्धस्थैर्यस्य । अन्याय्यमयोग्यम् । **अत एवेति** । अचिरोपनीतापि कां शिक्षां ग्राहितेति स्वमुपदेशदानकौशलं दर्शयितुकामस्येत्यर्थः । निर्बन्ध आग्रहः । दोषाय दोषास्पदं स्यादित्यर्थः । मूढे अज्ञातमत्स्वभावे । जाग्रतीं मालविकाया राज्ञो दृष्टेर्निगूहने सावधानां दक्षामिति यावत् । सुप्तामनवहितां प्रमत्तामित्यर्थः । सासूयमसूयया सहितं यथा स्यात्तथा ॥ **अनिमित्तमित्यादि** । हे इन्दुवदने चन्द्रमुखि । इन्दुरिव वदनं यस्याः सा इन्दुवदना । तत्सम्बुद्धिः । अनि·

विदूषकः—श्रुतमार्याभ्यां भगवत्या वचनम् । एष पिण्डितार्थ उपदेशदर्शनेन निर्णय इति । (क)

हरदत्तः—परमुचितं[1] नः ।

गणदासः—देवि एवं स्थितम्[2] ।

देवी—यदा पुनर्मन्दमेधा शिष्योपदेशं मलिनयति तदाचार्यस्य दोषो नु । (ख)

राजा—देवि एवमापद्यते[3] । विनेतुरद्रव्यपरिग्रहो[4]ऽपि बुद्धिलाघवं प्रकाशयति[5] ।

देवी—(स्वगतम् ।) कथमिदानीम् । अलमार्यपुत्रस्योत्साहकारणं[6] मनोरथं पूरयित्वा । (गणदासं विलोक्य । प्रकाशम् ।) विरम निरर्थकादारम्भात् । (ग)

विदूषकः—सुष्ठु भवती भणति । भो गणदास संगीतापदेशेन सरस्वत्युपायनमोदकान्खादतः किं ते सुलभनिग्रहेण विवादेन । (घ)

(क) सुदं अज्जेहिं भअवदीए वअणं । एसो पिण्डितत्थो उवदेसदंसणेण णिण्णओत्ति (ख) जदा उण मन्दमेधा[8] सिस्सा उवदेसं मलिणेदि[9] तदा आअरिअस्स दोसो णु । (ग) कहं दाणीं । अलं अज्जउत्तस्स ऊसाहकारणं मणोरहं पूरिअ । विरम णिरत्थआदो आरम्भादो । (घ) सुट्ठु भोदी भणादि । भो गणदास संगीदावं[10]-देसेण सरस्सईउवाअणमोदआणं खादमाणस्स किं ते सुलह[11]णिग्गहेण विवादेण ।

मित्तं न विद्यते निमित्तं यस्मिन्कर्मणि तद्यथा तथा । कारणं विना किं अत्रभवतः पूज्यात् राज्ञः पराङ्मुखी विमुखी भवसि । तव अकारणकोपो न युक्त इति भावः । हि यतः कुटुम्बिन्यः कुलस्त्रियः भर्तृषु प्रभवन्त्यः प्रभुत्ववत्योपि कारणेन कोपो यासा ताः कारणकोपा भवन्ति । अकारणं न कुप्यन्तीत्यर्थः । अत्र कुलीनस्त्रीणां सकारणः कोप इति वैधर्म्येण सामान्येन राज्ञीकोपानुचितत्वं समर्थ्यते इति वैधर्म्येण सामान्येन विशेष-

---

१ परमभिमतः परमरुचितम्. २ देव...स्थितमेव. ३ उपपद्यते, आपद्यते. ४ ग्रह एव, गण०—विनेतु; इ. ५ तीति. ६ (गणदासं विलोक्य) (जनान्तिकम्) अलं ७ ०णादो, ०णे अ. ८ अमेहात्रिणी. मलिणेति. १० देसपदं लम्भिअ (लब्ध्वा) सरस्सइए, ०देसं आरहिअ. ११ सु-मु-ह (सु-मु-ख).

Vidūṣaka:—Sirs, you have heard the revered lady's speech; this is the gist of it:—The decision can be arrived at by practical display of your teaching.

Haradatta:—We quite approve of it.

Gaṇadāsa:— Queen, it has come to this.

Queen:—But when a dull-headed pupil disgraces the instruction of a teacher, is that the fault of the teacher?

King:—Queen, it is thus explained. The acceptance of an unpromising (*lit.* unfit) pupil shows a want of discernment on the part of the teacher.

Queen:—(*To herself*) How now (*i. e.* what shall I do now)? Away with fulfilling the desire of my husband which will only increase the ardour of his passion. (*looking at* Gaṇadāsa, *aloud*) Desist from this useless attempt.

Vidūṣaka:—Your Highness speaks properly. Gaṇadāsa! What have you, who are eating the sweetmeats offered to Sarasvatī on the pretence of (being a teacher of dancing, to do with a contest in which you may be easily defeated?

समर्थनरूपः अर्थान्तरन्यासोऽलंकारः। आर्यावृत्तम्। ॥ १८॥ दिष्ट्येति गणदासमुत्तेजयितुं विदूषकस्योक्तिः। अत्र देवीकोपेन वस्तुविच्छेदे प्राप्ते विदूषककृतं प्रोत्साहनमुत्तराङ्कोपयोगित्वेनाविच्छेदकारणत्वाद्बिन्दुरित्यनुसन्धेयम्। एवं जनो गृह्णाति यथा विदूषकेणोक्तं तथा अवधारयति। उपदेशदर्शनानैपुण्यं मयि आरोपयेदित्यर्थः। **विवादे इत्यादि।** विवादे उपस्थिते वादे आत्मनः क्रियायाः संक्रान्तिं शिष्यजने उपदेशसंक्रमणशक्तिं दर्शयिष्यन्तं दर्शयितुमिच्छन्तम्। अनुजानासि अनुमन्यसे। परित्यक्तोऽस्मीति मन्ये ॥१९॥ अपदे अस्थाने। देवी कदाचित् शिष्याशिक्षादर्शनान्म निवारयेदिति अकारणमेव जातशङ्कोऽस्मीत्यर्थः। किमपि देव्या इति कपटमूल एष प्रयोगो मालविकादर्शनार्थं इति। चतुर्भ्यः पदेभ्य उद्भवो यस्य तत्। चतुष्पदोत्थमिति पाठे चतुर्भ्यः पदेभ्य उत्तिष्ठतीति तथोक्तम्। दुःखेन प्रयोजयितुं शक्यं दुष्प्रयोज्यम्। उदाहरन्ति नाट्यवेदिन इति शेषः। एकः अभिन्नः अर्थः अभिधेयं वस्तु संश्रय आश्रयो यस्य तथाभूतम्। तरतमयोर्भावः तारतम्यं न्यूनाधिकभावः। उपदेशान्तरमिति पाठे उपदेशयोरन्तरं वैशिष्ट्यमित्यर्थः। प्रेक्षागृहं संगीतशाला।

गणदासः—सत्यमयमेवार्थो देवीवचनस्य[1]। श्रूयतामवसरप्राप्तमिदम्[2]।

लब्धास्पदोऽस्मीति विवादभीरो-
स्तितिक्षमाणस्य परेण निन्दाम्।
यस्यागमः केवलजीविकायै[3]
तं ज्ञानपण्यं वणिजं वदन्ति ॥ १७ ॥

देवी—अचिरोपनीता ते शिष्या। तदपरिनिष्ठितस्योपदेशस्यान्याय्यं प्रकाशनम्। (क)

गणदासः—अत एव मे निर्बन्धः।

देवी—तेन हि द्वावप्युपदेशं भगवत्यै दर्शयतम्। (ख)

परिव्राजिका—देवि नैतन्न्याय्यम्। सर्वज्ञस्याप्येकाकिनो निर्णयाभ्युपगमो दोषाय।

देवी—(आत्मगतम्[4]।) मूढे किं मां जाग्रतीमपि सुप्तामिव करोषि। (ग)

(इति सासूयं परावर्तते।)

(राजा देवीं परिव्राजिकायै दर्शयति।)

परिव्राजिका—

अनिमित्तमिन्दुवदने किमत्रभवतः पराङ्मुखी भवसि।
प्रभवन्त्योऽपि हि भर्तृषु कारणकोपाः कुटुम्बिन्यः ॥ १८ ॥

(क) अइरोवणीदा[5] दे सिस्सा। ता अवरिणिट्ठिदस्स उवदेसस्स[6] अण्णअं पआसणं। (ख) तेण हि दुवेवि उवदेसं भअवदीए दंसेध। (ग) मूंढे[7] किं म जागत्ति वि सुत्तं विअ करेसि।

निर्णयाधिकारे निर्णयविषयकोऽधिकारस्तमवलम्ब्येत्यर्थः। **सर्वाङ्गेत्यादि**। सर्वेषामङ्गानां नाट्यस्य शरीरस्य च अभिव्यक्तये। मालविकायां राज्ञोनुरागस्य वृद्ध्यर्थं तस्याः सर्वाङ्गावलोकनस्यावश्यकत्वादिति गूढाभिसन्धिः। अत्र गुणवत्त्वस्य गम्यमानत्वाद्विलोभनं नाम सन्ध्यङ्गमुक्तं भवति। उपायाः सामादयः पक्षे स्वाभिलषितसि-

---

१ वाक्यस्य. २ इदानीम्. ३ ०कैव. ४ जनान्तिकम्. ५ णीदाए सिस्साए उण पडिट्ठिदस्स (नीतायां शिष्यायां पुनः प्रतिष्ठितस्य). ६ सस्स पुण अणज्जं (अनार्यं) आवेदणं- ७ मुद्दे (मुग्धे),–मूढे–परिव्वाजिए.

Gaṇadāsa—In truth, this comes to be the meaning of the Queen's speech. Hear this, which I have to say as necessitated by the occasion.

The man who shrinks from a controversy because he has gained a footing, and patiently endures disparagement from a rival,—he whose learning is merely for (a means of gaining) a livelihood, is called a trader that traffics in knowledge. (17)

Queen:—Your pupil was but lately handed over to you; so it is unadvisable to exhibit instruction, that is not yet firmly implanted.

Gaṇadāsa:—It is for this very reason that I am so importunate.

Queen:—Then exhibit both of you, your skill in instruction to the revered lady (alone).

Parivrājikā :—Queen, this is not right. The arriving at a decision (of a particular question) by one person, omniscient though he be, is liable to be faulty (or erroneous).

Queen:—(*To herself*) You silly recluse, do you treat me like one asleep, when I am wide awake? (*Turns aside angrily*)

(*The King points out* the Queen *to the* Parivrājikā).

Parivrājikā :—(*Having looked at her*),

Why do you, O moon-faced one, causelessly turn away your face from His Majesty? For house-wives, though ever domineering over their husbands, get angry (or offended) with them, (only) when they have some cause for it. (18).

द्विसाधनानि । अत्र गूढार्थोद्भेदनाद्दुद्भेदो नाम संध्यङ्गमुक्तं भवति । **अलमन्यथेति** । हे मनस्विनि प्रशस्तं मनः अस्या अस्तीति मनस्विनी तत्सम्बुद्धिः । प्रशस्तमनस्के देवि । अन्यथा गृहीत्वा इममर्थमन्यथा संभाव्य अलम् । तदेव स्पष्टयति–न खल्वित्यादिना । इदं विवादकरणम् । यतः समानविद्याः विद्वांसः परस्परस्य यशसि पुरोभागाः दोषैकदर्शिनः । अन्योन्ययशोदूषणे उद्युक्ता भवन्तीत्यर्थः । अर्थान्तरन्यासोऽलंकारः । आर्या छन्दः । ॥ २० ॥ **जीमूतस्तनितेत्यादि** । जीमूतस्तनितविशङ्किभिर्जीमूतस्य स्तनितं गर्जितं विशङ्कन्त इति

विदूषकः—ननु सकारणमेव । आत्मनः पक्षो रक्षितव्य इति । (गणदासं विलोक्य ।) दिष्टया कोपव्याजेन देव्या परित्रातो भवान् । सुशिक्षितोऽपि सर्व उपदेशदर्शने न निपुणो भवति । (क)

गणदासः—देवि श्रूयताम् । एवं जनो गृह्णाति । तदिदानीम्

> **विवादे दर्शयिष्यन्तं[1] क्रियासंक्रान्तिमात्मनः ।**
> **यदि मां नानुजानासि परित्यक्तोऽस्म्यहं त्वया ॥ १९ ॥**

(आसनादुत्तिष्ठति[2] ।)

देवी—(स्वगतम् ।) का गतिः । (प्रकाशम् ।) प्रभवत्याचार्यः शिष्यजनस्य । (ख)

गणदासः—चिरम[3]पदे शङ्कितोऽस्मि । (राजानमवलोक्य ।) अनुज्ञातं देव्या । तदाज्ञापयतु देवः क[4]स्मिन्नभिनेय[5]वस्तुन्युपदेशं दर्शयिष्यामि ।

राजा—यदादिशति भगवती ।

परिव्राजिका—किमपि देव्या मनसि वर्तते । तच्छ[6]ङ्कितास्मि ।

देवी—भण विस्रब्धम् । ननु प्रभविष्याम्यात्मनः परिजनस्य । (ग)

राजा—मम चेति ब्रूहि ।

(क) णं सका[7]रणं एव्व । अत्तणो पक्खो रक्खिदव्वोत्ति । दिट्ठिआ कोवव्वाजेण देवीए परित्तादो भवं । सुसिक्खिदो वि सव्वो उव[8]देसदंसणे ण णिउणो होदि । (ख) का गई । पहवं[9]दि आआरिओ सिस्सजणस्स । (ग) भण विस्सद्धं । [10]णं पहविस्सं अत्तणो परिअणस्स ।

तथोक्तास्तैरुद्ग्रीवैरुत्कण्ठैर्मयूरैः शिखण्डिभिरनुरसितस्यानुध्वनितस्य पुष्करस्य वाद्यभाण्डमुखस्य मायूरी मयूरप्रिया मार्जना मनांसि मदयति हर्षयति । कीदृशी मार्जना । उपहितमध्यमस्वरोत्था उपहितो योजितो मध्यमस्वरो मध्यमसंज्ञकस्वरस्तस्मादुत्तिष्ठत्युदेतीति तथोक्ता । उपचितेति पाठे उपचितेन पूर्णतां प्राप्तेनेत्यर्थः ।

---

१ दर्शयिष्यामि. २ दुत्थातुमिच्छति. ३ अपदेश-शे. ४ कतमस्मि०···तमस्मिन्नुपदेशवस्तुनि प्रयोगं. ५ अभिनय. ६ ततः श०. ७ कारणादो. ८ उपदेसे, ०सणेण, ०सेण णिण्हादो (उपदेशेन निष्णातः). ९ पहवदि क्खु अज्जो. १० पहवदि पहू (प्रभवति प्रभुः)

Vidūṣaka:—Why, she does so with cause. She has to watch the interest of (lit. protect) her own party. (*Looking at* Gaṇadāsa) Luckily, you have been saved by the Queen under the pretext of being angry. Every person, though well-educated, has not the skill to impart instruction to others.

Gaṇadāsa :—Queen, listen. This is how people will interpret it. Therefore, now,

If you do not permit me, who am now desirous of showing, in the present contest, my power of imparting instruction, then (I must say) I am given up by you. (19)

(*So saying he rises from his seat.*)

Queen:—(*To herself*) What help is there ! (*Aloud*) You have full mastery over your pupil.

Gaṇadāsa :—My doubts for so long a time were quite out of place. (*Looking at the* King) I am granted permission by the Queen. Your Majesty, therefore, will kindly tell me in what subject-matter of dramatic representation I should show my ability to impart instruction.

King :—Just as her Reverence would direct.

Parivrājikā :—But, there is something in the mind of the Queen. I am, therefore, in suspense (whether I should name the subject or not).

Queen :—Say what you have to say, without reserve. Surely, I shall still have power over my attendants.

King :—And say—over me too (*i. e.*, you are as well the mistress of me also).

निर्ह्रादिन्यतिशयनिनादा । मार्जना नाम पुष्करवाद्यनामविशेषः । तथोक्तं भारतीये 'षोडशाक्षरसंपन्नं चतुर्मार्गं तथैव च ॥ द्विलेपनं षट्करणं त्रियति त्रिलयं तथा । त्रिगतं त्रिप्रचारं च त्रिसंयोगं त्रिपाणिकम् ॥ दशार्धपाणिप्रहतं त्रिप्रहारं त्रिमार्जनम् । एभिरङ्गैस्तु संपन्नं वाद्यं पुष्करजं भवेत् ॥' तथाच 'मायूरी चार्धमायूरी तथा कार्मारवीति च । तिस्रस्तु मार्जना ज्ञेयाः पुष्करेषु स्वराश्रयाः । गान्धारो वामके कार्यः षड्जो दक्षिणपुष्करे । मध्यमश्चोर्ध्वगः कार्यो मायूर्यास्तु स्वरास्त्वमी ॥ वामके पुष्करे षड्ज ऋषभो दक्षिणे तथा । धैवतश्चोर्ध्वगोत्रार्धमायूर्यां निर्दिशेद् बुधः ॥ ऋषभः पुष्करे वामे षड्जो दक्षिणपुष्करे । पञ्चमश्चोर्ध्वगः कार्यः कार्माख्याः स्वरा अमी ॥'

देवी—भगवति भणेदानीम्। (क)

परिव्राजिका—देव चतुष्पदोद्भवं चलितं दुष्प्रयोज्यमुदाहरन्ति। तत्रैकार्थसंश्रयमुभयोः प्रयोगं पश्यामः। तावता ज्ञायत एवात्रभवतोरुपदेशतारतम्यम्।

आचार्यौ—यदाज्ञापयति भगवती।

विदूषकः—तेन हि द्वावपि वर्गौ प्रेक्षागृहे संगीतरचनां कृत्वात्रभवतो दूतं प्रेषयतम्। अथ वा मृदङ्गशब्द एव न उत्थापयिष्यति। (ख)

हरदत्तः—तथा। (इत्युत्तिष्ठति।)

(गणदासो देवीमवलोकयति।)

देवी—(गणदासं विलोक्य।) विजयी भव। न खलु विजयप्रत्यर्थिन्यहमाचार्यस्य। (ग)

(उभौ प्रस्थितौ।)

परिव्राजिका—इतस्तावदाचार्यौ।

उभौ—(परिवृत्य।) इमौ स्वः।

परिव्राजिका—निर्णयाधिकारे ब्रवीमि। सर्वाङ्गसौष्ठवाभिव्यक्तये विरलनेपथ्ययोः पात्रयोः प्रवेशोऽस्तु।

(क) भअवदि भण दाणिम्। (ख) तेण दि दुवेवि वग्गा पेक्खाघरे संगीदरअणं करिअ अत्तभवदो दूदं पेसअह। अह वा मुदङ्गसद्दो एव्व णो उत्थावइस्सदि। (ग) विअई होहि। ण हु विअअपचत्थिणी अहं आअरिअस्स।

इति। प्रहर्षिणी वृत्तम्।॥ २१॥ सामाजिकाः समाजं समवयन्तीति सभ्याः। सामवायिका इति पाठे स एवार्थः सामयिका इति पाठे समयः प्राप्त एषां समयमनुवर्तन्ते इति वा। अविनयो धाष्ट्र्यं मालविकादर्शनाभिलाषप्रकटनादिति भावः। धीरं स्तिमितगत्या। विसंवादयिष्यति विप्रतिपत्स्यते।

---

१ देवेति नास्ति क्वचित्. २ शर्मिष्ठायाः कृतिं चतुष्पदोत्थं छलिकं-तं. ३ संगतं. ४ देशान्तरम्. ५ विलो०, धारिणीभव०. ६ आचार्यौ. ७ नास्त्येतत्क्वचित्. ८ विगत. ९ पेसअन्दु (प्रेषयताम्).

Queen :—Revered lady, speak out now (*i. e.* mention the subject).

Parivrājikā :—My Lord, they (experts) consider the Calita dance, based on the Catuṣpada, (a song of four parts) the most difficult to be enacted. Therefore, we shall see the representation of the same part of that same dance by both of them. By that much will, of course, be known the relative worth of their power of instruction.

The Preceptors :—Just as your Reverence desires.

Vfdūṣaka :—Well then, let both the parties go to the representation-hall (theatre), and having made the necessary arrangements for the musical concert, send a messenger here ; or rather the sound of the tabor itself will make us rise.

Haradatta :—All right. (*Gets up from his seat*).

(Gaṇadāsa *looks up to* Queen Dhāriṇī).

Queen :—(*Looking' at* Gaṇadāsa) May you come out victorious. I am not at all hostile to your success.

Parivrājikā :—Come here a moment.

Both :—(*Turning round*) Here we are.

Parivrājikā :—I speak in my capacity as judge (or by virtue of my power to decide). Let the two pupils enter, dressed in fine attire, that the elegance of movement of all their limbs might be clearly displayed.

तव मालविकागतं मनोरथमूहित्वा सकलमेव तन्त्रमाकुलयिष्यतीत्यर्थः। **धैर्येत्यादि**। अयं मुरजवाद्यस्य नादः शब्दः रागः रञ्जकत्वं धैर्यावलम्बिनमपि मया धीरमकृतत्वरेण गन्तव्यमिति कृतनिश्चयमपि मां त्वरयति संभ्रमयति। सिद्धेः इष्टलाभस्य पन्थाः सिद्धिपथः तं सिद्धिपथं सिद्धिमार्गमवतरतः प्राप्नुवतः स्वमनोरथस्यात्मवाञ्छितस्य शब्द इव ध्वनिरिव। अत्रोत्तरार्धे उत्प्रेक्षालंकारः। तस्य मनसि रथत्वारोपाद्रूपकमङ्गम्। एवं तयोरङ्गाङ्गिभावेन संकरः॥ आर्या छन्दः। ॥२२॥ अत्र बीजस्य पुनरावर्तनात्समाधानं नाम संध्यङ्गमुक्तं भवति।

उभौ—नेदमप्यावयोरुपदेश्यम्[1]। (इति निष्क्रान्तौ।)

देवी—(राजानमवलोक्य।) यदि राजकार्येष्वपीदृश्युपायनिपुणतार्यपुत्रस्य ततः शोभनं भवेत्। (क)

राजा—

अलमन्यथा गृहीत्वा न खलु मनस्विनि मया प्रयुक्तमिदम्।
प्रायः समानविद्याः परस्परयशःपुरोभागाः ॥ २० ॥

(नेपथ्ये मृदङ्गशब्दः[2]। सर्वे कर्णं ददति।)

परिव्राजिका—हन्त। प्रवृत्तं संगीतकम्[3]। तथा ह्येषा

जीमूतस्तनितविशङ्किभिर्मयूरैरुद्ग्रीवैरनुरसितस्य[4] पुष्करस्य।
निर्ह्रादिन्युपहितमध्यमस्वरोत्था[5] मायूरी मदयति मार्जना मनांसि ॥२१॥

राजा—देवि सामाजिका[6] भवामः।

देवी—(स्वगतम्।) अहो अविनय आर्यपुत्रस्य। (ख)

(सर्वे उत्तिष्ठन्ति।)

विदूषकः—(अपवार्य।) भोः धीरं गच्छ। मा खल्वत्रभवती धारिणी विसंवादयिष्यति। (ग)

राजा—

धैर्यावलम्बिनमपि त्वरयति मां मुरजवाद्यनादोऽयम्।
अवतरतः सिद्धिपथं शब्दः स्वमनोरथस्येव ॥ २२ ॥

(इति निष्क्रान्ताः सर्वे।)

इति प्रथमोऽङ्कः।

(क) जइ राअकज्जेसु वि ईरिसी उवाअणिउणदा अज्जउत्तस्स तदो सोहणं भवे। (ख) अहो अविणओ अज्जउत्तस्स। (ग) भो धीरं गच्छ। मा क्खु अत्तभोदी धारिणी विसंवादइस्सदि।

अत्रैव सुखागमस्य गम्यमानत्वात्प्राप्तिर्नाम संध्यङ्गमुक्तं भवति। अत्रोपक्षेपादिषु संध्यङ्गेषु कतिचिदेव कविनोक्तानि नेतराणि तथापि न दोषः। 'न्यूनमप्यत्र यैः

---

१ मावयोः. २ ध्वनिः. ३ संगीतम्. ४ अनुगमितस्य. ५ निर्णादिन्यु०; उपचित. ६ तस्याः सामयिकाः, सामवायिकाः, साह्यवादिकाः. ७ रागः. ८ कज्जेसु एवं णिउ० ९ गच्छम्ह. १० तत्त०

Both :—We need not be told this.

(*Exeunt the* two teachers).

Queen :—(*Looking at the* King) If my lord shows such skill in devising expedients in state-affairs, the result will be splendid.

King :—Do not take it otherwise (enough of misconstruing the matter); indeed, this was not brought about by me, O high-minded one : generally, men of equal learning are envious of each other's fame. (20).

(*The sound of a tabor is heard behind the scenes. All listen*).

Parivrājikā :—Ah, the music has begun. For, this

Deep resonant sound, so dear to peacocks, and having the pitch of the middle tone for its basis, of the tabor, followed by the notes of the peacocks with necks erect, suspecting it to be the thunder of rain-clouds, delights the mind. (21)

King :—Queen, let us join the assembly.

Queen :—(*To herself*) Oh, the indecorous behaviour of my husband !

(*All rise up*).

Vidūṣaka :—(*Aside to the* King) Oh, walk patiently and slowly, let not the queen find you inconsistent with yourself (or, thwart the plan).

King :—

Though I resort to firmness (try to be patient), this sound of the music of the tabor makes me hasten, as if it is the sound of my own desire descending to the path of fulfilment. (22)

(*Exeunt omnes.*)

HERE ENDS THE FIRST ACT.

कैश्चिदङ्गैर्नाट्यं न दुष्यति । यद्गुणात्तेषु संपत्तिराराधयति तद्विदः ॥' इति वचनात् । अत्र नृत्यदर्शननिश्चयान्ते प्रथमाङ्कार्थे समाप्तेऽपि तमसमाप्यैवोत्तराङ्कादौ विष्कम्भादौ प्रतिपाद्यायाः संगीतरचनाया अत्रैव निपातनादङ्कावतरणं नामार्थोपक्षेपक उक्तो भवति । यथोक्तम्—'अङ्कावतारस्त्वङ्कान्ते पात्रेणाङ्कस्य सूचनात्' इति ॥

इति श्रीकाटयवेमभूपविरचिते कुमारगिरिराजीये
मालविकाग्निमित्रव्याख्याने प्रथमोऽङ्कः ॥

द्वितीयोऽङ्कः ।

(ततः प्रविशति संगीतरचनायां कृतायामासनस्थः सवयस्यो राजा धारिणी परिव्राजिका विभवतश्च परिवारः ।)

राजा—भगवति अत्रभवतोराचार्ययोः कतरस्य प्रथममुपदेशं द्रक्ष्यामः ।

परिव्राजिका—ननु समानेऽपि ज्ञानवृद्धभावे वयोवृद्धत्वाद्गणदासः पुरस्कारमर्हति ।

राजा—तेन हि मौद्गल्य एवमत्रभवतोरावेद्य स्वनियोगमशून्यं कुरु ।

कञ्चुकी—यदाज्ञापयति देवः (इति निष्क्रान्तः ।)

(प्रविश्य ।)

गणदासः—देव शर्मिष्ठायाः कृतिर्लयमध्या चतुष्पदा । तस्याश्चतुर्थवस्तुनः प्रयोगमेकमनाः श्रोतुमर्हति देवः ।

राजा—आचार्यबहुमानादवहितोऽस्मि ।

(निष्क्रान्तो गणदासः ।)

राजा—(जनान्तिकम् ।) वयस्य ।

कविरिदानीमङ्कान्तरं प्रस्तौति—ततः प्रविशतीत्यादि । 'भगवति अत्रभवतोः' इत्यादिना 'गणदासः पुरस्कारमर्हति' इत्यन्तेन प्रतीयमानं राज्ञ उपायतो मालविकादर्शनप्रवर्तनं प्रयत्नो नाम द्वितीयावस्थितिरिति मन्तव्यम् । अत्र बिन्दुप्रयत्नयोः समन्वयात्प्रतिमुखसंधिरित्यनुसंधेयम् ॥ ज्ञानेन वृद्धः ज्ञानवृद्धः तस्य भावः तस्मिन् । उभयोस्तुल्यज्ञानत्वेपीत्यर्थः । पुरस्कारं उपदेशदर्शने अग्रमानम् । देव शर्मिष्ठाया इत्यादि । शर्मिष्ठा नाम वृषपर्वणो राक्षसराजस्य दुहिता ययातिभार्या । तस्याः कृतिः काव्यम् । लयमध्या लयेन तालकालेन मध्या मध्यमानयुक्ता । चतुष्पदा चत्वारि पदानि खण्डानि यस्याः सा तथोक्ता । तस्याः कृतेः संबन्धिनश्चतुर्थवस्तुनश्चतुर्थस्य तुर्यस्य वस्तुनः प्रबन्धस्य प्रयोगमभिनयं एकस्मिन् मनो यस्य सः एकमना अवहितः सन् श्रोतुमर्हति । अत्र शृङ्गारस्य प्रतिपाद्यमानत्वाल्लयमध्येत्युक्तम् । तथा चोक्तं भारतीये—'शृङ्गारहास्ययोर्मध्यलयः । करुणे विलम्बितः । वीररौद्राद्भुतबीभत्सभयानकेषु द्रुतः ॥' बहुमानात् वस्तुबहुमानाद्

---

१ नायामासनस्थः, २ वयोधिकत्वात्. ३ एवमेव. ४ ०दास्ति ५ तस्यास्तु च्छलिकप्र०

ACT II

(*Then enter after the orchestral arrangements are completed, the* King *with his* friend, *seated on a throne*, Dhāriṇī, Parivrājikā *and the* retinue *in order of rank*).

King:—Revered Lady! Out of the two revered professors, whose instruction shall we see first?

Parivrājikā :—I say, although their great attainments are equal, Gaṇadāsa deserves precedence on account of his seniority of age.

King :—Well, then, Maudgalya, inform thus the two revered preceptors and then attend to your business.

Chamberlain :—As your Majesty commands.

(*Entering*)

Gaṇadāsa :—My lord, there is a composition of S'armiṣṭhā, consisting of four parts, in which the time kept is the middle tone. Your Majesty will be pleased to hear (behold) with undivided attention the representation of the fourth part of it.

King :—Preceptor, I am attentive out of the high respect I have for you.

(*Exit* Gaṇadāsa.)

King:—(*Aside to* Vidūṣaka) Friend,

आचार्यबहुमानाद्वा। यद्वा आचार्यबहुमानादित्येकं पदम्। जनान्तिकम् जनस्याभीष्टस्य अन्तिकं समीपे। यदभीष्टजन एव शृणुयादिति कृत्वा तत्समीप उच्यते तत्। तदुक्तं 'त्रिपताककरेणान्यानपवार्यान्तरा कथाम्। अन्योन्यामन्त्रणं यत्स्याज्जनान्ते तज्जनान्तिकम्॥' इति। **नेपथ्यपरिगताया इति**। नेपथ्यपरिगताया जवनिकान्तरस्थितायास्तस्या मालविकाया दर्शनसमुत्सुकमवलोकनोत्कण्ठितं मे चक्षुरधीरतया तरलतया अकालक्षमतयेत्यर्थः तिरस्करिणीं जवनिकां संहर्तुमपनेतुं व्यवसितमिवोद्युक्तमिव। उत्प्रेक्षालंकारः। आर्या छन्दः। ॥ १ ॥ अत्रेष्टार्थविषयेच्छाया गम्यमानत्वाद्विलासो नाम संध्यङ्गमुक्तं भवति। उपस्थितं नयनयोः मधु मालविकारूपं नयनमधु संनिहिता मक्षिका धारिणीरूप यस्य तत् संनिहितमक्षिकं च। **ततः प्रविशतीत्यादि**। आचार्याविक्ष्यमाणाङ्गसौष्ठवा आचार्येण गणदासेनावेक्ष्यमाणमङ्गानां सौष्ठवं यस्याः सा तथोक्ता। सौष्ठवं नामाङ्गानां शोभनावस्था॥ यथोक्तम्—'अनुच्चनीचचलतामङ्गनां समपादताम्। कटिकूर्परशीर्षा-

नेपथ्यपरिगतायाश्चक्षुर्दर्शनसमुत्सुकं तस्याः।
संहर्तुमधीरतया व्यवसितमिव मे तिरस्करिणीम् ॥ १ ॥

विदूषकः—(अपवार्य।) भो उपस्थितं नयनमधु संनिहितमक्षिकं च। तदप्रमत्त इदानीं प्रेक्षस्व। (क)

(ततः प्रविशत्याचार्यप्रत्यवेक्ष्यमाणाङ्गसौष्ठवा मालविका।)

विदूषकः—(जनान्तिकम्।) प्रेक्षतां भवान्। न खल्वस्याः प्रतिच्छन्दात्परिहीयते मधुरता। (ख)

राजा—(जनान्तिकम्।) वयस्य।

चित्रगतायामस्यां कान्तिविसंवादशङ्कि मे हृदयम्।
संप्रति शिथिलसमाधिं मन्ये येनेयमालिखिता ॥ २ ॥

(क) भो उवट्ठिदं णअणमहु संणिहिदिमक्खिअं अ। ता अप्पमत्तो दाणिं पेक्ख।
(ख) पेक्खदु भवं। ण खु से पडिच्छन्दादो परिहीअदि महुरदा।

सकण्ठानां समरूपताम् ॥ रम्यां प्रतीकविश्रान्तिमुरसश्च समुन्नतिम्। अभ्यासोपहितामाहुः सौष्ठवं नृत्यवेदिनः ॥' इति। प्रतिच्छन्दात् चित्रगतरूपादित्यर्थः परिहीयते न्यूना भवति मधुरता ॥ अत्रापवार्येत्येतन्नियतश्राव्यार्थभेदस्यापवारितस्य विवक्षितत्वे कविना प्राक्प्रयुक्तमिति मन्तव्यम्। यथोक्तं वसन्तराजीये—'अर्थस्त्वेकेन विज्ञेयो नियतश्राव्य इष्यते। द्विविधः स परिज्ञेयो जनान्तश्चापवारितः ॥' अत्र 'परैरलक्ष्यव्यापारे कथितोऽर्थोऽपवारितः। उक्त्वा प्रागपवार्येति पश्चादेनं प्रयोजयेत् ॥' इति ॥ **चित्रगतायामित्यादि** । मे हृदयं मनश्चित्रगतायामालेख्यगतायामस्यां मालविकायां कान्तिविसंवादशङ्कि कान्तेः शोभाया विसंवादं विपर्यासं शङ्कते इति तथोक्तं अस्या रूपं प्रतिकृतिशोभासदृशं भवेन्न वेति शंकाकुलमित्यर्थः आसीत्। संप्रतीदानीम्। साक्षाद्दर्शनवेलायामित्यर्थः। इयं मालविका येन चित्रकारेणालिखिता तं चित्रकारं शिथिलसमाधिं शिथिलप्रयत्नं शिथिलचित्तैकाग्र्यं वा मन्ये न तेनास्या रूपं यथार्थतो लिखितमिति जानामि ॥ २ ॥ मुक्तसाध्वसा परित्यक्तभया सभाकम्परहितेत्यर्थः। सत्त्वे चित्तस्याविकृत्यवस्थायां तिष्ठतीति सत्त्वस्था सत्त्वगुणयुक्ता। अविकृता भवेत्यर्थः। यथोक्तम्—'चित्तस्याविकृतिः सत्त्वं विकृतेः कारणे सति' इति। अत्र विकृतिकारणं नायकसंनिधिः। अहो इत्याश्चर्ये। सर्वस्थानान-

१ गृह; परिणतायाः. २ अपवार्य. ३ ता इत्यादि नास्ति पुस्तकान्तरे. ४ पेक्खदु भवं. ५ दोवि (दपि), हीअदि.

My eye, eager to behold her who is hidden by the tiring-room, seems, through impatience, to be endeavouring to draw up the curtain. (1)

Vidūṣaka :—(*Aside*) Ha! the honey of your eyes has approached, but the bee is near; therefore, look on without being careless (*i. e.* cautiously).

(*Then enters* Mālavikā *with the* teacher *of dancing carefully marking the elegance of her limbs*).

Vidūṣaka :—(*Aside*) May your Highness observe. Her loveliness does not, indeed, fall short of the picture.

King :—(*Aside*) Friend,

When she was only a picture to me, my mind apprehended that her (real) beauty might not come up to that of the picture (lit. was inconsistent with the reality); but now, I think that the painter, by whom she was drawn, was slack in his concentration (or was furnished with insufficient or imperfect materials). (2)

वद्यता सर्वेषु स्थानेषु सर्वावयवेष्वनवद्यता निर्दोषता । रमणीयतेत्यर्थः । **दीर्घाक्षमित्यादि** । वदनं मुखं दीर्घाक्षं दीर्घे आयते अक्षिणी लोचने यस्य तत्तथोक्तम् । शरदिन्दुकान्ति शरदिन्दोः शरच्चन्द्रस्य कान्तिरिव कान्तिर्यस्य तत्तथोक्तम् । बाहू भुजावंसयोः स्कन्धयोर्नतौ नम्रौ । निबिडौ अन्योन्यश्लिष्टौ उन्नतौ तुङ्गौ स्तनौ यत्र तत्तथा । अत एव संक्षिप्तं जातसंक्षेपमुरः । पार्श्वे प्रमृष्टे श्लक्ष्णीकृते इव । मध्योऽवलग्नं पाणिमितः पाणिना हस्तेन मितः परिमितः । मुष्टिग्राह्य इति यावत् । जघनं प्रशस्तो नितम्बोस्यास्तीति नितम्बि नितम्बातिशययुक्तम् । अमितमिति पाठे विशालमित्यर्थः पादौ चरणावरालाङ्गुली अराला आकुञ्चिता अङ्गुलयो ययोस्तौ तथोक्तौ । अस्या मालविकाया वपुः शरीरं नर्तयितुर्नृत्ताचार्यस्य छन्दोऽभिप्रायो यथा यादृशस्तथा तेन प्रकारेण श्लिष्टं संगतम् । अनेन नर्तक्या नृत्तारम्भोचितावस्थानविशेष उक्तः । तथा चोक्तं वसन्तराजीये—'अङ्गस्य चतुरस्रत्वसमपादौ लताकरौ । आरम्भे सर्वनृत्तानामेतत्सामान्यमिष्यते ॥' इति । शार्दूलविक्रीडितं वृत्तम् । ॥ ३ ॥ गानात्पूर्वं कर्तव्यं वसन्तादिरागानुगतं स्वरविशेषपरिशीलनम् । उपगानं रागलपितं (दीप्तं-इ पा) कृत्वा । उरवहनमिति पाठे 'उपोह्यते स्वरो यस्मात्तत्तूरवहनं स्मृतम्' इत्युक्तलक्षणं पूर्वगानम् । चतुष्पदवस्तु चतुष्पदसंज्ञकं प्रबन्धं गायति । वस्त्विति प्रबन्धः । 'प्रबन्धो रूपकं वस्तु निबन्धस्याभिधात्रयम्'

गणदासः—वत्से मुक्तसाध्वसा सत्त्वस्था[1] भव।

राजा—(आत्मगतम्।) अहो सर्वस्थानानवद्यता[2] रूपस्य[3]। तथा हि।

दीर्घाक्षं शरदिन्दुकान्ति वदनं बाहू नतावंसयोः
संक्षिप्तं निबिडोन्नतस्तनमुरः पार्श्वे प्रमृष्टे इव।
मध्यः पाणिमितो नितम्बि जघनं पादावरालाङ्गुली
छन्दो नर्तयितुर्यथैव मनसः[5] श्लिष्टं तथास्या वपुः ॥ ३ ॥

मालविका—(उपगानं[6] कृत्वा चतुष्पदवस्तु गायति।)

दुर्लभः प्रियस्तस्मिन्भव हृदय निराश-
महो अपाङ्गको मे प्रस्फुरति किमपि वामः।
एष स चिरदृष्टः कथमुपनेतव्यो
नाथ मां पराधीनां त्वयि गणय सतृष्णाम् ॥ ४ ॥ (क)

(इति। ततो यथारसमभिनयति।)

(क) दुल्लहो पिओ[7] तस्सिं भव हिअअ णिरासं अह्मो[8] अपङ्गओ मे पप्फुरइ[9] किं पि वामो[10]। एसो सो चिरदिट्ठो[11] कहं उवणइदव्वो णाह मं पराहीणं तुइ[12] गणअ सतिण्हम् ॥

इत्युक्तत्वात् दुर्लभ इति। हृदय निराशं निरभिलाषं भव। अभिलाषं मा कुरु इत्यर्थः। अहो इत्याश्चर्ये। मम वामः अपाङ्गो नेत्रप्रान्तः किमपि अज्ञातहेतुकं प्रस्फुरति स्पन्दते। स्त्रीणां वामाङ्गस्य शुभसूचकत्वादभीष्टसमागमं सूचयतीति भावः। अत एवाश्चर्यम्। एष स प्रियः कथमुपनेतव्यः समीपं प्रापणीयः। चिन्तोपस्थितं नाथमाह मां पराधीनां परवशामपि त्वयि सतृष्णां सानुरागां गणय कलय। जानीहीत्यर्थः। ॥ ४ ॥ ततो गानानन्तरं यथारसं रसानुकूलमभिनयति। अत्र रसोऽयोगविप्रलम्भशृङ्गारः। यथोक्तम्—'अप्राप्तिर्विप्रलम्भः स्याद्यूनोर्जाताभिलाषयोः। विप्रलम्भस्य भेदाः स्युरयोगो विरहस्ततः॥ प्रवासः शापः करुणा मानश्चेति च षण्मताः॥' तत्र 'संप्राप्तेः प्रागसङ्गो यस्तमयोगं प्रचक्षते' इति। अत्र चतुष्पद्यां क्रमेण पादचतुष्टये निर्वेदः सविस्मयो हर्षश्चिन्ता दैन्यं चेति संचारिभावास्तत्तदनुभावैर्मुखरागादिभिः सम्यक्प्रकाशिता इत्युनुसंधेयम्। तेषां लक्षणमुक्तं वसन्तराजीये—इष्टार्थविरहव्याधिनिन्दापदवमाननैः। दारिद्र्यताडनाक्षेपपरवृद्धय-

---

१ ०संस्था. २ सर्वास्ववस्थासु. ३ रूपविशेषस्य. ४ ०तोऽमितं च, नतं च. ५ मनसि, मनसा. ६ ०वहनम्. ७ पिओ मे. ८ अम्महे. ९ परिप्फु. १० वामओ. ११ कहं उण दठ्ठव्वो (द्रष्टव्यः) १२ परिगणअ.

Gaṇadāsa :—My dear child, leave off your timidity, and be steady-minded.

King :—(*To himself*) Oh, the perfection (lit. flawlessness) of her beauty in every limb ! For,

Her face has long eyes and the lustre of the autumnal moon; and her two arms are smoothly curved at the shoulders; her chest is compact, having closetouching, elevated breasts; her sides are as if planed off; her waist can be spanned by the hand; her hips are expansive; her feet have toes slightly curved; (her body thus) seems to be moulded just according to the ideal in the mind of the teacher of dancing. (3)

Mālavikā :—(*having hummed the preparatory tune, sings the fourth part of the song consisting of four parts*)

The beloved is difficult to obtain; be without hope about him, O my heart ! Oh ! The outer corner of my left eye throbs on some account; here is he seen after a long time; how is he to be approached? My lord, reckon (know me); dependent as I am, to be ardently longing for thee. (4)

(*After singing the song she dances with gesticulations in accordance with the sentiments contained therein*)

वलोकनैः । निष्फलत्वमतिर्नृणां निर्वेदो जीवितादिषु ॥' अत्रेष्टार्थविरहजनितो निर्वेदः ॥ 'अन्तर्बाष्पोद्गमध्याननिःश्वासस्वावमाननैः । दैन्यगद्गदवैवर्ण्यैरभिनेयो भवेदयम् ॥ हर्षो मनःसमुल्लासो गुरुदेवमहीभुजाम् । प्रसादात्प्रियसङ्गाच्च भवेदिष्टार्थलाभतः ॥' अत्रेष्टार्थलाभजनितो हर्षः । अपाङ्गस्फुरणस्येष्टार्थलाभहेतुत्वात् । 'मुखनेत्रप्रसन्नत्वप्रियोक्तिपुलकोद्गमैः । दानत्यागपरीरम्भैरभिनेयो भवेदयम् ॥ इष्टालाभादिष्टनाशादनिष्टाप्तेश्च दैन्यतः । चित्तस्यैकाग्रता चिन्ता ॥' अत्र चिन्ता इष्टालाभजनिता । 'स्मरणं चानुपस्मृतिः ॥ संतापोच्छ्वासनिःश्वासा मान्द्यमिन्द्रियकर्मणाम् । अधोमुखत्वमित्याद्यैरभिनेया भवेदियम् ॥ अनौजस्त्वं तु मनसो दैन्यमित्यभिधीयते । मनःसंतापदारिद्र्यचिन्तौत्सुक्यादिभिर्भवेत् ॥' अत्रौत्सुक्यजनितं दैन्यम्।' अङ्गानामपि शैथिल्यं देहसंस्कारवर्जनम् । अञ्चितं च शिरस्तस्मिन्ननुभावाः प्रकीर्ति (दर्शि) ताः'इति । [द्वारीकृत्य तद्द्वारेण उपस्थापितः न्यस्त इव । हृदयमभिप्रायः] जनमिममित्यादि । नाथ स्वामिन् इमं जनम् । मामित्यर्थः । अनुरक्तं स्निग्धम् । त्वयीति शेषः । विद्धि जानीहि । इत्येवंविधे गेये गीते । वचनं 'णाह मं पराहीणं' इत्यादिवाक्यं स्वाङ्गनि-

विदूषकः—(जनान्तिकम् ।) भोः चतुष्पदवस्तुकं द्वारीकृत्य त्वय्युपस्थापित इवात्मा तत्रभवत्या । (क)

राजा—(जनान्तिकम् ।) सखे [1]एवमेव मम[2]पि हृदयम् । अनया खलु

जनमिममनुरक्तं विद्धि नाथेति गेये
वचनमभिनयन्त्या स्वाङ्गनिर्देशपूर्वम् ।
प्रणयगतिमदृष्ट्वा धारिणीसंनिकर्षा-
दहमिव[2] सुकुमारप्रार्थनाव्याजमुक्तः ॥ ५ ॥

(मालविका गीतान्ते निष्[3]क्रमितुमिच्छति ।)

विदूषकः—भवति तिष्ठ । किमपि वो विस्मृतः क्रमभेदः । तं तावत्प्रक्ष्यामि । (ख)

गणदासः—व[4]त्से स्थीयताम् । उपदेशविशुद्धा यास्यसि ।

(मालविका निवृत्य स्थिता ।)

राजा—(आत्म[5]गतम् ।) अहो सर्वास्ववस्थासु चारुता [6]शोभां पुष्यति । तथा हि ।

वामं संधिस्तिमितवलयं न्यस्य हस्तं नितम्बे
कृत्वा श्यामाविटपसदृशं स्रस्तमुक्तं द्वितीयम् ।
पादाङ्गुष्ठालुलितकुसुमे कुट्टिमे पातिताक्षं
नृत्तादस्याः स्थितमतितरां कान्तमृज्वायतार्धम् ॥ ६ ॥

(क) भो[7] चउ[8]ष्पदवत्थुअं दुवारीकरिअ तुइ उ[9]वट्ठाविदो विअ अप्पा तत्तहोदीए ।
(ख) भोदि चिट्ठ । किंपि[10] वो विसुमरिदो कमभेदो । तं दाव पुच्छिस्सम् ।

र्देशपूर्वमात्मशरीरप्रदर्शनपूर्वं यथा भवति तथाभिनयन्त्या हस्तादिभिः प्रकाशीकुर्वत्या अनया मालविकया धारिणीसंनिकर्षाद्धेतोः प्रणयगतिं मम स्नेहप्रवृत्तिं [यद्वा मयि तस्याः प्रणयगतिमनुरागप्रसरम्] अदृष्ट्वा अज्ञात्वा । अनुभावानामप्रकाशनादिति भावः ।

---

१ एवमावयोर्हृ. २ मपि. ३ गन्तुम्. °मितुमारब्धा. ४ भद्रे उपदे° यातुमर्हसि; °विशुद्धौ या°; क्षणमात्रं स्थित्वा उप° ५ स्वर्ग° ६ शोभान्तरम्. ७ भो वअस्स. ८ चउप्पदं, ° प्पदावत्थअं (पदावस्थाकं) ९ उवक्खित्तो (उपक्षिप्तः) १० किंचि (किंचित्)...तत्त कम्म°; कम्भ (कर्म) भेदो.

Vidūṣaka :—(*Aside*) Friend! The lady has, through the medium of the *catuṣpada* song, resigned herself to you, as it were.

King :—(*Aside*) Friend, my heart too tells me the same. Certainly, by her

Gesticulating with expressive action the words of the song, "Lord, know me to be devoted to you", by pointing at her own body, I was, it seems, addressed under the pretence of a gentle request, seeing no other way of showing her love owing to the presence (lit. neighbourhood) of Dhāriṇī. (5)

(Mālavikā *at the end of the singing wishes to go away*).

Vidūṣaka :—Stop, lady! You have somehow forgotton some particular action. I will just ask you about it.

Gaṇadāsa :—Dear child, stop a while; you may go after the instruction is declared free from fault.

(Mālavikā *turns round and stands still.*)

King :—(*To himself*) Ah! Her beauty gains fresh splendour in every posture. For,

Far lovelier than her dancing is her standing attitude in which the upper half of her body is straight drawn up, and in which she, having placed on her hip her left hand, with its bracelets sticking motionless to the joint of the wrist, made the other hang down loosely like a branch of the S'yāmā-creeper, is casting her eye on the pavement, the flowers on which are being gently pushed aside by her with her toe. (6)

सुकुमारप्रार्थनाव्याजं सुकुमारा मृदुला । रसनीयेत्यर्थः । सा चासौ प्रार्थना सैव व्याजोऽपदेशो यस्मिन्कर्मणि तत्तथोक्तम् । अहमुक्त इवोदित इव इत्युत्प्रेक्षा । मालिनीवृत्तम् । ॥ ५ ॥ क्रमभेदः क्रमविशेषः । कर्मभेदः इति पाठे क्रियाङ्गम् । उपदेशविशुद्धा उपदेशे विशुद्धा अनवद्या इत्युक्ता सती । पाठान्तरे उपदेशस्य विशुद्धौ निर्दोषतायां अभ्युपगतायामित्यर्थः । शोभां कान्तिविशेषम् । अनेन माधुर्यं नाम नायिकालंकार उक्तः । तदुक्तं–'सर्वावस्थाविशेषेषु माधुर्यं रमणीयता' इति । **वाममित्यादि** । संधिस्तिमितवलयं संधौ मणिबन्धे स्तिमितं निश्चलं वलयं कङ्कणं यस्य स तथोक्तः । तं वामं सव्यं हस्तं नितम्बे न्यस्य निधाय । श्यामाविटपसदृशं श्यामायाः विटपेन सदृशं फलिनीशाखासंनिभं द्वितीयं दक्षिणं हस्तं स्रस्तमुक्तं स्रस्तं शिथिलं यथा भवति तथा

देवी—ननु गौतमवचनमप्यार्यो हृदये करोति । (क)

गणदासः—देवि मैवम्[1] । देवप्रत्ययात्संभाव्यते सूक्ष्मदर्शिता गौतमस्य ।

मन्दोऽप्यमन्दतामेति संसर्गेण विपश्चितः ।
पङ्कच्छिदः फलस्येव निकषेणाविलं[2] पयः ॥ ७ ॥

(विदूषकं विलोक्य ।) तच्छृणुमो[3][4] विवक्षितमार्यस्य ।

विदूषकः—(गणदासं विलोक्य ।) साक्षिणीं तावत्पृच्छ । पश्चाद्यो मया क्रमभेदो लक्षितस्तं भणिष्यामि । (ख)

गणदासः—भगवति यथादृष्टमभिधीयतां । गुणो वा दोषो वा[5] ।

परिव्राजिका—यथादृष्टं[6] सर्वमनवद्यम् । कुतः ।

अङ्गैरन्तर्निहितवचनैः सूचितः सम्यगर्थः
पादन्यासो लयमनुगतस्तन्मयत्वं[7] रसेषु ।
शाखायोनिर्मृदुरभिनयस्तद्विकल्पानुवृत्तौ
भावो भावं नुदति[8] विषयाद्रागबन्धः स एव ॥ ८ ॥

(क) णं गोदमवअणं वि अज्जो हिअए करोदि । (ख) सक्खिणीं दाव पृच्छ । पच्छा जो मए कंमभेदो लक्खिदो तं भणिस्सं ।

मुक्तं विसृष्टम् लम्बितमित्यर्थः । कृत्वा विधाय । पादाङ्गुष्ठालुलितकुसुमे पादाङ्गुष्ठेनालुलितमामृष्टं कुसुमं यस्य तत्तथोक्तं तस्मिन्कुट्टिमे स्फटिकादिखचित-स्थले पातिते व्यापारिते अक्षिणी यस्मिन्कर्मणि तथोक्तम् । ऋज्वायतार्धम् ऋजु अवक्रमायतं दीर्घं अर्धं शरीरस्योर्ध्वभागो यस्य तत्तथोक्तम् । अस्याः स्थितं निष्क्रियतया अवस्थानं नृत्तान्नर्तनादतितरामत्यर्थं कान्तं मनोहरं भवति । अत्र वाक्यस्य विशेषितत्त्वात्पुष्पं नाम संध्यङ्गमुक्तं भवति । वाक्यार्थहेतुकं काव्यलिङ्गमलंकारः । मन्दाक्रान्ता वृत्तम् । ॥ ६ ॥ मन्दोऽपीति । विपश्चितः पण्डितस्य संसर्गेण संगत्या मन्दो जडबुद्धिरपि अमन्दतां बुद्धिवैशद्यमेति भजते । पङ्कच्छिदः मलहरस्य फलस्य कतकबीजस्य निकषेण घर्षेण आविलं पङ्किलं पयः इव । तद्यथा नैर्मल्यं याति तद्वत् । पथ्यावक्त्रं वृत्तम् । अस्य वाक्यस्योपपत्तिमत्त्वादुपन्यासो नाम संध्यङ्गमुक्तं भवति ॥७॥

---

१ मा मैवम्. २ कर्षेणा. ३ ततः; ४ ०मो वयं. ५ वेति. ६ यथाशास्त्रं. ०दर्शनम्. ७ सुप. ८ तुदति. ९ कोसिह (कौशिकी). १० कम्म (कर्म) ११ दिट्ठो.

Queen :—Does your Honour mind (take seriously) the words even of Gautama ?

Gaṇadāsa :—Queen, do not say so. From the knowledge (he must be getting from) his Majesty (as he is constantly in his company), Gautama is likely to have become sharp-sighted ; observe,

Even a dull person becomes clever by association with the wise, as turbid water becomes clear by contact with the powder of the mud-removing fruit. (7)

(*Looking at* vidūṣaka). Let us then hear what your Honour has got to say.

Vidūṣaka :—(*Looking at* Gaṇadāsa). In the first place ask the Umpire (*lit.* the lady who has witnessed the performance) ; afterwards I will mention the omission (in the performance) which I have observed.

Gaṇadāsa :—Revered one, give your opinion according to what you have observed—whether it (the performance) was faultless (a success) or was faulty.

Parivrājikā :—All was faultless as I observed it. For,

The meaning was well brought out by her limbs which were eloquent with expression ; the placings of her feet were in perfect unison with time ; there was complete identification with the sentiments conveyed ; the acting made by means of (the movements of) the hands was gentle, while in its successive stages chased away emotion (gave rise to another) from its substratum ; still the interest remained just the same. (8)

अनवद्यमदोषम् । अवद्यपण्य-इति निपातनात्साधु । **अङ्गैरित्यादि ।** अन्तर्निहितवचनैरन्तर्निहितान्यभ्यन्तरस्थापितानि वचनानि पदानि विक्षेपविशेषैः स्वाभिप्रायस्य प्रकटनात् यैस्तैरङ्गैर्हस्तादिभिः । अत्राभ्यासपाटवादङ्गानां स्वत एवान्तर्निहितवचनत्वमुत्प्रेक्षितमिति मन्तव्यम् । अर्थो गीतार्थः सम्यक् साधु सूचितः प्रकाशितः । पादन्यासः पादस्य न्यासो विन्यासः । लयमनुगतोऽनुसृतः लयो नाम तालमानम् । 'तालवर्ती तु यः कालः स काललयनाल्लयः' इत्युक्तत्वात् । (तालान्तरालवर्ती यः कालोऽसौ लय ईरितः । इ. पा.) 'छन्दोक्षरपदानां हि समत्वं यत्प्रकीर्तितम् । कलाकलान्तरकृतः स लयो मानसंज्ञितः ॥' इति भरतः । अत्र पादन्यासस्य स्वतो लयानुसरणभ्यासपाटवादिति मन्तव्यम् । रसेषु

गणदासः—देवः कथं वा मन्यते।

राजा—गणदास वयं स्वपक्षे[1] शिथिलाभिमानाः संवृत्ताः।

गणदासः—अद्य नर्तयितास्मि।

उपदेशं विदुः शुद्धं सन्तस्तमुपदेशिनः।
श्यामायते न युष्मासु[2] यः काञ्चनमिवाग्निषु॥ ९॥

देवी—दिष्ट्या परीक्षकाराधनेनार्यो वर्धते। (क)

गणदासः—देवीपरिग्रहः[3] एव मे वृद्धिहेतुः। (विदूषकं विलोक्य।) गौतम वदेदानीं यत्ते मनसि वर्तते।

विदूषकः—प्रथमोपदेशदर्शने प्रथमं ब्राह्मणस्य पूजा कर्तव्या। सा ननु वो विस्मृता। (ख)

परिव्राजिका—अहो प्रयोगाभ्यन्तरः प्राश्निकः[4]।

(सर्व प्रहसिताः[5]। मालविकापि स्मितं करोति।)

राजा—(आत्मगतम्[6]) आत्तसारश्चक्षुषा[7] मे स्वविषयः। यदनेन

स्मयमानमायताक्ष्याः किंचिदभिव्यक्तदशनशोभि मुखम्।
असमग्रलक्ष्यकेसरमुच्छ्वसदिव[8] पङ्कजं दृष्टम्॥ १०॥

(क) दिट्ठिआ परिक्खआराहणेण[9] अज्जो वड्ढइ।
(ख) पुढमोपदेसदंसणे पुढमं बह्मणस्स पूआ कादव्वा[10]। सा[11] णं वो विसुमरिदा।

रसविषयेषु तन्मयत्वं तादात्म्यम्। रसात्मता भवतीत्यर्थः। अत्र रसशब्देनोपचारात्परितो (पो) षातिशयवन्तो भावाः कथ्यन्ते। प्रकृतरसस्यैकत्वाद्रसेष्विति बहुवचनानुपपत्तिप्रसङ्गात्। अभिनयः प्रयोगः। यथोक्तम्—'प्रयोगो यस्तु

---

१ स्वपक्षशि०. २ युष्मासु. ३ ग्रहश्च, ग्रहोपि मे. ४ प्रश्नः। अतः परं–अयि पण्डितमन्ये। किम यत्। मोदकखण्डेनेऽप्यसमर्थो त्वं किं जानासि। प्रसन्नचन्द्रपादसदृशैः केशपाशैरेतान् भीष से। (अयि पडितंमण्णे। किं अण्ण। मोदअखण्डणेवि असमत्था तुमं किं जाणासि। पसण्णचन्दपादसरिसेहिं केसपासेहिं एदाणं भौसिअसि।) ५ परिहसन्ति। मा० च मन्दस्मितं. ६ स्वगतं. ७ उपात्त. ८ अपरि० (अपरिक्षतारा०), परिसदा (परिषदा०); अहिअं (अधिकं) ९० अज्जो. ९ सस्स. १० इच्छिदव्वा (एष्टव्या). ११ सा उण; ण वोपलक्खिदा.

Gaṇadāsa :—What does His Majesty think?

King :—Gaṇadāsa, we have become slack in our enthusiasm about the success of our protege (*lit.* side).

Gaṇadāsa :—To-day, I am a (real) dancing preceptor.

Wise men know (regard) that instruction of a teacher to be faultless which does not turn black (prove faulty) before (in the presence of) learned men, like gold in the fire. (9)

Queen :—I congratulate you, sir, upon your having satisfied the examiners.

Gaṇadāsa :—But Your Majesty's favour is the cause of this my good fortune. (*Looking towards* Vidūṣaka) Gautama, now say what you have in your mind.

Vidūṣaka :—The first time that instruction is exhibited, a complimentary worship must first be offered to a Brāhmaṇa; that, I say, you forgot.

Parivrājikā :—Oh! An Umpire thoroughly conversant with the details of acting!

(*They all laugh. Mālavikā, too, smiles*).

King :—(*To himself*) My eye has perceived the best part of its proper object, since, by it

Was seen the smiling face of the large-eyed one, graceful by the teeth slightly displayed, like an opening lotus with its filaments not yet fully visible. (10)

नाट्यादेर्भवेदभिनयो हि सः' इति । शाखायोनिः शाखा योनिः प्रभवो यस्य स तथोक्तस्तथाविधः सन् । मृदुः सुकुमारः । 'प्रयोगो द्विविधश्चैव विज्ञेयो नाट्यमाश्रितः । सुकुमारस्तथा विद्धो नानाभावरसाश्रयः ॥' इति भरतः । शाखा नाम नृत्तहस्तानां मानप्रचारः । यथोक्तम्—'शाखा तु नृत्तहस्तानां या मात्रा चित्रनर्तने' इति । तद्विकल्पानुवृत्तौ तस्याभिनयस्य विकल्पो भेदस्तस्यानुवृत्तिरनुगतिः प्राप्तिः । तस्याम् । भावः अभिनीयमानो निर्वेदादिः । विषयादाश्रयात् । प्रकृतात्स्थायिन इत्यर्थः । पूर्वाभिनीतं संचारिणं नुदति [प्रेरयति] अपाकरोति । रागबन्धो रञ्जनत्वयोगः स एव पूर्वं यादृशस्तादृश एवेत्यर्थः ॥ मन्दाक्रान्तावृत्तम् ॥८॥ नर्तयितास्मि यथार्थो नाट्याचार्योस्मि । तदेव विशदयति । **उपदेशं विदुरित्यादि** । सन्तः सदसद्विवेकिनः उपदेशिनः शिक्षकस्य । तमुपदेशं शिक्षां शुद्धं निर्दोषं विदुः जानन्ति । यः उपदेशः ।

गणदासः—महाब्राह्मण न खलु [1]प्रथमं नेपथ्यसंगीतकमिदम्। अन्यथा कथं त्वाम[2]र्चनीयं नार्चयिष्यामः।

विदूषकः—मया नाम मुग्धचातकेनेव शुष्कघनगर्जितेऽन्तरिक्षे जलपानमिष्टम्। (क)

परिव्राजिका—एवमेव।

विदूषकः—तेन हि पण्डितपरितोषप्रत्यया ननु मूढा जातिः। यतोऽत्रभवत्या शोभनं भणितं ततोऽस्या इदं पारितोषिकं प्रयच्छामि। (ख)

(इति राज्ञो हस्तात्कटकमाकर्षति।)

देवी—तिष्ठ तावत्। गुणान्तरमजानन्किमिति त्वमाभरणं ददासि। (ग)

विदूषकः—परकीयमिति कृत्वा। (घ)

देवी—(आचार्यं विलोक्य।) आर्य गणदास ननु दर्शितोपदेशा ते शिष्या। (ङ)

(क) मए णाम [3]मुद्धचादएण वि[4]अ सुक्खघणगज्जिदे अन्तरिक्खे जलपाणं इच्छि[5]दं। (ख) तेण हि पण्डिदपरितोसपच्चया णं [6]मूढा जादी। [7]जदो अत्तहोदीए सोहणं भणिदं तदो से इमं पारितोसिअं पअच्छामि। (ग) चिट्ठ दाव। गुणन्तरं अआणन्तो [8]किंति तुमं आहरणं देसि। (घ) [9]परकेरअंति करिअ। (ङ) अज्ज गणदास णं दंसिदोवदेसा दे[10] सिस्सा।

विद्वत्सु युष्मासु युष्मादृशेषु। विवेकिष्वित्यर्थः। अग्निषु काञ्चनमिव न श्यामायते। मलिनीभवति। लोहितादिडाज्भ्यः क्यष्'। 'वा क्यषः' इति विकल्पादात्मनेपदम्। अनुक्तहेतुको व्यतिरेकालंकारः। उपमानात्काञ्चनादपेक्षयोपदेशस्याधिक्यबोधनात्। 'आधिक्यमुपमेयस्योपमानान्न्यूनताथ वा। व्यतिरेक एक उक्ते हेतौ नोक्ते स च त्रिधा॥' इत्युक्तः इति अ. रा.॥ ९॥ प्रथमोपदेशेत्यादि। अत्र परिहासस्य गम्यमानत्वान्नर्मेति संध्यङ्गमुक्तं भवति। प्रयोगे अभ्यन्तरः प्रयोगाभ्यंतरः प्रयोगरहस्यज्ञ इत्यर्थः। आत्तः

---

१ प्रदर्शनमि०, सवनमि० २ दक्षिणीयं. ३ मुद्दा (मुधा); णाम सुक्ख० पाणं इच्छदा. जलपाणेन. नाय चादआइदं (चातकायितं). ४ एतन्नास्ति क्वचित्. ५ कादुं इच्छिअदि (कर्तुमिष्यते). ६ मूढजादी. ७ जइ, जइ भअवदीए. ८ किंणिमित्तं. ९ परकीअं. १० वः.

Gaṇadāsa :—Great Brāhmaṇa, this, indeed, is not the first concert (rehearsal) in the tiring room; otherwise how should we not have honoured you, who are worthy of honour ?

Vidūṣaka :—I, indeed, like a silly *Cātaka* longed for a drink of water from a sky resounding with empty (waterless) clouds.

Parivrājikā :—Exactly so.

Vidūṣaka :—Then, indeed, dull persons (like myself) have to be guided by the satisfaction of the wise. Since your Reverence has called the performance excellent I will bestow upon Mālavikā this reward. (*So saying he draws off a bracelet from the* King's *wrist*).

Queen :—Stop ! Why do you give away the ornament, ignorant as you are of the difference in merits ?

Vidūṣaka :—Because it belongs to another (and not to me).

Queen :—(*Looking towards the teacher of dancing*) Noble Gaṇadāsa, your pupil has exhibited her skill (in the instruction she has received).

गृहीतः सार उत्कृष्टांशो यस्य। **स्मयमानमित्यादि**। यस्मादनेन चक्षुषा आयते दीर्घे अक्षिणी यस्याः सा आयताक्षी तस्याः स्मयमानं कृतस्मितं अत एव किंचिदीषदभिव्यक्ता ये दशनाः तैः शोभते इति तथोक्तं मुखं उच्छ्वसत् विकसदत एव संपूर्णविकासाभावात् असमग्रं लक्ष्याणि केसराणि यस्य तदसमग्रलक्ष्यकेसरमसमस्ताभिव्यक्तकिञ्जल्कं पङ्कजं कमलमिव दृष्टम्। 'अत्र दशनकेसराणां मुखकमलयोः स्मितविकासयोर्बिम्बानुबिम्बभावेनोपन्यासाद्बिम्बानुबिम्बभावेनोपमा।' अ. रा. ॥ १० ॥ महाब्राह्मण इति निन्दागर्भम्। संगीतकमित्यत्र सवनमिति अर्चनीयमित्यत्र दक्षिणीयमिति पाठौ। तत्र सवनं नाट्यमण्डपे विघ्नोपशान्तये आदौ क्रियमाणो यज्ञः भरतेन नाट्यशास्त्रारम्भे प्रोक्तः। दक्षिणामर्हतीति दक्षिणीयः। कडङ्गरदक्षिणाच्छ च इति छः। नेपथ्यसेवनमिति पाठे नेपथ्यपरिग्रह इत्यर्थः। मुग्धोऽज्ञः। शुष्का जलहीना घनास्तेषां गर्जितं यस्मिन्। तैर्गर्जिते वा जलपानमिष्टं यथा शुष्कमेघगर्जितमाकर्ण्य जलं याचमानो चातको वञ्चितो भवति तथा भवतः प्रयोगाडम्बरमालोक्य स्वस्तिवाचनादिकमपेक्षमाणोहं भग्नेच्छः संवृत्त इत्यर्थः। चातकायितमिति पाठे चातकवदाचरितमित्यर्थः। कर्तुः क्यङ् सलोपश्च इति क्यङ् ततः क्तश्च। पण्डितानां परितोषः

गणदासः—वत्से । एहि गच्छाव इदानीम् ।

(मालविका सहाचार्येण निष्क्रान्ता ।)

विदूषकः—(राजानं विलोक्य । जनान्तिकम् ।) एतावान्मे मतिविभवो भवन्तं सेवितुम् । (क)

राजा—(जनान्तिकम् ।) अलमलं परिच्छेदेन । अद्य हि

भाग्यास्तमयमिवाक्ष्णोर्हृदयस्य महोत्सवावसानमिव ।
द्वारपिधानमिव धृतेर्मन्ये तस्यास्तिरस्करणम् ॥ ११ ॥

विदूषकः—(जनान्तिकम् ।) साधु त्वं दरिद्र इवातुरो वैद्येनोपनीयमानमौषधमिच्छसि । (ख)

(प्रविश्य ।)

हरदत्तः—देव मदीयमिदानीं प्रयोगमवलोकयितुं क्रियतां प्रसादः ।

राजा—(आत्मगतम् ।) अवसितो दर्शनार्थः । (दाक्षिण्यमवलम्ब्य । प्रकाशम् ।) हरदत्त ननु पर्युत्सुका एव वयम् ।

हरदत्तः—अनुगृहीतोऽस्मि ।

(नेपथ्ये ।)

वैतालिकः—जयतु जयतु देवः । उपारूढो मध्याह्नः । तथा हि ।

(क) एत्तिओ मे मदिविहवो भवन्तं सेविदुं । (ख) साहु तुमं दलिद्दो विअ आदुरो वेज्जेण उँवणीअमाणं ओसहं इच्छसि ।

पण्डितपरितोषस्तेन प्रत्ययो यस्याः । अस्यै मालविकायै । गुणान्तरं गुणविशेषम् । आर्य गणदास । दर्शितोपदेशा ते शिष्या । अनेन मालविकानिर्गमनहेतुना देवीवचनेन राज्ञो हितरोधनान्निरोधो नाम संध्यङ्गमुक्तं भवति । परिच्छेदेन एतावान्मतिविभव इति मर्यादाकरणेन । अतः परं समधिकं मम तव साहाय्येन प्रयोजनमिति भावः । **भाग्यास्तमयमित्यादि** । तस्या मालविकायास्तिरस्करणं तिरोधानमक्ष्णोर्नेत्रयोर्भाग्यास्तमयमिव भाग्यस्य भागधेयस्यास्तमयमिव नाशमिव । हृदयस्य

---

१ प्रतिष्ठस्व इ० २ अहं ३ करिणीम् . ४ मे दर्श० ५ विजयतां देवः. ६ मध्यमहः सविता; सुखाय भवतु माध्यन्दिनीसन्ध्या देवस्य. ७ ओसदं दीअमाणं.

Gaṇadāsa :—Dear child, come, let us now retire.

(*Mālavikā departs with her* teacher.)

Vidūṣaka :—(*Looking at the* King, *aside*) Thus far is the power of my intellect to serve your Majesty.

King :—Do not, do not (thus) set limits (to your power). For now,

I consider her disappearance behind the curtain to be like the termination of the good luck of my eyes, like the end of the great festivity of my heart, and like the closing of the door of happiness. (11)

Vidūṣaka :—(*Aside*) Bravo! Like a poor patient you desire the medicine to be brought to you by the physician himself.

Haradatta :—(*Entering*) My lord, now you should do me the favour of looking at my representation.

King :—(*To himself*) My object in being a spectator is now at an end. (*Aloud, resorting to politeness*) Haradatta, we are, indeed, anxious to behold it.

Haradatta :—I am highly favoured.

(*Behind the Scenes*)

A Bard :—All prosperity to the King! The sun has risen to mid-day. For,

---

मनसो महोत्सवस्यावसानमन्तमिव। धृतेः प्रीतेर्द्वारपिधानमिव द्वारस्य प्रवेशमार्गस्य पिधानं निरोधं तिरोधानमिव। मन्ये संभावयामि। सर्वं शून्यमिव जातमित्यर्थः। उत्प्रेक्षालंकारः। आर्यावृत्तम् ॥ ११ ॥ अत्रार्तेर्गम्यमानत्वाद्विधुतं नाम संध्यङ्गमुक्तं भवति। दरिद्र इवातुर इति। अयं भावः—त्वं स्वयं किमपि न करोषि। मया त्वत्संनिधावानीयमानां मालविकामिच्छसि। **पत्रच्छायास्विति**। दीर्घिका उद्यानवापी तत्र याः पद्मिन्यः कमलिन्यस्तासां पत्रच्छायासु हंसा मुकलिते नयने येषां ते मुकुलितनयनाः संमीलितलोचनाः स्थिता इति शेषः। अत्यर्थतापादतिमात्रसूर्योष्मणः सौधानि राजसदनानि। वलभ्यः गोपानस्यः ताभिः परिचयः तासां संश्रयः तं द्विषन्तीति द्वेषिणः पारावता यत्र तथाभूतानि। शिखी मयूरः बिन्दूत्क्षेपान् उत्क्षिप्तजलबिन्दून् तृषाकुलत्वात् पिपासुः पातुमिच्छुः सन् भ्रान्तिमत् भ्रमणःशीलं वारियन्त्रं जलोद्गारियन्त्रं परिपतति परितो भ्रमति। सप्त सप्तयः अश्वा यस्य स

पत्रच्छायासु हंसा मुकुलितनयना दीर्घिकापद्मिनीनां
सौधान्यत्यर्थतापाद्वलभिपरिचयद्वेषिपारावतानि।
बिन्दूत्क्षेपान्पिपासुः परिपतति शिखी भ्रान्तिमद्वारियन्त्रं
सर्वैरुस्रैः समग्रैस्त्वमिव नृपगुणैर्दीप्यते सप्तसप्तिः॥ १२॥

विदूषकः—अविहा अविहा। ब्राह्मणस्य भोजनवेला संवृत्ता। अत्रभवतोऽपि। उचितवेलातिक्रमे चिकित्सका दोषमुदाहरन्ति। हरदत्त किमिदानीं भणसि। (क)

हरदत्तः—नास्ति मद्वचनस्यावकाशोऽत्र।

राजा—(हरदत्तमवलोक्य।) तेन हि त्वदीयमुपदेशं श्वो वयं द्रक्ष्यामः। विश्राम्यतु भवान्।

हरदत्तः—यदाज्ञापयति देवः। (इति निष्क्रान्तः।)

देवी—निर्वर्तयत्वार्यपुत्रो मज्जनविधिम्। (ख)

विदूषकः—भवति विशेषेण पानभोजनं त्वरय। (ग)

परिव्राजिका—(उत्थाय।) स्वस्ति भवते। (इति सपरिजनया देव्या सह निष्क्रान्ता।)

(क) अविहा अविहा। बह्मणस्स भोअणवेला संवुत्ता। अत्तहोदोवि। उइदवेलादिक्कमे चिइच्छआ दोसं उदाहरन्ति। हरदत्त किं दाणिं भणसि। (ख) णिव्वट्टेदु अज्जउत्तो मज्जणविहिम्। (ग) भोदि विसेसेण पाणभोअणं तुराववेहि।

सप्तसप्तिः सूर्यः समग्रैः समग्राणि येषां तैः संमुखपातिभिः सर्वैः उस्रैः किरणैः त्वमिव समग्रैः सर्वव्यापिभिः नृपगुणै राजतेजोभिः दीप्यते। 'गोपानसी तु वलभिः' इति। 'पारावतः कलरवः' इति। 'किरणोस्रमयूखांशु-' इति चामरः। उपमालंकारः। स्रग्धरावृत्तम्॥ १२॥ उचितेलाया योग्यकालस्यातिक्रमः तस्मिन्सति। चिकित्सका वैद्याः। मज्जनविधिं स्नानविधिम् मध्याह्नविधिमिति पाठे मध्यम-

---

१ बिन्दुक्षे. २ सरति. ३ समग्र. ४ वचनावसरोत्र; वचनस्यान्यस्यः नास्ति चान्यस्य वचना०. ५ विरमतु. ६ यथा. ७ अह्माणं ठण भोअणवेला उपठ्ठिदा. ८ (हरदत्तं विलोक्य।). ९ अज्जो. १० एतन्नास्ति कचित्. ११ ०वेदु (त्वरयतु).

The geese have their eyes half closed under the shade of the leaves of the lotus-plants in the pleasure-tank; the mansions on account of the extreme heat, have become such as have their sloping roofs shunned by pigeons; the peacock, desirous of drinking the drops of water thrown up, flies round the revolving water-wheel (fountain): and the sun blazes with all his rays falling perpendicularly in their fulness, as thou with all thy princely qualities. (12)

Vidūṣaka :—Oh! HO! the Brāhmaṇa's time of dining has arrived. The physicians declare that it is injurious (to health) when the usual time (of dining) is allowed to pass (*lit.* transgressed), Haradatta, what do you say now?

Haradatta :—There is no room for my words (*i.e.* I cannot say anything now).

King :—(*Looking towards* Haradatta) Then we shall see your skill in teaching exhibited to-morrow. You may take rest in the meanwhile.

Haradatta—As your Majesty commands.

(*Exit* Haradatta)

Queen :—Let your Majesty finish the ceremony of bath.

Vidūṣaka :—Lady, let the arrangements for eating and drinking be hurried on with special care.

Parivrājikā :—(*Rising up*) Hail to Your Majesty!

(*Exit with the* Queen, *accompanied by her attendants.*)

दिनकृत्यमित्यर्थः । पानं च भोजनं च तयोः समाहारः पानभोजनम् । अद्वितीया नास्ति द्वितीयं उपमानं यस्याः सा निरुपमा । **अव्याजेति** । अव्याजेन भूषणाद्युपचाराभावेन सुन्दरीम् । अकृत्रिमलावण्यामित्यर्थः । तां ललितेन सुभगेन विज्ञानेन संगीतकलापरिज्ञानेन । योजयता युक्तां कुर्वता विधात्रा विषेण दिग्धः विषदिग्धः विषाक्तशल्यः कामस्य बाणः परिकल्पितः उपस्थापितः । अत्र विज्ञानयोजनबाणोपकल्पनरूपवस्तुनोः संबन्धः असंभवन् मालविकाशिल्पज्ञानयोर्बाणविषसादृश्यमुपकल्पयतीति निदर्शनालंकारः । आर्या छन्दः ॥ १३ ॥ विपणिकन्दुर्नाम पण्यवीथिकायां व्रीहि(पिष्ट)-पचनपात्रम् । 'कन्दुर्ना स्वेदनी स्त्रियाम्' इत्यमरः । विपणिकन्दोरिव ममोदराभ्यन्तरं बुभुक्षया पीड्यते इति भावः ॥ **एवमेवेत्यादि** । एवमेवेत्थमेव यथा भवान्भोजनरूपे स्वकार्ये त्वरते तथा सुहृदर्थे मदर्थे मालविकापुनर्दर्शने त्वरताम् । अत्र दृष्टनष्टस्य बीजस्यानूपसर्पणात्परिसर्पो नाम संध्यङ्गमुक्तं भवति ॥ गृहीतक्षणोऽस्मि तवार्थसाधने

विदूषकः—भो न केवलं रूपे शिल्पेऽप्यद्वितीया मालविका। (**क**)

राजा—वयस्य

अव्याजसुन्दरीं तां विज्ञानेन ललितेन योजयता।
[1]परिकल्पितो विधात्रा बाणः कामस्य विषदिग्धः॥ १३॥

किं बहुना। चिन्त[2]यितव्योऽस्मि।

विदूषकः—भवताप्यहम्। दृढं विपणिकन्दुरिव म उदराभ्यन्तरं दह्यते। (**ख**)

राजा—एवमेव भवान्[3]सुहृदर्थे त्वरताम्।

विदूषकः—गृहीतक्षणोऽस्मि। किं तु मेघावलीनिरुद्धा ज्योत्स्नेव पराधीनदर्शना तत्रभवती। भवानपि सूनोपरिचरो विहङ्गम इवामिषलोलुपो भीरुकश्च। तस्मादनातुरो भूत्वा कार्यसिद्धिं प्रार्थयमानो मे रोचसे। (**ग**)

राजा—सखे [4]कथमनातुरो भविष्यामि।

सर्वान्तःपुरवनिताव्या[5]पारप्रतिनिवृत्तहृदयस्य।
सा वामलोचना मे स्नेहस्यैकायनीभूता॥ १४॥

(इति निष्क्रान्ताः सर्वे)

इति द्वितीयोऽङ्कः।

(**क**) भो[6] ण केवलं रूवे सिप्पेवि अद्दुदीआ मालविआ (**ख**) भवदावि अहं। दिढं[7] विपणिकन्दु विअ मे उदर[8]ब्भन्तरं दज्झ[9]इ। (**ग**) [10]गहीदक्खणोम्हि। किं दु मेहा[11]वलीणिरुद्धा जोण्हा विअ पराहीणदंसणा त[12]त्तहोदी। भवं वि स[13]ूणोपरिच्चिरो विहंगमो[14] विअ आमिसलोलुओ भीरुओ अ। ता [15]अणादुरो भविअ कज्जसिद्धिं पत्थअन्तो मे रो[16]असि।

निश्चितमतिरस्मि। क्षणो निर्व्यापारस्थितिः आवश्यकं मनःस्वास्थ्यमित्यर्थः। निरुद्धा अन्तरितदर्शना। परस्मिन्नधि पराधीनं परतन्त्रम्। 'सप्तमी शौण्डैः' इति समासः। 'अषड-

---

१ उप. २ सखे चि० ३ र्थेपि, अस्मदर्थे. ४ कथं नातुरः. ५ व्यापारं. ६ भो वअस्स. ७ दिढं खु. ८ हिअअ. ९ ढ·भज्जइ. १० गहीदो क्खणो. ११ मेहोवरुद्धाजोण्हा. १२ ०होदी मालविआ. १३ सूणापरिसरचरो, ०णापरिच्चरो. १४ गिद्धो. १५ अच्चादुरो (अत्यातुरः) १६ रुच्चइ, रुचेसि.

Vidūṣaka :—Ha ! Not only in beauty but in artistic skill also is Mālavikā without a second (unsurpassed).

King :—Friend,

The Creator, by endowing her, who is artlessly (naturally) beautiful, with attractive accomplishments, has prepared an arrow for the god of love, steeped in poison. (13)

Why should I say more? You must think about me (*i. e.* my helpless condition.)

Vidūṣaka :—You ought also to take thought for my comfort. Surely the inside of my stomach burns like an oven in the market place.

King :—You should also in a similar way speedily exert yourself for the sake of your friend.

Vidūṣaka :—I am determined to do it. But her ladyship is such that her sight is dependant on others like the moon-light obscured by a line of clouds. As for your Honour, you are like a bird hovering round a slaughter-house, desirous of meat, but timid. Therefore I should like you to seek the accomplishment of your object without being impatient.

King :—Friend, how can I help being impatient? since, affection of me whose heart is averse to all dealings with the beauties of my harem. (14)

(Exeunt Omnes).

HERE ENDS THE SECOND ACT.

क्षाशितङ्ग्वलंकर्मालंपुरुषाध्युत्तरपदात्खः ' इति खः । दर्शनं यस्याः सा । धारिणीप्रतिबन्धादिति भावः । सूना वधस्थानं तस्याः परिसरे चरतीति तथोक्तः । आमिषे मांसे पक्षे अभिलषितवस्तुनि लोलुपः अतिशयेन लुब्धः । अनातुरः नातिपर्याकुलः नात्युत्सुको वा । अत्र सान्त्वनस्य गम्यमानत्वात्पर्युपासनं नाम संध्यङ्गमुक्तं भवति ॥ **सर्वान्तः–पुरेत्यादि** । सा वामलोचना चारुनयना मालविका सर्वा या अन्तःपुरवनितास्तासु यः व्यापारः अवलोकनालपनालिङ्गनादिस्तस्मात्प्रतिनिवृत्तं हृदयं यस्य तस्य मे स्नेहस्य प्रेम्ण एकायनीभूता । एकं केवलमयनं स्थानम् । आश्रय इत्यर्थः । तद्भूता तद्विरहितो न क्वापि निर्वृतिं लभे इत्यर्थः । आर्याछन्दः । ॥ १४ ॥ अत्राङ्के मालविकानिष्क्रमणेन कथाविच्छेदे सति सर्वान्तःपुरेत्यादिना गम्यमानो राज्ञोऽभिलाषातिशय उत्तराङ्ककथाहेतुत्वाद्बिन्दुरित्यनुसंधेयम् ॥

इति श्रीकाटयवेमभूपविरचिते कुमारगिरिराजीये मालविकाग्निमित्रव्याख्याने द्वितीयोऽङ्कः ॥

तृतीयोऽङ्कः ।

(ततः प्रविशति परिव्राजिकायाः परिचारिका ।)

परिचारिका—आज्ञप्तास्मि भगवत्या उपायनार्थं बीजपूरकं गृहीत्वा-गच्छेति । तद्यावत्प्रमदवनपालिकां मधुकरिकामन्विष्यामि । (परिक्रम्यावलोक्य च ।) एषा तपनीयाशोकमवलोकयन्ती मधुकरिका तिष्ठति । यावदेना मुपसर्पामि । (क)

(ततः प्रविशत्युद्यानपालिका ।)

प्रथमा—(उपसृत्य ।) मधुकरिके अपि सुखस्त उद्यानव्यापारः । (ख)

द्वितीय—अहो समाभृतिका । सखि स्वागतं ते । (ग)

समाभृतिका—सखि भगवत्याज्ञापयति । अरिक्तपाणिनास्मादृशजनेन तत्रभवती देवी द्रष्टव्या । तद्बीजपूरकेण शुश्रूषितुमिच्छामीति । (घ)

मधुकरिका—ननु संनिहितं बीजपूरकम् । कथय तावदन्योन्यसंघर्षि-तयोर्नाट्याचार्ययोरुपदेशं दृष्ट्वा कतरो भगवत्या प्रशंसित इति । (ङ)

(क) आणत्तह्मि भअवदीए उ[2]वाअणत्थं बीअऊरअं गेण्हिअ आअच्छत्ति । ता जाव पमदवणपालिअं महुअरिअं अण्णसामि । एसा तवणीआसोअं ओलोअ[3]न्ती महुअरिआ चिट्ठदि । जाव णं उ[4]वसप्पामि । (ख) म[5]हुअरिए अवि सुहो दे उज्जाणव्वावारो । (ग) अह्मो स[6]मामुदिआ । सहि सागदं ते । (घ) हला भगवदी आण्णवेदि । अरित्तपाणिणा अह्मारिसजणेण तत्तहोदी देवी देक्खिदव्वा । ता बीअपूरएण सुस्सूसिदुं इच्छामित्ति । (ङ) णं संणिहिदं बी[8]अपूरअं । कहेहि दाव अण्णोण्णसंघ[9][10]रिसिदाणं णट्टाअरिआणं उवदेसं देक्खिअ कदरो भअवदीए पसंसिदोत्ति ।

कविरिदानीमङ्कान्तरमारभमाणः कथासंघटनार्थं प्रथमं प्रवेशकं नामार्थोपक्षेपकं प्रस्तौति—**ततः प्रविशतीत्यादिना** ॥ भगवत्या उपायनार्थं उपायनमुपहारस्तदर्थम् । बीजपूरकं मातुलिङ्गफलम् । 'फलपूरो बीजपूरो रुचको मातुलुङ्गके ।' इत्यमरः । तपनीयाशोकः तपनीयमग्नितप्तं सुवर्णं तेन पीतरक्तत्वं लक्ष्यते । तादृशकुसुमः अशोकः ।

---

१ ०का समाहितिका. २ जहा समाभुदिए. समाहिदिए दवीए उवा०, देवस्स उववणन्थं (उपवनस्थ). ३ अन्ती चिट्ठदि, आलो अन्ती (आलोकमाना) ४ संभावेमि. ५ आलि. ६ परहुदिआ (परभृतिका). ७ पेक्खिदं (प्रेक्षितुं). ८ जेव्व बीअ. ९ अस्मात्परं—दुवेणंवि संगीदओवदेसणिमित्तं इत्यधिकं पुस्तकान्तरे. १० संघट्टितयोः.

ACT III

(*Enter* a female attendant *of the* Parivrājikā).

First Attendant:—I have received the following order from the revered lady: "Get me a citron and bring it here that I may present it, as a token of respect, to the queen". So I will go and look for Madhukarikā, the keeper of the pleasure-garden. (*Walking round and looking*)—Ah! Here she stands looking at the golden Aśoka tree. I will approach her then.

(*Enters* the keeper of the garden.)

First:—(*Going up to her*):—Madhukarikā, do you find your duty of looking after the garden pleasant?

Second attendant:—Oh, here is Samābhṛtikā. Welcome to you, my friend.

Samābhṛtikā:—Friend, the revered lady says–"Her Highness the Queen should be approached by people like us with hands not empty; I, therefore, wish to wait on her with (by presenting) a citron."

Madhukarikā:—Why, here is a citron near you. But tell me, first, which of the two preceptors of music, who were disputing with each other about their respective merits as teachers, was praised (declared superior) by the revered lady after beholding the performances of their pupils?

उद्यानव्यापारः उद्यानपालनकर्म । **अरिक्तपाणिनेति** । आचारप्राप्तमेतत् । तदुक्तम्-'रिक्तपाणिस्तु नोपेयाद्राजानं देवतां गुरुम् ।' इति । शुश्रूषितुं सभाजयितुमित्यर्थः । अन्योन्यसंघर्षितयोः अन्योन्येन स्पर्धमानयोः । संघर्षोऽनयोः संजातः संघर्षितौ । आगमः नाट्यशास्त्रज्ञानमनयोर्विद्यते तौ आगमिनौ । प्रयोगे लास्योपदेशे निपुणौ । उन्नमित उत्कर्षितः । मालविकागतं मालविकासंबद्धं । कौ पृथिव्यां लीन कुत्सितत्वात् कुलीनं तस्य भावः कौलीनं लोकवार्ता लोकापवाद इति यावत् । चित्तं चेतोविकारं रक्षन् हृदयव्यथां परिहरन्निति यावत् । प्रभुत्वं न दर्शयति देवीं विगणय्य मालविकां न परिगृह्णाति । आदौ अनुभूता उपभुक्ता शिरसि धारिता च पश्चान्मुक्ता उत्सृष्टा च अनुभूतमुक्ता । मालतीमाला जातिकुसुमस्रक् 'सुमना मालती जातिः' इत्यमरः । पेशलतरं सुन्दरतरम् । साधुजनः परिव्राजिका । शुश्रूषा तस्यै बीजपूरकदानम् ।

समाभृतिका—द्वावपि किलागमिनौ प्रयोगनिपुणौ च । किं तु शिष्यागुणविशेषेणोन्नमितो गणदासः । (क)

मधुकरिका—अथ मालविकागतं कौलीनं किं श्रूयते । (ख)

समाभृतिका—बलवत्खलु साभिलाषो तस्यां भर्ता । केवलं देव्या धारिण्याश्चित्तं रक्षन्नात्मनः प्रभुत्वं न दर्शयति । मालविकाप्येषु दिवसेष्वनुभूतमुक्तेव मालतीमाला म्लायमाना लक्ष्यते । अतः परं न जाने । विसृज माम् । (ग)

मधुकरिका—एतच्छाखावलम्बितं बीजपूरकं गृहाण । (घ)

समाभृतिका—(नाट्येन गृहीत्वा ।) सखि त्वमप्यतः पेशलतरं साधुजनशुश्रूषायाः फलमनुभविष्यसि । (इति प्रस्थिता ।) (ङ)

मधुकरिका—सखि सममेव गच्छावः । अहमप्यस्य चिरायमाणकुसुमोद्गमस्य तपनीयाशोकस्य दोहदनिमित्तं देव्यै विज्ञापयामि । (च)

(क) दुवेवि किल आअमिणा पओअणिउणा अ । किं तु सिस्सागुणविसेसेण उ[1]ण्णमिदो गणदासो । (ख) अह मालविआगदं कोलीणं[2] किं सुणीअदि । (ग) [3]बलियं क्खु साहिलासो तस्सिं भट्टा । के[4]वलं देवीए धारिणीए चित्तं रक्खन्तो[5] अत्तणो पहुत्तणं ण दंसेदि । मालविआवि इमेसु[6] दिअहेसु अणुहूदमूत्ता विअ मालदीमाला मिलाअमाणा लक्खीअदि[7] । अदो वरं ण जाणे । विसज्जेहि मं । (घ) एदं साहावलम्बिदं[8] बीअपूरअं गेण्ह । (ङ) हला[9] तुमं वि अदो पेसलदरं साहुजणसुस्सूसाए फलं अणुभविस्ससि[10] । (च) सहि[11] समं जेव्व गच्छह्म । अहं वि इमस्स चिराअमाणकुसुमोग्गमस्स तवणीआसोअस्स दोहलनिमित्तं देवीए विण्णवेम्हि[12] ।

चिरायमाणः विलम्बितः कुसुमोद्गमः पुष्पप्रसवो यस्य । दोहदनिमित्तं दोहदपूरणप्रयोजनम् । यद्वा । पूरणार्थम् । दोहदोऽत्र चरणताडनापेक्षा । तदुक्तम्–‘ पादाहतः प्रमदया विकसत्यशोकः ।’ इति । **प्रवेशकः**–‘यस्तु प्रयोगबाहुल्यादङ्केऽर्थो न समाप्यते । बहु-

---

१ उण्णमिदोपदेसो. गणदासो उण्णमिदो उवदेसे: मालविआए उवदेसो पसंसिदो; सिस्साए मालविआए गुणविसेसेण गणदासस्य उवदेसो पसंसिदो । २ कहं. ३ दिढं-बाढं किल; बाढं. ४ किं तु केवलं; चित्तं रक्खिदुं अहिलासदंसणेणः ५ रक्खमाणो. ६ अमूइं दिअहाइं. ७ देवीए राक्खीअदि इत्य० ८ लम्ब. ९ तह (इति नाट्येन बीजपूरकं गृहीत्वा ।) हला. १० पावेह (प्राप्नुहि); पाविदा होदि (प्राप्ता भव). ११ हला. १२ णिवेदेमि.

Samābhṛtikā :—Both of them are adepts in the science of dancing, and clever in execution. But Gaṇadāsa was ranked the higher (of the two) on account of the superior excellence of his pupil.

Madhukarikā :—Now, what is the gossip that is heard about Mālavikā ?

Samābhṛtikā :—To be sure His Lordship is desperately in love with her ; it is only to spare the feelings of Queen Dhārinī, that he does not exercise his royal power (to satisfy his desire). Mālavikā, too, is observed in these days to be fading like a *jasmine* garland that has been worn and left off. More than this I do not know. Give me leave to depart.

Madhukarikā :—Take the citron hanging on this branch.

Samābhṛtikā :—(*Shows that she takes it*). Friend, you too will obtain the fruit, more precious than this, of your service of the saintly lady. (*So saying she starts to go*).

Madhukarikā :—Friend, we will go together. I also have to give the Queen information about the necessity of gratifying the longing of this golden As'oka tree, which has delayed to burst into blossom.

वृत्तान्तोऽल्पकथैः स विषेयः प्रवेशकैः ॥' तल्लक्षणम्—'प्रवेशकोऽनुदात्तोक्त्या नीचपात्रप्रयोजितः। अङ्कद्वयान्तर्विज्ञेयः शेषं विष्कम्भके यथा' ॥ इति साहित्यदर्पणे। 'नोत्तममध्यमपुरुषैराचरितो नाप्युदात्तवचनकृतः। प्राकृतभाषाचारः प्रवेशको नाम विज्ञेयः ॥' इति भरतश्च। ततः प्रविशतीत्यादि। कामयमानावस्थः कामयमानानां कामिनामवस्थेवावस्था दशा यस्य स तथोक्तः ॥ शरीरमित्यादि। दयितालिङ्गनसुखे प्रियाभिष्वङ्गसौख्येऽसत्यविद्यमाने सति शरीरं वपुः क्षामं स्यात्कृशं भवेत्। क्षणमपि क्षणमात्रमपि सा मालविका न दृश्यत इति न लक्ष्यत इति चक्षुः सास्रबाष्पं भवेत्स्यात्। हे हृदय चित्त सारङ्गस्य इव अक्षिणी यस्याः सा तया सारङ्गाक्ष्या हरिणनेत्रया तया मालविकया कदाचिज्जातु विरहितं वियुक्तं नासि न भवसि। अतस्तस्मात्कारणान्निर्वाणे सुखे प्रसक्ते प्रस्तुते सति किं किमर्थं परितापं संतापं वहसि धारयसि व्रजसि प्राप्नोषि। एतेन चिन्ता नाम व्यभिचारी भाव उक्तः। तदुक्तं—'ध्यानं चिन्तेहितानाप्तेः शून्यताश्वासतापकृत्। इति शिखरिणी वृत्तम् ॥ १ ॥ धीरतां मनःस्थैर्यं त्यक्त्वा धीरतयाऽवसरपरिपालनमकृत्वेत्यर्थः। परिदेवितेन विलापेन। नागरक्षितः नागेन सर्पेण रक्षितः निधिः

समाभृतिका—युज्यते। अधिकारः खलु तव। (क)

(इति निष्क्रान्ते।)

प्रवेशकः।

(ततः प्रविशति कामयमानावस्थो राजा विदूषकश्च।)

राजा—(आत्मानं विलोक्य।)

शरीरं क्षामं स्यादसति दयितालिङ्गनसुखे
भवेत्सोस्रं चक्षुः क्षणमपि न सा दृश्यत इति।
तया सारङ्गाक्ष्या त्वमसि न कदाचिद्विरहितं
प्रसक्ते निर्वाणे हृदय परितापं वहसि किम्॥१॥

विदूषकः—अलं भवतो धीरतामुज्झित्वा परिदेवितेन। दृष्टा खलु मया तत्रभवत्या मालविकायाः प्रियसखी बकुलावलिका। श्राविता च मया यद्भवता संदिष्टम्। (ख)

राजा—ततः किमुक्तवती।

विदूषकः—विज्ञापय भर्तारम्। अनुगृहीतास्म्यनेन नियोगेन। किं तु सा तपस्विनी देव्याधिकृततरं रक्ष्यमाणा नागरक्षित इव निधिर्न सुखं समासादयितव्या। तथापि घटयिष्यामीति। (ग)

(क) जुज्जइ। अहिआरो क्खु तुह। (ख) अलं भवदो धीरदं उज्झिअ परिदेविदेण। दिट्ठा क्खु मए तत्तहोदीए मालविआए पिअसही बउलावलिआ। सुणाविदा[३] अ मह जं भवदा संदिट्ठं। (ग) विण्णवेहि भट्टारं। अणुगहिदम्हि इमिणा णिओएण। किं दु सा तवस्सिणी देवीए अहिअदरं[४] रक्खीअमाणा[५] णाअरक्खिदो विअ[६] णिही ण सुहं समासादइदव्वा। तहवि घटइस्सं ति।

भूम्यादौ निहितः द्रव्यसंचयः। अतिलुब्धो हि मरणादूर्ध्वं नागो भूत्वा स्वद्रव्यनिधे रक्षणं करोतीति लोकवादः। **सा तपस्विनी** इति–अत्र तपस्विनीति करुणापात्र-मुच्यते। 'तपस्वी करुणापात्रम्' इति हलायुधः। अत्र प्राप्तिसंभावनया प्राप्त्याशा-नाम तृतीयावस्था सूचिता। अनया प्राप्त्याशया: बिन्दो समन्वयाद्गर्भसंधिरिति मन्त-

---

१ मन्दं. २ व्रजसि, भजसि. ३. सुणाविदो अअं अत्थो; सुणाविदा अ तं अत्थं भवदा संदिट्ठम्। ४ अहिअं. ५ रक्खन्तीए. ६ भणा विअ.

Samābhṛtikā :—Quite proper. It is, indeed, your duty.
(*Exeunt.*)

(*Here ends the* Interlude.)

(*Enter the* King *in a love-sick state, and* Vidūṣaka).

King :—(*Looking at himself*) The body may be lean when it has not obtained the pleasure of embracing the beloved; my eye may be filled with tears for the reason that she is not to be seen by it even for a moment; but thou, my heart, art not separated for a single instant from that fawn-eyed one; why then dost thou suffer anguish, when the highest bliss is ever near thee? (1)

Vidūṣaka :—Let your Highness cease lamenting having set aside all firmness of mind. I have seen Bakulāvalikā, lady Mālavikā's dear friend, and have delivered to her (lit. made her hear) the message desired to be communicated by Your Highness.

King :—What did she say then ?

Vidūṣaka :—"Inform His Majesty that I am favoured by having this duty entrusted to me. But that poor girl, who is being guarded by Her Majesty with greater care than before, is not easily to be got at like a treasure guarded by a *Nāga* ; nevertheless I will try to bring about a union".

व्यम् ॥ संकल्पः योनिरुद्भवो यस्य स संकल्पयोनिः मदनः तत्संबुद्धिः । प्रतिबंधनन्तु विघ्नयन्तु । अभिनिवेशय बलवन्नियोज्य । कालान्तरक्षमः विलम्बासहः । क रुजेत्यादि । हृदयं प्रमथ्नातीति हृदयप्रमाथिनी चित्तस्थैर्योन्माथिनी रुजा व्यथा क । तव विश्वसनीयं कुसुममयत्वादपीडाकरत्वेन विश्वासार्हं आयुधं क । कशब्दद्वयमुभयोरत्यन्तं विरुद्धत्वं दर्शयति । लोके मृदु सुकुमारं वस्तु तीक्ष्णतरं अतिप्रखरमिति यदुच्यते तदिदं त्वयि दृश्यते प्रतीयते । तवायुधस्य मृदुत्वेऽपि कार्यस्य तीक्ष्णत्वादिति भावः । अत्र हेतुकार्ययोः मृदुत्वसंतापरूपविरुद्धगुणोत्पत्तिप्रतिपादनाद्विषमालङ्कारः । वियोगिनी (वैतालीयं) वृत्तम् ॥ २ ॥ साधनीये मालविकाप्राप्तिरूपे । उपक्षेपः आरम्भः । पर्यवस्थापयतु संस्तम्भयतु । धैर्यमवलम्ब्यति शेषः । अत्र 'कृत उपक्षेपः' इत्यनेन कपटोपायकल्पनया गम्यमानत्वेन अभूताहरणं नाम संध्यङ्गमुक्त भवति ॥ पाठान्तरे सुभगाणि सुन्दराणि । कुरवकाणि

राजा—भगवन् संकल्पयोने प्रतिबन्धवत्स्वपि[1] विषयेष्वभिनिवेश्य[2] किं तथा प्रहरसि यथा जनोऽयं कालान्तरक्षमो न भवति।

(सविस्मयम्।)

क रुजा हृदयप्रमाथिनी क च ते विश्वसनीयमायुधम्।
मृदु तीक्ष्णतरं यदुच्यते तदिदं मन्मथ दृश्यते त्वयि ॥ २ ॥

विदूषकः—ननु भणामि तस्मिन्साधनीये कृत उपक्षेप इति। तत्पर्यवस्थापयतु भवानात्मानम्। (क)

राजा—अथेमं दिवसशेषमुचितव्यापारपराङ्मुखेन[3] चेतसा क नु खलु यापयामि[4]।

विदूषकः—नन्वद्यैव प्रथमं वसन्तावतारसूचकानि रक्ताशोककुसुमान्युपायनं प्रेष्य नववसन्तोत्सवापदेशेन इरावत्या निपुणिकामुखेन प्रार्थितो भवानिच्छाम्यार्यपुत्रेण सह दोलाधिरोहणमनुभवितुमिति। भवताप्यस्यै प्रतिज्ञातम्। तत्प्रमदवनमेव गच्छावः। (ख)

राजा—न क्षममिदम्।

विदूषकः—कथमिव। (ग)

(क) णं भणामि तस्सिं साहेणिज्जे[5] किदो उवक्खेओत्ति। ता पज्जवत्थावेदु भवं अप्पाणं। (ख) णं अज्ज एव्व पुढमं[7] वसन्दावदारसूअआणि[8] रत्तासोअकुसुमाइं[9] उवाअणं[6] पेसिअ णववसन्दूसवावदेसेण[10] इरावदीए णिउणिआमुहेण पत्थिदो भवं इच्छामि अज्जउत्तेण सह दोलहिरोहणं अणुहविदुं ति। भवदावि से पडिण्णादं। ता पमदवणं एव्व गच्छम्ह। (ग) कहं विअ।

कुरण्टकपुष्पाणि। अपदेशेन मिषेण। क्षमं कर्तुं योग्यम्। निसर्गनिपुणाः प्रकृत्या पटुमतयः परभावावबोधे कुशला इत्यर्थः। अन्यस्यां संक्रान्तं हृदयं प्रेम यस्य तम्। उपलालयन्तमुपच्छन्दयन्तं बाह्यतः प्रीत्याविष्करणेनानुकूलयन्तामित्यर्थः। उचित इति। प्रणय इरावत्या प्रार्थना विहन्तुं प्रतिषेद्धमुचितोऽर्हो वरं मनाक्प्रियम्। अयं

---

१ वत्सु चापि, वस्तुष्वपि. २ वेशकारी, निवेशिनं मां. ३ विमुखेन. ४ गमयामि० ५ साह० कज्जे. ६ उवाओप० (उपायोप.) ७ वसन्दपुढभाव०; वसन्त इति नास्ति क्वचित्. ८ सुहआणि; (सुभगानि) ९ सोअक्रोरआणि. १० दावदाराव०; न्दारव्ववदेसेण,

King :—O revered God of Love, born of the mind, having caused this person strongly to set his heart on objects beset with obstacles, why dost thou smite him in such a way that he is unable to brook any delay ?

(*With an expression of astonishment*).

Where (on the one hand) is this heart-torturing agony and where (on the other) thy gentle weapon (*lit.* which deserves confidence) ? What is said as being soft and exceedingly sharp as well–here is that (illustrated) in thee–O god of Love ! (2)

Vidūṣaka:—Here I say, that I have made a beginning in the matter of achieving the object desired to be attained. Your Honour should, therefore, compose yourself.

King:—Well, where shall I pass the rest of the day with a mind averse to the usual occupations ?

Vidūṣaka :—Why, Irāvatī sent you just to-day some flowers of the red Aśoka indicative of the first appearance of spring, and under the pretext of enjoying the fresh spring festival, made this request through Nipuṇikā,–"I wish to enjoy the pleasure of sitting in (riding) the swing in company with your Lordship." Your Highness, too, promised (to gratify her wish). To the pleasure-garden itself then let us go.

King :—This is not practicable.

Vidūṣaka:—How so ?

पक्षः किंचित्साधुरित्यर्थः । हि यस्मात्कारणात्खण्डनहेतव ईर्ष्याकोपकारणानि बहवोऽनेके दृष्टाः । मया लक्षिताः । प्रणयभङ्गे बहूनि कारणानि कथयितुं सुलभानीति भावः । खण्डनहेतुदर्शनेऽप्युपचारविशेषैः प्रलोभ्यतामित्यत आह–उपचारेति । भावशून्यः प्रेमरहित उपचारविधिरिष्टाचरणं पूर्वाभ्यधिकोऽपि मनस्विनीनां तु प्रशस्तमनसां पुनः । विवेकवतीनामित्यर्थः । उपचारविधिर्न भवति । किं त्वपचारविधिरित्यर्थः । अत्र नञर्थ-स्तद्विरोधः । यद्वा तु किं तु पूर्वाभ्यधिकोपि मनस्विनीनामुपचारविधिः सेवाप्रकारः भावशून्यः वास्तवप्रेमरहितः न वरमिति योज्यम् । अत्र मनागपि प्रियत्वाभावे भावशून्य इति पदं हेतुरिति पदार्थहेतुकं काव्यलिङ्गमलंकारः। औपच्छन्दसिकं वृत्तम् ॥ २ ॥ अन्तःपुरप्रतिष्ठितमवरोधस्त्रीषु चिररूढम् । दक्षिणस्य छन्दोवर्तिनः भावः दाक्षिण्य-

राजा—वयस्य निसर्गनिपुणाः स्त्रियः । कथं मामन्यसंक्रान्तहृदयमुपलालयन्तमपि ते सखी न लक्षयिष्यति । अतः पश्यामि ।

उचितः प्रणयो वरं विहन्तुं बहवः खण्डनहेतवो हि दृष्टाः ।
उपचारविधिर्मनस्विनीनां न तु पूर्वाभ्यधिकोऽपि भावशून्यः ॥ ३ ॥

विदूषकः—नार्हति भवानन्तःपुरप्रतिष्ठितं दाक्षिण्यमेकपदे पृष्ठतः कर्तुम् । (क)

राजा—(विचिन्त्य ।) तेन हि प्रमदवनमार्गमादेशय ।

विदूषकः—इत इतो भवान् । (ख)

(उभौ परिक्रामतः ।)

विदूषकः—वसन्तः किलैताभिः पवनचलिताभिः पल्लवाङ्गुलीभिस्त्वरयतीव भवन्तमेतत्प्रमदवनं प्रविशेति । (ग)

राजा—(स्पर्शसुखं रूपयित्वा ।) अभिजातः खलु वसन्तः । सखे पश्य ।

आमत्तानां श्रवणसुभगैः कूजितैः कोकिलानां
सानुक्रोशं मनसिजरुजः सह्यतां पृच्छतेव ।
अङ्गे चूतप्रसवसुरभिर्दक्षिणो मारुतो मे
सान्द्रस्पर्शः करतल इव व्यापृतो माधवेन ॥ ४ ॥

(क) णारुहदि भवं अन्तेउरपडिट्ठिदं दक्खिण्णं एक्कपदे पिट्ठदो कादुम् । (ख) इदो इदो भवं । (ग) वसन्दो किल एदाहिं पवणचलिदाहिं पल्लवङ्गुलीहिं तुवरेदि विअ भवन्तं एदं पमदवणं पविसत्ति ।

मनुवृत्तिः । तदुक्तं–'दाक्षिण्यं चेष्टया वाचा परचित्तानुवर्तनम् ।' इति । पृष्ठतः कर्तुं विहातुमित्यर्थः । अभिजातः कुलीनस्य दाक्षिण्यात् । यद्वा पण्डितः सेवावसरज्ञानात् । 'अभिजातः कुलीने स्यान्न्याय्यपण्डितयोस्त्रिषु ।' इति मेदिनी । **आमत्तानामित्यादि** । आमत्तानां मधुरवृत्तेः प्रीतानामीषत्क्षीबाणां वा । 'हृष्टो मत्तस्तृप्तः प्रह्लन्नः प्रमुदितः प्रीतः ।' 'मत्ते शौण्डोत्कटक्षीबाः' इति चामरः । कोकिलानां परभृ-

---

१ नु. २ स्पर्शं निरूप्य. ३ उन्म०. ४ भवं सव्वं. ५ एदं पमदवणं पवणदरचलाहिं...भवन्दं पवेसिदुं, णं एदं मन० पवणबल–पवनदर–चलाहिं ..भवं पवि—सदुत्ति; णं एदं पम० पवणबलच०; ण एदं......पवणचलिदाहिं...भवन्तं । ता पविसदु भवं.

King :—Friend, women are by nature very shrewd. How will your friend (Irāvatī) not mark me as one whose heart is devoted to another, even when I shall be caressing her ? Therefore, I see that

It is better to decline her request, though fit to be complied with ; for many are the reasons (or excuses) seen for disappointing her ; but not the ministration to their wishes in the case of high-minded ladies which though done with greater attention than before, is void of real affection. (3)

[Or, it is better to ignore the request of high-minded ladies though fit &c. than formally to show greater attention to them, if it is &c.]

Vidūṣaka :—It does not behove you suddenly to cast aside your invariable (lit. firmly fixed) courtesy to the ladies of the harem.

King :—(*Reflecting*) Then show me the way to the pleasure-garden.

Vidūṣaka :—This way, this way, Your Highness.

(Both *walk* on.)

Vidūṣaka :—The Spring, by means of these finger-like shoots, agitated by the wind, is asking Your Highness, as it were, to enter this pleasure-garden with haste.

King :—(*Gesticulating the pleasurable sensation caused by touch*) The Spring is noble, indeed ! Observe, my friend,

Compassionately asking me, as it were, by the notes of intoxicated cuckoos, agreeable to the ear, how I bear the anguish of love, the southern wind, fragrant with mango-blossoms and of agreeable touch has been employed by the Spring to pass along my body, like the palm of hand. (4)

तानां श्रवणसुभगैः श्रुतिसुखैः कूजितैः रुतः मनसिजरुजः कामव्यथायाः सह्यतां सोढुं शक्यतां कियत्सह्यते इति यावत् । अनुक्रोशेन सहितं यथा तथा सानुक्रोशं सदयम् । ‘ कृपा दयाऽनुकम्पा स्यादनुक्रोशोऽपि ’ इत्यमरः । पृच्छता माधवेन वसन्तेन । चूतानामाम्रवृक्षाणां प्रसवैः कुसुमैः सुरभिः रम्यगन्धः सान्द्रः घनः स्निग्धो वा स्पर्शो यस्य स तथा । दक्षिणः मारुतः पवनः करतल इव व्यापृतः व्यापारितः । संचारित

विदूषकः—प्रविश निर्वृतिलाभाय। (क)

(उभौ प्रविशतः।)

विदूषकः—भो वयस्य अवधानेन तावद् दृष्टिं देहि। एतत्खलु भवन्तमिव विलोभयितुकामया मधुलक्ष्म्या युवतिवेषलज्जयितृकं वसन्तकुसुमनेपथ्यं गृहीतम्। (ख)

राजा—[1]ननु विस्मयादवलोकयामि।

रक्ताशोकरुचा [2]विशेषितगुणो बिम्बाधरालक्तकः
प्रत्याख्यातविशेषकं कुरबकं श्यामावदातारुणम्।
आक्रान्ता तिलकक्रिया च तिलकैर्[3]लग्नद्विरेफाञ्जनैः
सावज्ञेव मुखप्रसाधनविधौ श्रीर्माधवी योषिताम्॥ ५॥

([4]उभौ उद्यानशोभां निर्वर्णयतः।)

(ततः प्रविशति पर्युत्सुका मालविका।)

मालविका—अविज्ञातहृदयं भर्तारमभिलषन्त्यात्मनोऽपि तावल्लज्जे। कुतो विभवः स्निग्धस्य सखीजनस्येमं वृत्तान्तमाख्यातुम्। न जानेऽप्रतीकारगुरुकां वेदनां कियन्तं कालं मदनो मां नेष्यतीति। ([5]कतिचित्पदानि गत्वा।) कुत्र नु प्रस्थितास्मि। ([6]विचिन्त्य।) आम् संदिष्टास्मि देव्या। गौ[7]तमचापलाद्दोला

(क) पविसं णिव्वुदिलाहाअ। (ख) भो वअस्स अवहाणेण दाव दिट्ठिं देहि। एदं खु भवन्तं विअ विलोहइदुकामाए [9]महुलच्छीए जुवइवेसलज्जइत्तिअं वसन्तकुसुमणेवत्थं गहीदं।

इत्यर्थः। रुग्णस्य हि करतलेन स्पर्शः सुखावहः। "अत्र मारुते सखिकार्येण तद्यवहारारोपणात्समासोक्तिः। पृच्छतेवेत्यत्र क्रियोत्प्रेक्षा करतल इति द्रव्योत्प्रेक्षा चेत्येतेषां संकरः" इति अ० राघ०। मन्दाक्रान्ता वृत्तम्॥ ४॥ दृष्टिं देहि विलोकय। विलोभयितुमाक्रष्टुं कामो यस्याः सा तया। युवतिवेषस्य लज्जायितृकं लज्जाकरम्। ततोपि चारुतरमित्यर्थः। वसन्तकुसुमान्येव नेपथ्यं वेषः वसन्तकुसुमनेपथ्यं गृहीतम्।

१ (विस्मयात्) एतद०. २ लतावि०. ३ लीन. ४ उभौ नाट्येनो०: निरूपयतः ५ इति कति०. ६ इति स्मृतिमभिनीय, आत्मगतम्. ७ यथा...मालविके गौतमचापल्या. दोलायाः परिभ्रष्टाहम्। तस्मान्न शक्नोमि चरणौ चालयितुम्। त्वं...दर्शयेत्ततोऽहं अभिलाषदापयितृपदं दास्यामि. ८ एहि पविस. ९ पमदवणल० १० लज्जापइत्तअं.

Vidūṣaka :—Enter, that you may get ease of mind.

(*Enter* both.)

Vidūṣaka :—O friend, direct your eyes with attention. Here, indeed, has Vernal Beauty, as if desirous of attracting you, donned the robe of spring flowers that puts to shame the dress of young ladies.

King :—Why, I behold it with astonishment :

The red dye of the *bimba*-like lip is surpassed in excellence by the splendour of the red Aśoka ; the *kurabaka*-flower, darkish and white-red, throws into the background the painting on the face (*Viśeṣaka)* ; while the ornamental mark on the forehead is transcended by the *tilaka* flowers dotted with collyrium in the form of bees : Vernal Beauty seems thus to treat with contempt (not to care for) the way in which women decorate their faces. (5)

(Both *carefully observe the beauty of the garden*).

(*Enter* Mālavikā *in a state of agitation*).

Mālavikā :—I am ashamed even of myself for loving the king whose heart I do not know. Whence can there be the power then to communicate the matter to my dear friend ? I do not know for how long a time Love will make me suffer the torment heavy (unbearable) on account of its being irremediable. (*Having advanced some steps*) Where am I going now ? (*After reflecting*) Ah ! I have been commi-

---

रक्ताशोकत्यादि । बिम्बाधरे । बिम्बमिवाधरस्तस्मिन् 'विशेषणं विशेष्येण बहुलम्' इति विशेषणसमासः । 'उपमितं व्याघ्रादिभिः सामान्याप्रयोगे' इत्युपमितसमासस्तु कविभिरत्र प्रायेण नाङ्गीकृतः । अलक्तको लाक्षा । रक्ताशोकरुचा रक्ताशोककुसुमस्य रुचा कान्त्या विशेषितगुणः । विशेषितोऽतिशयितस्तिरस्कृतो गुणो रागो यस्य स तथोक्तः । श्यामावदातारुणम् । श्यामं च तदवदातं [सितं] अरुणं च तत्तथोक्तम् । 'वर्णो वर्णेन' इति कर्मधारयः । कुरवकं कुरवकपुष्पं प्रत्याख्यातविशेषकं प्रत्याख्यातं तिरस्कृतं विशेषकं पत्रभङ्गो येन तथोक्तम् । लग्नद्विरेफाञ्जनैः लग्नः सक्तो द्विरेफो भ्रमर एवाञ्जनं येषु तैस्तिलकैस्तिलककुसुमैस्तिलकक्रियापि तिलकस्य ललाटिकायाः क्रियापि आक्रान्ता उल्लङ्घिता परिभूतेत्यर्थः । माधवी मधुसंबन्धिनी श्रीर्लक्ष्मीः शोभेत्यर्थः । योषितां स्त्रीणां मुखप्रसाधनविधौ मुखालंकारकरणे

परिभ्रष्टायाः सरुजौ मे चरणौ। त्वं तावद्गत्वा तपनीयाशोकस्य दोहदं निर्वर्तय। यद्यसौ पञ्चरात्राभ्यन्तरे कुसुमं दर्शयति ततोऽहं—(अन्तरा निःश्वस्य।)-अभिलाषपूरयितृकं प्रसादं दास्यामीति। यावन्नियोगभूमिं प्रथमं गता भवामि। यावदनुपदं मम चरणालंकारहस्तया बकुलावलिकया-गन्तव्यं परिदेवयिष्ये तावद्विस्रब्धं मुहूर्तकम्। (इति परिक्रामति।) (क)

विदूषकः—(दृष्ट्वा।) ही ही इयं खलु शीधुपानोद्वेजितस्य मत्स्यण्डिका उपनता। (ख)

राजा—अयि किमेतत्।

विदूषकः—एषा खलु नातिपर्याप्तवेषा पर्युत्सुकेवैकाकिनी मालविका अदूरे वर्तते। (ग)

राजा—(सहर्षम्।) कथं मालविका।

विदूषकः—अथ किम्। (घ)

(क) अविण्णाहहिअअं भट्टारं अहिलसन्ती अत्तणो वि दाव लज्जेमि। कुदो विहवो सिणिद्धस्स सहीजणस्स इमं वुत्तन्तं आचक्खिदुं। ण जाणे अप्पडिआर-गुरुअं वेअणां केत्तिअं कालं मअणो मं णइस्सदित्ति। कहिं णु पत्थिदह्मि। आम्। संदिट्ठह्मि देवीए। गोदमचावलादो दोलापरिभट्टाए सरुजा मे चलणा। तुमं दाव गदुअ तवणीआसोअस्स दोहलं णिव्वट्टेहि। जदि सो पञ्चरत्तब्भन्तरे कुसुमं दंसेदि तदो अहं अहिलासपूरइत्तअं पसादं दाइस्सं ति। जाव णिओअभूमिं पुढमं गदा होमि। जाव अणुपदं मम चलणालंकारहत्थाए बउलावलिआए आअन्तव्वं परिदेवइस्सं ताव वीसद्धं मुहुत्तअं। (ख) ही ही इअं खु सीहुपाणुव्वेजिदस्स मच्छण्डिआ उवणदा। (ग) एसा क्खु णादिपज्जत्तवेसा पज्जुसुआ विअ एआइणी मालविआ अदूरे वट्टदि। (घ) अह इं।

सावज्ञेव अवमानेन सहितेव। अवमाननां कृतवतीवेत्यर्थः। उत्प्रेक्षालंकारः। शार्दूल-विक्रीडितं वृत्तम् ॥५॥ अविज्ञातं हृदयं हृद्गतो भावः यस्य तम्। आत्मनः स्वहृदयादपीत्यर्थः लज्जे। धाष्ट्र्यादिति भावः। विभवः सामर्थ्यम्। सखीजनस्य चतुर्थ्यर्थे षष्ठी। अविद्यमानः प्रतीकारः प्रतिक्रिया यस्याः सा अप्रतीकारा अत एव

---

१ अणभिण्णाद. २ भट्टारअं. ३ सिणद्धसही. ४ क्खु, णु क्खु. ५ आदि॰ ६ ताजाव, ताव. ७ वअस्स एदं खु. ८ परिक्खिद (परिष्कृत).

ssioned by the Queen :—"Having had a fall from a swing, owing to the carelessness of Gautama, my feet are paining; therefore, do thou go and fulfil the longing of the golden As'oka-tree. If in five nights from this time it displays flowers, I will-*(she stops and heaves a sigh)*-bestow on thee a favour which will gratify thy desires." Well, I will then go first to the place where I am to perform this duty. Until Bakulāvalikā comes close upon my heels with the decorations for the feet in hand, I will, for a moment, weep *(lit.* give vent to my grief) undisturbed. *(She walks around).*

Vidūṣaka :—Ha ! Ha ! Here is fine (granulated) sugar come to one disgusted with liquor drink.

King :—Ah ! What is that ?

Vidūṣaka :—There stands Mālavikā at no great distance, not fully dressed, looking quite uneasy and all alone.

King :—*(Delighted)* What ! Mālavikā !

Vidūṣaka :—Certainly.

गुरुका दुःसहा । अप्रतीकारा चासौ गुरुका च इति वा । ताम् । आमिति स्मरणे । गौतमस्य विदूषकस्य चापलात् चपलत्वेन हेतुना । रुजया पीडया रुजा वा सहितौ सरुजौ । पञ्चानां रात्रीणां समाहारः पञ्चरात्रम् । 'संख्यापूर्वं रात्रम्'–इति क्लीबत्वम् । तस्याभ्यन्तरे । तपनीयाशोकः पीतरक्ताशोकः । नियोगस्य दोहदपूरणस्य भूमिं स्थानम् । यत्राशोकः स्थितः तां भूमिमित्यर्थः । यावत् गता भवामि गमिष्यामि । 'यावत्पुरानिपातयोर्लट्' इति भविष्यदर्थे लट् । चरणयोः अलंकाराः यावकनूपुरादयः हस्ते यस्याः सा तथोक्ता तया । परिदेवयिष्ये विलपिष्यामि । विस्रब्धं निःशङ्कं यथा तथा । केनाप्यलक्षितेत्यर्थः । सीधुपानेन आसवपानेन उद्वेजितस्य उद्भ्रान्तस्य । 'उद्वेग उद्भ्रमः' इत्यमरः । मत्स्यण्डिका नाम शर्कराविशेषः । तदुक्तं वैद्यके- 'मत्स्यण्डिका खण्डसिताः क्रमेण गुणवत्तमाः । वालुकेव भृशं सूक्ष्मः सुस्निग्धा सितपिङ्गला ॥ मत्स्याण्डाकृतिसादृश्ययोगान्मत्स्यण्डिका स्मृता ॥' इति । अजीर्णामृतमञ्जर्यां च-'मदयति न हि मद्यं जातु चेत्पीतमद्यं पिबति घृतममंतां शर्करामेव सद्यः ।' इति । नातिपर्याप्तः विपुलः वेषो यस्याः सा नातिपर्याप्तवेषा परिमितालंकारयुतेत्यर्थः । नातिपरिष्कृतवेषेति पाठे नातिपरिष्कृतः नात्युज्ज्वलः वेषो यस्याः इत्यर्थः । शीधुपानमासवपानं तेन उद्वेजितस्य निर्विण्णस्य । त्वदुपलभ्येत्यादि ।

राजा—शक्यमिदानीं जीवितमवलम्बितुम्[1] ।

त्वदुपलभ्य समीपगतां प्रियां हृदयमुच्छ्वसितं मम विक्लवम् ।
तरुवृतां[2] पथिकस्य जलार्थिनः सरितमारसितादिव सारसात् ॥ ६ ॥

अथ क्व तत्रभवती ।

विदूषकः—एषा ननु तरुराजिमध्यान्निष्क्रान्ता इत एव परिवर्तमाना दृश्यते । (क)

राजा—(विलोक्य सहर्षम् ।) वयस्य पश्याम्येनाम् ।

विपुलं नितम्ब[3]बिम्बे मध्ये क्षामं समुन्नतं कुचयोः ।
अत्यायतं नयनयोर्मम जीवितमेतदायाति ॥ ७ ॥

सखे पूर्वस्मा[4]दवस्थान्तरमुपारूढा[5] तत्रभवती । तथा हि ।

शरकाण्डपाण्डुगण्डस्थलेयमाभाति परिमिताभरणा ।
माधवपरिणतपत्रा कतिपयकुसुमेव कुन्दलता ॥ ८ ॥

विदूषकः—एषापि भवानिव मदनव्याधिना परामृष्टा भविष्यति । (ख)

(क) ए[6]सा णं तरुराइमज्झादो णिक्कन्ता इदो एव्व प[7]रिवट्टन्ती दीसइ ।
(ख) एसा वि भवं विअ मअणव्वाहिणा परामि[8]ट्ठा भविस्सदि ।

समीपगतां प्रियां प्रिया आसन्नवर्तिनीति त्वदुपलभ्य ज्ञात्वा मम विक्लवं मदनव्यथाविह्वलं हृदयमुच्छ्वसितं समाश्वासितम् । हर्षेण स्फीतमिति वाचस्पतिः । जलार्थिनो जलपानेच्छोः पथिकस्य पान्थस्य आरसितात् शब्दितात् । सरसि भवः सारसः पक्षिभेदः तस्मात्तरुवृतां वृक्षच्छन्नां सरितमुपलभ्य इव यथा हृदयं उच्छ्वसितं प्रसन्नं भवति तथा । उपमालंकारः । द्रुतविलम्बितं वृत्तम् ॥ ६ ॥ अत्र संचिन्त्यमानार्थस्य प्राप्तेः क्रमो नाम संध्यङ्गमुक्तं भवति ॥ **विपुलमिति** । नितम्बबिम्बे श्रोणिफलके विपुलं विशालम् । विपुलनितम्बवदित्यर्थः । एवमग्रेऽपि । मध्ये क्षामं कृशम् । क्षायो मः इति निष्ठातस्य मः । तनुमध्यमित्यर्थः । एतज्जीवितमेवायाति इत्युत्प्रेक्षा ॥ ७ ॥ **शरेति** । शरः तृणविशेषस्तस्य काण्डः स्तम्बः तद्वत्पाण्डु धवलं गण्डस्थलं यस्याः सा । पाण्डुकपोला इत्यर्थः ।

---

१ आत्मानम्. २ तरुवृतं पथिकस्य पिपासतः सलिलमुद्रसिता०. ३ म्बदेशे- ४ स्मादतिमनोहरमवस्था०. ५ मारुढा. ६ एसा तरु०. ७ आअच्छदि. ८ परिमिट्ठा.

King :—Now my life can be sustained.

Hearing from you that my beloved is near, my distressed heart feels relieved, like the heart of a traveller longing for water, when he learns from the cry of the Sārasas (cranes) that a tree-covered river is near. (6)

Where is the lady ?

Vidūṣaka :—Here she is coming in this very direction, having emerged from the midst of a row of trees.

King :—My friend, I behold her,—

Expansive in the round hips, thin in the waist, elevated in the bosom, and very long in the eyes, here comes my very life. (7)

Friend, her ladyship has reached a condition far more charming than (what she was in) before ; for,

With her broad cheeks pale like the stalk of a reed, and wearing but a few ornaments, she appears like a *Kunda* creeper having its leaves ripened by the spring, and with only a few flowers. (8)

Vidūṣaka :—She too, like Your Honour, may have been affected by love-sickness.

परिमितानि आभरणानि यस्याः सा । अल्पाभरणभूषितेत्यर्थः । इयं मालविका माधवेन वसन्तेन वैशाखेन वा परिणतानि जीर्णानि पत्राणि यस्याः सा । कतिपयानि कुसुमानि आभरणस्थानीयानि यस्याः सा कुन्दलतेवाभाति । पूर्णोपमालंकारः ॥ ८ ॥ परामृष्टा उपसृष्टा क्लिष्टेत्यर्थः । परिमृष्टेति पाठे अभिभूता । सौहार्दमिति-त्वं सुहृद्भावादेवं मन्यसे । ललितः चारुः दोहदः चरणताडनप्राप्तिरूपस्तमपेक्षत इत्यसौ । मालविकापक्षे दोहदः राज्ञा संगमः स्यादिति मनोरथः । अगृहीतं कुसुमान्येव नेपथ्यं येन । मालविकापक्षे अगृहीतं कुसुमनेपथ्यं पुष्पभूषणं यया । उत्कण्ठा अस्याः संजाता असौ उत्कण्ठिता । उत्कण्ठा सस्पृहा चिन्ता । 'चिन्ता तु स्मृतिराध्यानं स्मरणं सस्पृहे पुनः । उत्कठोत्कलिके' इति शब्दार्णवः । प्रकृष्टा छाया यत्र तत्प्रच्छायमत एव शीतलं यत् शिलापट्टकं तस्मिन् । प्रसन्नः विशदः । यथार्थज्ञानवानिति यावत् । तर्क ऊहो यस्य तम् । मदर्थमेवास्या उत्कण्ठेति न निश्चिनोमीत्यर्थः । वोढेत्यादि । कुरबकाणां कुरण्टकपुष्पाणां

राजा—सौहार्दमेवं पश्यति।

मालविका—अयं स ललितदोहदापेक्षी अगृहीतकुसुमनेपथ्य उत्कण्ठिताया मामनुकरोत्यशोकः। यावदस्य प्रच्छायशीतले शिलापट्टके निषण्णात्मानं विनोदयामि। (क)

विदूषकः—श्रुतं भवता। उत्कण्ठितास्मीति तत्रभवत्या मन्त्रितम्।(ख)

राजा—नैतावता भवन्तं[1] प्रसन्नतर्कं मन्ये। कुतः।

वोढा कुरबकरजसां किसलयपुटभेदशीकरानुगतः।
अनिमित्तामुत्कण्ठामपि[2] जनयति मलयवातोऽयम्॥ ९॥

(मालविकोपविष्टा।)

राजा—वयस्य[3] इतस्तावत्। आवां लतान्तरितौ भवावः।

विदूषकः—इरावतीमिव दूरे समर्थये (ग)।

राजा—न हि कमलिनीं दृष्ट्वा[4] ग्राहमवेक्षते[5] मतङ्गजः। (इति विलोकयन्स्थितः।)

(क) अअं सो ललिअ[6]दोहलावेक्खी अग्गहीदकुसुमणेवत्थो उक्कण्ठदाए[7] मह अणुकरेदि असोओ। जाव से[8] पच्छाअसीदले सिलापट्टए णिसण्णा अत्ताणं विणोदेमि। (ख) सुदं भवदा। उक्कण्ठिदम्हित्ति तत्तहोदीए[9] मन्तिदं। (ग) इरावदिं विअ दूरं[10] समत्थेमि।

रजसः परागस्य वोढा वाहकः। अनेन तस्य सौगन्ध्यं ध्वनितम्। किसलयपुटानां भेदात् गलन्तः ये शीकरा अम्बुकणास्तैरनुगतः। अनेन तस्य जडत्वं शीतत्वं च सूचितम्। मलयवातो दक्षिणवातः। नास्ति निमित्तं यस्याः सा अनिमित्ता तादृशीमुत्कण्ठाम्। प्रियाविरहाद्दृते इत्यर्थः। जनयति। तस्योन्मादयितृकत्वात्। आर्या छन्दः॥९॥ कमलिनीं दृष्ट्वा तया आकृष्टः सन्नित्यर्थः। मतङ्गजः हस्ती ग्राहं नक्रं नावेक्षते न गणयति तथा मालविकागतमनोरथः अहमपि इरावतीं न गणयामीति भावः। निर्गतोऽवलम्बो यस्य स निरवलम्बोऽनाधारस्तस्मात्। अतिभूमिलङ्घनः अतिभूमिं गताम्। मामायास्य

---

१ भवतः प्रसन्नतर्कतां. २ अनिमित्तोत्कण्ठमपि जनयति मनसो मलयवातः ३ सखे. ४ लब्ध्वा, कमलिनीं सरतं. ५ अपेक्षते, गणयति. ६ मउमाल (सुकुमार); ललिदसुउमार. ७ ठक्कण्ठिदं मं. ८ एदस्स. ९ तत्तहोदी मन्तदि (मन्त्रयते). १० अदूरे.

King :—It is only (your) friendship (for me) that sees thus (takes this view).

Mālavikā :—This As'oka, that is waiting for the fulfilment of its longing in a graceful way, and has not put on its robe of flowers imitates me in my state of longing. Let me, therefore, sit down on this stone-slab cool with the shade on the tree, and divert myself.

Vidūṣaka:—Did Your Honour hear? The lady said "I am in a state of longing."

King :—Even this much does not make me think you a man of unerring (right) conjecture. For,

The wind from the Malaya mountain, bearing along the pollen of the Kurabaka flowers, and accompanied with drops of water issuing from the opening folds of tender leaves, produces longing in the mind even without a (definite) cause. (9)

(Mālavikā *sits down*)

King:—My friend, come this way; let us hide ourselves behind the creeper.

Vidūṣaka :—I seem to see Irāvatī in the distance.

King :—But when he sees a lotus-plant, the elephant does not surely care for the alligator. (*He stands gazing.*)

कस्ते लाभः इत्यर्थः । **औत्सुक्येत्यादि** । औत्सुक्यहेतुमुत्कण्ठाकारणं त्वं न विवृणोषि प्रकाशयसि । तर्कः अनुमानमपि तत्त्वस्य वस्तुस्वरूपस्यावबोधो ज्ञानं स एव एको मुख्यो रसो यस्य तथा वस्तुतत्त्वनिश्चायको न भवति । तथापि हे रम्भोरु रम्भे इव ऊरू यस्याः सा तत्संबोधनम् । एषां तव परिदेवितानां विलापानामात्मानं लक्ष्यं करोमि । मामुद्दिश्यैवैतानि इति मन्ये । उपजातिर्वृत्तम् ॥ १० ॥ निःसंशयं संशयस्याभावः । तत्र सर्वः संशयः नश्येदित्यर्थः । आर्पितः मया निवेदित-मदनविषयः संदेशो यस्यै सा तादृशि । विविक्ते विजने । योग्यतया अस्मिन् दोहदपूरणः कर्मणि योग्या इति । सालक्तकमलक्तकेन सहितं यावत्सालक्तकम् । सनूपुरं मञ्जीरयुक्तम् । सुखिततया सुखमस्य संजातमिति सुखितं तस्य भावः सुखितता तया अलम् । मा सुखितं भव । अयं पुरोवर्ती विभवः दोहदपूरणार्थक आलक्तकरसनूपुरादिः उपस्थितः इति कृत्वा । मोचयेयं नियोगं कथं साधु निर्वाहयेयमित्यर्थः । मृत्युमण्डनं मृत्युकाले धारणीयोऽलंकारः

मालविका—हृदय निरवलम्बादतिभूमिलङ्घिनो मनोरथाद्विरम। किं मामायासयसि। (क)

(विदूषको राजानमवेक्षते।)

राजा—प्रिये पश्य वाम[1]तां स्नेहस्य।

औत्सुक्यहेतुं विवृणोषि न त्वं तत्त्वावबोधैकरसो न तर्कः।
तथापि रम्भोरु करोमि लक्ष्यमात्मानमेषां परिदेवितानाम्॥ १०॥

विदूषकः—सांप्रतं भवतो निःसंशयं भविष्यति। एषार्पितमदनसंदेशा विविक्ते ननु बकुलावलिकोपस्थिता। (ख)

राजा—अपि स्मरेदस्मे[2]दभ्यर्थनाम्।

विदूषकः—किमिदानीमेषा दास्या दुहिता तव गुरुकं संदेशं विस्मरिष्यति। अहमपि तावन्न विस्मरामि। (ग)

(प्रविश्य चरणालंकारहस्ता।)

बकुलावलिका—अपि सुखं सख्याः। (घ)

मालविका—अहो बकुलावलिका। सखि स्वागतं ते। उपविश। (ङ)

बकुलावलिका—(उपविश्य।) सखि त्वमिदानीं देव्या योग्यतया नियुक्ता तस्मादेकं चरणमुपनय। यावत्सालक्तकं सनूपुरं च करोमि। (च)

(क) हिअअ णिरवलै[3]म्बादो अदिभूमि[4]लंघिणो मणोरहादो विरम। किं मं आओ[5]सेसि। (ख) संपदं भवदो णिस्संस[6]अं भविस्सदि। एसा अप्पिदमअणसंदेसा विविचे णं बउलावलिआ उवट्ठिदा। (ग) किं दाणिं एसा दासीए दुहिदा[7] तुह[8] गुरुअं संदेसं विसु[9]मरिस्सदि। अहं वि दावँ[10] ण विसुमरेमि। (घ) अवि सुहं सहीए। (ङ) अम्हो बउलावलिआ। सहि साअदं ते। उववि‍स। (च) हला तुमं दाणिं देवीए जीग्गदाए णिउत्ता एकं[11] चलणं उवणेहि। जाव[12] सालत्तअं सणूउरं च करेमि।

---

१ वामत्वं; महत्वं. २ दसाव. ३ णिप्फलादो: ०म्बणादो मणोरहादो. ४. एतन्नास्ति बहुषु पुस्तकेषु. ५ आआसिअ (आयास्य). ६ सओ. ७ सुदा. ८ दाव गुरुअं. ९ विसुमरेदि. १० ताव दाणिं एदं ण. ११ दाव दाणिं; दे चलणं दोहलकरणजो०. १२ जाव णं.

Mālavikā :—Cease, my heart, from entertaining a desire that has no support and has reached its climax. Why dost thou torture me ?

(Vidūṣaka *looks at the* King.)

King :—My darling, observe the perverseness of love.

Thou dost not reveal the cause of thy pining, nor is conjecture solely devoted to the perception of (able to disclose) the real truth: Still, O thou with plantain-like thighs, I consider myself to be the object of these lamentations. (10)

Vidūṣaka :—Now your doubts will be cleared, indeed; for here comes Bakulāvalikā, whom I gave the message of love, to wait upon her in private.

King :—Will she remember my request ?

Vidūṣaka :—What ! Will that slave's daughter forget such a weighty message from Your Highness ? Why, even I do not forget it.

(*Enters* Bakulāvalikā *with the ornaments for the feet in her hand*).

Bakulāvalikā :—Is my friend happy ?

Mālavikā :—Oh ! Bakulāvalikā ! Welcome, my friend ; sit down.

Bakulāvalikā :—(*Sitting down*) Friend, on the present occasion you are charged with an appropriate duty by the Queen ; therefore, give me one of your feet, that I may paint it with lac, and put the anklet on it.

भविष्यति। अस्य मदनोद्दीपकत्वाद्दुर्लभमनोरथाप्राप्तेश्च मे मरणमेव भवेदिति भावः। कथमिति प्रश्ने संभ्रमे वा। अन्तःपुरनेपथ्येन राजस्त्र्युचितवेषेण। इति जानासि इति नर्मोक्तिः। मर्षय एनं पादम्। त्वदङ्के मत्पादनिवेशनमित्यर्थः। शरीरमसि मे अतो मदङ्के पादार्पणं न दोषायेति भावः। **चरणान्तेति**। प्रियायाः चरणान्ते निवेशितां च पादाग्रप्रयुक्तां सरसामार्द्रां रागस्य लाक्षारसस्य रेखां हरदग्धस्य मनोभवः काम एव-द्रुमो वृक्षस्तस्य प्रथमामग्रजातां पल्लवप्रसूतिं किसलयाङ्कुरमिव पश्य। उत्प्रेक्षालंकारः। स च मनोभवे द्रुमत्वारोपाद्रूपकेण संमिश्रः। औपच्छन्दसिकं वृत्तम्। ॥ ११ ॥

मालविका—(आत्मगतम्।) हृदय अलं सुखिततया अयं विभव उपस्थित इति। कथमिदानीमात्मानं मोचयेयम्। अथवैतदेव मम मृत्युमण्डनं भविष्यति। (क)

बकुलावलिका—किं विचारयसि। उत्सुका खल्वस्य तपनीयाशोकस्य कुसुमोद्गमे देवी। (ख)

राजा—कथमशोकदोहदनिमित्तोऽयमारम्भः।

विदूषकः—किं खलु न जानास्यकारणादेवीमामन्तःपुरनेपथ्येन न संयोजयिष्यतीति। (ग)

मालविका—सखि मर्षय तावदेनम्। (इति पादमुपहरति।) (घ)

बकुलावलिका—अयि शरीरमसि मे। (नाट्येन चरणसंस्कारमारभते।) (ङ)

राजा—

चरणान्तनिवेशितां प्रियायाः सरसां पश्य वयस्य रागरेखाम्।
प्रथमामिव पल्लवप्रसूतिं हरदग्धस्य मनोभवद्रुमस्य॥ ११॥

विदूषकः—चरणानुरूपः खलु तत्रभवत्या अधिकार उपक्षिप्तः। (च)

(क) हिअअ अलं सुहिदिदाए अअं विहवो उवट्टिदोत्ति। कहं दाणीं अत्ताण मोचएअं। अह वा एदं एव्व मम मिच्चुमण्डणं हविस्सदि। (ख) किं विआरेसि। उत्सुआ खु इमस्स तवणीआसोअस्स कुसुमुग्गमे देवी। (ग) किं खु ण जाणासि अकालणादो देवी इमं अन्तेउरणेयच्छेण संजोअइस्सदित्ति। (घ) हला मरिसेहि दाव णं। (ङ) अइ सरीरअं सि मे। (च) चलणाणुरूवो क्खु तत्तहोदीए अहिआरो उवक्खित्तो।

नवकिसलयेत्यादि। बाला मालविका नवकिसलयस्य प्रत्यग्रप्रवालस्य इव रागो रक्तिमा यस्य तेन। स्फुरिता प्रसृता नखानां रुक् यस्य तेन। अनेन। अग्रश्चासौ पादश्च तेन अग्रपादेन पादाग्रेण। द्वौ हन्तुं प्रहर्तुमर्हति। दोहदापेक्षया। कुसुमान्यस्य संजातानि असौ कुसुमितः न कुसुमितः अकुसुमितः तमशोकम्।

---

१ (पादमुपहरन्ती) हला. २ शोभाम्. ३ अह वा दाणिं. ४ मसमु०, मुउलु० (मुकलो.) ५ णु खु; णु खु जाणासि तुमं मह कालणादो...णेवच्छेण जोअइ०. ६ दाणीं. ७ अलंकारो.

Mālavikā :—(*To herself*) Heart! do not consider thyself happy, because this good fortune (the office of gratifying the longing of the Aśoka tree) has come to me. How can I now extricate myself (from this difficulty)? Or why? This very (painting) will be my funeral adornment.

Bakulāvalikā :—Why do you hesitate? The Queen is, indeed, anxious that the golden Aśoka-tree should put forth flowers.

King :—How, is it that all this preparation is for the sake of fulfilling the longing of the Aśoka?

Vidūṣaka :—What, do you not, indeed, know that the Queen would not without reason cause her to be adorned with the decorations of the harem?*

Mālavikā :—(*Holds out her foot*) Friend, I beg your pardon (please excuse me for holding out my foot to you).

Bakulāvalikā :—Why, you are as dear to me as my own body. (*She gesticulates the painting of Mālavikā's foot*).

King :—Friend! Behold the glossy (lit. moist) streak of colour placed upon the extremity of my darling's foot, as if it were the first appearance (peeping out) of the sprouts of the tree of love (after it was) consumed by Śiva. (11)

Vidūṣaka:—Truly, a duty, befitting her feet, has been imposed upon her ladyship (or, a duty worthy of the feet, indeed, has been assigned to her by the Queen).

आर्द्रः प्रत्यग्रः प्रणयकृतो वा अपराधो यस्य तं प्रणमितं पादयोः अवनमितं शिरो यस्य तं कान्तं प्रियं च। परिसंख्यालंकारः। मालिनी वृत्तम् ॥ १२ ॥ सिद्धिं द्रष्टुं शीलमस्यासौ सिद्धिदर्शी तस्य। युक्तः संक्रान्तः मदः क्षीबता यस्याः सा। लोकवादो लोकोक्तिरेव। सांप्रतं त्वयि प्रत्यक्षदृष्टत्वाद्यथार्थः संवृत्तः। अलं स्नेहभणितेन प्रियोक्त्या। अखण्डितादविच्छिन्नात्प्रणयात् प्रेम्णः अनुमीयते प्रथमं गत इति। अलं सेवया मत्प्रियार्थं चाटूक्त्या। मध्यस्थतामपक्षपातित्वम्। यथार्थं ब्रूहीत्यर्थः। वसन्ते दीयमानमुपायनं स्वस्तिवाचनं वसन्तोपायनं तत्र लोलुपेन अतिलुब्धेन। अवस्थासदृशं मदानुभवदशाया योग्यं यथा तथा। न प्रसरतः मदविक्लवत्वादिति भावः। भट्टिनी अनभिषिक्ता राजभार्या एवमुच्यते। देवी कृताभिषेकायामितरासु तु

---

* What, did you think that it was on your account that the Queen, etc. (V. l.)

राजा—सम्यगाह भवान्।

नवकिसलयरागेणाग्रपादेन बाला
स्फुरितनखरुचा द्वौ हन्तुमर्हत्यनेन।
अकुसुमितमशोकं दोहदापेक्षया वा
प्रणमितशिरसं वा कान्तमार्द्रापराधम्॥ १२॥

विदूषकः—प्रहरिष्यति तत्रभवती त्वामपराद्धम्। (क)

राजा—प्रतिगृहीतं वचः सिद्धिदर्शिनो ब्राह्मणस्य।

(ततः प्रविशति युक्तमदा इरावती चेटी च।)

इरावती—हञ्जे निपुणिके श्रृणोमि बहुशो मदः किल स्त्रीजनस्य विशेषमण्डनमिति। अपि सत्यो लोकवादोऽयम्। (ख)

निपुणिका—प्रथमं लोकवाद एव। अद्य सत्यः संवृत्तः। (ग)

इरावती—अलं स्नेहभणितेन। कुत इदानीमवगतं दोलागृहं प्रथमं गतो भर्ता इति। (घ)

निपुणिका—भट्टिन्या अखण्डितात्प्रणयात्। (ङ)

इरावती—अलं सेवया। मध्यस्थतां परिगृह्य भण। (च)

(क) पहरिस्सदि तत्तहोदी तुम अवरद्धम्। (ख) हञ्जे णिउणिए सुणामि बहुसो मदो किल इत्थिआजणस्स विसेसमण्डणं ति। अवि सच्चो लोअवादो अअं। (ग) पुढमं लोअवादो एव्व। अज्ज सच्चो संवुत्तो। (घ) अलं सिणेहभणिदेण। कुदो दाणिं अवगदं दोलाघरं पुढमं गदो भट्टेति। (ङ) भट्टाणीए अखण्डिदादो पणआदो। (च) अलं सेवाए। मज्झत्थदं परिगहिअ भणाहि।

भट्टिनी। इत्यमरः। प्रियङ्गुलता श्यामाख्या वल्ली तया परिक्षिप्तम्। अशोकतले शिलापट्टमशोकशिलापट्टम्। चूताङ्कुरमिति—दष्टं दंशः कृतः। भावे क्तः। भर्तारं मृगयमाणयोरावयोः चूताङ्कुरान्वेषणपरस्य पिपीलिकादंश इव पीडाकरं माल-

---

१ सम्यगभिहितं भवता. २ णार्द्र. ३ दोहला. ४ प्रणिहित. ५ मूर्ध्ना प्रति० ६ उन्मत्तवेषा. ७ चटि. ८ परिहससि तत्तहादीए अवरध्दं. ९ अज्ज उणं, दाणिं सच्चं संवुत्तं १० अलं मइ सिणेहेण. संकित्तणासंसि (संकीर्तनशंसिना) अलं सिणेहेण। कहेहि कुदो- ११ दाणिं ओगमिदव्वो,० दव्वं...गदो भट्टा न वेत्ति।

King :—You have spoken the exact truth.

With the forepart of her foot, of the hue of a young sprout and with the gleam of the nails flashing about it, this young maiden deserves to strike two, *viz.*, the Aśoka that has not yet flowered owing to the desire of having its longing gratified, and her lover standing with bowed head, having recently committed an offence. (12)

Vidūṣaka :—Her ladyship will strike you, when guilty of an offence. (*V. l.*, You will have an opportunity of offending the lady).

King :—I accept the words of a Brāhmaṇa who foresees the accomplishment of my desired object.

(*Enter* Irāvatī *in a state of intoxication, and her* Attendant).

Irāvatī :—Nipuṇikā, my girl, I have often heard that intoxication lends a special charm to women. Do you think that this popular saying is true ?

Nipuṇikā :—It was formerly a mere popular saying (to me) ; to-day it has been found to be true.

Irāvatī :—Away with this talk of affection. Whence did you come to know, on the present occasion, that the King had gone before me to the swing-house ?

Nipuika :—I inferred it from his unceasing affection for you, his queen.

Irāvatī :—No more of flattery ; speak as if you were a person unconcerned.

विकादर्शनं जातमिति भावः । अभूमिः अनुचिता भूमिः स्थानम् । उत्तमस्त्रीणामेव तत्र भ्रमणाधिकारात् । रुजया सहितौ सरुजौ चरणौ यस्याः सा तथोक्ता तया । दोहदाधिकारे दोहदपूरणकर्मणि । नियुक्ता अधिकृता । अनुज्ञास्यति तद्वारणे परिजनं कथमधिकरिष्यतीत्यर्थः । संभावना बहुमानदर्शनम् । अन्यतः अस्मात्स्थानादन्यत्र । विकारयति शङ्कामुत्पादयतीत्यर्थः । आशङ्कितस्य नपुंसके भावे क्तः । मालविकायां राज्ञीपक्षपातशङ्काया इत्यर्थः । अन्तं गमिष्यामि निर्णेष्यामि । निरूप्य वीक्ष्य । स्थाने मालविकायास्तादृग्रूपसम्पत्तेः । कातरं तस्यां राजानुरागसम्भावनयेति भावः ।

निपुणिका—वसन्तोपायनलोलुपेनार्यगौतमेन कथितम्। त्वरतां भट्टिनी। (क)

इरावती—(अवस्थासदृशं परिक्रम्य।) हञ्जे[1] मदेन क्लाम्यमानां मामार्यपुत्रदर्शने हृदयं त्वरयति। चरणौ पुनर्न मार्गे प्रसरतः (ख)

निपुणिका—ननु प्राप्ते स्वो दोलागृहम्। (ग)

इरावती—निपुणिके नात्र आर्यपुत्रो दृश्यते। (घ)

निपुणिका—भट्टिन्यवलोकयतु। परिहासनिमित्तं कुत्रापि गूढेन भर्त्रा भवितव्यम्। आवामपीमं प्रियङ्गुलतापरिक्षिप्तमशोकशिलापट्टकं प्रविशावः। (ङ)

(इरावती तथा करोति।)

निपुणिका—(परिक्रम्य विलोक्य च।) अवलोकयतु भट्टिनी। चूताङ्कुरं विचिन्वत्योरावयोः पिपीलिकाभिर्दष्टम्। (च)

इरावती—कथमिव। (छ)

निपुणिका—एषा बकुलावलिका अशोकपादपच्छायायां मालविकायाः चरणालंकारं निवर्तयति। (ज)

(क) वसन्तोवाअणलोलुवेण[2] अज्जगोदमेण कहिअं। तुवरदु भट्टिणी। (ख) हञ्जे मदेण किलमिअमाणं[3] मं अज्जउत्तदंसणे हिअअं तुवरेदि। चलणा उण ण मग्गे[4] पसरन्ति[5]। (ग) णं पत्तह्म दोलाघरं। (घ) णिउणिए ण एत्थ अज्जउत्तो दीसहि। (ङ) भट्टिनी ओलोएदु। परिहासणिमित्तं कहिं वि गूढेण[6] भत्तुणा होदव्वं। अम्हे वि इमं पिअङ्गुलदापरिक्खित्तं असोअसिलापट्टअं पविसामो। (च) ओलोअदु भट्टिणी। चूदङ्कुरं विचिण्णन्तीणं अम्हाणं पिपीलिआहिं दंसिदं। (छ) कहं[7] विअ (ज) एसा बउलावलिआ असोअपाअवच्छाआए मालविआए चलणालंकारं णिव्वट्टेदि।

प्रसाधनकला अलंकरणकला। अभिविनीता शिक्षिता। गुरुदक्षिणा राज्ञे देया दक्षिणा मालविकाप्राप्तिरूपा। चरणौ लब्ध्वा रञ्जनार्थमिति शेषः। लम्भयितव्यः आर्द्ररागशोषणार्थमित्यर्थः। प्रवातं प्रकृष्टो वात यत्र तत्। मुखवातमन्तरेणापि रागः शुष्येदि-

---

१ चेटि. २ णं वसंतोस्सवुपा०. ३ मिलाअमाणं, गिलाअमाणं (ग्लायमानं) अत्ताणं ४ मह ५ ओसलन्ति. ६ अदिठ्ठेण. ७ किं विअ एदं.

Nipuṇikā :—It was told by the worthy Gautama ever eager for the spring-gifts. Let Your Highness come quickly.

Irāvatī :—(*Walking around as well as her state would permit*) Maid! My heart urges me on to behold my husband, though I am overpowered by intoxication, but my feet will not advance on the path.

Nipuṇikā :—Now, indeed, we have arrived at the Swing-House.

Irāvatī :—Nipuṇika, I do not see my husband in it.

Nipuṇikā :—Your Ladyship should see carefully. His Lordship must be hiding somewhere wishing to play a trick. Let us, on our part, repair to this stone-slab under the As'oka tree which is overgrown by the Priyaṅgu creeper.

(Irāvatī does so.)

Nipuṇikā :—(*Walking round and looking*) Observe, Your Highness! While searching for the mango-blossom, we are bitten by red ants.

Irāvatī :—What do you mean?

Nipuṇikā :—Here is Bakulāvalikā decorating the foot of Mālavikā in the shade of the As'oka tree.

त्यर्थः। **आर्द्रालक्तकामित्यादि**। आर्द्रः अलक्तकः यावकरसरेखाविन्यासः यस्य तमस्या मालविकायाः चरणं मुखमारुतेन वीजयितुं शोषयितुं मे मम प्रथमतरो मुख्यतरः सेवावकाशः सेवनावसरः प्रतिपन्नः पात्रः॥ १२॥ अनुशयः चिन्ता। शतं पत्राण्यस्य शतपत्रम्। अरुणं च तत् शतपत्रं च अरुणशतपत्रं तदिव विकसित। रक्ताम्भोजमिवेत्यर्थः। अभिनिवेशिनः आसक्तिमतः दृढपक्षपातिनो वा। अलीकमनृतम्। एतदेव त्वं भर्तुः प्रियेति यत्त्वयोक्तं तत्। भर्तुः कृशेषु इति। दरपाण्डरेषु इति पाठे ईषत्पाण्डुरेषु। त्वयि बद्धभावस्य त्वामेव चिन्तयतो भर्तुरङ्गानि कृशानि जातानि। अतः तेभ्यः स्फुटं ज्ञायत एव यत्त्वं तस्य प्रियेति। **अनुराग** इति। यथा त्वं तस्मिन्ननुरागवती तथा सोपि त्वयीति जानीहीत्यर्थः। छन्दन स्वचित्तानुवृत्या। बिम्बान्तरितानि शरीरान्तरसंक्रान्तानि। बिम्बं मुखं वा। भ्रमरैः सम्बाधः संकुल इति। भ्रमरपीडा स्यादिति हेतोरित्यर्थः। चूतप्रसवः आम्र-

इरावती—(शङ्कां रूपयित्वा ।) अभूमिरियं मालविकायाः । कथमत्र तर्कयसि । (क)

निपुणिका—तर्कयामि दोलापरिभ्रष्टया सरुजचरणया देव्या अशोकदोहदाधिकारे नियुक्ता मालविकेति । अन्यथा कथं देवी स्वयं धारितं नूपुरयुगुलं परिजनस्यानुज्ञास्यति । (ख)

इरावती—महती खल्वस्याः संभावना । (ग)

निपुणिका—किं पुनर्नान्विष्यते भर्ता । (घ)

इरावती—हञ्जे न मे चरणावन्यतः प्रवर्तेते । मनो मम किमपि विकारयति । आशङ्कितस्य तावदन्तं गमिष्यामि । (मालविकां निर्वर्ण्य आत्मगतम् ।) स्थाने खलु कातरं मे हृदयम् । (ङ)

बकुलावलिका—(चरणं दर्शयन्ती ।) अपि रोचते तेऽयं रागरेखाविन्यासः । (च)

मालविका—सखि आत्मनश्चरणगत इति लज्जे एनं प्रशंसितुम् । केन प्रसाधनकलायामभिविनीतासि । (छ)

(क) अभूमी इअं मालविआए । कहं[1] एत्थ तक्केसि । (ख) तक्केमि दोलापरिब्भट्टाए सरुअचलणाए देवीए असोअदोहलाहिआरे णिउत्ता मालविएति । अण्णहा कहं देवी सअं[3] धारिअं णूउरजुउलं परिअणस्स अणुं[4]जाणिस्सदि । (ग) महदी क्खु से संभावणा (घ) किं उण ण अण्णेसीअदि भट्टा । (ङ) हञ्जे ण मे चलणा अण्णदो पवट्टन्ति । मणो[5] मह किंवि विआरेदि आसङ्किदस्स दाव अन्तं गमिस्सं । ठाणे क्खु कादरं मे हिअअं । (च) अवि[6] रोअदि ते अअं राअरेहा[7]विण्णासो । (छ) हला अत्तणो चलणगदोत्ति लज्जेमि णं पसंसिदुं । केण पसहिण[8]कलाए अहिविणीदासि ।

---

१ मालविकायै च०. २ किं तक्कसि. ३ असाधारणं णूउर. ४ अब्भंणु. ५ मणोविः मदो मं विओरदि. ६ हला मालविए अवि. ७ चलणराअ. ८ सिप्पसाहणकलाए एव्वं ।

Irāvatī :—(*Exhibiting signs of fear*) This is not the proper place for Mālavikā. What conjecture do you form in this matter ?

Nipuṇikā :—I conjecture that the Queen, whose feet are painful (injured) owing to her fall from the swing, has appointed Mālavikā to the office of supplying its desire to the Aśoka tree; otherwise, how could she have allowed her attendant to put on the pair of anklets worn by herself ?

Irāvatī :—It is certainly a great honour to her.

Nipuṇikā :—Why do you not search for His Lordship ?

Irāvatī :—Maid, my feet refuse to go elsewhere. My mind leads me to suspect something. I will, in the first place, definitely satisfy myself with regard to my suspicions. (*Observing* Mālavikā, *to herself*) Rightly, indeed, was my mind apprehensive.

Bakulāvalikā :—(*Calling* Mālavikā's *attention to her foot*) Are you pleased with the way in which the lines of colour are arranged on your foot ?

Mālavikā :—As it is on my own foot, I am ashamed to praise it (your handiwork). Tell me, who instructed you in the art of decoration ?

मञ्जरी। न अवतंसयितव्यः कर्णपूरीकर्तव्यः किम्। अपि तु कर्तव्य एव। यथा-चूतप्रसवमवतंसयितुकामः भ्रमरपीडां न गणयति तथा राजन्यनुरक्ता त्वं भारिणीं मा चिन्तयेति भावः। दुर्जाते दुःखे [देव्या व्यसने उत्पन्ने]। 'दुर्जातं व्यसने क्लीबमसम्यग्जातवस्तुनि।' इति केशवस्वामी॥ विमदसुरभिः विमर्देन परिमलनेन सुरभिः सुगन्धिः बकुलानां माला। पक्षे विमर्दे सति आपदि आपतितायां सुरभिः मनोज्ञा साहाय्यकरणात्। **भावज्ञानेत्यादि**। कस्यान्यस्य प्रिया। अलीकं मन्त्रयसे। एतदेव मयि नास्ति इति वाक्यैः मालविकायाः भावस्य प्राथमिकस्य मदन-विकारस्य। निर्विकारात्मके चित्ते भावः प्रथमविक्रिया।' इत्युक्तेः। अनुरागस्य इति यावत्। ज्ञानान्तरं भर्तुः कुशेषु इत्यादिना सुजनवचनं प्रमाणीकुरु इति प्रस्तुतेन

बकुलावलिका—अत्र खलु भर्तुः शिष्यास्मि । (क)

विदूषकः—त्वरय तावदेनां गुरुदक्षिणायै । (ख)

मालविका—दिष्ट्या न गर्वितासि । (ग)

बकुलावलिका—उपदेशानुरूपौ चरणौ लब्ध्वाद्य गर्विता भविष्यामि । (आत्मगतम् ।) हन्त सिद्धं मे दौत्यम् । (रागं विलोक्य प्रकाशम् ।) सखि एकस्य ते चरणस्यावसितो रागनिक्षेपः । केवलं मुखमारुतो लम्भयितव्यः । अथवा प्रवातमेवैतत्स्थानम् । (घ)

राजा—सखे पश्य पश्य ।

आर्द्रालक्तकमस्याश्चरणं मुखमारुतेन वीजयितुम् ।
प्रतिपन्नः प्रथमतरः संप्रति सेवावकाशो मे ॥ १३ ॥

विदूषकः—कुतस्तेऽनुशयः । चिरं भवता एतत्क्रमेणानुभवितव्यम् । (ङ)

बकुलावलिका—सखि अरुणशतपत्त्रमिव शोभते ते चरणः । सर्वथा भर्तुरङ्कपरिवर्तिनी भव । (च)

(इरावती निपुणिकामुखमवेक्षते ।)

राजा—ममेयमाशीः ।

मालविका—सखि अवचनीयं मन्त्रयसे । (छ)

(क) एत्थ क्खु अहं भत्तुणो सीसह्मि । (ख) तुवरेहि दाव णं गुरुदक्खिणाए । (ग) दिट्ठिआ ण गव्विदासि । (घ) उवदेसाणुरूवा चलणा लम्भिअ अज्ज गव्विदा भविस्सं । हन्त सिद्धं मे दोच्चं । सहि एक्कस्स दे चलणस्स अवसिदो राअणिक्खेवो । केवलं मुहमारुदो लम्भइदव्वो । अहवा पवादं एव्व एदं ठाणं । (ङ) कुदो दे अणुसओ । चिरं भवदा एवं कमेण अणुहविदव्वं । (च) सहि अरुणसदपत्तं विअ सोहदि दे चलणो । सव्वहा भत्तुणो अङ्कपरिवट्टिणी होहि । (छ) हला अवअणीअं मन्तेसि ।

१ शोषयितुम्, शोषयतः. २ कामवेक्षते. ३ अहं. ४ दाणिं गुरु० ५ चलणं दाणीं ६ अज्ज दाव. ७ विक्खेवी. ८ पवादो एव्व अअं पदेसो. ९ चलणं. १० मा ख. मन्तेहि.

Bakulāvalikā :—In this I am a pupil, of course, of His Majesty.

Vidūṣaka :—Then hasten her for (as) the teacher's remuneration.

Mālavikā :—I am glad to see that you are not proud.

Bakulāvalikā :—Having obtained feet worthy of displaying my skill upon, I shall become proud to-day. (*To herself*) I have accomplished my commission. (*Looking at the colour, aloud)* My friend, I have finished painting one of your feet. It is only necessary to breathe on it (for the purpose of drying it); but this place is windy.

King :—My friend, observe, observe.

Now there has arrived an excellent opportunity for me to serve her by fanning with the breath of my mouth her foot, the red dye on which is wet. (13)

Vidūṣaka :—Why do you regret ? You will soon be able to enjoy this privilege for a long time.

Bakulāvalikā :—Friend, your foot shows like a red lotus. May you certainly repose upon the lap of His Majesty !

(Irāvatī *looks at the face of* Nipuṇikā).

King :—This is my prayer (ardent longing).

Mālavikā :—Ah ! Friend, you are saying what ought not to be said (you are talking nonsense).

वाक्येन । पुनश्च किमात्मनः छंदेन मन्त्रयसे इति तस्य प्रत्याख्याने निराकरणे कृते भर्तुः खलु एतानि इत्यादिवाक्येन दत्तमुचितं युक्तमुत्तरं यस्मिन् येन वा । तेन वाक्येन इयं मालविका स्वे निदेशे मदर्थकरणरूपे स्थापिता । भूयान् काम एषामस्तीति कामिनस्तेषां प्राणाः दूत्यधीना दूत्यायत्ता इति यदुच्यते तत्स्थाने युक्तमेव । निसृष्टार्था इयं दूती । तदुक्तं साहित्यदर्पणे–उभयोर्भावमुन्नीय स्वयं वदति चोत्तरम् । सुश्लिष्टं कुरुते कार्यं निसृष्टार्था तु सा स्मृता ॥ इति । शालिनी वृत्तम् ॥ १४॥ पदं कारिता भर्तुरनुरागमधिकृत्य विश्वासमुत्पाद्य राजसमागमकर्मणि प्रवर्तिता इत्यर्थः । एतत्पदमिति पाठे इमं व्यवसायम् । पदं व्यवसितत्राण-इत्यमरः ॥

बकुलावलिका—मन्त्रयितव्यमेव मया मन्त्रितम् । (क)

मालविका—प्रिया खल्वहं तव । (ख)

बकुलावलिका—न केवलं मम । (ग)

मालविका—कस्य वाऽन्यस्य । (घ)

बकुलावलिका—गुणेष्वभिनिवेशिनो भर्तुरपि । (ङ)

मालविका—अलीकं मन्त्रयसे । एतदेव मयि नास्ति । (च)

बकुलावलिका—सत्यं त्वयि नास्ति । भर्तुः कृशेषु ईषत्परिपाण्डुरेषु दृश्यते अङ्गेषु । (छ)

निपुणिका—प्रथमगणितमिव हताशाया उत्तरम् । (ज)

बकुलावलिका—अनुरागोऽनुरागेण परीक्षितव्य इति सुजनवचनं प्रमाणीकुरु । (झ)

मालविका—किमात्मनश्छन्देन मन्त्रयसे । (ञ)

बकुलावलिका—नहि नहि । भर्तुः खल्वेतानि प्रणयमृदुकान्यक्षराणि बिम्बान्तरितानि । (ट)

मालविका—सखि देवीं विचिन्त्य न मे हृदयं विश्वसिति । (ठ)

(क) मन्तिदव्वं एव्व मए मन्तिदं । (ख) पिआ खु अहं तुह । (ग) ण केवलं मह । (घ) कस्स वा अण्णस्स । (ङ) गुणेसु अहिणिवेसिणो भत्तुणो वि । (च) अलीअं मन्तेसि । एदं एव्व मइ णत्थि । (छ) सच्चं तुइ णत्थि । भत्तुणो किसेसु इसि[2]परिपण्डरेसु दसिइ अङ्गेसु । (ज) पुढमग[3]णिदं विआ हदासाए उत्तरं । (झ) अणुराओ अणुराएण परिक्खि[4]दव्वो त्ति सुअणवअणं पमाणीकरेहि । (ञ) किं अत्तणो छन्देन मन्तेसि । (ट) णहि णहि । भत्तुणो खु इदाइं पणअमि[5]दुलाइं अक्खराइं विम्ब[6]न्तरिदाइं । (ठ) हला देविं विचिन्तिअ ण मे हिअ[7]अं विस्ससदि ।

---

१ खु. २ दर-वर पण्डु., सुन्दरप० ३ भ-ग-णिदं. ४ पच्चेट्ठव्वो (प्रत्येष्टव्यः), पडिच्छिदव्वो (प्रतिच्छेत्तव्यः). ५ मिदुआइं (मृदुकानि).: पणअमआई, पणअसू-अआइं. ६ वन्तत्त (वक्त्रान्त०) ७ हिअअस्स पहविस्सं.

Bakulāvalikā :—I have said exactly what has to be said.

Mālavikā :—I am surely loved by you (and so you say so).

Bakulāvalikā :—I am not the only person who loves you

Mālavikā :—Who else then loves me ?

Bauulāvalikā :—The King also, who always admires (*lit.* fixes his mind upon) merits.

Mālavikā :—You are saying what is false. That fortune s not mine.

Bakulāvalikā :—Really it is not yours ! It is seen in the emaciated and slightly pale limbs of the King.

Nipuṇikā :—The wretch gives her answer as if she had got it ready beforehand.

Bakulāvalikā :—Conform yourself to (lit. admit the authority of) the maxim of the experts that love must be tested by love.

Mālavikā :—Why do you chatter (*also*, are you talking this) at your own sweet will ?

Bakulāvalikā :—No, indeed ; these are but the words, sweet with love, of His Majesty spoken through me (lit. hidden from him by a different body or mouth).

Mālavikā :—Ah ! When I think of the Queen, my heart feels quite diffident.

निर्विकारस्य स्वस्थचित्तस्यापि । उत्सुकताजनक उत्कण्ठाकारी । गृहीतार्था ज्ञातयथावद्वृत्तान्ता । निर्वृत्तं समाप्तं परिकर्म प्रसाधनम् । रागरेखानिवेशनमिति यावत् यस्य । उपारूढः वृद्धिं प्राप्तः रागः त्वद्विषयकोऽनुरागः पक्षे रक्तिमा यस्य सः । उपभोगक्षमः संभोगयोग्यः । पक्षे शरीरधारणयोग्यः । एष किं भर्ता । न तावद्भर्ता । इत्यत्र द्व्यर्थोक्त्या चतुर्थं पताकास्थानमुक्तं भवति। तदुक्तं दर्पणे–द्व्यर्थो वचनविन्यासः सुश्लिष्टः काव्ययोनितः । प्रधानार्थान्तरापेक्षी पताका स्थानकं परम् ॥ इति । **पर्याप्तमिति** एतावता पर्याप्तं पर्याप्तिः । यद्वा पर्याप्तमलम् । एतन्मात्रश्रवणमपि कामिजनस्य तुष्ट्यै अलमित्यर्थः । **अनातुरेत्यादि** । अनातुरोत्कण्ठितयोः । अनातुरोऽनार्तः ।

बकुलावलिका—मुग्धे भ्रमरसंबाध इति वसन्तावतारसर्वस्वं किं न चूतप्रसवोऽवतंसयितव्यः। (क)

मालविका—त्वं तावद्दुर्जातेऽत्यन्तं सहाया भव। (ख)

बकुलावलिका—विमर्दसुरभिर्बकुलावलिका खल्वहम्। (ग)

राजा—साधु बकुलावलिके साधु।

भावज्ञानानन्तरप्रस्तुतेन प्रत्याख्याने दत्तयुक्तोत्तरेण।
वाक्येनेयं स्थापिता स्वे निदेशे स्थाने प्राणाः कामिनां दूत्यधीनाः॥१४॥

इरावती—हञ्जे पश्य। कारितैव बकुलावलिकयैतस्मिन् पदं मालविका। (घ)

निपुणिका—भट्टिनि निर्विकारस्याप्युत्सुकताजनक उपदेशः। (ङ)

इरावती—स्थाने खलु शङ्कितं मे हृदयम्। गृहीतार्था अनन्तरं चिन्तयिष्यामि। (च)

(क) मुद्दे भमरसंबाधोत्ति वसन्तावदारसव्वस्सं किं ण चूदप्पसवो ओदंसिदव्वो। (ख) तुमं दाव दुज्जादे अच्चन्तं सहाया होहि। (ग) विमद्दसुरही बउलावलिआ खुं अहं। (घ) हञ्जे पेक्ख। कारिदा एव्व बउलावलिआए एदस्सिं पदं मालविआ। (ङ) भट्टिणि णिव्विआरस्सवि उस्सुअदाजणओ उवदेसो। (च) ठाणे खु संकिदं मे हिअअं। गहीदत्था अणन्तरं चिन्तइस्सं।

कामोत्कण्ठारहित इत्यर्थः। उत्कण्ठा कामाभिलाषः अस्य सञ्जाता असौ उत्कण्ठितः कामी। अनातुरः च एकः पक्षः। उत्कण्ठितः च अन्यः पक्षः। तौ अनातुरोत्कण्ठितौ। यद्वा अनातुरा नायिका च उत्कण्ठितः नायकश्च तयोः। प्रसिद्धयता संभवता समागमेनापि संपर्केणापि मां प्रति मामनु। मत्पक्ष इत्यर्थः। रतिर्न शृङ्गारो न भवति। एकानुरागस्य रसाभासत्वात्। तथा चोक्तम्–'एकत्रैवानुरागश्चेद्बहुसक्तिश्च योषितः। अनौचित्यप्रवृत्तिश्च शृङ्गाराभास उच्यते॥' इति। किंतु समः तुल्यं अनुरागो ययोस्तयोः। अन्योन्यमुत्कण्ठितयोः इत्यर्थः। परस्परस्य

---

१ कामिनः २ सम्बन्धो, संपादो भविस्सदित्ति ३ सव्वस्सभूदो. ४ पल्लवो ५ ओदंसणिज्जो. ६ अच्चन्तसहाइणी. गच्छन्तस्स सहाइणा. ७ णु. ८ कारिदं...एवं पदं मालविआए. ९ अहिआरस्स उइदो उव. (अधिकारस्य उचित उप०)

Bakulāvalikā :—Foolish girl ! Is not a mango-shoot, the whole essence of the manifestation of the spring, to be used as an ear-ornament, just because it has been clinging to it ?

Mālavikā :—Well, do you then help me to the utmost, in case calamity ensues.

Bakulāvalikā :—I am, indeed, Bakulāvalikā that becomes the more fragrant (helpful), the more it is pressed.

King :—Bravo ! Bakulāvalikā, Bravo !

By means of a speech (conversation) which was commenced as soon as she knew the state of her mind, and in which proper answers were given to contradictions, this one here (Mālavikā) has been made to follow her counsel (or brought within the scope of her *i. e.* Bakulāvalikā's commission) ; rightly (indeed) are the lives of lovers dependent upon female go-betweens. (14)

Irāvatī :—Observe, my girl, Bakulāvalikā has but induced Mālavikā to take the step in this direction.

Nipuṇikā :—Queen ! Her instruction is (words are) such as would produce a longing even in one free from passion.

Irāvatī :—Not without reason, indeed, was my heart apprehensive. When I shall have got at the facts, I shall consider what to do.

प्राप्तिः तत्र निर्गता आशा ययोस्तयोः निराशयोः। शरीरनाशोपि मरणमपि वरं मनागभीष्टः। न तु विषमानुरागयोः संगम इति भावः। वंशस्थविलं वृत्तम् ॥ १५ ॥ **आदायेत्यादि**। कर्णकिसलयं कर्णपूरार्थं किसलयम्। अत्र कर्णशब्देन कर्णपूरो लक्ष्यते ॥ इयं मालविका अस्मादशोकात् कर्णकिसलयमादाय अत्र अस्मै चरणमर्पयति। अशोके पादं न्यस्यति। एवमुभयोः मालविकाऽशोकयोः सदृशयोः पल्लवगुच्छचरणयोः विनिमयात् विनिमयः परिवृत्तिः। न जातः तथा मम इति आत्मानं वञ्चितमकृतार्थं मन्ये ॥ १६ ॥ निर्गुणः गुणरहितः कुसुमोद्भेदे पुष्पदर्शने मन्थरः मन्दः भवेत्। झटिति पुष्पाणि न दर्शयेत्। **अनेनेत्यादि**।

बकुलावलिका—एष द्वितीयोऽपि ते निर्वृत्तपरिकर्मा चरणः। यावद्-द्वावपि सनूपुरौ करोमि। (इति नाट्येन नूपुरयुगलमामुच्य।) हला उत्तिष्ठ अनुतिष्ठ देव्या अशोकविकासयितृकं नियोगम्। (क)

(उभे उत्तिष्ठतः।)

इरावती—श्रुतो देव्या नियोगः। भवत्विदानीम्। (ख)

बकुलावलिका—एष उपारूढराग उपभोगक्षमः पुरतस्ते वर्तते (ग)

मालविका—(सहर्षम्।) किं भर्ता। (घ)

बकुलावलिका—(सस्मितम्।) न तावद्भर्ता। एषोऽशोकशाखावलम्बी पल्लवगुच्छकः। अवतंसयैनम्। (ङ)

विदूषकः—अपि श्रुतं भवता। (च)

राजा—सखे पर्याप्तमेतावता कामिनाम्।

अनातुरोत्कण्ठितयोः[1] प्रसिध्यता समागमेनापि रतिर्न मां प्रति।
परस्परप्राप्तिनिराशयोर्वरं शरीरनाशोऽपि समानुरागयोः[2] ॥ १५ ॥

(मालविकारचितपल्लवावतंसा सलीलम[3]शोकाय पादं प्रहिणोति।)

राजा—वयस्य[4]।

आदाय कर्णकिसलयमस्मादियमत्र चरणमर्पयति।
उभयोः सदृशविनिमयादात्मानं वञ्चितं मन्ये ॥ १६ ॥

(क) एसो दुदीओवि दे णिव्वुतप[5]रिकम्मा चलणो। जाव दुवे[6]वि सणूउरे करोमि। हला उट्ठेहि। अणुचिट्ठ देवीए असोअविआसइत्तअं णिआअं। (ख) सुदो देवीए णिओओ[7]। होदु दाणिं। (ग) एसो उवारूढाओ उअभोअक्खमो पुरदो दे वट्टइ[8]। (घ) किं भट्टा। (ङ) ण दाव भट्टा। एसो असोअसाहावलम्बी पल्लवगुच्छओ। ओदंसेहि[9] [10] णं। (च) अवि सुदं भवदा।

१ अनादरो०. २ समानरागयोः. ३ एतन्नास्ति क्वचित्. ४ वयस्य पश्य. ५ समत्त (समाप्त). ६ णं सणूउरं, णूउरशोभिदं. ७ णिओओत्ति, सुदं...णिओओत्ति दाणिं. ८ उओढ (उवोढ). ९ चिठ्ठइ दिसइ. १० दाव णं.

Bakulāvalikā :—Here is your second foot with its decoration completed. Now, I will put the anklets on both. (*Shows that she puts on the anklets*). Friend, rise up and execute the duty imposed on you by the Queen of causing the Aśoka to blossom. (*Both rise up*).

Irāvatī:—Oh, the Queen's order is heard (V. *l.* Oh, we have heard that it is the Queen's order) : let it be executed now.

Bakulāvalikā:—Here stands in front of you, with the *Rāga* (1 redness—2 love) increased and fit for enjoyment,—

Mālavikā :—(*Delighted*) Who ! Is it his Lordship ?

Bakulāvalikā :—(*Smiling*) No, not his Lordship, but this bunch of leaves hanging down from the bough of the Aśoka ; make an ear-ornament of it.

Vidūṣaka :—Did your Highness hear ?

King :—This much is enough for lovers.

I would not be pleased with the union, though sure to be accomplished, of two lovers, one of whom is ardent, and the other indifferent (cold) ; better would be the destruction of the bodies of an equally loving pair hopeless of mutual obtainment. (15)

(Mālavikā *having made an ear-ornament of the As'oka-buds, in a playful manner puts forth her foot to strike the tree*).

King :—Friend,

Having taken from the As'oka-tree a shoot for her ear, she presents to it her foot; since the two have exchanged similar gifts, I consider myself as one defeated in my object. (16)

हे अशोक तनुः कृशः मध्यः कटिः यस्यास्तया तनुमध्यया । मुखरः शब्दायमानः यः नूपुरः तेन आरौति इति आरावी तेन । नवं सद्योविकसितं यदम्बुरुहं कमलं तद्वत्कोमलेन सुकुमारेण अनेन चरणेन संभावितः स्पर्शनेन कृतसत्कारः त्वं यदि सद्यः सपद्येव कुसुमैः न सम्पत्स्यसे युक्तो भविष्यसि तर्हि ललितकामिभिः विलासिकामुकैः साधारणं समानं दोहदं चरणताडनापेक्षारूपं वृथा व्यर्थं वहसि धारयसि । कृतमेतादृशेन दोहदधारणेनेत्यर्थः । पृथ्वीवृत्तम् । अत्र द्वितीयचरणे कोमलेनेत्यत्र यतिभङ्गो न दोषाय ।

मालविका—अपि नाम आवयोः सम्भावना सफला भवेत् । (क)

बकुलावलिका—सखि नास्ति ते दोषः । निर्गुणोऽयमशोको यदि कुसुमोद्भेदमन्थरो भवेद्य ईदृशं चरणसत्कारं लभते । (ख)

राजा—

> **अनेन तनुमध्यया मुखरनूपुरारांविणा**
> **नवाम्बुरुहकोमलेन चरणेन संभावितः ।**
> **अशोक यदि सद्य एव कुसुमैर्न संपत्स्यसे**
> **वृथा वहसि दोहदं ललितकामिसाधारणम् ॥ १७ ॥**

सखे वचनावसरपूर्वं प्रवेष्टुमिच्छामि ।

विदूषकः—एहि । एनां परिहासयिष्यामि । (ग)

(उभौ प्रवेशं कुरुतः ।)

निपुणिका—भट्टिनि भर्तात्र प्रविशति । (घ)

इरावती—एतत्प्रथमं मम चिन्तितं हृदयेन । (ङ)

विदूषकः—(उपसृत्य ।) भवति युक्तं नाम अत्रभवतः प्रियवयस्यः अयमशोकः वामपादेन ताडयितुम् । (च)

उभे—(ससंभ्रमम् ।) अहो भर्ता । (छ)

(क) अवि णाम अह्माणं संभावना सफला भवे । (ख) हला णत्थि दे दोसो णिग्गुणो अअं असोओ जइ कुसुमब्भेदमन्थरो भवे जो इरिसं चलणसक्कारं लहेइ । (ग) एहि । णं परिहासइस्सं । (घ) भट्टिणि भट्टा एत्थ पविसदि (ङ) एदं पुढमं मम चिन्तिदं हिअएण । (च) होदि जुत्तं णाम अत्तहोदो पिअवअस्सो अअं असोओ वामपादेण तादिदुं । (छ) अम्हो भट्टा ।

---

१ पुरोद्वाहिना. २ मुकुलैः. ३ मुधा. ४ वचनानुसरण०, पूर्वकं. ५ उपेत्य. ६ अग्गुणो ७ मुणोम्भेद, मोग्गम. ८ अलभत, लंभिदो (लम्भितः) जो चल० लम्भिअ (लब्ध्वा). ९ भट्टिणि भट्टिणि; एत्थ एव्व. १० एव्वं, इदं. ११ ण जुत्तं; अअं वाम०, अत्तभोदि पिअवअ—(अत्रभवति प्रियवयस्ये) असोओ. १२ णं वाम०.

Mālavikā :—Do you think our expectation will be fulfilled ?

Bakulāvalikā :—Friend, it will not be your fault ; devoid of merits (unappreciative) would be this Aśoka, that has obtained such an honour of being touched by (your) foot, if it should be slow in putting forth flowers.

King :—

O, Aśoka, if after having been honoured by the slender-waisted one with this foot of hers, tender like a young lotus and loud-tinkling with noisy anklets, you do not become immediately laden with a wealth of flowers, in vain do you cherish a desire shared by you in common with sportive lovers. (17)

Friend, I wish to present myself, taking a favourable opportunity for speaking.

Vidūṣaka :—Come along. I shall make fun of her.

(Both *enter.*)

Nipuṇikā :—Madam, here is His Lordship appearing on the scene.

Irāvatī :—This was contemplated (anticipated) by my mind at the outset.

Vidūṣaka :—(*Advancing*) My lady, proper, indeed, it is on your part to strike with your left foot the Aśoka tree, the dear friend of His Lordship !

Both:—(*In a state of confusion*) Oh ! His Lordship.

प्रतिपदिकप्रत्यययोर्मध्यपातित्वे तस्यादोषत्वात् । तृतीयचरणे तु एवेत्यत्र यतिभङ्गो केषांचिन्मते दोष एव ॥ १७ ॥ वचनस्यावसरः वचनावसरः स पूर्वः यस्मिन् कर्मणि । युक्तं नामेत्यत्र काकुरनुसंधेया । गृहीतार्थया ज्ञाततदाशयया । भयं रूपयतीति । अत्र भयकथनात्संभ्रमो नाम संध्यङ्गमुक्तं भवति ॥ किसलयेत्यादि । हे विलासिनि विलासः शृङ्गारभावजा क्रिया अस्या विद्यते इति तथोक्तातत्सम्बुद्धिः। अत इनिठनौ इति मत्वर्थीयः इन् । ऋन्नेभ्य इति ङीप । यानस्थानासनादीनां मुखनेत्रादिकर्मणाम् । विशेषस्तु विलासः स्यादिष्टसंदर्शनादिना ॥ इति विलासलक्षणमुक्तं साहित्यदर्पणे । कठिणे कठोरस्पर्शे

विदूषकः—बकुलावलिके गृहीतार्थया त्वया अत्रभवती ईदृशमविनयं कुर्वती कस्मान्न निवारिता। (क)

(मालविका भयं रूपयति।)

निपुणिका—भट्टिनि पश्य। किं प्रवृत्तमार्यगौतमेन। (ख)

इरावती—कथं खलु ब्रह्मबन्धुरन्यथा जीविष्यति। (ग)

बकुलावलिका—आर्य एषा देव्या नियोगमनुतिष्ठति। एतस्मिन्नतिक्रमे परवतीयम्। प्रसीदतु भर्ता। (इत्यात्मना सहैनां प्रणिपातयति।) (घ)

राजा—यद्येवमनपराद्धासि। उत्तिष्ठ भद्रे। (इति हस्तेन गृहीत्वोत्थापयति।)

विदूषकः—युज्यते। देव्यत्र मानयितव्या। (ङ)

राजा—(विहस्य।)—

किसलयमृदोर्विलासिनि कठिने निहितस्य पादपस्कन्धे।
चरणस्य न ते बाधा संप्रति वामस्य वामोरु॥ १८॥

(मालविका लज्जां नाटयति।)

इरावती—(सासूयम्।) अहो नवनीतहृदय आर्यपुत्रः। (च)

मालविका—बकुलावलिके एहि। अनुष्ठितमात्मनो नियोगं देव्यै निवेदयावः। (छ)

बकुलावलिका—तेन हि विज्ञापय भर्तारं विसर्जयेति। (ज)

(क) बउलावलिए गहीदत्थाए तुए अत्तहोदी ईरिसं अविणअं करन्ती कीस ण णिवारिदा। (ख) भट्टिणि पेक्ख। किं पउत्तं अज्जगोदमेण (ग) कहं खु बह्मबन्धु अण्णहा जीविस्सदि। (घ) अज्ज एसा देवीए णिओअं अणुचिट्ठदि। एदस्सिं अदिक्कमे परवदी इअं। पसीददु भट्टा। (ङ) जुज्जइ। देवी एत्थ माणइदव्वा। (च) अहो णवणीदहिअओ अज्जउत्तो। (छ) बउलावलिए एहि। अणुट्ठिदं अत्तणो णिओअं देवीए णिवेदेह्म। (ज) तेणहि विण्णवेहि भट्टारं विसज्जेहित्ति।

---

१ समम्. २ त्वेनाम् ३ रूपयति. ४ सखी. ५ णीदकप्पो अविणीदहिअओ क्खु (अविनीतहृदयः खलु).

Vidūṣaka :—Bakulāvalikā ! Why did you, who knew her object (that she was going to strike the tree), not prevent the lady from committing such an ill-bred act ?

(*Mālavikā shows fear.*)

Nipuṇikā :—Madam, see what the revered Gautama has begun !

Irāvatī :—How else could that wretch of a Brāhmaṇa earn his livelihood ?

Bakulāvalikā :—Sir, she is executing the order of the Queen. In this transgression she is the instrument of (lit. dependent upon) another. Your Lordship will be pleased (to excuse us). (She *makes* Mālavikā *prostrate herself and falls prostrate at the same time before the King.*)

King :—If this is the case, you are not guilty. Rise up, gentle maiden. *(He takes her by the hand and raises her up).*

Vidūṣaka :—Quite right. In this matter the Queen must be respected.

King :—*(Smiling)*

Charming one, with graceful thighs, I hope your left foot, soft as a shoot, does not now feel pain, being planted on (struck against) the hard trunk of the tree. (18)

(Mālavikā *blushes.*)

Irāvatī :—*(Spitefully)* Ah ! my lord has a heart as soft as a fresh butter !

Mālavikā :—Come, Bakulāvalikā, let us inform the Queen that we have executed her command.

Bakulāvalikā :—Then, ask His Lordship to give you leave to depart.

पादपस्कंधे अशोकप्रकाण्डे निहितस्य दत्तस्य। किसलयमिव मृदुः किसलयमृदुः तस्य प्रवाल-सुकुमारस्य ते वामस्य चरणस्य हे वामोरु वामौ अतिसुन्दरौ ऊरू यस्याः सा वामोरूः तत्सम्बुद्धिः। संहितशफलक्षणवामादेश्च। इति ऊङ्। सम्प्रति बाधा पीडा न कच्चित्। आर्या जातिः॥ १८॥ अत्र प्रसक्त्या संग्रहो नाम सन्ध्यङ्गमुक्तं भवति॥ नवनीतमिव अत्यन्तं

राजा—भद्रे यास्यसि । मम तावदुत्पन्नावसरमर्थित्वं श्रूयताम् ।

बकुलावलिका—अवहिता शृणु । आज्ञापयतु भर्ता । (क)

राजा—

धृतिपुष्पमयमपि जनो बध्नाति न तादृशं चिरात्प्रभृति ।
स्पर्शामृतेन पूरय दोहदमस्याप्यनन्यरुचेः ॥ १९ ॥

इरावती—(सहसोपसृत्य ।) पूरय पूरय । ननु अशोकः कुसुमं दर्शयति । अयं पुनः पुष्प्यति फलति च । (ख)

(सर्वे इरावतीं दृष्ट्वा संभ्रान्ताः ।)

राजा—(अपवार्य ।) वयस्य का प्रतिपत्तिरत्र ।

विदूषकः—किमन्यत् । जङ्घाबलमेव । (ग)

इरावती—बकुलावलिके साधु त्वयोपक्रान्तम् । मालविके त्वं तावत् सफलप्रार्थनं कुर्वार्यपुत्रम् । (घ)

उभे—प्रसीदतु भट्टिनी । के आवां भर्तुः प्रणयपरिग्रहस्य । (इति निष्क्रान्ते ।) (ङ)

इरावती—अहो अविश्वसनीयाः पुरुषाः । मया खलु आत्मनो वञ्चनावचनं प्रमाणीकृत्य व्याधगीतरक्तया हरिण्येवाशङ्कितयैतन्न विज्ञातम् । (च)

(क) अवहिदा सुणाहि । आणवेदु भाट्ठ (ख) पूरेहि पूरेहि । [1]णं असोओ कुसुमं दंसेदि । अअं उण [2]पुप्फेदि फलदि अ । (ग) किं अण्णं । जंघा[3]बलं [4]एव्वं । (घ) बउलावलिए साहु तुए उवक्कन्तं । मालविए तुमं दाव [5]सफलपत्थणं करेहि अज्जउत्तं । (ङ) पसीददु भट्टिणी । का अह्मे भत्तुणे पणअपरिग्गहस्स । (च) अहो अविस्ससणीआ पुरिसा । मए क्खु अत्तणो वञ्चणावअणं पमाणीकरिअ[6] वाहगीदरत्ताए हरिणीए विअ असङ्किदाए एहं ण विण्णादं ।

---

१ असोओ कुसुमं णं. २ पुप्फदि एव्व. ३ जंघावलम्बणं. ४ एव्व सरणं. ५ दाणिं सफलब्भत्थणं. ६ करिअ अक्खिताए (आक्षिप्तया) वाहजणगीदगहीदचित्ताए विअ हरिणीए एदं; अत्ताणो वञ्चणा वाहजणगीदिरत्ताए...० किदाए ण विण्णादा; पमाणीकरिअ अक्खिताए पिअधरिणीए हिअअसल्लं किदं एव्वं ण विण्णादं मए वाह० अविसंकिदाए हरिणीए विअ विणासोत्ति.

King :—Fair damsel, you will go (indeed). But hear first my supplication, for which the proper opportunity has come.

Bakulāvalikā :—Listen attentively! Your Lordship will be pleased to speak out.

King :—

This person (*i. e.* I) too has not (been able to) put forth a blossom in the form of happiness for a long time. With the nectar of your touch gratify, therefore, the longing of him also, who has no liking for anything else (is devoted to you alone). (19)

Irāvatī :—(*Suddenly approaching*) Gratify it, gratify it; the As'oka shows flowers only, while this displays flowers and yields fruit also.

(All *are confused on seeing* Irāvatī).

King :—(*Aside*) My friend, what recourse is there now?

Vidūṣaka :—Only (what else than) taking to our heels (*lit.* the strength of our legs)!

Irāvatī :—Bakulāvalikā! Well you have begun. Mālavikā! Grant the request of His Lordship.

Both Girls :—Madam, excuse us. Who are we that we should have the favour of his Lordship's affection?

(*Exeunt* Bakulāvalikā and Mālavikā).

Irāvatī :—Oh, how faithless are men! I, indeed, relying upon your deceitful speech, unsuspicious like the deer that is attracted by the tunes of the hunter, did not (anticipate) know this.

मृदु हृदयं यस्य सः। इति सोल्लुण्ठं वचः। उत्पन्नः अवसरः यस्य तत्। लब्धावकाश-मित्यर्थः। धृतिपुष्पेति। अयमपि जनः अहमपि चिरात्प्रभृति दीर्घकालमारभ्य तादृशं धृतिरूपमभीष्टप्राप्तिजन्यपरितोषरूपं पुष्पं धृतिपुष्पं न बध्नाति। अतः न विद्यते अन्यस्य रुचिर्यस्य। यद्वा न अन्या त्वत्स्पर्शामृतादन्या रुचिर्यस्य। तस्य अनन्याभिलाषिणः अस्यापि ममापि स्पर्शं एवामृतं तेन स्पर्शामृतेन आलिङ्गनादिनेत्यर्थः। दोहदं पूरय॥ १९॥ पूरयेति अत्र संरब्धवचनात्तोटकं नाम संध्यङ्गमुक्तं भवति॥

विदूषकः—(जनान्तिकम्।) प्रतियोजयेदानीं किमपि। कर्मगृहीतेन कुम्भीलकेन सन्धिच्छेदने शिक्षितोऽस्मीति वक्तव्यं भवति। (क)

राजा—सुन्दरि न मे मालविकया[1] कश्चिदर्थः। मया त्वं चिरयसीति यथाकथंचिदात्मा विनोदितः।

इरावती—विश्वसनीयोऽसि। मया न विज्ञातमीदृशं विनोदवस्तु आर्यपुत्रेणोपलब्धमिति। अन्यथा मन्दभागिन्यैवं न क्रियते। (ख)

विदूषकः—मा तावदत्रभवती अत्रभवतो दाक्षिण्यस्योपरोधं भणतु। समापत्तिदृष्टेन देव्याः परिजनेन संकथापि यदि अपराधः स्थाप्यते अत्र त्वमेव प्रमाणम्। (ग)

इरावती—ननु संकथा नाम भवतु। किमित्यात्मानमायासयिष्यामि। (इति रुषा[2] प्रस्थिता।) (घ)

राजा—(अनुसरन्।) प्रसीदतु भवती।

(इरावती रशनासंदित[3]चरणा व्रजत्येव)

राजा—सुन्दरि न शोभते प्रणयिनि[4] जने निरपेक्षता।

इरावती—शठ अविश्वसनीयहृदयोऽसि। (ङ)

(क) पडिजाएहि[5] दाणिं किंपि। कम्मग्गहीदेण[6] कुम्भीलएण संधिच्छेदे[7] सिक्खिओम्मित्ति वत्तव्वं होदी। (ख) विस्सणीओसी। मए[8] ण विण्णादं ईरिसं[9] विणोदवत्थुं[10] अज्जउत्तेण उवलद्धंति। अण्णहा मन्दभाइणीए[11] एव्वं ण करीअदि। (ग) मा दाव अत्तहोदा अत्तहोदो दक्खिण्णास स उअरोहं[12] भणदु। समावत्तिदिट्ठेण[13] देवीए परिअणेण[14] संकहावि जइ अवराहो ठावीअदि[15] एत्थ तुमं एव्व पमाणं। (घ) णं संकहा णाम होदु। किंति[16] अत्ताणं आआसइस्सं। (ङ) सठ अविस्ससणीअहिअओसि[17]।

---

१ ०कायां. २ रुष्टा. ३ संदानित. ४ प्रणयिजन, प्रणयिजननिरपे०. ५ भोपडिवज्जेहि किंवि उत्तरं. ६ ०देण विअ. ७ ०च्छेदे, चछेदणं च्छेदणशिक्खिओ (शिक्षकः). ८ मंए णाम. ९ एतारिसं. वत्थुअं, वुत्तन्तं (ईदृशोवृत्तान्तः). ११ अण्णहा दुक्खरं (दुष्करं-दक्खतरं दुक्ख्व्वावारिणी. १४ (व्यापारिणी) एव्वं ण करोमि. १२ अवराहं (अपराधं). १३ समोवट्ठिदेण. १४ परिचारिइत्थिअजणेण. १५ वारिअदि, क्खमीअदु. १६ केंच्चि. अकालं. १७ विस्सस०

Vidūṣaka :—(*Aside*) Advance something in reply. A burglar, caught in the act red-handed, has to say that he is a student of (simply practises) the art of house-breaking.

King :—Beautiful one ! I had no interest in Mālavikā. Because you delayed, I diverted myself somehow.

Irāvatī :—You are—(indeed) to be trusted ! I did not know that my Lord had obtained such an object of diversion. Otherwise, unfortunate that I am, I would never have done this (presumed to annoy you by this intrusion).

Vidūṣaka :— Your Ladyship ought not to consider (call) His Majesty's conduct a breach of politeness. If mere conversation with the attendants of the Queen, when met by chance, be considered a crime, then in this case you are the best judge (and we must acquiesce).

Irāvatī :—Well, let it be conversation (as you say ; or, let this pleasant (सं) conversation go on). Why should I torture myself (for nothing) ? (*She goes off in anger*).

King :—(*Going after her*) Let your Ladyship be appeased.

(*Irāvatī, with her feet, though entangled by her girdle, keeps on going*).

King :—O charming one, such an indifference towards a loving person is not proper for you.

Irāvatī :—O rogue, your heart is not to be relied on.

वयस्येत्यादि। का प्रतिपत्तिः को विचारः। क उपाय इत्यर्थः। अत्र भीतेर्गम्यमानत्वादुद्वेगो नाम संध्याङ्गमुक्तं भवति ॥ जङ्घाबलमेव जङ्घाबलमाश्रित्य शीघ्रमितः पलायनमेवेति परिहासोक्तिः। साधु उपक्रान्तमभीष्टार्थस्य निपुणतयोपक्रमः कृतः। के आवां नहि इत्यर्थः। वञ्चनावचनं त्वया सह दोलाधिरोहणमनुभवितुमागच्छामीति प्रतारणावचनम्। प्रमाणीकृत्य सत्यत्वेन स्वीकृत्य अशङ्कितया अन्यतो भयमशङ्कमानया। एतदित्यनेन राज्ञः कपटाचरणं परामृश्यते। किमपि प्रतियोजय उपपन्नमनुपपन्नं वा उत्तरं कुर्वित्यर्थः। कर्मगृहीतेन कर्मणि चौर्यकर्मणि गृहीतेनापि कुम्भीलकेन चोरेण सन्धिच्छेदने पिहितभूमिः सन्धिस्तस्याः छेदने भेदने। सुरङ्गाकरणे इत्यर्थः।

राजा—

शठ इति मयि तावदस्तु ते परिचयवत्यवधीरणा प्रिये।
चरणपतितया न चण्डि[1] तां विसृजसि मेखलयापि याचिता ॥ २० ॥

इरावती—इयमपि[2] हताशा त्वामेवानुसरति। (इति रशनामादाय राजानं ताडयितुमिच्छति।) (क)

राजा—एषा।

बाष्पासारा हेमकाञ्चीगुणेन श्रोणीबिम्बादव्यपेक्षाच्युतेन[3]।
चण्डी चण्डं हन्तुमभ्युद्यता मां विद्युद्दाम्ना मेघराजीव विन्ध्यम् ॥ २१ ॥

इरावती—किं मामेवं भूयोऽप्यपराद्धां करोषि। (इति सरशनं[4] हस्तमवलम्बते।) (ख)

राजा—

अपराधिनि मयि दण्डं संहरसि[5] किमुद्यतं कुटिलकेशि।
वर्धयसि विलसितं त्वं दासजनायात्र[6] कुप्यसि च ॥ २२ ॥

नूनमिदमनुज्ञातम्[7]। (इति पादयोः पतति।)

(क) इअं पि हदासा तुमं एव्व अणुसरदि। (ख) किं मं एवं भूओ वि अवरद्धं करेसि।

शिक्षितः अभ्यसितोसीति वक्तव्यम्। विश्वसनीयोसीत्यत्र विपरीतलक्षणानुसंधया ॥ ईदृशं विनोदवस्तु मालविकारूपं। एवं न क्रियते युवयोर्विनोदे उपरोधो न क्रियेत। मा तावदिति। अत्रभवता मालविकया सह संकथा कुर्वता आत्मनः दाक्षिण्यमेव दर्शितम्। तत्र मया उपरोधः कृत इति मा ब्रूहि। यन्मालविकां प्रति उक्तं तदुपचारमात्रमेव। अतस्त्वदागमनं नोपरोध इति भावः। समापत्तिदृष्टेन यदृच्छादृष्टेन। स्था-

---

१ चण्डतां, चण्डितां. २ इयं इरावती; वयस्यैषा हि. ३ दप्युपे० ४ रशनां हस्तेनावलम्बते; ०मालम्बते. ५ हरसि किमभ्युः मय तं. ६ अद्य. ७ अस्मात्प्राक्-(आत्मगतं) इति क्वचित्

King :—

O dear one, let your slight, indicated by the (use of the) word 'Rogue', be shown towards me who am so familiar with you; but, O wrathful one, you do not give up your anger even though entreated by your girdle lying prostrate at your feet. (20).

Irāvatī :—Even this cursed girdle sides with you. *(She takes up the girdle and shows her readiness to strike the* King *with it).*

King :—This lady,—

in a passion, shedding a profusion of tears, is prepared to strike me with the string of her golden girdle slipped down through carelessness from her round hips, like a row of clouds pouring down vapoury showers of water and ready to strike the Vindhya mountion with a streak of lightning. (21).

Irāvatī :—Why do you thus prove me to be guilty again? *(Hangs down her hand with the girdle in it).*

King :—

Why do you withdraw the intended punishment from me, who am guilty, O curly-haired one ? You increase your gracefulness, and still you are angry with this your slave here. (22)

Surely I am allowed to do this. *(Falls at her feet).*

प्यते प्रतिपाद्यते । गण्यते इत्यर्थः । रसनया मेखलया स्वस्थानात् च्युतया संदितौ बद्धौ । उपरुद्धौ इति यावत् । चरणौ यस्याः सा । बद्धे संदानितं मूतमुद्दितं सीदेतं सितम् । इत्यमरः । शठः गूढविप्रियकारी । तदुक्तं साहित्यदर्पणे-'शठोयमेकत्र बद्धभावो यः । दर्शितबहिरनुरागो विप्रियमन्यत्र गूढमाचरति ॥ ' इति । **शठ इत्यादि**-हे प्रिये । परिचयवति परिचयः [संस्तवः] यस्य स परिचयवान् । अतिशायने मतुप् । तस्मिन्मयि शठ इति गूढविप्रियकारीति अवधीरणा तिरस्कारः [तावत्साकल्येन] अस्तु । यतः 'अतिपरिचयादवज्ञा' इति वदन्ति तस्मादियमवधीरणा युक्तैवेत्यर्थः । हे चण्डि अत्यन्तकोपने । चरणपतितया मेखलया रशनया याचितापि प्रार्थितापि तामवधीरणां न विसृजसि न त्यजसि । किमिदं युक्तमिति शेषः । अपरवक्त्रं वृत्तम् ॥ २० ॥ **बाष्पासारेत्यादि** । बाष्पाणामासारो यस्याः सा बाष्पासा-

इरावती—न खल्विमौ मालविकायाश्चरणौ यौ ते स्पर्शदोहदं पूरयिष्यतः । (इति निष्क्रान्ता [1]सचेटी ।)   (क)

विदूषकः—उत्तिष्ठ । कृतप्रसादोऽसि ।   (ख)

राजा—(उत्थाय । इरावतीमपश्यन् ।) कथं गतैव प्रिया ।

विदूषकः—वयस्य दिष्टया अनेनाविनयेनाप्रसन्ना गतैषा । तद्वयं शीघ्रमपक्रमामः । यावदङ्गारको राशिमिवानुवक्रं प्रतिगमनं न करोति ।   (ग)

राजा—अहो [2]मदनस्य वैषम्यम् ।

> **मन्ये प्रियाहृतमनास्तस्याः प्रणिपातलङ्घनं सेवाम् ।**
> **एवं हि प्रणयवती सा शक्यमुपेक्षितुं कुपिता ॥ २२ ॥**

(इति निष्क्रा[4]न्तः सह वयस्येन ।)

इति तृतीयोऽङ्कः ।

(क) ण क्खु इमे मालवि[5]ओए चलणा जा दे फरिसदोहलं पूरइस्सन्ति । (ख) उठेहि । किदप्पसादोसि । (ग) वअस्स दिट्ठिआ [6]ईमस्स अविणअस्स अप्पस[7]ण्णा गदा एसा । ता वअं सिग्घं अवक्कमाम । जाव अङ्गारओ रासिं विअ अणुवक्कं पडिगमणं ण करेदि ।

रा अश्रुवर्षा चण्डी अत्यन्तकोपना इयं इरावती श्रोणीबिम्बात् नितम्बमण्डलात् अत्यपेक्षया कोपप्रस्थानसंरम्भादित्यर्थः । च्युतेन गलितेन हेमकाञ्चीगुणेन सुवर्णमेखलया । चण्डम् । कृतापराधत्वादित्यर्थः यद्वा चण्डमुग्रं यथा तथा । मां बाष्पासारा सबाष्पवर्षा मेघराजी मेघपंक्तिः विद्युद्दाम्ना सौदामनीगुणेन विंध्यमिव हन्तुं प्रहर्तुमभ्युद्यता । उपमालंकारः । शालिनी वृत्तम् ॥ २१ ॥ अपराद्धां कृतापराधाम् । ताडनं कुर्यामिति संभावनयेति भावः । **अपराधिनीत्यादि** । हे कुटिलकेशि अरालकेशि अपराधिनि कृतापराधे मयि उद्यतं दण्डं रशनया ताडनरूपं किं

---

१ सह चेट्या, ससखा निष्क्रान्ता. २ मनसिजैव; मदनवै० ३ एवं प्रणयवती सा मयि–न हि. ४ परिक्रम्य निष्क्रान्ताः सर्वे. ५ मालविआच०...हरिस (हर्ष) दो० देवेहिं इमस्स अविणअस्स अपसारिता णिअन्तणा (नियन्त्रणा) जाव सिग्घं–सिदरग्घं अव० ७ अप्पसादिता. ८ एतन्नास्ति बहुषु पुस्तकेषु.

Irāvatī :—These, indeed, are not the feet of Mālavikā that will gratify your longing for (the felicitous) touch. (*She departs with her attendant*).

Vidūṣaka :—Rise ; you are favoured (by Irāvatī).

King :—(*Rising up and not seeing* Iravatī) What, is the dear one really gone ?

Vidūṣaka :—I am glad that she has gone without being reconciled—with such an impropriety of conduct. Therefore, let us make off quickly, before she returns like the planet Mars retrogressing to the zodiacal sign.

King :—Oh the inconsistency of love !

With my mind attracted by my beloved, I consider her (Irāvatī's) rejection of my humble supplication a veritable service ; for, thus I can neglect the angry one, (though) so full of love for me. (23)

(Both *walk round and exeunt*).

HERE ENDS THE THIRD ACT.

किमर्थं संहरसि निवर्तयसि। एवं दण्डसंहरणेन विलसितं विलासं वर्धयसि अत्र अस्मै दासजनाय कुप्यसि च। क्रुधद्रुहेति चतुर्थी। आर्या छन्दः ॥ २० ॥ **नूनमिति**। इदमेतद्रशनासंहरणमनुज्ञातमनुमतम्। मत्प्रार्थनया इति शेषः। नूनमसंशयमिदं पादयोः पतनं त्वया अनुज्ञातम्। स्पर्शरूपं दोहदम्। हर्षदोहदेति पाठे हर्षहेतुं दोहदम्। अनया परुषोक्त्या अस्या अधीरत्वं सूचितम्। तदुक्तम्-'प्रियं सोत्प्रासवक्रोक्त्या मध्याधीरा दहेद्रुषा। धीराऽधीरा तु रुदितैरधीरा परुषोक्तिभिः ॥' इति। अप्रसन्ना कलुषिताशया। कुपितेति यावत्। अङ्गारकः मङ्गलग्रहः। अनुवक्रं कुटिलगत्या मङ्गलग्रह इव प्रत्यावृत्य किमप्यनिष्टं यावत् न कुर्यात्तावदपक्रमाम इति भावः। **मन्य इत्यादि**। प्रियाहृतमना मालविकाहृतमनाः प्रणिपातलंघनं प्रणामातिक्रमं तस्या इरावत्याः सेवामनुकूलाचरणं मन्ये। सेवायाः फलमाह प्रणयवती प्रेमवती सा इरावती कुपिता क्रुद्धा [अपि] एवमनेन क्रमेण प्राणिपातलंघनरूपेणोपेक्षितुमौदासीन्येन वर्तितुं शक्यं हि शक्या खलु। शक्यमिति निपातः अत्र बीजानुसंधानादाक्षपो नाम संध्यङ्गमुक्तं भवति। इदमनुसंधानमेवोत्तराङ्ककथोपयोगित्वाद्बिन्दुरित्यनुसंधेयम् ॥ २३ ॥

इति श्रीकाटयवेमभूपविरचिते कुमारगिरिराजीये
मालविकाग्निमित्रव्याख्याने तृतीयोऽङ्कः ॥

चतुर्थोऽङ्कः ।

(ततः प्रविशति पर्युत्सुको राजा प्रतीहारी च ।)

राजा—(आत्मगतम् ।)

तामाश्रित्य श्रुतिपथगतामास्थया बद्धमूलः
संप्राप्तायां नयनविषयं रूढरागप्रवालः ।
हस्तस्पर्शे मुकुलितं इव व्यक्तरोमोद्गमत्वा-
त्कुर्यात्क्लान्तं मनसिजतरुर्मां रसज्ञं फलस्य ॥ १ ॥

(प्रकाशम् ।) सखे गौतम ।

प्रतिहारी—जयतु भर्ता । असंनिहितो गौतमः । (क)

राजा—(आत्मगतम् ।) आम् । मालविकावृत्तान्तज्ञानाय मया प्रेषितः ।

(प्रविश्य ।)

विदूषकः—वर्धतां भवान् । (ख)

राजा—जयसेने जानीहि तावत्क्व देवी धारिणी कथं वा सरुज- चरणत्वाद्विनोद्यत इति ।

(क) जेदु भट्टा । असंणिहिदो गोदमो । (ख) वड्ढदु भवं ।

कविरिदानीमङ्कान्तरमारभते—**ततः प्रविशतीत्यादिना** ॥ **तामिति** । श्रुतेः पन्थाः श्रुतिपथः । तमागतां कर्णमार्गोपस्थितां वाक्श्रवणविषयीभूतामित्यर्थः । तां मालविकाम् । आश्रित्यावलम्ब्य आशया । तत्प्राप्त्यभिलाषेण बद्धं मूलं येन स बद्धमूलो गृहीतमूलः । ततो नयनविषयं नेत्रगोचरं संप्राप्तायां दृष्टायामित्यर्थः । तस्यां रूढरागप्रवालः रूढा रागरूपाः प्रवालाः किसलया यस्य स तथाभूतः । ततः पश्चात् हस्तस्पर्शे सति । व्यक्तरोमोद्गमत्वात् रोम्णां पुलकानामुद्गमः आविर्भावः रोमोद्गमः । व्यक्तः रोमोद्गमः तस्य भावः व्यक्तरोमोद्गमत्वं तस्मात् । मुकुलित इव संजातमुकुल इव । तारकादित्वादितच् । मनसिजतरुः मदनरूपवृक्षः । क्लान्तं

---

१ लब्ध. २ स्पर्शैः. ३ कुसुमित. ४ कान्तं. ५ आः; अये. ६ क्वासौ. ७ जेदु जेदु.

ACT IV

(Enter the* King *in a love-affected state and a
***Female* Door-Keeper.)**

King :—*(To himself)*

May the tree of (my) love which struck root in the form of hope when she crossed the path of my ears (I heard of her), which, when she came within the range of my eyes, put forth the sprouts of passion and which was covered with buds, as it were, at the touch of her hand, on account of my hair having stood prominently erect—may that tree make me, who am languid, taste the flavour of its fruit ! (1)

***(Aloud)* Friend Gautama !**

Female Door-keeper :—Prosperity to my Lord ! Gautama is not present here.

King :—*(To himself)* Ah, yes ! I sent him to learn the news about Mālavikā.

(Entering)

Vidūṣaka :—Prosperity to your Honour !

King :—Jayasenā, (go and) see where Queen Dhāriṇī is and how she is diverted, as her foot is painful.

विरहव्यथापर्याकुलं मां फलस्य मालविकाप्राप्तिरूपस्य रसज्ञं आस्वादज्ञं कुर्यात्। मुकुलित इव संजातमुकुल इव कान्तं कामनायुक्तं कुर्यादिति प्रार्थनायां लिङ्। अत्र मूलरोहणादीनां लोकप्रसिद्धेनैव क्रमेणोपन्यासाद् रत्नावल्यलंकारः। तदुक्तं- 'क्रमिकं प्रकृतार्थानां न्यासं रत्नावली विदुः।' इति। मन्दाक्रान्ता वृत्तम्। ॥ १ ॥ अत्र प्रसञ्जितं बीजं प्रकरीस्थाने कृतमिति मन्तव्यम्॥ असंनिहितः न समीपवर्ती। आमिति स्मरणे। सरुजचरणत्वात् रुजया सहितौ सरुजौ चरणौ यस्याः सा सरुजचरणा तस्या भावः सरुजचरणत्वं तस्मात् पीडायुक्तपादत्वात्। विनोद्यते विस्मृतदुःखा क्रियते इत्यर्थः। बिडालगृहीताया मार्जारातिक्रान्तायाः। परभृतिकायाः कोकिलायाः। परैः काकैः भृता परभृता सा एव परभृतिका। स्वार्थे कः। कप्रत्यय अजादित्वात् टापि च प्रत्ययस्थात्कात् इत्यत इत्वम्। तपस्विनी अनुकम्प्या। पिङ्गलाक्ष्यां क्रोधात्पिङ्गलत्वम्। यद्वा पिङ्गलाक्ष्या इति निन्दावचनम्। सारभाण्डानां उत्कृष्टद्रव्याणां भूगतगृहे। मत्संपर्कं मत्संबन्धम्। चण्डीकृता अत्यन्तं

प्रतिहारी—यद्देव आज्ञापयति । (इति निष्क्रान्ता ।) (क)

राजा—सखे[1] को वृत्तान्तस्तत्र भवत्यास्ते सख्याः ।

विदूषकः—यो बिडालगृहीतायाः परभृतिकायाः । (ख)

राजा—(सविषादम् ।) कथमिव ।

विदूषकः—सा खलु तपस्विनी तया पिङ्गलाक्ष्या सारभाण्डभूगृहे मृत्युमुख इव निक्षिप्ता । (ग)

राजा—ननु मत्संपर्क[2]मुपलभ्य ।

विदूषकः—अथ किम् । (घ)

राजा—कः[3] एवं विमुखोऽस्माकं येन चण्डीकृता देवी ।

विदूषकः—शृणोतु भवान् । परिव्राजिकया मे कथितम् । ह्यः किल तत्रभवतीरावती रुजाक्रान्तचरणां देवीं सुखं प्रष्टुमागता । (ङ)

राजा—ततस्ततः ।

विदूषकः—ततः सा देव्या पृष्टा । किं न्वत्रलोकितो वल्लभजन इति । तयोक्तम् । मन्दो व उपचारो यत्परिजने संक्रान्तं वल्लभत्वं न ज्ञायते । (च)

(क) जं देवो आणवेदि । (ख) जो बिडालगहीदाए परहुदिआए । (ग) सा खु तवस्सिणी ताए पिङ्गलच्छिए सारभण्डभूघरए मिच्चुमुहे[4] विअ णिक्खित्ता । (घ) अह इं । (ङ) सुणादु भवं । परिव्वाजिआए[5] मे कहिदं । हिओ किल तत्तहोदी इरावदी रुजा[6]क्कन्तचलणं देविं सुहं[7] पुच्छिदुं आअदा । (च) तदो सा देवीए पुच्छिदा । किं[8] ण्णु ओलोइदो वल्लहजणो त्ति । ताए उत्तं । मन्दो वो उवआरो जं परिजणे संकंतं वल्लहत्तणं ण जाणीअदि ।

---

१ गौतम, सखे गौ० २ मत्सम्बन्धमुपलक्ष्य. ३ गौतम कः ४ गुहाए (गुहायां) ५ ०जिआ मे कहेइ (कथयति). ६ रुजाविहत्य, रुजाअन्त (रुजायमान). ७ सुहं पुच्छिआ. ८ किं णु ण; किं ण लक्खिदो जणो वल्लहोत्ति। ताए उत्तं मदो वा उवआरो वा जं दे परिअणस्स वल्लहत्तंगं जाणन्ती त्ति पुच्छसि त्ति; किं उण लक्खिदो...। तदो ताए उत्तं कुदो वा दे उवआरो जं द परिअणस्स...। तदो ताए उत्तमन्तीए कुदो वा उपआरो जं...। परि...त्तणं जाणिस्सदित्ति ।

Female Door-Keeper :—As your Majesty commands. *(Exits)*

King :—How is your esteemed friend (Mālavikā) faring ?

Vidūṣaka:—In the same way as a female cuckoo in the grip of a cat.

King :—*(With sorrow)* How do you mean ?

Vidūṣaka :—That poor girl has, indeed, been thrown (confined) into the subterranean store-house, as if in the mouth of death, by that tawny-eyed one (the Queen).

King :—Was it on knowing about her meeting with me ?

Vidūṣaka :—Just so.

King :—Who was thus adversely disposed towards me that set the Queen against me (*lit.* made the Queen angry) ?

Vidūṣaka:—May your Honour hear. (This) the Parivrājikā told me—Yesterday, as I was told, the lady Irāvatī went to the Queen, whose foot has been sorely paining, to ask if there was any relief.

King:—What followed then ?

Vidūṣaka :—Then she was asked by the Queen—Was the beloved one (yourself) seen by His Majesty ? She replied—Idle is this formality of yours, since you do not know that the 'being the beloved' has passed to your maid-servant.

कोपिता । ह्यः पूर्वेद्युः । रुजया पीडया आक्रान्तश्चरणो यस्याः सा ताम् । वल्लभजनः प्रेमपात्रं भवतीत्यर्थः । मन्दः असमञ्जसः उपचारः उपचारपदम् । यद्यस्मात्कारणात् । परिजने मालविकायामिति भावः । निर्भेदाद्दतेऽति स्फुटीकरणं विनापि । उपन्यासः वागारम्भः । 'उपन्यासस्तु वाङ्मुखम्' इत्यमरः । मालविकायां शङ्कयति मालविकाविषयां शङ्कामुत्पादयतीत्यर्थः । अनुबध्यमानया साग्रहं पृच्छयमानया । अविनयमन्तरेण मालविकोपसर्पणरूपादाक्षिण्यवर्तनमधिकृत्य । परिगृहीतार्था ज्ञातवृत्तान्ता । धारिणी राज्ञोऽविनयमिरावत्याः सकाशाज्ज्ञातवतीत्यर्थः ॥ निगडः शृंखला पदयोः ययोः ते निगडपदौ । स्वाङ्गाच्चोपसर्जनादसयोगोपधात् इति ङीष् । अदृष्टाः सूर्यपादाः रविकिरणाः याभ्यां ते अदृष्टसूर्यपादे । पाताले पा-

राजा—निर्भेदाद्दतेऽपि मालविकायामयमुपन्यासः शङ्कयति ।

विदूषकः—ततस्तयानुबध्यमानया भवतोऽविनयमन्तरेण परिगृहीतार्था कृता देवी । (क)

राजा—अहो दीर्घरोषता तत्रभवत्याः । अतः परं कथय ।

विदूषकः—किमतः परम् । मालविका बकुलावलिका च निगडपद्मावदृष्टसूर्यपादं पातालवासं नागकन्यके इवानुभवतः । (ख)

राजा—कष्टं कष्टम् ।

मधुरस्वरा[1] परभृता भ्रमरी च विबुद्धचूतसङ्गिन्यौ ।
कोटरमकालवृष्ट्या प्रबलपुरोवातया गमिते ॥ २ ॥

अप्यत्र कस्यचिदुपक्रमस्य गतिः स्यात् ।

विदूषकः—कथं भविष्यति । यत्सारभाण्डगृहे व्यापृता माधविका देव्या संदिष्टा । ममाङ्गुलीयकमुद्रामदृष्ट्वा न मोक्तव्या त्वया हताशा मालविका बकुलावलिका चेति । (ग)

राजा—(निःश्वस्य । सपरामर्शम् ।) सखे किमत्र कर्तव्यम्[3] ।

विदूषकः—(विचिन्त्य ।) अस्त्यत्रोपायः । (घ)

राजा—क इव ।

(क) तदो ताए अणुबन्धिज्जमाणाए[4] भवंदो अविणअं अन्तरेण परिगहीदत्था किदा देवी । (ख) किं अदो वरं । मालविआ बउलावलिआ । अ णिअलवदीओ[5] अदिट्ठसुज्जपादं पादालवासं णाअकण्णआओ विअ अणुहोन्ति । (ग) कहं भविस्सदि । जं सारभण्डघरए[6] वाउदा माहविआ देवीए संदिट्ठा । मह अङ्गुलीअअमुद्दं अदेक्खिअ ण मोत्तव्वा तुए हदासा मालविआ बउलावलिआ अ त्ति । (घ) अत्थि एत्थ उवाओ ।

---

१ मधुररवा परभृतिका; ०स्वरा परभृतिः. २ एतन्नाति क्वचित्. ३ प्रतिकर्तव्यम्, ४ अणुखिज्जमाणा...परिगदत्था (परिगतार्था) किदा. ५ लवदिओ (लवल्यौ). ६ भाण्डे भाण्डवाउदा, गिहव्वावारिदा.

King:—This way of putting it causes suspicion to be pointed to Mālavikā, even without explicit mention (of her).

Vidūṣaka :—Then she, when continuously pressed, fully acquainted the Queen with your misdemeanour.

King :—Oh the unforgiving disposition (*lit.* long continued resentment) of her ladyship ! Tell what happened next.

Vidūṣaka :—What can happen next ? Mālavikā and Bakulāvalikā, with their feet fettered, are experiencing, like two Nāga-damsels, a residence in the nether region, where the rays of the sun never meet the eye.

King :—Pity, O pity !

The sweet-voiced cuckoo and the bee, as they came in contact with the mango-tree in blossom, have been driven to the hollow by an untimely shower accompanied by a sharp (*lit.* slashing), driving wind. (2)

Can there be scope for some remedy in this case ?

Vidūṣaka :—How can there be ? Mādhavikā, the keeper of the store-house, had this order from the Queen—You are not to set free the cursed Mālavikā and also Bakulāvalikā, unless you see my seal ring.

King :—(*Sighing, and stroking him*) Friend, what should be done here ?

Vidūṣaka :—(*Musing*) There is a remedy for this.

King :—What, pray ?

तालब्धदशभूरुहे च वासः तम् । **मधुरस्वरेत्यादि** ॥ मधुरः स्वरो यस्याः सा मधुरस्वरा कोकिला स्त्री । अजादित्वात् टाप् । विबुद्धः विकसितः यः चूत आम्रस्तस्य सङ्गिन्यौ सङ्गते । प्रबलः पुरोवातः अग्रवायुर्यस्याः सा तया अकालवृष्टया कोटरं वृक्षरन्ध्रं गमिते प्रापिते । अत्र अप्रस्तुतेन भ्रमरीपरभृतयोः कोटरप्रवेशवृत्तान्तेन प्रस्तुतस्य मालविकाबकुलावलिकयोः निरोधस्य गम्यमानत्वादप्रस्तुतप्रशंसालंकारः । तदुक्तम्—'अप्रस्तुतप्रशंसा सा या सैव प्रस्तुताश्रया ।' इति ॥ २ ॥ उपक्रमस्य उपायारम्भस्य । गतिः प्रसरः । व्यापृता अधिकृता । कर्णे ते कथयामि एवमिव । अत्र राज्ञः कर्णे विदूषकोक्त उपायो नियमेन

विदूषकः—(सदृष्टिक्षेपम् ।) कोऽप्यदृष्टः शृणोति । कर्णे ते कथयामि । (इत्युपश्लिष्य कर्णे ।) एवमिव । (इत्यावेदयति ।) (क)

राजा—(सहर्षम् ।) सुष्ठु चिन्तितम् । प्रयुज्यतां सिद्धये ।

(प्रविश्य ।)

प्रतीहारी—देव प्रवातशयने देवी निषण्णा रक्तचन्दनधारिणा परिजनहस्तगतेन चरणेन भगवत्या कथाभिर्विनोद्यमाना तिष्ठति । (ख)

राजा—तेन ह्यस्मत्प्रवेशयोग्योऽयमवसरः ।

विदूषकः—तद्गच्छतु भगवान् । अहमपि देवीं द्रष्टुमरिक्तपाणिर्भविष्यामि । (ग)

राजा—जयसेनायास्तावत्संवेद्य गच्छ ।

विदूषकः—तथा । (कर्णे ।) भवति एवमिव । (इत्यावेद्य निष्क्रान्तः ।) (घ)

राजा—जयसेने प्रवातशयनमार्गमादेशय ।

प्रतीहारी—इत इतो देवः । (ङ)

(ततः प्रविशति शयनस्था देवी परिव्राजिका विभवतश्च परिवारः ।)

देवी—भगवति रमणीयं कथावस्तु । ततस्ततः । (च)

(क) को वि अदिट्ठो सुणोदि । कण्णे दे कहेमि । एव्वं विअ । (ख) देव पवादसॅअणे देवी णिसण्णा रत्तचन्दणधारिणा परिअणहत्थगदेण चलणेण भअवदीए कहाहिं विणोदिज्जमाणा चिट्ठदि । (ग) ता गच्छदु भवं । अहं वि देवीं पेक्खिदुं अरित्तपाणी भविस्सं । (घ) तह । होदि एव्वं विअ । (ङ) इदो इदो देवो । (च) भअवदि रमणिज्जं कहावत्थु । तदो तदो ।

मालविकाप्राप्तिहेतुत्वान्नियताप्तिर्नाम चतुर्थावस्था सूचिता । अत्र पूर्वं प्रकरीस्थानोक्तबीजस्यानया नियताप्त्या समन्वयादवमर्शो नाम चतुर्थसंधिः प्रतिपादित इति मन्तव्यम् ॥ प्रकृष्टः वातः यस्मिन् तत्स्थानं प्रवातं तस्मिन्

---

१ साधु प्रयु. २ प्रयाण. ३ अस्मद्रहस्यं विदितं कुरु. ३ सअणीए. ५ गहीदेन (गृहीतेन). ६ ०दीए पडिवाजिआए.

Vidūṣaka :— *(Glancing about)* Some one unseen may hear. I will whisper it in your ear. (So *saying he gets close to him and whispers in the ear).* Of this sort. *(He communicates it.)*

King :— *(Rejoicingly)* Cleverly conceived! Put in into execution for success (*i. e.* that it may lead to success.)

Female Door-keeper – *(Entering)* Sir, the Queen is reclined on a couch set in a very airy place with her foot covered with rubbed red sandal and held in their hands by her maids, and is being diverted with tales by the venerable lady (Parivrājikā).

King :—Then this is the proper time for me to visit her.

Vidūṣaka :—Your Honour may go. I, too, will have some present in my hand with which to see the Queen.

King :—Inform Jayasenā of it (your plan) and then go.

Vidūṣaka :—Very well. *(Approching her ear)* Lady, it is thus. *(Whispers it and exits).*

King :—Jayasenā, show me the way to the couch in the windy place.

Female Door-keeper—This way, my Lord.

(Then are discovered, the Queen *lying on a couch, the* Parivrājikā *and the* Attendants *in order of their rank.)*

Queen :—Revered lady, the subject-matter of the story is charming. What next ?

शयनं तत्र। **रक्तेति।** शोघापनोदार्थं निषिक्तं रक्तचन्दनं तद्धारिणा परिजनहस्तं गतेन चरणेन उपलक्षिता। संवेद्य अस्मद्रहस्यं निवेद्य। उपचारयन्त्रणया आचारपालनक्लेशेन। **अनुचितेति।** हे कलभाषिणि कलं मधुरं भाषितुं शीलं यस्यास्तथाभूते। अनुचितः नूपुरस्य मञ्जीरस्य विरहः यस्य तथाभूतं नूपुरविश्लेषानर्हमित्यर्थः। तपनीयस्य सुवर्णस्य पीठकमालम्बते तथाभूतं सुवर्णपादपीठनिहितमित्यर्थः रुजा वेदनया परीतं व्याप्तम्। चरणं मां च पीडयितुं नार्हसि। तवोत्थानेन तव चरणस्य पीडा स्यात्। तदवलोकयतः ममापि। अतो मा उत्तिष्ठति भावः। अत्र रुजा परीतमिति वाक्यार्थस्याग्निमित्रपीडां प्रति हेतुत्वात्काव्यलिङ्गमलंकारः। ॥ ३ ॥ **तत इति।** यज्ञोपवीतेन बद्धोऽङ्गुष्ठो यस्य स तथोक्तः।

परिव्राजिका—(सदृष्टिक्षेपम् ।) देवि अतः परं पुनः कथयिष्यामि । अत्रभवान्विदिशेश्वरः संप्राप्तः ।

देवी—अहो आर्यपुत्रः । (इत्युत्थातुमिच्छति ।) (क)

राजा—अलमलमुपचारयन्त्रणया ।

अनुचितनूपुरविरहं नार्हसि तपनीयपीठकालम्बि ।
चरणं रुजा परीतं कलभाषिणि मां च पीडयितुम् ॥ ३ ॥

धारिणी—जयत्वार्यपुत्रः । (ख)

परिव्राजिका—विजयतां देवः ।

राजा—(परिव्राजिकां प्रणम्योपविश्य ।) देवि अपि सह्या ते वेदना ।

धारिणी—अस्ति मे विशेषः । (ग)

(ततः प्रविशति यज्ञोपवीतबद्धाङ्गुष्ठः संभ्रान्तो विदूषकः ।)

विदूषकः—परित्रायतां परित्रायतां भवान् । सर्पेण दष्टोऽस्मि । (घ)

(सर्वे विषण्णाः ।)

राजा—कष्टं कष्टम् । क्व भवान्परिभ्रान्तः ।

विदूषकः—देवीं द्रक्ष्यामीत्याचारपुष्पग्रहणकारणात्प्रमदवनं गतोऽस्मि । (ङ)

देवी—हा धिक् हा धिक् । अहमेव ब्राह्मणस्य जीवितसंशयनिमित्तं जातास्मि । (च)

(क) अह्मो अज्जउत्तो । (ख) जेदु अज्जउत्तो । (ग) अत्थि मे विसेसो । (घ) परित्ताअदु परित्ताअदु भवं । सप्पेण दट्ठेह्मि । (ङ) देविं देक्खिस्सं त्ति आआरपुप्फग्गहणकारणादो पमदवणं गदोह्मि । (च) हद्धि हद्धि । अहं एव्व बह्मणस्स जीविदसंसअणिमित्तं जादह्मि ।

---

१ तत्रभवान् ईश्वरः. २ पीठिका०; लम्बम्. ३ अज्ज अत्थि. ४ गहणार्थ. ५ अत परं-परित्ताअदु परित्ताअदु इत्य० क्वचित्.

Parivrājikā :—(*Casting a glance about*) From this point I will tell it afterwards; (for) here comes His Honour, the Lord of Vidiśā.

Queen :—Oh, my husband! (*She tries to rise up.*)

King :—Enough, enough of troubling yourself with this formality.

You should not, O sweet-voiced one, give pain to your aching foot unaccustomed to separation from its anklets and usually resting on a gold pedestal, and to me also (thereby.) (3)

Dhāriṇī :—Victory to my Lord!

Parivrājikā :—Prosperity to the King!

King :—(*Sits down having bowed to the* Parivrājikā.) Queen, do you find the pain sufferable?

Dhāriṇī :—I feel better.

(*Enters* Vidūṣaka *in a state of fright, with his thumb tied up with his sacred thread*).

Vidūṣaka :—Save me, save me, your Honour! I am bitten by a snake!

(*All are dejected*).

King :—Alas, alas! Where have you been wandering listlessly?

Vidūṣaka :—As I wished to see the Queen, I went to the Pramada-garden to gather flowers (to present them to her), as is required by custom.

Queen :—Alas, alas! I have become the cause of peril to the Brāhmaṇa's life.

अत्र कल्पनाया गम्यमानत्वाचलनं नाम संध्यङ्गमुक्तं भवति ॥ आचारार्थं रिक्तपाणिना देवी न द्रष्टव्या इति य आचारस्तदर्थं तत्परिपालनार्थं पुष्पाणि तेषां कारणात् स्तबककारणात्स्तबकग्रहणार्थम्। पूर्वकर्म प्रथमप्रतिक्रिया। छेदो दंशस्येत्यादि। दंशस्य दंशस्थानस्य च्छेदः। क्षतेः व्रणात्। रक्तस्य मोक्षणं स्रावणम्। दष्टमात्राणां दष्टा एव दष्टमात्राः तेषाम्। दंशक्षण एव इत्यर्थः। आयुष्याः आयुषे हिताः आयुर्दा इत्यर्थः। प्रतिपत्तयः उपायाः। तदुक्तं वैद्यचन्द्रोदये–' आदौ तु

विदूषकः—तस्मिन्नशोकस्तबककारणात्प्रसारिते दक्षिणहस्ते कोटरनिर्गतेन सर्परूपेण कालेन दष्टोऽस्मि। नन्वेते द्वे दंशपदे। (क)

परिव्राजिका—तेन हि दंशच्छेदः पूर्वकर्मेति श्रूयते। स तावदस्य क्रियताम्।

छेदो दंशस्य दाहो वा क्षतेर्वा[1] रक्तमोक्षणम्।
एतानि दष्टमात्राणामायुष्याः[2] प्रतिपत्तयः ॥ ४ ॥

राजा—संप्रति विषवैद्यानां कर्म। जयसेने क्षिप्रमानीयतां ध्रुवसिद्धिः।

प्रतीहारी—यदेव आज्ञापयति। (इति निष्क्रान्ता)। (ख)

विदूषकः—अहो पापेन मत्युना गृहीतोऽस्मि। (ग)

राजा—मा कातरो भूः। अविषोऽपि कदाचिद् दंशो भवेत्।

विदूषकः—कथं न भेष्यामि। सिमसिमायन्ति मेऽङ्गानि। (घ)

(इति विषवेगं रूपयति।)

देवी—हा दर्शितमशुभं विकारेण (विषारेण)। अवलम्बध्वं ब्राह्मणम्। (ङ)

(परिजनः[3] ससंभ्रममवलम्बते।)

विदूषकः—(राजानं विलोक्य।) भोः भवतो बाल्यात्प्रियवयस्योऽस्मि। तद्विचार्यापुत्राया मे जनन्या योगक्षेमं वह। (च)

(क) तहिं असोअत्थ[4]वअकारणादो पसारिदे दक्खिणहत्थे कोडरणिग्गदेण सप्परूवेण कालेण दट्ठोह्मि। णं एदाइं दुवे दंसणपदाइं। (ख) जं देवो आणवेदि। (ग) अहो पावेण मिच्चुणा गहिदोह्मि। (घ) कहं ण भाइस्सं। सिमसिमाअन्ति मे अङ्गाइं। (ङ) हो दंसिदं असुहं विआरेण। अवलम्भध बह्मणं। (च) भोः भवदो बालत्तणादो पिअवअस्सोह्मि। तं विआरिअ अपुत्ताए मे जणणीए जोगक्खेमं वहेहि।

---

१ क्षतस्यारक्त०, मोचनम्. २ आयुष्यः. ३ परिव्राजिका; पारिपार्श्विका. ४ अत्थत्रअस्स; असोअत्थपुप्फका०. ५ पसारिदो....तदो. ६ ही ही; हा...आहिअं (आधिक्यं) ७ हला अव०. ८ बाल्लादो वे; बालवअस्सोम्हि। ता अविआरेण बुध्धाए (बालवयस्योऽस्मि तदविचारेण वृद्धायाः)

Vidūṣaka :—There (*i.e.* in the garden), as I stretched out my hand to pluck a bunch of Aśoka-blossoms, I was bitten by the god of Death in the form of a snake, that came out of a hollow. See, here are the two marks of the bite. *(He shows the bite).*

Parivrājikā :—If so, then excision of the bitten parts is the first remedy, as they say. Let that be done in the first place in this case.

Excision or cauterization of the bitten part or letting off of blood from the wound—these are the remedies for saving the lives of persons, to be adopted as soon as they are bitten. (4)

King :—Now this is a case for poison-doctors. Jayasenā, let Dhruvasiddhi be immediately sent for.

Female Door-keeper :—As your Majesty commands. (*Exits*).

Vidūṣaka:—Alas, I am seized by wicked Death.

King:—Be not alarmed ; the bite may possibly be non-venomous.

Vidūṣaka :—How can I not be alarmed ? My limbs shake convulsively. (*Gesticulates that the poison is taking effect.*)

Queen :—Alas ! The affection threatens a calamitous end. (दशितं विषारेण–Oh, a calamitous snake-bite !) Support the Brāhmaṇa.

(The attendants support him hastily.)

Vidūṣaka:—(*Looking at the* King) Friend, I have been your dear friend from infancy. Taking that into consideration, look to the maintenance and protection of my sonless mother.

स्रावयेद्रक्तं छित्त्वा शस्त्रेण दंशतः । बहिर्वगीकृते रक्ते विषं तस्माद्विनश्यति ॥ उर्ध्वं-स्रोतोनुगे क्ष्वेडे न मन्त्रा नौषधिक्रिया ।' इति ॥ वाग्भटे च–'दंश मण्डलिनां मुक्त्वा पित्तलत्वादथापरम् । प्रतप्तैर्हेमलोहाद्यैर्दहेदाशून्मुखेन वा ॥ करोति भस्मसात्सद्यो वह्निः किं नाम न क्षणात् । निष्पीड्यानूद्धरेद्रक्तं मर्मसन्ध्यगतं तथा ॥ न जायते विषावेगो बीजनाशादिवाङ्कुरः । विषे प्रविसृते विध्येच्छिरां सा परमा क्रिया । शिरास्वदृश्यमानासु योज्याः शृङ्गजलौकसः ॥' इति । पथ्यावक्त्रं वृत्तम् ॥४॥

राजा—मा भैषीः । स्थिरो भव । अचिरात्त्वां वैद्यश्चिकित्सते[1] ।

(प्रविश्य ।)

जयसेना—देव आज्ञापितो ध्रुवसिद्धिर्विज्ञापयति । इहैवानीयतां गौतम इति । (क)

राजा—तेन हि वर्षवरपरिगृहीतमेनं तत्रभवतः सकाशं प्रापय ।

जयसेना—तथा । (ख)

विदूषकः—(देवीं विलोक्य ।) भवति जीवेयं वा न वा । यन्मयात्रभवन्तं सेवमानेन तेऽपराद्धं तन्मर्षय । (ग)

देवी—दीर्घायुर्भव । (घ)

(निष्क्रान्तौ विदूषकः प्रतीहारी च ।)

राजा—प्रकृतिभीरुस्तपस्वी । ध्रवसिद्धेरेपि[2] यथार्थनाम्नः सिद्धिं न मन्यते ।

(प्रविश्य ।)

जयसेना—जयतु भर्ता । ध्रुवसिद्धिर्विज्ञापयति । उदकुम्भविधाने सर्पमुद्रितं किमपि कल्पयितव्यम् । तदन्विष्यतामिति । (ङ)

(क) देव आणाविदो धुवसिद्धी विण्णावेदि । इह एव्व आणीअदु[3] गोदमोत्ति । (ख) तह । (ग) भोदि जीवेअं वा ण वा । जं मए अत्तभवन्तं सेवेमाणेण ते अवरद्धं तं मॅरिसेहि[4] । (घ) दीहाऊ होहि । (ङ) जेदु भट्टा । धुवसिद्धी विण्णावेर्दि । उदकुम्भविहाॅण[5] सप्पमुद्दिअं किंपि कप्पइदव्वं । तं अण्णेसीअदु त्ति ।

कर्म उपायकरणकौशलम् । सिमसिमायन्ति सिमसिमेति कम्पनादिविकारस्यानुकरणवाचि । ततः सिमसिमशब्दात् अव्यक्तानुकरणाद्यजवरार्धात् इति डाचि लोहितादिडाज्भ्यः इति क्यषि वा क्यष इति आत्मनेपदविकल्पात्परस्मैपदम् । ध्रुवसिद्धिरिति तस्य वैद्यस्य नाम । सिमसिमायन्ति मेऽङ्गानि । अनेन संतापः सूच्यते । विषवेगं विषप्राप्तिं रूपयति प्रकाशयति । विषवेगास्तु वसन्तराजीये कथिताः—

---

१ विषवैद्यः चिकित्सिष्यति–त्सयिष्यति. २ सिद्धिमपि यथार्थनामानं सिद्धिमन्तं न. ३ अदु सो ४ सव्वं अवराहं मरि० ५ विहाणेण.

King :—Do not be frightened. Be calm. The physician will soon cure you.

Jayasenā :—(*Entering*) My Lord, Dhruvasiddhi being summoned requests—Let Gautama be brought here.

King :—If so, then take him to the physician supported by eunuchs.

Jayasenā :—As Your Majesty commands.

Vidūṣaka :—(*Looking at the* Queen) My lady, I may live or not; pardon the faults that I might have committed while serving His Honour.

Queen :—May you live long!

(*Exeunt* Vidūṣaka and Pratihārī)

King :—The poor fellow is timid by nature. He has no confidence even in the unfailing success of Dhruvasiddhi of a truly significant name.

Jayasenā :—(*Entering*) Victory to the Lord! Dhruvasiddhi begs to say,—something bearing the image of a snake on it must be (provided, or) endowed with magical virtue in connexion with the performance of the rite called 'Udakumbhavidhāna.' So let such a thing be found.

'वैवर्ण्यं वेपथुर्दाहः फेनः स्कन्धस्य भञ्जनम् । दुःखं जाड्यं मृतिश्चेति विषवेगाः स्युरष्टधा' इति हा कष्टम् । अशुभममङ्गलं मरणरूपं विषवेगाधिक्यात् । बाल्याद्बाल्यप्रभृति । अपुत्राया मयि मृते इति भावः । योगक्षेमं योगः अप्राप्तस्य प्राप्तिः तेन सहितं क्षेमं लब्धस्य परिपालनम् । जीवनयात्राचिन्तामित्यर्थः । चिकित्सते विषप्रतिक्रियां करिष्यतीत्यर्थः । कितव्यीधिप्रतिकार गुप्तिज्किद्भयः इति सन् । प्रकृत्या स्वभावतः भीरुः । तपस्वी दीनः । ध्रुवाः निश्चयेन भाविनी सिद्धिर्यस्य तस्य । सिद्धिं न मन्यते विषप्रतीकारं कुर्यादित्यत्र विश्वासं न गच्छति । उदकुम्भविधानं नाम विषदोषशमनार्थः कर्मविशेषः । तस्मिन्कर्तव्ये । उदकुम्भविधानं भैरवतन्त्रोक्तं यथा । "भैरवी उवाच–देवदेव जगन्नाथ जगतां हितकारक । केनोपायेन भगवन्मर्त्यः सर्पविषं जयेत् ॥ ईश्वर उवाच–श्रुणु देवि प्रवक्ष्यामि यन्नोक्तं कस्यचित्पुरा । उदकुम्भविधानेन विषं राजिमतां जयेत् ॥ घटमेकं समादाय मृन्मयं चाव्रणं शुभम् । कन्याकर्तितसूत्रेण वेष्टनं तद्गले चरेत् ॥ कोशातक्यग्निकः पाठा सूर्यवल्यमृताभयाः । शेलुः शिरीषः किणिहीहरिद्रे क्षौद्रसाह्वया ॥ पुनर्नवा

देवी—इदं सपमुद्रितमङ्गुलीयकम्। पश्चान्मम हस्ते देहि तत्। (इति प्रयच्छति[1]।) (क)

(प्रतीहारी गृहीत्वा प्रस्थिता[2]।)

राजा—जयसेने कर्मसिद्धावाशु प्रतिपत्तिमानय[3]।

प्रतीहारी—यद्देव आज्ञापयति। (ख)

परिव्राजिका—यथा मे हृदयमाचष्टे तथा निर्विषो गौतमः।

राजा—भूयादेवम्।

(प्रविश्य।)

जयसेना—जयतु देवः। निवृत्तविषवेगो गौतमो मुहूर्तेन प्रकृतिस्थः संवृत्तः। (ग)

देवी—दिष्ट्या वचनीयान्मुक्तास्मि। (घ)

प्रतीहारी—एष पुनरमात्यो वाहतको विज्ञापयति। राजकार्यं बहु मन्त्रयितव्यम्। तद्दर्शनेनानुग्रहमिच्छामीति। (ङ)

(क) इदं सप्पमुद्दिअं अङ्गुलीअअं। पच्छा मम हत्थे देहि णं। (ख) जं देवो आणवेदि। (ग) जेदु देवो। णिवुत्तविसवेगो गोदमो मुहुत्तेण पकिदित्थो संवुत्तो। (घ) दिट्ठिआ वअणीआदो मुत्तह्मि। (ङ) एसो उण अमच्चो वाहतओ विण्णावेदि। राअकज्जं बहु मन्तिदव्वं। ता दंसणेण अणुग्गहं इच्छामि त्ति।

त्रिकटुकं बृहत्यौ सारिवे बला। कल्कमेषां कुमार्याश्च रसेन परिकल्पयेत्॥ घटान्तर्लेपयेत्तेन बहिर्भागं तु धूपयेत्। तद्वन्मधूकमधुकपद्मकेसरचन्दनैः॥ मौनेन जलमाहृत्य नद्यास्ताम्रघटेन वै। तं घटं पूरयेन्मन्त्रमिममुच्चार्य यत्नतः॥ ॐ नमः पुरुषसिंहाय नमो नारायणाय च। यथासौ नाभिजानाति रणे कृष्णः पराजयम्॥ एतेन सत्यवाक्येन सलिलं चामृतायताम्। हस्तेन तं घटं स्पृष्ट्वा उत्तराभिमुखः स्थितः॥ एतेन मन्त्रराजेन जलं तदभिमन्त्रयेत्। नमो वैडूर्यमाते हुलु हुलु रक्ष मां सर्वविषेभ्यः॥ गौरि गान्धारि मातङ्गि चाण्डालि स्वाहा। अनूरुनुजाय विनतानन्दनाय

---

1 इत्युङ्गुलीयकं ददाति. 2 जयसेना नाट्येन गृह्णाति. 3 प्रतिपादय.

Queen :—Here is a ring with the impression of a snake on its real. Give it into my hand after (the purpose is served). (*So she hands it over*).

(Pratīhārī *takes it and starts to go.*)

King :—Jayasenā, when the business is successfully accomplished (*i. e.* Gautama's cure is effected), bring us quickly the news.

Female Door-keeper :—Your Majesty's order will be obeyed. (*Exit*)

Parivrājikā :—As my heart tells me, Gautama is free from the effects of the poison (by now.).

King :—May it be so !

Jayasenā :—(*Entering*) Victory to the King ! The effect of his poison being counteracted, Gautama was restored to health in half an hour.

Queen :—Thank God, I am freed from the blame !

Female Door-keeper :—Now the minister Vāhataka here respectfully submits—'There are many state-affairs on which I have to take counsel with Your Majesty. So I wish to be favoured with an interview.'

काश्यपाय पक्षिराजाय नारायणवाहनायामृतहरणाय । ॐ नमो गरुडायेदं जलममृतरूपं कुरु कुरु दर्वीकराद्यखिलपन्नगानां विषं संहर । ॐ नमो नारायणायेति । पिप्पल्यो श्यामकं मांसी खपूरः कुन्दरुस्तथा । पञ्चवल्कवरायष्टीनागपुष्पैलवालुकम् ॥ जीवकर्षभकोशीरं सितापद्मकमुत्पलम् । कुमार्या स्नातया कुम्भे क्षिपेदर्ध-चूर्ण्य भैरवी ॥ सुरसामार्कवकुशशिरीषाम्बुदनिम्बकैः । बद्धकूर्चेन तत्तोयं सेचयेच्छतवारकम् ॥ सर्पदष्टप्रदेशं तु मन्त्रमेनं पठन्पुनः अनूर्वनुज इत्यादि यावद्रोमाग्रहर्षणम् ॥ विषमुक्तो भवेज्जन्तुस्तक्षकेणापि दंशितः । अपमृत्युविनाशार्थं सिञ्चेच्छिरसि मानवः ॥ सर्पबाधाप्रशमनं विषरोगनि । णम् । उदकुम्भविधानं ते मया देवी प्रकीर्तितम् ॥ गृहे सिञ्चज्जलमिदं पलायन्ते भुजंगमाः । स्मरणादोषधीनां तु सकृन्मन्त्रस्य कीर्तनात् ॥" इति ॥ नागमुद्राविधिस्तु रसरत्नावल्याम्—"नागार्जुन महाबाहो वद मे गुह्यमुत्तमम् । उरगाणां महाघोरविषबाधापकर्षणम् ॥ नागार्जुन उवाच—शृणु विप्र प्रवक्ष्यामि लोकानां हितकाम्यया । नागमुद्राविधानं तु रहस्यं परमं

देवी—गच्छत्वार्यपुत्रः कार्यसिद्धये । (क)

राजा—आतपाक्रान्तोऽयमुद्देशः । शीतक्रिया चास्या रुजः प्रशस्ता । तदन्यत्र नीयतां शयनीयम्[1] ।

देवी—बालिकाः आर्यपुत्रवचनमनुतिष्ठत । (ख)

परिजनः—तथा । (ग)

(निष्क्रान्ता देवी परिव्राजिका परिजनश्च !)

राजा—जयसेने गूढेन[2] पथा मां प्रमदवनं प्रापय ।

प्रतीहारी—इत इतो देवः । (घ)

राजा—जयसेने समाप्तकृत्यो[3] ननु गौतमः ।

प्रतीहारी—अथ किम् । (ङ)

राजा—

इष्टाधिगमनिमित्तं प्रयोगमेकान्त[4]साधुमपि मत्वा ।
संदिग्धमेव सिद्धौ[5] कातरमाशङ्कते चेतः[6] ॥ ५ ॥

(प्रविश्य ।)

विदूषकः—वर्धतां भवान् । सिद्धानि ते मङ्गलकर्माणि । (च)

राजा—जयसेने त्वमपि स्वनियोगमशून्यं कुरु ।

प्रतीहारी—यद्देव आज्ञापयति । (इति निष्क्रान्ता ।) (छ)

राजा—वयस्य[7] क्षुद्रा[8] माधविका । न खलु किंचिद्विचारितमनया ।

(क) गच्छदु अज्जउत्तो कज्जसिद्धीए । (ख) बालिआओ अज्जउत्तवअणं अणुचिट्ठह । (ग) तह । (घ) इदो इदो देवो । (ङ) अह इं । (च) वड्ढदु भवं । सिद्धाइ द[10] मङ्गल[11]कम्माइं । (छ) जं देवो आणवेदि ।

---

१ शयनम्. २ गूढपथेन. ३ करणीयो. ४ साध्यंः मत्वा–लब्ध्वा. ५ सिद्धः ६ हृदयम्. ७ गौतम. ८ क्षुद्रमाधविका. ९ जेदु. १० मे. ११ सव्व.

Queen :—My Lord may go to accomplish the business.

King :—This plaee is now covered with the sun, while a cooling treatment is recommended for this ailment. So let the bed be removed to another place.

Queen :—Girls, execute the order of my Lord.

(*Exeunt the* Queen, Parivrājikā *and the attendants.*)

King :—Jayasenā, take me to the Pramada-grove by a secret path.

Female Door-Keeper :—This way, this way, my Lord.

King :—Jayasenā, can Gautama have finished his business ?

Door-Keeper :—Ay, Sire.

King :—

Although I think the plan adopted for the attainment of the desired object is sure to lead to the intended result, yet my timid heart, feeling quite diffident of success, entertains a doubt. [Or, my timid mind feeling doubtful as to the success of the plan ...... object, though extremely good, is apprehensive.] (5)

(Entering)

Vidūṣaka :—My congratulations to your Honour ! Your auspicious affairs have been accomplished.

King :—Jayasenā, you too attend to your business.

Female Door-Keeper :—As Your Majesty commands. (*Exit*)

King :—Friend, silly must that Mādhavikā be ! Did she not hesitate even in the least ?

स्फुटम् ॥ सपादपलमानेन सुवर्णेन सुशोभनम् । नागं विधाय मतिमानग्न्युत्तारण-पूर्वकम् । नाग करेण संस्पृश्य मन्त्रानेनांस्त्रिरुच्चरेत् ॥ श्रीनागस्य प्राणाः इह प्राणाः । श्रीनागस्य जीव इह स्थितः । श्रीनागस्य सर्वेन्द्रियाणि इह स्थितानि । श्रीनागस्य वाङ्मनःप्राणा इहायान्तु स्वाहा । इति प्रतिष्ठापितप्राणं श्रीनागं नमस्कुर्यात् ॥ एवं प्राणप्रतिष्ठां वै कृत्वा नागं निधापयेत् । उदकुम्भमुखे रम्ये पात्रे ताम्रमय शुभे ॥

विदूषकः—देव्या अङ्गुलीयकमुद्रां दृष्ट्वा कथं विचारयति। (क)

राजा—न खलु मुद्रामधिकृत्य ब्रवीमि। एतयोर्द्वयोः[1] किंनिमित्तोऽयं मोक्षः। किं[2] देव्याः परिजनमतिक्रम्य भवान्संदिष्ट इत्येवमनया प्रष्टव्यम्।

विदूषकः—ननु पृष्टोऽस्मि। पुनर्मन्दस्यापि मे तस्मिन्प्रत्युत्पन्ना मतिः। (ख)

राजा—कथ्यताम्।

विदूषकः—भणितं मया। दैवचिन्तकैर्विज्ञापितो राजा सोपसर्गं वो नक्षत्रं सर्वबन्धनमोक्षः क्रियतामिति। (ग)

राजा—(सहर्षम्।) ततस्ततः।

विदूषकः—तच्छ्रुत्वा देव्येरावतीचित्तं रक्षन्त्या राजा किल मोचयतीत्यहं संदिष्ट इति। ततो युज्यत इति तया संपादितोऽर्थः। (घ)

राजा—(विदूषकं परिष्वज्य।) सखे प्रियोऽहं तव।

न हि बुद्धिगुणेनैव सुहृदामर्थदर्शनम्।
कार्यसिद्धिपथः सूक्ष्मः[3] स्नेहेनाप्युपलभ्यते[4] ॥ ६ ॥

(क) देवीए अङ्गुलीअअमुद्दिअं देक्खिअ कहं विआरेदि। (ख) णं पुच्छिदोह्मि। पुणो मन्दस्स वि मे तस्सिं[5] पच्चुप्पणा मदी (ग) भणिदं[6] मए। देव्वचिन्तएहिं विण्णाविदो राआ सोवसग्गं वो णक्खत्तं सव्वबन्धणमोक्खो करीअदु त्ति। (घ) तं सुणिअ देवीए[9] इरावदीचित्तं रक्खन्तीए राआ किल मोएदि त्ति अहं संदिट्ठो त्ति। तदो जुज्जदि त्ति ताए[10] संपादिदो अत्थो।

सर्षपैः पूरित रक्तसूत्रवेष्टितकन्धरे। स्थापयेद्दक्षहस्तेन संस्पृश्य मन्त्रमुच्चरेत् ॥ अथ मन्त्रः-ॐ फ्लः सर्पकुलाधिपतये श्रीनागायामृतमूर्तये हुलु हुलु सर्वविषं शमय

---

१ द्वयोः. २ किं वा. ३ पदं सूक्ष्मं. ४ उपलक्ष्यते. ५ तह पच्चुप्पण्णं उत्तरं आसि. पच्चुप्पण्णबुद्धिणा मए कहिदं देव्वचिं०. ६ भणिदा. ७ राआ भणिओ. ८ ता सव्व०. ९ देवीए धारिणीए...किल मोचेदि मालविअंति; तुमं एव्व मोचेहिदि त्ति संदि. १० ताए माहविआए वि.

Vidūṣaka:—How could she hesitate after seeing the Queen's seal-ring ?

King:—I do not speak with respect to the seal-ring. Why is (*lit.* what is the occasion for) this release of these two, when they were (purposely) put into custody ? Why were you deputed with the message, leaving aside all the personal attendants of the Queen ?—Questions like these she should have asked.

Vidūṣaka:—Why, I *was* asked (such questions). But dullwitted as I am, my intellect gave me a ready tongue to reply to her.

King :—Tell it then.

Vidusaka :—I said to her—'The King was respectfully informed by the astrologers that his star was maliciously disposed and that therefore (as the means of averting its bad influence) he should order the release of all prisoners.'

King :—*(Joyfully)* And what further ?

Vidūṣaka :—'When the Queen heard this, she, wishing to spare Irāvatī's feelings, sent me with the order, making it appear that the King set them at liberty.' Then saying 'That is proper', she granted our object.

King :—(*Embracing* Vidūṣaka) Friend, you (really) love me. For,

Not only by virtue of the acuteness (or, excellence) of intellect do friends see the (way to the) accomplishment of the desired object, but the subtle path leading to the accomplishment of a business is discerned by affection also. (6)

शमय नमस्ते स्वाहा ॥ इति मन्त्रेणाभिमन्त्र्य चाष्टोत्तरशतं सुधीः। नागमुद्रां ततः कृत्वा पूजयेत्संस्तुवीत च॥ नागराज नमस्तुभ्यं गरदोषनिबर्हण। भूतेशाभरणश्रेष्ठ विषं संहर ते नमः॥ तत उद्वास्य तं नागं तोयेनानेन सेचयेत्॥ विषं निर्विषतां याति सर्पदष्टस्य तत्क्षणात्॥ इति गुह्यं मया विप्र तव स्नेहात्प्रकाशितम्। विषदोषहरं नृणां किमन्यत्कथयामि ते॥" इति॥ सर्पमुद्रितं सर्पप्रतिमायुक्तमित्यर्थः। पश्चान्नाममुद्राविधाने समाप्ते। कर्मणो नागमुद्राविधानस्य सिद्धौ। कर्मणः मालविकामोचनरूपस्येति गूढार्थः। हृदयमाचष्टे अन्तःप्रसन्नतयेत्यर्थः। प्रकृतौ गुणसाम्ये

विदूषकः—त्वरतां भवान्। समुद्रगृहे सखीसहितां मालविकां स्थापयित्वा भवन्तं प्रत्युद्गतोऽस्मि। (क)

राजा—अहमेनां संभावयामि। गच्छाग्रतः।

विदूषकः—एतु भवान् (परिक्रम्य।) इदं समुद्रगृहम्। (ख)

राजा—(साशङ्कम्।) वयस्य एषा कुसुमावचयव्यग्रहस्ता सख्यास्ते इरावत्याः परिचारिका चन्द्रिका संनिकृष्टमागच्छति। इतस्तावदावां भित्तिगूढौ भवावः।

विदूषकः—अहो कुम्भीलकैः कामुकैश्च परिहरणीया खलु चन्द्रिका। (ग)

(उभौ यथोक्तं कुरुतः।)

राजा—गौतम कथं नु ते सखी मां प्रतिपालयति। एहि। एनां गवाक्षमाश्रित्य विलोकयावः।

विदूषकः—तथा। (घ)

(उभौ विलोकयन्तौ तिष्ठतः।)

(ततः प्रविशति मालविका बकुलावलिका च।)

बकुलावलिका—सखि प्रणम भर्तारम्। (ङ)

राजा—मन्ये प्रतिकृतिं मे दर्शयति।

मालविका—(सहर्षम्।) नमस्ते। (द्वारमवलोक्य। सविषादम्।) सखि मां विप्रलम्भयसि। (च)

(क) तुवरदु भवं समुद्दघरए सहीसहिदं मालविअं ठाविअ भवन्तं पच्चुग्गदोह्मि। (ख) एदु भवं। ईदं समुद्दघर। (ग) अहो कुम्भीलएहि कामुएहिं अ परिहरणीआ खु चन्दिआ। (घ) तह। (ङ) सहि पणम भट्टारी। (च) णमो दे। हला मं विप्पलम्भेसि।

---

१ यथासमर्थितं. २ स्थितौ. ३ शङ्कु निर्दिशति. ४ समाहिं ५ एदु एदु. ६ एदं. ७ अस्मात्परं–जो पस्सदो पिट्ठदो देक्खीअदि (यः पार्श्वतः पृष्ठतो दृश्यते), जं पिट्ठदो पासदो देक्खसि; इत्यधिकं क्वचित्.

Vidūṣaka :—Your Honour should make haste. Having placed Mālavikā with her friend in the summer-house, I have come to greet you.

King :—I will go to welcome her. Proceed on the way.

Vidūṣaka :—Your Honour should follow. (*Having walked on*) Here is the summer-house.

King :—(*With apprehension*) Here is advancing towards us Candrikā, the maid-servant of your friend Irāvatī, with her hands busily engaged in gathering flowers. So let us at once hide ourselves behind the wall.

Vidūṣaka :—Thieves and gallants must, iudeed, avoid Candrikā (moon-light) !

(*Both act as suggested.*)

King :—Gautama, how (eagerly), indeed, must your friend (Mālavikā) be waiting for me ! Come, let us stand close to the window and see.

(*Both stand looking on.*)

(*Then enter* Mālavikā *and* Bakalāvalikā.)

Bakulāvalikā :—Friend, bow to your Lord.

King :—I think she is showing to her my picture.

Mālavikā :—(*Joyfully*) I bow to you.

(*Looking at the door, with dejection*)

Friend, you deceive me.

तिष्ठतीति तथोक्तः। वचनीयात् निन्दारूपदोषात्। मन्त्रयितव्यं गूढं विचारणीयम्। समाप्तकृत्यं मालविकामोचनरूपं यस्य। समाप्तकार्यः इति पाठे कार्यं इष्टं कर्म इति स एवार्थः। इष्टाधिगमेत्यादि। इष्टं वाञ्छितं वस्तु मालविकारूपं तस्य अधिगमे प्राप्तौ निमित्तं साधनभूतम् प्रयोगमुपायं एकान्तसाधुं निश्चयेन कार्यस्य साधकं मत्वापि कातरं मे चेतः सिद्धौ इष्टसम्पादने संदिग्धं संदेहयुक्तमेव सत् आशङ्कते बिभेति। यद्वा–०निमित्तमेकान्तसाधुमपि प्रयोगं सिद्धौ संदिग्धमेव मत्वा मे चेतः इत्यादि। नियोगमुचितं कर्म। अशून्यं कुरु अनुतिष्ठेत्यर्थः। तदनुष्ठानार्थं गच्छेति भावः। क्षुद्रा नीचा। मन्दप्रज्ञा वा। विचारितमाशङ्कया पृष्टमित्यर्थः। अतिक्रम्य मुक्त्वेत्यर्थः। प्रत्युत्पन्ना मतिः मया समयोचितमुत्तरं दत्तमित्यर्थः। दैवचिन्तकैः ज्योतिः–

राजा—सखे हर्षविषादाभ्यामत्रभवत्याः प्रीतोऽस्मि ।

सूर्योदये भवति या सूर्यास्तमये च पुण्डरीकस्य ।
वदनेन सुवदनायास्ते समवस्थे क्षणादूढे ॥ ७ ॥

बकुलावलिका—नन्वेष चित्रगतो भर्ता । (क)

उभे—(प्रणिपत्य ।) जयतु भर्ता । (ख)

मालविका—सखि तदा संमुखस्थिता भर्तू रूपदर्शनेन न तथा वितृष्णास्मि यथाद्य । मया विभावितश्चित्रगतदर्शनो भर्ता । (ग)

विदूषकः—श्रुतं भवता । अत्रभवती चित्रे यथा दृष्टस्तथा न दृष्टो भवानिति मन्त्रयते । मुधेदानीं मञ्जूषेव रत्नभाण्डं यौवनगर्वं वहसि । (घ)

राजा—सखे कुतूहलवानपि निसर्गशालीनः स्त्रीजनः । पश्य ।

कार्त्स्न्येन निर्वर्णयितुं च रूप-
मिच्छन्ति तत्पूर्वसमागमानाम्[1] ।
न च प्रियेष्वायतलोचनानां
समग्रपातीनि[2] विलोचनानि ॥ ८ ॥

(क) णं एसो चित्तगदो भट्टा । (ख) जेदु भट्टा । (ग) हला तदा संमुहट्ठिदा भट्टिणो रूवदंसणेण ण तह वितिण्ह'म्हि जह अज्ज । मए विभाविदो चित्तगददंसणो भट्टा । (घ) सुदं भवदा । अत्तहोदी चित्ते जह दिट्ठो तह ण दिट्ठो भवं त्ति मन्तेदि । मुहा दाणिं मञ्जूसा विअ रअणभण्डअं जोव्वणगव्वं वहेसि ।

शान्त्यैः । सोपसर्गं उपसर्गेण सह सोपसर्गं पापग्रहादियुक्तत्वात् । मोचयति इति हेतुना । यद्वा इति प्रकाशने । इति प्रकाशयन्त्या । 'इति हेतौ प्रकाशने' इति मेदिनी । न हि बुद्धीत्यादि । सुहृदां मित्राणाम् । 'सुहृद्दुर्हृदौ मित्रामित्रयोः' इति निपातनात्साधुः । अर्थदर्शनं अभीष्टसिद्ध्युपायदर्शनं बुद्धिगुणेन बुद्धेः प्रकर्षेण एव केवलेन न । किं तु कार्यसिद्धेः पन्थाः कार्यसिद्धिपथः । 'ऋक्पूरब्धूःपथामानक्षे'

---

१ समागतानाम्. २ वृत्तीनि ३ संभमदिट्ठं भट्टिणो रूवे जहा ण वितिण्हम्हि तहा अज्ज वि मए भाविदो अवितिण्हदंसणो भट्टा (संभ्रमदृष्टे भर्तू रूपे यथा न वितृष्णास्मि तथा अद्यापि मया भावितो अवितृष्णदर्शनो भर्ता). ४ तत्त०, अत्तहोदीए...मन्तिदं (मन्त्रितं)

King :—Friend, I am amused by the joy and dejection of her ladyship.

In a moment, have heen possessed (exhibited) by the face of the lovely-faced one, the two states (appearances) of the white lotus, *viz.* the one it assumes at sunrise and the one it presents at sunset. (7)

Bakulāvalikā :—Why, here is His Lordship drawn in a picture!

Both :—(*Having bowed down*) Victory to the King!

Mālavikā :—Friend, on the occasion when I stood before the King, I was not gratified by (enjoying) the sight of his beauty so much as I have been to-day; (for) I have attentivelly gazed at him in the picture.

Vidūṣaka :—Did your Honour hear? Her ladyship says that she did not see you (in the bodily form) so well (find you so handsome when bodily present), as she did you in the picture. In vain have you now the pride of youth, like a casket containing a treasure of jewels.

King :—Friend, women, though full of curiosity, are naturally bashful. See,—

They wish to observe fully the form (beauty) of their lovers and yet the eyes of the long-eyed ones meeting them for the first time do not fall fully on the objects of their love. (8)

इत्यप्रत्ययः समासान्तः । यद्वा पथशब्दः अदन्तोऽप्यस्ति स ग्राह्यः । तथा च त्रिकाण्डशेषः — वाटः पथश्च मार्गश्च' इति । सूक्ष्मः दुर्ग्राह्योऽपि स्नेहेनापि उपलभ्यते । स्नेहबलादपि दृश्यते इत्यर्थः । तदुक्तं विक्रमोर्वशीये-'अतिस्नेहः खलु कार्यदर्शी इति॥७॥ समुद्रगृहं जलयन्त्रगृहं । 'समुद्रगृहमित्युक्तं जलयन्त्रनिकेतनम्' इति हारावली । मुद्रायुक्तं गृहमिति केचित् । संभावयामि गत्वा संमानयामि । अहो इत्यामन्त्रण । कुम्भीलकैश्चौरैः । कामुकैः कामिभिः । प्रियागृहमभिसरद्भिरिति शेषः । चन्द्रिका ज्योत्स्ना । राज्ञा चन्द्रिकेत्युक्ते ज्योत्स्नेति अर्थान्तरं गृहीतं परिहासार्थं विदूषकेण । ते सखी मालविकेत्यर्थः । गवाक्षं वातायनम् । भट्टारं पूज्यं राजानं भर्तारमिति वा । 'भट्टारो भगवान् पूज्य' इति त्रिकाण्डशेषः । सूर्योदय इत्यादि । पुण्डरीकं सूर्यविकासि कमलं तस्य सूर्योदये या अवस्था विकासरूपा भवति । अस्तमये च या अवस्था

मालविका—सखि कैषा पार्श्वपरिवृत्तवदनेन भर्त्रा स्निग्धया दृष्टया निध्यायते। (क)

बकुलावलिका—नन्वियं पार्श्वगतेरावती। (ख)

मालविका—सखि अदक्षिण इव भर्ता मे प्रतिभाति यः सर्वं देवीजनमुज्झित्वैकस्या मुखे बद्धलक्ष्यः। (ग)

बकुलावलिका—(आत्मगतम्।) चित्रगतं भर्तारं परमार्थतो गृहीत्वासूयति। भवतु। क्रीडिष्यामि तावदेतया। (प्रकाशम्।) सखि भर्तुर्वल्लभैषा। (घ)

मालविका—ततः किमिदानीमात्मानमायासयिष्यामि। (इति सासूयं परावर्तत।) (ङ)

राजा—सखे पश्य।

भ्रूभङ्गभिन्नतिलकं स्फुरिताधरोष्ठं
सासूयमाननमितः परिवर्तयन्त्या।
कान्तापराधकुपितेष्वनया विनेतुः
संदर्शितेव ललिताभिनयस्य शिक्षा॥ ९॥

(क) हला का एसा पासपरिउत्तवअणेण भट्टिणा सिणिद्धाए दिट्ठिए णिज्झाईअदि। (ख) णं इअं पासगदा इरावदी। (ग) सहि अदक्खिणो विअ भट्टा मे पडिभादि जो सव्वं देवीजणं उज्झिअ एक्काए मुहे बद्धलक्खो। (घ) चित्तगदं भट्टारं परमत्थदो गेण्हिअ असूअदि। होदु। कीडिस्सं दाव एदाए। हला भट्टिणो वल्लहा एसा। (ङ) तदो किं दाणिं अत्ताणं आआसेमि।

म्लानतारूपा भवति। ते उभे अवस्थे सुवदनाया वदनेन क्षणादूढे धृते। हर्षान्मुखविकासः विषादान्म्लानता जातेत्यर्थः। आर्याच्छन्दः॥ ७॥ सखीति—न वितृष्णा स्म न तथा मे रूपदर्शनतृष्णा गता यथाद्य। यतो मया अद्य विभावितः सावधानेन दृष्ट इत्यर्थः। अत्रभवतीति यथा चित्रे तव रूपं ममाकर्षकं तथा न प्रत्यक्षतया दृष्टमिति।

१ पर। ने सवथा मुखम्. २ हविनेषु, विषयेष्य० ३ ईसपरिउत्तवअणा, ०उत्तमुहेण. ४ भट्टिणो पास. ५ एव्व. ६ परमत्थं. ७ संकप्पिअ.

Mālavikā :—Who is this, with her face a little turned aside, that is being intently looked at by the Lord with an affectionate glance ?

Bakulāvalikā :—Ah, it is Irāvatī standing by his side.

Mālavikā :—His Majesty seems to me to be somewhat impolite, since he, leaving the other Queens, has fixed his gaze on the face of one alone.

Bakulāvalikā:—(*To herself*) She has shown jealousy, taking (the action of) the Lord in the picture for the reality. Well, I shall enjoy some fun out of her. (*Aloud*) Friend, she is the King's favourite.

Mālavikā :—Then why shall I trouble myself now ? (*Turns away in jealousy.*)

King :—Friend, observe :

By her jealously turning away from the direction her face, the frontal mark on which is furrowed by the knitting of the eye-brows and the lower lip of which is throbbing, was exhibited, as it were, the instruction received from her preceptor in graceful acting when under fits of anger at the fault of a lover. (9)

मञ्जूषा पेटा । मुखेति यथा भाण्डस्थरत्नानि मञ्जूषाया अनुरञ्जकाणि तथामौज्ज्वल्यस्य बहिरप्रकटनात्तथा भवतो तारुण्यं न कस्मैचिदपि गुणायेति । कुतूहलवान् प्रियालोकने उत्सुकोपि । 'रम्यवस्तुसमालोके लोलता स्यात्कुतूहलम् ।' इति सा द. । निसर्गेण प्रकृत्या शालीनोऽधृष्टः । कार्त्स्न्येनेति । आयतलोचनाः प्रियाणां रूपं कार्त्स्न्येन साकल्येन निर्वर्णयितुमालोकयितुमिच्छन्ति च । स पूर्वः प्रथमः समागमो यासां तासां तत्पूर्वसमागमानाम् । आयते दीर्घे लोचने यासां ता आयतलोचनास्तासां विलोचनानि प्रियेषु वल्लभेषु समग्राणि पतन्तीति तानि तथोक्तानि न भवन्ति । प्रियस्वरूपं साकल्येन द्रष्टुमनसोपि नवसंगमोत्थलज्जायोगात्तथा कर्तुं न प्रभवन्तीत्यर्थः । उपजातिर्वृत्तम् ॥ ८ ॥ पार्श्वे परिवृत्तं वदनं येन स तथा तेन । स्निग्धया प्रेमयुक्तया । निध्यायते विलोक्यते । अदक्षिणः सर्वासु स्त्रीषु समरागो न भवति तथा । ततः किमिति-यतो मय्यपि एवमस्थिरप्रेमा भवेदिति भावः । सासूयम् असूया परप्रेमासहत्वं तया सहितं यथा स्यात्तथा । भ्रूभङ्गेत्यादि । भ्रुवोर्भङ्गेन

विदूषकः—अनुनयसज्ज इदानीं भव। (क)

मालविका—आर्यगौतमोऽप्यत्रैव सेवत एनम्। (पुनः स्थानान्तराभिमुखी भवितुमिच्छति।) (ख)

बकुलावलिका—(मालविकां रुद्ध्वा।) न खलु कुपितेदानीं त्वम्। (ग)

मालविका—यदि चिरं कुपितामेव मां मन्यस एष प्रत्यानीयते कोपः। (घ)

राजा—(उपेत्य।)

कुप्यसि कुवलयनयने चित्रार्पितचेष्टया किमेतन्मे।
ननु तव साक्षादयमहमनन्यसाधारणो दासः ॥ १० ॥

बकुलावलिका—जयतु भर्ता। (ङ)

मालविका—(आत्मगतम्।) कथं चित्रगतो भर्ता मयासूयितः। (इति व्रीडावदनाऽञ्जलिं करोति।) (च)

(राजा मदनकातर्यं रूपयति।)

विदूषकः—किं भवानुदासीन इव। (छ)

राजा—अविश्वसनीयत्वात्सख्यास्तव।

विदूषकः—अत्रभवत्यामयं तवाविश्वासः। (ज)

राजा—श्रूयताम्।

(क) अणुणअसज्जो दाणिं होहि। (ख) अज्जगोदमो वि एत्थ एव सेवदि णं। (ग) ण खु कुविदा दाणिं तुमं। (घ) जइ चिरं कुविदं एव्व मं मण्णेसि एसो पच्चाणीअदि कोवो। (ङ) जेदु भट्टा। (च) कहं चित्तगदो भट्टा मए असूइदो। (छ) किं भवं उदासीनो विअ। (ज) अत्तहोदीए अअं तुह अविस्सासो।

---

१ किमवमयि, २ सव्रीड-प्रणय-वदनं. ३ निरूपयति. ४ गोदमो एत्थं णं संसं॰

Vidūṣaka :—Be now ready to propitiate her.

Mālavikā :—The revered Gautama is also waiting upon him just here! (*Wishes to turn her face towards another place.*)

Bakulāvalikā :—(*Preventing* Mālavikā) Surely, you are not angry now?

Mālavikā :—If you think I can simply be angry for a long time, here I recall my anger.

King :—(*Approaching*)

What is this, O lotus-eyed one, that you get angry with me for an action represented in a picture? Surely, here I am, in person, your servant exclusively devoted to you. (10)

Bakulāvalikā :—Victory to the Lord!

Mālavikā :—(*To herself*) How strange that I showed jealousy towards the Lord in a picture! (*She folds her hands in supplication, her face full of blushes.*)

(*The King exhibits the nervousness of love.*)

Vidūṣaka :—How is it that Your Honour seems to be apathetic?

King :—Because your friend cannot be trusted.

Vidūṣaka :—You betray such distrust of the lady!

King :—Listen.

कुटिलतापादनेन भिन्नो विकृतः तिलको विशेषको यत्र तादृशम्। स्फुरितः अधरोष्ठः यत्र तत्। 'ओत्वोष्ठयोः समासे वा' इति वा पररूपम्। आननं सासूयं इतः चित्रप्रदेशात् परिवर्तयन्त्या अनया मालविकया विनेतुः आचार्यस्य गणदासस्य। कर्तरि षष्ठी। कान्तापराधकुपितेषु कान्तस्य प्रियस्य अपराधे अन्यस्त्रीसंगमादिरूपे कुपितानि क्रोधकरणानि। नपुंसके भावे क्तः। तेषु विषये ललितः रमणीयः यः अभिनयः कोपव्यञ्जकचेष्टाविशेषः तस्य। कर्मणि षष्ठी। शिक्षा संदर्शिता इव इत्युत्प्रेक्षा। वसन्ततिलकं वृत्तम् ॥ ९ ॥ अनुनयाय सान्त्वनाय सज्जः संनद्धः। उद्युक्त इति यावत्। भव। प्रत्यानीयते। विगतोपीति शेषः। कुप्यसीत्यादि। हे कुवलयनयने

पथि नयनयोः स्थित्वा स्वप्ने[1] तिरोभवति क्षणा-
त्सरति[2] सहसा बाह्वोर्मध्यं गतापि[3] सखी तव।
मनसिजरुजा क्लिष्टस्यैवं[4] समागममायया
कथमिव सखे विश्रब्धं स्यादिमां प्रति मे मनः ॥ ११ ॥

बकुलावलिका—सखि बहुशः किल भर्ता विप्रलब्धः। इदानीं तावदात्मा विश्वसनीयः क्रियताम्। (क)

मालविका—सखि मम पुनर्मन्दभाग्यायाः स्वप्नसमागमोऽपि भर्तुर्दुर्लभ आसीत्। (ख)

बकुलावलिका—भर्ता कथयत्वस्या उत्तरम्। (ग)

राजा—

उत्तरेण किमात्मैव पञ्चबाणाग्निसाक्षिकम्।
तव सख्यै मया दत्तो न सेव्यः सेविता रहः ॥ १२ ॥

बकुलावलिका—अनुगृहीते स्वः। (घ)

(क) सहि बहुसो किल भट्टा विप्पलद्धो। दाणिं दाव[5] अत्ता विस्ससणिज्जो करीअदु। (ख) सहि मह उण मन्दभग्गाए सिविणसमाअमो वि भट्टिणो दुल्लहो आसि। (ग) भट्टा कहेदु[6] से उत्तरं। (घ) अणुग्गहीदम्ह।

कमलेक्षण चित्रे अर्पिता लिखिता या चेष्टा इरावत्यवलोकनरूपा तया मे मह्यं कुप्यसि किमेतत्। सर्वथाऽयुक्तमिदमित्यर्थः। ननु अयमहं अन्यासां स्त्रीणां साधारणो न भवतीति तथा। त्वदेकचित्त इत्यर्थः। तव साक्षात् प्रत्यक्षतया स्थितः दासोऽस्मि। आर्या ॥ १० ॥ असूयितः असूत्र् उपतापे इत्यतः कण्ड्वादेः क्तः। व्रीडया व्रीडनं वा सहितं सव्रीडं सलज्जं वदनं यस्याः सा। वदनमिति पाठे सव्रीडं वदनं यस्मिन् कर्मणि तद्यथा तथा। मदनेन कामविकारेण कातर्यं धैर्याभावम्। उदासीनो निरुत्साहः। अत्र भवत्यामयं तवाविश्वासः। अस्मिन्वाक्ये काकुरनुसंधेया। पथि नयनयोरित्यादि। तव सखी स्वप्ने नयनयोः पथि मार्गे स्थित्वा दृग्गोचरीभूय क्षणात् तिरोभ-

---

१ स्थित्वा. २ रहसि...गतापि पलायते. ३ गताऽप्यबला सती. ४ क्लिश्यत्येव, क्लान्तस्य, आविष्टस्य. ५ दाव तुए अत्ता. ६ देहि, करेदु.

Having stood, in a dream, within the range of my eyes, your friend vanishes in a moment; and though clasped within the arms, she slips off all at once; how possibly, then, O friend, can the mind of me who am tormented by love with such delusion of a union, feel confidence in her ? (11)

Bakulāvalikā :—Friend, often, indeed, has the Lord been deceived; now make yourself an object of confidence.

Mālavikā :—Friend, but to me, unfortunate that I am, a union with the Lord, even in a dream, was a thing hard to obtain.

Bakulāvalikā :—My lord should give an answer to this.

King :—

What is the use of giving a reply ? I have given my own self to your friend in the presence of the fire of Love (the five-arrowed god), to be one not the served (master), but a servant in private. (12)

Bakulāvalikā :—We are obliged.

वति दृष्टिपथान्नश्यति । बाह्वोर्मध्यं गतापि आलिङ्गनार्थं धृतापि सहसा अकस्मात्सरति अपगच्छति । अबला सतीति पाठे सहसा बलादित्यर्थः । एवं हे सखे समागममायया समागमे संगमे या माया प्रतारणा तया हेतुभूतया मनसिजरुजा कामव्याधिना क्लिष्टस्य पीडितस्य मम मनः इमां मालविकां प्रति कथं विश्रब्धं विश्वासयुक्तं स्यात् । न कथंचिदपीत्यर्थः । अनेन अस्या नायिकाया मुग्धात्वं ध्वनितम् । तदुक्तं साहित्यदर्पणे–'प्रथमावतीर्णयौवनमदनविकारा रतौ वामा । कथिता मृदुश्च माने समधिकलज्जावती मुग्धा ॥' इति । हरिणी वृत्तम् ॥ ११ ॥ विश्वसनीयो विश्वासार्हः । उत्तरेणेत्यादि । उत्तरेणोत्तरदानेन कोऽर्थः । अत्र कर्तव्यनिर्देश एव समर्थमुत्तरमित्याशयेनाह–पञ्चबाण एव अग्निः पञ्चबाणाग्निः स साक्षी यस्मिन् कर्मणि तद्यथा तथा । मया आत्मा एव तव सख्यै दत्तः । मदनाग्निसाक्षिकं भार्यात्वेनाङ्गीकृतेत्यर्थः । स च ममात्मा रहः रहसि न सेव्यः मालविकया किं तु तस्याः सेवक एव । अद्यप्रभृति तस्याः सेवापर एव स्यामिति भावः । 'अत्र मदन वह्नित्वारोपस्य प्रकृते मालविकायै देहसमर्पणरूप कार्ये उपयुक्तत्वात्परिणामालंकारः' अ. रा. ॥ १२ ॥

विदूषकः—(परिक्रम्य ससंभ्रमम्।) बकुलावलिके एष बालाशोक-वृक्षस्य पल्लवानि लङ्घयति हरिणः। एहि निवारयाव एनम्। (क)

बकुलावलिका—तथा। (इति प्रस्थिता।) (ख)

राजा—वयस्य एवमेवास्मिन्रक्षणक्षणेऽवहितेन त्वया भवितव्यम्।

विदूषकः—एवमपि गौतमः संदिश्यते। (ग)

बकुलावलिका—(परिक्रम्य।) आर्य गौतम अहमप्रकाशे तिष्ठामि। त्वं द्वाररक्षको भव। (घ)

विदूषकः—युज्यते। (ङ)

(निष्क्रान्ता बकुलावलिका।)

विदूषकः—इदं तावत्स्फटिकस्थलमाश्रितो भवामि। (तथा कृत्वा।) अहो सुखस्पर्शता शिलाविशेषस्य (इति निद्रायते।) (च)

(मालविका ससाध्वसं तिष्ठति।)

राजा—

विसृज सुन्दरि संगमसाध्वसं
तव चिरात्प्रभृति प्रणयोन्मुखे।
परिगृहाण गते सहकारतां
त्वमतिमुक्तलताचरितं मयि॥ १३॥

मालविका—देव्या भयेनात्मनः प्रियं कर्तुं न पारयामि। (छ)

(क) बउलावलिए एसो बालासोअरुक्खस्स पल्लवाइं लङ्घेदि हरिणो। एहिणिवारेम णं। (ख) तह। (ग) एव्वं वि गोदमो संदिसेअदि। (घ) अज्ज गोदम अहं अप्पआसे चिट्ठामि। तुमं दुवाररक्खओ होहि। (ङ) जुज्जइ। (च) इमं दाव फलिहत्थलं अस्सिदो होमि। अहो सुहप्फरिसदा सिलाविसेसस्स। (छ) देवीए भएण अत्तणो पिअं कादुं ण पारेमि।

---

१ अस्मद्रक्षणे, अस्मिन्नक्षेण. २ तथा त्वया. ३ ससाध्वसा. ४ ननु. ५ लंघिदुं इच्छेदि-आअच्छाद. ६ वखम्भं. ७ संसिदो (संश्रितः). ८ अत्तणोवि.

Vidūṣaka :—*(Walking about in a hurry)* Bakulāvalikā, here is a deer about to browse the sprouts of the young Aśoka tree. Come, let us drive it off.

Bakulāvalikā :—Very well. (*Exit*).

King :—Friend, you should be vigilant just in this way at this hour, when we ought to be guarded.

Vidūṣaka :—Is Gautama required to be thus instructed ?

Bakulāvalikā :—(*Walking about*) Revered Gautama, I shall wait in a shade; you guard the door.

Vidūṣaka :—That is proper.

(*Exit* Bakulāvalikā).

Vidūṣaka :—I will just recline on this crystal pavement. *(Doing so)* O the pleasant touch of this excellent stone ! (He *sleeps*.)

(Mālavikā stands full of nervous agitation.)

King :—

Give up, O fair one, this fear of union (with me); act the part of the Atimukta creeper towards me, who having long sought your love, have come to be in the position of a Sahakāra (mango-tree). **(13)**

Mālavikā :—Through the fear of the Queen, I am not able to do what is dear to me.

लङ्घयति भक्षणार्थमाक्रामति । अयं राज्ञे रहो दातुमपसरणार्थं व्याज इति स्फुटमेव । रक्षणक्षणे इरावत्याद्यागमे रहस्यरक्षणावसरे । संदिश्यते कार्यज्ञस्य मम नैतदावश्यकमिति भावः । **विसृजेत्यादि** । हे सुन्दरि संगमसाध्वसं संगमे यत्साध्वसं भयं तद्विसृज । चिरात्प्रभृति बहुकालादारभ्य तव प्रणयोन्मुखे प्रणयः प्रेम याञ्चा वा तस्य उन्मुखे उत्सुके मयि सहकारतामाम्रवृक्षत्वं सहचरत्वं च गते त्वमतिमुक्तलता माधवीलता तस्याश्चरितं कृत्यं परिगृहाण प्रतिपद्यस्व । अतिमुक्तलता यथा विगतसाध्वसा सर्वात्मना सहकारमालिङ्गति तथा मामालिङ्गेति भावः । अत्र मामालिङ्गेत्यस्य पर्यायेण भङ्ग्यन्तरेणाभिधानात्पर्यायोक्तमलङ्कारः । द्रुतविलम्बितं वृत्तम् ॥ १३ ॥

राजा—अयि न भेतव्यम् ।

मालविका—(सोपालम्भम् ।) यो न बिभेति स मया भट्टिनी-दर्शने दृष्टसामर्थ्यो भर्ता । (क)

राजा—

दाक्षिण्यं नाम बिम्बोष्ठि बैम्बिकानां कुलव्रतम् ।
तन्मे दीर्घाक्षि ये प्राणास्ते त्वदाशानिबन्धनाः ॥ १४ ॥

तदनुगृह्यतां चिरानुरक्तोऽयं जनः । (इति संश्लेषमभिनयति ।)

(मालविका नाट्येन परिहरति ।)

राजा—(आत्मगतम् ।) रमणीयः खलु नवाङ्गनानां मदनविषये-व्यापारः । तथा हि ।

हस्तं कम्पयते रुणद्धि रशनाव्यापारलोलाङ्गुलिं
हस्तौ स्वौ नयति स्तनावरणतामालिङ्ग्यमाना बलात् ।
पातुं पक्ष्मलचक्षुरुन्नमयतः साचीकरोत्याननं
व्याजेनाप्यभिलाषपूरणसुखं निर्वर्तयत्येव मे ॥ १५ ॥

(क) जो ण भाअदि सो मए भट्टिणीदंसणे दिट्ठसमत्थो भट्टा ।

सोपालम्भं सोल्लुण्ठम् । भट्टिनीदर्शने इरावतीदर्शने । दृष्टसामर्थ्यः इति । भर्तापि भीतः किमुताहमिति अर्थापरयोक्तम् ।० समवस्थ इति पाठे दृष्टा समा अवस्था यस्येति तथोक्तः । दाक्षिण्यमित्यादि । बैम्बिकास्तद्वंश्या राजानः । हे बिम्बोष्ठि बिम्बं पक्वतुण्डीफलमिव ओष्ठो यस्यास्तथाभूते । दाक्षिण्यं सर्वासु दयितास्वनुकूलाचरणं नाम । नामेति प्रकाशये । कुलव्रतं सर्वैरवश्यं पालनीयो नियमः । तत्तो हे दीर्घाक्षि दीर्घे अक्षिणी यस्यास्तथाभूते । 'बहुव्रीहौ । सक्थ्य-क्ष्णोः ।' इति समासान्ते षचि 'षिद्गौरादिभ्यः' इति ङीष् । मे ये प्राणास्ते त्वदाशा-

---

१ न भे० न भेतव्यं. २ नायकानां. ३ रक्तहृदयः. ४ उपजनयति. ५. विषयावतारः ६ कम्पयते. ७ ङ्गुलीः. ८ नेत्रमु०. ९ संभवत्थो.

King :—Dear one, you should not be afraid.

Mālavikā :—*(Tauntingly)* I have seen the power of my Lord who does not get afraid, when in the presence of the young Queen (Irāvatī).

King :—

Politeness, indeed, O you with bimba-like lips, is the family-vow of the descendants of Bimbaka; therefore (that being the case), O long-eyed one, all my life depends (hangs) upon the hope of getting you. (14)

Favour, therefore, this person, long-devoted to you. *(Acts as if going to embrace her.)*

(Mālavika *gesticulates avoiding it.*)

King :—(*To himself*) Charming, indeed, are the actions of young maidens under the influence of love ! For,

She, trembling, obstructs (stays) my hand the fingers of which are active in the work of (unclasping) the girdle ; she makes her hands serve as coverings for her breasts, when being forcibly embraced ; and turns away her face, having eyes with bushy (beautiful) eyelashes, as I raise it in order to kiss it; even under the pretext (of refusals), she does bring pleasure to me, such as accrues from the fulfilment of one's longing. (15)

निबन्धनाः तव या प्राप्त्याशा सा निबन्धनमाधारो येषां ते तथोक्ताः । इतरास्वानुकूल्येन वर्तमानस्यापि मे जीवितं त्वदधीनम् । त्वं मम प्राणभूतेत्यर्थः । पथ्यावक्त्रं वृत्तम् । ॥ १४ ॥ **हस्तमित्यादि** । कम्पवती जातकम्पा रशनायां यो व्यापारः नीवीविश्लेषणार्थं चालनरूपस्तत्र लोला अङ्गुल्यो यस्य तम् । मम करं रुणद्धि प्रतिबध्नाति । बलात्प्रसह्य आलिङ्ग्यमाना आत्मनः हस्तौ स्तनयोः आवरणतामावरकत्वं नयति । हस्ताभ्यां कुचावाच्छादयतीत्यर्थः । प्रशस्तानि पक्ष्माणि अक्षिलोमानि ययोस्तादृशे चक्षुषी यत्र तत्तथोक्तम् । सिध्मादित्वात्प्रशंसायां मत्वर्थे लच् । आननं पातुं चुम्बितुमुन्नमयतोभिमुखमूर्ध्वं कुर्वतो मे । उन्नमयन्तं मामनादृत्येत्यर्थः ।

(ततः प्रविशतीरावती निपुणिका च ।)

इरावती—हञ्जे निपुणिके सत्यं त्वं परिगतार्था चन्द्रिकया समुद्रगृहालिन्दे शयित एकाकी आर्यगौतमो दृष्ट इति । (क)

निपुणिका—अन्यथा कथं भट्टिन्यै विज्ञापयामि । (ख)

इरावती—तेन हि तत्रैव गच्छामः संशयान्मुक्तमार्यपुत्रस्य प्रियवयस्यं प्रष्टुं च । (ग)

निपुणिका—सावशेषमिव भट्टिन्या वचनम् । (घ)

इरावती—चित्रगतमार्यपुत्रं प्रसादयितुं च । (ङ)

निपुणिका—अथ कथमिदानीं भर्तैव न प्रसाद्यते । (च)

इरावती—मुग्धे यादृशश्चित्रगतस्तादृश एवान्यसंक्रान्तहृदय आर्यपुत्रः । केवलमुपचारातिक्रमं प्रमार्जितुमयमारम्भः । (छ)

निपुणिका—इत इतो भट्टिनी । (ज)

(उभे परिक्रामतः ।)

(क) हञ्जे णिउणिए सच्चं तुमं[1] परिगदत्था चन्दिआए समुद्दघरअलिन्दे[2] सइदो एआई अज्जगोदमो दिट्ठोत्ति (ख) अण्णहा[3] कहं भट्टिणीए विण्णावेमि । (ग) तेण हि तहिं एव्व गच्छामो संसआदो मुत्तं अज्जउत्तस्स पिअवअस्सं पुच्छिदुं अ । (घ) सावसेसं विअ भट्टिणीए वअणं । (ङ) चित्तगदं[4] अज्जउत्तं पसादेदुं अ । (च) अह कहं[5] दाणिं भट्टा एव्व ण प्पसादीअदि । (छ) मुद्धे जारिसो चित्तगदो तारिसो[6] एव्व अण्णसंकन्तहिअओ अज्जउत्तो । केवलं उवआरादिक्कमं पमज्जिदुं अअं आरम्भो । (ज) इदो इदो भट्टिणी ।

---

१ तुए संदिट्ठं. २ लिन्दे एआई. ३ अण्णहा भट्टिणीए ण विण्णावीअदि. ४ अण्णं अ; आम । चित्त०. ५ अह दाणिं भट्टा एव किं ण पच्चणूणीअदि (प्रत्यनुनीयते); कहं भट्टा एव्व ण अणुणीअदि. ६ भट्टा ण तारिओ एव्व अण्ण० इत्य०.

(Enter Irāvatī *and* Nipuṇikā.*)*

Irāvatī :—Nipuṇikā, my girl, did Candrikā really tell you that she saw the revered Gautama sleeping alone on the verandah of the summer-house ?

Nipuṇikā :—How shall I falsely inform your ladyship ? (Or, otherwise how shall I tell it) ?

Irāvatī :—If so, let us go there to ask (about the well-being of) my husband's dear friend rescued from peril, and—

Nipuṇikā :—Your ladyship's speech appears to be incomplete.

Irāvatī :—To propitiate my husband drawn in a picture.

Nipuṇikā :—Now, why do you not propitiate the King himself ?

Irāvatī :—Foolish girl, my husband, whose heart (affection) is transferred to another, is just like (no better than) one drawn in a picture. This my attempt is only to atone for my incivility (*lit.* breach of propriety) to him.

Nipuṇikā :—This way, your Highness.

(Both *walk forth.*)

षष्ठी च अनादरे इति षष्ठी। तत् साचीकरोति तिर्यग्धारयति। एवं व्याजेन प्रतिषेधरूपेणापि मे अभिलाषपूरणेन संगमेच्छापूर्त्या यत्सुखं तन्निर्वर्तयति विदधात्येव। शार्दूलविक्रीडितं वृत्तम् ॥ १५ ॥ चन्द्रिकया करणभूतया परिगतो ज्ञातोऽर्थो यया। यद्वा चन्द्रिकया दृष्ट इति योज्यम्। अर्थमाह समुद्रेति। संशयात्सर्पदंशोत्पन्नमरणभयात्। इरावत्या भाषणे चकारप्रयोगादाह सावशेषमिवेति। भट्टा एव साक्षाद्भर्ता। किमिति चित्रगतः प्रसाद्यते इत्यर्थः। मुग्धे मनुष्यस्वभावानभिज्ञे। यादृश इति। अधुना अन्यसंक्रान्तहृदयत्वाच्चित्रगतस्य इव भर्तुःमत्सान्निध्ये भावानुदयादित्यर्थः। मत्सरस्य नायिकान्तरेण सह द्वेषस्य। वयस्यया बकुलावलिकया। निगडबन्धने कृता शृङ्खलया निगृहीता। अयं जनः अहमित्यर्थः। कस्य वान्यस्य अपि तु तवैवेत्यर्थः। वर्धते उत्कर्षवान्भवति। विपणिगतः पण्यवीथिकास्थः। प्रसन्नः जीवत इव अकलुषः मुखवर्णो यस्य। चिकित्सितः कृतविषविकारप्रतिकारः। पापं मृत्युरूपम्। अत्याहितं नाम जीवानपेक्षि कर्म। 'अत्याहितं महाभीतिः कर्म जीवानपेक्षि च।' इत्यमरसिंहः।

(प्रविश्य ।)

चेटी—जयतु भट्टिनी । देवी भणति । न मे एष मत्सरस्य कालः तव खलु बहुमानं वर्धयितुं वयस्यया सह निगडबन्धने कृता मालविका । यद्यनुमन्यसे आर्यपुत्रस्य प्रियं कर्तुं तथा करोमि । यत्तवेष्टं तन्मे भणेति । (क)

इरावती—नागरिके विज्ञापय देवीम् । का वयं भट्टिनीं नियोजयितुम् । परिजननिगडनेन दर्शितो मय्यनुग्रहः । कस्य वान्यस्य प्रसादेनायं जनो वर्धत इति । (ख)

चेटी—तथा । (इति निष्क्रान्ता ।) (ग)

निपुणिका—(परिक्रम्यावलोक्य च ।) भट्टिनि एष द्वारदेशे समुद्रगृहस्य विपणिगत इव बलीवर्द आर्यगौतम आसीन एव निद्रायते । (घ)

इरावती—अत्याहितम् । न खलु सावशेषो विषविकारो भवेत् । (ङ)

(क) जेदु भट्टिणी । देवी भणादि । ण मे एसो मच्छरस्स कालो । तुह खु बहुमाणं वड्डेदुं वअस्सिआए सह णिअलबन्धणे किदा मालविआ । जइ अणुमण्णसि अज्जउत्तस्स[2] पिअं कादुं तह करेमि । जं तुह इच्छिअं तं मे भणाहित्ति । (ख) णाअरिए विण्णावेहि देविं । का वअं भट्टिणिं णिओजेदुं । परिअणणिअलणेण[3] दंसिदो मइ अणुग्गहो । कस्स वा अण्णस पसादेण अअ जणो वड्ढदित्ति । (ग) तह । (घ) भट्टिणि एसो दुवारदेसे[4] समुद्दघरस्स विपणिगदो[5] विअ बलीवद्दो अज्जगोदमो आसीणो एव्व णिद्दाअदि । (ङ) अच्चाहिदं[6] । ण खु सावसेसो विसविआरो हवे ।

---

१ केवलं तुह खु, तेण खु तुह. अज्जउतं वि तुह किदे विण्णविस्सं; विण्णावइस्सम्. ३ निगगहेण. ४ दुवारोच्छङ्गे (द्वारोत्सङ्गे); दुवारुद्देसे (द्वारोद्देशे); दुवारे. ५ कुसहो विअ विसड्ढो; णिवुत्तविसवेअ विअ. ६ अम्हो । अच्चा०; किं णु खु अच्चा० । सावसेसो विअ विस०; सावसेसविसो, सावसेसे विसे विरतो भवे.

(*Enter a maid.*)

Maid :—Victory to your Highness ! The Queen says—'This is not the (proper) time for me to show jealousy; verily, then, it was to increase the great respect (you command) that Mālavikā was put in fetters along with her friend. If you will consent to do good to our husband, I will do it. Tell me what your wish is.'

Irāvatī :—Nāgarikā, say to the Queen-'Who am I to direct the Queen ? You have shown favour to me by putting your servants in irons. By the favour of what other person can this person (myself) prosper ? '

Maid :—I will say so. (*Exit.*)

Nipuṇikā :—(*Walking round and looking on*) Your Highness, here is the revered Gautama, at the door of the summer-house, gone to sleep while just sitting up, like a bull in a market-street.

Irāvatī :—Oh calamity ! I hope, no bad effects of the poison still remain.

उत्स्वप्नायते निद्रावशो नरो यत्किंचित्स्वमनोगतं प्रकटयति तदुत्स्वप्नायितमित्युच्यते । स्वस्तिवाचने लब्धा मोदकाः स्वस्तिवाचनमोदकास्तैः । कस्यैष ···उत्स्वप्नायते । अत्र दोषोद्घाटनादपवादो नाम संध्यङ्गमुक्तं भवति । अत्रैव रोषभाषणात्संफेटो नाम संध्यंगमुक्तं भवति । अतिक्रामन्ती अतिशयाना । इरावत्या अपि भर्तुः प्रेयसी । भाययिष्यामि भयाकुलं करिष्यामि । भियो णिच् । भीतेर्हेतुजन्यत्वाभावान्न षुक् । नाप्यात्मनेपदम् । 'उवद्दवस्स' इत्यत्र कश्चित् । 'अर्हतेः' इति प्राकृते कर्मणि षष्ठी ॥ उपरि पतितः । अत्रोद्वेजनाद्युक्तिर्नाम संध्यङ्गमुक्तं भवति ॥ कुटिलगतिः कुटिला वक्रा गतिर्यस्य । पक्षे गतिः प्रवृत्तिः अनेन इरावत्यागमनं सूचितम् । दिवासंकेतः-दिवा दिवसे संकेतः समागमार्थं कृतः समयः । दूतस्य भावो दूत्यं स एवाधिकार दूत्याधिकाराः स विषयो यस्याः । दूत्यभिसार इति पाठे दूत्या अभिसारः संगमार्थं नायकनायिकयोः संकेतस्थलं प्रत्यानयनं स विषय उद्देश्यं यस्याः । दर्दुरा व्याहरन्त्याक्रोशन्तीति । इति हेतोः देवः इन्द्रः पृथिवीं विस्मरति

निपुणिका—प्रसन्नमुखवर्णो दृश्यते । अपि च ध्रुवसिद्धिना चिकित्सितः । तदस्याशङ्कनीयं पापम् । (क)

विदूषकः—(उत्स्वप्नायते ।) भवति मालविके— (ख)

निपुणिका—श्रुतं भट्टिन्या । कस्यैष आत्मनीनो हताशः कितवः । सर्वकालमित एव स्वस्तिवाचनमोदकैः कुक्षिं पूरयित्वा सांप्रतं मालविकामुत्स्वप्नायते । (ग)

विदूषकः—इरावतीमतिक्रामन्ती भव । (घ)

निपुणिका—एतदत्याहितम् । इमं भुजंगभीरुकं ब्रह्मबन्धुमनेन भुजंगकुटिलेन दण्डकाष्ठेन स्तम्भान्तरिता भाययिष्यामि । (ङ)

इरावती—अर्हत्येव कृतघ्न उपद्रवस्य । (च)

(निपुणिका विदूषकस्योपरि दण्डकाष्ठं पातयति ।)

विदूषकः—(सहसा प्रबुध्य ।) अविधा अविधा । भो वयस्य सर्पो म उपरि पतितः । (छ)

राजा—(सहसोपसृत्य ।) सखे न भेतव्यं न भेतव्यम् ।

मालविका—(अनुसृत्य ।) भर्तः मा तावत्सहसा निष्क्राम । सर्प इति भण्यते । (ज)

(क) पसण्णमुह[1]वण्णो दीसइ । अवि अ धुवसिद्धिणा चिइच्छिदो । तास्से असङ्कणिज्जं पावं । (ख) भोदि मालविए (ग) सुदं भट्टिणीए । कस्स एसो [2]अत्तणीणो हदासो किदवो । सव्वकालं इदो एव्व सोत्थिवाअणमोदएहिं कुच्छिं पूरिअ संपदं मालविअं उस्सिविणावेदि । (घ) इरावदिं अदिक्कमन्ती होहि । (ङ) एदं[3] अच्चाहिदं । इमं भुअङ्गभीरुअं बह्मबन्धुं इमिणा भुअङ्गकुडिलेण दण्डकट्ठेण खम्भन्तरिदा भाअइस्सं[4] । (च) अरुहदि एव्व किदं[5]घो उवद्दवस्स । (छ) अविहा अविहा । भो वअस्स [6]सप्पो मे उवरि पडिदो । (ज) भट्टा मा दाव सहसा णिक्क[7]म । सप्पोत्ति भ[8]णीअदि ।

---

१ मुहो. २ अत्तणिओअसंपादणे विस्ससणिज्जो हदासो; अब्भवहारसंवादापेक्खी ओदरिओ. ३ सुदं एदं. ४ भाअआमि, ताडइस्सं ५ किदवो (कितवः), किदवो सप्पदंसस्स. ६ दव्वीकरो (दर्वीकरः) ७ णिक्कमिस्ससि. ८ भणादि.

Nipuṇikā :—The expression of his face appears to be bright; moreover, he was treated by Dhruvasiddhi; so no evil can be feared in his case.

Vidūṣaka:—(*Speaks in his sleep*) Lady Mālavikā—

Nipuṇikā :—Did your Highness hear? To whom can this cunning wretch ever attach himself? Having at all times filled his belly with the sweet-meats accompanying auspicious presents obtained just from us, he is now addressing Mālavikā in a dream.

Vidūṣaka :—Do you outshine Iravatī.

Nipuṇikā :—This is the calamity (Your Highness feared). Hidden behind the pillar, I will frighten, with this stick, crooked like a serpent, this wretch of a Brāhmaṇa who (always) dreads serpents.

Irāvatī :—The ungrateful rogue deserves such molestation.

(Nipuṇikā *throws the stick on* Vidūṣaka.)

Vidūṣaka :—(*Suddenly waking up*) Help, help! O friend, a serpent has fallen upon me.

King :—(*Rushing to him at once*) Friend, be not afraid, be not afraid!

Mālavikā :—(*Following him*) My lord, do not rush forth all at once (heedlessly). He speaks of a serpent being there.

पृथिव्यां वर्षणं कर्तुं विस्मरति। अपितु न। तथा मम जल्पितं श्रुत्वा देवः भट्टिनीं न विस्मरिष्यतीति भावः। पृथिवीं वर्षितुं स्मरतीति पाठे यथा महेन्द्रकृतवृष्टौ दर्दुराक्रोशितानां न कश्चित्संबन्धः तथा मालविकापरिग्रहे न मदुक्तानां कश्चित्संबन्धः। यथा भेकशब्दं श्रुत्वा इन्द्रो न वर्षति तथा मदुक्तानि श्रुत्वा भर्ता मालविकां न परिग्रहीष्यतीति भावः। अस्थाने अकारणाम्। कदेत्यादि। हे वरतनु वरा श्रेष्ठा तनुः यस्यास्तत्संबुद्धौ। तव मुखं कारणादृते कारणं विना कदा क्षणमपि कोपगात्रतां क्रोधास्पदत्वं आगतम्। न कदापीत्यर्थः। तदेव दृष्टान्तेन विशदयति। विभावरी रात्रिः अपर्वणि पूर्णिमाभिन्नकाले ग्रहेण राहुणा कलुषं धूसरमिन्दुमण्डलं चन्द्रबिम्बं यस्यां तथा कथं भविष्यति। न थमपीत्यर्थः। अत्र चन्द्रो रात्रेर्मुखस्थानीयः।

इरावती—हा धिक् हा धिक्। भर्तेत एव धावति। (क)

विदूषकः—(सप्रहासम्।) कथं दण्डकाष्ठमेतत्। अहं पुनर्जाने यन्मया केतकीकण्टकैर्दंशं कृत्वा सर्पस्य इव दंशः कृतस्तन्मे फलितमिति। (ख)

(प्रविश्य [1]पटाक्षेपेण।)

बकुलावलिका—मा तावद्भर्ता प्रविशतु। इह कुटिलगतिः सर्प इव दृश्यते। (ग)

इरावती—([2]स्तम्भान्तरिता राजानमुपेत्य।) अपि निर्विघ्नमनोरथो दिवासंकेतो मिथुनस्य। (घ)

(सर्वे इरावतीं दृष्ट्वा संभ्रान्ताः।)

राजा—प्रिये [3]अपूर्वोऽयमुपचारः।

इरावती—बकुलावलिके दिष्ट्या दूत्याधिकारविषया संपूर्णा ते प्रतिज्ञा। (ङ)

बकुलावलिका—प्रसीदतु भट्टिनी। किं नु खलु दर्दुरा व्याहरन्तीति देवः पृथिवीं विस्मरति। (च)

विदूषकः—मा तावत्। भवत्या दर्शनमात्रेणात्रभवान्प्रणिपातलङ्घनं विस्मृतः। भवती पुनरद्यापि प्रसादं न गृह्णाति। (छ)

(क) हद्धि हद्धि। भट्टा इदो एव्व धावदि। (ख) कहं दण्डकट्ठ एदं। अहं उण जाणे जं मए केदईकण्टएहिं दंसं करिअ [4]सप्पस्स इव दंसो किदो तं मे फलिदंति। (ग) मा [5]दाव भट्टा पविसदु। इह कुडिलगई सप्पो विअ दीसदि। (घ) [6]अवि णिव्विग्घमणोरहो दिवासंकेदो मिहुणस्स। (ङ) बउलावलिए दिट्ठिआ दुद्याहिआरविसआ संपुण्णा दे पडिण्णा। (च) पसीददु भट्टिणी। किं णु खु दद्दुरा वाहरन्तित्ति [7]देवो पुढवीं विसुम[8]रदि। (छ) मा दाव। होदीए दंसणमत्तेण अत्तभवं पणिवादलङ्घणं विसुमरिदो। [9]होदी उण अज्जवि पसादं ण गेण्हेदि।

---

१ ससंभ्रमम्-मा. २ एदन्नास्ति क्वचित्. ३ प्रिये. ४ सप्पस्स उवरि अअसो (अयशः) किदं. ५ खु. ६ आवि सिद्धा मणोरहा दिवासंकेदमिहुणस्स, दिवससंगमो. ७ दवीए पुढवीए देव्वो वरिसिदुं विरमति (देव्यां पृथिव्यां देवो वर्षितुं विरमति); पुढवि वरिसिदुं सुमरेदि ८ अस्मात्पर-कि मए किदंति दवो पुच्छिदव्वो-इत्यधिकं क्वचित्. ९ तुमम्...गेण्हेसि.

Irāvatī :—Woe, woe! The King is running just hitherwards.

Vidūṣaka :—(*Smiling aloud*) What, it is only a stick! I, however, thought that I reaped the fruit of my producing a bite by means of the Ketakī thorns and giving it the semblance of a serpent's bite (*i. e.* got a true bite).

(*Entering with a toss of the curtain.*)

Bakulāvalikā :—Let not my Lord advance: here is seen something like a serpent that moves tortuously.

Irāvatī :—(*Approaching the* King *from behind the pillar*) Is the appointed day-meeting of the couple such as has the desired object accomplished without an obstacle?

(*All are confounded on beholding* Irāvatī.)

King :—My darling, strange is this from of greeting (or courtesy).

Irāvatī :—Bakulāvalikā, I congratulate you on the entire fulfilment of your promise with regard to your mission as a go-between.

Bakulāvalikā :—May your Highness be pleased. Does Indra forget the earth because the frogs croak?

Vidūṣaka :—Let not your ladyship act thus. Merely at your sight his Honour has forgotten your slighting of his prostration. Your ladyship, however, is not yet reconciled.

दृष्टान्तालंकारः। रुचिरा वृत्तम् ॥ १६ ॥ अन्यसंक्रान्तेषु मालविका गतेषु। हास्या उपहासार्हा। मम कोपस्याकिंचित्करत्वात्। स्थाने एव कोपो युज्यते इति भावः। नार्हतीत्यादि। परिजनः सेवकजनः कृतः अपराधः मया सह भाषणरूपो येन स कृतापराधोपि उत्सवदिवसेषु बन्धं बन्धनं नार्हति इति अतो हेतोः एते मालविका-बकुलावलिके मया बन्धान्मोचिते। मां प्रणिपतितुमुपगते च। केवलं कृतज्ञतादर्शनार्थ-मागते नान्यस्मात्कारणादिति कृतमन्यथा कल्पनयेति भावः ॥ १७ ॥ पक्षपातो

इरावती—कुपितेदानीमहं किं करिष्यामि। (क)

राजा—अस्थाने कोप इत्यनुपपन्नं त्वयि। तथा हि।

कदा मुखं वरतनु कारणादृते
तवागतं क्षणमपि कोपपात्रताम्।
अपर्वणि ग्रहकलुषेन्दुमण्डला
विभावरी कथय कथं भविष्यति॥ १६॥

इरावती—अस्थान इति सुष्ठु व्याहृतमार्यपुत्रेण। अन्यसंक्रान्तेष्वस्माकं भागधेयेषु यदि पुनः कुप्येयं ततो हास्या भवेयम्। (ख)

राजा—त्वमन्यथा कल्पयसि। अहं पुनः सत्यमेव[1] कोपस्थानं न पश्यामि। कुतः।

नार्हति कृतापराधोऽप्युत्सवदिवसेषु परिजनो बन्धम्[2]।
इति मोचिते मयैते प्रणिपतितुं[3] मामुपगते च[4]॥ १७॥

इरावती—निपुणिके गच्छ देवीं विज्ञापय। दृष्टो भवत्याः पक्षपातो नन्वद्येति। (ग)

निपुणिका—तथा। (इति निष्क्रान्ता।) (घ)

विदूषकः—(आत्मगतम्।) अहो अनर्थः संपतितः। बन्धनभ्रष्टो गृहकपोतो चिल्लाया मुखे पतितः। (ङ)

(क) कुविदा दाणिं अहं किं करिस्सं। (ख) अट्ठाणेत्ति सुट्ठु वाहरिदं[5] अज्जउत्तेण। अण्णसंकन्तेसु अह्माणं भाअहेएसु जदि उण कुप्पेअं[6] तदो हस्सा भवेअं। (ग) णिउणिए गच्छ। देवीं विण्णवेहि। [7]दिट्ठो भवदीए पक्खवादो णं अज्जत्ति। (घ) तह। (ङ) अहो अणत्थो संपडिदो। बन्धणब्भट्ठो गिहं[8]कवोदो[9] चिल्लीए[10] मुहे पडिदो।

---

१ मेवात्र. २ बन्दुम्; दण्डम्. ३ सभाजयितुम्. ४ अस्मात्परं—विदू०-दयालु खु एसो भौरुओ अ। इत्याधिकं क्वचित्. ५ भणिदं. ६ कुपिदा भविस्सं. ७ दिट्ठं भ० पक्खवादित्तणं. ८ भो. ९ कवोदओ. १० बिडालिआए आलोए; मन्दा-रलतालग्गो...चिल्लिआलोए.

Irāvatī :—What can I do now, though I get angry ?

King :—Anger without cause, is a thing not compatible with you (your disposition). To be clear—

When, O fair-bodied one, did your face become, even for a moment, the object of anger ? Tell me, how will the night have the orb of the moon dimmed (eclipsed) by the planet (Rāhu) except on the full-moon-day ? (16)

Irāvatī :—(Anger) 'without cause' is rightly said by my husband. When our good fortune has passed to another, if I were to be angry again, I should make myself ridiculous.

King:—You take a different view. I, on my part, really see no cause for anger. For,

Servants, even though they have committed a crime, ought not to be kept in confinement on festive days.—With this thought I got them set free ; and they came to bow down to me (in gratitude). (17)

Irāvatī : Nipuṇikā, go to the Queen and say to her—I have really seen to-day your partiality to me (how you side with me.)

Nipuṇikā—So I will. (*Exit.*)

Vidūṣaka :—(*To himself*) Oh, an undesirable thing (calamity) has happened. The house-pigeon, having escaped from confinement, has fallen into the mouth of a kite.

मयि अनुकूला वृत्तिः । अद्य राज्ञो मालविकया संगमदिवसे । मालविका धारिण्यैव बन्धनान्मोचिता इति मन्वानाया इवं विपरीतलक्षणया निन्दोक्तिः बन्धनाद्भ्रष्ट इति आपद आपदन्तरमापतितमित्यर्थः । यदृच्छया अतर्कितम् । निर्वृत्तं निष्पन्नम् । कामतन्त्रे मदनरहस्ये सचिवः साहाय्यकारी तस्य । यदि नीतेरिति । यदि नीतिज्ञानस्य गन्धोपि मयि स्यात्तर्हि गायत्रीमपि विस्मरेयम् । यथा गायत्रीविस्मरणं मय्यसंभाव्यं तथा नीतिज्ञानमपीत्यर्थः । पाठान्तरे–प्रेषितो भवेत् नीतिज्ञोहं चेद्राज्ञः मालविकायाश्च संगमं कुर्यामेव किं तु नैतदेवमित्यर्थः । अनुधावन्ती अनुसृत्य

(प्रविश्य ।)

निपुणिका—(अपवाय ।) भट्टिनि यदृच्छादृष्टया माधविकया आख्यातम् । एवं खल्वेतन्निर्वृत्तमिति । (इति कर्णे कथयति ।) **(क)**

इरावती—(आत्मगतम् ।) उपपन्नम् । सत्यमयमत्र ब्रह्मबन्धुना कृतः प्रयोगः । (विदूषकं विलोक्य । प्रकाशम् ।) इयमस्य कामतन्त्रसचिवस्य नीतिः । **(ख)**

विदूषकः—भवति यदि नीतेरेकमप्यक्षरं पठेयं तदा गायत्रीमपि विस्मरेयम् । **(ग)**

राजा—(आत्म[1]गतम् ।) कथं नु खल्वस्मात्संकटादात्मानं मोचे[2]यिष्यामि ।

([3]प्रविश्य ।)

जयसेना—(सावेगम् ।) देव कुमारी वसुलक्ष्मीः कन्दुकमनुधावन्ती पिङ्गलवानरेण बलवत्-त्रासिताङ्कनिषण्णा देव्याः प्रवातकिसलयमिव वेपमाना न किमपि प्रकृतिं प्रतिपद्यते । **(घ)**

राजा—कष्टम् । कातरो बालभावः ।

इरावती—(सावेगम् ।) त्वरतामार्यपुत्र एनां समाश्वासयितुम् । मास्याः संत्रासजनितो विकारो वर्धताम् । **(ङ)**

(क) भट्टिणि जदिच्छादिट्ठाए माहविआए आचक्खिदं । एव्वं खु एदं णिव्वुत्तंति । (ख) उर्व[4]वण्णं । सच्चं अअं एत्थ बम्हबन्धुणा किदो पओओ । इअं इमस्स कामतन्तसचिवस्स णीदी । (ग) भोदि जदि[5] णीदिए एक्कंवि अक्खरं पढेअं त[6]दो गाअत्तिं वि विसुमरेअं । (घ) देव कुमारी वसुलच्छी कन्दुअं [7]अणुधावन्ती पिङ्गलवाणरेण बलिअं त[8]ासिदा [9]अङ्कणिसण्णा देवीए प[10]वादकिसलअं विअ वेवमाणा ण किंवि पकिदिं पडिवज्जइ । (ङ) तुवरदु अज्जउत्तो णं [11]समस्सासइदुं । मा से संतासजणिदो विआरो वड्ढदु ।

---

१ अपवार्य. स्वगतम्. २ मोक्ष्यामि, मोचयामेह-वेहे. ३ प्र० सावेगं, सावेगा जय० ४ वण्णं एव्व । ब्रम्हबन्धणा किदो अअं; ०वण्णं सव्वं बम्ह० उब्भिण्णो दुप्पओओ (उद्भिन्नो दुष्प्रयोगः). ५ णीदिगदं. ६ तदो णं,-णं मए अत्तभवं पेसिदो हवे; ण मए अत्तभवं संसिदो (संश्रितः) भवे, णीदावेक्कमपि अक्षरं पठितं तदात्मानं गोहत्यां प्रापितो भवेयम् (टी.). ७. अणुहोन्ती. ८ ताडिदा, उत्तासिता. ९ अङ्के. १० पवादचल; पवादे. ११ समस्सासेदुं.

(*Entering*)

Nipuṇikā :—Queen, Mādhavikā, who met me accidentally, told me—'This came to pass in this way.' (*Whispers it in her ear*).

Irāvatī :—(*To herself*) It is all explained now. Truly, the knavish Brāhmaṇa must have employed this device here! (*Looking at the* Vidūṣaka, *aloud*) This is the policy of this minister of the department of love-affairs!

Vidūṣaka :—Lady, if I ever read one syllable of policy, I should forget even the Gāyatrī.

King :— (*To himself*) How shall I extricate myself from this difficulty ?

(*Entering*)

Jayasenā :—(*In excitement*) My Lord, the princess Vasulakṣmī, while running after the ball (with which she was playing,), was greatly frightened by the brown ape (or the ape Pingala) ; and though seated on the Queen's lap, she, trembling like a tender leaf (waving) in a strong wind, does not, anyhow, regain her natural composure (of mind).

King :—Alas ! Childhood is attended with timidity (children are naturally timid).

Irāvatī :—(*With agitation*) Let my Lord hasten to cheer her up, that her affliction caused by the fright may not increase.

ग्रहणार्थं त्वरया गच्छन्ती । प्रवाते प्रकृष्टवातस्थले स्थितं किसलयं पल्लव इव वेपमाना कम्पमाना । न किमपि प्रकृतिं प्रतिपद्यते कथमपि स्वास्थ्यं न लभते । मोहं न जहातीति भावः । संज्ञापयामि संज्ञां चेतनां लम्भयामि । स्वपक्षः चापलकारित्वात्त्वत्पक्षोऽहमिति परिहासोक्तिः । अथ वा सपक्षः साहाय्यकारित्वादहं नृपश्च । देवीं चिन्तयित्वा यदेमं वृत्तान्तं देवी ज्ञास्यति तदा तस्याः कोपप्रकारं चिन्तयित्वेत्यर्थः । दोहदस्य मालविकाकृतस्य पादताडनरूपस्य । तस्मादारभ्य पञ्चरात्रेऽपूर्णे असमापिते

राजा—अयं[1]मेनां संज्ञापयामि। (इति सत्वरं परिक्रामति।)

विदूषकः—(आत्मगतम्।) साधु रे पिङ्गलवानर। साधु परित्रातस्त्वया संकटात्स्वपक्षः। (क)

(निष्क्रान्तः[2] सवयस्यो राजा इरावती निपुणिका प्रतिहारी च।)

मालविका—सखि देवीं चिन्तयित्वा वेपते मे हृदयम्। न जानेऽतः परं किं वानुभवितव्यं भविष्यतीति। (ख)

(नेपथ्ये।)

आश्चर्यमाश्चर्यम्। अपूर्ण एव पञ्चरात्रे दोहदस्य मुकुलैः संनद्धस्तपनीयाशोकः। यावद्देव्यै निवेदयामि। (ग)

(श्रुत्वा प्रहृष्टे[3]।)

बकुलावलिका—आश्वसितु सखी। सत्यप्रतिज्ञा देवी (घ)

मालविका—तेन हि प्रमदवनपालिकायाः पृष्ठतो भवावः। (ङ)

बकुलावलिका—तथा। (च)

(इति निष्क्रान्ते[4]।)

इति चतुर्थोऽङ्कः।

(क) साहु[5]रे पिंगलवाणर। साहु परित्तादो तुए[6] संकटादो सपक्खो। (ख) हला देविं चिन्तिअ[7] वेवदि मे हिअअं। ण जाणे अदो वरं [8]किं वा अणुहविदव्वं हविस्सदित्ति। (ग) अच्चरिअं अच्चरिअं। अपुण्णे एव्व पञ्चरत्ते दोहलस्स मुउलेहिं संणद्धो तवणीआसोओ। जाव देवीए णिवेदेमि। (घ) आससिदु सही। सच्चप्पइण्णा देवी। (ङ) तेण हि पमदवणपालिआए पुट्ठदो होम। (च) तह।

---

१ अयमहं. २ निष्क्रान्तौ राजा विदूषकश्च; निष्क्रान्तो वयस्येन. ३ प्रहृष्टे भवतः. ४ निष्क्रान्ताः सर्वे. ५ सुट्ठु. ६ तुए सप०, ७ चिन्तअन्तीए. ८ किं अणुहोदव्वं.

King :—Here I go to bring her to her senses. (*He walks hastily.*)

Vidūṣaka :—(*To himself*) Well done, yon brown ape; well have you rescued your party from the difficulty.

(*Exeunt the* King *with his* Companion, Irāvatī, Nipuṇikā, *and the* Female door-keeper.)

Mālavikā :—Friend, my heart trembles, when I think of the Queen. I do not know what I shall have to experience next.

(*Behind the scenes*)

Wonder, Oh, Wonder! Before the expiry of the five nights from the (time of the) gratification of its desire, the yellow Aśoka is thickly covered with buds. I will then go and inform the Queen.

(*Both are greatly delighted on hearing this.*)

Bakulāvalikā :—Let my friend take heart. The Queen is (always) true to her promise.

Mālavikā :—If so, let us be at the back of the keeper of the Pramada-grove.

Bakulāvalikā :—Let us do so. (*Exeunt both.*)

Here *ends the* FOURTH ACT.

एव ॥ **सत्यप्रतिज्ञेति** । सत्या प्रतिज्ञा यद्यशोकः पञ्चरात्राभ्यन्तरे कुसुमं दर्शयति ततस्तवाभिलाषपूरयितृकं प्रसादं दास्यामीत्येवंरूपा यस्याः सा तथोक्ता । स्वप्रतिज्ञानुरूपमाचरिष्यत्येवेति भावः । इदमाश्वासे हेतुः । अत्र देव्यनुग्रहरूपकार्यसंग्रहणादादानं नाम संध्यङ्गमुक्तं भवति ॥ **तेन हीति** । इदं मालविकाकृतमुद्यानपालिकानुसरणमुत्तराङ्कोपयुक्तत्वाद्बिन्दुरित्यनुसंधेयम् ।

इति श्रीकाटयवेमभूपविरचिते कुमारगिरिराजीये
मालविकाग्निमित्रव्याख्याने चतुर्थोऽङ्कः ॥

पञ्चमोऽङ्कः।

(ततः प्रविशत्युद्यानपालिका।)

उद्यानपालिका—उपक्षिप्तो मया कृतसत्कारविधेस्तपनीयाशोकस्य वेदिकाबन्धः। यावदनुष्ठितनियोगमात्मानं देव्यै निवेदयामि। (परिक्रम्य।) अहो दैवस्यानुकम्पनीया मालविका। तस्यां तथा चण्डी देव्यनेनाशोककुसुमवृत्तान्तेन प्रसादसुमुखी भविष्यति। कुत्र नु खलु भवेद्देवी। (विलोक्य।) अहो एष देव्याः परिजनाभ्यन्तरः किमपि जतुमुद्रालाञ्छितां मञ्जूषां गृहीत्वा चतुःशालातः कुब्जः सारसको निष्क्रामति। प्रक्ष्यामि तावदेनम्। (क)

(ततः प्रविशति यथानिर्दिष्टः कुब्जः।)

उद्यानपालिका—(उपसृत्य।) सारसक कुत्र प्रस्थितोऽसि। (ख)

सारसकः—मधुकरिके विद्यापारगामिनां ब्राह्मणानां नित्यदक्षिणा दातव्या। तामार्यपुरोहितस्य हस्तं प्रापयितुम्। (ग)

उद्यानपालिका—किंनिमित्तम्। (घ)

(क) उवक्खित्तो मए किदसक्कारविहिणो[1] तवणीआसोअस्स वेदिआबन्धो[2]। जाव अणुट्ठिदणिओअं अत्ताणं देवीए णिवेदेमि। अहो देव्वस्स अणुकम्पणीआ मलाविआ। [3]तस्सि तह चण्डिआ देवी इमिणा [4]असोअकुसुमवुत्तन्तेण पसादसु[5]मुही हविस्सदि। कहिं णु खु हवे देवी। अह्मो एसो देवीए[6] परिअणब्भन्तरो किंवि जदुमुद्दालञ्छदं मञ्जूसं[7] गेण्हिअ चदुस्सालादो कुज्जो [8]सारसओ णिक्कमदि। पुच्छिस्सं दाव णं। (ख) सारसअ कहिं पत्थिदोसि। (ग) महुअरिए विज्जापा[9]रगामिणं बह्मणाणं णिच्चदक्खिणा दादव्या। तां अज्जपुरोहिदस्स हत्थं पाविदुं। (घ) किंणिमित्तं।

कविरिदानीमङ्कान्तरमारभमाणः कथासंघटनार्थं प्रथमं प्रवेशकं नामार्थोपक्षेपकं प्रस्तौति—**ततः प्रविशतीत्यादिना**। कृतः सत्कारसंबद्धः विधिः संमार्जनरङ्गवल्लीरचनादिः। दोहदादि सत्कारकर्म इति केचित्। यस्य तस्य। वेदिकाबन्धो मूलं परितो वेदिकारचना। दैवस्य अनुकम्पनीया दयार्हा। दैवं दयाप्रवणं जातमित्यर्थः।

---

१ त्रिहिणा. २ भितिबन्धो ३ ज तास्सि तह चण्डोकिदा. ४ हरिसदोहलवुत्त० ५ दाभिमुह्रो. ६ देवीपरि० ७ चौरम०; चौरबन्धं. ८ सारसिओ. ९ भरिआणं. १० दक्खिणा मासिआ इमाइं दक्खिणाणिक्काणि। ताइं पुरो०.

ACT V

(Enter the Female Keeper of the garden.)

Female Garden-Keeper:—I have finished the construction of a dais round the yellow As'oka whose decoration has been performed. I will then first inform the Queen that her order has been executed. (*Walking about*) Oh, fate is disposed to take pity on Mālavikā. The Queen, who was angry with her to that extent, will now look upon her with a favourable countenance owing to this information about the blossoming of the yellow As'oka. Where can the Queen be ? (*Looking forth*) Oh, here is the hunchback Sārasaka, one of the attendants of the Queen, issuing forth from the quadrangle with some object in view, taking with him a box marked with the seal of red lac. I shall just ask him.

(*Enter the* Hunch-back *as described above.*)

Female Garden-Keeper :—(*Approaching him*) Sārasaka, where are you going to ?

Sārasaka :—Madhukarikā, Dakshiṇā is to be daily given to the Brāhmaṇas, who have mastered the Vedic lore. (I am going) to give the same into the hands of the revered family-priest.

Female Garden-Keeper :—What is the occasion ?

किमपि कमप्यर्थमुद्दिश्य । जतुनो लाक्षाया मुद्रया लाञ्छितां चिह्नितां मञ्जूषां पेटिकाम् । चतुःशालातः संजवनात् । विद्यापारगामिनामधीतवेदवेदाङ्गानाम् । नित्यदक्षिणा प्रतिदिनदेया दक्षिणा । दक्षिणां मासिकीमिति पाठे मासस्येयं मासिकी तावत्कालपर्याप्ता । कालात् ठञ् इति ठञ् । ततः टिड्ढाणञ्० इत्यादिना ङीप् । पुरोहितस्य राज्ञः पुरोधसः । श्रुतं देव्या इति शेषः । भर्तृदारकः राजपुत्रः । आयुर्निमित्तमायुषा वृद्ध्यर्थम् । अष्टादश सुवर्णाः स्वर्णकर्षाः परिमाणं यस्यास्ताम् । 'सुवर्णो ना स्वर्णकर्षे' इति विश्वः । दक्षिणीयो दक्षिणार्हः । 'कडङ्करदक्षिणाच्छ च' इति छप्रत्ययः । विजयन्ते शत्रूनिति विजयाः । एरच् इत्यच् । विजयाश्च ते दण्डाः सैन्यानि च तैः । 'दण्डः सैन्ये दमे यमे'। इति हैमः। मोचितो बन्धादित्यर्थः। महान्सारो येषां तानि महासाराणि महार्घाणि । तद्वा महान्ति च तानि साराणि श्रेष्ठानि च तानि। ततः प्रविशतीत्यादि ।

सारसकः—यदाप्रभृति श्रुतं सेनापतिना यज्ञतुरंगरक्षणे नियुक्तो भर्तृदारको वसुमित्र इति तदाप्रभृति तस्यायुर्निमित्तमष्टादशसुवर्णपरिमाणां दक्षिणां देवी दक्षिणीयैः परिग्राहयति । (क)

उद्यानपालिका—युज्यते । अथ कुत्र देवी । किं वानुतिष्ठति । (ख)

सारसकः—मङ्गलगृहे आसनस्था भूत्वा विदर्भविषयाद्भ्रात्रा वीरसेनेन प्रेषितं लेखकरैर्वाच्यमानं लेखं शृणोति । (ग)

उद्यानपालिका—कः पुनर्विदर्भराजवृत्तान्तः । (घ)

सारसकः—वशीकृतः किल वीरसेनप्रमुखैर्भर्तुर्विजयदण्डैर्विदर्भनाथः । मोचितश्चास्य दायादो माधवसेनः । दूतश्च तेन महासाराणि रत्नवाहनानि शिल्पकारिकाभूयिष्ठं परिजनं चोपायनीकृत्य भर्तुः सकाशं प्रेषितः श्वः किल भर्तारं पश्यतीति । (ङ)

उद्यानपालिका—गच्छ । अनुतिष्ठात्मनो नियोगम् । अहमपि देवीं प्रेक्षिष्ये । (इति निष्क्रान्तौ ।) (च)

प्रवेशकः ।

(ततः प्रविशति प्रतीहारी ।)

(क) जं[1]प्पहुदि सुदं सेणावइणा जण्णतुरंगरक्खणे णिउत्तो भट्टिदारओ वसमित्तोत्ति तदप्पहुदि तस्स [2]आऊसणिमित्तं [3]अट्ठादमसुवण्णपरिमाणं दक्खिणं देवी दक्खिणीएहिं परिग्गाहेदि । (ख) जुज्जइ । अह कहिं देवी । किं वा अणुचिट्ठदि । (ग) मङ्गलघरे आसणत्था भविअ विजब्भविसआदो भादुणा वीरसेणण पेसिदं लेह[4]करेहिं वाइअमाणं लेहं सुणादि । (घ) को उण विदब्भराअवु[5]त्तन्तो । (ङ) वसीकिदो किल वीरसेणप्पमुहेहिं भत्तुणो विजअदण्डेहिं विदब्भणाहो । मोइदो अ[6] से दाआदो माहवसेणो । दूदो अ तेण महासाराणि र[7]अणवाहणाणि सिप्पआरि[8]आभूइट्ठं परिअणं अ उवाअणीकरिअ भट्टिणो सआसं पेसिदो सुवो किल भट्टारं देक्खिस्सदित्ति । (च) गच्छ । अणुचिट्ठ अत्तणो णिओअं । अहं वि दे[9]वीं पेक्खिस्सं ।

---

१ जदप्पहुदि सेनापदी (०पतिः) वसुमित्रो तद०. २ आउसो णि०. ३ णिक्कसदसु० ४ लिपिअरैः; ०अरेहिं. ५ वुत्तन्तो सुणिअदि (श्रूयते). ६ किल. ७ रअणाणि, ८ सिप्पिदारिआ. ९ देवीए सआसं गच्छह्मि । तुमं वि अत्तणो णिओअं अणुचिट्ठ.

Sārasaka :—Ever since the Queen heard that Prince Vasumitra was appointed the guardian of the sacrificial horse by the General, she has been bestowing on worthy (Brāhmaṇas) *Dakshiṇā* amounting to eighteen *suvarṇas* of gold with the object of securing him long life.

Female Garden-Keeper :—That is proper. But where is the Queen, and what is she engaged in ?

Sārasaka :—Seated on a seat in the sacred Hall, she has been listening to a letter sent to her by her brother, Vīrasena, from the country of the Vidarbha, and read out to her by the clerks (*lit.* writers).

Female Garden-Keeper :—What, then, is the news about the Vidarbha-King ?

Sārasaka :—I hear that the Vidarbha-King has been subjugated by the King's victorious army commanded by Vīrasena and his relation, Mādhavasena, released from captivity ; and the report goes that the ambassador, sent by him to the King with a present of very costly jewels and vehicles and a body of servants consisting mostly of accomplished girls, will see his Majesty to-morrow.

Female Garden-Keeper :—Go ; attend to your mission. I, too, will see the Queen.

(*Exeunt the two.*)

End of the Praveśaka.

अशोकस्य सत्कारः संमानकरणं तत्र व्यापृतया । प्रसूनलक्ष्मीं पुष्पशोभाम् । धर्मासनगतं न्यायासनस्थितम् । वैतालिकौ राज्ञः कालादः बोधकरौ बन्दिविशेषौ । दण्डेन शासनेन ॥ परभृतेत्यादि । हे वरद अभीष्टद । अङ्गवान् शरीरवान् अनङ्ग मदन इव परभृतानां कोकिलानां कलेषु मधुरेषु व्याहारेषु रुतेषु आत्ता कृता रतिः प्रीतिर्येन स आत्तरतिः त्वम् । राजपक्षे परभृतानां सेवकानाम् । बन्दिनामित्यर्थः । व्याहारेषु स्तुतिषु इत्यपि योज्यम् । विदिशा नाम नदी तस्याः तीरयोर्यानि उद्यानानि उपवनानि तेषु मधुं वसन्तं नयसि । यद्वा अङ्गवान् प्रशस्तशरीरवान् त्वम् । अनङ्गः काम इव । आत्ता गृहीता रतिः संतोषः तन्नाम्नी पत्नी च येन सः । विदिशातीरोद्यानेषु परभृतानां

प्रतीहारी—आज्ञप्तास्म्यशोकसत्कारव्यापृतया देव्या । विज्ञापय आर्यपुत्रम् । इच्छाम्यार्यपुत्रेण सहाशोकवृक्षस्य प्रसूनलक्ष्मीं प्रत्यक्षीकर्तुमिति । तद्यावद्धर्मासनगतं देवं प्रतिपालयामि। (इति परिक्रामति ।) (क)

(नेपथ्ये वैतालिकौ ।)

प्रथमः—दिष्टया [1]दण्डेनारिशिरःसु वर्तते देवः।

परभृतकलव्याहारेषु त्वमात्तरतिर्मधुं
नयसि विदिशातीरोद्यानेष्वनङ्ग इवाङ्गवान्।
विजयकरिणामालानत्वं गतैः प्रबलस्य ते
वरद वरदारोधोवृक्षैः सहावनतो रिपुः ॥ १ ॥

द्वितीयः—

विरचितपदं वीरप्रीत्यासुरोपम सूरिभि-
श्चरितमुभयोर्मध्येकृत्य स्थितं क्रथकैशिकान्।
तव हृतवतो दण्डानीकैर्विदर्भपतेः श्रियं
परिघगुरुभिर्दोर्भिः शौरेः[3] प्रसह्य च रुक्मिणीम् ॥ २ ॥

(क) आणत्तह्मि असोअसक्कारवावुदाए देवीए । विण्णावेहि अज्जउत्तं । इच्छम्हि अज्जउत्तेण सह असोअरुक्खस्स पसूनलच्छिं पचक्खीकादुंति । ता जाव धम्मासणगदं देवं पडिवालेमि ।

कोकिलानां बन्दिनीं च कलव्याहारेषु मधुं वसन्तं माधुर्यं च नयसि । परभृतेति उद्यानविशेषणं वा । किं च प्रबलस्य ते तव विजयकरिणां विजयहस्तिनां आलानत्वं बन्धनस्तम्भत्वं गतैः । आलानांकैरुपोढबलस्येति पाठे उपोढबलस्य उपोढं वृद्धिं गतं बलं सामर्थ्यं यस्य तस्य प्रकृष्टसामर्थ्यस्य ते आलानमङ्कः चिह्नं येषां तैः । आलानांकैर्बन्धनः शृंखलचिह्नितैः । इत्यर्थः । 'आलानं बन्धस्तम्भेऽथ शृंखले' इत्यमरः । वरदारोधोवृक्षैर्वरदा नाम विदर्भदेशस्था काचिन्नदी तस्या रोधसि स्थिता वृक्षा रोधोवृक्षास्तैस्तीरस्थतरुभिः सह रिपुः वैदर्भः अवनतः नम्रतां गतः। उत्तरार्धे सहोक्तिरलंकारः। हरिणी वृत्तम् ॥ १ ॥ विरचितेत्यादि । हे सुरोपम देवतुल्य । परिघगुरुभिः

---

१ दण्डेनैव, दण्डैरेव रिपुशि०. २ मालानांकैरुपोढबलस्य. ३ विष्णोः. ४ एतन्नास्ति क्वचित्. ५ वत्सलाए. ६ रुक्खप्पसू०. ७ कुसुम.

(*Enter the* Female Door-keeper.)

Female Door-Keeper:—I am ordered by the Queen engaged in the work of doing honour to the As'oka, thus—'Inform my husband that I wish to see, accompained by him, the wealth (or, the beauty) of flowers of the Aśoka tree.' I will then just wait for His Majesty now seated on his judgement-seat (engaged in dispensing justice). (*She walks about.*)

(Two Bards *behind the scenes*)

First Bard :—

Happily your Majesty tramples upon the heads of your enemies by means of your army (or, by inflicting punishment on them) alone.

You, taking delight in (delightfully enjoying) the sweet notes of the cuckoos, pass your time, like the god of love in a bodily form, in the gardens on the banks of the Vidis'ā; while your enemy, O you bestower of boons, has bent down, together with the trees on the banks of the Varadā, which served as tie-posts to the victorious elephants of you, the mighty one. (1)

Second Bard :—

O god-like one (*lit.* one comparable to a god), the exploits of the two, achieved over the Kratha-Kais'ikas, have been reduced to composition (celebrated in song) by poets through their love of heroes (heroic valour) : Of you, who have taken away the royalty of the King of Vidarbha by means of your military forces, and of S'auri (Krishna) who forcibly carried away Rukmiṇī by his arms as strong (or stout) as the fastening bars of a city-gate. (2)

परिघास्त्रवद् दृढैः अर्गलादीर्घैरिति वा। प्रसह्य हठात् रुक्मिणीं हृतवतः शौरेः। शूरस्य गोत्रापत्यं पुमान् शौरिः कृष्णः तस्य। दण्डानीकैः शासकसेनाभिः विदर्भपतेः श्रियं प्रसह्य बलात् हृतवतः तव च। उभयोः चरितं सूरिभिः कविभिः वीरप्रीत्या शूरप्रीत्या विरचितानि पदानि शब्दाः यत्र तथाभूतं सत्। क्रथकैशिकान् विदर्भदेशान् मध्येकृत्य। आक्रम्येत्यर्थः। 'मध्ये पदे निवचने च' इति गतिसंज्ञायां 'कुगतिप्रादयः' इति समासः। समासानन्तरं 'समासेऽनञ्पूर्वे क्त्वो ल्यप्' इति ल्यबादेशः

प्रतीहारी—एष जयशब्दसूचितप्रस्थानो भर्तेत एवागच्छति। अहमपि तावदस्य प्रमुखात्किंचिदपसृत्यैतन्मुखालिन्दतोरणं समाश्रिता भवामि। (इत्येकान्ते स्थिता।) (क)

(ततः[1] प्रविशति सवयस्यो राजा।)

राजा—

कान्तां विचिन्त्य सुलभेतरसंप्रयोगां
श्रुत्वा विदर्भपतिमानमितं बलैश्च।
धाराभिरातप इवाभिहतं सरोजं
दुःखायते च[2] हृदयं सुखमश्नुते च॥ २॥

(क) एसो जअसद्दसूइदप्पत्थाणो भट्टा इदो एव्व आअच्छदि। अहं वि दाव इमस्स पमुहा[3]दो किंवि ओसरिअ[4] एदं मुहालिन्दतोरणं समस्सिदा होमि।

"अत्र गुणोत्कृष्टेन विष्णुना राज्ञः समीकरणात्तुल्ययोगितालंकारः। तदुक्तं-'गुणोत्कृष्टैः समीकृत्य वचोऽन्या तुल्ययोगिता।' इति। रत्नाकरदर्पणकारादीनां मते तु अत्र प्रकृताप्रकृतयोः समस्तत्वान्नायमलंकारः। तैरिह व्यस्तयोरेव प्रकृताप्रकृतयोः प्रयोजकतास्वीकारात्। अतस्तेषां मते दीपकमेवेदम्। तदुक्तं-प्रकृतानां चेतरेषामौपम्यं गम्यते यदि। समानधर्मसम्बन्धात् दीपकम्" 'इति' इति अ० रा०। हरिणी वृत्तम्॥ १॥ जय इति शब्दो जयशब्दः तेन सूचितं प्रस्थानं यस्य सः। मुखे स्थितमलिन्दं मुखालिन्दं तस्य तोरणम्। कान्तां विचिन्त्येत्यादि। कान्तां मालविकां सुलभेतरसंप्रयोगां सुलभादितरो दुर्घट इत्यर्थः संप्रयोगः प्राप्त्युपायो यस्याः ताम्। दुर्लभसमागमाम्। विचिन्त्य विदर्भपतिं मम बलैः सैन्यैः आनमितं वशीकृतं च श्रुत्वा। आतपे सूर्यप्रकाशे स्थितं धाराभिः वृष्टिपातैः अभिहतं ताडितं च सरोजमिव मम हृदयम्। एकस्य विषादहेतुत्वात् दुःखायते। 'सुखादिभ्यः कर्तृवेदनायाम्' इति क्यङ्। अपरस्य हर्षहेतुत्वात् सुखमश्नुते अनुभवति च। उपमासंकीर्णः यथासंख्यमलंकारः। वसन्ततिलका वृत्तम्॥ २॥

---

१ प्रविश्य सवयस्यः. २ मम मनः ३ हालोआदो (आलोकात्) ४० रिखम्भान्तरिदा होमि.

Female Door-keeper :—Here is the King coming just in this direction, his departure being indicated by the words of victory (wishing); I, on my part, will move a little out of his direct path and will station myself under the arch of this front terrace. *(She stands aside.)*

(Enter the **King** *with his* **Friend.)**

King :—

As I think of my beloved as being one, union with whom is other than easy (hard to attain), and hear that the King of the Vidarbhas is subdued by my armies, my heart, like a lotus in the sun beaten by showers, experiences pain and at the same time enjoys pleasure. (3)

अत्र मालविकारूपबीजानुसंधानात्संधिर्नाम निर्वहणसंध्यङ्गमुक्तं भवति । एकान्तमत्यन्तं सुखमस्य संजातमिति सुखितः । कथमिवेति प्रश्ने । अत्र कार्यान्वेषणाद्विरोधो नाम संध्यङ्गमुक्तं भवति । प्रसाधनगर्वमहमेव प्रसाधिका अलंकर्त्रीत्येवंरूपम् । वैदर्भं विदर्भदेशीयम् । विदर्भदेशीयानां प्रसाधनविधौ प्रसिद्धत्वात् । विवाहसंबन्धि नेपथ्यमलंकरणम् । तत्रभवती धारिणीत्यर्थः । अत्र कार्योपदर्शनात्पूर्वभावो नाम संध्यङ्गमुक्तं भवति । मदपेक्षानुवृत्त्या मदिच्छानुकूलवर्तनेन । निवृत्ता ईर्ष्या यस्याः तस्याः । यथार्हश्चासौ संमानश्च तेन सुखितम् । मालविका पुरोगा अग्रेसरी यस्य तेन । परिवृत्तं गतं यौवनं तारुण्यं यस्य स तथोक्तः । **अग्रे विकीर्णेत्यादि ।** अग्रे पुरतः । विकीर्णानि कुरबकाणि कुरण्टकपुष्पाणि यत्र तत् विकीर्णकुरबकं च फलजालकेन भिद्यमानाः भिन्ना दृश्यमानाः सहकारा यत्र तच्च तथोक्तम् । यद्वा विकीर्णानां कुरबकाणां फलजालकेन भिद्यमानाः सहकारा यत्र तच्च तथोक्तम् । परिणामस्य अभिमुखं समाप्तमध्यावस्थं ऋतोः यौवनं चेतः उत्सुकयति सोत्कण्ठं करोति । आर्या वृत्तम् ॥४॥ दत्तनेपथ्यः कृतभूषणः । प्रसवमन्थरः प्रसवे पुष्पधारेण मन्थरः अलसः । **सर्वाशोकेत्यादि ।** प्रथमं वसन्तावतारारम्भे सूचितः ज्ञापितः वसन्तस्य विभवः पुष्पादिसंपत्तिर्यैः तेषाम् । सर्वे च ते अशोकतरवस्तेषां कुसुमानि । निर्वृत्तः दोहदः नारीपादाघातरूपः यस्य स निर्वृत्तदोहदः तस्मिन् अस्मिन् पुरो दृश्यमाने तपनीयाशोके संक्रान्तानि इव । अस्य कुसुमातिशये सर्वेषां पुष्पाणामेकत्र समावेशकल्पनया क्रियो-

विदूषकः—यथाहं पश्यामि तथैकान्तसुखितो भवान्भविष्यति। (क)

राजा—कथमिव।

विदूषकः—अद्य किल देव्या पण्डितकौशिकी भणिता। भगवति यत्त्वं प्रसाधनगर्वं वहसि तद्दर्शय मालविकायाः शरीरे वैदर्भ विवाहनेपथ्यमिति। तया च सविशेषालंकृता मालविका। तत्रभवती कदाचित्पूरयेद्भवतोऽपि मनोरथम्। (ख)

राजा—सखे मदपेक्षानुवृत्त्या[1] निवृत्तेर्ष्याया धारिण्याः पूर्वचरितैः संभाव्यते[2] एतत्।

प्रतीहारी—(उपगम्य।) जयतु भर्ता। देवी विज्ञापयति। तपनीयाशोकस्य कुसुमसौभाग्यदर्शनेन ममारम्भः सफलः क्रियतामिति। (ग)

राजा—ननु तत्रैव देवी[3]।

प्रतीहारी—अथ किम्। यथार्हसंमानसुखितमन्तःपुरं विसृज्य मालविकापुरोगेणात्मनः परिजनेन सह देवं प्रतिपालयति। (घ)

(क) जह अहं पेक्खामि[4] तह एकन्त[5]सुहिदो भवं हविस्सदि। (ख) अज्ज किल देवीए[6] पण्डितकोसिकी भणिदा। भअवदि जं तुमं पसाहणगव्वं[7] वहसि तं दंसेहि मालविआए सरीरे वेदब्भ[8]अं विवाहणेवच्छन्ति[9]। तोए[10] अ[11] सविसेसालंकिदा मालविआ। तत्तहोदी कदावि पूरेइ भवदोवि मणोरहं। (ग) जेदु[12] भट्टा। देवी विण्णावेदि। तवणीआसोअस्स कुसुमसोह[13]ग्गदंसणेण मह आरम्भो सफलो[14] करीअदुत्ति। (घ) अह इं। जहारहसंमाण[15]सुहिअं अन्तेउरं[16] विसज्जिअ मालविआपुरोएण अत्तणो परिअणेण सहं[17] देवं पडिवालेदि।

---

१ मदपेक्षानुवृत्त्याप्यनया धारिण्या पूर्वा०; मदपेक्षामनुसृत्य-प्राप्य. २ एवैतत्. ३ तिष्ठति. ४ देक्खामि. ५ सव्वहा ए०. ६ देवीए एव्वं धारिणीए. ७ णेउणं (नैपुण्यं). ८ तत्तभोदीए मा०. ९ नास्त्येतत्क्वचित्. १० तदो ताए. ११ वि. १२ जेदु जेदु. १३ सोहा (शोभा); कुसुमोग्गमसिरिं अज्जउत्तेण सह पच्चक्खीकादुं इच्छामित्ति. १४ सफलीक. १५ संमाणण; यथार्हं संमान्य सर्वं. १६ उरजणं. १७ पण्डिदकोसिकीए समं.

Vidūṣaka :—As far as I see, your Highness will be entirely happy.

King :—How do you mean ?

Vidūṣaka :—To-day, as I hear, the Queen said to the learned Kaus'ikī—'Revered lady, since you pride yourself upon (your skill in) decoration, display on Mālavikā's person the wedding-dress in the fashion that prevails in the Vidarbha country.' She too decked Mālavikā in a special style. Her ladyship may perhaps gratify your desire.

King :—Friend, this seems to be possible, judging from the past acts of Dhāriṇī, who has forgone her jealousy on account of her acting (her desire to act) in a way conformable to my wishes.

Female Door-Keeper :—(*Approaching*) Victory to your Majesty ! The Queen sends this message—'May my endeavour be brought to a successful termination by your beholding the splendour of flowers of the golden As'oka'.

King :—Is the Queen *there* ?

Door-Keeper :—Yes (Sire). Having dismissed the ladies of the harem who were happy at their being honoured in accordance with their ranks, she has been waiting for Your Majesty, accompanied by her attendants with Mālavikā as the foremost of them.

त्प्रेक्षालंकारः । आर्याजातिः ॥ ५ ॥ विश्रब्धः मालविकाप्राप्तिविषये विश्वस्तः । संनिहितेषु समीपस्थेषु । पार्श्वपरिवर्तिनीं तस्याः पार्श्वे अवस्थानमित्यर्थः । **मामियमित्यादि** । इयं देवी धारिणी प्रियया मालविकया विनयात्सविनयमुपस्थिताऽनुवर्तमाना । अनूत्थिता इति पाठे देवीमुत्थितामनूत्थितेत्यर्थः । विस्मृतं हस्ते वर्तमानं कमलं यया तया विस्मृतहस्तकमलया नरेन्द्रलक्ष्म्या राजलक्ष्म्या उपस्थिता वसुमती भूदेवी इव मामभ्युत्तिष्ठति अभ्युत्थानेनं संभावयति । विस्तृतहस्तकमलयेति पाठे विस्तृतं हस्त एव कमलं यस्याः । पक्षे विस्तृतं हस्तवर्ति कमलं

राजा—(सहर्षं[1] विदूषकं विलोक्य ।) जयसेने गच्छाग्रतः ।

प्रतीहारी—इत इतो देवः । (सर्वे परिक्रामन्ति ।) (क)

विदूषकः—(विलोक्य ।) भो वयस्य किंचित्परिवृत्तयौवन इव वसन्तः प्रमदवने लक्ष्यते । (ख)

राजा—यथाह[1] भवान् ।

> **अग्रे विकीर्णकुरबकफलजालकैर्भिद्यमानसहकारम्[2] ।**
> **परिणामाभिमुखमृतोरुत्सुकयति यौवनं चेतः ॥ ४ ॥**

विदूषकः—(परिक्रम्य ।) भो अयं स दत्तनेपथ्य इव कुसुमस्तबकैस्तपनीयाशोकः । अवलोकयतु भवान् । (ग)

राजा—स्थाने खल्वयं प्रसवमन्थरोऽभूत् । यदिदानीमनन्यसाधारणीं शोभामुद्वहति । पश्य ।

> **सर्वाशोकतरूणां[3] प्रथमं सूचितवसन्तविभवानाम् ।**
> **निर्वृत्तदोहदेऽस्मिन्संक्रान्तानीव कुसुमानि[4] ॥ ५ ॥**

विदूषकः—भोः विस्रब्धो भव । अस्मासु संनिहितेष्वपि धारिणी पार्श्वपरिवर्तिनीं मालविकामनुमन्यते । (घ)

(क) इदो[5] इदो देवो । (ख) भो वअस्स किंचि[6] परिवुत्तजोव्वणो विअ वसन्तो पमदवणे लक्खीअदि । (ग) भो[7] अअं सो दिण्णणेवच्छो विअ कुसुमत्थवएहिं तवणीआसोओ । ओलोअदु भवं । (घ) भो[8] विसद्धो होहि । अह्मेसु संणिहिदेसु[9] वि धारिणी पासपरिवट्टिणीं मालविअं अणुमण्णेदि[10] ।

---

१ यथावृत्तं भवानाह. २ विभि०, विभज्य०, कहीय०. ३ लतानां. ४ मुकुलानि. ५ एदु, एदु, ६. किंवि. ७ अहो. ८ तह । भो. ९ उवगतेसु. १० अणुणेदि.

King :—(*Looking joyfully at the* Vidūṣaka) Jayasenā, lead the way.

Female Door-Keepr :—This way, this way, Your Majesty. (*All walk on*).

Vidūṣaka:—(*Looking on*) Friend, the Spring appears to be a little past his youth in the pleasure-garden.

King:—It is as you say.

The youth of the season, in which the Kurabaka flowers are scattered here and there and the Mango-trees are bursting out with their fruit in the front, and which is approaching its end, creates longing in the mind. (4)

Vidūṣaka :—(*Turning round*) Oh! Here is the golden Aśoka, furnished with ornaments as it were by (in the form of) its bunches of flowers. May Your Honour look at it.

King :—Rightly, indeed, was this Aśoka slow in putting forth flowers, since it presents an uncommon beauty (of flowers) now. Observe—

The flowers of all (other) Aśoka trees, which first indicated the glory of Spring, are, as it were, transferred to it, its longing being gratified. (5)

Vidūṣaka :—Oh, be of good cheer. Though we are near, Dhāriṇī allows Mālavikā to be by her side.

यस्या इति योज्यम् । नरेन्द्रलक्ष्म्येत्युपमानेन मालविकाया भाग्यातिशयो ध्वनितः । वसुमतीवेति धारिण्याः क्षमाशीलता सूचिता । उपमालंकारः । आर्याजातिः ॥ ६ ॥ कौतुकं विवाहोत्सवस्तत्संबन्धी अलंकारो नेपथ्यविधानं तस्य । बिसिन्यः कमलिन्याः पत्रगतं पत्रस्थितम् । दक्षिणादितरद् दक्षिणेतरद् वाममित्यर्थः । वामनयनस्फुरणे-नेष्टलाभः सूचितः । **अनतिलम्बीत्यादि** । नातिलम्बिते इत्यनातलम्बि यद् दुकूलं क्षौमं तन्निवस्ते परिधत्त इति निवासिनी । इयं मालविका बहुभिः आभरणैः युक्ता मे प्रतिभाति । केवेत्याह । गतमपसृतं हिमं कान्तिप्रतिबन्धकं तुहिनं येषां

राजा—(सहर्षम् ।) सखे पश्य ।

मामियमभ्युत्तिष्ठति देवी विनयादुपस्थिता[1] प्रियया ।
विस्मृत[2]हस्तकमलया नरेन्द्रलक्ष्म्या वसुमतीव ॥ ६ ॥

(ततः प्रविशति धारिणी[3] परिव्राजिका मालविका विभवतश्च परिवारः ।)

मालविका—(आत्मगतम् ।) जानामि निमित्तं कौतुकालंकारस्य । तथापि बिसिनीपत्रगतमिव सलिलं वेपते मे हृदयम् । अपि च दक्षिणेतरदपि मे नयनं बहुशः स्फुरति । (क)

विदूषकः—भो वयस्य विवाहनेपथ्येन सविशेषं खलु शोभते अत्रभवती मालविका । (ख)

राजा—पश्याम्येनाम्[4] । यैषा

अनतिलम्बिदुकूलनिवासिनी बहुभि[5]राभरणैः प्रतिभाति मे ।
उडुगणैरुदयोन्मुखचन्द्रिका[6] गत[7]हिमैरिव चैत्रविभावरी ॥ ७ ॥

देवी—(उपेत्य[8] ।) जयत्वार्यपुत्रः । (ग)

(क) जाणामि णिमित्तं कोदु[9]आलंकारस्स । तह वि बिसिणीपत्त[10]गदं विअ सलिलं वेवदि मे हिअअं । अवि अ दक्खिणेदरं वि मे णअणं[11] बहुसो फुरदि । (ख) भो[12] वअस्स विवाहणेवच्छेण सविसेसं खु सोहदि अत्तहोदि मालविआ । (ग) जेदु अज्जउत्तो ।

तैः उडुगणैः नक्षत्रसमूहैः युक्ता । उदयोन्मुखी आसन्नोदयोत्यर्थः । चन्द्रिका यस्य तथाभूता चैत्रविभावरी चेत्ररात्रिः इव । उपमालंकारः । द्रुतविलम्बितं वृत्तम् ॥ ७ ॥

---

१ अनूत्थिता, वचनादनुस्थिता. २ विस्तृत. ३ देवी. ४ पश्याम्याभरणालंकृतामेनाम्. ५ लघुभि. ६ कामुदी. ७ हत. ८ उपसृत्य. ९ मह कोदु०. १० पुक्खरपत्तगम्भगअसलिलं; पुक्खरपत्तगअं. ११ णअणं पप्फु०. १२ भो असंदेहं वेबाहिअ.

King :—*(Joyfully)* See, friend,

Here is the Queen rising up to receive me, respectfully waited upon by my beloved, like the earth attended by the goddess of royalty that has forgotten to take the (sportive) lotus in her hand. (6)

(Enter Dhāriṇī, Parivrājikā, Mālavikā, *and the* Attendants *according to their respective ranks.)*

Mālavikā :—*(To herself)* I know the reason of my (being decked with the) wedding dress; and yet my heart trembles like the water lying on a lotus-leaf, and at the same time my left eye throbs repeatedly.

Vidūṣaka :—O friend, her ladyship Mālavikā appears all the more beautiful in her nuptial dress.

King :— I see her, who,—

Clothed in a silk garment not much hanging down, appears to me with her many ornaments like a night in the month of Caitra, with the constellations of stars (clearly displayed) being free from frost and with the moon about to rise. (7)

Queen :—*(Approaching)* Victory to my husband!

तरुणीजनः सहायः सहचरः यस्य तस्य तव । संकेतगृहं रतिसंकेतस्थानम् । त्वामत्र प्रियजनेन संगमयितुमिच्छाम इति ध्वनितोर्थः । व्रीडया व्रीडेन वा सहितं यथा तथा सव्रीडं सलज्जम् । अशोकमिति 'अभितःपरित' इत्यादिना द्वितीया । **नायं देव्या इत्यादि** । अयमशोकः देव्या ईदृशानां सत्काराणां संकेतकरणरूपसंमानानां भाजनत्वं पात्रतां न नेय इति न । अपि तु नेय एव । द्वौ नञौ प्रकृतार्थदार्ढ्यं गमयतः । यः अशोकः माधवश्रिया वसन्तलक्ष्म्या नियोगे कुसुमधारणरूपे सावज्ञः कृतावमाननः सन् त्वत्प्रयत्ने दोहदपूरणरूपे पुष्पैः प्रसमृद्धया आदरं शंसति । त्वत्प्रयत्ने दर्शितादरस्यास्य त्वया संमानकरणमत्यन्त-

विदूषकः—वर्धतां भवती । (क)

परिव्राजिका—विजयतां देवः ।

राजा—भगवति अभिवादये ।

परिव्राजिका—अभिप्रेतसिद्धिरस्तु ।

देवी—(सस्मितम् ।) आर्यपुत्र एष तेऽस्माभिस्तरुणीजनसहायस्याशोकः संकेतगृहं कल्पितः । (ख)

विदूषकः—भोः आराधितोऽसि । (ग)

राजा—(सव्रीडमशोकमभितः परिक्रामति ।)

नायं देव्या भाजनत्वं न नेयः सत्काराणामीदृशानामशोकः ।
यः सावज्ञो माधवश्रीनियोगे पुष्पैः शंसत्यादरं त्वत्प्रयत्ने[1] ॥ ८ ॥

विदूषकः—भो विस्रब्धो भूत्वा त्वं यौवनवतीमिमां पश्य । (घ)

देवी—काम् । (ङ)

विदूषकः—भवति तपनीयाशोकस्य कुसुमशोभाम् । (च)

(सर्वे उपविशन्ति ।)

राजा—(मालविकां विलोक्य । आत्मगतम् ।) कष्टः खलु संनिधिवियोगः[2] ।

(क) वड्ढदु भोदी । (ख) अज्जउत्त एस ते अह्मेहिं तरुणीजणसहाअस्स असोओ संकेदघरो[3] कप्पिदो । (ग) भो आराहिओसि । (घ) भो वीसद्धो भविअ तुमं जोव्वणवदिं इमं पेक्ख । (ङ) कं । (च) भोदि तवणीआसोअस्स कुसुमसोहम् ।

---

१ यत्प्रयत्ने. २ वियोगो ममाद्य; कष्टं खलु ममाद्य संनिहितस्यापि विप्रयोगः । ३ घरअं, गेहक्को.

Vidūṣaka :—May Your Highness prosper !

Parivrājikā :—May the King be victorious !

King :—Revered lady, I bow to you.

Parivrājikā :—May you gain your desired object !

Queen :—(*With a smile*) My lord, this Aśoka here is intended by us a rendezvous for you, accompanied by the young ladies (of the harem).

Vidūṣaka :—Oh, you are propitiated.

King :—(*Walking round the Aśoka bashfully*)

It is not that this Aśoka should not be made the object of such honours by your ladyship; this (Aśoka) though treating with contempt the command of the goddess of vernal beauty, has shown its regard for your effort by bursting into flowers. (8)

Vidūṣaka :—O friend, being free from apprehension, look at this, full of youth.

Queen :—At whom ?

Vidūṣaka :—Lady, (I mean) the splendour of the blossom of the golden Aśoka.

(All *sit down.*)

King :—(*Looking at* Mālavikā ; *to himself*) Painful, indeed, is separation-in-presence.

मुचितमेवेति भावः। अत्र पूर्वार्धार्थे उत्तरार्धार्थस्य हेतुत्वात्काव्यलिङ्गमलंकारः। शालिनी वृत्तम् ॥ ८॥ इमां मालविकामिति विदूषकस्याभिप्रेतोर्थः। संनिधिवियोगः संनिधौ सामीप्ये वियोगः। अहं रथाङ्गेत्यादि। अहं रथाङ्गस्य चक्रस्य नाम यस्य स रथाङ्गनामा चक्रवाक इव। मे प्रिया मालविका सहचरी चक्रवाकी इव। नौ आवयोः अननुज्ञातसंपर्का अननुज्ञातः अननुमतः संपर्कः संगमो यया सा धारिणी रजनीव। उपमालंकारः। सा च पूर्वार्धे सामान्यधर्मानुपादानात् लुप्ता।

अहं रथाङ्गनामेव प्रिया सहचरीव मे ।
अनुज्ञातसंपर्का धारिणी रजनीव नौ ॥ ९ ॥

(प्रविश्य[1] ।)

कञ्चुकी[2]—विजयतां[3] देवः । देव अमात्यो विज्ञापयति । तस्मिन् विदर्भविषयोपायने[4] द्वे शिल्पकारिके मार्गपरिश्रमादलघुशरीरे[5] इति[6] पूर्वं न प्रवेशिते । संप्रति देवोपस्थानयोग्ये[7] संवृत्ते । तदाज्ञां देवो दातुमर्हतीति ।

राजा—प्रवेशय ते ।

कञ्चुकी—यदाज्ञापयति देवः । (इति निष्क्रम्य ताभ्यां सह पुनः प्रविश्य ।) इत इतो भवत्यौ ।

प्रथमा—(जनान्तिकम् ।) सखि मदनिके अपूर्वमपीदं राजकुलं प्रविशन्त्याः प्रसीदति मे हृदयम् । (क)

द्वितीया—ज्योत्स्निके ममाप्येवमेव । अस्ति खलु लोकप्रवादः आगामि सुखं दुःखं वा हृदयसमवस्था कथयतीति । (ख)

प्रथमा—स सत्य इदानीं भवतु । (ग)

कञ्चुकी—एष देव्या सह देवस्तिष्ठति । उपसर्पतां भवत्यौ ।

(उभे उपसर्पतः ।)

(मालविका परिव्राजिका च चेट्यौ दृष्ट्वा परस्परमवलोकयतः ।)

(क) हला मदणिए[8] अपुव्वंवि इमं राअउलं पविसन्तीए पसीददी मे हिअअं । (ख) जोसिणीए[9] महवि एव्वं एव । अत्थि खु लोअप्पवादो[10] [11] आआमि सुहं दुक्खं वा हिअअसमवत्था कहेदित्ति । (ग) सो सच्चो दाणिं[12] होदु ।

---

१ ततः प्रविशति कञ्चुकी. २ काञ्चुकेयः. ३ जयतु जयत. ४ विदर्भराजोपायने. ५ अलसशरीरे. ६ इति कृत्वा. ७ स्थाने. ८ रअणिए. ९ अब्भन्तरगदो अप्पा. १० हंजे जो०. ११ कोअवादो. १२ दाणिं णो.

I am like the bird Cakravāka ; my beloved is like my mate ; while Dhāriṇī, who does not permit our union, is like the night (that separates us). (9)

(*Enter* Chamberlain.)

Chamberlain :—Victory to Your Majesty ! My Lord, the minister begs to say—'Two girls skilled in arts, out of the present sent from the Vidarbha country, were not sent to Your Majesty, as they were thought not to be in good trim of body owing to the fatigue of the journey. Now, they have become (are in a state) fit for appearing before Your Majesty. Your Majesty, therefore, will be pleased to give the order with respect to them.'

King :—Introduce them.

Chamberlain :—As your Majesty commands. (*Going out and returning with them*) This way, this way, ladies.

First :—(*Aside*) Friend, Madanikā, my inner soul is pleased (delighted), as I enter this novel royal palace.

Second :—Jyotsnikā, mine too feels (delighted) in the same way. There is a popular saying that the state of the heart indicates the coming happiness or misery.

First :—May it prove true now !

Chamberlain :—Here is His Majesty sitting with the Queen. Your ladyships may now enter.

(*Both go forth.*)

(Mālavikā *and the* Parivrājikā look *at each other on seeing the maids.*)

उत्तरार्धे पूर्णा । पथ्यावक्त्रं वृत्तम् ॥ ९ ॥ विदर्भविषयाद्विदर्भदेशादागते उपायने । अलघु असुन्दरं जडं वा शरीरं ययोस्ते । देवोपस्थानयोग्ये देवस्य राज्ञस्तव उपस्थाने सेवायां योग्ये । हृदयसमवस्था हृदयस्य दशा । सत्यो भवतु सुखप्राप्त्येत्यर्थः । अभिविनीते शिक्षिते । अभ्यन्तरे लब्धशिक्षे । निपुणे इत्यर्थः । विजयदण्डेजयिनीभिः सेनाभिः । कनीयमी । 'युवाल्पयोः कनन्यतरस्याम्' इति युवशब्दस्य कनादेशः । ईयसुन उगित्वात् ङीप् । पादुकापरिभोगेण उपानहमिवोपयुज्येत्यर्थः । यथा सुरभिचन्दनस्य पादुकात्वनोपयोगोऽत्यन्तं गर्ह्यस्तथा अस्या

उभे—(प्रणिपत्य।) जयतु भर्ता। जयतु भट्टिनी। (क)

(राजाज्ञया उभे उपविष्टे।)

राजा—कस्यां कलायामभिविनीते भवत्यौ।

उभे—भर्तः संगीतेऽभ्यन्तरे स्वः। (ख)

राजा—देवि गृह्यतामनयोरन्यतरा।

देवी—मालविके इतः पश्य। कतरा ते संगीतसहकारिणी रोचते। (ग)

उभे—(मालविकां दृष्ट्वा।) अहो भर्तृदारिका। (प्रणम्य।) जयतु जयतु भर्तृदारिका। (इति तया सह बाष्पं विसृजतः।) (घ)

(सर्वे सविस्मयमवलोकयन्ति।)

राजा—के भवत्यौ। का वेयम्।

उभे—देव इयमस्माकं भर्तृदारिका। (ङ)

राजा—कथमिव।

उभे—शृणोतु भर्ता। यः स भर्त्रा विजयदण्डैर्विदर्भनाथं वशीकृत्य बन्धनान्मोचितः कुमारो माधवसेनो नाम तस्येयं कनीयसी भगिनी मालविका नाम। (च)

देवी—कथं राजदारिकेयम्। चन्दनं खलु मया पादुकापरिभोगेण दूषितम्। (छ)

(क) जेदु भट्टा। जेदु भट्टिणी। (ख) भट्टा संगीदे अब्भन्तरेह्म। (ग) मालविए इदो पक्ख। कदरा ते संगीदसहआरिणी रुच्चदि। (घ) अह्मो भट्टिदारिआ। जेदु जेदु भट्टिदारिआ। (ङ) देव इअं अह्माणं भट्टिदारिआ। (च) सुणादु भट्टा। जो सो भट्टिणो विजअदण्डेहिं विदब्भणाहं वसीकरिअ बन्धणादो मोइओ कुमारो माहवसेणो णाम तस्स इअं कणीअसी भइणी मालविआ णाम। (छ) कहं राअदारिआ इअं। चन्दणं खु मए पादुआपरिभोएण दूसिदं।

---

१ राजनिर्देशात्. २ अभियोगो भवत्योः. ३ प्रणिपत्य. ४ विकिरतः. ५ वा भवत्यौ का चेयम् ६ अस्मात्परं-राजा। स्वागतम्। इतो निषीदतम्। इत्यभिकं काचित्. ७ अभिविर्णादे. ८ देक्ख. ९ ०सहाइणी. १० भट्टा एसा. ११ भट्टिणो. १२ अम्हो. १३ पादुओवणोएण (०कोपयोगेन).

Both :—Victory to the King! Victory to the Queen! *

(Both *sit down by royal order.*)

King :—What are you instructed in?

Both :—Lord, we have got an insight in music.

King :—Queen, take one of these.

Queen :—Mālavikā, look here; which of these you like to have for your companion in music?

Both :—(*Looking at* Mālavikā) Ah, the Princess! *(Bowing)* Victory, victory to the Princess! *(They shed tears along with her.)*

(All *look on in amazement.*)

King :—Who are you, and who is this (lady)?

Both :—Lord, she is our Princess.

King :—What do you mean?

Both :—May Your Majesty listen. This is the younger sister, named Mālavikā of the Prince, Mādhavasena by name, who was released from confinement by Your Majesty, having subdued with your victorious forces the King of Vidarbha.

Queen :—Oh! She is a Princess! I, indeed, defiled sandal wood, then, by using it as (for the purpose of) shoes!

अपि परिचारिकासु नियोजनमिति भावः। इत्थंभूता एतामवस्थां गता। अस्मादृशं दासीरूपम्। उज्झित्वा त्यक्त्वा। गूढमप्रकाशम्। स्वरसंयोगः स्वरसंघटना। तस्या इव अस्याः स्वर आभातीत्यर्थः। दुःखेन असौकर्येण। विभाव्यते अभिज्ञायत। तथागतभ्रातृकां तथागतो बन्धनं प्राप्तो भ्राता यस्यास्ताम्। अपवाह्य अपनीय। भवत्संबन्धापेक्षया भवता यः संबन्धो वैवाहिकस्तदपेक्षया तमुद्दिश्य। पथिकसार्थमध्वगसमूहम्। विदिशा अग्निमित्रस्य राजधानी तां गच्छतीति गामी तम्। गताध्वा गतः आक्रान्तः अध्वा मार्गो येन सः। तूणीरपट्टेत्यादि। तूणी

---

* Some read before this—'King, Welcome to you; sit down.'

राजा—अथात्रभवती कथमित्थंभूता।

मालविका—(निःश्वस्य। आत्मगतम्।) विधिनियोगेन। (क)

द्वितीया—शृणोतु भर्ता। दायादवशंगतेऽस्माकं भर्तृदारके माधवसेने तस्यामात्येन आर्यसुमतिना अस्मादृशं परिजनमुज्झित्वा गूढमपनीतैषा। (ख)

राजा—श्रुतपूर्वं मयैतत्। ततस्ततः।

द्वितीया—एतावदेव। अतः परं न जानीमः। (ग)

परिव्राजिका—अतः परमहं मन्दभाग्या कथयिष्यामि।

उभे—भर्तृदारिके आर्यकौशिक्या इव स्वरसंयोगः। (घ)

मालविका—ननु सैव। (ङ)

उभे—यतिवेषधारिण्यार्यकौशिकी दुःखेन विभाव्यते। भगवति वन्दावहे। (च)

परिव्राजिका—स्वस्ति भवतीभ्याम्।

राजा—कथमाप्तवर्गोऽयं भगवत्याः।

परिव्राजिका—एवमेतत्।

विदूषकः—तेन हि कथयतु भगवत्यत्रभवत्या वृत्तान्तावशेषम्। (छ)

परिव्राजिका—(सवैक्लव्यम्।) श्रूयतां तावत्। माधवसेनसचिवं सुमतिं ममाग्रजमवगच्छ।

(क) विहिणिओएँण। (ख) सुणादु भट्टा। दाआदवसंगदे अम्हाणं भट्टिदारए माहवसेणे तस्स अमच्चेण अज्जसुमदिणा अह्मारिसं परिअणं उज्झिअ गूढं अँवणीदा एसा। (ग) एत्तिअं एव्वँ अदो वरं ण आणीमो। (घ) भट्टिदारिए अज्जकोसिइंए विअ सरसंजोओँ। (ङ) णं सा एव्व। (च) जदिवेसधारिणी अज्जकोसिई दुक्खेण विभावीअदि। भअवदि वन्दाँमो। (छ) तेण हि कहेदुँ भअवदी अत्तहोदीए उत्तँन्तावसेसं।

---

१ एतावत्. २ भागिनी. ३ भवत्याः. ४ विहिणो णि०. ५ आणीदा. ६ भट्टा, भट्टा. एत्तिअं जाणीमो न अदो परम्. ७ जोओ सुणीअदि. ८ णमो दे. ९ कहेदु दाणिं. १० उत्तान्तसेसं, उत्तान्तं दाव असेसम्.

King :—Now, how was her ladyship reduced to this state ?

Mālavikā :—(*Having sighed, to herself*) By the decree of fate.

Second :—May Your Majesty listen. When our Prince Mādhavasena fell into the power of his kinsman, his minister, the revered Sumati, secretly bore her away, leaving off attendants like us.

King :—This was heard by me before. What happened next ?

Second :—Lord, we do no not know what happened after that.

Parivrājikā :—What happened afterwards, I, unlucky that I am, will relate.

Both :—Princess, this voice strikes our ears like that of the revered Kauśikī.

Mālavikā :—Why, this is, indeed, she.

Both :—The revered Kauśikī wearing the dress of an ascetic is recognized with difficulty. Revered lady, we both salute you.

Parivrājikā :—May you fare well !

King :—How now, this is the circle of your Reverence's friends !

Parivrājikā :—It is so.

Vidūṣaka :—Then, your Reverence should narrate the remaining part of her ladyship's account.

Parivrājikā :—(*With emotion*) Listen, then. Know Sumati, the minister of Mādhavasena, to be my elder brother.

रानां शरधीनां पट्टैर्बन्धनवध्रीभिः परिणद्धानि विशालतां गतानि भुजान्तरालानि भुजमध्यभागा यस्य। आकर्णं कर्णौ मर्यादीकृत्य लम्बते इति लम्बी शिखिपिच्छानां कलापस्तस्य धरतीति धारि। कोदण्डानि धनूंषि पाणिषु यस्य तत्कोदण्डपाणि। निनदत् शब्दायमानम्। आपाते प्रथमाभिगमे एव दुष्प्रसहं दुःखेन सोढुं शक्यम्। एवंविधं प्रतिरोधकानां मार्गप्रतिरोधिनामनीकं सैन्यमाविरभूत् प्रादुरासीत्। पिच्छबर्हे नपुंसकम्' इति, 'कलापो भूषणे बर्हे तूणीरे संहतावपि' इति, 'प्रतिरोधि

राजा—उपलब्धम्[1] । ततस्ततः ।

परिव्राजिका—स इमां तथागतभ्रातृकां मया सार्धमपवाह्य भवत्सं-बन्धापेक्षया पथिकसार्थं विदिशा[2]गामिनमनुप्रविष्टः ।

राजा—ततस्ततः ।

परिव्राजिका—स चाटव्य[3]न्ते निविष्टो गताध्वा वणिग्जनो[4] विश्रमितुम् ।

राजा—तत[5]स्ततः ।

परिव्राजिका—ततः ।

तूणीर[6]पट्टपरिण[7]द्धभुजान्तराल-
मार्कर्ण[8]लम्बिशिखिपिच्छ[9]कलापधारि ।
कोदण्डपाणि नि[10]नदत्प्रतिरोधकाना-
मापातदुष्प्रसहमाविरभूदनीकम् ॥ १० ॥

(मालविका भयं रूपयति ।)

विदूषकः—भवति मा बिभेहि । अतिक्रान्तं खलु भगवती कथयति । (क)

राजा—ततस्ततः ।

परिव्राजिका—ततो मुहूर्तं ब[11]द्धयुद्धास्ते पराङ्मुखीकृताः सार्थवाहयो-द्धारस्तस्करैः ।

(क) भोदि मा भआहि । अदिक्कंतं खु भअवदी[12] कहेदि ।

परास्कन्दि' इति चामरः । वसन्ततिलका वृत्तम् ॥ १० ॥ बद्धयुद्धाः बद्धं कृतं युद्धं यैस्ते । कृतयुद्धा इत्यर्थः बद्धायुधा इति पाठे बद्धानि युद्धार्थमायुधानि यैस्ते । सार्थवाहयोद्धारः वणिक्पक्षीया योधाः । इमामित्यादि । दुर्नाते आपदि पराभिम-

---

१ उपलक्षितं-तः; अस्मात्परं-विदू० । एत्तिअं सच्चं । राजा-इत्य० क्वचित्. २ वैदिश ३ ०व्यन्तरे. अटव्यामन्तरे. ४ जनोऽध्वश्रमार्तः; अध्वश्रमान्मार्गे. ५ किं चान्यत्; किं नु भूयः. ६ बन्ध; बद्ध. ७ ०परिबद्ध. ८ आपार्ष्णि. ९ बर्हकलापशोभि. १० विनदत् ११ प्रतिबद्ध-बद्धायुधाः. १२ अत्र-तत्त-भोदी.

King :—Known, proceed.

Parivrājikā :—He having carried off this Princess, whose brother had fared in that way, together with me, joined a body of travellers (caravan) that were going to Vidiśā, with the object of forming a matrimonial alliance with you.

King :—What next ?

Parivrājikā :—That body of merchants, after having performed the day's journey, encamped in a forest to rest.

King :—And then ?

Parivrājikā :—Then,

There appeared a host of waylayers, bow in hand and shouting, whose chests (*lit.* spaces between the arms) were covered with the quiver-straps, who wore plumes of peacock's feathers that hung down to their ears and who were irresistible at the first onset (or, charge). (10)

(Mālāvikā *manifests fear.*)

Vidūṣaka :—Do not be afraid; the revered lady is relating a past event.

King :—What next ?

Parivrājikā :—Then the warriors on the side of the merchants, after fighting for a short while, were repulsed by the robbers.

वकातराम् । परेषां शत्रूणां शत्रुकृत इत्यर्थः । यद्वा परैः अभिभवः आक्रमणं तस्मात्कातरां भीतामिमां मालविकां परीप्सुः पर्याप्तुं परित्रातुमिच्छुः । 'आप्ज्ञप्यृधामीत्' इतीत्वम् । 'अत्रलोपोऽभ्यासस्य' इत्यभ्यासलोपः । 'पर्याप्तिः स्यात्परित्राणं हस्तधारणमित्यपि' इत्यमरः । भर्तृप्रियः स्वामिभक्तः । प्रियैरिष्टैः प्रयत्नेन रक्षणीयैरपि आसुभिः प्राणैर्भर्तुः अनृणस्य भावः आनृण्यमनृणत्वं गतः प्राप्तः । आत्मनः भर्तृदत्तं पालनरूपमृणं तद्दुहितृरक्षणे स्वप्राणव्ययेन निरयातयत् । मृत इति भावः ॥ ११ ॥ तनुभृतां देहिनाम् । तनुत्यजामिति पाठे तनुं त्यजन्ति म्रियन्ते इति तनुत्यजो मर्त्यास्तेषामित्यर्थः । लोकयात्रा लोकस्थितिः । सफलीकृतो भर्तृपिण्डो भर्तृदत्तं

राजा—भगवति अतः परमिदानीं कष्टं श्रोतव्यम्।

परिव्राजिका—ततः स मत्सोदर्यः।

इमां परीप्सुर्दुर्जाते पराभिभवकातराम्।
भर्तृप्रियः प्रियैर्भर्तुरानृण्यमसुभिर्गतः ॥ ११ ॥

प्रथमा—हा हतः सुमतिः। (क)

द्वितीया—अतः खलु भर्तृदारिकाया इयं समवस्था संवृत्ता। (ख)

(परिव्राजिका बाष्पं विसृजति।)

राजा—भगवति तनुभृतामीदृशी लोकयात्रा। न शोच्यस्तत्रभवान्सफलीकृतभर्तृपिण्डः। ततस्ततः।

परिव्राजिका—ततोऽहं मोहमुपगता यावत्संज्ञामुपलभे तावदियं दुर्लभदर्शना संवृत्ता।

राजा—महत्खलु कृच्छ्रमनुभूतं भगवत्या।

परिव्राजिका—ततो भ्रातुः शरीरमग्निसात्कृत्वा पुनर्नवीभूतवैधव्यदुःखया मया त्वदीयं देशमवतीर्येमे काषाये गृहीते।

राजा—युक्तः सज्जनस्यैष पन्थाः। ततस्ततः।

परिव्राजिका—तत इयमप्याटविकेभ्यो वीरसेनं वीरसेनाच्च देवीं गता देवीगृहे लब्धप्रवेशया मया पुनर्दृष्टा। इत्येतदवसानं कथायाः।

(क) हा हदो सुमती। (ख) अदो खु भट्टिदारिआए ईअं समवत्था संवुत्ता।

वेतनं येन सः दुर्लभं दर्शनं यस्यास्तथाभूता। केनाप्यपहृतेत्यर्थः कृच्छ्रं कष्टम्। अग्निसात्कृत्वा दग्ध्वेत्यर्थः। पुनः भ्रातृमरणेन। काषाये कषायेण वर्णेन रञ्जिते वाससी परिगृहीते परिव्राजिकात्वं स्वीकृतम्। आटविकेभ्यः वनचरेभ्यः। तस्क-

---

१ हन्त इतः परं कष्टतरं. २ सुमतिः. ३ दुर्जातेः. ४ विकिरति. ५ लज्जां. ६ शोचितव्यः. ७ प्रतिज्ञः. ८ कष्टं. भ्रातृ. १० ०कुत. ११ त्वदीयदेश. १२ सेयं. १३ अहो; हंहो गदो तादो मरणम्; हदो तादो अज्जसुमदी अम्हाणम्. १४ एआरिसी.

King :—Revered lady, what followed must be painful to hear now.

Pavrājikā :—Then that brother of mine—

Who loved his master, wishing to rescue in calamity this Princess who was afraid of an insult (or defeat) at the hands of the enemy, paid off the debt due to his Master with his dear life. (11)

First (Maiden) :—Alas, Sumati was killed!

Second :—Hence it is that such has been the conditions of the Princess.

(Parivrājikā *sheds tears.*)

King :—Such (so to terminate) is the course of life of embodied beings. Your honoured brother who proved true to his master's salt ought not to be lamented for. What happened next ?

Parivrājikā :—Then, by the time I, who had fainted, regained consciousness, this (Mālavikā) was not to be seen.

King :—Great, indeed, was the affliction suffered by Your Reverence !

Parivrājikā :—Then, having consigned the body of my (dead) brother to flames, I, whose grief of widowhood was renewed, came down to your country and put on these brown garments (took to an ascetic's life).

King :—Such a course is proper for a good person. What next ?

Parivrājikā :—Then, this (lady) who passed from the hands of the foresters into those of Vīrasena and from him to the Queen, was seen again by me, when I got admission into the Queen's palace. This is the end of my tale.

रेस्य इति यावत् । अवसानं समाप्तिः । विनिपाता आपदः । परिभवमपमानमुपहरन्तीति परिभवोपहारिणः । **प्रेष्यभावेनेत्यादि** देवीशब्दक्षमा देवीशब्दयोग्या सती इयं मालविका प्रेष्यभावेन परिचारकत्वेन उपयुज्यते नाम नियुज्यते किल । पत्त्रोर्णं वा धौतकौशेयमिव । वेत्युपमायाम् । 'उपमायां विकल्पे वा' इत्यमरसिंहः । स्नानीयवस्त्रक्रियया स्नानीयवस्त्रकरणेन । स्नात्यनेनेति स्नानीयं स्नानोपयुक्तं वस्त्रम् ।

मालविका—(आत्मगतम् ।) किं नु खलु सांप्रतं भर्ता भणति । (क)

राजा—अहो परिभवोपहारिणो[1] विनिपाताः कुतः ।

प्रेष्यभावेन नामेयं देवीशब्दक्षमा सती ।
स्नानीयवस्त्रक्रियया पत्रोर्णं[2] वोपयुज्यते ॥ १२ ॥

देवी—भगवति त्वयाभिजनवतीं मालविकामनाचक्षाणयाऽसांप्रतं कृतम् । (ख)

परिव्राजिका—शान्तं पापं शान्तं पापम् । कारणेन[3] खलु मया नैभृत्यम्[4]-वलम्बितम् ।

देवी—किमिव तत्कारणम् । (ग)

राजा—यदि वक्तव्यं कथ्यताम् ।

परिव्राजिका—श्रुयताम् । इयं पितरि[5] जीवति केनापि लोक[6]यात्रागतेन सिद्धादेशेन[7] साधुना मत्समक्षम्[8]आदिष्टा संवत्सरमात्रमियं प्रेष्यभावमनुभूय ततः सदृशभर्तृगामिनी भविष्यतीति । तद[9]वश्यंभाविनमादेशमस्यास्त्वत्पादशुश्रूषया परिणमन्तमवेक्ष्य कालप्रतीक्षया मया साधु[10] कृतमिति पश्यामि ।

राजा—युक्ता प्रतीक्षा[11] ।

(क) किं णु खु संपदं भट्टा भणादि । (ख) भअवदि तुए अभिजनवदिं मालविअं अणाचक्खन्तीए असंपदं किदम् । (ग) किं विअ[12] तं कारणम् ।

पत्रोर्णं धौतकौशेयमित्यमरः । नामेति कुत्सायां वा । मालविका दासीत्वेनोपयुक्तेति अयुक्तं कृतमित्यर्थः । उपमालंकारः । पथ्यावक्त्रं वृत्तम् । ॥ १२ ॥ अभिजनवतीमुन्नतवंशसंभवाम् । असांप्रतमयुक्तम् । शान्तं पापम् । परोक्तानङ्गीकारार्थमेतत् । कारणेन विशिष्टहेतुना । नैभृत्यं मौनमिति यावत् । नैर्घृण्यमिति पाठे निर्दयत्वम् । लोकयात्रा जीवनार्थं भ्रमणम् । सिद्धादेशेन सिद्धो निश्चयेन भावी आदेशो यस्य

---

१. परिभवप्रहारिणः २ पत्रोर्णंवो०; पत्रोर्णमुप०. ३ केन च का०. ४ नैर्घृण्यं, नैर्भृत्यं ५ परिदीप्यन्ती. ६ देव. ७ ०देशेकेन. ८ ०मक्षं समा. ९ एवंभावि०. १० तत्साधु. ११ उपेक्षा. १२ विअ एव्व का०.

Mālavikā :—*(To herself)* What, indeed, will his Lordship say now ?

King :—Oh, how calamities bring on humiliation ! For,

This lady being worthy of the title of 'Queen,' has been used in the capacity of a servant, like a silk garment used for the purpose of a bathing-garment. (12)

Queen :—Revered lady, you acted improperly in not telling that Mālavikā was of noble descent.

Parivrājikā :—Heaven forbid ! Not so. It was, indeed, on purpose that I maintained (*lit.* had recourse to) silence.

Queen :—What can that purpose be ?

King :—If it is fit to be told, then tell it.

Parivrājikā :—Listen. This lady, while her father lived, was told, in my presence, by a certain sage whose words (prophecies) always came true and who had come (there) in the course of his wandering for livelihood, that she would be united to a worthy husband after having experienced servitude for a year. Seeing that that infallible prophecy in connexion with her was being fulfilled by her serving your feet, I waited for the time to run, and I think I acted rightly in doing so.

King :—Your waiting was proper.

तेन । प्रेष्यभावं दास्यमित्यर्थः । परिणमन्तं सिध्यन्तम् । कालस्य प्रतीक्षया संवत्सरावसानं प्रतीक्षमाणया । विदर्भगतं विदर्भनृपसंबद्धम् । अनुष्ठेयं करणीयं कार्यम् । द्वैराज्यं द्वयो राज्ञोर्भावः कर्म वा । ब्राह्मणादित्वात् ष्यञ् । अवस्थापयितुं कामः यस्य सः । 'तुं काममनसोरपि' इति मकारलोपः । **तौ पृथगित्यादि** । तौ यज्ञसेनमाधवसेनौ पृथक्पार्थक्येनोत्तरदक्षिणे वरदाकूले । वरदा नाम तत्रत्या नदी तस्याः कूले उभे तीरे शिष्टां रक्षताम् । वरदाया दक्षिणोत्तरयोस्तयोः पार्थक्येन राज्यमस्तु । काविवेत्याह–शीतकिरणश्चन्द्रः उष्णकिरणः सूर्यस्तौ । द्वंन्द्वान्ते श्रूयमाणः किरणशब्दः प्रत्येकं संबध्यते । नक्तंदिवं रात्रिदिने । 'अचतुरविचतुर…' इति निपातनात्साधु । विभज्य पृथक् कृत्वा इव । उपमालंकारः ॥ १३ ॥ दर्शनं विचार्य निश्चितं मतम् । **द्विधेत्यादि** । द्विधा विभक्तां धुरम् उद्वहन्तौ धारयन्तौ

कञ्चुकी[1]—देव कथान्तरेणान्तरितम्[2]। अमात्यो विज्ञापयति । विदर्भगतमनुष्ठेयमवधारितमस्माभिः[3] । देवस्य तावदभिप्रेतं[4] श्रोतुमिच्छामीति ।

राजा—मौद्गल्य तत्रभवतोर्भ्रात्रोर्यज्ञसेनमाधवसेनयोर्द्वैराज्यमिदानीमवस्थापयितुकामोऽस्मि[5] ।

तौ पृथग्वरदाकूले शिष्टामुत्तरदक्षिणे ।
नक्तंदिवं[6] विभज्योभौ शीतोष्णकिरणाविव ॥ १३ ॥

कञ्चुकी—देव एवममात्यपरिषदे निवेदयामि[7] ।

राजा—(अङ्गुल्या अनुमन्यते ।)

(निष्क्रान्तः कञ्चुकी ।)

प्रथमा—(जनान्तिकम् ।) भर्तृदारिके दिष्टया भर्तृदारकोऽर्धराज्ये प्रतिष्ठां गमिष्यति । (क)

मालविका—एतत्तावद्बहु मन्तव्यं यज्जीवितसंशयान्मुक्तः । (ख)

(प्रविश्य ।)

कञ्चुकी—विजयतां देवः । देव अमात्यो विज्ञापयति । कल्याणी[8] देवस्य बुद्धिः । मन्त्रिपरिषदोऽप्येवमेव दर्शनम् । कुतः ।

द्विधा विभक्तां श्रियमुद्वहन्तौ धुरं रथाश्वाविव संग्रहीतुः ।
तौ स्थास्यतस्ते नृपती[10] निदेशे परस्परावग्रहनिर्विकारौ[11] ॥ १४ ॥

(क) भट्टदारिए दिट्ठिआ भट्टिदारओ[12] अद्धरज्जे पडिट्ठं गमिस्सदि । (ख) एवं दाव बहु मन्तव्वं जं जीविदसंसआदो मुक्तो ।

---

१ अस्मात्प्राक्-प्रविश्य कञ्चुकी । इत्य० २ ०रितमिदम्. ३ अनुष्ठितमभूत. ४ अभिमतं, अभिप्रायं. द्वयो राज्यं स्थापयितुमिच्छामि. ६ नक्तंदिनं. ७ विज्ञापयामि. ८ अहो देवस्य. ९ एतदेव. १० नृपते, नृपतेः, ११ ० रोपगृह. १२ भट्टिणा भट्ट...गमइस्सदि.

Chamberlain :—My Lord, the introduction of another matter did not allow me to tell it. The minister begs to say—'We have decided how matters in connexion with Vidarbha are to be settled; we just wish to know Your Majesty's opinion (or wish).'

King :—Maudgalya, I wish to establish a double monarchy with respect to those honoured cousins, Yajñasena and Mādhavasena.

Let the two govern separately the (territory laying on the) Northern and Southern banks of the Varadā, as the moon and sun rule, dividing between themselves, the night and the day. (13)

Chamberlain :—My Lord, I shall thus inform the council of ministers.

(King consents by a motion of his finger.)

(Exit Chamberlain.*)*

First Maiden :—(*Aside*) Princess, it is a matter for congratulation that the Prince will be established in half the kingdom.

Mālavikā :—This should be considered a great thing, in the first place, that he has been rescued from peril to his life.

(Having entered)

Chamberlain :—Victory to your Majesty! My Lord, the minister respectfully says—'Happy is your Majesty's idea; such is the view of ministers also. For,

The two Kings possessing royalty divided (equally) between them, and causing no disturbance owing to mutual restraint, will abide by your command, as the two horses bearing the yoke (of a chariot, the weight of which is) equally divided, and harmless, being mutually restrained, follow the will of the charioteer.' (14)

रथाश्वौ रथस्य वोढारौ अश्वौ संग्रहीतुः संयन्तुः। सारथेरित्यर्थः। इव द्विधा विभक्तां श्रियं राज्यलक्ष्मीमुद्वहन्तौ तौ नृपती परस्परस्यावग्रहेण नियन्त्रणेन निर्विकारौ निर्बाधौ। यद्वा परस्परबाधाशून्यौ। रथाश्वयोऽपि एतद्योज्यम्। तव निदेशे स्थास्यतः आज्ञानुरोधेन वर्तिष्यते। उपमालंकारः। वृत्तमुपजातिः।॥ १४ ॥ प्राभृतमुपायनमेव

राजा—तेन हि मन्त्रिपरिषदं ब्रूहि। सेनापतये वीरसेनाय लिख्यतामेवं क्रियतामिति।

कञ्चुकी—यदाज्ञापयति देवः। (इति निष्क्रम्य सप्राभृतकं लेखं गृहीत्वा पुनः प्रविष्टः।) अनुष्ठिता प्रभोराज्ञा। अयं पुनरिदानीं देवस्य सेनापतेः पुष्पमित्रस्य सकाशात्संप्राभृतको लेखः प्राप्तः प्रत्यक्षीकरोत्वेनं देवः।

(राजा सहसोत्थाय सोपचारं गृहीत्वा प्राभृतकं परिजनायार्पयति।)

(लेखं च नाट्येनोद्वेष्टयति।)

देवी—(आत्मगतम्।) अहो ततोमुखमेव नो हृदयम्। श्रोष्यामि तावद्गुरुजनस्य कुशलानन्तरं वसुमित्रस्य वृत्तान्तम्। अधिकारे खलु मे पुत्रकः सेनापतिना नियुक्तः।

राजा—(उपविश्य वाचयति।) स्वस्ति। यज्ञशरणात्सेनापतिः पुष्पमित्रो वैदिशस्थं पुत्रमायुष्मन्तमग्निमित्रं स्नेहात्परिष्वज्यानुदर्शयति। विदितमस्तु। योऽसौ राजयज्ञदीक्षितेन मया राजपुत्रशतपरिवृतं वसुमित्रं गोप्तारमादिश्य संवत्सरोपावर्तनीयो निरर्गलस्तुरगो विसृष्टः स

(क) अह्महे तदोमुहं एव्व णो हिअअं। सुणिस्सं दाव गुरुअणस्स कुसलाणन्तरं वसुमित्तस्स वुत्तन्तं। अहिआरे खु मे पुत्तओ सेणावदिणा णिउत्तो।

प्राभृतकम्। स्वार्थे कः। प्राभृतकेन सहितं सप्राभृतकम्। 'प्राभृतं तु प्रदेशनम्। उपायनम्' इत्यमरः। सोत्तरीयप्रा० इति पाठे उत्तरीयं संव्यानम्। उत्तरस्मिन्देहभागे भवमुत्तरीयम्। सोपचारं उचितसमानसहितम्। ततोमुखं ततो लेखश्रवणे एव मुखं यस्य तत्। तच्छ्रवणोत्सुकमित्यर्थः अतिघोरे इति पाठे अतिसंकटे सैनापत्यरूपे कर्मणि। अह्महे इति हर्षे। स्वस्ति लेखस्याग्रे मङ्गलार्थे एतत्प्रयुज्यते यज्ञशरणाद्यज्ञगृहात्। वैदिशस्थ विदिशास्थम्। अनुदर्शयति आत्मवृत्तान्तं पुरतो लिखिति। राजयज्ञो नामाश्वमेधः। राजयज्ञो राजसूयाख्यः। 'राजसूयो नृपाध्वरः' इति त्रिकाण्डशेषः। तत्र

१ सेनान्ये. २ लेख्यताम्. ३ सोत्तरीयप्रा. ४ उपसृत्य. सप्राभृतकं लेखं सोप० परिजनायार्पयति। परिजनो लेखं नाट्येनोद्घाटयति. ६ लेखं सोपचारं गृहीत्वा वाचयति. ७ वैदिशस्तत्रत्यं; वैदिश्यम्. ८ च्त्रज्येदं. ९ राजसूय १० वत्सरोपात्तनियम. ११. तुरंग. १२ विसर्जितः, १३ स सिद्धार्थः, १४ अणकुस०. १५ अदिघोरे, तुरगक्षाधिकारे

King :—Tell the cabinet then to send a despatch to General Vīrasena to this effect.

Chamberlain :—As your Majesty commands. (*He goes out; but enters again with a letter accompanied with a present*) Your Majesty's order has been executed. But here has arrived a letter together with a present from His Majesty, Puṣpamitra, the General. Your Majesty should look inio it.

(*The* King rises at once, *takes it with due respect, hands over the present to the attendants, and shows that he opens the letter.*)

Queen :—(*To herself*) Oh! Our heart is directed to the same (the news from Puṣpamitra). I shall now get some information about Vasumitra after hearing about the well-being of the elders. To a responsible post, indeed, has my son been appointed by the General.

King :—(*Sits down and reads*) My blessing to you. Puṣpamitra, the General, having affectionately embraced his son, Agnimitra, of long life, writes from the sacrificial enclosure as follows. 'The horse, which was let loose to go about unobstructed by me, consecrated for the Rāja (horse) sacrifire, having appointed Vasumitra, protected (*lit.* surrounded) by a hundred princes, its guardian, and which was to return

---

दीक्षितेन गृहीतदीक्षेण । राजपुत्रशतपरिवृतं राजपुत्राणां शतेन परिवेष्टितम् । तथा च श्रुतावश्वमेधप्रकरणे ' शतेन राजपुत्रैः सह ' इति । संवत्सरेण एकेन वर्षेण उपावर्तनीयो निवर्तनीयः । ०पात्तनियम इति पाठे संवत्सरं यावदुपात्तो गृहीतः नियमः प्रतिनिवर्तनरूपो येनेति स एवार्थः । निरर्गलः निर्गता अर्गला निरोधो यस्मात् । निष्प्रतिबन्धचारीत्यर्थः । सिन्धोर्नाम नद्स्य । दक्षिणरोधसि दक्षिणतीरे । अश्वानीकेन अश्वारोहसैन्येन । प्रार्थितः युद्धचिकीर्षया निगृहीतः । संमर्दो युद्धम् । ततः परानित्यादि । ततो जाते युद्धे धन्विना प्रशस्तधनुर्धरेण वसुमित्रेण परान् शत्रून् पराजित्य प्रसह्य बलान्नीयमानो मे वाजिराजः अश्वश्रेष्ठः निवर्तितः प्रत्याहृतः । ॥ १५ ॥ अनेन स्वपुत्रजयवृत्तान्तेन । सगरः सूर्यवंशसंभवो नृपविशेषः । अंशु-

सिन्धोर्दक्षिणरोधसि चरन्नश्वानीकेन यवनानां प्रार्थितः। तत उभयोः सेनयोर्महानासीत्संमर्दः।

(देवी विषादं नाटयति।)

राजा—कथमीदृशं संवृत्तम्। (शेषं पुनर्वाचयति।)

ततः परान्पराजित्य वसुमित्रेण धन्विना।
प्रसह्य ह्रियमाणो मे वाजिराजो निवर्तितः॥ १५॥

देवी—अनेनाश्वस्तं मे हृदयम्। (क)

राजा—(लेखशेषं वाचयति।) सोऽहमिदानीमंशुमतेव सगरः पौत्रेण प्रत्याहृताश्वो यक्ष्ये। तदिदानीमकालहीनं विगतरोषचेतसा भवता वधूजनेन सह यज्ञसेवनायागन्तव्यमिति।

राजा—अनुगृहीतोऽस्मि।

परिव्राजिका—दिष्ट्या पुत्रविजयेन दंपती वर्धेते। (देवीं विलोक्य।)

भर्त्रासि वीरपत्नीनां श्लाघ्यानां स्थापिता धुरि।
वीरसूरिति शब्दोऽयं तनयात्त्वामुपस्थितः॥ १६॥

विदूषकः—भवति परितुष्टोऽस्मि यत्पितरमनुगतो वत्सः। (ख)

(क) इमिणा आससिदं मे हिअअं। (ख) भोदि परितुट्ठोम्हि जं पिदरं अणुगदो वच्छो।

मान् तस्य पौत्रः। अकालहीनं कालेन हीनं न भवति तथा अकालक्षेपम्। अविलम्बितमित्यर्थः। विगतो रोषो यस्मात्ताद‍ृक् चेतो यस्य तेन। यज्ञसेवनाय यज्ञसेवार्थम्। **भर्त्रासीत्यादि**। भर्त्रा श्लाघ्यानां प्रशस्तानां वीरः पतिर्यासां तासां वीरस्त्रीणां धुरि अग्रे स्थापितासि। तव पतिर्वीरश्रेष्ठ इति त्वं सर्वासु वीरपत्नीषु

---

१. यवनेन. २ विमर्दः. ३ नि—रूपयति. ४ समरं पवु०. ५ संगृह्य ६ ०शेषं पुनः ७ अंशुमता सगरपुत्रेणेव प्र० ८ संदर्शनाय ९ वर्तेते. १० श्लाघ्यायां. ११ देवी भअवदि परितुट्ठम्हि (तुट्ठास्मि). १२ दाणिं आस्ससदि.

after one year, was seized while wandering on the Southern bank of the Sindhu by a cavalry squadron of the Yavanas. Then there was a fierce fight between the two armies.'

(*The* Queen *exhibits dejection.*)

King :—How could it come to this! (*Reads the remaining part of the letter.*)

'Then Vasumitra, the mighty archer, having defeated the enemies, rescued my noble horse that was being forcibly led away.' (15)

Queen :—My heart feels consoled on hearing this.

King :—(*Reads the rest of the letter*) 'I, then, whose horse has been brought back by my grandson, will offer the sacrifice now, like Sagara who had his horse brought back by Amśumat. You should therefore come, without delay, to witness the sacrifice with my daughters-in-law and with a mind free from anger.'

King :—Oh, I am favoured.

Parivrājikā :—I congratulate you two (*lit*, husband and wife) on the victory of your son. (*Looking at the* Queen)—

By your husband you have been placed at the head of the noble wives whose husbands are heroes; and (now) the title 'mother of a hero' has come to you from your son. (16)

Vidūṣaka :—Lady, I am greatly pleased that the dear son has followed his father.

श्रेष्ठासीति भावः। अधुना च तनयात् पुत्राद्धेतोः वीरं सूते असौ वीरसूर्वीरमातेति शब्दः अपि त्वामुपस्थितः प्राप्तः। अतो धन्या त्वमिति निष्कर्षः ॥ १६ ॥ कलभेन करिपोतेन । यूथपतिः अनुकृतस्तत्सदृशः पराक्रमः कृतः । **नैतावदित्यादि ।** एतावता एतत्परिमाणेन वीरविजृम्भितेन शत्रुपराजयपूर्वमश्वप्रत्याहरणरूपेण शूर-चेष्टितेन नः चित्तस्य विस्मयं न आदधाति । तत्र हेतुमाह—यस्य अप्रधृष्यः परैः प्रधर्षयितुं पराभवितुमशक्यः उच्चैः महान् त्वम् । अपां समुद्रजलानां दग्धुः

परिव्राजिका—कलभेन खलु यूथपतिरनुकृतः।

कञ्चुकी—देवं अयं कुमारः।

नैतावता वीरविजृम्भितेन
चित्तस्य नो विस्मयमादधाति।
यस्याप्रधृष्यः प्रभवस्त्वमुच्चै-
र्वह्नेरपां दग्धुरिवोरुजन्मा ॥ १७ ॥

राजा—मौद्गल्य यज्ञसेनश्यालमुरीकृत्य मुच्यन्तां सर्वे बन्धनस्थाः।

कञ्चुकी—यदाज्ञापयति देवः। (इति निष्क्रान्तः।)

देवी—जयसेने गच्छ। इरावतीप्रमुखेभ्योऽन्तःपुरेभ्यः पुत्रस्य विजयवृत्तान्तं निवेदय। (क)

प्रतीहारी—तथा। (इति प्रस्थिता।)

देवी—एहि तावत्। (ख)

प्रतीहारी—(परिवृत्य।) इयमस्मि। (ग)

देवी—(जनान्तिकम्।) यन्मयाशोकदोहदनियोगे मालविकायै प्रतिज्ञातं तदस्या अभिजनं च निवेद्य मम वचनेनेरावतीमनुनय। त्वयाहं सत्यान्न परिभ्रंशयितव्येति। (घ)

(क) जयसेणे गच्छ। इरावदिप्पमुहाणं अन्तेउराणं पुत्तस्स विअअवुत्तन्तं णिवेदेहि। (ख) एहि दाव। (ग) इअं ह्मि। (घ) जं मए असोअदोहल-णिओए मालविआए पइण्णादं तं से अहिजणं च णिवेदिअ मह वअणेण इरावदि अणुणेहि। तुए अहं सच्चादो ण परिब्भंसइदव्वेत्ति।

---

१ राजा-मौद्गल्य ननु कलभेन यूथे० २ देवेत्यादि नास्ति कुत्रचित् ३ पुत्रस्य. ४ वह्नेः, उररी. ६ तं एव्वम्.

Parivrājikā :—The young elephant has, indeed, imitated the lordly elephant (*lit.* the chief of the herd).

Chamberlain :—Sire, this prince,—

Does not produce astonishment in our minds by such a display of heroic power, whose source (father) your lofty and unassailable self is, as the thigh-born one (the sage Aurva) is of the fire that consumes water. (17)

King :—Maudgalya, let all the prisoners, including Yajñasena's brother-in-law, be set free.

Chamberlain :—As Your Majesty commands. (*Exit*)

Queen :—Jayasenā, go and communicate the news of my son's victory to the ladies of the harem headed by Irāvatī.

Female Door-keeper :—So I will do. (*Begins to go.*)

Queen :—Come back a moment.

Female Door-Keeper :—(*Turning back*) Here I am.

Queen :—(*Aside*) Inform Irāvatī of what I promised to Mālavikā when I appointed her to gratify the longing of the Aśoka, and also of her noble parentage, and persuade her, at my instance, that she should not make me fall off (swerve) from truth.

दाहकस्य अग्नेः और्वाग्नेः ऊरुजन्मा ऊरोजन्म यस्य स ऊरुजन्मा मुनिः इव त्वं प्रभवः । इतोऽप्यधिकस्य पराक्रमस्य स्थानमयं यस्य त्वं पिता इति भावः । इन्द्रवज्रा वृत्तम् ॥ १७ ॥ यज्ञसेनश्यालं मौर्याख्यं मौर्यसचिवं वा । ऊरीकृत्य अङ्गीकृत्य । तत्प्रभृतय इत्यर्थः । अन्तःपुरेभ्यः अन्तःपुरस्थस्त्रीभ्यः । दोहदनियोगे दोहदं पूरयेति नियोगदानावसरे । अनुनय प्रवणीकुरु । कस्मिन्नर्थे इत्यादि—स्वयाहमिति । मञ्जूषास्मीति सर्वाभिरन्तःपुरस्त्रीभिर्दत्तानामाभरणानां मञ्जूषेवैकनिवासोहं जातेत्यर्थः ।

प्रतीहारी—यद्देव्याज्ञापयति । (इति निष्क्रम्य पुनः प्रविश्य ।) भट्टिनि पुत्रविजयनिमित्तेन परितोषेणान्तःपुराणामाभरणानां मञ्जूषास्मि संवृत्ता । (क)

देवी—किमत्राश्चर्यम् । साधारणः खलु तासां मम चायमभ्युदयः । (ख)

प्रतीहारी—(जनान्तिकम् ।) भट्टिनि इरावती पुनर्विज्ञापयति । सदृशं खलु देव्याः प्रभवन्त्या वचनं । प्रथमसंकल्पितं न युज्यतेऽन्यथा कर्तुमिति । (ग)

देवी—भगवति त्वयानुज्ञातेच्छाम्यार्यसुमतिना प्रथमसंकल्पितां मालविकामार्यपुत्राय प्रतिपादयितुम् । (घ)

परिव्राजिका—इदानीमपि त्वमेवास्याः प्रभवसि ।

देवी—(मालविकां हस्ते गृहीत्वा ।) इदमार्यपुत्रः प्रियनिवेदनानुरूपं पारितोषिकं प्रतीच्छतु । (राजा सव्रीडं[1] जोषमास्ते ।) (ङ)

(क) जं देवी आणवेदि । भट्टिणि पुत्तवि[2]जअणिमित्तेण परितोसेण अन्तेउराणं आहरणाणं सञ्जूसह्मि संवुत्ता । (ख) किं[3] एत्थ अच्चरिअं । सा[4]हारणो खु ताणं मह अ अअं अब्भुदओ । (ग) भट्टिणि इरावदी उण विण्णवेदि । सरिसं क्खु[5] देवीए पहवन्तीए वअणं पुढमसंकप्पिदं ण जुज्जदि अण्णहा कादुं ति । (घ) भअवदि तुए अ[6]णुण्णादा इच्छामि अज्जसुमदिणा पुढमसंक[7]प्पिदं मालविअं अज्जउत्तस्स पडिवादेदुं । (ङ) ई[8]दं अज्जउत्तो पिअणिवेदणाणुरूवं पारितोसिअं पडिच्छदु ।

---

१ व्रीडां नाटयति. २ विजएण अविभत्तपरितोसाणं (अविभक्तपरितोषाणां); अविहद-अस्सन्त (अश्रान्त) परि०; दिण्णपारितोसिआणं. ३ एदं किं अच्च० ४ णं साधा० ५ खु पहव० तुह वअणं. ६ अणुमदा. ७ संभाविदं. ८ इमं...सिअं मालविअं.

Female Door-Keepr :—As the Queen commands. (*Exit and re-enter*) Queen, I have become (as it were) the box of the ornaments of (given to me as presents by) the ladies of the harem owing to the satisfaction felt by them at the victory of your son.

Queen :—Where is the wonder in this? This good fortune is, indeed, common to them as well as to me.

Female Door-keeper :—(*Aside*) Queen, Irāvatī again begs to say—'Befitting are the words of the Queen who is all-powerful; what is determined upon, it is not proper to change afterwards.'

Queen :—Revered Lady, permitted by you I wish to bestow Mālavikā on my husband as originally intended by the revered Sumati.

Queen :—(*Holding* Mālavikā *by the hand*) Let my Lord accept this reward, befitting the communication of the happy news.

कल्पितां दातव्यतया मनसा निश्चिताम्। प्रतिपादयितुं दातुम्। प्रियनिवेदनं लेखवाचनेन पुत्रस्य विजयप्राप्तिवृत्तान्तकथनम्। पारितोषिकं प्रतीच्छतु अङ्गीकरोतु। अत्र प्रीत्युत्पादनात् प्रसादो नाम संध्यङ्गमुक्तं भवति॥ लज्जातुरः लज्जाकुलः। प्रणयस्यानुरागस्य विशेषो यस्मिन्कर्मणि तद्यथा तथा। **अप्याकरेत्यादि**। हे कल्याणि शोभने। आकरसमुत्पन्ना रत्नाकरजातापि मणिजातिः रत्नजातं असंस्कृता अनुत्तेजिता सती जातरूपेण सुवर्णेन संस्कारं नार्हति। महाकुलसंभूतापि एषा देवीशब्देन अनलंकृता राज्ञा संयोगं नार्हतीति भावः। अत्र लब्धार्थस्य स्थिरीकरणात्कृतिर्नाम संध्यङ्गमुक्तं भवति॥ १८॥ अभ्युदयकथया उत्कर्षकथाव्यापृततया उत्सवे क्वचित्प्रमादः क्षन्तव्य एवेति भावः। कौशेयस्य कृमिकोशोत्थस्य पत्रोर्णं धौतवस्त्रम्। हन्त हर्षे। प्रतिगृहीता वशीकृता। अत्र वाञ्छितावाप्तेरानन्दो नाम संध्यङ्गमुक्तं भवति। जयतु भट्टिनी। अत्र बहुमानप्राप्तेर्भाषितेति संध्यङ्गमुक्तं भवति॥ **प्रतिप-**

देवी—(सस्मितम् ।) किमवधीरयति मामार्यपुत्रः । (क)

विदूषकः—भवति एष लोकव्यवहारः सर्वोऽपि नववरो लज्जातुरो भवति । (ख)

(राजा विदूषकमवेक्षते ।)

विदूषकः—अथ वा देव्या प्रणयविशेषं दत्तदेवीशब्दां मालविकामत्रभवान्प्रतिग्रहीतुमिच्छति । (ग)

देवी—एतस्या राजदारिकाया अभिजनेनैव दत्तो देवीशब्दः । किं पुनरुक्तेन । (घ)

परिव्राजिका—मा मैवम् ।

अप्याकरसंमुत्पन्ना मणिजातिरसंस्कृता ।
जातरूपेण कल्याणि न हि संयोगमर्हति ॥ १८ ॥

देवी—(स्मृत्वा ।) मर्षयतु भगवती । अभ्युदयकथयोचितं मया न लक्षितम् । जयसेने गच्छ तावम् । कौशेयपत्त्रोर्णमुपनय । (ङ)

प्रतीहारी—यद्देव्याज्ञापयति । (इति निष्क्रम्य पत्त्रोर्णं गृहीत्वा पुनः प्रविश्य ।) देवि एतत् । (च)

देवी—(मालविकामवगुण्ठनवतीं कृत्वा ।) आर्यपुत्र इदानीमिमां प्रतीच्छतु ।

(क) किं अवधीरेदि मं अज्जउत्तो । (ख) भोदि एसो लोअव्ववहारो सव्वो वि णववरो लज्जादुरो होदि । (ग) अह वा देवीए प्पणअविसेसं दिण्णदेवीसद्दं मालविअं अत्तभवं पडिग्गहीदुं इच्छदि । (घ) एदाए राअदारिआए अहिजणेण एव्व दिण्णो देवीसद्दो । किं पुणरुत्तेण । (ङ) मरिसेदु भअवदी । अब्भुदअकहाए उइदं मए ण लक्खिदं । जअसेणे गच्छ दाव । कोसेअपत्तोण्णं उवणेहि । (च) जं देवी आणवेदि । देवी एदम् । (छ) अज्जउतो दाणि इमं पडिच्छदु ।

---

१ ०त्पत्रो रत्नजातिपुरस्कृतः...मणिः संयोग०. २ स. ३ अवगुण्य. ४ लज्जलुओ (लज्जालुः). ५ देवीए एव्व किदप्प०. ६ ₹ा राज० इअं...नदा दिण्णो. ७ पत्तोण्णअलं, ०ण्णणेवच्छं से सिग्घं उव०.

(The King remains silent and bashful.)

Queen :—(*Smiling*) What, then, does my Lord disregard me ?

Vidūṣaka :—Lady, it is the custom of the world that every new bridegroom is bashful.

(The King looks at the Vidūṣaka.)

Vidūṣaka :—Or rather, His Honour would like to accept Mālavikā having the title of Queen given to her by Your Majesty as a mark of special affection (or favour).

Queen :—As she is a Princess, the title of Queen has been given to her by her exalted birth ; what is the use of repetition ?

Parivrājikā :—Not so, not so !

A jewel of any class, though produced in a mine, is not fit, O blessed one, to be united with gold, if unpolished. (18)

Queen :—(*Remembering*) Your Reverence should forgive me. Owing to the talk about the joyous event, I was not mindful of what was fit to be done. Jayasenā, go and bring for her a washed silk-garment.

Female Door-Keeper :—As Your Highness commands. (*Exit and re-enter with the garment.*) Queen, here it is.

Queen :—(*Having veiled* Mālavikā *with it*) My husband should now finally accept her.

क्षेणेत्यादि । भर्तृवत्सलाः भर्तरि प्रिये वत्सलाः प्रेमवत्यः साध्व्यः पतिव्रताः । प्रतिपक्षेणापि आत्मनः सपत्नीवर्गेणापि भर्तारं सेवन्ते । तस्य सपत्नीकरणमनुमन्यन्ते इत्यर्थः । अत्र दृष्टान्तमाह । समुद्रगा महानद्यः हि अन्यसरितां शतानि अब्धि उदधिं प्रापयन्ति आत्मना सह प्रवेक्षयन्ति । दृष्टान्तालंकारः । आर्याछन्दः ॥ १९ ॥ उपचारातिक्रमेण उपचारस्य तृतीयाङ्कावसाने कृतस्य प्रणिपातरूपस्य अतिक्रमेणोल्लंघनेन । भर्तुरनुकूलं मालविकाया समागमे विघ्नभूतमात्मन आगमनं परि-

राजा—देवि त्वच्छास[1]नादप्रत्युत्तरा वयम् ।

परिव्राजिका—हन्त प्रतिगृहीता ।

विदूषकः—अहो देव्या अत्रभवतोऽनुकूलता । (क)

(देवी[2] परिजनमवलोकयति ।)

परिव्राजिका—(मालविकामुपेत्य ।) जयतु भट्टिनी । (ख)

(देवी परिव्राजिकाम[3]वेक्षते ।)

परिव्राजिका—नैतच्चित्रं त्वयि ।

प्रतिपक्षेणापि पतिं सेवन्ते भर्तृवत्सलाः साध्व्यः ।
अन्यसरि[4]तां शतानि हि समुद्रगाः प्रापयन्त्यब्धिम् ॥ १९ ॥

(प्रविश्य ।)

निपुणिका—जयतु भर्ता । इरावती विज्ञापयति । यदुपचारातिक्रमेण तदा भर्तुरपराद्धं तत्स्वयमेव भर्तुरनुकूलं नाम मयाचरितम् । सांप्रतं पूर्णमनोरथेन भर्त्रा प्रसादमात्रेण संभावयितव्येति । (ग)

देवी—निपुणिके अवश्यं तस्याः संदेशमनुज्ञास्यत्यार्यपुत्रः । (घ)

निपुणिका—अनुगृहीतास्मि । (ङ)

(क) अहो देवीए अत्तहोदो अणुऊलदा । (ख) जेदु भट्टिणी । (ग) जेदु भट्टा । इरावती विण्णावेदि । जं उवआरादिक्कमेण तदा भट्टिणो अवरद्धं[5] तं सअं एव्व भत्तुणो अणुऊलं णाम मए आअरिदं । संपदं पुण्णमणोरहेण भत्तुणो[6] पसादमेत्तेण संभावइदव्वत्ति । (घ) णिउणिए अवस्सं ताँए संदेसं अणुजाणिस्सदि अज्जउत्तो । (ङ) अणुगहीदह्मि ।

---

१ नात्प्रवृत्ता एव, शासनंप्रत्यनुरक्ता वयम् । (अपवार्य ।) हन्त प्रतिगृहीतम्. २ धारिणी. ३ निरी०, निर्वर्णयति. ४ सरितामपि जलं;...न्त्युदधिम्. ५ तं भट्टिणो अणुऊलं ण मे आ०, जह हि उवआरादिक्कमेण किदावराधाए ण मए भट्टिणो अणु०; अणुरूवं. ६ अहं वि भट्टिणा. ७ से सेविदं...जाणि०; रोषं आर्यपुत्रो हास्यति. ८ जं देवी आणवेदि.

King :—Queen, as it is your order, I am without answer.

Parivrājikā :—Oh, she is accepted *(*as a wife) !

Vidūṣaka :—Oh, the favourableness of the Queen towards Your Honour !

(*The* Queen *casts a meaning glance at her attendants.)*

Attendants :—*(Having approached* Mālavikā) Victory to the Queen !

(*The* Queen *looks at the* Parivrājikā.)

Parivrājikā :—This is not astonishing in you.

Good wives, who dearly love their husbands, serve them by (allowing them) even a rival wife ; for, rivers take hundreds of other streams to the sea (their husband). (19)

(Entering)

Nipuṇikā :—Victory to the king ! Irāvati sends this message–'In making myself guilty towards my husband on that occasion by slighting his prostration, I, forsooth, myself acted favourably towards him (as it now turns out*)*. Now, I should be honoured by being merely favoured by my Lord who has gained his object.'

Queen :—Nipuṇikā, my husband will necessarily grant her request.

Nipuṇikā :—I thank you.

हृत्येति । भावः नामेत्यभ्युपगमे । संदेशमनुज्ञास्यसि संदेशानुरूपमाचरिष्यति । चरितः अर्थः येन स चरितार्थः कृतार्थः तम् । सभाजयितुं अभिनन्दितुम् । दिष्टिवृद्धया संभावयितुमित्यर्थः । सभाजनाक्षराणि अभिनन्दनशब्दान् । स्नेहेन परवान्स्नेहाधीन इत्यर्थः । युवयोः स्नेहं मनसि कृत्वा गन्तुं न पारयामीति भावः । **त्वं मे प्रसादेत्यादि** । हे देवि त्वं मे मम नित्यं सर्वदा प्रसादसुमुखी प्रसादेन प्रसन्नतया शोभनं मुखं यस्यास्तथोक्ता भव भूयाः । एतावदेवेदमेव हृदये मनसि प्रतिपालनीयमपेक्षणीम् । इतः परं भरतवाक्यम् । **आशास्यमित्यादि** । प्रजान जनानाम् ईतीनामवृष्टयादिमहानर्थानां विगमो दूरीभवनं स प्रभृति

परिव्राजिका—देवाहममुना भवत्संबन्धेन चरितार्थं[1] माधवसेनं सभाजयितुमिच्छामि यदि मे तव प्रसादः।

देवी—भगवति न युक्तमस्मान्परित्यक्तम्। (क)

राजा—भगवति मदीयेषु[2] लेखेषु तत्रभवते त्वामुद्दिश्य सभाजनाक्षराणि पातयिष्यामि।

परिव्राजिका—युवयोः स्नेहेन[3] परवानयं जनः।

देवी—आज्ञापयत्वार्यपुत्रः किं भूयोऽपि प्रियमनुतिष्ठामि। (ख)

राजा—किमतः[4] परमपि प्रियमस्ति। तथापीदमस्तु।

त्वं मे प्रसादसुमुखी भव देवि[5] नित्य-
मेतावदेव हृदये[6] प्रतिपालनीयम्।

(भरतवाक्यम्।)

आशास्य[7]मीतिविगमप्रभृति प्रजानां
संपद्यते[8] न खलु गोप्तरि नाग्निमित्रे ॥ २० ॥

(इति निष्क्रान्ताः सर्वे।)

इति श्रीकालिदासस्य कृतौ मालविकाग्निमित्रे पञ्चमोऽङ्कः।

(क) भअवदि[9] ण जुत्तं अह्मे परिच्चइदुं। (ख) आणवेदु[10] अज्जउत्तो किं भूओवि पिअं अणुचिट्ठामि।

यस्य तत्। ईतयस्तु, "अतिवृष्टिरनावृष्टिः शलभा मूषकाः शुकाः। प्रत्यासन्नाश्च राजानः षडेता ईतयः स्मृताः॥" इत्युक्ताः। पाठान्तरे अभ्यधिगमात्संप्राप्तेः। परिग्रहादित्यर्थः। तस्मात्प्रभृत्यारभ्याग्निमित्रेऽस्मिन्नायके गोप्तरि रक्षके सति तासां प्रजानामाशास्यमपेक्ष्यवस्तु न संपद्यत इति न न संभवतीति न। संभवत्येवेत्यर्थः। अनेन आशास्यसिद्ध्यनुरूपेण शुभशंसनेन प्रशस्तिर्नाम संध्यङ्गमुक्तं भवति। यदुक्तम्—'प्रशस्तिः शुभशंसनम्' इति। सर्वनाटकप्रयोगान्ते भरतेन सर्वकालसाधारणे आशीर्वचने

---

१ देव अमुना युक्तसं० जयितुं गच्छामि...२ ष्वेव...भवतः ३ स्नेहात्. ४ अतः परम्—तथापि भवत्वेवं तावत्. ५ चण्डि. ६ मृगये प्रतिपक्षहेतोः. ७ स्यमित्यमभ्यधिगम०; मभ्यधिगमात्. ८ संपत्स्यते. ९ भअवदीए. १० अज्जउत्त किं त...उपहरामि.

Parivrājikā :—King, I wish to offer my congratulations to Mādhavasena who has obtained his desired object by being thus connected with you, if you will show me so much favour (*i. e.* favour me by granting me permission to go).

Queen :—Revered lady, it is not proper for you (thus) to leave us.

King :—Venerable lady, in my letters I shall drop words of compliment from you to His Honour.

Parivrājikā :—Owing to this affection of you both, I am entirely at your disposal (*lit.* not independent to act).

Queen :—Let my lord tell me, what other agreeable service I should render unto him.

King :—Is there anything further that I can wish for ? Still let there be this—

Be you, O Queen, always favourably disposed towards me; this much I should ever cherish in my mind :

(*Bharatavākya*)

As for my other object of wish on the part of the subjects such as the removal of public calamities, there is none that cannot be accomplished, while Agnimitra is their protector. (20)

(*Exeunt omnes.*)

End of Act V of the Play MĀLAVIKĀGNIMITRA, composed by Kālidāsa.

(सर्वकालसाधारण्येनाशंसावचने इ. पा.) कर्तव्ये सति अत्र प्रधानामाशास्यसिद्धिं प्रति गोप्तुरग्निमित्रस्य कथनं तत्कालराजोपलक्षणमिति मन्तव्यम् ॥ २० ॥

श्रीमत्काटयवेमस्य कृतिर्विज्ञानशालिनः ।
कुमारगिरिराजीया जीयादाचन्द्रतारकम् ॥

इति श्रीकाटयवेमभूपविरचिते कुमारगिरिराजीये मालविकाग्निमित्रव्याख्याने पञ्चमोऽङ्कः ।

NOTES

NOTES.

ACT I

P. 2. मालविकाग्निमित्रम्—For explanation, see note on the word at p. 4. The poet begins his work with a benediction (नान्दी), referring to his favourite deity, Śiva. This is usually known as the *Mańgala* which is thought by Sanskrit writers to be necessary for the safe completion of the work undertaken, by the removal of obstacles. Patañjali in his Mahābhāṣya thus describes the efficacy of *Mańgala*—मङ्गलादीनि [मङ्गलमध्यानि मङ्गलान्तानि च] शास्त्राणि प्रथन्ते वीरपुरुषकाणि च भवन्ति आयुष्मत्पुरुषकाणि च। अध्येतारश्च प्रवक्तारो भवन्ति सिद्धार्था यथा स्युरिति। Bharata says—यद्यप्यङ्गानि भूयांसि पूर्वरङ्गस्य नाट्के। तथाप्यवश्यं कर्तव्या नान्दी विघ्नप्रशान्तये ॥

Verse 1. Construe :—

प्रणतबहुफले एकैश्वर्ये स्थितः अपि यः स्वयं कृत्तिवासाः, कान्तासंमिश्रदेहः अपि यः अविषयमनसां यतीनां परस्तात्, अष्टाभिः तनुभिः कृत्स्नं जगत् बिभ्रतः अपि यस्य अभिमानः न, सः ईशः वः तामसीं वृत्तिं सन्मार्गालोकनाय व्यपनयतु।

एकैश्वर्ये—See com. एकैश्वर्य-supreme, unique power. एक 'supreme, all-comprehending' (such as is possessed by no one else.) ऐश्वर्य is an abstract noun from ईश्वर (ईष्टे असौ one who rules over all things. ईश् + वरच्). Śiva has the eight superhuman powers, *viz.* अणिमा लघिमा प्राप्तिः प्राकाम्यं महिमा तथा। ईशित्वं च वशित्वं च तथा कामावसायिता ॥ *i. e.* the power to be (1) as small as an atom ; (2) to be as light as one likes ; (3) to attain every object ; (4) supreme or perfect will-power ; (5) the power of becoming as great as one likes : (6) the power to control all things ; (7) perfect mastery over the senses ; and (8) the power to subdue passion or the attainment of all desires. *Cf.* यस्मिन्नीश्वर इत्यनन्यविषयः शब्दो यथार्थाक्षरः। Vik. I. 1. ; अणिमादिगुणोपेतमस्पृष्टपुरुषान्तरम्। शब्दमीश्वर इत्युच्चैः सार्धचन्द्रं बिभर्ति यः॥ Kum. VI. 75 ; तमीश्वराणां परमं महेश्वरं &c. *S've Up.* &c. VI. 7.

प्रणतबहुफले—For comp. see com. ; yielding manifold fruit to (fulfilling the desires of all kinds, of) those who bow down to him (with an object in view). कृत्तिवासाः—Wearing an antelope's or tiger's skin for a garment (as is done by ascetics). *Cf.* स कृत्तिवासास्तपसे यतात्मा &c. Kum. I. 54; or there may be a reference here to the skin of the elephant-demon (son of महिषासुर) killed by Śiva and ever after worn as a trophy by him at the demon's request. *Cf.* गजासुर उवाच–त्रिशूलपाणे देवेश जाने त्वां स्मरहारिणम्। तव हस्ते मम वधः श्रेयानेव पुरांतक ॥ यदि प्रसन्नो दिग्वासास्तदा नित्यं वसान मे। इमां कृत्तिं विरूपाक्ष त्वत्त्रिशूलाग्निपाविताम्। नामास्तु कृत्तिवासास्ते प्रारभ्याद्यतनं दिनम् ॥ Kas'īkhaṇḍa.

Some think that there is विरोध, or rather विरोधाभास as it is more generally called (apparent verbal opposition), between एक (of one kind) in एकैश्वर्ये and बहु in the epithet बहुफले, (which is removed by taking एक to mean 'supreme'); it may or may not have been intended by the poet, but there is such opposition between प्रणतबहुफले एकैश्वर्ये स्थितः and स्वयं कृत्तिवासाः, as shown by अपि, intended to magnify the greatness of Śiva. Though in full possession of the power which is peculiarly his, and which enables him to grant every desire of his devotees, he has a mere skin for his garment. The *Virodha* is removed by saying that Śiva, as supreme lord, is free to act as he likes. *Cf.* गजाजिनालम्बि दुकूलधारि वा न विश्वमूर्तेरवधार्यते वपुः। Kum. V. 78. The reading एकैश्वर्यस्थितोपि ०फलः is equally good, if not better. In this case, the विरोध is between स्वयं कृतिवासाः ऐकश्वर्यस्थितः and प्रणतबहुफलः; how can one, who is himself poor and possessed of one thing, give many things to others? again, how can one who has एकैश्वर्य (wealth or excellence of one kind) confer many blessings on others? The विरोध is removed as above, or by taking एक to mean not 'one' but 'supreme'. कान्तासंमिश्रदेहोऽपि—'Though such a passionate lover as to have his wife forming half the part of his body' refers to Śiva's अर्धनारीश्वरत्व. The quality-in-unity of Śiva and his wife Pārvatī is represented by their one body, the right half being male and the left one female. *Cf.* समादिदेशैकवधूं भवित्रीं प्रेम्णा शरीरार्धहरां हरस्य। Kum. I. 50. अपि—shows opposition as in the first line. अविषय०—Whose minds are entirely free from (the desire for) worldly pleasures, free from passion; or the अ may have the sense of उपरम or cessation,– 'turned away from.' परस्तात्—far beyond; the highest of. *V. l.* पुरस्तात्—at the head of, foremost of. यतीनां—self-restrained persons, ascetics. The *Virodha* is removed by referring to Śiva's influenced by the presence of a woman). For this power of Śiva *Cf.* अथेन्द्रियक्षोभमयुग्मनेत्रः पुनर्वशित्वाद्बलवन्निगृह्य। Kum. III. 69 ; also I, 59 ; for the line *cf.* एको रागिषु राजते प्रियतमादेहार्धहारी हरो नीरागेषु जनो विमुक्तललनासङ्गो न यस्मात्परः ॥ Bhar. Vair.

अष्टाभिः &c.—The eight forms of Śiva are the five elements (पृथ्वी, अप्, तेजस्, वायु and आकाश), the sun, the moon, and the sacrificer (for the time being). *Cf.* जलं वह्निस्तथा यष्टा सूर्याचन्द्रमसौ तथा। आकाशं वायुरवनी मूर्तयोऽष्टा पिनाकिनः॥ and Śāk. I. 1. See also Malli. on *Ragh.* II. 35 or Kum. I. 57. कृत्स्नं जगत् &c.—The five elements constitute the world. The sun being the centre of activity supports the world. *Cf.* the Śrutis: सूर्य आत्मा जगतस्तुषश्च; मित्रो दाधार पृथिवीमुत द्याम्; &c. The moon also sustains the world. *Cf.* सोमेनादित्या बलिन: सोमेन पृथ्वी मही &c. Rig. X. 85, 2. The sacrificer also adds to the power of the sun and thereby sustains the universe. *Cf.* Manu अग्नौ प्रास्ताहुतिः सम्यगादित्यमुपतिष्ठते &c. Thus Śiva supports the world by his eight visible manifestations. *Cf.* कलितान्योन्यसामर्थ्यैः पृथिव्यादिभिरात्मभिः। येनेदं ध्रियते विश्वं &c. Kum. VI. 76 ; and the Śruti यो रुद्रो अग्नौ योऽप्सु य ओषधिषु। यो रुद्रो विश्वा भुवना विवेश। Taittirīya, samh. V. 5. 9. न अभिमानः—Ordinary persons are proud of their greatness ; but Śiva, though the supporter of the whole world, is not touched by pride ; because he is quite aloof from the world ; *cf.* the Śruti असङ्गो ह्ययं पुरुषः Bṛih. IV. 3, 15.

सन्मार्गा०—That you may see, *i. e.* know, the path of virtue or righteousness ; or it may mean the path leading to final emancipation (मोक्ष). तामसीं वृत्तिं–तमस इयं तामसी तां ; the operation or influence of the तमस् quality, the removal of which is necessary for the obtainment of true knowledge. The removal of darkness is also necessay for obtaining the sight of a thing. Śiva being the god of *Tamas* (*cf.* प्रजानां प्रलये तमःस्पृशे Kād. Intro. śl. 1) can remove the तामसी वृत्ति. तमः is defined as गुरुवरणकमेव तमः प्रदीपवच्चार्थतो वृत्तिः। Sāmkhya-Kārikā, 13.

The figures of speech in this śl. are विरोध and विशेषोक्ति. There is विशेषोक्ति inasmuch as the हेतु or cause of अभिमान (जगद्भरण) is stated and there is absence of the effect (अभिमान).

The commentator discovers in the Nāndi an indication of the subject-matter of the play. See his remarks अत्र प्रणतबहुफलैश्वर्यं &c. In सन्मार्गा० he sees a covert reference to the dance called मार्ग, which forms the chief incident of the play. The commentator also remarks that the Nāndi here does not conform to the convention about the number of *Padas* in it. यत्राष्टभिर्द्वादशभिरष्टादशभिरेव वा is the usual convention about the length of the Nāndi; but it appears from Kālidāsa's plays that he does not take cognizance of it in the construction of his Nāndis. Probably, the convention is of later growth; at least, it did not settle down into rule in Kālidāsa's time. नान्दी—नान्दी is defined as आशीर्वचनसंयुक्ता स्तुतिर्यस्मात्प्रयुज्यते। देवद्विजनृपादीनां तस्मान्नान्दीति संज्ञिता। Sāh.-D. VI. 24. नन्दन्ति देवता अस्यामिति (that in which the gods delight) नान्दी; fr, नन्द् + अ, the वृद्धि being irregular (पृषोदरादित्वात्); Jag. on the Māl.-Mādh. derives it as नन्दयतीति नन्दः। पचाद्यच्। नन्द एव नान्दः प्रज्ञादित्वादण्। and then स्त्रियां नान्दी. This Nāndi formed the concluding part of the elaborate theatrical preliminaries (called पूर्वरङ्ग) which were thought necessary to be gone through for the removal of obstacles in the performance of the play; *cf.* यन्नाट्यवस्तुनः पूर्वं रङ्गविघ्नोपशान्तये। कुशीलवाः प्रकुर्वन्ति पूर्वरङ्गः स उच्यते ॥ D.-R.

नान्द्यन्ते सूत्रधारः—This expression has caused much difficulty to many critics; for, as these words occur after the Nāndi, the question arises-who repeats the Nāndi, and different explanations have been given. But the simple explanation seems to be this. The Sūtradhāra repeats the Nāndi, as is distinctly said by Bharata—सूत्रधारः पठेन्नान्दीं मध्यमं स्वरमाश्रितः। नान्दीं पदैर्द्वादशभिरष्टभिर्वाप्यलंकृताम् ॥. But as the Nāndi contains a benediction and is thus auspicious, the words सूत्रधारः प्रविश्य &c. are not put before it, as none but auspicious words can begin a composition. Again the Nāndi was probably recited by the Sūtradhāra along with other actors; and as the real business of the drama began after that, it was the Sūtradhāra who, as the chief stage-manager, spoke after its recital. For other particulars see our note on the same in Śāk. or Vik.

सूत्रधारः—The principal manager 'who held the thread of the drama' *i. e.* directed the stage-business; he was a Brāhmaṇa, and thus qualified to recite the Nāndi. *Cf.* नाट्यस्य यदनुष्ठानं तत्सूत्रं स्यात्सबीजकम्। रङ्गदैवतपूजाकृत् सूत्रधार उदीरितः ॥

नेपथ्ये—नेपथ्य here means 'the tiring room' or the room behind the principal curtain where the actors attired themselves and remained in readiness to enter the stage. Also, any room used for a similar purpose ; see p. 46. नेपथ्य is irregularly derived as ने: नेतुः पथ्यं ; निनः नेत्रस्य वा पथ्यं what is agreeable to the eye. It also means dress, decoration; as in नेपथ्यविधानं Śāk. I ; or further on in विरलनेपथ्ययोः पात्रयोः p. 40. *Cf.* Ragh. V. 16; Kum. VII. 7.

मारिष—मृष्यतीति मर्षणान्मारिषः irregularly formed from मृष् 1st. or 4th conj. to bear patiently ; or मा न (the prohibitive particle) रेषतीति ; fr. रिष् 1 conj. + अ (कः). A respectful term used by the Sūtradhāra to address his assistant. **पारिपार्श्विक**—परिपार्श्वे वर्तते इति ; fr. परिपार्श्व + इक (ठक); the ठक् is obtained by the addition of च in the सूत्र 'परिमुखं च' (परिमुखं वर्तते पारिमुखिकः। चात्पारिपार्श्विकः Sid.-Kau.); it is sometimes written as ०र्श्वक ; in that case it should be explained as परिपार्श्वे भवः पारिपार्श्वः । तत्र भवः इत्यण् । पारिपार्श्व एव पारिपार्श्वकः by adding क स्वार्थे. भाव—The Sūtradhāra is addressed as भाव by his assistants. See com.

P. 4. **अभिहितोऽस्मि** & c.—This short dialogue is meant to introduce the author of the piece to the audience. **विद्वत्परिषदा**—परिषीदन्ति अस्यामिति परिषद्—that where the people sit ; hence secondarily 'the audience'. The omission of विद्वत् before परि० in some MSS. is not in good taste. Kālidāsa uses some laudatory epithet in such cases : *cf.* अभिरूपभूयिष्ठा परिषद् Śāk I. It seems that in ancient times the learned were consulted as regards the merit of a play and the one declared to be the best was brought to the notice of the king and rewarded ; *cf.* Bh. Nāṭya. XVII. 65, 66—धाता यस्य त्वल्पाः संख्याताः सिद्धयश्च बहुलाः स्युः विदितं कृत्वा राज्ञस्तस्मै देया पताका हि ॥ Hence the allusion to the learned in the assembly. **वस्तु**—The subject-matter or plot of the piece. *Cf.* सद्वस्तुपुरुषबहुमानात् Vik. I. ; the word is used in a different sense further on; see p. 14 (अनूनवस्तुकां). **मालविका०**—मालविका च अग्निमित्रश्च मालविकाग्निमित्रौ तावधिकृत्य कृतं नाटकम् अभेदोपचारात्तथा by transference of an epithet ; or अण् may be added in the sense of अधिकृत्य कृते ग्रन्थे by taking मालविकाग्निमित्र as a comp. of the शाकपार्थिवादि class. See com. नाटक–one of the ten Rūpakas. For its description, see Introduction.

वसन्तोत्सवे—In ancient India, it seems, dramatic performances were exhibited at the time of some fair or festival. See prologue to Bhavabhūti's Uttar. or Māl.-Mādh.

The Vasantotsava, celebrated to signalize the advent of the vernal season, and originally probably to welcome back the victorious Āryan heroes who usually started on their tour of conquest on the Dasarā day after the cessation of the rains, comes annually on the first of the dark half of the month of Phālguna and generally lasts till the 5th day. It was freely enjoyed by people of all classes, with men and women mingling together, and though some excesses were indulged in (see the opening scene of the 1st Act of the Ratnāvalī), it was free from the vulgar obscenities that characterize the modern *Holī*-festival as celebrated by the lower classes. "The observances enjoined for the Vasantotsava-day are :—(1) That a man shall touch a Mahār and shall then bathe, to secure freedom from all sin, from sorrows and diseases. (2) That he shall worship the *holī* spot to secure the destruction of all pain, with this mantra—वन्दितासि सुरेन्द्रेण ब्रह्मणा शंकरेण च अतस्त्वं पाहि नो देवि भूते भूतिप्रदा भव ॥. (3) That he shall eat the blossom of the Mango-tree mixed with sandal-wood, to secure the highest happiness, with this mantra-चूतमग्र्यं वसन्तस्य माकन्द कुसुमं तव। सचन्दनं पिबाम्यद्य सर्वकामार्थसिद्धये ॥ See Nirṇayasindhu under Vasantotsava. During the *holī*-festival dramatic representations of all sorts are still very common. "—S. P. Pandit.

"The burning of the *holī*" says Mr. Pandit, "is the mythological burning of the body of Kāma, and the loud lamentations represent the cries of Kāma's beautiful widow Rati, and the obscene words are exclamations of despair of Rati uttered to ask herself—What is the use now of my youth and beauty ?"

संगीतकं—The triple symphony of song, instrumental music and dancing.

मा तावत्—This should not be; it should not be acted. He means—We should set right the view of the audience in that respect and represent a play composed by &c. The Pārī. expresses this disapproval of the Sutradhara's proposal, only to give greater prominence to the greatness of Kālidāsa by giving to the Sūtra. thereby an occasion to eulogize the poet.

भाससौमिल्लक॰—Names of play-wrights who preceded Kālidāsa. Nothing was known about Bhāsa beyond a bare reference to his name and works by Bāṇabhaṭṭa in his introduction to his Harṣacarita, * or by Rājaśekhara in this Sūktimuktāvali †, until some of his works were recently discovered by Pandit T. Gaṇapati Śāstrī of Trivendrum while on his tour in Southern Travancore in search of Sanskrit MSS. The number of his dramas as yet discovered is thirteen ; they are स्वप्नवासवदत्त, प्रतिज्ञायौगन्धरायण, पञ्चरात्र, दूतवाक्य, चारुदत्त, दूतघटोत्कच, अविमारक, बालचरित, मध्यमव्यायोग, कर्णभार, ऊरुभङ्ग, अभिषेकनाटक and प्रतिमानाटक. Bhāsa was the most celebrated of all the dramatic poets that preceded Kālidāsa, and it seems he was a great favourite with the actors and the public and his plays were often represented on the stage. It was only after centuries that his fame must have been eclipsed by the superior genius of Kālidāsa and Bhavabhūtī and his plays must have gradually fallen into disuse. As regards his age there is a great diversity of opinion and no date has yet been fixed with exactness. Pandit Gaṇapati Śāstrī places him before Buddha and even Pāṇini. Prof. Bhide places him between 500 B. C. and 321 B. C.–making him live under the Magadha King Udayi or his successor. While Mr. Dhruva after an elaborate discussion of the different views, places him in the 2nd century B. C. (Gujarātī Introd. to his Gujr, translation of स्वप्नवासवदत्त). About Kaviputra and Saumillaka not much is known as yet. Prof. Bhide identifies them with Rāmila and Somila, the court-poets of S'ūdraka, who ascended the throne in 220 B.C. and died in 197 B.C., and mentioned in the well-known verse of Rājaśekhara–तौ शूद्रककथाकारौ रम्यौ रामिलसौमिलौ। काव्यं ययोर्द्वयोरासीदर्धनारीनरोपमम् ॥, Rāmila being the Kaviputra of Kālidāsa. See his Intro. to Svapnavāsavadatta, pp. 36–37.

प्रबन्ध—बध्यते काव्यवस्तु अस्मिन् असौ बन्धः a composition, poetic work ; *cf.* प्रकीर्यते काव्यबन्ध एषोऽत्र । Venī. 1. 5; प्रकृष्टः बन्धः प्रबन्धः an excellent composition. **अतिक्रम्य**—Passing over or setting aside, disregarding. **क्रिया**—work, composition ; *cf.* शृणुत मनोभिरवहितैः क्रियामिमां कालिदासस्य। Vik. I, 2 : for a different sense see *infra* I. 16. **पारिषदः बहुमानः**—is equivalent to परिषद्

---

* सूत्रधारकृतारम्भैर्नाटकैर्बहुभूमिकैः। सपताकैर्यशो लेभे भासो देवकुलैरिव ॥

† भासनाटकचक्रेऽपि च्छेकैः क्षिप्ते परीक्षितुम्। स्वप्नवासवदत्तस्य दाहकोऽभून्न पावकः ॥

बहु मन्यते shows a great regard for, attaches great importance to, to the exclusion of the excellent works &c.; *i.e.* shows a greater regard for. This implies that the audience had already approved of the play, as is clearly shown by the words of the Sūtradhāra further on–सन्तः परीक्ष्यान्यतरद्भजन्ते.

अयि—Ah, dear one; it is a term of tender address (कोमलामन्त्रेण). **विवेक०**—विवेकः विश्रान्तः यस्मात् तद्यथा तथा. Properly this should be विश्रान्तविवेक; but the परनिपात (coming latter in a comp.) of the p. p. विश्रान्त may be explained by classing it under the आहिताग्न्यादि group, which is an आकृतिगण (*i. e.* words requiring a similar explanation may be classed under it). "Thoughtlessly, without due consideration of the matter'.

Verse 2. Construe :—

सर्वं (काव्यं) पुराणं इति एव साधु न, काव्यं नवं इति अपि च अवद्यम् न, सन्तः परीक्ष्य अन्यतरत् भजन्ते, मूढः परप्रत्ययनेयबुद्धिः (अस्ति)।

पुराणं—पुरा भवं, from पुरा; or पुरा नवं (what was new in former times, not new, hence old); both formed irregularly. **अवद्यं**—Fit to be spoken of badly, censurable, य (यत्) is added to वद् with the neg. particle in the sense of कुत्सिते or reproach (कुत्सिते वदेर्नञि यत् Sid.-Kau. on Unādi 54); **सन्तः**—learned men, men able to discern merit and demerit (like those composing the present audience); *cf.* तं सन्तः श्रोतुमर्हन्ति सदसद्व्यक्तिहेतवः। Rag. I 10. **मूढः**—opp. of सत्; not having discerning power; unable to judge for himself. **परप्रत्यय**—प्रत्यय experience, judgment.

आर्यमिश्राः—The respectable audience. आर्याश्च ते मिश्राः पूज्याश्च; मिश्र is added as an honorific suffix and used always in the plural. पूज्ये मिश्रपदं नित्यं बहुवचनान्तं; मरीचिमिश्रैर्दक्षेण इति विष्णुपुराणात्। Jag. on Māl. Mādh. I. **प्रमाणं**—The authority *i. e.* their judgment must be followed, is final.

P. 6. **तेन**—If so, *i. e.* if you accept their judgment as unimpeachable.

Verse 3. Construe :—

शिरसा प्रथमगृहीतां परिषदः आज्ञां कर्तुं इच्छामि, देव्याः धारिण्याः अयं सेवादक्षः परिजनः इव।

शिरसा गृहीतां—Accepted implicitly and with profound respect (*lit.* with a respectful inclination of the head); *cf.* अशेषनरपतिशिरः समभ्यर्चितशासनः। Kād.; गुणानुरागेण शिरोभिरुह्यते नराधि-

वैमल्यमिवास्य शासनम्। Kir. I. 21; also Kum. III. 22. धारिण्या:—Dhārinī, the chief queen of Agnimitra, the Hero of the play. सेवादक्षः—सेवायां दक्षः (diligent in); ever ready to serve. परिजनोऽयं—The servants, here entering. Mark how simply and imperceptibly the dialogue between the Sūtradhāra and his assistant glides into the commencement of the action of the play.

The प्रस्तावना, which employs this mode of introducing the character or characters to enter the stage, is techincally called प्रयोगातिशय; *i. e.* when a character enters immediately after the Sūtradhāra has directly referred to his or her appearance. The प्रस्तावना, of the S'āk. is also of this kind. एषोऽयमित्युपक्षेपात्सूत्रधारप्रयोगतः। पात्रप्रवेशो यत्रैष प्रयोगातिशयो मतः॥ D.-R. III. 11. प्रस्तावना—Every Sanskrit play is introduced by what is called आमुख or प्रस्तावना (a dramatic prelude) which is a dialogue between the Sūtra. and the actress, or his assistant, or विदूषक, bearing on the business to be introduced; see com. The introduction to Bhāsa's plays is called स्थापना wherein the Sūtradhāra alone establishes the topic of the piece.

चेटी—A female servant (who is sent out on some errand. चेट्यते sent out as a servant इति, fr. चिट् 10 conj). देव्या—The chief queen is addressed as देवी. अचिरप्रवृत्तो॰—Instruction in which has been lately begun.

चलितं—(also written as छलिकं-तं) a kind of dance; see com. and *infra* p. 44. नाट्यं—dance; it is defined as अवस्थानुकृतिर्नाट्यं, a pantomimic representation of situations. अन्तरेण—with regard or respect to; Kāṭa. says—'with regard to receiving instruction in' (उपदेशार्थे). कीदृशी—का इव दृश्यते or कामिव इमां पश्यन्ति जनाः इति कीदृशी; what aptitude she shows for, or what progress she has made in; how she is faring in.

हला—A female friend is to be addressed as such; see com. धीरता—steadiness, fixity of mind on one thing (which does not allow it to be diverted to anything else), gravity. अम्हो—a particle showing surprise at something happening unexpectedly. "Oh Bak."-means—'I did not expect to see you here'. शिल्पिन्—शिल्पमस्यास्तीति one expert or skilled in an art; an artisan; here, 'a goldsmith'. नागमुद्रा॰—with a seal having the figure of a snake inscribed on it. The poet has an object in making the ring bear a serpent's figure on its seal. It is made to play an important part in the fourth Act, where it is covertly used as the means of procuring Mālavikā's release from custody by the Vidūṣaka who pretends to suffer from snake-bite.

स्निग्धं—with affection (*i.e.* attraction due to the gloss and workmanship of the ring); hence, admiringly (so as to have the eyes riveted on it). निध्यायन्ती—looking at with deep attention; with a steadfast look or gaze; *cf.* विद्याधरदारिका तेन राजर्षिणा चिरं निध्याता। Vik. IV. P. 93; मन्त्रान्या मुहुरभिलष्यता निदध्ये। Śiś. VIII. 69; Kir. X. 46. निभालयन्ती *v. l.*—looking at; pres. p. of भल with नि 10 cl. to see, to behold.

P. 8. स्थाने—on the right place or object; it is proper that. सज्जति—remains attached to or fixed on. उद्भिन्नकिरण॰—With filaments in the form of rays shooting forth from it. कुसुमितः—putting forth a flower; *fr.* कुसुम + इत (which is added to words of the तारकादि group in the sense of तदस्य संजातं 'this has got that;' as तारकाणि अस्य संजातानि तत् तारकितं नभः); पुष्पित, सुखित &c. are to be similarly explained. The streaming rays of the ring being compared to the filaments of flowers, the hand is said to have a flower. अग्रहस्तः—Karm. comp.; see com. The compound must be taken as such; see Malli. on Kum. V. 63. In a Karm. having an adjective for its first member, such as नीलोत्पल, उत्पल and नीलत्व are identical; but in the present case अग्र and हस्त are not identical; but अग्र as the part of the hand may be regarded as identical with it by the relation of the अवयव and the अवयविन्; see com.; for a fuller discussion of the point see our notes to Śāk. p. 92. प्रस्थिता—The p. p. participles of roots implying motion and of intransitive roots (see Pāṇ. III. 4. 72) have an active sense. See Apte's *Guide* § 152.

उपदेशग्रहणे—Receiving instruction and carrying it out. ईदृशेन व्या॰—by means of such employment (as dancing, singing &c., *i. e.* being kept confined in the dancing house) असंनिहिता—*lit.* not near, hence, kept out of his sight. किल—It is said, I hear. She means—In spite of the special care taken by the queen to keep Māl. out of the sight of the king, she was seen by the latter. The reading दिट्ठा कहं एसा is bad. For the reply given to this question by Bakul. begins with आम्, which expresses assent and which, therefore, is quite improper after the question कथं &c. आम्—An interjection expressing assent; 'oh', 'yes'. It has also the sense of 'recollection'. पार्श्वगता—Acc. Tat.; पर्शूनां समूह: पार्श्वं a collection (arrangement) of ribs; the part of the body below the arm-pit; hence, 'side' in general.

चित्रशाला—The hall set apart for painting work. प्रत्यग्रवर्णरागा—The colour of the paint of which was fresh (vivid). Elsewhere राग is used in the sense of the paint; *cf.* III. 11; रागरेखाविन्यास: p. 90; see also p. 92. चित्रलेखा—A painting or pictures. उपचार—Formalities of reception such as rising up, speaking words of welcome, making the customary bow &c. *Cf.* उपचारविधिर्मनस्विनीनां *infra.* III, 3, and गुरुपरितापानि न ते गात्राण्युपचारमर्हन्ति। Śāk. III. 16. It also means 'the customary salutation' or obeisance; *cf.* तयोपचाराञ्जलिखिन्नहस्तया Rag. III. 11. आसन्नतरां—Very close to her.

P. 10. अपूर्वा—new one; one not seen before; and hence the ground for the question. It also means 'extraordinary', 'wonderful', in which sense it was understood by the Queen, as is clear from her hesitation to answer the question further on. The reading अपूर्वरूपा is to be rejected, as the king cannot be expected directly to say anything that would indicate his admiration of her and rouse the Queen's jealousy. किंनाम०—किं नामधेयं name यस्या:। नाम एव नामधेयं; धेय is added to रूप, नाम and भाग without any alteration of the meaning; so we have रूपधेय and भागधेय.

आकृतिविशेषेषु—आकृतीनां विशेषा: remarkable or extraordinary patterns of forms; hence, persons of eminently noble appearance; or आकृति: विशेष: येषां ते those distinguished by their forms. पदं कृ—To set foot in or on, as a matter of course; hence 'to be naturally or spontaneously felt'; the whole means 'lovely forms command respect'. Bakulā. thought that the King's question proceeded from his admiration of Mālavikā's exquisitely beautiful form, and made the remark. अवधीरित०—*i. e.* by not replying to him. शङ्कित:—शङ्का अस्य संजाता असौ। by adding इत:; see कुसुमित supra p. 8. अनुबन्द्धुं—To ask persistingly, to importune. *Cf.* पुन: पुनश्चानुबध्यमाना Kād. वसुलक्ष्मी—is understood to be the younger sister of Dhāriṇī. आवुत्त:—The sister's husband (used in dramas only); *cf.* Amara.—नाट्योक्तौ गणिकाज्जुका। भगिनीपतिरावुत्त:।

सविशेष—With greater precaution, with special care. Mark the stages of the Queen's jealousy. She had already fears about Māla.'s charms captivating the King's mind, in case he saw her. Her fears were confirmed by the King's question, after he saw her in a picture; and when the King knew her name, she took special care to keep her out of his sight. **दर्शनपथः**—The range of sight; *cf.* श्रवणपथः; see com. the last word may also be पथः a road; वाट पथश्च मार्गश्च इति त्रिकांडशेषः। **अनुतिष्ठ आत्मनो नि०**—execute or attend to your business—said as a courteous way of saying 'you may go now', even when the other person has no special business to attend to; *cf.* त्वमपि स्वनियोगमशून्यं कुरु constantly occurring in dramas. **दर्शयामि**—Pres. in the sense of immediate future.

P. 12. **कामं**—I grant that (with a degree of unwillingness on the part of the speaker; अकामानुमतौ कामं Amara.); meaning to say, 'though not always with reason'. **कुलविद्या**—hereditary lore, the knowledge of an art or profession handed down from father to son. **सर्वस्य बहुमता**—*cf.* सहजं किलं यद्विनिन्दितं &c. Śāk VI. 1. The p. p. participle, of the roots मन् to think, बुध् to know and पूज् to worship, and others having the same sense are used in the sense of the present tense and are then construed with the genitive, by मतिबुद्धिपूजार्थेभ्यश्च and क्तस्य च वर्तमाने। Pān. III. 2. 188; II. 3. 67. **पुनः**—but again, however. *Cf.* तथापि न पुनरस्ति विश्वासः Vik. IV. **नाट्यं प्रति**–for नाट्य see next śl. **मिथ्या**—false, groundless; *i. e.* we are justly proud of.

Verse 4. Construe :—

मुनयः इदं (नाट्यं) देवानां कान्तं चाक्षुषं क्रतुम् आमनन्ति, रुद्रेण इदम् उमाकृतव्यतिकरे स्वाङ्गे द्विधा विभक्तम्, अत्र त्रैगुण्योद्भवं नानारसं लोकचरितं दृश्यते, नाट्यं भिन्नरुचेः अपि जनस्य बहुधा एकं समाराधनम्।

आमनन्ति—म्ना with आ, to lay down as in a sacred text; hence, to state authoritatively; *cf.* त्वामामनन्ति प्रकृतिं Kum. II. 13; तं हि धर्मं धर्मसूत्रकाराः समामन्ति Uttar. IV. **मुनयः**—Bharata (see Nāt. Śā. I. 91) and others, the original writers on the scenic art. **कान्तं**—charming, as it produces a pleasurable sensation by giving rise to different feelings. **क्रतुं**—a sacrifice, (originally meant 'wisdom', or strength; see our note on शतक्रतु Rag. III. 38. *Cf.* Greek 'Kratos'). **चाक्षुषं**—चक्षुषा ग्राह्यं 'fit to be enjoyed by the eye,' it being the province of the eyes. Nāṭya is poetically called a *kratu* because it not only gives satisfaction to the gods as a sacrifice does, but is also of sacred character. See com. By कान्त and चाक्षुष the poet simply means that the sacrifice presents scenes varied and charming, and this provides a feast for the eyes; while an ordinary sacrifice is too formal and rigid to please the eyes and spreads over a wearisome length.

Mr. Pandit, however, has the following note on this— "The epithets कान्त and चाक्षुष 'lovely and agreeable for the eye to see', doubtless are intended to imply that the Kratu proper was neither *Kānta*, nor *Chākshusha*, and refer us to a time when animal sacrifices had come to be regarded with disfavour, as being horrid and disagreeable to the eye; a time, that is to say, when Buddhistic ideas of the vedic sacrifice predominated".

उमाकृत०—उमा Pārvati; ओः शिवस्य मा लक्ष्मीरिव; उं शिवं माति मन्यते पतित्वेन इति वा; Kālidāsa thus accounts for the name—उ मेति मात्रा तपसो निषिद्धा पश्चादुमाख्यां सुमुखी जगाम। Kum. I. 26. व्यतिकर—properly 'blending, or mixture'; कृतव्य०—lit. in which a mixing up is brought about by Umā; *i. e.* which is shared in half by Umā. *Cf. supra* कान्तासंमिश्रदेह: śl. 1. द्विधा विभक्तं—divided in two ways or styles of dancing, the one called ताण्डव and the other लास्य. Rudra or Śiva who has a passion for music is represented as dancing and singing with his consort. ताण्डव is the frantic or violent dance of Śiva; *cf.* Mud. I. 2., Māl-Mād. 22, 23. लास्य-a dance; 'consisting chiefly of gesticulation with a shuffling movement of the feet (seldom lifted from the ground) forwards and backwards as invented by Pārvatī ,and opposed to the boisterous masculine dance called Tāṇḍava practised by Śiva and his followers'.

Hence also, a gentle dance accompanied with instrumental music and singing and representing the emotion of love. *Cf.* Daś.-R.—मधुरोद्धतभेदेन तद् द्वयं द्विविधं पुनः। लास्यताण्डवरूपेण नाटकाद्युपकारकम् ॥ I. 10. त्रैगुण्यो०—We get त्रैगुण्य (three qualities) by adding अ (ष्यञ्) in its own sense to त्रिगुणं a Dvigu (see com.). The three qualities, the constituents of Māyā (of Prakṛti according to the Sāṃkhya philosophy), are सत्त्व the quality of purity or goodness, रजस् the quality of foulness or passion, and तमस् the quality of darkness. The life of man (in whom Rajas predominates) chequered by its virtues and vices, passions and aspirations, and actions of all kinds, is the result of the influence of these in a more or less degree. **अत्र**—in this *i. e.* Nāṭya. **नानारसं**—of various aspects, or giving rise to different sentiments, Śṛṅgāra, Vīra and others.

नाट्यं—used here in the wider sense of 'the whole scenic art', as in Bharata's नाट्यशास्त्र. In the second line it has the restricted sense of 'नृत्य'. बहुधा-may be taken with भिन्नरुचेः, 'whose tastes widely differ'; or, better still, it should be taken with समाराधनं as is done by the com., as the idea of variety is already expressed by भिन्न; 'gratifier in many ways,' *i. e.*, by giving delight to the eyes, the ears, the mind &c. The figure of speech in this śl. is Kāvyaliṅga, as the third line serves as the हेतु which explains the statement in the fourth line.

अपि—goes with भिन्नरुचेः. **उपदेशग्रहणे**—is **वैषयिकसप्तमी**, 'in the matter of'. **अतिक्लेशयति**—अतिकिलिस्सदि (क्लिश्यति ते) *v. l.* (where क्लिश् is intrans.) means—does she find it very hard to receive instruction? Some translate it by क्लिश्नाति which is trans. and means 'does she not trouble you' &c.

विज्ञाप्यतां—be informed or told. When a person in an inferior position addresses or says something to a person in a superior position, the verb विज्ञापय् is used; and when one in a higher station says something to a person in a lower station आज्ञापय् is used (without there being any idea of actual request or command). विभाव्यतां *v. l.* is not good. It will at the best mean—'let the Queen be made to bring to her mind' (be convinced of or assured), a sense which is obscure, the usual sense of विभावय् being 'to revolve in or bring before the mind'. मेधाविनी—Here विन् has the sense of प्राशस्त्य or excellence (see com.); gifted with great intelligence.

Verse 5. Construe :—

प्रयोगविषये मया तस्यै यत् यत् भाविकम् उपदिश्यते तत् तत् बाला विशेषकरणात् मे प्रत्युपदिशति इव।

भाविकं—भावाय हितं; from भाव+इक (ठक्) favourable to भाव; gesticulations or movements of the body calculated to bring out, or contributing to the manifestation of a feeling (भाव)-भाव, is the being affected of the mind by different emotions

(विकारो हृद्गतो भावः Amara.); it is defined as सुखदुःखादिकैर्भावैर्भावस्तद्भावभावनं the entire pervasion of the mind by any feeling, such as that of pleasure or pain arising from the object under sight. See com. also. विशेषकरणात्—By performing the same in a better style or exhibiting it with superior excellence प्रत्युपदि०-She returns my instruction, as it were, by teaching me how to do the same in a better manner. The figure is उत्प्रेक्षा. बाला—बाल is one who is ग्रहणधारणपटुः able (by age and intelligence) to understand and remember what is taught.

P. 14. अतिक्रामन्तीं—Surpassing, excelling. See p. 150. इव—The figure is उत्प्रेक्षा. इरावती-name of the second (uncrowned) queen of Agnimitra. According to Paṇḍit Tārānātha it means an Apsaras of that name. But there is no reason why Baku. should refer to a heavenly nymph here. Baku. says this to herself in order that Gaṇadāsa should not notice her partiality for Mālavikā, lest he might speak about it to Irāvati. कृतार्था—*lit.* one who has fulfilled the mission of her life; hence, blessed, happy; or one who has gained her object; successful. यस्य—see com.; the instrumental is more usual; *cf.* रत्नैर्महार्हैस्तुतुषुर्न देवाः । Bhar.; आत्मन्येवात्मना तुष्टः Bg. II. 55. तद्विधानां—सा विधा यासां ताः तद्विधाः persons of her type or description (so clever). असुलभत्वात्—सुखेन लभ्या सुलभा, न सुलभा असुलभा, तस्या भावः असुलभत्वं तस्मात्। पात्रं—a proper object, a fit person; some assign a technical meaning to this, for which see com.

वर्णावरः—वर्णेन (by caste) अवरः Instr. Tat.; inferior to her by reason of his caste. The Varṇas (so called probably from the contrast of colour between the dark aboriginal tribes of India and their fair conquerors) are four as recognized by Manu and other ancient writers; viz. ब्राह्मण, क्षत्रिय, वैश्य and शूद्र. Of these a man of the higer class could marry a girl of his own class, as well as one of any of the lower classes (if he chose to do so). Thus a Brāhmaṇa could marry a girl of his own class, and also one of the Kṣatriya, Vaiśya or S'ūdra class; a Kṣatriya, a girl of the Kṣatriya class, as also one of the Vaiśya or S'udra class; and so on. Manu. III. 12, 13. So Vīrasena seems to have been the son of Dhārinī's father by a Vaiśya or S'ūdra wife.

अन्तपालदुर्गे—Antapāla may have been the name of a fort on the border of the kingdom of Agnimitra, or it may mean a fort on the frontier of his territory (अन्तं पालयतीति अन्तपालः स चासौ दुर्गश्च). **नर्मदातीर**—Narmadā, also called रेवा ('the roaring one') is one of the sacred rivers of India, and a bath in its water is as purifying as a bath in the Ganges *Cf.* गङ्गास्नानेन यत्पुण्यं तद्रेवादर्शनेन च। See our note on Megh. I. 19. It rises in the mountain Amarakaṇṭaka in Gondavana and after a westerly course of about 800 miles falls into the gulf of Cambay below Broach. In some editions the reading मन्दाकिनीतीरे is found for नर्मदा॰; now मन्दाकिनी usually signifies the heavenly Ganges and sometimes its tributary (See Megh. II. 6); but this will not do here. It is also the name of an actual river flowing, according to the Vāyu-Purāṇa from the Riksha mountain, or near the mountain Chitrakūṭa in Bundelkhand (probably the modern Pisuni). See Ragh. XIII. 48. "There is no doubt," remarks Mr. Paṇḍit, "that the Mandākinī of the present passage is a river of the Deccan. And further, it is probable that it may here stand for the Narmadā, in conformity with a practice, still very common all over India, of designating any sacred river by the most sacred river-name, as Gaṅgā."

शिल्पाधिकार—Capacity or ability to learn an art; here the fine arts. शिल्प also means skill or proficiency in; *See infra* I. 6, for अधिकार see pp. 40, 90,152. **उपायनं प्रेषिता**—It seems it was customary in those days to send such presents. *Cf.* infra p. 162.

आकृतिविशेषप्रत्ययात्—Lit. on account of the conviction brought home (to me) by her extraordinary from; hence, judging from, etc. आकृति (amiable form). प्रत्ययात् has also the same meaning. **॰विनयप्र॰** *v. l.* means— आकृतिश्च विनयश्च (modest demeanour, polite manners) तयोः प्र॰. But विनय is unnecessary as आकृति itself is supposed to imply possession of merits; *cf.* यत्राकृतिस्तत्र गुणा वसन्ति। Subh; आकृतिमनुगृह्णन्ति गुणाः। Vid. Bha; न ह्याकृतिः सुसदृशं विजहाति वृत्तम्। Mrich. IX. 16. **अनूनवस्तुकां**—Of excellent character (Kāṭa.); made of no inferior stuff (वस्तु stuff, materials of which a thing is made; hence वस्तु-कुलादिकं high descent and such other things;) न ऊनवस्तुकां :निकृष्टाभिजनां Nīlakaṇṭha. **यशस्विना भवितव्यं**—I am sure to be succesful.

Verse 6. Construe :—

आधातुः पात्रविशेषे न्यस्तं शिल्पं गुणान्तरं व्रजति पयोदस्य समुद्रशुक्तौ न्यस्तं जलं मुक्ताफलतां इव ।

पात्रविशेष :—(विशिष्टं पात्रं) an excellent recipient, a worthy pupil. ०विशेषे—विशेषन्यस्तं *v. l.* the former is better, as न्यस्त left out of the comp. can also be taken with शुक्तौ. **गुणान्तरं**—अन्यः (तत उत्कृष्टः) गुणः गुणान्तरं a higher excellence: *cf.* न स्म वेद न गुणान्तरं च सः । S'is. XIV. 47. **शिल्पं**—Skill or proficiency in an art. **जलमिव** etc.—This is a श्रौती पूर्णोपमा, all the four things necessary for a comparison (the उपमेय, उपमान, साधारणधर्म and उपमाप्रतिपादक शब्द) being stated. It is a belief that the rain-drops falling into the open oyster-shells while the sun is in the asterism Svāti (the star Arcturus), are converted into pearls. The *svāti* annually comes on the ecliptic about the 22nd of October; see Var. Bṛih.-Sam. Ch. XV. 13. *Cf.* Bhar. Nit. 67 स्वात्यां सागरशुक्तिमध्यपतितं सन्मौक्तिकं जायते ।

P. 16. **पञ्चाङ्गाभिनय** :—Acting, exhibited by means of (or consisting of) five parts. अभिनय or acting is of four kinds, भवेदभिनयोऽवस्थानुकारः स चतुर्विधः । आंगिको वाचिकश्चैवमाहार्यः सात्त्विकस्तथा ॥ Sāh.-Dar. VI 2; (1) *Āṅgika* or gestural, *i. e.* conveyed by bodily movements; (2) *Vācika* or vocal, *i. e.* conveyed by words; (3) *Āhārya* or extraneous, *i. e.* expressed by dress, ornaments, decorations; etc. and (4) *Sātvika*, *i. e.* conveyed by the manifestation of internal feelings, such as perspiration, horripilation, etc. The five *Aṅgas* referred to here are the mind, the eye, the eyebrows, the hands and the feet, which are used in the pantomimic representation of situations (see com). Nīlakaṇṭha quotes—कराभ्यां चरणाभ्यां च शिरसा चाभिनीयते । यत्र वस्त्वति विज्ञेयो पञ्चाङ्गाभिनयो हि सः ॥ According to Kāṭa. the mode of dancing called प्रेरण is referred to here, for which see com.

दीर्घिका०—दीर्घिका an oblong well or tank with lotus-plants in it, in a garden attached to a mansion or palace. See II. 12. **अवलोकन**—overlooking, commanding the view of. **गवाक्षे**-गोः अक्षि इव a round window, originally probably resembling in shape a bull's eye. **प्रवात** *n.*—a strong current of wind. **से**—**(अस्याः)**—The genitive may be the object of निवेदन or be connected with उत्साह. Properly the form is *mas.* and here stands for ताए, but such *mas.* pronominal forms are often found used in plays. **यावद् वर्धयामि**—यावत् when used with a form of the present tense gives it the sense of the future (यावत्पुरानिपात्-योर्लट्). **लब्धक्षणः**—क्षण a moment, hence one's own moment of time; leisure, recess; the Marāṭhi word **सण** a festival (day of leisure) is derived from this.

विष्कम्भकः—is an interlude at the beginning of an act of a play enacted by minor characters (*i. e.* **मध्यम** or middling and **नीच** or low ones) who by their conversation succinctly indicate parts of the story gone by or that are to follow. It is **शुद्ध** when performed by one or more of middling characters, and मिश्र or संकीर्ण when performed by characters middling and low. It is necessary for acquainting the audience with incidents which are not actually represented on the stage but the knowledge of which is necessary for the proper understanding of the plot.

Thus in the foregoing interlude we are told that a beautiful girl, Mālavikā by name, was presented to the Queen by her brother, and that she was placed under Gaṇadāsa to learn dancing and singing, to prevent her being seen by the king. The king, however, we are further told, sees her picture and being attracted by her exquisitely lovely form inquires about her and learns from the Queen's sister that her name was Mālavikā. The queen, thereafter, takes all the greater care to guard her from the king's sight.

लेखहस्ते०—A Vyadhikaraṇa Bah. **अन्वास्यमानः**—attended upon by; *lit.* seated behind (as a mark of respect). **आस्** with **अनु** is trans. *Cf.* Ragh. 1. 56 (अन्वासितमरुन्धत्या). **अनुवाचित०**—अनुवाचितः लेखो येन. अनुवाचय् means 'to read silently to oneself'. *Cf.* **अनुवाचय तावदेतत्।** Vik. p. 57. **किं प्रतिपद्यते**—what does he propose or undertake to do ? What terms does he accept ? The meaning of प्रतिपद् is 'to undertake to do'; *cf.* निर्वाहः प्रतिपन्नवस्तुषु सतामेतद्धि गोत्रव्रतम्। Mud. II. 18. **वैदर्भः**—The king of Vidarbha, Yajñasena by name and cousin of Mālavikā. Vidarbha is the modern Berar, which was a great kingdom in ancient times, lying to the north of Kuntala and extending from the banks of the Kṛṣṇā to about the banks of the Narmadā; on account of its great size it was also called Mahārāṣṭra. Kuṇḍinapura (probably the modern Bedar) was its ancient capital. The river Varahā (Warhā) divided Vidarbha into two parts, Amarāvati being the capital of the northern, and Pratiṣṭhāna of the southern part.

अमात्य:—अमा सह समीपे वा भवः, fr. अमा *ind.* meaning 'together' and त्य by the Vārttika अमेहक्वतसित्रेभ्य एव; so इहत्य, क्वत्य, ततस्य and तत्रत्य. *Lit.* it means 'a constant companion of', hence, a minister. **देव**—a king is to be so addressed by his servants and subjects. *Cf.* देवेति नृपतिर्वाच्यो भृत्यैः प्रकृतिभिस्तथा। **आत्मविनाशं**—(प्रतिपद्यते). He means–by the insolent tone of his reply he is simply seeking his own destruction or drawing down ruin on himself.

P. 18. **संदेशं**—निर्देशं *v. l.* will mean—what is dictated to us (निर्दिश्यते इति), the terms proposed. **निर्देश**—'a definite statement', means the same thing. Tārānātha also translates this by अभिसंधि or पण; this reading is better suited to the minister's reply 'आत्मनो विनाशम्'.

पूज्येन—The revered one *i. e.* Agnimitra. **पितृव्य** पुत्रः &c.—The words from पितृव्य॰ to मोचयितव्यः are a quotation from Agnimitra's letter to the Vidarbha king. **भवतः**—*i. e.* of Yajñasena. **पितृव्यः**—पितुः भ्राता formed from पितृ by adding व्य (व्यत्) in the sense of 'father's brother' पितुर्भ्रातरि व्यत् Vārttika **प्रतिश्रुतसंबन्धः**—who had promised a family-connexion to me (*i. e.* by giving Mālavikā in marriage to me). **अन्तपालेन**—may be a proper name, or what is more likely, a frontier guard or the keeper of a fort on the frontier. **अवस्कद्य**—*Ger.* of स्कन्द् with अव to attack. मदपेक्षया—Out of regard for me (*i. e.* if you wish to keep up your good relations with me). **तत्र वो** &c.—Here begins the reply of the Vidarbha King. This sentence is variously read and it is difficult to determine the original reading. The reading adopted in the text seems to be the best, as its tone is more offending. तत्र वो means—It is not un-known to you, *i. e.*, it is well known to you. **वः**—*pl.* to show respect. **तुल्याभि॰**—तुल्यः अभिजनः descent येषां; of equal descent, who claim an equal pedigree or high descent. **भूमिहरेषु**—lit. those who take a share of the kingdom; *dāyādas*. **वृत्तिः ईदृशी**—Their conduct is such, *i.e.*, they can take such a one prisoner or keep one in custody. Another should not interfere in such matters. He means to say—I have a perfect right to act inimically or otherwise as will suit my purpose towards Mād., an undesirable relative of mine; and you should not meddle in our affairs. For the double negative *cf.* further on—न च परिचितो न चाप्यगम्यः p. 24. The Com. seems to read तन्न वो विदितं, and remarks that there is a *kāku* here, *i. e.*, the negative particle should be read in such a way as to imply the contrary (as in a question of appeal). Is it not known to you? Certainly it is. एतन्ननु वो विदितं *V. l.*—it is certainly (ननु) known to you &c.—is also a good reading. Mr. Paṇḍit reads the passage as तन्न वो विदितं यत्तुल्याभिजनेषु भूमेरिव राज्ञां प्रवृत्तिः which means—Do you not know then that the conduct of kings towards kings who belong to the same family....should be like that of earth, *i. e.* one of perfect impartiality, (and therefore, you should not be partial to Mādhavasena)? But this quality of the earth is nowhere referred to by Kālidāsa, though the idea itself is good. **अतोऽत्र** &c.—Construe अत्र (in the matter of Mādhavasena's release) पूज्यः the revered one *i. e.* Agnimitra, मध्यस्थः भवितुं अर्हति should be pleased to be &c.

सोदर्या—समाने उदरे शयिता सोदर्या *Pāṇ* IV. 4. 108; by विभाषा उदरे we get समानोदर्या also; the aff. य is added by the rule सोदराद्यः, Pān. IV. 4. 109. **ग्रहण०**—ग्रहणे विप्लवः (tumult, confusion caused) ग्रहणविप्लवः. **अथ**—is used here पक्षान्तरे; 'but if, supposing on the other hand that'. **मोचयितव्य** :—*pot. p. p.* of the causal of मुच्; should be caused to be set at liberty. मया is the primitive agent. **अभिसंधिः**—purpose, the object aimed at; hence the terms or conditions securing such an object.

Verse 7. Construe :—

यदि पूज्यः संयतं मम श्यालं मौर्यसचिवं विमुञ्चति ततः अहम् अपि सद्यः माधवसेनं बन्धनात् मोक्ता।

मौर्यसचिवं—Kāṭayavema takes this as the name of the brother-in-law of the Vidarbha king. If this supposition is not correct, he would appear to be the minister of the last of the Maurya kings of Pāṭaliputra imprisoned by gnimitra probably to prevent him, as Mr. Pandit supposes from exciting the people against his father, Puṣpamitra, who had murdered the Maurya King, Bṛihadratha, and usurped his throne. The imprisonment of Mādhavasena, the intended brother-in-law of Agnimitra, by his cousin, the King of the Vidarbhas, could then be explained as only a retaliation for his brother-in-law's imprisonment by Agnimitra. Tāranātha reads आर्यसचिवम्. सचिव is derived from सचि companionship (fr. सच्, 1st conj. to be associated with &c.) and वा to go (सचिं वाताति). मोक्ता—1st Fut.; the Com. reads मोक्ता माधवसेनस्ततो मया &c. where मोक्ता must be taken as Pass. 1st Fut.; but symmetry requires the Active form. Here मोक्ता cannot be taken as a noun in तृ denoting the agent; for a noun in तृ is used with the Acc. only when it implies habit; see Pān. II. 3. 69; III. 2. 134.

कार्यविनिमयेन—by (proposing) an exchange of duties or acts. **व्यवहृ**—to deal with. Verbs meaning 'to deal with, behave' &c. govern their object in the loc., as आर्योऽस्मिन् विनयेन वर्तताम्। Uttar. VI., तस्यां त्वं साधु नाचरः। Ragh. I. 76. **अनात्मज्ञ**:—आत्मानं जानातीति आत्मज्ञः; न आत्मज्ञः अनात्मज्ञः; one who does not know oneself, *i. e.* where one's good or safety lies; hence, foolish. *Cf.* मा तावदनात्मज्ञे Śāk. VI. **प्रकृत्यमित्र**:—प्रकृत्या अमित्रः प्रकृ०, a natural enemy, *i.e.* one who has his kingdom situated close on the border of one's country. See Malli. on Śiś. II. 36. अमित्र is derived from अम् to go and the aff. इत्र added in the sense of enemy by the Unādi sūtra अमेर्द्विषति चित् (IV. 174) and is *mas.* The Com. says विषयानन्तरत्वात् *i. e.* owing to his being in close proximity with Agni.'s territory. **प्रतिकूलचारी**—प्रतिकूलं *lit.* 'against the current', चरतीति one who has acted inimically, who has given offence. **यातव्यपक्षे**—On the side (under the category of), those who deserve to be marched against or attacked (by having given provocation). यातुमभियातुं योग्याः यातव्याः तेषां पक्षः तस्मिन्. **पूर्वसंकल्पित०**—पूर्वसंकल्पितं च तत्समुन्मूलनं च तस्मै, his total destruction that was previously determined upon. Agnimitra had made up his mind to root out the Vidarbha king but waited for some excuse to invade his territory; the present reply to his letter furnished that. The reading पूर्वसंकल्पितं is rejected because if adopted, it can qualify दण्डचक्रं, but there is no reason why the army should have been kept ready when Vidarbha had not yet given direct provocation. **वीरसेन०**—वीरसेनः (see p. 14) प्रमुखः यस्य. दण्डचक्रं—दण्ड्यते शत्रुरनेन इति दण्डः an army; तस्य चक्रं the whole body of, *i. e.* an army consisting of all its constituents.

P. 20. **शास्त्रदृष्टं**—may be taken as (1) **शास्त्रेण दृष्टं**—seen by, approved of by the political science; or (2) **शास्त्रे दृष्टं** what is seen in *i. e.* found prescribed in the S'āstras; what is in keeping with the teaching of the S'āstras.

Verse 8. Construe—

अचिराधिष्ठितराज्यः शत्रुः प्रकृतिषु अरूढमूलत्वात् नरसंरोहणशिथिलः तरुः इव समुद्धर्तुं सुकरः।

अचिरा॰—अचिर not long ago अधिष्ठितं obtained राज्यं येन; a new king. **प्रकृतिषु**—the subjects. **अरूढमूल॰**— रूढमूल means what has taken firm root, and can apply properly only to the tree; when referring to the enemy it must be taken in the secondary sense of who has gained a firm hold on the affections of the people, whose rule is firmly established among his subjects'. *Cf.* अथ वीक्ष्य रघुः प्रतिष्ठितं प्रकृतिष्वात्मजमात्मवत्तया Ragh. VIII. 10.

अवितथं—विगता तथा यस्मात्तत् वितथं what is removed from truth, untrue, false; न वितथं अवितथं true, what conforms to truth or stands to facts. He means the words of the तन्त्र॰ are bound to come true and we are sure to succeed. **तन्त्रकार**—The writer of a treatise on political science. तन्त्र is used here in the sense of a शास्त्र or its branch or सिद्धान्त (settled principles); cf. कामतन्त्र (p. 156), कन्दुकतन्त्र &c.; it also means a work (generally in the form of a dialogue between S'iva and Durgā) teaching magical and mystical formularies for the attainment of superhuman power of securing the favour of a deity, &c.; *e. g.* the भैरवतन्त्र referred to in the notes on उदकुम्भविधाने p. 124. **वचनं**—authoritative statement, a tenet, rule or dictum. **इदं**—*i. e.* the insolent reply given. **समुद्योज्यतां**—should be made to proceed or commence operations against; should be set against.

तथा—Is elliptical for यथा देव आज्ञापयति तथा करिष्ये; **यथाव्यापारं**—According to their duties: engaged in their respective occupations. **विदूषकः**—The jocose companion and confidential friend of the hero of a play; his duty is to excite mirth by his quaint dress, speech, gestures &c.; he takes pleasure in quarrels and is one who knows his business well. He is required to be a Brāhmaṇa. *Cf.* कुसुमवसन्ताद्यभिधः कर्मवपुर्वेषभाषाद्यैः। हास्यकरः कलहरतिर्विदूषकः स्यात्स्वकर्मज्ञः॥ S.-D. III. 42. See

Introduction. यदृच्छा-येन केनापि ऋच्छनं यदृच्छा; *fr.* यद्+ऋच्छा a noun *fr.* ऋच्छ् to go+अ affix; the act of taking a eourse anyhow; accident. प्रत्यक्ष०—अक्षं (इन्द्रियं) प्रतिगतं, अक्ष्णोः प्रति इति वा प्रत्यक्षं दर्शनं यस्याः 'will be one whose actual sight is obtained' *i. e.*, who will be seen face to face. सचिवः—The king humorously calls the Vidū. this. अन्यत्कार्यं कार्यान्तरं a Nitya Samāsa; तत्र सचिवः a minister in a business other than political; an assistant in love-matters. The Vidū. is often called नर्मसचिव. कच्चित्—asks a question in the hope of getting an expected answer; 'is it employed'—I hope it is. *Cf.* Ragh, V. 8, 9. उपेयोपाय०-उपेय what is to be reached as one's goal; the object aimed at; the variant उपायोपेयदर्शने must be explained as उपायैः उपेयस्य दर्शनं तत्र—in the matter of obtaining a sight of the object to be gained by means of remedies. प्रज्ञाचक्षुः—प्रज्ञैव प्रज्ञारूपं वा चक्षुः the eye in the form of your intellect; your mental eye.

प्रयोगसिद्धं &c.—The Vidūṣaka gives a curt reply, instead of giving a direct answer to the King's question, to please him at once. The particle आः found in some editions is dropped, as it implies 'anger or dissatisfaction'. प्रयोग means here in scheme, a remedy devised, an artifice'. The word is used in two other senses by our poet in this work, *viz.* practice or the experimental part of a subject, as opposed to its theory (see *infra* p. 26 शास्त्रे प्रयोगे च &c.), and outward exhibition, representation, as in प्रयोगप्रधानं हि नाट्यशास्त्रं *infra* p. 30.

एत्तामित्त—Although the Vidūṣaka utters these two words audibly, he whispers in the king's ear the remedy devised by him to have his object accomplished; his plan was, as will subsequntly appear, to stir up a quarrel between the two dancing masters, Gaṇadāsa and Haradatta, as to their comparative merits, resulting in an actual exhibition by their pupils of their sklll in dancing, and thereby to cause Mālavikā to be brought before the king.

P. 22. उपक्रान्तं—उपक्रमः कृतः made a beginning. उपक्रम —first beginning. दुरधिगम०—दुःखेन अधिगम्यते इति दुरधिगमा; दुर० सिद्धिर्यस्य in which success is difficult to obtain. आरम्भ—आरम्यते इति आरम्भः an undertaking. *Cf.* आरम्भेऽस्मिन्स्वामिनो वृद्धिहेतौ Rat. 1.6; आगमैः सदृशारम्भः &c. Ragh. I.15.

Verse 9. Construe :—

सहायवान् एव सप्रतिबन्धं अर्थं अधिगन्तुं प्रभुः (भवति) सचक्षुः अपि दीपेन विना तमसि दृश्यं न पश्यति ।

सप्रतिबन्धं—Full of, hampered by, impediments. By this he refers to his two queens धारिणी and इरावती.. सहाय-वानेव—Only when one has a friend to help him. सचक्षुः—one having one's power of vision or good eyes. Shāstrī Rashivde-kar suggests the reading सुचक्षुरपि, but this is not necessary. The figure of speech here is दृष्टान्त (by व्यतिरेक), as there is nothing in the उपमेयवाक्य to correspond to सचक्षुरपि in the उपमानवाक्य. It will be better to construe the first line as प्रभुः अपि सहायवानेव.........न्तुं समर्थः भवति ।

समक्षं—अक्ष्णोः समीपे, Avya : the final अ is added by the rule प्रतिपरसमनुभ्योऽक्ष्णः। अधरो०—अधरस्य उत्तरस्य व्यक्तिः the manifestation of (it will clearly appear) which of us is inferior and which superior. सुनीति०—शोभना नीतिः सुनीतिः (a plan cleverly or wisely devised) एव पादपः तस्य पुष्पं—which is the sign of the future fruit *viz.* Mālavikā's personal appearance.

कञ्चुकी—so called from the long cloak worn by him (कञ्चुकः अस्यास्तीति); he was the chief attendant of the harem in ancient India. He is represented as a Brāhmaṇa, old, possess-ed of a number of good qualities such as truthfulness, and a clever man of business. *Cf.* अन्तःपुरचरो राज्ञां वृद्धो विप्रो गुणान्वितः। सर्वकार्यार्थकुशलः कञ्चुकीत्यभिधीयते ॥ See also note on Vikr. III. 1.

Verse 10. Construe :—

साक्षात् शरीरिणौ भावौ इव परस्परजयोद्यतौ उभौ अभिनयाचार्यौ त्वां द्रष्टुं इच्छतः।

अभिनयाचार्यौ—Masters of the art of gesticulation. आचार्य is one who knows a subject thoroughly well. जयोद्यतौ—जयाय उद्यतौ bent or intent on getting victory over each other. जयैषिणौ *v. l.* wishing to get, etc. भावौ—internal feelings or emotions. शरीरिणौ—शरीरं विद्यते अनयोस्तौ incarnate, appearing in a bodily form. दुरासदः-दुःखेन आसादयितुं शक्यः difficult to be approached; striking one with awe. राजमहिमा—the king's majesty, *i. e.*, the majestic king.

Verse 11. Construe :—

P. 24. न परिचितः न च अपि च अगम्यः न, तथापि अस्य पार्श्वं चकितं उपैमि, सः एव अयं सलिलनिधिः इव मे अक्ष्णोः प्रतिक्षणं नवः नवः भवति ।

न अगम्यः—One not to be not approached *i. e.*, approachable (on account of his good qualities)! *cf.* भीमकान्तैर्नृपगुणैः स बभूवोपजीविनाम्। अधृष्यश्चाभिगम्यश्च। Ragh. I 16. रम्य—*v. l.* attractive, inviting by his appearance. चकितं—adv., with fear or awe. सलिलनिधिरिव—Like the ocean which presents a new surface to view every moment on account of its surging waves and has to be entered into with care. नवो नवः—He ever appears charming to the eyes; *cf.* क्षणे क्षणे यन्नवतामुपैति तदेव रूपं रमणीयतायाः। The figures of speech in this *śloka* are विभावना, and a fusion of अतिशयोक्ति and उपमा. There is विभावना, in as much as there is fear mentioned in the second line while its cause is not stated. There is अति० as the same man is said to be new every moment (अभेदे भेदप्रतिपादनरूपा). सलिलनिधिरिव is उपमा..

पुरुषाकारं—Appearing in human form. ज्योतिः—The king on account of his pre-eminent position and bodily effulgence is considered as a portion of the Supreme Being and is called here ज्योतिस् which is a form of Brahman; *cf.* ज्योतिषामपि तज्ज्योतिः। Bg. XIII. 17; तद्देवा ज्योतिषां ज्योतिरायुर्होपासतेऽमृतम्। Brih. Up. IV. 4. 16. पुरुषाधिकरणं—*v. l.* means residing in a man (पुरुषः अधिकरणं स्थानं यस्य), *i. e.* in a human form. The reading पुरुषाधिकारं is not good; it may mean पुरुषेषु अधिकारो यस्य, exercising its authority or influence over men; पुरुषः अधिकारः अधिकरणं residence यस्य.

Verse 12. Construe :—

द्वारे (प्रथमं प्रतिवारितोऽस्मि) नियुक्तपुरुषानुमतप्रवेशः सिंहासनान्तिकचरेण सह उपसर्पन् अस्य विनिवर्तितदृष्टिपातैः तेजोभिः वाक्यात् ऋते पुनः प्रतिवारितः इव अस्मि।

द्वारे नियुक्त०—Although द्वार is not connected with नियुक्तं which it should be, the comp. is allowed as the connexion can be easily known, there being नित्यापेक्षा. *Cf.* for a similar use तां सैव वेत्रग्रहणे नियुक्ता Ragh. VI. 26; नियुक्ता प्रतिहारभूमौ VI. 31 *ibid.* Or द्वारे may be taken separately; at the door'. विनिवर्तित० which repel the casting of a glance at him, which make me withdraw my eyes. पुनः—must be taken here in the sense of 'in a different way', and not in that of 'again', a second time as he was not repelled at the door for the first time. अस्य तेजोभिः वाक्यादृते पुनः भेदेन (प्रकारान्तरेण) प्रतिवारितोऽस्मि इव, 'पुनरप्रथमं भेदे', इत्यमरः। The fig. is Utprekṣā. किमिदं......पस्थानम्—Notice how the king feigns ignorance of the matter. तीर्थ—An expert preceptor : *fr*, तॄ + the Uṇādi aff. थ (थक्); तीर्यते अनेन इति तीर्थम्; the reading सुतीर्थ is better in this respect. दत्तप्रयोग:—One who has given practical lessons (in the art of theotrical representation). He means—'I am both an expert and experienced teacher'

P. 26. दृढं—firmly, so as not to forget it. —सोऽहं I who am such, having such antecedents, प्रधान०—प्रधानाश्च ते पुरुषाश्च तेषां समक्षं (which makes the case worse); he could have abused me in private. परिवादरत:—*V. l.* He took pleasure in, was given to, abusing or reproaching me; परिवाद *fr.* वद् with परि + अ (घञ्); also परीवाद by the rule उपसर्गस्य घञ्यमनुष्ये; the vowel of a preposition is optionally lengthened before the aff. घञ् when the word does not denote a man; as परिपाक, परीपाक; but निषाद only अत्रभवत:—is used ironically; or अत्र may be taken separately—अत्र अभिनयविज्ञायाम्. किल—verily, certainly. समुद्रप०—is ironical. विशेषज्ञ:—one able to find out the special merit or the superiority of. प्राश्निक:—(*fr.* प्रश्न + इक; see com.) lit. one authorized to ask questions; hence an examiner, a judge. With the reading विशेषज्ञः (a noun) प्राश्निकश्च the meaning will be—Your Majesty is a judge and an examiner as well. समर्थं—reasonable or favourable (to your object); समर्थस्त्रिषु शक्तिस्थे सबद्धार्थे हितेऽपि च। Amara. प्रतिज्ञातं—a declaration, proposal; here त is added भावे (प्रतिज्ञातं = प्रतिज्ञा).

प्रथम—First-rate, most reasonable, excellent. कल्प:—proposal, plan; (the best) course suggested. This occurs constantly in Bhāsa ; see Madhyamavyā., Pancharātra &c. उदार कल्प: Śāk. VII. तावत्—For a while. पक्षपातमत्र &c.—Here the student should remember that Haradatta was patronized by the King and Gaṇadāsa by the Queen. Now the King, wishing to appear perfectly indifferent in the matter, desires that the question should be decided in the presence of the Queen, accompained by the learned Kauśikī to assist her in the matter, so that the Queen should not have any ground for complaint in case the question was decided in favour of Haradatta. The real object, however, of the king in calling Kauśikī is that she, who was taken into the secret by his friend Vidūṣaka, should so direct the course of events that it would be necessary for the two dancing masters to produce their pupils before the party for examination, so that Mālavikā would be brought before the king. It does not appear from the context that the two dancing masters also were taken into confidence by the Vidūṣaka. They seem to know nothing about the plot.

पण्डित०—पण्डिता चासौ कौशिकी च; पण्डिता becomes पण्डित by the rule स्त्रियाः पुंवत् etc. Pāṇ. VI. 3. 34. न्याय्यः—not departing from justice (see com.); just, proper. य is added to न्याय in this sense by the Sutra धर्मपथ्यर्थन्यायादनपेते Pāṇ. IV. 4, 92; so धर्म्यं, पथ्यं, अर्थ्यम्. व्यवहार—here means the decision of a case after investigation. प्रस्तावं—matter in dispute or hand; occasion.

P. 28. संरम्भ—emulation, contest. कथं पश्यसि—what do you foresee to be the issue or result of the contest? who will win? स्वपक्ष—Your *protege* or favourite, *viz.* गणदास. अवसाद—lit. ruin or loss; hence, giving way, defeat. परिहीयते—Pass. of हा 3 Par. (used with the Abl.) to be inferior to, to fall short of. *Cf.* न प्रतिच्छन्दात्परिहीयते मधुरता *infra* p. 46 न परिहीयते शच्या ओजस्वितया Vikr. III. p. 79. प्रतिद्वंद्विन्—द्वंद्व a duel, a contest between two; द्वंद्वमस्यास्तीति द्वंद्वी; प्रतिगतो द्वंद्वी प्रति०; an antagonist, a rival. राजपरिग्रहः—राज्ञः परिग्रहः His being patronized or favoured by the king, उपहरति—brings, *i. e.* gives him superiority (advantage over). अपहरति *v. l.*-deprives him of; in this case से (अस्य) would refer to गणदास. राज्ञी०— you too enjoy the title of 'Queen; *i. e.* Gaṇadāsa being *your* favourite is also equally great.

Verse 13 Construe

अनलः भानोः परिग्रहात् अतिमात्रभासुरत्वं पुष्यति, चन्द्रः अपि निशापरिगृहीतः महिमानं अधिगच्छति।

अतिमात्र०—मात्रामतिक्रान्तं Prādi. Tat.; or अतिशयिता मात्रा यस्य तत् Bah; that the measure of which is great'; now see com. भासुरत्वं—भासुरस्य भावः. भासुर—shining, splendid; *fr.* भास् + affix उर (घुरच्) which is added to भञ्ज्, भास् and मिद्; so भङ्गुर and मेदुर (fat, thick) by भञ्जभासमिदो घुरच् Pāṇ. III. 2. 161. भानोः परिग्रहात्—It is a belief that the sun deposists his lustre in the fire when setting; see com. and Ragh. IV. 1; *cf.* also प्रभा हि सौरी

पादेन ह्रस्तं याति दिवाकरे। अभिमाविशते रात्रौ तस्माद् दूरात्प्रकाशते ॥ The reading भानुः परिग्रहादहः is bad. In the first place it is absurd to speak of the sun being favoured by the day; for the sun can never appear at night so that he can be मन्दप्रभ (in fact he is the maker of the day); but the moon does appear by the day and is मन्दप्रभ; like the fire during day-time. Secondly, the illustration is intended to support the statement that one can attain greatness when supported by a female as one does when supported by a male. Here भानु and निशा correspond to the King and the Queen respectively, and अनल and चन्द्र to Haradatta and Gaṇadāsa. The fig. of speech is दृष्टान्त in each line.

अविहा—May be translated by (1) अपिहा in the sense of Ah, hush (हा meaning जुगुप्सा); it does not show surprise; for the Queen's arrival was expected; or (2) by अविहा which is short for अव इह protect, take care; here meaning 'do not say or do anything that will rouse the Queen's suspicion'. The Vidūṣaka utters these words to give a warning to the king.

पीठमर्दिका—The Nāyaka or Hero of a dramatic piece has for his assistants पीठमर्द, विट, चेट, and विदूषक. Of these the last three assist him in love-matters, while the first possessing qualities somewhat short of the hero, is his assistant in some important and extensive matter of which he has the charge (कार्यविशेषेऽधिकृतत्वात्पीठं मृद्नातीति पीठमर्दः) and is also his adviser. He is one of the principal advisers and ranks second to the minister when a king is the hero. It is a mistake to suppose that he assists the hero in securing his mistress. He may do it incidentally; but that is not his chief office. See com. and Sāh-D. III. 32, 40. Writers on dramaturgy provide a separate person for that, viz. the निसृष्टार्थ दूत or निसृष्टार्था दूती (*e. g.* Kāmandakī in the Māl.-Mād.) The heroine too has assistants corresponding to those of the hero. And it is in the sense given above that the term पीठमर्दिका is used here. She is a companion of the Queen (not of Mālavikā) and is her adviser. Being, however, previously instructed by the Vidūṣaka as to what part she was to play in the decision of the case of the two dancing masters, she suggested that it would be no sufficient test to ask the teachers to enter into disputation and to decide their respective merit, but that they should be judged by the performances of their pupils; and further, that the pupils should give their performance before herself and the King, as the decision of one individual was likely to be erroneous. She thus helps the King (and Mālavikā also) indirecly in gaining their object.

Verse 14. Construe—

मङ्गलालंकृता (धारिणी) यतिवेषया कौशिक्या समं त्रयी विग्रहवत्या अध्यात्मविद्यया इव भाति ।

मङ्गलालंकृता—See com.; better dissolve **मङ्गलैः अलंकृता** 'decked with auspicious ornaments;' for the use of **मङ्गल** as a noun *cf.* मङ्गलमात्रभूषणा Vik. III. 12. **यतिवेषया—यतेर्वेषो** यस्याः साः तया. **त्रयी—त्रयः** अवयवा यस्याः सा त्रयी. This word is restricted to the three Vedas collectively. त्रय means a collection of three; the aff. तय is optionally changed to अय after द्वि and त्रि; so द्वय, द्वितय (fem. ॰यी); त्रय, त्रितय (fem. ॰यी). The Vedas are sometimes spoken of as three, the fourth अथर्व being left out, either because it is a later addition, as Western scholars think, or because its subject-matter is of a different type. The Vedas (exclusive of the Upaniṣads) point out the ways to obtain happiness and hence धारिणी is compared to them. **अध्यात्मविद्यया**—आत्मानं ब्रह्म अधिकृत्य या विद्या सा अध्यात्मविद्या knowledge of the supreme spirit or ब्रह्म (and the connexion of the individual soul with it) leading to **मोक्ष** as propounded in the Upaniṣads. Or by अध्यात्म we may take the individual soul. *Cf.* अक्षरं ब्रह्म परमं स्वभावोऽध्यात्ममुच्यते। Bg. VIII. 3, and Śridhara on it-स्वस्यैव ब्रह्मण एव अंशतया जीवस्वरूपेण भावो भवनं स एव आत्मानं देहमधिकृत्य भोक्तृत्वेन वर्तमानः अध्यात्मशब्देनोच्यते. अध्यात्मविद्या is the विद्या that teaches the true nature of the individual soul, *i. e.* its being one with ब्रह्म when freed from अविद्या or the operation of माया. This requires the total annihilation of Karman (good or bad); so Kauśiki who is a संन्यासिनी is fitly compared to अध्यात्मविद्या. **विग्रहवत्या**—may also be taken with त्रयी (विग्रहवती) by changing the case. The Fig. of speech here is उपमा.

Verse 15. Construe—

महासारप्रसवयोः सदृशक्षमयोः धारिणीभूतधारिण्योः द्वयोः भर्ता शरच्छतं भव।

P. 30. **महासार॰** &c.—The epithets महासारप्रसवा and सदृशक्षमा go with both धारिणी and भूतधारिणी (the earth). The Com. takes these in the same sense applying to both (as instances of अभङ्गश्लेष),

viz. (1) having great and excellent progeny; (2) yielding abundant and excellent produce. We may take the first, however, as (1) having progeny of great valour (see com.); (2) महान् सारो धनं यस्मात्तादृक् प्रसवो यस्याः yielding produce of great value, or yielding rich crops, there being abundant rain; *i. e.* of the earth having plentiful rain and rich in produce. **सदृश०**—(1) having forgiveness or forbearance worthy for her exalted rank; the compliment is intentional as the queen will have occasions to show क्षमा as the plot develops; (2) having power of endurance in keeping with its onerous office, *viz.* to support all the creatures. These two epithets are doubtless intended to flatter the queen. Her son is called महासार; and women are never better pleased than when their sons are praised. **धारिणी—भूतधारिण्योः**—of Dhāriṇī and the earth (and of no one else).—The Parivrājikā cunningly says this to show to the queen that she is quite ignorant of the king's love-intrigue, much less she could be a party to it. **भर्ता**—kings are spoken of by poets as the husbands of the earth; *cf.* वसुमत्या हि नृपाः कलत्रिणः Ragh. VIII. 83; Śāk. III. 17 &c. **शरच्छतं**—For शरद् meaning a year *cf.* शरदामयुत ययौ Ragh. X, 1; परःसहस्राः शरदः Uttar I. 15; पश्येम शरदः शतं जीवेम शरदः शतं। Ṛgveda (Saura).

आर्यपुत्रः—Lit. 'the son of the honoured one, *i. e.* the father-in-law,' the husband is always so addressed by his wife in dramas. **विज्ञानसंघर्षः**—a contest about superiority in the knowledge of the art of dancing. विज्ञान is the knowledge of the arts and worldly sciences (as opposed to knowledge of the supreme soul); मोक्षे धीर्ज्ञानमन्यत्र विज्ञानं शिल्पशास्त्रयोः Amara. **उपालम्भ**—is used here in the sense of 'joke'. **पत्तनं** &c.—She means to hint—just as a village is not the proper place for a jewel to be examined when a city (where alone good jewellers are found) is at hand, so she was not the fit person to take the place of an umpire or judge when the king or queen was at hand to do it. To this the king replies by advancing two reasons, *viz.* (1) **पण्डितकौ०**-You are the learned Kaus'ikī (who cannot be compared to a ग्राम) and therefore perfectly qualified to take the post of a judge in the present case; (2) **पक्षपातिनौ**—पक्षे पातः अनयोः तौ interested parties (and therefore unable to be impartial judges). **गुणदोषतः**—Here तस has the sense of the loc = ०दोषविषये, 'as regards' &c. **परिच्छेत्तुं**—

परिच्छिद् to cut all round; hence, to know a thing thoroughly; to judge or form an estimation of the merits or demerits properly and fully. प्रयोगम०—has for its chief factor (essentially depends on) प्रयोग actual exhibition or representation. कथं वा &c.—In some editions the words are put in the mouth of the King. But they are out of place there. For the king appears from the tenor of his speeches studiously to refrain, from saying anything that will rouse the queen's suspicion about his being at the bottom of the plot. Besides, the following reply of the queen is to the परि० and not to the King. Also, the particle वा has no force if the King is the speaker.

P. 32. समानविद्यतः—परिभू is used with the abl. of the agent; कस्मात्तेः परिभवः। दयादिभ्यः। Pt; or तस् may be taken in the sense of the Instr., ०विद्येन परिभवितुं योग्यम्. Gaṇadāsa is polite to Haradatta in the presence of the king and calls him his समानविद्य. The reading ०विद्यात: means, 'since I possess the same degree of knowledge'. The readings ०विद्यतः परिहीनं and परिभवनीयं-अनुमन्तुं mean 'your ladyship will not, please, consent to my being reckoned inferior to or as one capable of being beaten by one whose knowledge is the same as mine (*i. e.* who is not at all superior to me),' The reading अवगमयितुं means 'you will please not make others (give ground to others to) believe that I am capable of being defeated &c.'

उरभ्रसंपातं—The fight between two rams. Vidūṣaka in his usual jocose way calls the contest between the two dancing masters a fight of rams, probably on account of their fatness. उदरंभरिसं०—(the fight between two gluttons) *V. l.* is also suitable in the mouth of the Vidū., though not so jocular as the first; but it is slightly insulting. Again, if they are उदरंभरिs (men given to the filling up of their bellies only, greedy) the remark किं मुधा &c. becomes out of place, while the first has some point in it. 'They have grown fat like rams by the wages they get; let us enjoy a sight of &c.' वेतन—(वीयते अनेन fr. वी 2 P. to go and the Uṇādi aff. तन) wages; also, means of subsistence. Mr. Pandit derives this word from वर्तन, 'which word' he says, 'also seems to be the origin of the Marāṭhī term वैरण or वेरण 'fodder.' कलहप्रियोऽसि—*cf.* with this the def. of Vid. मा एवं &c.—Some read चण्डि

for एवं ; but Vid. can never be expected to be so audacious as to address the queen as चण्डि, whatever freedom he may enjoy in his conversation with her. He has always a proper regard for the queen and he generally tries not to displease her. It is the king who can thus address the queen as a gentle rebuke for her getting angry with him. See *infra* III. 23. कलहितयोः—कलहः अनयोः संजातः इति कलहितौ तयोः This is emphatic. The Vidū. means to say—It is unjust to call me कलहप्रिय; they had already quarrelled. कथमुपशमः—How can their ardour be put down ? *i. e.* how can they sit quiet ?

स्वाङ्गसौष्ठ०—Dissolve—स्वमङ्गं स्वाङ्गं तस्य सौष्ठवं (see com.) तेन, स्वाङ्गसौष्ठवयुक्तो वा अभिनयः acting exhibited by means of the graceful build of their bodies. सौष्ठव has a technical meaning. It is the particular build of the body suited to dancing, natural or acquired by bodily exercise. For it see com. on आचार्येणावेक्ष्यमाणाङ्गसौष्ठवा p. 46. Bharata has the following on this— न हि सौष्ठवहीनाङ्गः शोभते नाट्यनृत्ययोः। अचंचलमकुब्जं च सन्नमात्रं तथैव च। नात्युग्रचलपादं च सौष्ठवांगं प्रयोजयेत्॥ कटी कर्णसमा यत्र कूपरोंसशिरस्तथा। समुन्नतमुरश्चैव सौष्ठवं नाम तद्भवेत्॥ अत्र नित्यं प्रयत्नो हि विधेयो मध्यमोत्तमैः। नाट्यं नृत्यं च सर्वं हि सौष्ठवे संप्रतिष्ठितम्॥ Nātyaśāstra Ch. 10. तदिदानीं &c.—प्रयाययितव्यं (pot. *p. p.* of the cau. of इ with प्रति) 'what is there that they have to convince as about *i. e.* what further proof of their skill have they to give us ? Mark how the King outwardly shows his indifference by asking this question. Apparently it means 'then nothing more remains to be shown by them,' 'let the matter end here.' But really he means—What more do you want them to show?

Verse 16. Construe—

कस्यचित् आत्मसंस्था क्रिया शिष्टा। अन्यस्य संक्रान्तिः विशेषयुक्ता, यस्य उभयं साधु सः एव शिक्षकाणां धुरि प्रतिष्ठापयितव्यः।

क्रिया—Practical display of the knowledge (of some art &c.) ; here, acting or dancing. आत्मसंस्था—as existing in or confined to one's person; personal. संक्रान्ति—the power of transferring, *i. e.* imparting it. विशेषयुक्ता—विशेषेण युक्ता–joined with excellence or distinction, peculiarly excellent. धुरि—at the yoke *i. e.* head of; धुर् properly the yoke of a carriage, and as it is the foremost part of a carriage, it secondarily means–

'what is foremost', or 'is at the head of.' *Cf.* अपांगुलानां धुरि कीर्तनीया। Ragh. III. 2.

P. 34. पिण्डितार्थः—The meaning summed up, the gist or sum and substance of the whole. एवं स्थितं—It has come to this, *i. e.* we must give practical proof of our skill in teaching. मन्दमेधा—the reading मन्दमेधाविनी is bad, as विन् shows प्राशस्त्य and so मन्द cannot be prefixed; it should be अमेधाविनी. आचार्यस्य दोषो नु—The queen means to say—You cannot test the ability of a teacher by examining his pupil. Suppose a bad pupil brings discredit on the instruction received, you cannot blame the teacher for that. Here the queen is trying to bring forward an objection against the decision of the Pari. to have the dispute settled by examining the pupils. She wants to have it set aside; but she cannot openly say that.

आपद्यते—happens, comes to be. उपपद्यते *v. l.*—is (thus) explained. अद्रव्य०—द्रव्य a fit object, worthy pupil; न द्रव्यमद्रव्यं. Cf. नाद्रव्ये विहिता काचित्क्रिया फलवती भवेत्। Hit.; तद्द्रव्यं जिगीषुमधिगम्य &c. Mud. VII. 14; and क्रिया हि वस्तूपहिता प्रसीदति। Ragh. III. 29. बुद्धिलाघवं—want of good sense, error of judgment. These words of the King, who had maintained an attitude of indifference so long, are intended to meet the queen's argument, कुशिष्या उपदेशं मलिनयति &c.; they have no further bearing on the discussion. The king means—the very acceptance of a bad pupil shows want of judgment on the part of a teacher; it is his fault and he must suffer for that. So you should not take your stand on this argument. The queen, however, misunderstands him and thinks that the words are intended to fire the spirit of Gaṇa., and says to herself अलमार्यपुत्रस्योत्साह &c. In some editions these words are put in the mouth of Gaṇadāsa. In this case they must be taken to mean 'the acceptance of an unworthy pupil also shows the acuteness' &c. (*i. e.* bespeaks confidence in his own power to impart instruction even to such a pupil.) But this is not proper. In the first place, they are not a direct reply to the Queen's उपदेशं मलिनयति; the queen did not say शिष्यां परिगृह्णति. Secondly, Gaṇadāsa cannot say a thing that would offend the queen; nor is he expected to admit that Mālavikā is an अद्रव्य (*Cf.* 1.5 *supra*). Again लघु, from which

लाघव is derived has to be taken in an obscure sense. Apart from the context the reading is not bad. कथमिदानीं &c.—How now? What shall I do to prevent this ? Mark the queen's anxiety to prevent giving things a turn that would bring Māla. directly before the king's eyes. Some read the stage direction (गणदासं विलोक्य जना०) after this. This would make the following speech intended for Gaṇadāsa, which does not seem to be correct from Gaṇadāsa, reply to Vidūṣaka's next speech. अलं—enough of; I should not allow &c. उत्साहकारणं—that will encourage him or fire his spirit. निरर्थकात्—fruitless; which will bring you no gain, even if the matter be decided in your favour (for, she means—you have already been enjoying my favour ; what more are you to gain ?).

संगीत०—Under the pretext of (teaching) संगीत ; see p. 6 and notes. संगीतकपदं (the position of a teacher of) लब्ध्वा *v. l.* सरस्वत्यु०—उपायनभूता: मोदकास्तान्. *Modakas* (generally a dishful of them) or other sweetmeats are offered as a present to the goddess Sarasvati and then given to the preceptor, her minister, when the ceremony of the first initiation in an art or lore is performed, and also on subsequent occasions when the goddess is worshipped. सुलभ०—where defeat is easily got, *i. e.* wherein you are sure to be defeated. मुखनिग्रहेण—*v. l.* means you being defeated no *Modakas* will be presented to you and so you cannot get them to eat (you will have to close up your mouth). Mark how Vidūṣaka is trying by his remarks to work up Gaṇadāsa gradually into giving an exhibition.

P. 36. अयमेवार्थ:—This is (so it will be understood to be) the meaning &c. Stung by the remark of the Vidū., Gaṇadāsa, who had already been smarting under the insult offered by Haradatta, makes bold to say to the queen that her words would be interpreted that way by the people, and declares his determination not to submit tamely to the aspersions cast on him by others.

Verse 17. Construe—

लब्धास्पदः अस्मि इति विवादभीरो परेण (कृतां) निन्दां तितिक्षमाणस्य यस्य आगमः केवलजीविकायै तं ज्ञानपण्यं वणिजं वदन्ति ।

लब्धास्पद:—One who has got a footing (*i. e.* a position and there is no danger of losing that). तितिक्ष०—Pres. par. of the desid. of तिज् but without a desiderative force ; स being added in the sense of ' to bear, ' 'to put up with' or 'to suffer'; see com. ज्ञानपण्यं—पण्य may be an adj. or a noun here ; ज्ञानं पण्यं विक्रेयं यस्य ; or see com. ; पण्य in the sense of a commodity or article for sale is *mas.* (see A. Dic.).

अचिरोपनीता—उपनीत has a technical sense ; brought (to a preceptor) for instruction or initiation ; *cf*, उपनयनं आचार्यकरणं (Pāṇini). अचिरोपनीता—This is corroborated by the words of Bakulāvalikā अचिरप्रवृत्तोपदेशं &c. on pp. 6, also. अपरिनिष्ठित॰—not well-fixed or properly imbibed. निर्बन्धः—pressing for it ; importunity ; *cf.* अत एव खलु निर्बन्धः । Śāk. III. p. 70. He means—when my pupil is found so well-grounded in the art in such a short space of time, it will redound all the more to my credit. तेन हि भगवत्यं &c.—Stress is to be laid on the word भगवत्यै. This is the last attempt of the queen to defeat the object of the King. She failed to persuade Gaṇadāsa not to give his consent to the decision arrived at. She therefore says—If an exhibition is to be given, let it be before the Parivrājikā alone—thinking that here she was on firm ground. The Pari., however, rises equal to the occasion. The queen's proposal was one to which no reasonable objection could have been taken, and the whole plot would thus have come to nothing. At such a juncture the Pari. says नैतन्न्याय्यं &c. and saves the situation.

एकाकिनः—Because when the judge is one, he is likely to be sometimes unconsciously misled by prejudice, मूढे &c.—She means-do you think that I do not know what you are really about and expect me to sit idle in the matter ? This speech of the queen is आत्मगत. She had from the very beginning a suspicion about the Parivrājikā's being privy to the intrigue set on foot by Vidūṣaka to have Māla. brought in person before the king. The preceding speech of the Pari. strengthened that. But as she could not speak it out, she merely turned away her face with an angry frown or an air of jealousy.

Verse 18 Construe—

इन्दुवदने, अनिमित्तं अत्रभवतः किं पराङ्मुखी भवसि, कुटुम्बिन्यः प्रभवन्त्यः अपि भर्तृषु कारणकोपाः हि ।

इन्दुवदने—It is difficult to see the propriety of this epithet when put in the mouth of a female addressing another female. Perhaps it is intended to suggest that her face ought to be always delight-giving like the moon. It should not be disfigured by anger. पराङ्मुखी-पराक् turned back (पराञ्चतीति fr. परा+अञ्च्+क्विप्) मुखमस्याः प्रभवन्त्यः भर्तृषु—भू with प्र 'to have power over', generally governs the *genitive*, see A. G. § 113. भर्तृषु may also be taken with कारणकोपाः. कारणकोपा—Vyadh. Bah.; see com. The Parivrājikā knew that the queen really frowned at her, but she cunningly represents her anger as directed against the king, to show that she was not privy to the plot. *Cf. infra* IV. 16.

P. 38. दिष्ट्या—(Properly the instr. sing. of दिष्टि fortune) fortunately; thank God.' उपदेशदर्शने न—This remark of the Vid. is intended to serve as the last stroke to excite Gaṇadāsa to the pitch of insisting upon proving his skill by actual representation at any cost. Some read °दर्शनेन (becomes clever, acquires skill by giving an exhibition); but it has no propriety here; it loses the Vidū's point altogether. एवं जनो गृह्णाति—People will understand the matter thus, *i. e.* will consider me unable to give practical proof of my skill.

Verse 19. Construe—

यदि विवादे आत्मनः क्रियासंक्रान्ति दर्शयिष्यतं मां न अनुजानासि त्वया अहं परित्यक्तः अस्मि।

विवादे—supply उपस्थिते; now that a dispute has arisen. परित्यक्तोऽस्मि—I shall regard myself as given up by you, *i. e.* I shall leave you and go away, my services being no longer needed.

का गतिः—what course is left to me *i. e.* I am helpless. Foiled in her efforts to direct the course of things otherwise, and finding Gaṇadāsa obdurate, the queen is at last forced to give her consent to the representation by Mālavikā. अपदे—in a wrong place, *i. e.* without proper ground. I was wrong in thinking that the queen would come in my way. Tārānātha reads अपदेशशङ्कितोऽस्मि which may mean—I was afraid of the thing being ordered away (countermanded). अभिनयवस्तु—the matter (theme) to be represented by acting.

किमपि देव्याः—&c. According to the settled programme, she wanted to refer to the *Chhalita* dance which Mālavikā alone could perform; but she was afraid of the queen whose anger she expected to be still more excited, and said किमपि देव्या मनसि &c. meaning to say—the queen has formed some wrong idea about the matter and so I am afraid to say what I wish to say.

ननु प्रभविष्यामि—I shall have mastery over, *i. e.* control my servants as I like. The queen, who seems to have penetrated the whole mystery, now means to say 'you may bring Mālavikā before the king now; it will be for me to prevent her from coming in contact with him again'. मम चेति ब्रूहि—A fine stroke of gallantry, as remarked by Mr. Pandit.

P. 40. चतुष्पदोद्भवं—arising from, based on or adopted to चतुष्पदा. Nilakaṇṭha explains this as चतुर्विधाभिनयोद्भूतम्। अथ वा चतुर्भिः पदैः संपन्नम्। See note on the word at p. 44, *Act* II. चालितम्—a dance in which the dancer while representing the sentiments of another gives expression to her own feelings. तत्र—In connexion with that, *i. e.* the same part of it should be pantomimically represented by both. तारतम्य—the respective worth of, the superiority or inferiority of each. प्रेक्षागृहे—Tārānātha reads वर्णप्रेक्षा० which he explains as 'the waiting-room of the actors.' गण०— अवलोकयति—This he did to learn the final wish of the queen in the matter, as she had shown herself to be not much in favour of the representation. विजयप्र०—विजयं प्रत्यर्थयते असौ or विजयस्य प्रत्यर्थिनी hostile to your success; *i. e.* I wish you all success. ननु विजयाभ्यर्थिनी—is another reading.

निर्णयाधिकारे—In virtue of the authority given to me to decide the case; in the capacity of a judge. सर्वाङ्ग०—(1) The apparent meaning is that the graceful acting may be seen in all the parts of the dance (to which the cumbrous full dress would be an impediment); the real meaning is (2) That the grace of all the limbs may be seen. The Pari.'s object in saying this is that Mālavikā should appear (before the king) in all her natural loveliness and win his heart finally. विरल०—thin or light dress; विगत०—*v. l.* means—not in the stage-dress (which might be a hindrance to the graceful movement of their limbs being seen); *i. e.* in their ordinary dress. The reading appears to be supported by न खलु नेपथ्यसंगीतकमिदम् on p. 56. But the former is better, as the point of the Pari. is that Mālavikā's graceful limbs should be seen by the king. **पात्रयोः**—Nīlakaṇṭha says मालविकेरावत्योः; Irāvatī cannot be the second पात्र. She was the second queen, next in rank to Dhāriṇī, and could not have been placed under Haradatta like an ordinary maid.

P. 42. **यदि, राजकार्येष्वपि** & c.—Here the queen administers a gentle rebuke to the king by clearly confessing to him her suspicion that the whole affair was cleverly planned and put into execution at his own instigation.

Verse 20. Construe :—

अन्यथा गृहीत्वा अलं, मनस्विनी इदं मया न खलु प्रयुक्तं, समानविद्याः प्रायः परस्परयशः पुरोभागाः।

अन्यथा गृहीत्वा—Viewing the matter in another light, do not put a wrong construction on the matter. **मनस्विनि**—O proud woman. He means—your jealous pride makes you think so; but I did not plan this. Or better still—O noble-minded one (see com.), you are a sensible lady and ought not to take such a view of the matter. **०पुरोभागाः**—पुरः भागः येषां ते—those who claim a share first; hence jealous of each other; or पुरः भजन्ते fr. पुरः + भज् + अ (घिणुन्); finding fault with, *i. e.* trying to throw each other's fame into the back-ground; envious of each other.

Verse 21. Construe :—

जीमूतस्तनितविशङ्किभिः उद्ग्रीवैः मयूरैः अनुरसितस्य पुष्करस्य निर्ह्रादिनी उपहितमध्यमस्वरोत्था मायूरी मार्जना मनांसि मदयति।

जीमूत०—जीवनस्य मूतः a bag, जीमूत; a comp. of the पृषोदरादि class; now see com. The deep sound of the Mrdaṇga is often represented as being mistaken for the rumbling of clouds by peacocks. *Cf.* Māl.-Mad. I, 1. **उद्ग्रीवैः**—उद्गता ग्रीवा येषां तैः। **अनुरसित**—The sound of which is responded to or followed (by peacocks) with their shrieks. **पुष्कर**—A kind of tabor (मृदंग); according to the Com. the mouth of a Mṛdaṇga.

निर्ह्रादिनी—sounding deeply. **उपहित**—adjusted. **उपचित**—*v. l.* brought to the pitch of. **मध्यमस्वर**—मध्ये भवः मध्यमः, fr.

मध्य + म. The fourth or middle note in the scale of Indian music, represented by म. The seven notes are—षड्जर्षभौ च गान्धारो मध्यमः पञ्चमस्तथा। धैवतश्च निषादश्च सप्त तन्त्र्युद्भवाः स्वराः॥ (Ak. adapted). These are symbolically represented by सा, रि, ग, म, प, ध, and नि. षड्जं रौति मयूरस्तु गावो नर्दन्ति चर्षभम्। अजाविकौ च गान्धारं क्रौञ्चो नर्दति मध्यमम्॥ पुष्पसाधारणे काले कोकिलो रौति पञ्चमम्। अश्वस्तु धैवतं रौति निषादं रौति कुञ्जरः॥–°°रोत्था—rising from, *i. e.* having the pitch of the fourth note. मायूरी मार्जना—मार्जना is a kind of deep sound produced by striking the right-hand mouth of a tabor with the extended palm of the hand and lifting up at once the upper portion of it (called थाप in Marathi). It is called मायूरी because peacocks delight to hear it; see com. The sense given in Apte's Dic. (following M.-W's Dic.), *viz.* 'belonging to or arising from a peacock' does not seem to be correct. It is a noun (that which is dear to peacocks) and not an adjective.

सामाजिकाः—Fr. समाज + इक (ठक्); members of an assembly, let us be members of the assembly *i. e.* let us join it. सामवायिक *v.l.*—has the same meaning (fr. समवाय a collection). सामयिक—*v.l.* means 'one who keeps an appointment or agreement (समय). अविनयः—Because the king plainly asked the queen to accompany him to witness the performance and showed his impatience therey. अपवार्य—See note on p. 44. विसंवादयिष्यति—will cause the thing to fail, *i. e.* knowing your real object, from your impatience to go there, she will withdraw her permission and stop the whole thing. In this case we must supply एतत्कार्यं as the object of विसं° *Cf.* for this sense रमणीयः खलु अवधिः विधिना विसंवादितः। Śāk. VI; तत्रभवती उर्वशी भवतो मनोरथानां कुसुमं दर्शयित्वा फले विसंवदति। Vik. II. p. 51. It may also mean 'will show you to be inconsistent with yourself (supplying त्वां as the object of विसं°); but this does not seem to be intended. The particle मा with the future or the potential has the sense of यथा न (that not, lest it should); *cf.* मा खलु (शकुन्तला) कस्यापि चिक्कणशीर्षस्य हस्ते पतिष्यति। Śāk. II

Verse 22. Construe :—

धैर्यावलम्बिन् अपि माम् अयं मुरजवाद्यरागः सिद्धिपथम् अवतरतः स्वमनोरथस्य शब्दः इव मां त्वरयति।

राजा—After this we should expect the stage-direction अपवार्य. But it seems to have been dispensed with, as the king's speech can easily be known to be such, being a reply to Vidūṣaka's speech, which is अपवार्य. मुरज—मुराद्वेष्टनात् जातः; fr. मुर् 6 conj. P. to cover, to encircle. स्वमनोरथस्य—mark the pun on the word मनोरथ which means 'the car (consisting) of the mind' (which can produce a sound), and a desire. The concluding portion of this act is an instance of अङ्कावतार or the hinting of the commencement of the succeeding Act at the end of the previous Act; see com. The reference to the sound of the drum here introduces the audience to the प्रेक्षागृह and the dancing with which the second Act opens. According to Śāh.—D. the commencing portion of the next Act would be Aṅkāvatāra.

Critical Appreciation of The Act I

The main scene of the Act I is preceeded by a मिश्रविष्कम्भक containing a dialogue between बकुलावलिका, कौमुदिका and गणदास. In this interlude, we learn that the king अग्निमित्र has seen मालविका in a picture and has shown unusual curiosity for her. The queen धारिणी is taking special care to keep मालविका out of the sight of the king. This indicates the queen's jealousy for मालविका. मालविका is described as a girl of uncommon intelligence and as a clever student of dancing. Her real identity is not revealed. We are only informed that मालविका was sent as a present to धारिणी, by her brother वीरसेन. Thus the seed of the main action in the play is introduced in this interlude. A ring with the snake-seal thereon which plays an important part in the play, is also introduced.

The main scene of the first act can be divided into four parts as follows :—

(i) The conversation between Agnimitra and वाहतक, the minister,

(ii) The conversation between the king and the विदूषक,

(iii) The quarrel between the two dance teachers in the presence of the king and the विदूषक and

(iv) The decision of परिव्राजिका.

From the conversation between the king and वाहतक, we learn that the king decides to send his army against the king of विदर्भ. The quick decision taken by अग्निमित्र reveals his spirited nature, political wisdom, intolerent spirit and self-confidence.

The conversation between the king and the विदूषक reveals that at the instance of the king, the विदूषक has devised a scheme in order that अग्निमित्र may see मालविका in person. The successful working of the scheme proves विदूषक to be a shrewd person. The king also pays him a compliment by calling him a कार्यान्तरसचिव.

The quarrel of the two dance teachers before the king brings out the grandure of the king's personality. The king pretends surprise at the untimely arrival of the dance teachers. He refuses to act as a judge in deciding their respective merits and cleverly suggests the name of पण्डिता कौशिकी for doing that job.

The परिव्राजिका, in a very clever way, suggests the staging of the dance by respective pupils of the dance teachers. The intelligence of परिव्राजिका is seen in her logical and convincing argument with which she included the king among the judges. The jealousy of the queen धारिणी is well revealed through her repeated attempts to avoid the performance of a dance by the pupils. She even openly taunts the king with the words यदि राजकार्येष्वपीदृश्युपायनिपुणतार्यपुत्रस्य तदा शोभनं भवेत्। However, it must be noted that she never leaves her magnanimity and modesty. The विदूषक with his witty and sarcastic remarks provokes गणदास and thus makes him insist on the contest. But for his taunts, the quarrel perhaps would have been settled without any contest. Amongst the two dance teachers, गणदास is sincere, sentimental, possessed of self-respect and loyal to the queen. The king successfully plays the part of a hypocrite.

मालविका does not appear on the stage in this act. Yet her presence is felt throughout on account of the intense jealousy of धारिणी and the unusual eagerness of the king to see her in person.

The seed of the main theme is, thus, well sown in the first act.

Act II

P. 44. ततः प्रविशति &c.—Such a beginning of an Act (*i.e.* without a प्रवेशक or विष्कम्भक) is called अङ्कावतार or अङ्कावतरण; *cf.*

Pratāparudra—यत्र स्यादुत्तराङ्कार्थः पूर्वाङ्कार्थानुसंगतः। असूचिताङ्कपात्रैश्च तदङ्कावतरणं मतम्॥ See also Sāh.-Dar. VI. 58-59. संगीतरचना—The arrangements for a musical concert, such as the setting of the musical instruments to the proper tune, the attiring of dancers, &c. विभवतश्च—According to their ranks; विभव—dignity, position.

तेन हि—If so; well then. अत्रभवती—*scil.* the two Āchāryas. पुरस्कारं—Lit. placing in the front; hence precedence. Mark how the Pari. finds some excuse to decide in favour of the king. स्वनियोगं &c.—अशून्यं not void, that is, executed. -कुरु—this phrase occurs constantly in dramas in the sense of 'go about or attend to your duty'. This is a formal way of saying 'you need not come back; you are no longer wanted here'. शर्मिष्ठायाः—Śarmiṣṭhā, the daughter of Vṛṣaparvan, the well-known demon king, and the second wife of Yayāti. See Śak. IV. 6. She was better accomplished than Uṣā, Chitralekhā, and others, and is said to have composed some musical pieces and laid down some rules on Saṃgīta. लय—is the agreement or correspondence (happening exactly at the same time) of song, instrumental music, the settings of feet by the dancers, &c.; *cf.* तालः कालक्रियामानं, लयः साम्यं Amara. (गीतवाद्यपादादिन्यासानां क्रियाकालयोः साम्यं com. on Amara). It is of three kinds—द्रुत or rapid, मध्य or middle and विलम्बित or slow. The मध्यलय is suited to Śṛṅgāra or love-matters; see com. चतुष्पदा——or the four-footed stanza, each foot consisting of a verse of four lines, *i.e.* a stanza, having for each quarter a verse of four lines. The Com. on प्राकृतपिङ्गलसूत्रs says—चतुष्पदीछन्दः। एतत्पदचतुष्टययुक्तमेकं चरणम्। एतादृशचरणचतुष्टयं तादृशं छन्दः। Each of the four component verses is called वस्तु so that the fourth verse is the चतुर्थवस्तु; see com.; or वस्तु may mean the subject-matter or theme of. *Cf.* Bharata—एकवस्तु ध्रुवा ज्ञेया द्विवस्तु परिगीतिका। त्रिवस्तु मद्रकं ज्ञेयं चतुर्वस्तु चतुष्पदा॥ Nāṭy. Ś. Ch. 32. 7. प्रयोग—The performance with proper gestures of. श्रोतुं—to hear and see; to behold. Mark the meaning of श्रु, which though primarily meaning 'to hear something explained or read out' means secondarily 'to gain knowledge either by reading or hearing or seeing.' *cf.* श्रुतो हितोपदेशोऽयं &c.; श्रुति the Veda. आचार्यबहुमा०—Some read as आचार्य बहु० but it is better to read this as one word. The king wants to show his indifference to the performance by this. He means to say–'I am attentive owing to my great regard for you and not on account of any great desire on my part to see the dance.' Tārānātha adds after this—तत्प्रवेशय पात्रम्। But the king is not expected directly to say so in the presence of the queen.

जनान्तिकम्—A speech meant to be heard by a particular person or persons (नियतश्राव्य) is of two kinds. जना॰ is one when an individual makes a secret communication to another (in the course of the conversation of a company) preventing, as it were, others from hearing by means of the three-bannered hand (holding up the palm of the hand with the fingers, but the thumb and the ring-finger raised so as to look like three banners as it were); while अपवार्य—(*Lit.* warding off the party meant to be kept out of hearing) is when a person turns aside and communicates a secret to another. See com.

Verse 1. Construe :—

नेपथ्यपरिगतायाः तस्याः दर्शनसमुत्सुकं मे चक्षुः अधीरतया तिरस्करिणीं संहर्तुं व्यवसितम् इव।

P. 46. **नेपथ्यपरिगता**—surrounded by *i. e.* hidden by the curtain. **सहर्तुं**—shows that there were more curtains than one, and that the front curtain was rolled up; for the king says संहर्तुं and not अपसारयितुम्. **तिरस्करिणी**—a curtain; तिरस्करोतीति, fr. कृ with तिरस्+इन् (णिनि); there is no Vṛddhi of the radical vowel in this sense (निपातनात् वृद्ध्यभावः). *Cf.* with this Duṣyanta's remarks—अहो चेष्टाप्रतिरूपिका कामिजनमनोवृत्तिः। अहं हि अनुयास्यन्मुनितनयां &c. Śāk. I. 26. **नयनमधु**—Lit. honey for the eyes; but as the Vidū. says पश्य while honey is a thing to be licked, we must take मधु in the secondary sense of a charming object, a treat for the eyes. **॰मक्षिकं च**—The मक्षिका meant here is Dhāriṇī. A man wishing to take honey from bee-hives ought to be careful enough to protect himself from the bees, lest he might be stung by them. So Vidū. asks the king to look at Mālavikā but cautiously so as not to give the least ground to the queen to suspect him. **॰प्रत्यवेक्ष्यमाण॰**—ईक्ष with प्रति and अव means 'to look into or examine carefully.' The preceptor saw that she was so attired as to have beauty of all her limbs well set off, before introducing her on the stage. *Cf.* प्रत्यवेक्षिताः प्रमदवनभूमयः Śāk. VI.

Verse 2. Construe :—

मे हृदयं चित्रगतायाम् अस्यां कान्तिविसंवादशङ्कि (अभूत्), संप्रति येन इयम् आलिखिता (तं) शिथिलसमाधिं मन्ये।

चित्रगतायां—When she was only a picture to me, *i. e.* when I saw her beauty as represented in the picture. **विसंवाद**—disagreement (between) her actual beauty and that delineated in the picture *i. e.* I doubted whether she might be really as beautiful as represented in the picture.

संप्रति—Now, when I have actually seen her. **शिथिल०**—He means—Now I find that the painter did not do full justice to her beauty, not having the necessary concentration of mind to be able to draw a life-like picture of her; for her real beauty far exceeds that of the picture; or समाधि may mean लेखनसामग्री or materials (समाधीयते उपात्यते अनेन इति) as in तं वेधा विदधे नूनं महाभूतसमाधिना। Ragh. I. 29. But the first sense is preferable.

P. 48. **सत्त्वस्था भव**—*Lit.* take your stand on सत्त्व your natural mental fortitude; *i. e.* be well-composed or steady-minded; do not allow yourself to be over-powered by awe or flurry.

सर्वस्थाना०—न उद्यते इति अवद्यं by the Uṇādi affix. य, not fit to be spoken of, censurable; अनवद्यं what is praiseworthy or faultless; **०ता**-faultlessness. **सर्वास्ववस्थासु**—*v. l.* is rejected because in the following śloka the beauty of the different limbs is described, and not beauty in different conditions. Again, the king sees her for the first time now, so he cannot refer to her beauty in different states. The reading occurs on. p. 50. and the poet cannot repeat the ideas shortly after.

Verse 3. Construe :—

वदनं दीर्घाक्षं शरदिन्दुकान्ति, बाहू अंसयोः नतौ, उरः निबिडोन्नतस्तनं संक्षिप्तं, पार्श्वे प्रमृष्टे इव, मध्यः पाणिमितः नितम्बि जघनं, पादौ अरालाङ्गुली, नर्तयितुः मनसः यथा एव छन्दः तथा अस्याः वपुः श्लिष्टम्।

नतौ—depressed, so as to have smooth joints. **प्रमृष्टे**—(as if they were) planed off, *i.e.* very smooth (the bones being well-covered by the flesh). **पाणिमितः**—Here पाणि by Lakṣaṇā means मुष्टि (that can be grasped between the tips of the thumb and the middle finger); *cf.* मुष्टिग्राह्यमध्यां kād. 'Of the measure (circumference) of the hand' would be more natural. **अराल**—a

little bent down and short. छन्दो—&c. *i. e.* her body is formed just as symmetrically as a dancing master would desire it to be.

उपगानं (उपवहनं) *v. l.*)—preliminary singing ; a tune hummed up previous to formal singing to adjust the voice to the proper *Rāga*, to the pitch of the instruments, &c. **चतुष्पदवस्तु**–is the same as चतुष्पदचतुर्थवस्तु ; for Gaṇadāsa had selected that for being exhibited (see p. 44) and we cannot expect Māla. to sing the full song. Explain चतुष्पदसंबद्धं वस्तु चतुष्पदवस्तु.

Verse 4. Construe :—

प्रियः मे दुर्लभः (हे) हृदय तस्मिन् निराशं भव, अहो मे वामः अपाङ्गकः किम् अपि प्रस्फुरति, एषः चिरदृष्टः सः कथम् उपनेतव्यः, (हे) नाथ पराधीनां मां त्वयि सतृष्णां गणय।

निराशं—When she gave expression to her despair at the thought that the lover was hard to obtain, her left eye throbbed creating hope in her. **अपाङ्गकः**—अपांगति तिर्यक् चलति नेत्रं यत्र सः। The outer corner or angle of the eye. **किमपि**—for some reason or another (I do not know how to account for it]. **वामः**—The throbbing of the left eye in the case of women is considered auspicious (as auguring union with a beloved (person). **प्रस्फुरति**—This creates hope in her. Rather read मे स्फुरति (फुरइ); as पप्फुरदि violates the metre ; for there are 22 mātrās in each of the other three lines, while with प० this the second line will have 24. **कथमुप०**—This implies चिन्ता or mental effort to secure the lover. **नाथ**—The use of the word shows that *he* only can save her from the torment of love. **त्वयि गणय** &c—Here she indirectly makes an offer of herself to him (आत्मार्पण). Māla. had already fallen in love with the king (*cf* अविज्ञातशीलं भर्तारमभिलषन्ती &c. Māla.'s soliloquy on p. 74). She knew she was offered to the king and was being brought to him by her brother Mādhavasena (as will appear from Act V.) and seized this opportunity to indicate her love for him. The Pari. also, who is none other than the younger sister of Sumati, Mādhavasena's minister, knew of this and purposely selected a love-song for being sung on this occasion. **ततो यथारसं** &c.—This refers to the practice of first singing a song and then dancing with gestures expressive of the ideas and sentiments contained therein. The *Rasa* meant here is

विप्रलम्भशृङ्गार or disappointed love ; see com. ; for the various technical terms used in the com. here and *passim,* see Intro. I. In the four lines of the foregoing stanza are mentioned respectively the four states of the heroine's mind *viz.* (2) वैराग्य (निर्वेद) or despair ; (2) आशा or hope : (3) संकल्प mental effort or resolution and (4) आत्मार्पण. See also com.

P. 50. चतुष्पद०—चतुष्पदावस्थाकं *v. l.* means चतुष्पदनिष्ठा अवस्था यस्मिन् containing four lines descriptive of four states. वस्तुकं—Here वस्तु may mean either the song चतुष्पदं or the subject-matter of, the meaning conveyed by. उपस्थापितं—placed near, offered or given over to. The other reading उपक्षिप्तं means the same thing. हृदयं—idea ; view of the matter. It does not mean 'such (affected by love) is my heart too'. For Vid. knows it already.

Verse 5. Construe :—

(हे) नाथ, इमं जनम् अनुरक्तं विद्धि इति गेये वचनं स्वाङ्गनिर्देशपूर्वम् अभिनयन्त्या धारिणीसंनिकर्षात् प्रणयगतिम् अदृष्ट्वा सुकुमारप्रार्थनाव्याजम् अहम् उक्तः इव।

अभिनयन्त्या—Representing or manifesting by gestures the import of. स्वाङ्गनि०—स्वस्याङ्गं स्वाङ्गं तस्य निर्देशः (pointing to) पूर्वः यस्मिन्कर्मणि तद्यथा तथा। Mālavikā had pointed her finger towards herself when uttering the word मां in नाथ मां पराधीनां &c.) प्रणयगतिमदृष्ट्वा—Not seeing her love reaching (*i.e.* the effect thereof on) my heart, *i. e.* any sign of corresponding love in me (as the Com. takes it). Or not seeing her way (not knowing how) to convey her love to me. सुकुमारप्रार्थना०—under the pretex of (repeating) the gentle or humble request (of some one to some one).

किमपि—somehow ; किंचित् *v. l.* slightly, to some extent. क्रमभेदः—क्रमविशेषः a particular act to be done in the proper order. For this meaning of क्रम *cf.* Bhāsa एह्येहि पुत्र। अयमक्रमः। दुर्योधनः—अथ कः क्रमः। Pañcharātra I. कर्मभेदः—*v. l.* a particular act, an item in the peformance of. This is also a good reading; but the former appears to be genuine from the word प्रथम in Vidū.'s (प्रथमं ब्राह्मणस्य पूजा) on p. 54. Though really there was no flaw in the performance, still the Vidū. makes this remark, which after all turns out to be a mere witticism (see his reply to Gaṇadāsa on p. 56) intended to detain Mālavikā on the stage so that the King might enjoy her sight for sometime more. उपदेश०—As one whose instruction (*i. e.* after the instruction imparted to you) has been found or declared to be entirely (वि) pure *i. e.* faultless. ०विशुद्धौ—*v. l.* when or after your performance &c. सर्वास्व०—Māla. looked even more lovely when she stood still after the dance was over. Hence the king's remark. चारुता—(चरति चित्ते इति चारु तस्य भावः). The beauty of structure or symmetrical make that impresses the mind of another; the natural attractiveness of form; शोभा—beauty in any one of its phases (fr. शुभ् to shine). शोभान्तरं—&c. *v. l.* presents different aspects of loveliness; *i. e.* true beauty appears lovely in a particular way in a particular state; gains fresh charm. This idea occurs constantly in Kāli.; *cf.* अहो सर्वास्ववस्थासु रमणीयत्वमाकृतिविशेषाणाम्, Śāk. VI p. 148 ; किमिव हि मधुराणं मण्डनं नाकृतीनाम्। *Ibid.* I.

Verse 6. Construe :—

संधिस्तिमितवलयं वामं हस्तं नितम्बे न्यस्य, द्वितीयं (हस्तं) श्यामाविटपसदृशं स्रस्तमुक्तं कृत्वा, पादाङ्गुष्ठालुलितकुसुमे कुट्टिमे पातिताक्षम् ऋज्वायतार्धम् अस्याः स्थितं नृत्तात् अतितरां कान्तम् ।

संधिस्तिमित०—संधि joint of the wrist. स्तिमित motionless, being close-fitted. This epithet is used to show that her hands were well-rounded and plump. न्यस्य हस्तं—The construction is वाम हस्तं नितम्बे न्यस्य द्वितीयं...... स्रस्तमुक्तं कृत्वा &c. अस्याः स्थितं; the agent of न्यस्य and कृत्वा is इयं got from अस्याः श्यामा—श्यामा also called प्रियङ्गु seems to be a favourite creeper with the Sanskrit poets and the body of a woman, on account of its delicacy and thinness (and sometimes of man) is often compared by them to this creeper; *cf.* श्यामास्वङ्गं &c. Megh. II. 44; श्यामा लताः कुसुमभारनतप्रवालाः स्त्रीणां हरन्ति धृतभूषणबाहुकान्तिम्। Rit. III. 18. प्रियङ्गुश्यामाङ्गप्रकृतिरपि Māl. -Mād. III. 9. स्रस्तमुक्तं—Let down so as to hang loosely. Tārānātha takes this in the sense of 'from which pearls have fallen'. But this is not possible, as Māla., who was after all a servant-girl then, cannot be expected to wear pearls.

पादाङ्गुष्ठा०—पादाङ्गुष्ठेन आलुलितानि (slightly pressed or stirred about gently) कुसुमानि (the flowers placed as decorations) यस्मिन्. कुट्टिमे पाति०—For she could not look up or look straightforward owing to bashfulness. ऋज्वायतार्धम्—In which the upper half (trunk) of the body is straight drawn up. The same idea occurs in Kum. III. 45 (पर्यङ्कबन्धस्थिरपूर्वकायमृज्वायतं संनमितोभयांसम् ।). स्थितं is a noun here (= स्थिति ; see com.) the posture assumed by Māla.

P. 52. ननु—may be प्रश्ने (I ask) or आमन्त्रणे. गौतमवचनमपि &c.-the queen here shows her surprise that Gaṇadāsa should have attached importance to the words of Gautama who is but a trifler and not likely to know much of the science of music and dancing and asked Mālavikā to stay. This indicates her anxiety to have Mālavikā removed from the king's sight as soon as possible. देवप्रत्ययात्—From his Majesty's knowledge or critical power ; or from the confidence he has in his judgment. संभाव्यते—He means—On account of his constant association with the king and his being guided by him in his judgment, the Vid. is likely &c. सूक्ष्मदर्शिता—Lit. the power to see or mark minute things, or mark the things minutely ; hence, acuteness or sharpness of perception.

Verse 7. Construe :—

विपश्चितः संसर्गेण मन्दः अपि अमन्दताम् एति पङ्कच्छिदः फलस्य निकषेण आविलं पयः इव ।

विपश्चित्—वि प्रकृष्टं निश्चिनोति चेतति चिन्तयति वा पृषोदरादिः । पङ्कच्छिदः—(पङ्कं छिनत्तीति पङ्कच्छिद्) is the tree called कतक, known in Marāthi as निवळी, the powder of whose fruit is used for clearing turbid water ; the powder causes the dust in the water to precipitate to the bottom and leaves out clear water. निकष—rubbing. आविलं—आविलति स्तृणाति (covers) दृष्टिं that which does not allow the eye to see through ; dusty, turbid.

विवक्षितं—*p. p. p.* of the desid. of वच् ; what is desired to be said ; साक्षिणीं तावत् &c.-mark how Vidū's ready wit yet helps him. He does not answer Gaṇa. but refers him to Pari. and thereby manages to keep Māla. longer on the stage. साक्षिणीं—साक्षाद् द्रष्टा साक्षी ; (an eye-witness) by the rule साक्षाद् द्रष्टरि संज्ञायाम् । Pāṇ. V. 2. 61 ; *i. e.* the aff. इन् is added to साक्षात् in the sense of 'a looker on' when the word so formed is a name. Here साक्षिणी means one who had to see the performance and pronounce judgment upon it ; hence an umpire, a judge.

N. B. In a transaction like a loan &c. three persons directly see the act, *viz.* one who gives, one who takes and a third party who witnesses the act; the word संज्ञा is used to show that the word साक्षिन् is restricted to the person merely looking on (and does not refer to the lender or the borrower).

अनवद्यं — see *supra* note on अवद्यं p. 4.

Verse 8. Construe :—

अन्तर्निहितवचनैः अङ्गैः अर्थः सम्यक् सूचितः, पादन्यासः लयम् अनुगतः, रसेषु तन्मयत्वं, शाखायोनिः अभिनयः मृदुः, तद्विकल्पानुवृत्तौ भावः भावं विषयात् नुदति, रागबन्धः सः एव ।

अङ्गैः—By her limbs *i. e.* the gesticulations made by means of the limbs. अन्तर्नि०—which, as if, had words suppressed therein; eloquent with expression—so distinctly was the meaning indicated or conveyed to the beholders. पादन्यासः &c.—The planting of her feet exactly agreed with the लय or musical halts in the song. तन्मयत्वं रसेषु—the representation of sentiments was so perfect that she seemed to be quite identified with or completely absorbed in them. By रस she means निर्वेद, हर्ष, चिन्ता and दैन्य referred to in श्ल. 4. When she represented निर्वेद, she looked the very image of despair; and so on.

अभिनयः—expression of feelings by mute action or gesticulation, शाखायोनिः अभि०—शाखा has a technical sense for which see com.; gesticulation by means of the movements of the hand in correspondence with musical time was cleverly done (मृदु). Tārānātha takes शाखा in the sense of 'the branch-like hand (*i. e.* with the fingers spread out); but this has no propriety. तद्विकल्पा०—As its different parts succeeded one another. भावो भावं &c.—*i. e.* one feeling drove another from the field; as one acting followed another, the feeling expressed by the previous one was lost into or gave place to another. So capital was the performance. Or this may mean 'one feeling propelled, gave rise to another,' as its subject was represented. नुदति—तुदति *v. l.* means strikes, comes hard upon, follows closely. नुदति is better. विषयात्—from its base or substratum (विषय); the permanent sentiment (here of love). रागबन्धः—'the delightful impression made upon the mind' or the interest created by the acting. *Cf.* रागबद्धचित्तवृत्तिः । Śāk. I. p. 8. Or राग may have the same meaning as in रसान्तरेषु प्रतिबद्ध-रागम् । Kum. VII. 91, where Malli. quotes शृङ्गारहास्यकरुणाः स्त्रीरागेण प्रकीर्तिताः । **स एव**—was the same, *i. e.* although she represented different feelings, the interest created remained at the same pitch.

P. 54. **स्वपक्ष**—*i. e.* **विषये** as regards our protégé or side. **शिथिल॰**-whose pride in or high opinion about it is slackened in other words–On account of the incomparably superior performance of your pupil, we acknowledge ourselves vanquished. The King says this apparently to please the queen but really to please Māla., Haradatta being absent. **अद्य नर्त॰**—To-day I am truly a dancing-master (my skill and ability being recognized by those most eminently qualified to pass judgment.)

Verse 9. Construe :—

सन्तः उपदेशिनः तम् उपदेशं शुद्धं विदुः, यः विद्वत्सु अग्निषु काञ्चनम् इव न श्यामायते ।

सन्तः—wise men, men of discrimination. **न श्यामायते**—does not turn black, does not get tainted ; *i. e.* does not prove defective; hence stands the test of. For the idea *cf.* हेम्नः संलक्ष्यते ह्यग्नौ विशुद्धिः श्यामिकापि वा । Ragh. I. 10 ; प्रायः प्रत्ययमाधत्ते स्वगुणे-षूत्तमादरः । Kum. VI. 20 ; and आपरितोषाद्विदुषां न साधु मन्ये प्रयोग-विज्ञानम् । Śāk. I. 2. **विद्वत्सु**—learned men, *i. e.* able to judge ; critics. *V. l.* **युष्मासु**-is bad as the śl. makes a general statement and does not refer to a particular case.

परीक्षका॰—आराधन pleasing, giving satisfaction to. **आर्यो वर्धते**—The Queen here apparently pays a compliment to Gaṇadāsa ; but her words are really meant to be slightly sarcastic. The word परीक्षक is used with a meaning in it. She means—You have well succeeded in pleasing the examiners by your bringing Mālavikā before the King, to see whom was his chief object in organizing this musical concert and dance. **अपरिक्षतारा॰**—*v. l.* means full (*lit.* without a flaw) or entire satisfaction. But this reading does not bring out the hidden sense as the other does. **देवीपरिग्रह एव**—Gaṇadāsa who knew what the queen really meant flatters her by this. He means 'My being favoured by the Queen alone I regard as the real cause of my prosperity and not so much the pleasure of the examiners'. **देवीपारिग्रहश्च**—*v. l.* fails to bring out this meaning.

प्रथमोप०—The Vidū. had really noticed no defect in the acting; his object was, as already remarked, to detain Māla. on the stage; and so he said that there was something wrong in the order. He knew that he would be asked to point out the defect he noticed and his humorous reply was also ready. **प्रयोगा०**—प्रयोगे अभ्यन्तरः (अभिगतमन्तरं येन) O the great critic, who has an insight into the art of dancing! अभ्यन्तर means initiated in; hence skilled or proficient in; with the loc. or sometimes with the gen.; *cf.* संगीतके अभ्यन्तरे स्वः। *infra* V.; मन्त्रेष्वभ्यन्तराःके स्युः Rāmā : अनभ्यन्तरे आवां मदनगतस्य वृत्तान्तस्य। Śāk. III. The reading प्रश्नः for प्राश्निकः has no meaning, as the Vidū's words constiute no question. The Parivrājikā's remark is of course ironical, and is meant to excite laughter; for the Vidū.'s remark had no connexion whatsoever with the art of dancing,

The speech of the Vidūṣaka meant as a retort to the Pari.'s remarks (given in some editions), *viz.* अयि पण्डितमन्ये &c. (see foot-note) does not appear to be genuine. In the first place, the Parivrājikā is nowhere else described, as remarked by Mr. Pandit, as being old and gray-haired, who had lost all her teeth. Secondly, even the Vid. cannot be expected to be so far discourteous to her as to forget the respect which she commanded from all, more especially when he had to get the King's object accomplished. Thirdly, there is no reason why we should suppose the Vidū. to be so sensitive as to lose his temper here when further on he bears the Parivrājikā's remark without the least sign of resentment, but on the contrary say पण्डितप्रत्यया मूढजातिः (see p. 56). Fourthly, the remark प्रसन्नचन्द्रपाद० is quite out of place here. Again, here form भाषयसि is not correct; it should be भाययसि; for by the rule भिया हेतुभये षुक् Pāṇ. VII. 3. 40, भी takes the augment ष् when the fear comes from the agent of the causative. **प्रहसिताः, मा० स्मितं करोति**—Mark the modesty of Māla. while others laugh heartily aloud, she only smiles gently which lends a charm to her face and the King is delighted to see that. See the next s'l.

आत्तसारः—the best part of which is taken, *i. e.*, enjoyed. उपात्तसार has the same meaning. **स्वविषयः**—its own object. The objects of the five senses are रूपं शब्दो गन्धरसस्पर्शाश्च विषया

अमी। (Amara.). The object of the eye is रूप or form, here Mālavikā; and the eye enjoyed the sight of her beauty in a position of advantage.

Verse 10. Construe :—

स्मयमानं किंचिदभिव्यक्तदशनशोभि आयताक्ष्याः मुखम् उच्छ्वसत् असमग्रलक्ष्य-केसरं पङ्कजम् इव दृष्टम्।

स्मयमानं—with a gentle blooming upon it. **किंचिदभि०**—graceful with the teeth slightly displayed. Here **मुख** is compared to a lotus and the corresponding epithets are **स्मयमानं** and उच्छ्वसत्, किंचिदभिव्यक्त० and असमग्रलक्ष्य० &c.

P. 56. **महाब्राह्मण**—is ironical. महत् when compounded with the word ब्राह्मण implies censure; *cf.* शंखे तैले तथा मांसे वैद्ये ज्यौतिषिके द्विजे। यात्रायां पथि निद्रायां महच्छब्दो न दीयते ॥ **नेपथ्यसंगीतकं**—may mean a musical concert in the tiring room of a theatre; or a (public) concert in stage-dress (नेपथ्योपलक्षितं संगीतकम्) such as dancing-girls wear (in which case Vidū. would have been worshipped). This is the meaning here. It was customary in ancient times, as it is also at the present day, to worship the tutelary deity and make presents to Brāhmaṇas with Dakṣiṇā when a person was initiated into some art or Śāstra or at any inaugural ceremony. **नेपथ्यसवन**—is another reading which means 'a sacrifice accompanied with musical entertainment performed when a dramatic company was formally opened.' See com. **अर्चनीयं**—This is also ironical. **दक्षिणीयं** *v. l.* means one who deserves Dakṣiṇā, hence learned and revered, worthy; दक्षिणामर्हति दक्षिणीयः fr. दक्षिणा + ईय (छः). **नाम**—Verily, forsooth. **मुग्धचातकेन**—a silly chātaka, silly because unble to distinguish between rain-showering clouds and empty ones. On a different occasion the poet has to say a different thing of the Chātaka *Cf.* (स्वस्त्यस्तु ते) निर्गलिताम्बुगर्भं शरद्घनं नार्दति चातकोऽपि। Ragh. V. 17. The Chātaka is a bird which, according to poetic descriptions, can have no access to water found on earth and hence it has entirely to depend upon rain-water for allaying its thirst. See our note on दिव्यरसाभिलाषिणा चातकव्रतं गृहीतं Vik. II. The Vidūṣaka means—As the chātaka expecting water from an empty cloud is disappointed, so I, not knowing that this was not the प्रथमसं०, expected a present of sweetmeats only to be disappointed. He says this only to pass off the matter somehow. जलपानमिच्छता चातकायितं *v. l.* where चातकायितं is the *p. p. p.* of the nominal verb fr. चातक (चातकवदाचरति चातकायते) by कर्तुः क्यङ् सलोपश्च । ततः क्तः ।

पण्डितपरितोष० &c.—*Cf. supra* मूढः परप्रत्ययनेयबुद्धिः; I. 2. He means—since you a good critic have expressed your satisfaction, I, too, knowing your judgment to be sound, must express my satisfaction. पारितोषिकं—परितोषः प्रयोजनं (फलं कारणं च) अस्य इति ठञ् (इक). राज्ञो हस्तात्कट०—Acting probably under the private instruction of the King, Vidūṣaka offered to give an ornament from the King's hand to Māl. meaning to show thereby that she had a place in the king's heart. This trick is a counterpart of that played by Māla. when she said in the song नाथ मां विद्धि &c. गुणान्तरं—the difference of merits (between Māla. and Haradatta's pupil), the respective merits of; or, better, the special merit of Māla; the Queen not liking the action of Vidū. which only served to keep Māla. yet longer on the stage, takes him to task for it. परकीयमिति कृत्वा—Vidū.'s failing to do it enables him thus to give a jocular turn to the matter. He says—I give it because it is not mine; it may be well-deserved or ill-deserved; I am not a loser either way. आर्य गणदास—&c.—This is a hint to Gaṇdāsa to withdraw with his pupil.

P. 58. एतावान् मे &c.—The *sevā* meant is 'managing to keep Māla. as long as possible before the king's eyes.' Cf. a similar expression in Vik. II. p. 47. परिच्छेद—*Lit.* cutting a thing all round, giving a definite shape to; hence setting a limit to.

Verse 11. Construe :—

तस्याः तिरस्करणम् अक्ष्णोः भाग्यास्तमयम् इव हृदयस्य महोत्सवावसानम् इव धृते द्वारपिधानम् इव मन्ये ।

भाग्या०—the word अस्तमय is made up of the *indec.* अस्तं and अय noun from इ to go. The genitives अक्ष्णोः and हृदयस्य are respectively connected with भाग्य and महोत्सव only (and should have been compounded); so these are instances of एकदेशीयान्वय. पिधानं—the अ of अपि may optionally be dropped, so अपिधानं also. धृतेः—धृति may here mean fortitude, steadiness of the mind; or that which keeps the mind steady; hence satisfaction, delight, pleasure; *cf.* (न) चक्षुर्बध्नाति धृतिं तद्रूपालोकदुर्ललितम्

Vik. II. 8; यदि मयि लघिमानमागतायां तव धृतिरस्ति &c. Śiś. VII, 14. तिरस्करणं—disappearance from view. तिरस्करिणीं—*v. l.* the veil separating her. The king implies by this that he will feel lonely and unhappy in the absence of Mālavikā, and Vidū., therefore, should not say that he would not be able to serve him any more, but should exercise his ingenuity still further; King Purūravas similarly depends wholly on the help of Vidūṣaka for the aquisition of his object. In fact the scene here much resembles that in Vik. Act II. and many ideas and expressions are common to both.

दरिद्र इवातुरो—&c.—Vidūṣaka means–You yourself sit idle in the matter and wish me to do everything just as a poor patient should wish his doctor to bring the medicine to him instead of his going himself to his house. In the Vik. also Vidūṣaka compares himself to a Vaidya (भो अहल्याकामुकस्य महेन्द्रस्य वैद्य उवशीपर्युत्सुकस्य भवतोऽहमपि &c. p. 40). दर्शनार्थः—दर्शनस्य अर्थः the object or motive of seeing (the performance); I have seen Māla., and have no further interest in the exhibition. वैतालिकः—विविधेन तालेन चरतीति; विविधः तालः प्रयोजनमस्य इति वा; विताल+इक (ढक्) a sort of bard or minstrel whose duty it was to announce fixed periods of the day by singing a verse or verses in praise of the king.

Verse 12. Construe :—

अत्यर्थतापात् हंसाः दीर्घिकापद्मिनीनां पत्रच्छायासु मुकुलितनयनाः, सौधानि वलभिपरिचयद्वेषिपारावतानि, बिन्दूत्क्षेपान् पिपासुः शिखी भ्रान्तिमत् वारियन्त्रं परिपतति, सर्वैः नृपगणैः (समग्रैः) त्वम् इव सर्वैः उस्रैः समग्रैः सप्तसप्तिः दीप्यते।

P. 60. पत्रच्छायासु—पत्राणां छायाः पत्रच्छायाः the shades severally afforded by leaves; and not पत्राणां छाया as in that case the comp. will be पत्रच्छाया. The swans rested each under the shade of a leaf. हंसाः - हंस is derived from हस्+अ (अच्); the nasal comes in irregularly; *cf.* भवेद्वर्णागमाद्धंसः। Some derive it fr. हन् to go (हन्तीति) and the Uṇādi aff. स. This bird is a great favourite with Sanskrit poets and is often referred to by them. The Haṃsas are said to have the power of separating milk from water. They, are described as feeding upon bits of lotus-stalks and as migrating to the Mānasa lake once a year in the rainy season. मुकुलित--closed, contracted;

p. p. p. of मुकुलय् (denom. fr. मुकुल—a bud) to close so as to look like a bud.

सौध—सुधया (with chunam plaster) लिप्तं निर्णिक्तं वा। fr. सुधा + अ (अण्); *lit.* a white-washed or chunam-plastered house; hence a mansion or palace. **वलभि०**—also वलभी; वलति what covers + अभिच्. (अभि); ई being optionally added. It is the sloping roof of a house (especially that part of it which stretches beyond the outer wall) where pigeons are wont to gather when the sun is not very hot. *Cf.* धूपैर्जालविनिःसृतैर्वलभयः संदिग्धपारावताः Vik. III. 2 and note thereon. **परिचय**—acquaintance, familiarity; hence being in contact with; **०द्वेषि** hating *i.e.* not liking to gather there. **बिन्दूत्क्षेपान्**—Tārānāth reads ०पात् connecting it with (परिपतति) because it throws up drops of water. But then we should expect ०क्षेपणात्. **भ्रान्तिमत्**—&c.—S. P. Pandit says "The वारियन्त्र here referred to is doubtless the Persian wheel" (a large wheel surrounded with buckets for raising water); but it does not seem to mean that. A water-wheel with buckets does not throw up or about drops of water; water trickles or drops down from the buckets. Besides, भ्रान्तिमत् cannot properly apply to such a wheel; भ्राम्यत् would be more appropriate. So a whirling fountain, with a motion of its own, seems to be meant here. The peacock lying after the drops as they flew forward had to hover and hover round the fountain to catch them.

उस्रः—a ray; वसन्ति रसा अत्र fr. वस् to dwell, and aff. र, व taking संप्रसारण. समग्रैः—समग्रः *v. l.* has no propriety, as the sun is always समग्र. **सप्तसप्तिः**—This is usually explained as सप्त सप्तयोऽश्वा अस्य having (*i. e.* whose chariot is drawn by) seven horses; *cf.* the Vedic passage सप्त त्वा हरितो रथे वहन्ति देव सूर्य। Saurasūkta. Some explain this as सप्त शीर्षण्याः प्राणा इति श्रुतेः सप्तप्राणानां सप्तिः प्रवृत्तिर्यस्मात्। सप्त in the Vedas often means 'spreading': and सप्ति a ray; he who has a string of spreading rays. **आविहा**—may be here खेद 'अविहाविह निर्वेदे' इत्युक्तः। Rāghavabhatta on Śāk. VI.

चिकित्सकाः—चिकित्सति इति चिकित्सकः; fr. कित् + अक (ण्वुल्); the root कित् in the sense of 'to treat or cure disease' takes the augment स् (not the desiderative स्) by the Vārt. कितेर्व्याधिप्रतीकारे &c. See Pāṇ III. I. 5. **हरदत्त किमि०** etc. —the Vidū. by his clever speech makes it impossible for

Haradatta to press his point, and relieves the King from a necessity which would have otherwise forced him to stay there to witness the performance of Haradatta's pupil. नास्ति वचनस्य &c.—Haradatta means :—As this is meal-time I cannot ask His majesty to stay here any longer. Rāśivadekar Śāstri reads अस्ति चान्यस्य वचनावकाशोऽत्र and interprets it thus अन्यस्य प्रतिपक्षिणो गणदासस्य। कर्तरि षष्ठी। वचनावकाशः वचनस्य 'त्वत्पक्षपातिनापि राज्ञा नावलोकितस्ते प्रयोग इति मदपेक्षया निकृष्टतरस्त्वम्' इतिरूपस्य निन्दावचनस्यावकाशोवसरः। तेन मदुपदेशमवलोक्यैव गमनं युक्तमिति भावः। But this has no propriety as we cannot expect Hara. to be so discourteous as to ask the King to stay there any longer after what was said by the Vidūṣaka. तेन हि.... श्वो द्रक्ष्यामः—It appears from the conversation of the two maid-servants in the Prelude to the third Act that the examination was resumed the next day (as was absolutely necessary) and Hardatta's pupil asked to perform the same piece that was gone through by Mālavikā, the result being declared in Gaṇadāsa's favour. मज्जनविधि—Bathing formed a part of mid-day duties; *cf.* समयः खलु स्नानभोजनं सेवितुं Vik. II. p. 63.. The reading मध्याह्नविधि would be better as it would refer to all that is to be done at mid-day. पानभोजनं—So in Vik. II., भवति त्वरयास्य भोजनं p. 60. The Vidūṣaka who is a good epicure is always represented as being anxious to have dinner expedited.

Verse 13. Construe

अव्याजसुन्दरीं तां ललितेन विज्ञानेन योजयता विधात्रा कामस्य विषदिग्धः बाणः परिकल्पितः।

P. 62. अव्याजसुन्दरीं—अव्याजेन without artificial means (which hide defects and improve beauty) सुन्दरी ; *cf.* इदं किलाव्याजमनोहरं वपुः Śâk. I बाणः—कामस्य—Bhavabhūti describes Mālati's person as इदमिह मदनस्य जैत्रमस्त्रम्। Māl.-Mād. II 6. विषदिग्धः—ललितविज्ञान is the poison. चिन्तयितव्योऽस्मि—I am wounded by the poisoned arrow of Mālavikā's beauty; and you ought to save me from its effects. Kāli. makes his heroes rely absolutely for help in love-matters on the Vidūṣaka. Duṣyanta similarly says to his friend सखे त्रायस्व माम्। Śāk VI. विपणि—विपणन्ते अत्र where people carry on business, a market-place; fr. पण् with वि + इ. कन्दु:—an oven or a frying-pan: fr. स्कन्द् (1 P. to rise, to go ; to dry &c.) and the aff. उ, स् being irregularly dropped. दह्यते मे &c.—Inability to bear hunger is a characteristic of the Vidū.); *cf.* कथं बुभुक्षया खादयितव्योस्मि। Śāk. VI.

एवमेव—*i. e.* just as you take great care to satisfy your hunger. सुहृदर्थे—*i. e.* to bring about his union with Mālavikā. गृहीतक्षणः—क्षणः that which destroys or removes pain; a festive occasion; *cf.* किं मोदकखण्डिकायां। तेन हि अयं सुगृहीतः क्षणः। Śāk. II. p. 47. (क्षणोति दुःखमिति ; fr क्षण्+अ (अच्); hence here leisure, patience necessary for doing anything. गृहीत०—means I have made up my mind to find leisure for (your work); hence I shall do my best or spare no pains to do your business (and will not attend to any other thing till I do that). The following extract from Mr. Pandit's long note on this word will be interesting to the student :—

"The word क्षण originally means 'a moment', hence one's own moment, or leisure, vacation, in which last sense our own Marāthi word सण 'a festival' is derived from it. The phrase गृहीतक्षण has its origin in the following formula addressed to a Brāhamaṇa, who, having been invited to a Śrāddha, has come, and is seated ceremoniously near the dish in which he is to dine at the end of the rite. The formula is...श्राद्धे तु वैश्वदेवार्थं करणीयः क्षणस्त्वया। इत्येवं श्राद्धकृद् ब्रूयात् तं प्राप्नोतु भवानिति। स वदेत्प्राप्तवानीति इतरस्तं प्रति द्विजः। &c. Śaunakasmṛti 96, 11. where we have to translate करणीयः क्षणस्त्वया by 'may it please you to be at leisure for the Śrāddha of' (*i e.* to be freed from your studies and from every other engagement, and attend the Śrāddha) .. &c.

मेघावली—Dhāriṇī is compared to a row of clouds that hides from them the moon-light of Mālavikā. This is preferable to the variant मेघो० as मेघावली, being fem. in gender, better agrees with धारिणी। सूना—(also written शूना) a slaughter-house. आमिष—(1) a bait, an object of attraction; (2) flesh. अनातुरः &c.— आतुर fr. तुर् 3rd conj. to hasten, with आ (आतुतोर्ति) + aff. अ (कः), means suffering from some torment, or disease; here, eager, over-anxious. अनातुर one who is not over-anxious, is patient. Vid. means :—I shall like to exert myself for you if you will not be over-anxious but will have patience. It will be noticed that the Vidū. always asks the king not to be impatient. *Cf.* अलं भवतो धीरतामुज्झित्वा परिदेवितेन p. 68.

कथं नातुरः—अनातुरः *v.l* the king means—How can I not be eager when my mind cannot find pleasure anywhere ?

Verse 14. Construe :—

सर्वान्तःपुरवनिताव्यापारप्रतिनिवृत्तहृदयस्य मे स्नेहस्य सा वामलोचना एकायनीभूता।

व्यापार—My doings *i.e.* amatory sports with ; *cf.* उचितव्यापार-पराङ्मुखे चेतसा p. 70, where व्यापार means 'occupations, duties.' **एकायनीभूता**—has become the one abode. *i. e.* sole object of my love. Kāṭyavema appears, from his explanation, to read एकायनं भूता. This closing part of the Act is technically called बिन्दु which is defined as अवान्तरार्थविच्छेदे बिन्दुरच्छेदकारणम् । Bindu is that which serves to keep up the connexion or as a link between the parts of the story when suddenly interrupted, as by the exit of Mālavikā in the present case. See com.

Critical Appreciation of The Act II

The second act is a continuation of the first act. It has only one scene viz. the dance of Mālavikā in the music hall of the palace. The act, with its eye-filling dance and enchanting music, arrests the mind of the audience. Mālavikā is, for the first time, presented before the king and the audience. Mālavikā, with her beauty and skill, wins the heart of the king and the audience as well. The king's love for Mālavikā becomes more intense after seeing her and she too expresses her feelings through the Chalita dance.

The king plays well the part of an hypocrite when he tells Parivrājikā to decide about the order of appearance of the pupils on the stage. His impatient curiosity to see Mālavikā, when she is yet behind the curtain, reveals his eagerness for her. He is much delighted to see Mālavikā in person and is so pleased with her dance that he gladly accepts the defeat of his party even without the actual dance performance by Irāvatī, the pupil of Haradatta. He, like a romantic lover, construes the gestures of Mālavikā in the dance as meant for himself. At the departure of Mālavikā, he feels as if without life. Though not eager, he is courteous enough to accede to Haradatta's request to see the dance of Irāvatī.

The queen Dhārinī quietly watches the dance of Mālavikā. When Vidūṣaka attempts to detain Mālavikā on the stage, she intervenes and successfully prevents Vidūṣaka from presenting the king's bracelet to मालविका. Her remarks like ननु दर्शितोपदेशा ते शिष्या। reveal her jealousy. She is rightly described as a wasp guarding the honey in the form of Mālavikā.

The Vidūṣaka, in this act, acts more as an affectionate friend of the king than as a mere jester. He warns the king to be cautious when he becomes very impatient to see Mālavikā even in the presence of the queen Dhārinī. He detains Mālavikā on the stage and thus offers an opportunity to the king to see Mālavikā for a longer time. He invites the appreciation of Mālavikā's dance from the two judges and thus intensifies the king's love and fans the jealousy of Dhārinī. By delaying Mālavikā, he indirectly helps the postponement of the dance by Irāvatī. In the end, he assures his best cooperation to the king.

Gaṇadāsa proves to be a sincere teacher by his careful attention, on every detail, at the time of the entry of Mālavikā on the stage. He, like a confident and a true teacher, is anxious to see that Mālavikā gets a clean certificate from the judges.

The Parivrājikā plays well her role of a judge. In a clever and convincing manner, she gives priority to the pupil of Gaṇadāsa.

The seed which is sown in the first act is developed in this act. The hero and the heroine, for the first time, see each other. They indirectly convey their feelings to each other. Mālavikā with her consummate skill wins the sympathy of the audience whereas the jealousy of Dhārinī leaves us in a suspense for the furthur progress of the love-affair. The Vidūṣaka, who has proved himself to be a shrewd companion of the king, encourages us for the happy culmination of the love-affair.

Act III

P. 64. The third Act opens with an Interlude which introduces the audience to the following facts :—(1) The Parivrājikā seeking an interview with the Queen; (2) the end of the contest between the two dancing-masters; (3) Mālavikā's pining for the King; and (4) the Queen's favourite *Aśoka* tree withholding its flowers and therefore standing in need of its flower-yielding-desire being gratified-and thus prepares the ground for the further development of the plot.

उपायनार्थः—That it should serve as a present to. सभाजनार्थं —For honouring the Queen (which she could do by taking a fruit with her). A rule of conduct requires that gods and great personages should be seen) with a present. बीजपूरकः— (बीजैः पूर्यते बीजपूरः। बीजपूर एव बीजपूरकः) also called मातुलुंग (महाळुंग or माळुंग in Marāthi) is a fruit that is auspicious like the coconut and fit to be presented to a great personage at a visit. यावत्—In the first place, before doing anything else. प्रमदवनं—प्रमदानां वनं प्रमदवनं ; the आ is shortened by the rule "In the case of words ending in आ and ई their final is shortened in most cases in a compound when the whole is a name or when it occurs in the Vedas;" *e. g.* रेवतिपुत्रः, अजक्षीरं &c. Sometimes the long vowel is retained; so we may have प्रमदावनं also. Or प्रकृष्टो मदो यत्र तत्प्रमदं that which greatly exhilarates; प्रमदं च तद्वनं च. तपनीयाशोक— see below. उपसर्पामि—संभावयामि *v. l.* greet her; honour her by asking how she is doing. This is a better reading, as it will show that there was great familiarity between them. समाभृतिका—The name of this maid varies in different editions. समाधिमतिका is probably better as better agreeing with her character as the attendant of the Parivrājikā. स्वागतं ते—for the Dat. see *A.* G. § 67 (*d*) शुश्रूषितुं—To wait upon her (used when one attends upon a great person with a desire to please him or her).

P. 66. किल—'Verily; or, 'as the report goes, as we hear'- आगमिनौ—Well-versed in the science; आगम is any lore traditionally handed down; here used for शास्त्र. कौलीनं—A scandal, evil rumour (see com: *lit* that which is so bad as to be fit to be buried under the earth). अतः पेशलतरं—nicer, handsomer than this (*i. e.* what you are enjoying at present).

It is a blessing, meaning 'you will prosper still more'. चिरायमाण० तपनीयाशोकस्य—There are two kinds of Aśoka, Red and White, so called from the colour of its flowers; प्रसूनकैरशोकस्तु श्वेतो रक्त इति द्विधा। बहुसिद्धिकरः श्वेतो रक्तोऽत्र स्मरवर्धनः॥ quoted by Malli. in his com. on Megh. II. 18. It is the Red Aśoka that is usually described by poets on account of its power to excite passion. See *infra*, sl. 5. p. 43 notes. The Aśoka mentioned here is a third kind of Aśoka, having flowers of a deep yellow-red colour, which must have been very rare and hence so much anxiety about its longing being satisfied, as it had not put forth flowers yet. दौहदनि०—दोहमाकर्षं ददातीति दोहद; that which draws away the mind; hence a longing, especially that of a pregnant woman. According to the convention of poets the Aśoka puts forth flowers when struck by a young woman with the foot decked with jingling anklets; see com.; *cf.* असूत सद्यः कुसुमान्यशोकः स्कन्धात्प्रभृत्येव सपल्लवानि। पादेन नापैक्षत सुन्दरीणां सम्पर्कमाशिञ्जितनूपुरेण॥ Kum. III. 26; and सनूपुररवेण स्त्रीचरणेनाभिताडनम्। दोहदं यदशोकस्य ततः पुष्पोद्गमो भवेत्॥ quoted by Malli. thereon; also Megh. II. 18.

P. 68. प्रवेशकः—An Interlude acted between any two Acts (and hence it can never come at the beginning of the first Act) by inferior characters such as servants, the buffoon &c. (see com.); it is intended like the Viṣkambhaka to connect the parts of the story by briefly referring to what has occurred in the interval or what is going to happen subsequently.

कामयमाना०—Kāṭayavema solves the comp. according to the Bhāṣya which says सप्तम्युपमानपूर्वपदस्य उत्तरपदलोपश्च वक्तव्यः *i. e.* in a Bah. comp. the word following a सप्तम्यन्तपद or an उपमानपद is dropped; here कामयमानावस्था is the उपमानपद, so the latter word अवस्था is dropped; the modern way is to dissolve it as कामयमानानामिव अवस्था यस्य like चन्द्रकान्तिः.

Verse 1. Construe :—

दयितालिङ्गनसुखे असति शरीरं क्षामं स्यात्, सा क्षणम् अपि न दृश्यते इति चक्षुः सास्रं भवेत्, हृदय, त्वं तया सारङ्गाक्ष्या कदाचित् विरहितं न असि, निर्वाणे प्रसक्ते परितापं किं वहसि।

क्षामं— p. p. of क्षै 4, P. to waste away, to be emaciated, **सास्रं चक्षुः**—For such an effect *cf.* न च...मम नयनयोरुद्बाष्पत्वं सखे न भविष्यते। Vik. II. 10. **प्रसक्ते निर्वाण**—प्रसक्त (p. p. p. of सञ्ज्

with प्र) closely attached or sticking, hence uninterrupted, continuous. निर्वाण—*Lit.* with all disturbance completely blown off; hence unmixed or complete happiness, supreme bliss. In Buddhistic philosophy the term signifies the Summum Bonum (Moksha) of the Buddhas. It is the p. p. p. of वा with निस् when वात or wind is not the subject (निर्वाणोऽवाते); as निर्वाण:, अग्नि:, मुनिश्च। *Cf,* अये लब्धं नेत्रनिर्वाणम्। Śāk. III. p. 68 and our note thereon. The King means to say—If my body is emaciated it is because it does not get the pleasure of her embrace; if my eyes overflow with tears, that is because they cannot enjoy her sight. So I can understand this. But I do not know why, you, my heart, should suffer anguish when you are in uninterrupted enjoyment of bliss (on account of your constant association with the fawn-eyed one). Some take प्रसक्त in the sense of 'near, close at hand, 'but this is against the context. The King is not sure as yet of his being able to secure Mālavikā. परिताप—there is an apparent contrast (विरोध) between निर्वाण (complete extinction of fire or heat) and परिताप. अलं परिदेवितेन—so in Vik. अलं परिदेवितेन। अचिरेण तवेष्टसंपादयिता अनङ्ग एव सुखदो भविष्यति। II. p. 38.

P. 69. तपस्विनी—Poor, helpless. Properly one practising penance and therefore necessarily depending upon others for maintenance, protection &c.; hence one deserving pity and protection. नागरक्षित इव निधि:—It is a general belief that a miser whose heart is set on his treasure throughout life, becomes a serpent after death and keeps guard over his treasure buried in the earth, so that no one can touch it without risk of life. मणिरिव is another reading which is also good, as the serpent having a gem in its hood is said to take special care of it. Large serpents are supposed to have gems in their hoods. अधिकतरं—She was already guarded; (see p. 10. सांप्रतं माल० सविशेषं &c.); now she is guarded with greater care on account of the suspicion caused by the events of the second Act.

P. 70. संकल्पयोनि:—संकल्प: योनि: (source) अस्य; the thought-born (Cupid) *Cf.* the names मनसिज, मनोभव &c. अभिनिविश्—(cau.) *lit.* to make one take to a thing with deep attachment. *Cf.* अहो नु खलु दुर्लभाभिनिवेशी मदन:। Vik. I. p. 25.

Verse 2. Construe :—

मन्मथ, हृदयप्रमाथिनी रुजा क, ते विश्वसनीयम् आयुधं च क, मृदु तीक्ष्णतरम् उच्यते यत् तत् इदं त्वयि दृश्यते।

क रुजा क आयुधं—the two कs (*i. e.* when repeated in two co-ordinate sentences) show great difference or incongruity between two things or assertions. विश्वसनीय—deserving to be trusted (on account of its being nothing more than a flower) as doing no harm; hence tender. *Cf.* त्वया चन्द्रमसा च विश्वसनीयाभ्यामतिसंधीयते कामिजनसार्थः। Sāk III. मृदु तीक्ष्णतरं—For a similar thought, *cf.* कुतस्ते कुसुमायुधस्य सततस्तैक्ष्ण्यमिदम्। Sāk. II.

साधनीयं—The object to be gained, *viz* Mālavikā. पर्यवस्थापय—To collect or compose oneself; so in Vik—चित्रलेखा-हला पर्यवस्थापयात्मानम्. उचित०—उचितः (proper to be done, usual) चासौ व्यापारश्च तस्मात् पराङ्मुखं यस्य तत्पराङ्मुखं (turned away from, averse to,) तेन.

वसन्तप्रथमावतार०—*Cf. Vik.* II. पश्यतु भवान्वसन्तावतारसूचकमभिरामत्वं प्रमदवनस्य। ०सुभगानि *v. l.*—beautiful, charming. रक्ताशोक०—The Aśoka is one of the plants that blossom early in the spring; *cf.* असूत सद्यः कुसुमान्यशोकः &c. Kum. III. 26. The reading कोकिकाणी is not good as there is no reason why the buds should have been sent instead of the full-blown flowers. रक्तकुरबकाणि *v. l.*—The Kurabaka also is a flower that blows in spring; *cf.* कुरबका रवकारणतां ययुः। Ragh. IX. 29. Its flowers also are red in colour ; *cf.* तत्र शोणे कुरबकः Ak. II. 4. 74. The reading रक्ताशोक०, however, is preferred as the Aśoka flowers are mentioned as exciting love and as being favourite with women; *cf.* रक्ताशोकश्चलकिसलयः &c. Megh. II. 18 and Malli. on it (रक्तविशेषणं तस्य स्मरोद्दीपकत्वात् &. रक्तोत्र स्मरर्धनः।). वसन्तो०—This is better than the reading वसन्तावतार as the दोलारोहण is spoken of in connexion with the Vernal festival and so is appropriate with it. °अपदेशेन–under the plea of, putting forth that as the ground for. प्रतिज्ञातम्—promised.

P. 72. निसर्गनिपुणाः स्त्रियः—*cf.* स्त्रियो हि नाम खल्वेता निसर्गादेव पण्डिताः। Mrich. IV. 19; स्त्रीणामशिक्षितपटुत्वं &c. Śak. V. 22. अन्यसंक्रान्तहृदयम्—हृदय heart *i. e.* affection, love. So in Śak. अन्यसंक्रान्तहृदयोऽपि प्रथमसंभावनां &c. VI. अन्या *f.* becomes अन्य *m.* by the rule सर्वनाम्नो वृत्तिमात्रे पूर्वपदस्य पुंवद्भावः।; *i. e.* a pronoun forming the first member of a compound takes the masculine form. **For संक्रान्त cf.** पुत्रसंक्रान्तलक्ष्मीकैः Uttar. I 22, and the word संक्रान्ति *supra* in I. 16. **ते सखी**—It is usual with heroes to call their wife the friend (सखी) of their friend; *cf.* निर्विनोदां सखीं ते। Megh. II. 25; एकः सख्यास्तव सह मया वामपादाभिलाषी। *ibid.* II. 15. उपलालय्—(*causal* of लल् with उप) to fondle, to humour.

Verse 3. Construe :—

उचितः प्रणयः विहन्तुं वरम्, बहवः खण्डनहेतवः हि दृष्टाः; पूर्वाभ्यधिकः अपि भावशून्यः उपचारविधिः मनस्विनीनां तु न (वरम्)।

उचितः प्रणयः &c.—Construe: प्रणयः उचितः अपि (though proper) विहन्तुं वरं; विहन्तु being used as Pass. inf. and वरं serving as the predicate, being equivalent in sense to यज्यते; *Cf.* विषवृक्षोऽपि संवर्ध्य स्वयं छेत्तुमसांप्रतम्। Kum. II. 55 and Mallinātha thereon; पवनः आलिङ्गितुं शक्यम् Śāk. III. 5. हि—*ind.* 'for'. **खण्डनहेतवः**—Reasons or excuses for breaking the promise given. That root खण्ड् occurs in the word खण्डिता which is the name given to a *Nāyikā* neglected by her lover. **दृष्टाः**—I have seen, I have in view. **मनस्विनीनां**—is objective genitive, **उपचारविधिः**—The act of attending to or ministering to their desires. **भावशून्यः**—void of real love or affection. *Cf.* ममात्र भावैकरसं मनः स्थितं। Kum. V. 82; बबन्ध सा नोत्तमसौकुमार्या कुमुद्वती भानुमतीव भावम्। Ragh. VI. 36. **न तु**-supply वरं as the predicate, which is better than supplying भवति as is done by Kāṭayavema (See com.). For the idea *cf.* प्रियवचनशतोऽपि योषितां दयितजनानुनयो रसादृते। प्रविशति हृदयं न तद्विदां मणिरिव कृत्रिमरागयोजितः॥ (Vik. II. 22. What the King means to say is this—If I do not keep my promise and disappoint her, I can explain away my action in various ways so as to satisfy her; but a mere show of courtesy without real inward affection is not at all good, as it will serve, since she is a high-minded woman (मनस्विनी), to make matters worse for me. The Com. take the latter half of the stanza somewhat differently. **अन्तःपुरप्रतिष्ठितम्**—is a locative Tatp. **दाक्षिण्यं**—*lit.* acting in a way to please; hence, loveful conduct; *cf.* दाक्षिण्यं नाम बिम्बोष्ठि बैम्बिकानां कुलव्रतम्। *infra.* IV. 14. **पृष्ठतः कर्तुं**—To do away with; *cf.* लज्जां पृष्ठतः कृत्वा Kād. The corresponding expression in the sense of 'not to do away with', 'to adopt', to follow' is पुरस्कृ; *cf.* स पुरस्कृतमध्यमक्रमो नमयामास नृपान्। Ragh. VIII. 9.

वसन्तः किल &c.—is preferred to ननु एतत्प्रमद्वनं as the King refers to वसन्त in the next speech. पवनदर०—*V. l.* here दर means 'a little' (ईषत्). पल्लवाङ्गुलीभिस्त्वरयतीव—*Cf.* वातेरिताभिः पल्लवाङ्गुलिभिः त्वरयतीव मां केसरवृक्षः। Śāk. III. अभिजातः—'nobly-born', *i. e.* noble in behaviour, such as readily welcomes a visitor and attends to his comforts. This is explained in the next Śloka.

Verse 4. Construe :—

आमत्तानां कोकिलानां श्रवणसुभगैः कुजितैः मनसिजरुजः सह्यतां सानुक्रोशं पृच्छता इव माधवेन चूतप्रसवसुरभिः दक्षिणः मारुतः सान्द्रस्पर्शः करतलः इव मे अङ्गे व्यापृतः।

कूजितैः पृच्छतेव—The notes of the cuckoos are the voice of the spring, as conceived by the poet. For a similar idea compare: परभृताभिरितीव निवेदिते स्मरमते रमते स्म वधूजनः। Ragh. XI. 47. आलोकशब्दं वयसां विरावैः। *ibid.* II. 9. सानुक्रोशं—*adv.* with sympathy; अनुक्रोश means अनुकम्पा; कारुण्यं करुणा घृणा। कृपा दयानुकम्पा स्यादनुक्रोशः। Ak. I. 6. 18. The derivation of the two words is very nearly similar; 'sympathy' is from *sym* (together) and *pathos* (feeling); while अनुक्रोश comes from अनु (after, together with, in succession) and क्रुश् (to cry)—'crying alone with another' in sympathy. The word occurs at Śak. IV. p. 89.–सानुक्रोशः कृतः। मनसिजरुजः सह्यतां—its bearableness, *i. e.* how far I can bear it, whether it pains me too much. दक्षिणो मारुतः The southern breeze, blowing from the Malaya mountain and wafting the smell of the blossoms of the sandal trees growing there, forms one of the stock items in the descriptions of spring by Sanskrit poets. *Cf.* मलयमारुतकम्पितपल्लवा Ragh. IX. 29. भगवन् वसन्तप्रिय दक्षिणवायो। Vik. II. It is sometimes described as itself welcoming a guest; *cf.* प्रत्युद्गतो भवान्दक्षिणमारुतेन *ibid.* II. It is here represented as the palm of the hand of spring with which he affectionately touches the body of the King. सान्द्र—'close', or better still, 'soothing'. माधव-the spring.

P. 74. निर्वृति—mental ease or happiness; *cf.* व्रजति निवृतिमेकपदे मनः। Vik. II. 9. विलोभयितुकामया—The final म् of the infinitive is elided when compounded with काम and मनस् (by तुं काममनसोरपि). मधुलक्ष्म्या—Vernal beauty (as appearing in the garden) considered as a young lady. The reading प्रमद०,

though justified by the context, does not appear to be the poet's reading. The poet has already referred to Vasanta as welcoming the King and naturally he refers here to मधुलक्ष्मी, as is clear from the following śl. and as he has done elsewhere; see Kum III. 30. quoted below. युवतिवेष०— The dress of the Vernal beauty is more gorgeous than that of a young and charming woman. This is explained in detail in the following Śloka.

Verse 5. Construe :—

विम्बाधरालक्तकः रक्ताशोकरूचा विशेषितगुणः, श्यामावदातारुणं कुरबकं प्रत्याख्यातं विशेषकम्, लग्नद्विरेफाञ्जनैः तिलकैः तिलकक्रिया च आक्रान्ता माधवी श्रीः योषितां मुख-प्रसाधनविधी सावज्ञा इव।

रक्ताशोक etc.—For the two varieties of Aśoka see *supra* note on तपनीयाशोकस्य, p. 66. The variety with the red blooms is specially noted as causing passion to inflame at its sight. विशेषितगुणः—whose quality (of redness) is surpassed or excelled by; for this sense of विशेषित *cf.* मदनमपि गुणैर्विशेषयन्ती। Mrich. VI. 4, विशेषको वा विशिशेष यस्याः श्रियं त्रिलोकीतिलकः स एव। Śiś. III. 63. The poet means that the redness of the As'oka flowers (which may be conceived as the lips of Madhu Lakshmī) is deeper and brighter than that of the lips of ladies even though when they are further reddened by means of the *alaktaka* paint. बिम्बाधरा०—In the com. read बिम्बभ-धरस्तस्मिन् instead of बिम्बमिवाधरस्तस्मिन्; the compound should be taken as a विशेषणसमास like नीलोत्पल, and not as an उपमित-समास; see com. प्रत्याख्यात०—'ordered back, thrown into the background, excelled.' विशेषक is an ornamental arrangement of dots to different colours on the face of a woman; *cf.* अभिनवा इव पत्रविशेषकाः। Ragh. IX. 29: मृष्टचन्दनविशेषकभक्तिभ्रष्टभूषण, &c Śiś. X. 84. विशेषितगुणः and प्रत्याख्यातविशेषकं are used as predicates in the first and in the second line respectively. अवदात—'white', fr. दै 1st. conj. with अव. तिलक०—The mark on the forehead of Hindu ladies (whose husbands are living) made generally with *kumkuma* or saffron (now with the powder of reddened turmeric) and sometimes with black sandle or musk. *Cf* कस्तूरिकातिलकमालि विहाय सायम्। Bhāmi. II. 4. When made with *kunkuma* it was sometimes ornamented with dots made with collyrium. तिलकैः—by the flowers of the तिलक tree. *Cf.* न खलु शोभयति स्म वनस्थलीं न तिलकस्तिलकः प्रमदामिव। Ragh. IX. 41. आक्रान्ता—Conquered overcome, surpassed. लग्न०—The bees perched on the *tilaka* flowers serve as collyrium for the purpose of the comparison with the Tilak-mark decked with collyrium; see above. For the idea comp. लग्नद्विरेफाञ्जनभक्तिचित्रं मुखे मधुश्रीस्तिलकं प्रकाश्य। रागेण बालारुणकोमलेन चतूप्रवालोष्ठमलंचकार ॥ Kum. III 30. माधवी—मधोरियं; *fem. adj.* fr. मधु; 'of the spring'. सावज्ञेव &c.—The idea is that all these blossoms excel in decorative beauty the materials used for decorating their faces by ladies and मधुश्री treats these with scorn as it were.

निर्वर्णयतः—look at it attentively. पर्युत्सुका—affected with love-longing, anxiously longing for the company of her lover; *cf.* पर्युत्सुकां कथयसि प्रियदर्शनां तामार्तं न पश्यसि पुरूरवसं तदर्थे। Vik. II. 15. अविज्ञात०—so in S'āk., तव न जाने हृदयं III. 14. भर्तारं—the master, the king. लज्जे—because of the folly of loving the king without knowing the state of his mind. विभवः—the power, *i.e.* the necessary courage of mind. स्निग्धस्य—to loving friends, who alone by their sympathy can mitigate the torment and help in these matters. *Cf.* शकुन्तला—सखि कस्य वान्यस्य कथयामि। आयासयित्रीदानीं वां भविष्यामि। उभे (सख्या)—अत एव खलु निर्बन्धः। स्निग्धजनसंविभक्तं हि दुःखं सह्यवेदनं भवति। Śāk. Act III. p. 70. अप्रतिकारगुरुकां—heavy and irremediable; or heavy because there is no remedy to it. कुत्र &c.—Mālavikā was so much engrossed and worried with her own thoughts that she almost forgot the purpose for which she was sent there. आम्—a particle of remembrance; 'Ah, I have it.' I remember it now. चापल—*n.* a hasty or rash act.

P. 76. दोहदं—see *supra* p. 66. पञ्चरात्राभ्यन्तरे—पञ्चरात्र is a *Dvigu*; see com. दर्शयति—in the sense of दर्शयिष्यति. Perhaps the condition is suggested to the poet by the similar condition imposed upon Droṇāchārya by Śakuni on behalf of Duryodhana in Bhāsa's Pancharātra; *cf.* यदि पञ्चरात्रेण पाण्डवानां प्रवृत्तिरुपनेतव्या राज्यस्यार्धं प्रदास्यति किल। Act I. अन्तरा—*ind.* in the middle, between the two parts of her speech. निःश्वस्य—The words which she was to speak immediately after (अभिलाष० &c) made her at once think of her love for the king, and the hopelessness of that love being successful. The only

अभिलाष which she cared to have satisfied was that; but what did the Queen mean by her words अभिलाषपूरयि० ? Would she consent to her being married to the king? She did not think she would, and the despair of the प्रसाद taking that direction makes her sigh. नियोगभूमि—the place where she had a mission to execute (*viz.* to strike the Asoka with her foot). अनुपदं—Adv. comn.; *lit.* after ', *i. e.* 'following my footsteps' (पदानां पश्चात्). 'On the heels of, immediately after' *Cf.* गच्छतां पुरो भवन्तौ। अहमप्यनुपदमागत एव Śāk. II. p. 59. विस्रब्धं—with freedom and confidence, since there is no one to interrupt me for a while.

सीधुपानो—'Here is fine sugar for one who is over-intoxicated with liquor'. The Vidūṣaka means that just as a man who was taken too much wine and become helpless under its influence is brought round if he eats मत्स्यण्डिका or fine sugar, so the king, whom his passion for Māla. has maddened, as with wine, will now be calmer when he finds Mālavikā alone as he can then feast his eyes with sight. मत्स्यण्डिका is a variety of sugar and it is so called because being soft and yellowish-white like sand, its crystals or granules resemble the eggs of fish. Ancient medical works prescribe the use of sugar as an antidote against over-intoxication in their sections devoted to मदात्ययचिकित्सा. See also Ajīrṇamanjarī quoted in the com. सीधु–*m.* rum, liquor (पक्वेक्षुरसप्रकृतिकः सुराविशेषः). The word is also written as शीधु and derived from शी to lie down, 'that which makes a man sleep when it is drunk' (शेरते जना अनेन पीतेन). मत्स्यण्डिका fr. मत्स्य + अण्ड + the affix इक (and the *fem.*) to be explained like शकन्धु; in the case of compound–words of the शकन्ध्वादि class; the initial vowel of the second member is retained, the final of the first being dropped, as in कुलटा (कुल + अटा), सारङ्ग (सार + अङ्ग); some derive this as मदं मुदं वा स्यन्दते इति.

अयि किमेतत्—The king was engaged in observing the beauty of the season and so he did not see Mālavikā arriving there. Hence Vidūṣaka's characteristic comment (सीधुपानो०) is not intelligible to him, and he seeks an explanation. This the Viduṣaka proceeds to give by paraphrasing his witticism into plain language—एषा खलु मालविका अदूरे वर्तते। नातिपर्याप्तवेषा —not fully attired; पर्याप्त full, entire. *Cf.* पर्याप्तचन्द्रेव शरत्त्रियामा।

Kum. VII. 26. शशीव पर्याप्तकलो नलिन्याः। Ragh. VI. 44. परिष्कृत—*V. l.* gorgeously decorated. पर्युत्सुका—this he infers from her drooping condition, as well as the fewness of her ornaments. For the latter *cf.* तस्य पाण्डुवदनाल्पभूषणा सावलम्बगमना मृदुस्वना राजयक्ष्मपरिहानिराययौ कामयानसमवस्थया तुलाम् ॥ Ragh. XIX. 50.

कथं—shows the king's surprise at knowing that Mālavikā was there when he did not expect her. अथ किम्—yes, quite so, she is here.

P. 78. शक्यमिदानीं &c.—He is delighted at the prospect of meeting her and becomes cheerful. For the passive construction in अवलम्बितुं शक्यं *cf. supra* उचितः प्रणयो वरं विहन्तुं p. 72, and our note thereon.

Verse 6. Construe :—

आरसितात् सारसात् तरुवृतां सरितम् उपलभ्य जलार्थिनः पथिकस्य विक्लवं हृदयम् इव त्वत् समीपगतां प्रियाम् उपलभ्य मम विक्लवं हृदयम् उच्छ्वसितम्।

विक्लव—depressed, helpless owing to despair, as it saw no chance of being united with Mālavikā or even of meeting her like this. उच्छ्वसित—*lit.* 'has breathed a sigh (of relief),' has become full of hope. *Cf.* कामस्योच्छ्वसितं मनः। Kum. VI. 14, where Malli. comments उच्छ्वसितं सप्रत्याशं अभूत् इत्यर्थः। तरुवृत्तां—The hope with which the king has been inspired he compares to the similar feeling of relief experienced by a traveller parched with thirst when he suddenly hears a water-fowl's cry and knows that a river must be in the vicinity. The simile is elaborate, त्वत् corresponding with आरसितात् सारसात्, and समीपगतां प्रियां with तरुवृतां सरितम्. Construe : आरसितात् सारसात् तरुवृत्तां सरितं (उपलभ्य) जलार्थिनः पथिकस्य विक्लवं (हृदयं) इव मम हृदयं त्वत् समीपगतां प्रियां उपलभ्य उच्छ्वसितम्। आरसित 'one who has uttered a cry'—*p. p.* participle used in an active sense. सारस is a kind of aquatic bird or water-fowl which is found in large numbers in northern India. The name is derived as सरसि भवः सारसः 'residing in lakes', as it generally inhabits ponds and rivers. त्वद्—abl. case.

तरुराजि०—The Marāthi student will observe in राजि the original of the word राई 'a grove,' *e. g.* आंबराई.

Verse 7. Construe :—

नितम्बबिम्बे विपुलं, मध्ये क्षामं, कुचयोः समुन्नतं, नयनयो अत्यायतम्, एतत् मम जीवितम् आयाति ।

विपुलं &c.—The king by a metaphor identifies his life with Mālavikā, which, therefore, like her, is broad and expansive in the region of the hips, thin in the waist, prominent at the breasts, and long in the eyes. These in Sanskrit literature are regarded as the marks of beauty in a woman. **नितम्बबिम्बे**—*Cf.* श्रोणीबिम्ब *infra* III. 20; मध्ये क्षामं and **अत्यायतं नयनयोः**—*cf.* मध्ये क्षामा Megh. II. 22; दीर्घापाङ्गा Vik. IV. 9. **एतत्**—*i. e.* Mālavikā. **पूर्वस्मादतिमनोहरं**—She has become more charming than when I last saw her at the dancing exhibition (Act. II.) This he explains in the next sloka. For such an effect on lovers, *cf.* सखि इदानीं प्रथमदर्शनात्सविशेषं प्रियदर्शनो महाराजः प्रतिभाति । Vik. Act II. p. 44; संप्रति रमणीयतरा मालती । Māl.-Mād. III. p. 67.

Verse 8. Construe :—

शरकाण्डपाण्डुगण्डस्थला परिमिताभरणा इयं माधवपरिणतपत्रा कतिपयकुसुमा कुन्दलता इव आभाति ।

शर०—With cheeks pale-white like the stalk of the *s'ara* grass when ripe. काण्ड (*m. n.*) also means a cluster, a bunch. For the idea *cf.* पाकभिन्नशरकाण्डगौरयोः...गण्डलेखयोः Kum. VIII. 74, and अथाधिकस्निग्धविलोचनेन मुखेन सीता शरपाण्डुरेण । Ragh. XIV. 26. **स्थल** in **गण्डस्थल** expresses excellence (प्रशस्तौ गण्डौ गण्डस्थले) consisting in their being expansive. **परिमिता०**—*Cf.* नातिपर्याप्तवेषा *supra* p. 76. **माधव०**—He compares her with the *Kunda* creeper whose leaves ripen and become yellow in the spring, and which then bears few or no flowers, its regular flowering season being हेमन्त and शिशिर (See Malli. on Megh. II. 2 बालकुन्दानुविद्धं). For कतिपय in the sense of a few, *cf.* वर्णैः कतिपयैरेव Śiś. II. 72. (कतिपयैः परिमितैः Malli.) **मदनव्याधिः**—*cf.* मनसिजरुजा *infra* IV. 11. **परामृष्टा**—*lit.* 'touched' affected, attacked by.

P. 80. **सौहार्दमेवं पश्यति**—एवं thus; that she loves me ('मदनव्याधिना परामृष्टा भविष्यति'). You being my friend and therefore interested in me naturally think of everything as turning out in my favour. *Cf.* संकीर्तनशंसिना अल स्नेहेन *v. l.* at p 49; सर्वः कान्तमात्मीयं पश्यति Śāk. Act II. **सौहार्द**—friendship; सुहृदो भावः

सौहार्दम् fr. सुहृद्+अ (अण्). In the case of compound bases ending in the words हृद्, भग and सिन्धु, the initial vowels of both the members of the compound take Vṛiddhi before affixes having ञ, ण् or क् as their indicatory letter; thus we have सौभाग्यं, साक्तसैन्धवः.

अयं सः—*scil.* यं प्रति अहं देव्या चरणप्रहारदाने नियोजिता. **ललितदोहदापेक्षी**—explain ललितं (graceful, charming) दोहदं (longing) अपेक्षते इति. See *infra.* śloka 17. सुकुमार *v. l.* is not good as it cannot refer to दोहद directly but only by उपचार, the property of the foot being transferred to the दोहद. **अगृहीत॰**—the flowers are part of his dress; hence कुसुमान्येव नेपथ्यं &c. **ममानुकरोति**—She means that just as she herself is pained and anxious on account of the non-fulfilment of her desire, the As'oka also has forgotten to bedeck itself with flowers and is pining away as it were. The verb अनु-कृ is used with the genitive (*cf.* अनुकरोति भगवतो नारायणस्य Kād.; ततोऽनुकुर्याद्विशदस्य तस्यास्ताम्रौष्ठपर्यस्तरुचः स्मितस्य। Kum. I. 44) which is explained as संबन्धमात्र विवक्षायां षष्ठी. The use with the accusative is also met with, but less frequently; *cf.* शैलाधिपस्यानुचकार लक्ष्मीं Bk. 2. 8. **प्रच्छायशीतले**-See com. The word प्रच्छाय is used here as an *adj.* and not as a noun (as in प्रच्छायसुलभनिद्रा Śāk. I. 3.). शिलापट्ट *m.* or शिलापट्टक (p. 88 below)—a slab or large, flat piece of stone.

श्रुतं भवता—Vidūṣaka is anxious to prove to the king that Mālavikā is pining away with love for him; (*cf.* मदनव्याधिना परामृष्टा above); and he points out that she has said she was उत्कण्ठना which, in his opinion, could only refer to her passion for Agnimitra. The king declines to accept this interpretation, for, as he explains in the next s'loka, उत्कण्ठा may be caused by various causes, as for instance, by the mere blowing of the Malaya breeze, and it was not right to jump to the conclusion that it was caused by her love for the king. **प्रसन्नतर्कं**—whose guess is correct; *cf.* सखे प्रसन्नस्ते तर्कः। Vik. II. p. 48.

Verse 9. Construe :—

कुरबकरजसां वोढा किसलयपुटभेदशीकरानुगतः अयं मलयवातः मनसः अनिमित्तोत्कण्ठां अपि जनयति।

वोढा &c.—Breezes from the Malaya mountains have a natural tendency to excite love and passion, in the same manner as the sight of clouds (Megh. 1. 3 मेघालोके भवति सुखिनोऽप्यन्यथावृत्तिचेतः) and similar other things causes yearning. कुरबक°—shows that the breeze is laden with fragrance. किसलय°—accompanied by (*i. e* full of) the moist spray of water-drops which were contained in the folded budlike cavities of leaves, which the breeze had caused to open; किसलयानां पुटानि तेषां भेदः (opening) तस्मात् गलन् or निर्गतः शीकरः &c. (*Madhyamapadalopi* comp.). For the idea in the same words *cf.* भिन्नपल्लवपुटो वनानिलः Ragh. IX. 68. This epithet shows that the breeze is moist and cool. आनिमित्तां—longing for which there appears to be no apparent cause. °मित्तोत्कण्ठामपि &c. V. I. (see foot-note) is not so good as the word मनस् becomes redundant, उत्कण्ठा being of the mind.

°अन्तरित—concealed behind. He wishes to look at Mālavikā while himself remaining unobserved by her. इरावतीमिव &c.—I fancy it is some one like Irāvatī at no great distance. (Read अदूरे for दूरे in the text). Vidūṣaka had caught a distant glimpse of Irāvatī coming with her maid-servant (p. 49) and warns the king, who was, however, so much elated with the good fortune before him that he did not care for her approach. दूरे *V. 1.* —is not supported by the subsequent speech of the King. Besides the Vid. would not have alarmed the King at such a time if he had seen Irāvatī at a great distance, but would have waited to see if she was approaching them. न हि कमलिनीं &c.—does an elephant, who is, so fond of the lotus-plant hesitate to go near it for fear of the alligators that may be in the pond? He means that with Mālavikā near him he feels courageous enough to brave Irāvatī's visit. कमलिनी—a lotus-plant. It may also mean a tank abounding in lotuses. For the fondness of elephants for lotuses *cf.* लीलोत्खातमृणालकाण्डकवलच्छेदेषु संपादिताः। &c Uttar. III. 16. Māl,- Mād. IX. 34; and रात्रिर्गमिष्यति भविष्यति सुप्रभातं भास्वानुदेष्यति हसिष्यति पङ्कजश्रीः। इत्थं विचिन्तयति कोशगते द्विरेफे हा हन्त हन्त नलिनीं गज उज्जहार ॥ (quoted by Mr. Pandit from the Kuv.) ग्राहः—an alligator (गृह्णाति seizes इति) Here Irāvatī is compared to a ग्राह which is mas.; but this is not a fault here, as the comparison suggests how hard-hearted and unyielding Irāvatī is. अवेक्षते—minds, cares for; अपेक्षते—*V. l.* where प seems to be a mislection for वे; for it means-the elephant does not except to meet with ; but this is against the context. Irāvatī was expected to go in search of the King in case he did not keep his appointment. **मतङ्गजः**—an elephant, so called because elephants are supposed to be descended from a sage named Mātanga (मतङ्गादृषेर्जातः इति). What the King says here is an idle boast, as will be seen later on when Irāvatī appears on the scene.

P. 82. **हृदय** &c.—Mālavikā is addressing her heart asking it not to have too high-soaring an ambition. **निरवलम्बात्**—which has no basis, nothing as support or foundation upon which to build hopes of its attainment. **अतिभूमिलङ्घिन्**—reaching the highest limit, beyond which there remains nothing to be obtained. **विदूषकः** राजानमवेक्षते—he looks significantly at the King, as much as to say, here is a further proof of my guess ('मदनव्याधिना मालविका परामृष्टा') being correct. **प्रिये पश्य वामतां स्नेहस्य**—Look at the perverse or crooked nature of Love. Why crooked, he explains in the next stanza. For वाम *cf*. तदहो कामस्य वामा गतिः । Gīt. 12; विधातुर्वामत्वाद्विपदि परिवर्तामह इमे। Māl. Mādh. IX. 8.

Verse 10. Construe :—

त्वम् औत्सुक्यहेतुं न विवृणोषि, तर्कः तत्त्वावबोधैकरसः न, तथापि रम्भोरु, आत्मानम् एषां परिदेवितानां लक्ष्यं करोमि।

औत्सुक्यहेतुं—&c.—Cupid is perverse and crooked because for whom you are pining still it leads me fondly to cling to that conclusion—I cannot help thinking, owing to my own love for you, that you must be referring to me in these lamentations of yours (हृदय किं मामायासयसि &c.). **तत्त्वावबोधैकरसो न तर्कः**—the guesses I may make may not always lead me to the truth. If I indulge in any conjecturings, it is as much possible that I may be wrong as that I may be right ; because a lover's guesses are always favourable to himself (*cf*. कामी स्वतां पश्यति। in Śāk. II. 2), and therefore they may not necessarily represent the truth as it is. तत्त्वस्य अवबोधः (knowledge) **स एव एकः** (sole) रसः (feature, property, quality) यस्य. **रम्भोरु**—voc. sing of रम्भोरू *fem*. 'having things smooth and tapering like the stem of a plantain tree (रम्भा).' The final उ of ऊरु is lengthened by ऊरूत्तरपदादौपम्ये Pān. IV, 1. 69 ; otherwise the Voc. sing. would have been रम्भोरो.—See Gr.

§ 322. **आत्मानं लक्ष्यं करोमि**—I think they are aimed at me, refer to me. **परिदेवित**—*p. p. p.* used as a noun in the sense of परिदेवन as गत for गति, भाषित for भाषण, by the rule नपुंसके भावे क्तः Pān. III. 3. 114.

निःसंशयं—is generally an *adv.* (निर्गतः संशयः यस्मिन्कर्मणि तद्यथा तथा), but here it is used as a noun equivalent to संशयस्याभावः. *cf.* मक्षिकाणामभावो निर्मक्षिकं, used in कृतं भवता निर्मक्षिकम्. Śāk. II. p. 50. **अर्पितसंदेशा**—to whom I have entrusted your message of love. Bakulāvalikā will proceed to discharge her duty in the sequel, and this epithet prepares us in a way to expect what follows. **विविक्त**—a lonely place, where lovers can contemplate or converse with their friends without fear of disturbance; *cf.* विविक्तादृते नान्यदुत्सुकस्य शरणमस्ति। Vik. II.

अपि स्मरेत्—I hope she will remember. दास्याः दुहिता is used like the corresponding दास्याः पुत्रः in the masculine (*cf.* दास्याः पुत्रैः शकुनिलुब्धकैः Śāk. II.), as a term of abuse; *cf.* Marāthi बटकीची पोर. **गुरुक**—of importance. **अहमपि तावत्** &c.—Mr. Pandit omits this part of Vid.'s speech treating it as spurious and remarks—'There is no humour in the remark as Bakulāvalikā is really not such a high personage as to make Vidūṣaka's speech witty'. But Mr. Pandit himself does not see the wit in this. Vid. humourously means to say—Although I am generally regarded as मृत्पिण्डबुद्धि, 'a cold-pated fellow' I do remember it. How can then a clever maid like Bāk. forget it? **अहो बकुलावलिका**—Mālavikā was indulging in reveries and she did not observe Bakulāvalikā approaching, till the latter actually questioned her. **त्वं योग्यतया नियुक्ता**—As you are the fit person by reason of your personal charms and youth, you have been appointed to this duty by the Queen. She pays a compliment to her by this. **सनूपुरं करोमि**—the Nūpuras are necessary; comp. असूत सद्यः कुसुमान्यशोकः स्कन्धात्प्रभृत्येव सपल्लवानि। पादेन नापैक्षत सुन्दरीणां संपकमाशिञ्जितनूपुरेण ॥ Kum. III. 26. यावत्करोमि is equivalent to करिष्यामि.

P. 84. **अलं सुखिततया** &c.—You need not feel happy, as you are likely to be tempted to do, because you are selected for this high office. The reading सुखितया found in the Nirn. Ed. means the same, and is supported by स्पृष्टस्य गात्रे सुखिता ममैवम्। Śāk. VII. 19. **मोचयेयम्**—free myself from this onerous task, viz. that of causing the Aśoka to blossom. अथ वा—or rather. She sees a way, *viz.* death, that will free her from all worries. She is certain that death would be her lot in case the Aśoka refused to flower, since there would be then no possibility of obtaining her desire. Hence she conceives the ornaments brought by Bakulāvalikā as part of the funeral decorations, so to say. मृत्युकाले मण्डनं मृत्युमण्डनम्. According to an ancient Hindu custom the dead body was decorated with ornaments and flowers before being consigned to the fire ; *cf.* विससर्ज कृतान्त्यमण्डनामनलायागुरुचन्दनैधसे। Ragh. VIII. 71; क्रियतां कथमन्त्यमण्डनं परलोकान्तरितस्य ते मया। Kum. IV. 22.

किं विचारयसि—As Mālavikā did not show any joy or cheerfulness at the sight of the trinkets, Bakulāvalikā tries to rouse her from her reveire. उत्सुका खलु—"The Queen, as you are aware, is anxious'. कथमशोक॰—the King had not grasped the purpose of Māl.'s coming there and her being decorated with those ornaments, and he shows a little surprise when he learns it from Bakulāvalikā's remark. आरम्भः—undertaking, business in hand. अन्तःपुर—here seems to be used in the sense of देवी—a queen. मर्षय तावदेनं (चरणं)—Pardon the fault I am committing in touching you with this foot. शरीरमसि मे—I love you so much that I consider your body as my own, and hence the touch does not become a fault at all. संस्कार—decoration; *cf.* असंस्कारपाटलोष्ठपुटं मुखम्। Sāk. VII. 23.

Verse 11. Construe :—

वयस्य, हरदग्धस्य मनोभवद्रुमस्य प्रथमां पल्लवप्रसूतिम् इव प्रियायाः चरणान्तनिवेशितां सरसां रागरेखां पश्य।

प्रथमा—new. हरदग्धस्य मनोभवद्रुमस्य—Cupid, who was burnt by Śiva, is conceived as a Tree. Just as a tree by putting forth new foliage gives signs of a new life, so is my love gathering additional strength at the sight of this line of paint (which being *red* is likened to new foliage). The allusion is to Madana being burnt by Śiva, when the former tried to produce love in the latter for the birth of a hero-son to vanquish the demon Tāraka. See Kum. III. अधिकारः—the duty (of kicking the Aśoka tree to make it bloom). उपक्षिप्तः—made over, assigned.

P. 86. **सम्यगाह भवान्**—because the beauty of the foot justifies your praise.

Verse 12. Construe :—

बाला नवकिसलयरागेण स्फुरितनखरूचा अनेन अग्रपादेन दोहदापेक्षया अकुसुमितम् अशोकं वा आर्द्रापराधं प्रणिहितशिरसं कान्तं वा द्वौ हन्तुम् अर्हति।

नवकिसलय० etc.—Dissolve **नवकिसलयस्य राग इव रागो यस्य तेन.** See *H. Gr.* §248†. **अग्रपादः**—'the forepart of the foot'. **अग्रश्चासौ पादश्च अग्रपादः।** For the compound, *cf.*, **अग्रहस्त** *supra* p. 4. where see our Note. **बाला**—a young lady of sixteen; *cf.* बाला स्यात् षोडशाब्दा. **स्फुरित०**—adj. to **अग्रपादेन. रुच्**–*fem.* "brilliance', rays of light shooting forth. **अकुसुमितं**—See note on कुसुमित p. 8. **वा—वा** either–or'; *cf.* सा वा शंभोस्तदीया वा मूर्तिर्जलमयी मम। Kum. II. 60. **प्रणमितशिरसं**—also प्रणमितंशिरस्कं; see *H Gr.* § 263 **आर्द्रापराधम्**—'whose fault is fresh, newly committed;' *cf.* कामीवार्द्रापराधः शमयतु दुरितं शांभवो वःशराग्निः। Amaru. 2. आर्द्र is put in because it is only under the first impulse of anger that a woman is expected to strike her lover, and not when the anger cools down. For this reason also the other meaning 'who has committed a gentle fault', i. e. in some delicate love-matter, which is suggested by Mr. Pandit, is inadmissible.

प्रहरिष्यति etc.—The King had referred to the two offices of the leg in the above śl., out of which the second is often coveted by lovers. Cf एकः सख्यास्तव सह मया वामपादाभिलाषी। Megh. II. 18. The Vidūṣaka takes up his words and says 'you will one day experience it,' meaning that your marriage will take place and there will soon come a time when she will lord it over you, and you will enjoy things like चरणप्रहार, as much as you like. This is Kāṭayavema's reading also, and is fit in the mouth of the Vid. who is always free with his master. The *v. l.* given in the foot-note, though more polite, does not refer to the King's words directly. **वचः**—I accept it as sure to come true. This refers not to any special qualifications of the Vidūṣaka in the art of foretelling events, but to the general notion that the words of a Brāhmaṇa are sacred and generally come true; *cf.* प्रतिगृहीतं ब्राह्मणवचनम्। Vik. II; and अमोघाः प्रतिगृह्णन्तावर्घ्यानुपदमाशिषः। Ragh. I. 44. Of course the King says this in a half-jocular tone.

युक्तमदा—in a state of intoxication. The introduction of Irāvatī here is for the dramatic purpose of causing obstruction in the King's love. The object of introducing her as intoxicated is to justify her somewhat extravagant and rash conduct in the next scene. मद: किल &c.—It is said that women take on especial beauty and charm when they are in a state of intoxication. The idea is elaborately expressed by Māgha—चारुता वपुरभूषयदासां तामनूननवयौवनयोगः। तं पुनर्मकरकेतनलक्ष्मीस्तां मदो दयितसंगमभूषः॥ Śis. X 33. *Cf.* also असति त्वयि वारुणीमदः प्रमदानामधुना विडम्बना। Kum. IV. 12; ललितविभ्रमबन्धविचक्षणं...... ..पतिषु निर्विविशुर्मधुमङ्गनाः। Ragh. IX. 36; रागकान्तनयनेषु नितान्तं विद्रुमारुणकपोलतलेषु। सर्वगाऽपि ददृशे वनितानां दर्पणेष्विव मुखेषु मदश्रीः॥ Kir. IX. 63.

प्रथमं&c —Nipuṇikā pays a dexterously-turned compliment to her mistress. She says that hitherto she thought it was mere talk, but now that she has actual proof of it in the enhanced beauty of her mistress, she can believe it as quite true. दोलागृह—a spacious recreation-room with swings provided in it for sport. अखण्डितात्प्रणयात्—अखण्डित—unbroken or unremitted, continued. प्रणय—affection, love. 'As the King has never been slack in loving you, he is sure to keep his appointment and go there to wait for you.' But in this case the gen. भट्टिण्या must be taken as संबन्धसामान्ये; else we should expect the loc. It is better to take प्रणय in the sense of 'request'; *cf.* for this sense *cf.* संबन्धिनो मे प्रणयं विहन्तुम्। Ragh. II. 58; Vik. IV. 13. Since the King has never refused your request in his faithful anxiety to please you, he must have already gone to the place of appointment. This is another compliment to Irāvatī, a bolder one than the last. अखण्डित—See note on खण्डन *supra* p. 72. अलं सेवया—enough of compliments, do not say things simply to please me, your mistress. मध्यस्थतां परिगृह्य—impartially, without being influenced by our relation as mistress and maid.

P. 88. वसन्तोपायन॰—This refers to the ancient practice of inviting a Brāhmaṇa, worshipping him, and offering him presents (उपायन, *cf.* Mar. वाण) of eatables &c. on the occasion of the advent of Spring which is regarded with deified personification. *Cf.* स्वस्तिवाचनमोदकैः *infra*, Act IV. आर्यगौतमेन कथितम्—Here the question is—Did the Vidū. actually tell this to Nipu. ? We know that he did not. For, ever since he persuaded the King to go to the garden, he was on the stage with him and had no opportunity to communicate the news to Nipunikā. So Nipu. must have told an innocent lie; or she must have meant to say—Why; Gautama is fond of sweetmeats, and, sure of getting an Upāyana, he must have taken the King to the garden. It need not be *actually* told. In this case वसन्ता० is emphatic; and the whole is equivalent to गौतमस्य ०लोलुपत्वेन कथितम्। **आर्यपुत्रदर्शने**—the locative is used in the sense of the dative आर्यपुत्रदर्शनाय. **परिहासनिमित्तं**-*Cf.* परिहासविजल्पितं सखे परमार्थेन न गृह्यतां वचः। Śāk. II. 18. **प्रियङ्गुलतापरिक्षिप्त**—surrounded by (a bower of) *Priyaṅgu* creepers: *cf.* वेतसपरिक्षिप्ते लतामण्डपे। Śāk. III. p. 66. **अशोकशिलापट्टक**—an oblong seat of stone beneath the Aśoka tree.

चूताङ्कुरं—&c. she means—'While we were looking for something pleasant (the King's presence) we have come upon something most unpleasant (the sight of Māla. and her companion)'. The sight of Māla. whom Irāvatī and her maid already suspected as a possible rival in the King's love, is compared to the attack of ants. "It is doubtless the red ants living on tress that are meant here. They are known in Konkan by the name of हुमले. Theman go-tree is a very favourite abode of them. They configure its leaves into hollow globular nests for themselves"—S. P. Pandit.

P. 90. **अभूमिः**—'the wrong place for'—*i. e.* where she could not properly be expected to be present (and this makes her suspicious). The expression अभूमिः is often used in a figurative sense; *cf.* अभूमिरियं अविनयस्य। Śāk— VII.; मनोरथानामप्यभूमिः विसर्जनावसरसत्कारः। *ibid.*; अभूदभूमिः प्रतिपक्षजन्मनां भियां। Śiś. I. 42; अभूमिरियस्यमद्विधानां। Priy. III. **कथमत्र तर्कयसि**—what is your conjecture or explanation of Mālavikā's presence in this place? **दोलापरिभ्रष्टया** &c.—*cf.* गौतमचापलात् &c. *supra* p. 74. **०अधिकारे**—*cf.* चरणानुरूपः अधिकारः उपक्षिप्तः। p. 84. **महती खलु** &c.—Irāvatī is jealous that Dhāriṇī did not ask *her* to fulfil the As'oka's desire. **संभावना**—honour; *cf.* अनुगृहीतोऽहमनया मघवतः संभावनया। Śāk. VI. **हञ्जे** (Voc. sing. of हञ्जा a female servant)—is often used in dramas as a particle of address to a **चेटी** (maid-servant), like

हला to a friend; *cf.* हण्डे हञ्जे हलाह्वाने नीचां चेटीं सखीं प्रति। Amara. I. 6. 15. किमपि विकारयति—raises some suspicion in me. आशङ्कितस्य तावदन्तं&c.—I must first see the end of, clear, my doubts in this matter (*i. e.* whether the King is in love with Māla. or not). स्थाने—with sufficient reason. She is struck by the beauty of Mālavikā.

०विन्यासः—The arrangement or laying out of the lines of the *alaktaka* paint. आत्मनश्चरण०—If I were to praise it, in a way I should be praising my own leg, which would be egoistic, hence I refrain from directly praising it. प्रसाधनकला—the art of decoration; *cf.* प्रसाधनविधेः प्रसाधनविशेषः। Vikr. II. 3. अभिविनीता—instructed, trained. केन अभिविनीता असि—who is your teacher in this art?—meaning, he must be very clever in it himself, that he could have produced such competence in his pupil.

P. 92. भर्तुः शिष्यास्मि—Bakulā, sees here an opportunity to carry out her promise to the Vidūṣaka about helping the king in his suit, and in replying to this apparently innocent question of Mālavikā, she skilfully introduces the King. It will be seen that from this point onwards she keeps on dwelling on the same topic; e. *g.* सर्वथा भर्तुरङ्कपरिवर्तिनी भव। गुणेष्वभिनिविशिनो भर्तुरपि। भर्तुः प्रणयमृदुकानि अक्षराणि। etc. गुरुदक्षिणा—when a pupil finished his course it was customary for him to reward his preceptor in some suitable manner (*c. f.* समाप्तविद्येन मया महर्षिर्विद्यापितोऽभुद्गुरुदक्षिणायै। Ragh. V. 20). The Vidūṣaka means-Since there is a relation of *guru* and *s'iṣya* between the King and yourself, your dutylies in arranging for the payment of his *dakṣinā.* The only valuable thing he cares for is Mālavikā, and you should therefore arrange so that he gets her as soon as possible. दिष्ट्या—Having learnt from so competent a master, you have a just cause for pride; however it is very creditable, indeed, that you are free from it. उपदेशा०—Bakulāvalikā again skilfully alludes to her *instruction,* indirectly bringing in the King; she means—I was not proud hitherto, because I could not get a suitable subject or model to try my skill upon. Now, to-day I have got it. This is an indirect compliment to the beauty of Mālavikā's legs.

सिद्धं मे दौत्यं—My embassy is (as good as) successful, because I have managed to introduce the name of the King to

Māla. and thereby prepared her mind for the communication of the King's message, दौत्य – an *abs. n.* from दूत with the affix ष्यञ्; the form दूत्य sometimes met with is also correct, being obtained by the addition of the affix य 'by दूतवणिग्भ्यां च' Vārt. **मुखमारुतो लम्भयितव्यः**–I must blow with my mouth so that the wind (breath) may dry the colour. लम्भयितव्य—*pot. p. part.* in तव्य from the causal of लभ् to get. **अथ वा** &c.—Or, that is not necessary, since this being an airy place the colour will easily dry of itself. **प्रवात**—used as an *adj.* here ; at p. 16 it is used as a substantive ('a current of air').

Verse 13. Construe:—

अस्याः आर्द्रालक्तकं चरणं मुखमारुतेन वीजयितुं संप्रति मे प्रथमतरः सेवावकाशः प्रतिपन्नः।

प्रतिपन्न—has arrived. **प्रथमतर**—the very first, the first of all ; hence, excellent, splendid. **सेवावकाशः**—an occasion when I can be of service to her.

कुतस्ते अनुशयः—'Why are you sorry that you are unable to take advantage of this present opportunity ?' The use by the Vidūṣaka of the word अनुशय in the ordinary sense of 'sorrow' is not very accurate ; it properly means 'sorrow for something which one should not have done or has omitted to do', *i. e.* repentance, remorse (पश्चात्ताप); *cf.* Śāk. अनुशयदुःखायेदं हतहृदयं संप्रति विबुद्धम्। VI. 7 ; अनुशयतप्तहृदयस्तावदनुकम्प्यतामयं जनः। VI. ; बाष्पं प्रमृज्य विगतानुशयो भवेयम्। VII. 25. In our text the sense is merely that of ताप, and not of पश्चात्ताप. **क्रमेण**—in due course (after you are married to her).

शतपत्र *n.*—lotus-flower ; *cf.* सहस्रपत्रं कमलं शतपत्रं कुशेशयम् Ak. I. 9. 40, where Kṣīrasvāmī remarks: शतसहस्रे बहूपलक्षणम्—the words शत and सहस्र in शतपत्र and सहस्रपत्र signify 'numerous' ('many') भर्तुरङ्कपरिवर्तिनी—*cf.* अङ्के निधाय करभोरु यथासुखं ते संवाहयामि चरणौ। Śāk. III. 19. **०परिवर्तिन्** *adj.* lit. 'rolling on;' hence 'sitting on, resting upon.' **निपुणिका०**—as she sees a further confirmation of her suspicions in the words of Bakulāvalikā. **ममेयमाशीः**—**आशीः**—a prayer, or wish ; *cf.* निराशिषः सतः। Kum. V. 76 ; Bg. III. 30 ; IV. 21. **अवचनीयं**—what ought not to be said, because of its impropriety, and also because of the impossibility of its coming true.

P. 94. **मन्त्रयितव्यमेव**— *i.e.* I have (not said anything improper, or absurd, but) what it is quite proper to say, or what I must (implying, what I am authorised to) say. **प्रिया खलु**—and hence you say so. *cf.* सौहार्दमेवं पश्यति *supra* p. 80; **गुणेष्वभिनिवेशिनः**—who has a strong liking for, who always appreciates, good qualities. She means–Since you are a गुणवती lady, it is quite natural that the King should love you. **अभिनिवेश**— *m.* great devotion, intense attachment to; *cf.* बलीयान्खलु मेऽभिनिवेश इदानीमपि। Śāk. III. **एतदेव**— *i. e.* the King's love for me; or एतद् may refer to the previous sentence—that I should be loved for my merits. **ईषत्परि०** slightly pale. She means—that the King does love you, can be known from the thinness and paleness of his limbs. This is how lovers are usually described in Sanskrit poetry; *cf.* शरीरं क्षामं स्यादसति दयितालिङ्गनसुखं *supra* p. 68; क्षामक्षामकपोलमाननमुरः काठिन्यमुक्तस्तनं मध्यः क्लान्ततरः प्रकामविनतावंसौ छविः पाण्डुरा। Śāk. III. 8: कथितमेव कमलनालायमानैरङ्गैः। *ibid.*

प्रथमगणितं—first calculated, studied—*i. e.*, she seems to have been coached up beforehand for giving such replies; otherwise how does she answer so deftly and readily? **हताशा**—(*lit.* one whose hopes are frustrated, a wretch) "is a slang word corresponding to the Marāṭhi मेली, so often used by our illiterate [and literate] women."—S. P. Pandit.

अनुरागो &c.—Regard as authority the words of the wise that love should be tested (ascertained) by love; *i. e.* know that he loves you the same way that you love him. प्रमाणीकृ—'to accept as authority' is a च्वि–formation; *cf.* तरुभिरपि देवस्य शासनं प्रमाणीकृतम्। Śāk. VI. आत्मनश्छन्देन—by your own wish, and not at the instance of any one else. For छन्द *cf* छन्दो नर्तयितुर्यथैव मनसः &c. *supra* II. 3; विज्ञापय देवीं यस्ते छन्द इति। Vik. III. बिम्बान्तरितानि—transferred to another person, *viz.* myself. It is the King who said that, and I am only repeating his words. बिम्ब—an image, another form. The whole may also mean, transmitted through the medium (बिम्ब) of the Vidū., (who, it may be remembered, had coached Bakulāvalikā in this part of the intrigue). देवीं विचिन्त्य—*i. e.* I am afraid of incurring the Queen's displeasure if I act up to your words. *Cf. infra* pp. 142 and 158, where she betrays a similar fear.

P. 96. **भ्रमरसंबाध** etc.—Bakulā. means—'It is foolish to be afraid of being molested by bees if one wishes to use a mango-blossom as an ear-ornament'. So if you wish to really obtain the King's love, you must not mind the Queen. **भ्रमर०** —The fondness of bees for the mango-blossom is well-known, and poets generally describe the two together, *Cf.* सद्यः प्रवालोद्गमशारुपत्रे नीते समाप्तिं नवसूतबाणे। निवेशयामास मधुर्द्विरेफान्नामाक्षराणीव मनोभवस्य ॥ Kum. III. 27. **संबाध**—thickly crowded or beset with. वसन्तावतारसर्वस्वं–the all-in-all of, *i. e.*, the best production of the early days of, Spring. For the idea *cf.* आताम्रहरितपाण्डुर जीवितसर्वं वसन्तमासयोः। दृष्टोऽसि चूतकोरक ऋतुमङ्गलं त्वां प्रसादयामि ॥ Śāk. VI. 2. अवतंसयितव्यः—to be used as in **अवतंस.** (*m. n.* an ear-ornament); pot. p. of the demon. from अवतंस *Cf.* कर्णकिसलयं *infra* III. 16. **दुर्जाते**—in case calamity would ensue. *Cf.* दुर्जातबन्धुरयमृक्षहरीश्वरो मे। Ragh. XIII. 72; सुरारिसंभवे दुर्जाते महाराजः शरण आसीत्। Vik. II. p. 52; and *infra* V. 11. **अत्यन्तं**—*indec.* 'to the last,' through thick and thin. Mr. Pandit proposes to interpret दुर्जात with a pun on it, in the sense of 'you ill-bred girl' taking it as Voc. sing. of दुर्जाता (an abusive term of endearment). It is, however, absolutely unnecessary and even unreasonable to do so, and Mr. Pandit seems to have felt it, as he gives as an alternative the explanation that we have here given of this and the next speech. Mālavikā has asked her help. To this Bakulāvalikā assents, with a pun on her own name. **विमर्दसुरभिः बकुलावलिका खल्वहम्**—'I will of course assist you; for, am I not बकुलावलिका, which, as you know, is always विमर्दसुरभि?' Bak. means—a garland of *bakula* flowers gives out fragrance when crushed; similarly, the more I am pressed by difficulty, the more helpful I shall be to you. Thus there is a pun on the word विमर्द; *lit.* it means 'crushing', and *fig.* 'pressing difficulty,' 'bad times', the latter sense being got from the former.

Verse 14. Construe :—

भावज्ञानानन्तरं प्रस्तुतेन प्रत्याख्याने दत्तयुक्तोतरेण वाक्येन इयं स्वे निर्दे । स्थापिता, कामिनां प्राणाः दूत्यधीनाः (इति) स्थाने।

भावज्ञाना०—In the preceding dialogue Bakulāvalikā has discharged her commission as an emissary of Cupid, and has also shown her power of persuasion and ready-wittedness.

The King compliments her upon these. Construe : भावज्ञानानन्तरं प्रस्तुतेन, प्रत्याख्याने दत्तयुक्तोत्तरेण (च) वाक्येन (त्वया बकुलावलिकया) इयं (मालविका) स्वे निदेशे (see com.) स्थापिता। स्वे निदेशे स्थापिता—'She is placed in, *i. e.* definitely brought within the scope of, the duty or commission entrusted to her'. This she did by means of her speeches which she commenced after she had ascertained Mālavikā's real state of heart (भावज्ञानानन्तरं प्रस्तुतेन) and in which she gave proper replies to Mālavikā's contradictions or halting, hesitating words (प्रत्याख्यान दत्तयुक्तोत्तरेण). For references to the speeches containing भावज्ञान, तदनन्तर प्रस्तवा, प्रत्याख्यान and युक्तोत्तर, see com. स्थाने प्राणाः &c.—lovers would be helpless if they cannot get suitable messengers like Bakulāvalikā. This kind of दूती is technically known as निसृष्टार्था (see *com.*); for another passage where the work of such a *dūtī* is briefly summed up, *cf.* संप्रति मया मालतीं प्रति निसृष्टार्थदूतीकृत्यस्य लघूकृतो भारः। तथा हि। वैरेऽन्यस्मिन्द्विषः पितरि विचिकित्सा च जनिता पुरावृत्तोद्गारैरपि च कथिता कार्यपदवी। स्तुतं तन्माहात्म्यं यदभिजनतो यच्च गुणतः प्रसङ्गाद्वत्सस्येत्यथ खलु विधेय परिचयः। Māl.—Mādh. II. 13. The occasion there (in the Māl.-Mādh.) is different, but the idea is common and we may compare the two scenes so as to get an insight into the methods of two masters of the subject.

कारितैव बकुला०—Mālavikā is made to take a definite step in this business (*i. e.* loving the king and becoming his wife) ; if we understand राज्ञि by एतस्मिन्, this would mean, 'made to love the King ; this is supported by other passages in Kālidāsa ; *cf.* धर्मेणापि पदं शर्वे कारिते पार्वतीं प्रति। Kum. VI. 14. काम इदानीं सकामो भवतु येन असत्यसंधे जने सखी पदं कारिता। Śāk. IV. p. 93. निर्विकारस्यापि &c.—teaching (*i. e.* of the kind we have now witnessed) can produce a desire even in the mind of one who is free from passion before. She means that since Mālavikā had been सविकार, there is no wonder that Bakulā. should have been able to induce her to love the King (पदं कारिता). This is said in reply to Irāvatī's remark above, and by the force of अपि we are able to supply it to Mālavikā (किमुत सविकाराया मालविकायाः।), The reading in the Nirn. Ed. is **अधिकारस्योचित उपदेशः** which means, Bakulā.'s advice is suited to the commission entrusted to her.

स्थाने खलु—Rightly, indeed, was my heart apprehensive. She means—it was not quite groundless that I had suspicions about Mālavikā's being loved by the King. *Cf. Supra* p. 90. रूपयित्वा। गृहीतार्था—When I shall have (in the immediate future) grasped the full meaning of this. अनन्तरं चिन्तयिष्यामि—अनन्तरं may be taken as an *adv.* or as an equivalent of अनन्तरकरणीयं,, object of चिन्तयिष्यामि, as is done by Mr. Ayyar.

P. 98. निर्वृत्तपरिकर्मा—परिकर्म decoration; for this meaning of परिकर्म *cf.* विबुधरसि यस्य दारुणैरसमाप्ते परिकर्मणि स्मृतः। Kum. IV. 19. आमुच्य—'having put on'. मुच् with आ has the special sense of 'putting on' as an ornament; *cf.* आमुच्यमानाभरणा चकासे। Kum. VII. 21; आमुक्ताभरणः स्रग्वी हंसचिह्नदुकूलवान्। Ragh. XVII. 25.

श्रुतो देव्या नियोगः। भवत्विदानीं—This she says in irritation and impatience. 'Yes, yes. We have heard the Queen's order. Let it be executed.' Mr. Pandit's interpretation of this is—"It is heard to be the Queen's order. There let it rest, Irāvatī has been suspecting that Dhāriṇī herself is at the bottom of the affair, and thinks she is now (इदानीं) satisfied that her suspicions are correct, and that she wants to know no more.' But this is hardly possible. There is a distinction between श्रुतो देव्या नियोगः and श्रुतं देव्या नियोग इति; but Mr. Pandit has apparently failed to notice it. Moreover, it is incorrect to presume that Irāvatī suspected Dhāriṇī to be at the bottom, because there is nothing to support it in Irāvatī's speeches in this Act. Irāvatī is rather incensed at what she considered to be a slight upon her own claims when Mālavikā was chosen for the *niyoga* in preference to herself (*cf.* महती खल्वस्याः संभावना p. 90). Again, if Irāvatī by भवत्विदानीम् had meant that she wanted to hear no more, we should have expected some such stage-direction as इति परावर्तते; *cf.* in a similar context इति सासूयं परावर्तते। after Mālavikā's words before sl. 9 Act IV. Mr. Ayyar reads श्रुतो देव्या नियोग इति which is meaningless. It should be श्रुत &c. But this reading will make Irāvatī tamely submit to the will of the Queen.

एष उपारूढ०—The sentence is deliberately so worded by Bakulāvalikā as to convey two senses the subject being reserved to the last. Ostensibly and primarily it refers to the पल्लवगुच्छक of the Aśoka—"Here is in front of you, (one) who is उपारूढराग (with a rich redness of colour) and उपभोगक्षम (capable of being enjoyed, fit for being used as an ornament)'— But before she could add it, Mālavikā, who solely thought of the King and her love for him, in her impatience understands उपारूढरागः as 'with his love matured or deepened' and उपभोगक्षमः as 'fit for enjoyment, or able to enjoy.', and interrupts her by asking किं भर्ता. Bakulāvalikā smiles at the success of her trick and explains that she meant the bunch of As'oka's foliage, and not the King. पर्याप्तमेतावता कामिनाम्–Here we should rather expect एतावत् for एतावता; as it is, पर्याप्त must be taken as a noun equivalent to पर्याप्ति. For पर्याप्त *cf.* श्रुतं न पुनः पर्याप्तं हृदयस्य। Vik. p. 47. Lovers are satisfied if they know that the object of their affection returns their love; they do not mind if they get nothing more. In the light of the next śl. एतावता may be paraphrased as किं भर्तेति वाक्यात्समानुरागत्वस्य ज्ञानेन।

Verse 15. Construe :—

अनातुरोत्कण्ठितयोः प्रसिध्यता समागमेन अपि मां प्रति रतिः न, परस्परप्राप्तिनिराशयोः समानुरागयोः शरीरनाशः अपि वरम्।

अनातुरोत्कण्ठित० etc.—Union of two persons who do not love each other equally is no real union. *Cf.* Nāg. II. 14; and यस्यां मनश्चक्षुषोः प्रवृत्तिस्तस्यामृद्धिः। Vātsyā. Kām. S. I. 14. The essence of all union should be intense mutual affection; where that exists, the lovers should be satisfied, even if there is no actual union. The King means that what he really cared for, *viz.* Mālavikā's love for him, he has obtained; her actual possession is now a thing of minor importance to him; प्रसिध्यता is in apposition to समागमेन; 'being accomplished,' 'coming about'; *cf.* शरीरयात्राऽपि च ते न प्रसिध्येदकर्मणः। Bg. III. 1. For the syntax of शरीरनाशोऽपि वरं see *H. S. Gram.* § 717.

अशोकाय प्रहिणोति—*lit.* 'sends to Aśoka,' *i. e.* touches or strikes As'oka with it; *cf.* रक्षस्तस्मै महोपलं प्रजिघाय। Ragh. XV. 21

Verse 16. Construe :—

इयम् अस्मात् कर्णकिसलयम् आदाय अत्र चरणम् अर्पयति, उभयोः सदृशविनिमयात् (अहम्) आत्मानं वञ्चितं मन्ये।

आदाय etc.—Mālavikā took a *pallava* from the As'oka's branch and wore it as an ear-ornament; in return for this the As'oka received a blow from her leg. The King conceives these two as mutual gifts and the exchange he calls सदृश 'of similar things', because both the leg and the *pallava* were *red* in colour. The King says that both Mālavikā and Aśoka have thus exchanged gifts and honoured each other, while he, the lover, having as yet exchanged nothing with the object of his passion, is unfortunate. वञ्चित—*lit.* deceived, cheated of what is one's due; hence, 'unfortunate,' as here. *Cf.* तद्वञ्चितवामनेत्रा। Ragh. VII. 8; मन्यते स्म पिबतां विलोचनैः पक्ष्मपातमपि वञ्चनां मनः। *ibid.* XI. 36. For a similar idea cf. Duṣyanta's words: वयं तत्त्वान्वेषान्मधुकर हतास्त्वं खलु कृती। Śāk. I. 20.

P. 100. संभावना—has here the sense of 'expectation'; it does not mean 'honour' as understood by some, as a modest girl like Mālavikā will not herself call her touching the Aśoka with her foot an honour to it. *Cf.* धारिण्याः पूर्वाचरितैः संभाव्यत एतत्। *infra* Act V.; for the sense of 'honour,' see संभावित in the next śl. and *cf.* महति खल्वस्याः संभावना। p. 90. Or with संभावना meaning 'honour,' we may take it as देवीकृता सं०; the honour done to us by the Queen in thus asking us to gratify the hankering of the Aśoka. This speech of Mālavikā is omitted in many editions. and MSS. and perhaps with better taste. It is not quite necessary in underlying the following speech of Bakulā. by नास्ति ते दोषः &c. Baku. simply means—after this ceremony and the honour done to it, the Aśoka is bound to show flowers; if it does not, it cannot be your fault; it would be the fault of the Aśoka: it must indeed be worthless (unappreciating), if it does not blossom. ०मन्थरः—'slow in'; *cf.* यदि स राजा प्रत्यभिज्ञानमन्थरो भवेत्। Śāk. VI. p. 110.

Verse 17. Construe :—

तनुमध्यया मुखरनूपुराराविणा नवाम्बुरुहकोमलेन अनेन चरणेन संभावितः। (त्वं) यदि सद्यः एव कुसुमैः न संपत्स्यसे (तदा) (हे) अशोक, ललितकामिसाधारणं दोहदं वृथा वहसि।

तनुमध्यया—'having a slender waist', which is considered as a mark of female beauty; *cf.* मध्ये क्षामं *supra* śl. 7. मुखर०—adj. to चरणेन; 'which is resounding with the jingling of anklets'. मुखर—*lit.* 'talkative', 'making a noise'; hence 'sounding'; *cf.* मुखरमधीरं त्यज मञ्जीरं। Gīt, 5; स्तम्बेरमा मुखरशृङ्खलकर्षिणस्ते। Ragh. V. 72. मुखर is derived from मुख with the possessive affix र; or मुखं मुखव्यापारं शब्दं राति ददाति. आराविन्—sounding, noisy. न संपत्स्यसे—संपन्नः (युक्तः) न भवसि; *cf.* स तस्यां कामसपन्नो यक्ष्मणा समपद्यत (with the

Inst.)—Mahābhārata, Adi. P. वृथा वहसि etc.—what is the good of your having a longing, if after it is fulfilled in the best possible way by the most competent person, you are still obstinate in withholding the blossoms ? ललित०—the longing which is common to (*i. e.* is possessed both by) you and gallant lovers. ललित–adj. to कामिनः generally described as longing to receive kicks from beloveds. Mr. Paṇdit explains it in a round-about way, as a desire common to person '*fond of the graceful actions of young women*'. For the यतिभङ्ग or faulty pause in metre in the 2nd and 3rd lines, see com.

वचनावसरपूर्वं—*adv.*—'making or finding a proper opportunity for speaking'. The King does not wish to enter abruptly, but wants a suitable opportunity to make his presence known to the girls. There is a similar scene in the Śāk. Act I. (अवसरोऽयमात्मानं प्रकाशयितुम्।) and again in Act III. (अवसरः खल्वयमात्मानं दर्शयितुम्। *v. l.* before śl. 15). Here the King addresses the remark to the Vidūṣaka, because he wants the latter to go forth and provide for the opportunity, which he soon does. इमां परिहासयिष्यामि—I will play a joke at her (and thus give you the अवसर which you require). भर्तात्र प्रविशति—Nipuṇikā is somewhat surprised to find the King paying a visit to the girls. प्रथमं चिन्तितं—Irāvatī says that *she* is not surprised, she had a suspicion of it already and knew that the King would be somewhere in the vicinity. युक्तं नाम &c.—This must be read with a K*ā*ku (*i. e.* in a tone implying the opposite); see com. 'It is, indeed, proper for you' (*i. e.* certainly improper &c.) *Cf.* युक्तं नाम भवतां....मम पितुः द्रुपदकुलकलङ्केन स्पृश्यमानमुत्तमाङ्गमुपेक्षितुम्। Venī. III. Mr. Paṇdit who reads न युक्तं नाम explains it as 'It is not at all proper; it does not deserve even the *name* of proper.' Or this may be taken as a question. Is it at all or in any way proper for you &c? In this case नाम must be taken as used to emphasize the question. ताडयितुं युक्तम्—for the construction, *cf.* note on वरं विहन्तु *supra* p. 72.

P. 102. गृहीतार्थया त्वया—You who knew the fact (of the A oka being the special favourite of the King). It is better, however, to take अर्थ to mean 'object'; why did you, who knew that Māl. was going to strike the tree, not prevent her from carrying out her intention? अविनय—a rude act, improper behaviour; *cf.* अयमाचरत्यविनयं मुग्धासु तपस्विकन्यासु। Śāk. I. 22. The hidden meaning here is:—Why did you, who knew the King's secret and further that he was here, allow her to strike the Aśoka while he was looking on? You ought to have asked her to strike His Majesty lovingly. For गृहीतार्था *cf. supra* p. 96.

किं प्रवृत्तं &c.—Nipuṇikā is surprised to find Vidū. taking sides with the King and blaming the girls, simply to please the King who would like to enjoy the fun. Nip. also sees Vidū.'s secret motive in this. By proving her guilty towards the King he would give the latter an opportunity to forgive her which would deepen her love for him. **ब्रह्मबन्धु**—*m.* an unworthy Brāhmaṇa; one only connected with a Brāhmaṇa. The word is used as a sort of contemptuous term, like the Marathi भटुर्गा; ब्रह्मबन्धुरधिक्षेपे। Ak. III. 3.104. It is explained as ब्रह्म एव (ब्राह्मणजातिरेव) बन्धुरस्य। जात्या ब्राह्मणः न तु कर्मणा आचारेण वा। Comp. also the term ब्राह्मणब्रुव. **एतस्मिन्व्यतिक्रमे** etc—It is true that she is guilty of the transgression; but she did it in obedience to the orders of the Queen (and not of her own will), and hence she may be forgiven; for परवती *cf.* भगवन्परवानयं जनः प्रतिकूलाचरितं क्षमस्व मे। Ragh. VIII. 81; महाराज परवशोऽयं जनः। Vik. II. p. 55.

देव्यत्र मानयितव्या—This may be explained either as (1) true that you struck the King's favourite tree; but *you had to obey* the queen's orders, and thus you did what was proper;—or as (2) Oh! yes, *we must respect* the Queen, and not mind our own tree being treated like that.

Verse 18. Construe :—

(हे) विलासिनि, वामोरु, कठिने पादपस्कन्धे निहितस्य किसलयमृदोः ते वामस्य चरणस्य संप्रति बाधा न।

किसलयमृदोः etc.—This is one of the gallant speeches of the King, who anxiously and tenderly inquires if her foot suffered any injury. **विलासिनी**—*voc. sing.*: 'O you charming girl'. **न ते बाधा**—is a question—'I hope you feel no pain in your foot?' **वामोरु**—'whose thighs are beautiful' (*i.e.* delicate, and hence the possibility of pain being felt)'; see com. for the comp. ऊरु becomes ऊरू in a Bahu. comp. by Pāṇ.

IV. 1. 70. *Cf.* also our note on रम्भोरु p. 82. **वामस्य चरणस्य**—because it is the *left* foot that is to be used in kicking the Aśoka; *cf.* एकः सख्यास्तव सह मया वामपादाभिलाषी। Megh. II. 17.

नवनीतहृदयः etc.—This is said ironically 'Yes, I know my lord's heart is soft like butter, indeed.' **अविनीतहृदयः**—*v. l.* whose heart is impolite; *i. e.* who has the immodesty to flirt with a maid. The first reading is better, being more sarcastic. 'What a tender heart he has; he fears injury to the foot of Mālavikā.' Again, विनीत does not fit in well with हृदय. **विज्ञापय विसर्जयेति**—*i. e.* you should take his leave and then go. Baku. purposely says this in order that Māl. should exchange some words with the King. She also wishes to keep her longer in his company.

P. 104. **यास्यसि**—'you will go', *i. e.* there is time enough for you to go; wait a while. It corresponds to the Marāthi 'जाशील तूं'. **मम तावत्**—first listen to what I have to ask of you, for which this is the proper opportunity which has presented itself. **आर्थित्व**—*n.* a request (याच्ञा); *lit.* 'the condition of one who wants something'. (अर्थः आस्यास्तीति अर्थी। अर्थः याचने, अर्थयते असौ अर्थी इति वा। अर्थिनः भावः अर्थित्वम्।); *cf* तेनार्थित्वं त्वयि विधिवशाद् दूरबन्धुर्गतोऽहं। Megh. I. 6.

Verse 19. Construe :—

अयं जनः अपि चिरात् प्रभृति तादृशं धृतिपुष्पं न बध्नाति अनन्यरुचेः अस्य अपि दोहदं स्पर्शामृतेन पूरय।

धृतिपुष्प०—Like the Aśoka, I too have a *dohada*, *viz*, that I have lost all joy and cheerfulness for a long time, and that can come back to me, like the blossoms in the case of the Aśoka, only if you will touch me धृति—*f.* joy, delight; *cf.* द्वारपिधानमिव धृतेः। *supra* II. 11; and न खल्विमौ मालविकाचरणौ यौ ते हर्षदोहदं पूरयिष्यतः *infra* p. 110. धृति is called पुष्प for sustaining the metaphor. बध्नाति—the root बन्ध् is used with the words पुष्प and फल in the sense of 'to put forth'; *cf.* फलं बध्नन्ति नीतयः। Ragh. XII. 69. **स्पर्शामृतेन**—*i e.* अमृतमिवाह्लादकरेण स्पर्शेन your touch is as pleasant to me as nectar; *cf.* for a more elaborate description of the idea: जीवयन्निव संमूढसाध्वसस्वेदबिन्दुरधिकण्ठमर्प्यताम्। बाहुरैन्दवमयूखचुम्बितस्यन्दिचन्द्रमणिहारविभ्रमः॥ Māl.-Mādh. VIII. 3. **अनन्य**—स्पर्शामृतात् अन्या रुचिः यस्य न भवति तस्य मम।

पूरय पूरय etc.—Irāvatī says that while the Aśoka can only show flowers which may serve as ornaments, the King, who has compared himself to Aśoka (in śl. 19) will not only show flowers (पुष्प् 4 P. *cf.* पुष्प्यत्पुष्करवासितस्य पयसः। Uttar. III. 16) but fruit also. Mr. Paṇdit explains—"This [sc. फलति] refers to the children that Mālavikā would bear to the king. The coarseness of the allusion is in keeping with the condition of Irāvatī. For we must remember that. she is under the influence of wine." We think it is quite unnecessary to understand a vulgar allusion here which, moreover, is quite farfetched. It is suggested that he will not only show her ordinary favours (*e. g* marrying her) but follow them up with further substantial rewards (*e.g.* making her a Patta-Mahiṣī), in the same manner that flowers are followed by (the more substantial) fruit on a tree. **अयं पुनः उत्तम्भित एव**—*V. l.* here उत्तम्भित means 'raised up,' standing ready or eager for (showing flowers *i. e.* favours). **का प्रतिपत्तिरत्र**—what is the course of action to be adopted here ; what is to be done now. प्रतिपत्ति here means 'course of action', 'procedure' *cf.* विषादलुप्तप्रतिपत्ति (सैन्यं) Ragh. III. 46 : मनस्विनीनां प्रतिपत्तिरीदृशी। Kum. V. 42; आयुष्मतः प्रतिपत्तयः *infra* IV. 4; किं प्रतिपद्यते वैदर्भः *supra* p. 16. For another sense of प्रतिपत्ति see note on the word at p. 126. **जङ्घाबलं**—lit. the strength of the legs. "The only way out of the difficulty is to take to our heels." Said in his usual jocular way. **साधु त्वया**—you have well taken the initiative in this matter; said ironically. **के आवां** &c.—*i. e.* we are too insignificant creatures for the King's love. We cannot presume to accept it.

आत्मनः वञ्चनावचनं—Note that आत्मनः which refers to Irāvatī herself is not to be construed with वचनं, but with the word वञ्चना in the compound, so that the phrase really means आत्मवञ्चनाकारकं वचनम्. Such a compound is called a *Sāpekṣa* Samāsa, though such splitting up is unusual, and only allowed when the sense is quite clear. Thus in Ragh. VI. 1. मल्लतामाकृष्टलीलान् is used in place of आकृष्टमल्लीलान्; in VI. 2. रतेर्गृहीतानुनयेन for गृहीतरत्यनुनयेन, and thus elsewhere. **प्रमाणीकृत्य**—believing it to be true. For the promise, see *supra* p. 70 (भवताप्यस्यै प्रतिज्ञातम् &c.). That promise is now proved to Irāvatī to be वञ्चनावचन, because, as she thinks, the King did not promise for *her* sake, but rather because he wanted to have an opportunity to see Mālavikā. एतच्च विज्ञातम्—that you would behave thus. व्याघ०—She compares the deceit practised upon her to the sweet songs that hunters sing in forests, by which innocent, unsuspecting female deer are attracted and drawn towards them, only to meet destruction. अशङ्कितया—i. e who came here without suspecting your design. (*i. e.* who came here only to find that I had lost your love.) The reading आत्मनो वञ्चना व्याध जनगीतिरक्तया ...तया न विज्ञाता is simpler. It means—I did not know that I was to be deceived, being unsuspicious like &c. Tārānātha reads आत्मनो वञ्चनवचनं प्रमाणीकृत्याधिक्षिप्ताया प्रियगृहिण्या हृदयशल्यं कृतं; a dart has been prepared for the heart of a beloved wife despised after being made to believe in words intended to deceive her.

P. 106. प्रतियोजय—Say now something in reply. प्रतियुज् (*cau.*) *lit.* 'to fix on, adjust, or devise, in opposition to.' कर्मगृहीतेन etc.,—Even a thief, caught in the act of entering a house by making a hole in the wall, can say that he broke into the house not because he wanted to take away anything, but because he wished to learn, (practise, and perfect himself in) the art of making holes (in the wall) The excuse is no doubt lame, but it is better to say something that has at least a remote possibility in it, than to observe silence and thus implicitly plead guilty to the charge. कर्म—the act of boring the hole; *cf.* एतेन मापयति भित्तिषु कर्ममार्गं। Mṛich. III. 16. कुम्भीलक—*m.* a robber, thief; irregularly derived from कु the earth and भिद् 6 P. to break; one who breaks into a house. See Śāk VI p. 138 and our note on the word there. संधि *m.* is a technical term of thieves, applied to the chasm or opening made in a wall or under a building for the purpose of obtaining entrance. That appears to have been a standard mode of house-breaking in ancient India, when thieving was a *S'āstra* in its own province; compare in this respect the third Act of the Mṛichchhakaṭika where the thief Śarvilaka has a long soliloquy from which interesting sidelight is obtained on चौरशास्त्र. A good man may learn the art as an accomplishment; he must not practise it. So the ten heroes ot the Daśak. were taught the art of thieving along with others. संधिच्छेद—*m.* making holes शिक्षितः—have received lessons in. For the simile, *cf.* लोत्रेण गृहीतस्य

कुम्भीलकस्य अस्ति वा प्रतिवचनम्। Vik. II. p. 60. Mr. Paṇḍit prefers the reading ०सिक्खिओ which he renders as शिष्यः.

मे मालविकया अर्थः—the reading मालविकायां (loc.) is unidiomatic, because अर्थ is always found used with the instr. in similar cases; *cf.* न हि मे जीवितेनार्थो नैवार्थैन च भूषणैः। Rāmā. V. 26. 5; नैव तस्य कृतेनार्थो नाकृतेनेह कश्चन। Bg. III. 18, etc. यथा कथंचित्—somehow or other. विश्वसनीयोऽसि—this is said ironically, meaning—really you are not at all to be trusted. अन्यथा मन्दभागिन्या &c. Had I known it I would not have acted thus, *i. e.* come here and interfered in this splendid diversion. She calls herself 'unfortunate', because she now finds that she has no longer the King's love. Mr. Paṇḍit notices the reading and says—दुष्करं in Sanskṛit means 'difficult to do,' hence 'a difficulty;' and it may in Prākṛit signify a difficulty or interruption (विघ्न); 'I would not have caused an interruption to you'.

अत्रभवतो दाक्षिण्यस्य etc.—You should not say that the King has proved himself अदक्षिण (wanting in attention to you) in acting in the way he has done, *i. e.* his talking to Māla. was not a breach of his duty to you. दाक्षिणस्योपरोधं—*lit.* an obstruction to his दाक्षिण्य. समापत्तिदृष्टेन—'seen accidentally' (समापत्ति accident, chance); *cf.* उर्वशी समापत्तिदृष्टेन केशिना दानवेन बन्दिग्राहं गृहीता। Vik. I. p. 10. संकथा—talking, conversing with. अत्र त्वमेव प्रमाणम्—"You only are an authority for such a doctrine" (Paṇḍit)—*i. e.* others will not think it to be an अपराध at all. Or, here you are the final authority and we cannot dispute the matter with you. संकथा नाम भवतु etc. Irāvatī's indignation rises to a high pitch when she hears Vid. call the King's dalliance with Māla. a mere संकथा and she says—"You call it a mere talk. All right. You can have your way. Why should I trouble myself by further interfering in the matter? Here I am going". रशनासंदितचरणा—in the hurry of going in anger, her girdle slips and comes down to her feet and obstructs her motion. संदित (*p. p. p.* of दो 4 p. with सम्)—fettered, bound. व्रजत्येव—*i e.* without paying attention to the King's request 'प्रसीदतु भवती'. निरपेक्षता—indifference, as shown by her going away without being pacified. शठ—'You Rogue!' In the language of lovers शठ

is a technical word applied to a husband or lover who professes to show affection to one wife or mistress while he secretly loves another; see com. Writers on Śṛṅgāra mention four kinds of lovers—अथ शृङ्गारविषयाश्चत्वारो नायका इमे। अनुकूलो दक्षिणश्च धृष्टः शठ इति स्मृताः ॥ (Pratāparudrīya).

Verse 20. Construe :—

(हे) प्रिये, परिचयवति मयि तावत् शठ इति ते अवधीरणा अस्तु (हे) चण्डि चरणपतितया मेखलया याचिता अपि तां न विसृजसि।

P. 108. **शठ इति** etc.—In this verse the King in an artistic manner draws the attention of Irāvatī to her slipping girdle and at the same time presses his suit. "You may show —let there be-your disregard for my entreaties, because you consider and call me a शठ; it does not matter much, as being directed against me, who am so familiar with you and who will not therefore mind it. But you should, at least, not disregard the entreaties of your girdle as it is of your sex and is your constant companion". **परिचयवति**—is significant and goes with मयि; see above. Some propose to take it as परिचयवती, and construe it with अवधीरणा, "Your usual disregard for me". It is not a good way, however. In the first place it does not fit in well with अवधीरणा; for then we should expect परिचिता. Secondly, as Mr. Paṇdit points out, we should then have to suppose that the King was always similarly upbraided by Irāvatī for his intrigues (which it is the King's object to deny). Or the King may mean—You may neglect my request, because I am अतिपरिचित to you, and अवज्ञा in such a case is natural (see com.) But the request which the girdle is making to you is not an ordinary kind of intercession, and it behoves you not to disregard it. **चरणपतितया**—there is an obvious pun on this, because like a lover falling at the feet of his mistress, the girdle had come down to her feet to make the request, as it were. तां—*scil.* अवधीरणाम्. **इयमपि हताशा त्वामेव अनुसरति**—follows you, imitates you; you try to stop me, and the girdle too is doing the same. हताशा is a term of abuse; see *supra* p. 94. **ताडयितुमिच्छति**—shows the pitch to which her intoxication and irritation had worked her up. She merely wished to strike at the first impulse of anger, but did not.

Verse 21. Construe :—

बाष्पसारा चण्डी श्रोणीबिम्बात् अव्यपेक्षाच्युतेन हेमकाञ्चीगुणेन मां चण्डं हन्तुम् अभ्युद्यतां मेघराजी विद्युद्दाम्ना विन्ध्यम् इव।

एषा goes with **चण्डी** in the next śl. **चण्डी**—This angry Irāvatī. **बाष्पासारा**—बाष्पाणां आसारः (shower) यस्याः: shedding tears in profusion. Irāvatī was weeping at that time, as she was stung to the quick by the insult and neglect. **हेमकाञ्चीगुणेन**—काञ्चीगुण *lit.* the band of the girdle, *i. e.* the girdle itself: *cf.* काञ्चीगणैः काञ्चनरत्नचित्रैर्नो भूषयन्ति प्रमदा नितम्बान्। Ṛitus. IV. 4. **श्रोणीबिम्ब**—*cf.* नितम्बबिम्ब śl. 7 *supra*, and शरणमथ वा श्रोणीबिम्बं रणन्माणमेखलम्। Vairāgya. 6. **अव्यपेक्षाच्युतेन**—which has fallen down because of her neglect or carelessness; **व्यपेक्षा** means 'care, regard'; *cf.* न व्यपेक्षन्त समुत्सुकाः प्रजाः। Ragh. XIX. 6; compare also the word सव्यपेक्ष in स्नेहश्च निमित्तसव्यपेक्षश्चेति विप्रतिषिद्धमेतत् Māl.-Mādh. I. Mr. Paṇdit is inaccurate in translating अव्यपेक्षाच्युतेन as 'dropped *unexpectedly*'. **चण्डं**—*adv.* violently, fiercely. **विद्युद्दा मेघराजीव** &c.—Irāvatī's action as described in the first three lines is compared to the showers and lightning with which clouds gathering in the sky visit the Vindhya mountains during a thunderstorm. Here, मां corresponds to विन्ध्यम्, चण्डी to मेघराजी and हेमकाञ्चीगुणेन to विद्युद्दाम्ना and we have a fine though elaborate simile. The golden bright colour of the girdle makes the comparison to lightning easily intelligible. बाष्पासारा, when taken with मेघराजी should be understood to refer to showers of rain. **विद्युद्दाम**—continued streaks of lightning (lit. a garland or mass of lightnings); *cf.* विद्युद्दामस्फुरितचकितैः Megh. I. 27. **मेघराजी**—note the word राजी with the (long) ई; the other form राजि has occurred *supra* p. 78. **विन्ध्यम्** This is the famous range of mountains which divides Hindustan proper from the Deccan. Kālidāsa twice refers to the Vindhyas in the Ritusaṃhāra (II. 8, 27) and also in the Ragh. VI. 61, and it is believed by some that he resided somewhere near it.

भूयोऽप्यपराद्धां—Her first fault was when she came there inoppertunely to disturb his dalliance with Mālavikā. To strike him now would being guilty towards him a second time which she did not mean to do. For अपराद्धां Tārānātha reads अवधीरितां 'insulted'. **अवलम्बयति**-hangs down her hand, *i. e.*

does not strike ; इति रशनां हस्तेनावलम्बते *v. l.* means supports or holds up the girdle in her hand.

Verse 22. Construe :—

(हे) कुटिलकेशि, अपराधिनि मयि उद्यतं दण्डं किं संहरसि, त्वं विलसितं वर्धयसि दासजनाय अत्र कुप्यसि च ।

अपराधिनि etc.—You were about to strike me ; why do you hold it (उद्यतं दण्डं) back (संहरसि) ? For this sense of हृ with सम्, compare: शङ्के संहरति स्मरोऽपि चकितस्तूणार्धकृष्टं शरम् । Śāk. VI. 4. कुटिलकेशि—(कुटिलाः curly केशाः यस्याः सा, तत्संबोधनं); this is considered as a mark of beauty ; *cf.* अरालकेशी Ragh. VI. 81. The comp. may be either ०केशा or केशी ; see H. Gr. § 329 वर्धयसि विलसितं त्वं—By not striking me actually, but remaining, in a posture or attitude of forbearance (*cf.* सरशनं हस्तमवलम्बयति above), you increase your fascination ; you appear the more charming in my eyes. दासजनायात्र कुप्यसि च—and still you are angry with this your slave (*i. e.* myself) ! He means that she should relent towards him. अत्र—Scil. अत्र एवं स्थिताय. The com. explains अत्र by अस्मै which ultimately comes to the same thing. नूनमिदमनुज्ञातम्—Surely you will now allow this *viz.* my falling at your feet. See com.

P. 110. यौ ते &c.—This has reference to the King's words स्पर्शामृतेन &c. *supra* p. 104. "How do you expect *my* feet to touch you so as to give you joy, since you have declared that Mālavikā's feet *alone* (अनन्यरुचेः) can do it ?" कृतप्रसादोऽसि—(1) said jestingly–you are favoured in that she did not strike you; (1) she has shown favour to you in as much as she has gone away without being *prasanna.* This is explained in his next speech.

दिष्टया अप्रसन्ना गतैषा—It is a matter for congratulation that she has gone without mitigating her anger. अनेन अविनयेन—Owing to this your act of impropriety in having shown attention to Mālavikā. Or better still, अनेन अविनयेन उपलक्षिता she has gone away unreconciled, having committed this act of discourtesy towards you by slighting your prostration The force of the word दिष्टया is, that it is good that she has gone away without being reconciled, she has thus furnished you with an excuse for remaining indifferent now, and thereby left you undisturbed to pay court to Mālavikā, if she had not done so, you would have had to give up Mālavikā, since it would then have been grossly improper on your part to further slight and offend her. This explanation is strengthened by the King's own admission in śl. 23 below. The reading दैवेनास्या विनयस्यापसारिता नियन्त्रणा is bad; what is the propriety of the pl. दैवैः or देवैः ? Again, how could Vid. call Irāvatī's presence नियन्त्रणा when Māl. had already left them and was not likely to meet the King immediately after ? Moreover, if अविनय was not on the part of इ०, why should the Vid. expect her to come back ? Evidently he thought that Irā. might feel remorse for her disregard of the King's prostration and would return to express her sorrow. Some read—अस्याविनयस्याप्रसादिता गता and translate—Fortunately (or luckily) she has gone away without giving a proper reward (अप्रसादिता) for this impropriety of yours ; but it is not easy to understand how अप्रसादिता means 'without giving a reward for'.

यावदङ्गारकः etc.—Let us then be off at once, otherwise she might return and further trouble us. Her return is compared to that of the planet Mars, because both are unfavourable. The comparison to Mars may also have been suggested by her being hot-tempered and resentful and so resembling Mars which is malignant (क्रूर). The allusion here is to astronomy and certain astrological beliefs. The planet Mars during its synodic revolution round the Sun in 760 days once appears to the observer to turn back *in a retrograde motion* for 60 days, after which it is seen again to resume its regular course; during the period of its retrograde motion it is popularly believed to exercise a malignant influence on the destinies of men. She Grahalāghava III. 20. Bṛihatsaṃhitā VI., and Muhūrtatantra XIX. 5. The zodiac is a belt of the heavens limited by lines about 8^0 on each side from the ecliptic (the sun's apparent path in the sky). It includes all the apparent orbits of the sun, the moon, and the planets as known to the ancients, and is divided into 12 equal parts called राशिs (राशि *m.* 'a sign of the zodiac,' an astrological house). It is with reference to these राशिs or 'mansions' that astrological calculations are generally made. Mars beginning its retrograde motion would, of course, appear to come back to the राशि which it had recently left in its orbit. The planet is called अङ्गारक because of its dull-red colour as seen in the sky, which resembles that of a heated charcoal (अङ्गार); अङ्गार इव अङ्गारकः, the क being added by 'इवे प्रतिकृतौ' Pān. V. 3. 96. अनुवक्रम्—*adv.* in an oblique course, retrogressively.

मदनस्य वैषम्यम्—The oddness, the strange conduct or working of Cupid. It consists, as explained in the next śl., in making the King consider प्रणिपातलङ्घन a सेवा which he could not have regarded as such before he saw Māla; but it is मदन who makes it so; hence his वैषम्य.

Verse 23. Construe :—

प्रियाहृतमनाः (अहं) तस्याः (इरावत्याः) प्रणिपातलङ्घनं सेवां मन्ये, एवं (मयि) प्रणयवती सा कुपिता (इति) उपेक्षितुं शक्यम्।

प्रियाहृतमनाः—My heart being captivated by my darling, Mālavikā. तस्याः—*scil.* इरावत्याः—is a subjective genitive तत्कृतं प्रणिपातलङ्घनं—her slighting my prostration, declining to accept my homage; *cf.* अप्रभवान्प्रणिपातलङ्घनं विस्मृतः *infra* Act IV. p. 152. सेवां मन्ये—I consider that a service done to me. The reason is made clear in the second line. It is because (हि) it is now possible for him with an easier conscience to neglect Irāvatī and to pay his addresses to Mālavikā. प्रणयवती सा—*sc.* इरावती. एवं—because she has gone away like that. For the idea *cf.* किं तु प्रणिपातलङ्घनादहमस्यां धैर्यमवलम्बिष्ये। Vikr. II. p. 63. सा उपेक्षितुं शक्यं—for the syntax see our note on उचितः प्रणयो वरं विहन्तुं *supra* p. 72. The reading एवं प्रणयवती सा न हि &c. means—It is not possible for me thus to neglect her who is attached to me, although she is angry. In this case वैषम्य will mean 'the difficulty created by love.' But in this reading the हि has no force (we should rather expect च in its place), unless we take it in the sense of अवधारणं 'certainty'; but that would go against the context. Again, the King never shows the least anxiety to please Irāvatī, when once she is out of sight.

Critical Appreciation of the Act III

The प्रवेशक, at the beginning of this act, informs us that the result of the contest in dancing was in favour of Gaṇadāsa. After seeing Mālavikā in person, the King's love for her becomes more intense. The तपनीयाशोक has not yet blossomed and hence its longing (दोहद) needs to be fulfilled. The Parivrājikā desires to see the queen.

By introducing this प्रवेशक, Kālidāsa has cleverly avoided the presentation of the dance performance by Hardatta's pupil. This reveals the dramatic skill of the dramatist. The dohada of the Aśoka tree, which plays a significant part in the development of the plot, is introduced here. The King's nobility and sense of courtsey, are seen in his restrain from expressing his feelings for Mālavikā to others in the royal palace. In short, the प्रवेशक informs us about the earlier incidents and scatters the seeds for the progress of the plot.

In this act, the main theme of the play progresses well. मालविका, in her soliloquy, expresses her love for the King. The assurance of Bakulāvalikā, the clever intrigue of the Vidūṣaka and the promise of the Queen Dhāriṇī assure us the smooth progress of the love affair. The king comes closer to Mālavikā whom he had seen earlier only from a distance, in act II. The jealousy and anger of Irāvatī create an obstacle in the way of lovers and leaves the progress of the plot in heart-breathing suspense.

The king Agnimitra is so strongly attracted towards Mālavikā that he is unable to perform his usual duties. He is courteous and hence he desires to avoid the meeting with Irāvatī as he is not confident about the success of his hypocrite behaviour, of a sincere lover. The presence of Mālavikā captivates the king so much that he is even prepared to disregard the arrival of Irāvatī. His jealousy for the Aśoka tree reveals his intense love for Mālavikā. Though caught red-handed, he gives a false reply and later on confesses his insincerity in falling at the feet of Irāvatī.

Mālavikā is an extremely shy girl who is afraid to admit even to herself that she loves the king. Inspite of the queen's promise, she is pessimistic for her future.

The Vidūṣaka proves himself to be a successful Kāmatantra Sachiva. He takes into confidence Bakulāvalikā and tells her to act as a love-messenger between the king and Mālavikā. He brings about the fall of Dhāriṇī from the swing and thus is responsible for Mālavikā's presence in the

Pramadavana. He facilitates the entry of the king when the later fails to find any pretext for appearing before Mālavikā in the Pramadavana. Like a true friend, the Vidūṣaka assists the King in pacifying the anger of Irāvatī.

Irāvatī, like a true beloved, is eager to meet her lord in the Pramadavana for a swing ride. She feels jealous when she learns that Dhārinī, has appointed Mālavikā to carry out the task of fulfilling the Dohada of the As'oka tree. She secretly overhears the talk of Bakulāvalikā and Mālavikā. When the King approaches Mālavikā with a request for love, Irāvatī being full of jealous anger rushes to the scene and thus puts the king into a very confusing position. She disregards the King's prostrations and retires in anger.

The main attraction in this act is the wonderful arrangement of the tri-focal scene on the stage. The main theme progresses further in as far as the lovers closely meet together for the first time. But immediately then the jealous anger of Irāvatī creates an impediment in the way of the lovers and leaves us in a suspense for the further development of the theme.

Act IV

P. 112. पर्युत्सुक—love-sick. प्रतीहारी—the female door-keeper; fr. प्रति-ती-हार m. a door (*lit.* 'that which keeps back' fr. हृ 1st conj. with प्रति).

Verse 1. Construe :—

श्रुतिपथगतां ताम् आश्रित्य आस्थया लब्धमूलः, नयनविषयं संप्राप्तायां रूढराग-प्रवालः, हस्तस्पर्शैः व्यक्तरोमोद्गमत्वात् मुकुलितः इव मनसिजतरुः क्रान्तं मां फलस्य रसज्ञं कुर्यात्।

तामाश्रित्य etc.—In this verse the King describes the growth of his passion for Mālavikā by means of an elaborate metaphor, and expresses a hope that it will get its fruit. Love he likens to a tree, a comparison which we have got before at III. 11 in a different context. Now, a tree has four stages in its growth. It first strikes root in the ground; then appear the sprouts; then it puts forth the buds or flowers;

and lastly it produces the fruit. The King says—The tree of his passion for Mālavikā first "struck root," *i. e.* had a definite existence, when he first heard of her. That was when he saw her in a picture and knew her name from Vasulakṣmī (p. 10). तामाश्रित्य बद्धमूलः—It took root with regard to her (she being the ground). आस्थया—हेतुना hopefully, *i. e.* in the form of hope. संप्राप्तायां etc.—It put forth leaves, *i. e.* grew one step further, when I actually saw her. This was during the exhibition in Act II. रूढरागप्रवालः—रूढाः रागरूपाः प्रवालाः यस्य, the affection which he felt for her being likened to leaves. हस्तस्पर्शे etc.—When I actually touched her with my hand (See Act III. p. 102 इति हस्तेन गृहीत्वा उत्थापयति) my hair stood on its end as I was thrilled with delight; *cf.* यदयं रथसंक्षोभादंसेनांसो रथोपमश्रेण्याः । स्पृष्टः सरोमविक्रियमङ्कुरितं मनसिजेनेव ॥ Vik. I. 11; this rising of hair is compared to buds. The sensation of रोमोद्गम is often compared to the मुकुलोद्गम of trees; *cf.* स्फुरत्पुलकेन संप्रति मया विडम्बते क्षणबद्धकुड्मलकदम्बडम्बरः ॥ Māl.-Mādh. III. 7. In erotic poetry, the standing of the hair on end is considered to be the first sign of love, produced by the first bodily touch. मुकुलितः—explain मुकुलानि संजातानि अस्य। fr. मुकुल+इत (च्) by तदस्य संजातं तारकादिभ्य इतच् Pān V. 2. 36. The reading मुकुलित is preferable to कुसु॰ (see it.-note) as the buds better resemble the hair than the opened flowers. व्यक्तरोमोद्गमत्वात्—should better be dissolved as व्यक्तरोम्णामुद्गमः रोमोद्गमः यस्य सः। तस्य भावस्तस्मात्। The tree of the King's love has thus gone through the first three stages. Now it remains for it to put forth the fruit; and he expresses a hope to that effect in कुर्यात् &c, क्लान्त—languid owing to love-sickness. रसज्ञं फलस्य—The fruit would of course be मालविकासमागमरूपम्. Mark the use of रसज्ञ with क्लान्त; a thing that is क्लान्त require रस (water) to refresh it. In this Śl. some critics find the fault of भग्नप्रक्रमत्व or disregard of the continuity of similar syntax. तामाश्रित्येति द्वितीयान्तत्वेन प्रक्रम्य संप्राप्तायामिति पुनः सप्तम्यन्तनिर्देशात् भग्नप्रक्रमत्वं दोषः।

सखे गौतम—The King is so absent-minded, being absorbed in his thoughts about Mālavikā, that he forgets that the Vidūṣaka is not there, being away on an errand at his own bidding. आम्—*Cf.* आम् संदिष्टास्मि देव्या *supra* p. 74. जयसेने—Jayasenā is now dismissed by the King as her presence is not desired during the confidential interview that will now begin. कथं वा विनोद्यते—*i. e.* diverted so as not to feel the pain.

P. 114. ते सख्या:—*i. e.* of Mālavikā; this shows that the King regards Māl. as his wife. यः—The same as that of a female cuckoo-bird pounced upon and captured by a cat परभृतिका or परभृता (*infra* V. 2) is a cuckoo; *lit.* it means 'nourished by another' (*cf.* अन्यपुष्टा), so called because it is supposed to leave its eggs in the nest of a crow to be hatched by it, the latter being therefore called परभृत् 'one that nourishes another'. The Vidușaka means that she is in the most miserable condition. तपस्विनी—the poor girl; see *supra* p. 68; *cf.* सा तपस्विनी निर्वृता भवतु। Śāk. IV. p. 95. पिङ्गलाक्ष्या—By that tawny-eyed lady, used of Dhāriṇī, to sustain the comparison to a cat; पिङ्गल refers to the reddish-brown colour of her eye when she way angry. But the expression would more appropriately refer to Irāvatī, who was both angry and intoxicated. The Vidū. never speaks disparagingly of Dhāriṇī. The reading is probably निक्षेपिता (caused to be thrown into the cellar through Dhāriṇī by Irā.). सारभाण्डभूगृहे—A subterranean cellar which is generally used for storing valuable things. भाण्ड—goods, merchandise; *cf.* रत्नभाण्ड *infra.* p. 134, Act IV. सारभाण्ड-valuable goods; ornaments &c. रुजाक्रान्त—रुजाविहस्त० *v. l.* means 'with her foot disabled by pain'. ननु etc.—ननु asks a question here. एवं विमुख:—so inimical as to; ill-disposed to such a degree. सुखपृच्छिका— *v. l.* सुखं पृच्छतीति one inquiring after good health.

किं न्ववलोकितो वल्लभजनः—Did the King see his beloved person (*i. e.* yourself)? We translate this to suit the context. The plain meaning would be 'did you see the beloved one (*i. e.* the King)? Dhāriṇī must have known that Irāvatī had an appointment with the King in the Pramadavana. (see p. 70), and hence her question. तयोक्तम्— This passage, like some others in the play, has suffered at the hands of copyists. The reading adopted in the text seems best to suit the context. Irāvatī replied to her in the following words मन्दो व: etc.—"The formality of this inquiry (*viz.* किं नु &c.) is idle (meaningless), because we are no longer his वल्लभाः; that title has now been transferred to one of your servants, who has captured his heart. You do not seem to be aware of that fact, and hence you inquire in this way". Irāvatī with a real retort here hints at the obvious passion of the King

20

for Mālavikā, without actually uttering her name. Mr. Paṇdit reads and translates as—किं न लक्षितो जनो वल्लभ इति—"Why have I not seen my beloved one *i. e.* you, Irāvatī? But this is to pre-suppose that Irāvatī had not seen Dhāriṇī for many days previous to her present visit. तया उक्तं—"She (Irāvatī) said." मदो वा उपचारो वा यत्ते परिजनस्य वल्लभत्वं जानत्यपि पृच्छसीति। "This is either an affront or an empty form, since you ask this question knowing that the belovedness belongs to your maid-servant." But we cannot expect Irāvatī to speak with such effrontery to the Chief Queen. In the reading कुतो वा ते उपचार: यत्तव परिजनस्य &c. वा has no propriety. Mr. Paṇdit's comments on the above is this—

Irāvatī means that Dhāriṇī must be aware that Mālavikā has taken her (Irāvatī's) place as the favourite young wife of the King. She thinks that Dhāriṇī must know this, as otherwise she must not have commissioned Māla. to perform the *dohada* of the Aśoka tree. Dhāriṇī's question must be due to मद, because she having known all must be insulting her by the question; or it must be उपचार (all empty formality), because while asking the question she is conscious that Irāvatī is no longer वल्लभजन.

P. 116. निर्भेदादृतेऽपि—निर्भेद—a clear giving out of; hence, explicit or distinct mention of. मालविका शङ्कयति—makes one suspect; *i. e.* leads one to suppose that Mālavikā is meant. अयमुप०—उपन्यास means the manner of putting a thing before another; introduction. *Cf.* अहो उपन्यासशुद्धिः। Māl.-Mādh. III. p. 69. तया अनुबध्यमानया—when pressed to make her meaning clear or to state the case fully. भवतः अविनयमन्तरेण &c. *i. e.* the details of your meeting (in Act III.) were fully reported to her.

अहो दीर्घरोषता—The King did not quite expect Irāvatī to be so resentful. निगडपद्यौ— *Nom. dual.* of निडगपदी fem. of निगडपद, 'with their feet put in chains;' (निगड *m. n.* chains, fetters). अदृष्टसूर्यपादं may either be an *adv.*, or an *adj.* to वासं; न दृष्टाः सूर्यस्य पादाः यस्मिन्कर्मणि तद्यथा or यस्मिन् वासे तं; the Com. explains the reading अदृष्टसूर्यपादे which is also good; the meaning is that the celler was very close and dark, where the sun's rays (पादा) could not penetrate. पातालवासं नागकन्यके इव—The subterranean celler is compared to *pātāla*, where *nāgas* reside. पाताल—also called *Nāga-Loka*, is supposed to be the residence of the *Nāgas* presided over by their chief, Ananta. They are popularly confounded with snakes, but they are differently spoken of in the Bg.; *cf.* सर्पाणामस्मि वासुकिः । अनन्तश्चास्मि नागानां । X. 27, 28. The नाग्स are described as semi-divine beings, having a human face with the tail of a serpent and the expanded neck of a cobra. Their females were particularly handsome and some of them intermarried with men, as Ulūpī with Arjuna. Such is their mythological account; but a people bearing the name Nāga once actually lived in India and are historical.

"Kings of this race reigned at Mathurā, Padmāvatī, etc., and the name survives in the modern Nāgpur. There are various speculations as to who and what they were, but it seems clear they were a race distinct from the Hindus. The mythological accounts are probably based upon the historical, but they have been mixed up together and confused. The favourite theory is that they were a Scythic race, and probably *obtained their name from worshipping serpents or holding them in awe and reverence*". (Dowson's Classical Dictionary.)

Verse 2. Construe :—

विबुद्धचूतसङ्गिन्यौ मधुरस्वरा परभृता भ्रमरी च प्रबलपुरोवातया अकालवृष्ट्या कोटरं गमिते ।

मधुरस्वरा etc.—Here Māla. is fitly compared to a cuckoo : but Baku.'s comparison to a bee only holds so far as the two were enjoying the blossoms of a mango-tree and were forced to hide themselves in a hollow of the tree by a violent storm; the storm here means the angry Irāvatī. **परभृता**—see परभृतिका, p. 114 above. **विबुद्ध**—'awakened', *i. e.* blossomed. **अकालवृष्टि**—*i. e.* coming suddenly when not expected. **प्रबलपुरोवातया**—*adj.* to वृष्ट्या. As dissolved in the com. this means—having a wind blowing from the contrary direction; it may also be taken as प्रबलः strong पुरोवातः यस्यां तया—पुरोवात is *lit.* the strong wind that generally *precedes* (पुरो भवतीत्येवंरूपो वातः) the actual bursting of a thunderstorm; *cf.* प्रबलपुरोवातताडितशिखण्डः Vik. IV. 8; आशाः पुरोवातमवाप्य मेघः Ragh. XVIII. 38. **गमिते**—governs कोटरं 'made to resort to, driven into'.

उपक्रम—*m.* a plan or remedy applicable in a particular case; 'is there a scheme which we can use here to help us out of this trouble ? कथं भविष्यति—'how can there be any'—*i. e.* 'I don't see any. यत्—because. He explains why he sees no way out of the difficulty. The Queen had taken good care to keep them under the most vigilant surveillance with strict orders to the keeper not to release them on any account unless a messenger came showing her own snake-seal ring as a proof of his *bona fides.* व्यापृता—*lit.* in charge of. न मोक्तव्या &c.—Prof. Tawney remarks on this—"It is clear that the head Queen exercised in some departments an amount of authority that would have delighted the soul of Mr. J. S. Mill." सपरामर्शम्—परामर्श means-touching him with his palm as a mark of affection ; *cf.* Kum. III 22. Or परामर्श may mean 'reflection,' 'thought,'; 'thoughtfully'.

P. 118 सदाष्टिक्षेपम्—*i. e.* to find out if any one was within hearing. अदृष्टः शृणोति—*i. e.* being himself concealed he may overhear us and spoil our plans. What the Vid. tells the King in his ear will appear in the course of the events that immediately follow. His plan was this—the main object was to get the Queen's ring with the serpent's image. He therefore, was to appear before the Queen in a frightened state while the King was there, and represent himself as bitten by a serpent. Then Dhruvasiddhi, the physician, was to be apparently sent for who, instead of coming himself, was to desire to have Vid. sent to him and thereafter the प्रतीहारी (who was already taken into confidence) as if coming from him was to ask for something having a serpent's image on it. On hearing this the Queen was sure to give her ring with a serpent's seal, which the प्रती० was to take to Vidū. who in his turn was to take it to माधविका, get Māla. and Bakulā, released and then to take them to the समुद्रगृह. When this was accomplished the प्रती० was to go to the King and tell him that the minister wished to see him on some state matters. The King was then to leave the Queen under that pretext and meet Mālavikā at the समुद्रगृह. उपाश्लिष्य—going near.

प्रवातशयने—for प्रवात *cf. supra.* pp. 16, 92. रक्तचन्दनधारिणा—(sc. चरणेन)—The leg was smeared with a paste of red sandal which is supposed to have a curative effect on sprains and similar pains. It is a remedy which is still in use in villages where no medical help is at hand. **परिजन॰**—So as to give it some relief from pain. **चरणेन**—*Sc.* उपलक्षिता; the instrumental here is of the kind known as उपलक्षणे तृतीया; see H. S. Gr. § 815. **भगवत्या**—by the Parivrājikā, who was relating her some tale so that her time may pass pleasantly. **देवीं द्रष्टुमरिक्तपाणिः**—this custom still survives among the orthodox people in India; compare also *supra* अरिक्तपाणिना देवी द्रष्टव्या p. 64. **संवेद्य**—*i. e.* after taking her into our confidence. The student will notice that in the scene of the pretended snake-bite which follows, Jayasenā's assistance was necessary to bring the sham message from Dhruvasiddhi, as also from the minister. **भवति**—This is addressed to Jayasenā just to please her. **कथावस्तु**—for वस्तु *cf.* कालिदासग्रथितवस्तुना p. 4.

P. 120. **विदिशेश्वरः**—the ruler of Vidiśā, a city situated on a river of the same name. It was the capital of Agnimitra and is the modern Bhilsa in Scindia's territory. See our remarks in the Introduction. **अलमलं**—you need not get up and put yourself to unnecessary pain. **उपचारयन्त्रणा**—For custom required every woman to show respect to her husband by getting up at his approach; *cf.* the Śloka अभ्युत्थानमुपागते गृहपतौ &c. quoted in the notes to Śāk. Act IV. 18. **यन्त्रणा**—check, restraint (imposed on by custom); *cf.* ह्रीयन्त्रणां तत्क्षणमन्वभूवन्नन्योन्यलोलानि विलोचनानि। Kum. VII. 75. **अलं**, meaning 'enough of', is either used with the *inst.* as here, or with the gerund in त्वा as at अलमन्यथा गृहीत्वा न खलु मनस्विनि मया प्रयुक्तमिदम् I. 20 *supra*.

Verse 3. Construe :—

(हे) कलभाषिणि, अनुचितनूपुरविरहं तपनीयपीठिकालम्बि रुजा परीतं चरणं मां च पीडयितुं (त्वं) न अर्हसि।

अनुचित॰—For, on account of the pain you are compelled to remove from your feet even the anklets which, being a part of the Mangalālaṃkaras, are not usually taken off. **तपनीयपीठिकालम्बि**—This must be translated here as 'which habitually rests on a gold foot-stool' (but is now being held by the attendants; see *supra* परिजनहस्तगतेन चरणेन). Such stools were used in ancient India by royal personages for resting the feet on; *cf.* पादेन हैमं विलिलेख पीठम्। Ragh. VI. 15. Or we must suppose that by the time the King came, the Queen had rested her foot on the gold foot-stool. तपनीय—*n.* gold; पीठक *n.* a foot-stool. रुजा परीतं—*lit.* 'encompassed by pain,' *i. e.* completely ailing. मां च पीडयितुम्—you will not only pain the leg, but me too, if you get up, as I shall be sorry to see you in pain; this is added gallantly.

अस्ति मे विशेषः—*Cf.* the passage in Śāk. III. p. 83.-गौतमी—जाते अपि लघुसंतापानि तेऽङ्गानि। शकुन्तला—अस्ति मे विशेषः। यज्ञोपवीतबद्धाङ्गुष्ठः—The Vidūṣaka now enters pretending to be bitten by a cobra, and loudly crying for help. He has tied his thumb (just above the place where he is supposed to be bitten) with the thread of his *Yajñopavīta*, to stop the poison spreading and circulating upwards; it is a kind of simple First Aid in the case of a snake-bite. The *Yajñopavīta* is the sacred thread with which every person of the 'twice-born' class is invested at a certain age. Being always worn on the body, it is the nearest thread one can find in an emergency and that it is used in that way will be apparent from the humorous remarks of Śarvilaka in Mṛich. III.—यज्ञोपवीतं हि नाम ब्राह्मणस्य महदुपकरणद्रव्यम्। कुतः-एतेन मापयति भित्तिषु कर्ममार्गमेतेन मोचयति भूषणसंप्रयोगान्। उद्घाटको भवति यन्त्रदृढे कपाटे दष्टस्य कीटभुजगैः परिवेष्टनं च। संभ्रान्तः—in great agitation. परिभ्रान्तः—Mark the difference in meaning of these words caused by prepositions; (*cf.* the root हृ in this respect—आहार, विहार, व्याहार, उपहार &c.), परिभ्रान्तः—implies carelessness—where were you wandering heedlessly (so that you came to be bitten in this way)? आचारपुष्प &c.—This custom has been already referred to. The compound is of the *Madhyamapadalopi* class (see com.); *cf.* आचारलाजाः Ragh. II. 10. जीवितसंशय *lit.* means 'a doubt whether life will be preserved or not'; hence, danger to life.

P. 122. अशोकस्तबक—a bunch of the As'oka flowers; because women love to wear one; *cf.* अशोकनिर्भर्त्सितपद्मरागं...... वसन्तपुष्पाभरणं वहन्ती। Kum. III. 53. दंशपदे—The (two) marks of the bite, the holes made by its teeth. It will be seen in the sequel that our bold schemer made these holes with a thorn of the *Ketakī* plant. दंशच्छेदः पूर्वकर्म—the first thing to be done, the primary curative treatment, is to amputate the part which is bitten. *Cf.* अङ्गुलीवोरगक्षता। Ragh. I. 28.

On this remark of the Parivrājikā Mr. S. P. Paṇdit has the following note :—"The proposal to amputate coming from the Parivrājikā, who is in the secret of Vidūṣaka, and is liable to be suspected by Dhāriṇī of participation in Vidūṣaka's intrigue, is intended to avoid that suspicion, so that the ascetic may appear to be quite disinterested in all that passes around her. It is also intended to give her a character for learning and knowledge of medicine. The Buddhist priesthood made medicine one of their special studies and practised it for the benefit of those whom they wished to influence on behalf of their religion." Mr. Paṇdit's first assumption that the Parivrājikā knew (this part of) the secret of Vidūṣaka is wrong. It does not appear from the play that she knew anything about the plot. It was formed in her absence and immediately put into execution, Jayasenā being the only person taken into confidence by the Vidūṣaka; and even if the Parivrājikā had remained silent, there was no reason why *she* of all persons should have been suspected. As the poet puts in the mouth of Irāvatī, the suspicion does not travel beyond the Vidūṣaka (p. 156—सत्यमयमत्र ब्रह्मबन्धुना कृतः प्रयोगः। इयमस्य कामतन्त्रसचिवस्य नीतिः।). As regards the remedy suggesting her learning, we think that Mr. Paṇdit need not have credited *the Buddhists only* with the knowledge of such a simple remedy; all the alternatives and cures given in the following Śloka are matters of common knowledge even among ordinary people and have long been practised in India.

Verse 4. Construe :—

दंशस्य छेदः दाहः वा क्षतेः रक्तमोक्षणं वा एतानि दष्टमात्राणाम् आयुष्याः प्रतिपत्तयः।

क्षतेः रक्तमोक्षणम्—क्षतस्यारक्तमोक्षणं *v. l.* means—completely draining off the blood from. एतानि—is *plural* because it refers to the three remedies combined, and *neuter* because one of the three is neuter; see *H. S. Grammar* § 789. आयुष्य—*adj.* 'preserving life ;' fr. आयुस्+य (यत्) added by तस्मै हितम् Pān. V. 1. 5. This reading is better than आयुषः which is meaningless with दष्टमात्राणां; it would suit दष्टानां प्रतिपत्तयः—remedies ; see note on the word at p. 104.

विषवैद्याः—physicians whose special branch is toxicology or treatment of poisons of all kinds. ध्रुवसिद्धिः—(lit. *one who invariably succeeds in curing*) the name of a poison-doctor attached to the court. **कथं न भेष्यामि**—He says, the bite must have been सविष, since already one symptom of the poison acting has made its appearance, *viz.*, सिमसिमायन्ति मेऽङ्गानि—My limbs are convulsively affected. सिमसिमाम् is a verb denoting a kind of convulsive sensation, corresponding to our Marāthi शिवशिवणें ; it is derived onomatopoetically.

दर्शितमशुभं—The original Prakrit विआरेण can be rendered in the *chhāyā* either by विकारेण (which is better) or by विषारेण (विषार *m.* a poisonous snake). The whole is rendered in Sanskrit also as दंशितमशुभं विषारेण–The serpent has ominously bitten him, *i. e.* the bite will prove fatal. **अपुत्रायाः**—as she will be, as I think I, her only son, will now die. **योगक्षेमं वह**—Look to her well-being ; see that she does not fare badly in food, clothes &c. **योगक्षेम**—See com. for dissolution. The word *lit.* means 'the securing (क्षेम) of what is obtained (योग),' hence general welfare, prosperity, livelihood. It is generally (but erroneously) explained as a Samāhāradvmadva comp.; *cf.* तेषां नित्याभियुक्तानां योगक्षेमं वहाम्यहम्। Bg. IX. 22.

P. 124. **चिकित्सते**—will treat you ; the present is used for immediate future. The reading चिकित्सिष्यति found in some editions is grammatically wrong, as it ought to Ā'tm. (चिकित्सिष्येत). Mark how cleverly the Vid. is playing his part so as to excite the pity of the Queen. **आज्ञापितो ध्रुवसिद्धिर्विज्ञापयति**—is a good illustration of the uses of the verbs आज्ञापय् and विज्ञापय् ; see note *supra* on विज्ञाप्यतां देवी (p. 12). **इहैवानीयतां** &c.-It was pre-arranged that Jaya. should bring such a message from Dhruvasiddhi. To give effect to the plan, Vidū.'s removal from the Queen's presence was absolutely necessary. For it was he who was to go with the ring to Mādhavikā and free the prisoners. Whether Dhruvasiddhi was really sent for is not clear from the context. Very probably he was not. Jayasenā, it appears, only pretended to go to him (as previously instructed) and kept on bringing messages as if from him. The King says वर्षवरपरिगृहीतं &c. simply to delude the Queen. When he said that, the eunuchs were not there ; and when the Vid. goes out, he does so with the प्रतीहारी only. The Vid., as soon as he was out of the Queen's sight, must have waited for Jaya. outside and she must have taken the ring to him.

वर्षवरपरिगृहीतं—surrounded (*i. e.* supported from all sides) by वर्षवरs or eunuchs (who were formerly generally employed as servants in women's apartments of the palace). Bhānuji Dikshit quotes a verse which describes them as ये त्वल्पसत्त्वाः प्रथमाः (?) क्लीबाश्च स्त्रीस्वभाविनः। जात्या न दुष्टाः कार्येषु ते वै वर्षवराः स्मृताः॥ **तपस्वी**–*Cf.* तपस्विनी p. 114 above. **ध्रुवसिद्धेः यथार्थनाम्नः**—of Dhruvasiddhi, whose name is truly significiant. ध्रुवसिद्धिः (ध्रुवा सिद्धिर्यस्य) literally means 'one who invariably and certainly cures'. For the idea *cf.* परंतपो नाम यथार्थनामा। Ragh VI. 21. तथैव सोऽभूदन्वर्थो राजा प्रकृतिरञ्जनात्। *bid.* IV. 12. यस्यार्थयुक्तं गिरिराजशब्दं कुर्वन्ति बालव्यजनैश्चमर्यः। Kum. I. 13; यस्मिन्नीश्वर इत्यनन्यविषयः शब्दो यथार्थाक्षरः। Vik. I. 1—examples which show how Kālidāsa was fond of this particular kind of word-analysis.

उदकुम्भविधाने—in performing the rite known as *Udakumbha.* उदकुम्भ *m. lit.* means a jar of water ; उदकस्य कुम्भः उदककुम्भः or उदकुम्भः, the क being optionally dropped by 'एकहलादौ पूरयितव्येऽन्यतरस्याम्' Pān. VI. 3. 59; see H. S. G. § 288 (b). **कल्पयितव्यम्**—it is necessary to provide or procure; get ready. सर्पमुद्रा संजाता अस्येति सर्पमुद्रितम्, by the affix इतच् added to words of the तारकादि class. The details of the rite for curing a snake-bite by using charmed water from a specially enchanted water-jar will be found in the passage quoted from the *Bhairavatantra* in the com.; Dhruvasiddhi's process seems, however, not to have been that of the *Nāgamudrā,* but rather that of the *Rasaratnāvali* (also quoted in the com.). We should, therefore, adopt the reading उदकुम्भविधानेन &c. and the meaning will be—something bearing a serpent's image should be duly encharmed (into an antidote). For according to the latter quotation the bitten part is to be sprinkled over with water by means of the enchanted serpent's figure.

P. 126. **कर्मसिद्धौ**—There is a play on कर्म—(1) when the rite is finished; (2) when Māla. is freed; see com.; समाप्तकृत्य p. 128. **प्रतिपत्तिमानय**—प्रतिपत्ति- *f.* news, intelligence. प्रतिपत्तिः पदप्राप्तौ प्रवृत्तौ गौरवेऽपि च। इति विश्वः। *Cf.* कियच्चिरेणार्यपुत्रः प्रतिपत्तिं दास्यति। Śāk. VI. The word has already occurred on p. 104 in the sense of 'a remedy.' **आचष्टे**—*i. e.* by its being unperturbed.

निर्विषः गौतमः—Gau. is free from the effect of the poison (by this time). Mr. Paṇḍit in his notes on this passage suggests that the poet puts this speech into the mouth of the Parivrājikā because he wishes to prevent the Queen suspecting her to be a party to the Vidūṣaka's plot. As we have pointed out above, there is not the least evidence for this suggestion, the possibility of which is negatived by Mr. Paṇḍit himself when he says the speech may have been "made" consistently with a belief that the bite is genuine. मुहूर्तेन—in a little while. It does not signify in such cases the definite period it generally expresses; *cf.* हला शकुन्तले अत्रैव तावन्मुहूर्तं तिष्ठ। Śāk. I. सप्तपर्णवेदिकायां मुहूर्तमुपविश्य *ibid.*; लतावलये मुहूर्तं स्थास्यामि *ibid.* III.

वचनीयात्—from the blame likely to be attached to me, since it was *on my account* that he had gone to pluck the flowers where he was bitten; *cf.* हा धिक् हा धिक्। अहमेव ब्राह्मणस्य जीवितसंशयनिमित्तं जातास्मि। *supra* p. 120. एष पुनः—this is also a sham message, being a contrivance meant to give the king an opportunity to leave the Queen without rousing her suspicion, and to enable him to go to visit Mālavikā. मन्त्रयितव्यम्—to be deliberated upon.

P. 128. शीतक्रिया—treatment with cool (*i. e.* cooling) remedies. प्रशस्ता—recommended, advisable, good. बालिकाः—*cf.* Eng. 'girls,' समाप्तकृत्यः—The "work" was the liberation of Mālavikā and Bakulāvalikā.

Verse 5. Construe :—

इष्टाधिगमनिमित्तं प्रयोगम् एकान्तसाधुम् मत्वा अपि सिद्धौ संदिग्धं कातरं चेतः आशङ्कते एव।

०काम्यः—*V. l.* काम्यं the desired object. प्रयोगं-the expedient, device, trick. एकान्तसाधुम्—infallibly effective; एकान्तं (*adv.*) or एकान्तेन (*instr.*) (invariably) साधुं leading to the result. साध्यं—*V. l.*-dissolve एकान्तं साध्यं the object यस्मात्. संदिग्धमेव सिद्धौ-still it is diffident as regards the success. ते मङ्गलकर्माणि—undertakings for your good; 'your auspicious business;' by the plural he refers to the success of the plan suggested by him, the liberation of the prisoners and the meeting arranged without a hitch in the Samudragṛha. मङ्गलकर्मन्—is a word generally used to denote ceremonies like marriage, thread-investiture &c.; but here it is used in the above sense. क्षुद्रा माधविका—क्षुद्रा-light-hearted, dull-headed. The King means that since she could be so easily tricked, she seems to be a dull-witted person, not to have suspected what on the face of it invited suspicion.

P. 130. अङ्गुलीयकमुद्रां—See p. 116 above. कथं विचारयति—When she actually saw the Queen's ring she could not hesitate, as her instructions stopped her at that point. मन्दस्यापि मे—dull-witted though I am; this he says humorously; really he was not so. तस्मिन्प्रत्युत्पन्ना मतिः—in replying to her question I found ready wit; प्रत्युत्पन्नमतिर्ज्ञेयस्तत्कालोत्पन्नधीर्नरः। इति हलायुधः। प्रत्युत्पन्न *lit.* 'existing at the moment' prompt, ready; *cf.* इदं तत्प्रत्युत्पन्नमति स्त्रैणमिति यदुच्यते Śāk. V. p. 131. दैवचिन्तकैः—(*lit.* those who make calculations about fate) astrologers. सोपसर्गं वो नक्षत्रम्—that the King's star is exercising a malignant influence (over his luck); *lit.* is bringing him some danger or calamity (उपसर्ग); for this meaning *cf.* प्रशमिताशेषोपसर्गाः प्रजाः। Rat. I. 10. सर्वबन्धनमोक्षः—Liberation of prisoners (which meant blessings from so many persons) was one of the ways to propitiate or counteract the influence of the evil star. इरावतीचित्तं रक्षन्त्या—As it was at Irāvatī's special request that Mālav. and Bakulāv. were imprisoned (says the Vidūṣaka to Mādhavikā), if the Queen were to appear (herself) to take the initiative in liberating them that would displease Irāvatī. Dhāriṇī, therefore, wishing to spare her feelings, did not send one of her own attendants, but sent me, so as to make it obvious to Irāvatī that it was not Dhāriṇī directly, but the King himself, who was ordering their release. For the phrase चित्तं रक्षन् *cf.* *supra* p. 66 धारिण्याश्चित्तं रक्षन्‌ &c.

Verse 6. Construe :—

सुहृदाम् अर्थदर्शनं बुद्धिगुणेन एव न हि, सूक्ष्मः कार्यसिद्धिपथः स्नेहेन अपि उपलभ्यते।

न हि etc.—The King means that although the Vidūṣaka was sharp-witted, it was more his love for him that spurred his wits. सुहृदां—is कर्तरी षष्ठी; अर्थदर्शनम्—*i. e.* friends find out a way to obtain the thing desired by their friend. सूक्ष्मः—very subtle *i. e.* only to be discerned by one taking deep interest in his friend; with the idea here compare : अतिस्नेहः खलु कार्यदर्शी। Vikr. II. p. 40. कार्यसिद्धिपथः—See note on श्रुतिपथ p. 112.

P. 132. **समुद्रगृह**—*n.* a summer-house built in an artificial lake (a *Madhyamapadalopi* comp.); or a pleasure-house surrounded by water-ejecting fountains on all sides. **प्रत्युद्गत**—come to meet; *cf.* प्रत्युद्गता पार्थिवधर्मपत्न्या। Ragh. II. 20. **संभावयामि**—honour her (by paying a visit). **अवचय**—*m.* 'collection'. The use of this word here is a grammatical irregularity according to Pāṇini. By the Sūtra हस्तादाने चेरस्तेये। (III. 3.40) the root चि takes the affix घञ् causing *Vṛddhi* of the radical vowel when the sense is 'taking with the hand' (except in the case of stealing); so we should have अवचाय:; अवचय: must, therefore, be taken as a deviation from Pāṇini. Kālidāsa has similarly used अवचय in Śāk. IV. (कुसुमावचयं नाटयन्त्यौ सख्यौ।) Rāghavabhaṭṭa there defends the form by supposing that the flowers were not collected with the hand directly, but being out of reach were gathered by means of sticks; हस्तादाने इत्यनेन प्रत्यासत्तिरादेयस्य लक्ष्यते। वृक्षाग्रस्थानां फलानां यष्ट्या प्रचयं करोति; Sid.-Kau.; but even that weak defence will not hold here, as the word हस्त is distinctly used. **सख्यास्ते**—*i. e.* of Irāvatī. The wives of the King are thus spoken of with reference to the Vidū. **चन्द्रिका**—this was her name.

अहो etc.—Vidūṣaka does not forego this opportunity of punning upon the name चन्द्रिका, which also signifies 'Moonlight'. "Oh! Lovers as well as thieves have to avoid *Chandrikā*". Mr. Paṇḍit quotes from one of his MSS. a marginal note which says विटचोरतमश्चक्रपद्माद्याश्चन्द्रशत्रव:।

प्रणम भर्तारं—Bakulāv. is referring to the portrait of the King with the ladies of the harem, hung up above the door, or more probably painted on one of the walls of the pleasure-house; but she purposely uses vague words, so that she may joke a little when Mālav. would misunderstand her, as she was sure to do, as she always thought of the King. Her expectation is fulfilled and Mālavikā readily falls into the trap thus jestingly set by her friend. Some read after भर्तारं, 'य: पार्श्वत: पृष्ठतश्च दृश्यते' who is seen at the sides and behind *i. e.* is always present in thought. Tārānātha reads this after Māla.'s speech **नमस्ते**. प्रतिकृति-likeness, picture; *cf.* स्वहस्तलिखित तत्रभवत्या: शकुन्तलाया: प्रतिकृति। Śāk. VI. **सहर्षम्**—Because she thought that the King was near. **सविषादम्**—*i. e.* at his actual absence, as she immediately finds out. After this some read क भर्ता। and विप्रलभसे for विप्रलम्भयसि.

Verse 7. Construe:—

पुण्डरीकस्य सूर्योदये या सूर्यास्तमये च या (समवस्था) भवति सुवदनायाः वदनेन ते समवस्थे क्षणात् ऊढे।

P. 134. **या**—*Sc.* समवस्था. **समवस्था**—Kālidāsa generally uses this word for अवस्था or state, condition; *cf.* प्रियायाः समवस्थामनुस्मृत्य। *S'ak.* VI.; also *infra* Act V. The Puṇḍarīka blooms at sun-rise and fades away at sunset. Māla.'s lotus-like face too beamed with joy when she thought that the King was there, but it was darkened with dejection when she found that he was not there. **तदा संमुखस्थिता** &c.—This refers to their meeting in Act III. near the Aśoka tree. She says that then she could not look at the King, though bodily present before her, as much as she liked, owing to natural bashfulness; she had then to be content only with stolen glances. But now, even though it may be a picture, she could gaze at it without interruption and hence she is fully satisfied. **विभावितः**—contemplated, hence looked at carefully, seen with attention; *cf.* तामिन्दुसुन्दरमुखीं सुचिरं विभाव्य। Māl.-Mādh I. 18. To make the sense clear, supply यतः before मया; for I have seen the King with undivided attention. This passage also seems to have been much tampered with by copyists. The reading in the foot-note संभ्रमाद्दते &c. also gives a good sense. It means—Even to-day (though I looked leisurely at him) I found the King one with whose sight one can never be fully satisfied, just as I did when I gazed upon his beauty in the confusion of hurry on a former occasion. But the reading adopted in the text appears to make the nearest approach to the original as the following speach of the Vidū. seems to be partly derived from it. Bollensen (as quoted by Prof. Tawney) reads: तस्मिन्संभ्रमे स्थिता भर्तू रूपदर्शनेन न तथा वितृष्णास्मि यथाद्य मया भावितो वितृष्णदर्शनो भर्ता। which must mean—Being then in a confused state, I was not &c. as I am to-day, having seen the King to my full satisfaction. (अवितृष्णदर्शनः विगता तृष्णा यस्मात्तत् वितृष्णं, वितृष्णं दर्शनं यस्य तादृशः विभावितः। seen so as to have all further desire to see him gone *i.e.* to full satisfaction). Prof. Tawney renders this as—the King has had a more satisfactory look at myself than I have had at his picture owing to my excitement. But this is not supported by the context.

चित्रे यथा: दृष्ट: etc.—True to his instinct Vid. wants to be a little jocular with the King and purposely distorting Māla.'s meaning says—she did not think you looked so handsome when seen personally as your picture did, *i. e.* she thinks that your picture is better-looking than your own personal form. Bollensen reads: अत्रभवती त्वया यथा दृष्टा तथा न दृष्टो भवान्। which Prof. Tawney explains as—'you had a much better look at her than she has had at you'. **सुधेदानीं**—He means:—As the jewels, however valuable they may be, are of no use to the casket, since they cannot raise its value, so your good look are of no use to you as you have failed to create a good impression on your beloved; (as the poet says elsewhere प्रियेषु सौभाग्यफला हि चारुता। (Kum. V. I). **रत्नभाण्ड**—*Cf.* our note on सारभाण्ड p. 114 **कुतूहलवान्**—the King now explains how Mālavikā must have come to say what she did. Although women possess curiosity, they are naturally very bashful; and hence, when the lover is actually before them, they are unable to look at his form and mark his features closely. **शालीन:**—शालां (लक्षणया शालाप्रवेशं) अर्हतीति। *Lit.* one fit to enter the inner apartment, hence, modest; शाला + ईन (खञ्) by Pāṇ. V. 2. 20.

Verse 8. Construe :—

(आयतलोचनाः) तत्पूर्वसमागमानां (प्रियाणां) रूपं कात्स्न्र्येन निर्वर्णयितुम् इच्छन्ति च आयतलोचनानां विलोचनानि प्रियेषु समग्रपातीनि न च।

कात्स्न्र्येन etc.—निर्वर्णयितुं to observe attentively; or mark closely; gaze upon. **रूपं**—*Scil.* प्रियाणां. **तत्पूर्वसमागमानां**—gives the reason or हेतु of न समग्रपातीनि. The use of च-च in two consecutive sentences signifies 'though-yet'; *cf.* न सुलभा सकलेन्दुमुखी च सा किमपि चेदमनङ्गविचेष्टितम्। Vik. II. 9. कात्स्न्र्य is an abstract noun meaning 'completeness, entirely' fr. कृत्स्न. According to a Calcutta commentator, the collection of so many harsh and conjunct consonants in the first pāda—**कात्स्न्र्येन निर्वर्णयितुं** etc. constitutes a poetical blemish known as दुःश्रवत्व or श्रुतिकटुत्व. **तत्पूर्वसमागमानाम्**—may also be explained as स पूर्वः (first) समागमः येषां तेषाम्। (*viz.* प्रियाणां, to be supplied from प्रियेषु in the third line) and construed with रूपं in the first line. But this is not a good way ; as in this case there is nothing left to account for the असमग्रपातित्व of the eyes. तत्पूर्वं —that first, that which has occurred for the first time *i. e.* 'occurring then for the first time'; *cf.* अकारि तत्पूर्वनिबद्धया तया सरागमस्या रशनागुणास्पदम्। Kum. V. 10; तत्पूर्वपाणिग्रहणानुरूपम् *ibid.* VII, 30; Ragh. II. 42; XIV. 38, etc. In the reading तत्पूर्वसमागतानां, तत्पूर्वं will have to be taken adverbially. आयतलोचनानां— *i. e.* of women (in whose case large eyes are a mark of beauty). This epithet is meant to give an antithesis with न समग्रपातीनि समग्रपातिन्-समग्रं यथा तथा पतन्तीति तानि.

P. 136. स्निग्धा दृष्टिः—affectionate gaze; *cf.* ननु सः राजर्षिरस्य स्निग्धदृष्ट्या सूचिताभिलाषः। Śāk. III. निध्यायते—is looked at with attention; *cf.* निध्यायन्ती p. 6 *supra*; विद्याधरदारिका तेन निध्यातेति कुपितोर्वशी। Vik. IV. p. 93. सर्वं देवीजनमुज्झित्वा leaving (उज्झ् 6th conj. to abandon, leave) all his other queens—as painted there. It appears that although other queens were drawn there, the King was painted as looking at Irāvatī to the exclusion of the rest. परमार्थतो गृहीत्वा—taking him to be real, *i. e.* present in person and steadfastly gazing upon Irāvatī which as a painted figure he appeared to do; *cf.* परमार्थेन न गृह्यतां वचः। Śāk. II. 18. क्रीडिष्यामि तावदेतया—*Cf.* भवतु क्रीडिष्यामि तावदेतया। Vik. III. p. 75. वल्लभा—*Cf.* किं न्ववलोकितो वल्लभजनः *supra* p. 114. आत्मानमायास०—She means-I cannot entertain hopes of securing his love, since it already appears to have been given to Irāvatī. सासूयं—in jealous indignation.

सखे पश्य—the addition of the words ते सख्या मुखं makes the sentence rather prosaic; the King admires her gesture in सासूयपरावर्तन. Mālavikā had been learning, among other things, the art of gesticulation (अभिनय). Her turning away her face in indignation was done with such a grace and naturalness that (says the King) it seemed she was as if exhibiting the instructions she had learnt from the teacher in *abhinaya*. The art of *abhinaya* was such a familiar thing with our poet that he repeatedly refers to it even outside his plays ; *cf.* अभिनयान्परिचेतुमिवोद्यता मलयमारुतकम्पितपल्लवा। अमदयत्सहकारलता मनः सकलिका कलिकामजितामपि॥ Ragh. IX. 32; लतां कौन्दीं च नर्तयन्। Vik. II. 4.

Verse 9. Construe :—

भ्रूभङ्गभिन्नतिलकं स्फुरिताधरोष्ठम् आननं सासूयम् इतः परिवर्तयन्त्या अनया कान्तापराधकुपितेषु ललिताभिनयस्य विनेतुः शिक्षा संदर्शिता इव।

भ्रूभङ्ग° and स्फुरिता°—may be taken adverbially (or as adj. to आननम्, as done in the com.); so as to cause the splitting of the *tilaka* mark (see notes on III. 5), and to make the lower lip throb'. कान्तापराधकुपितेषु—कुपित—used as an abs. noun in the sense of कोप; 'when they have to show anger with their lovers commit a fault'. विनेतुः is a subjective genetive. For a similar idea differently expressed, compare Duṣyanta's description of Śakuntalā यतो यतः षट्चरणोभिवर्तते ततस्ततः प्रेरितलोललोचना। विवर्तितभ्रूरियमद्य शिक्षते भयादकामापि हि दृष्टिविभ्रमम्। Śāk. I. *V. l.* between 20-21.

P. 138. अनुनयसज्जः—ready to propitiate her, as befits a lover. आर्यगौतमोऽपि &c.—Māla. does not like that the Vid. who should have had greater regard for Dhāriṇī should have connived at what she thinks is a breach of decorum on the King's part in showing partiality to Irāvatī. He should not have been in attendance there under the circumstances. यदि चिरं—if you think I can be angry for a long time (which, however I cannot), then, although my anger is by this time all gone, I will still bring it back for your sake.

Verse 10. Construe :—

(अयि) कुवलयनयने (मम) चित्रार्पितचेष्टया किम् एतत् मे कुप्यसि; ननु तव अयम् अहं साक्षात् अनन्यसाधारणः दासः।

कुप्यसि etc.—कुवलयनयने Voc. sing. कुवलय a blue lotus. चित्रार्पित— *cf.* चित्रार्पितारम्भ इवावतस्थे। Ragh II. 31. किमेतन्मे—Mr. Paṇdit reads किमेव मयि, where मयि is grammatically anomalous, मह्यं (dative) being required with the verb कुप्यसि; hence किमेवमयि should better be explained as किं-एवं-अयि, अयि being a particle of tender address. तव दासः—*cf.* न सेव्यः सेविता रहः। Śl. 12 *infra.* साक्षात्—in person (contrasting with चित्रार्पित).

कथं—Māla. was ashamed to discover that all along she, being overpowered by emotion, had been upbraiding the King in the picture. मदनकातर्यं—a nervous reserve caused by Love. What is meant is that the King stands hesitating and undecided, without advancing towards Mālavikā. उदासीन इव-as though indifferent, not sufficiently caring for Mālavikā. अविश्वसनीयत्वात्—the King, not wishing to betray his weakness, passes off the matter by setting forth this plea. Why he feels diffident and uncertain he explains in the next śloka. अयं—

this, of this sort, so much. This is also read as—मा तावत् अत्रभवत्यां तवाविश्वासः; अत्रभवती तवाविश्वसनीया।

Verse 11. Construe :—

सखे, तव सखी (मे) नयनयोः पथि स्वप्ने स्थित्वा क्षणात् तिरोभवति, बाह्वोः मध्यं गता अपि सहसा सरति, एवं समागममायया मनसिजरुजा क्लिष्टस्य मे मनः इमां प्रति कथम् इव विश्रब्धं स्यात्।

P. 140. स्वप्ने—स्थित्वा *V. l.* (स्थित्वा स्थित्वा) will mean having repeatedly stood &c.; but स्वप्ने is better and necessary as shown by Māla.'s remark further on स्वप्नसमागमोऽपि। &c. सखी तव —*i. e.* Mālavikā. अबला सती—*v. l.* has no other propriety than the antithesis it gives with सहसा. Again अबला is रूढ for a grown-up woman (स्त्री योषिदबला योषा &c. Ak.) while Māla. is a कन्या. मनसिजरुजा—by the disease of love. समागममायया—by means of the delusion of a union. The construction is—मनसिजरुजा समागममायया एवं क्लिष्टस्य (p. p. p. of क्लिश् 9th conj.) मे &c.; the instr. in ०रुजा is कर्तरि (showing the agent of paining) and that in ०मायया is करणे (showing the means of paining).

इदानीं तावत्—now, at least (even if you have not done it before). आत्मा विश्वसनीयः क्रियताम्—*i. e.* by showing that you really and truly love him, and are not playing with his affection. स्वप्नसमागमोऽपि भर्तुः—union with him even in dreams. The King cleverly expressed his love towards Mālavikā by saying that he used to see her vision in dreams. But Mālavikā's expression of her love towards him is done with greater skill. The king's dreaming showed that he used to get some sleep in spite of his love-torment; but Mālavikā declares that love's pangs tormented her so much that she got no sleep at all, even to be enabled to dream about him.

Verse 12. Construe :—

उत्तरेण किम् ? मया तव सख्यै पञ्चबाणाग्निसाक्षिकम् आत्मा एव दत्तः रहः सेविता सेव्यः न।

उत्तरेण, etc.—The King means—the best reply is this, that I have already offered myself to her. पञ्चबाणाग्निसाक्षिकं—It is essential at a marriage-ceremoney that the bridegroom should accept the hand of the bride in the presence of the sacred fire which is, therefore, said to 'witness' it. *Cf.* वधूं द्विजः प्राह तवैष वत्से वह्निर्विवाहं प्रति कर्मसाक्षी। Kum. VII. 83. The fire here is

21

that of love, the idea is common enough. Cupid is called पञ्चबाण or the *five arrowed God*, the arrows being enumerated as अरविन्दमशोकं च चूतं च नवमल्लिका। नीलोत्पलं च पञ्चैते पञ्चबाणस्य सायकाः ॥ न सेव्यः सेविता—that (आत्मा) is given by me, not as a master *to be served* by her, but rather as a servant *serving her* in private.

P. 142. बकुलावलिके, etc.—This is a contrivance of the poet to clear the stage so that the lovers may be left alone in each other's company; compare a similar device in the third Act of the Śāk. where Priyaṃvadā says—अनसूये एष इतोदत्तदृष्टिः उत्सुको मृगपोतकः मातरमन्विष्यति। एहि संयोजयाव एनम्। p. 80. पल्लवानि—the word is *masc.* or *neuter.* लङ्घयति-*lit.* 'attacking' (*cf.* एषा खलु केसरिणी त्वां लङ्घयति Śāk. VII.). Here it means 'eating, browsing.' अस्मिन् रक्षणक्षणे—at this time when we badly want protection, *i. e.* when you should be on the look-out whether Irāvatī or such intruders are in sight. एवमपि गौतमः etc.—He means that he knows it very well, and would have certainly done it untold. We shall soon see how cleverly the Vidūṣaka performed this part of his duty. *Cf.* a similar remark *supra* नेदमावयोरुपदेश्यं p. 42. अप्रकाशे—'Not in light,'—*i. e.* in some corner in the dark. सुखस्पर्शता—pleasant, *i. e.* cool, smooth to the touch. शिलाविशेषस्य—for विशेष at the end of a comp., *cf.* पात्रविशेष at I. 6. and our note *ad loc.* निद्रायते—goes to sleep. This is how he kept his word. निद्राय् is a denominative from निद्रा.

Verse 13. Construe:—

(हे) सुन्दरि, चिरात् प्रभृति तव प्रणयोन्मुखे (मयि) संगमसाध्वसं विसृज सहकारतां गते मयि त्वम् अतिमुक्तलताचरितं परिगृहाण।

संगमसाध्वसं—the fear entertained at being united with me (for the first time). The second line may also be taken with the first supplying मयि after (मयि विषये). प्रणयोन्मुखे—towards me who have been long desirous of your affection. त्वं अतिमुक्तलता०—As the *atimukta* creeper coils itself closely round the *sahakāra* tree, so you too should embrace me closely. अतिमुक्तलता is known in Marāṭhi by the name of कुसरी or कस्तूरी मोगरा. Its चरितं is the coiling itself by the plant round (or grasping with its tendrils) the mango-tree on which it is propped up. The अतिमुक्त creeper is so called because in brilliancy of whiteness its flowers excel pearls (अतिक्रान्तो मुक्तां शौक्ल्यात्). Compare for a similar idea : क्व इदानीं सहकारमन्तरेण अतिमुक्तलतां पल्लवितां सहते। Śāk. III. "The beauty and fragrance of the flowers of this creeper give them a title to all the praises which Kālidāsa.... bestows on them. It is a gigantic and luxurious climber; but when it meets with nothing to grasp, it assumes the form of a sturdy tree, the highest branches of which display, however, in the air, their natural flexibility and inclination to climb."—Sir W. Jones as quoted by M.-W.

P. 144. सोपालम्भम्—*Adv.* comp. with an implied censure on his conduct (उपालम्भ *m.* taunt, reproach). यो न बिभेति &c. She means—Although you ask me not to be afraid of the Queen, I know what sort of courage you yourself displayed before her—referring to the nervousness shown by the King in Act III. p. 104—सर्वे इरावतीं दृष्ट्वा संभ्रान्ताः। राजा (अपवार्य) &c दृष्टसामर्थ्यः—I have seen your strength (of mind), implying, the *want* of it. समवस्थः—*v. l.* I have seen my lord in the same state as myself—is not so sarcastic.

Verse 14. Construe :—

(हे) बिम्बोष्ठि, दाक्षिण्यं नाम बैम्बिकानां कुलव्रतम्, तत् (हे) दीर्घाक्षि, ये मे प्राणाः ते त्वदाशानिबन्धनाः।

दाक्षिण्यं—Polite behaviour; behaving in a manner to please all : *cf.* Ragh. I. 32. — नाम *ind.* 'As is well known.' बैम्बिकानां—'of the descendants of Bimbaka.' Bimbaka, according to Mr. Paṇdit, who gives no authority for this, was one of the forefathers of Agnimitra. The sense given in Apte's Dic. *viz.* 'a gallant,' seems to be a guess. Even if we adopt that sense (the word being somehow made to mean that) the poet will have to be understood as making a general statement with regard to every gallant; it cannot be regarded as his कुलव्रतं. Again, the King is not expected to drag himself to the level of ordinary gallants. The *v.l.* नायकानां also appears to be an emendation of some one who did not understand his text. कुलव्रत—'a family vow,' a custom descending from father to son through many generations, and observed by all members of the family; hence, what is binding on every one; *cf.* मुनिवनतरुच्छायां देव्या तया सह शिश्रिये गलितवयसामिक्ष्वाकूणामिदं हि

कुलव्रतम् ॥ Ragh. III. 70. The King means to say–As a man of the Bimbaka family I am bound to act as I did, before Irāvatī; it was merely an act of courtesy due to her. तत्— still, however (तथापि). दीर्घाक्षि—*cf.* आयतलोचनानि *supra* IV. 8; अत्यायतं नयनयोः III 7. *etc.* त्वदाशानिबन्धनाः—depending (for their continued existence) on the hope of getting you. *Cf.* प्रेमाबन्धविवर्धिताधिकरसा प्रीतिस्तु या सा त्वयि। Rat. III. 18.

मा० नाट्येन परिहरति—observe the delicate handling of a love-scene by the poet; compare in the Śāk. राजा—अपरिक्ष० इति मुखमस्याः समुन्नमयितुमिच्छति। शकुन्तला परिहरति नाट्येन। (p. 82). मदनविषयव्यापारः—the actions or gestures connected with Love. रमणीयः खलुः—this is explained in the next Śl.

Verse 15. Construe :—

(एषा) कम्पवती रशनाव्यापारलोलाङ्गुलिं (मम) हस्तं रुणद्धि, बलात् आलिङ्ग्यमाना स्वौ हस्तौ स्तनावरणतां नयति, पक्ष्मलचक्षुः आननं पातुम् उन्नमयतः (मे) आननं साचीकरोति व्याजेन अपि मे अभिलाषपूरणसुखं निर्वर्तयति एव।

रशनाव्यापार—the work of untying the knot of the girdle-band. पातुं उन्नमयतः, *sc.* मे—as I try to raise (her face) to kiss. The verb पा (to drink) is often used with words like मुख, वदन, poetically in the sense of 'kissing'. पक्ष्मलचक्षुः—the eyes whereof have hairy (*i. e.* beautiful) eyelashes, which is considered a mark of beauty. *Cf.* मुखमंसविवर्ति पक्ष्मलाक्ष्याः कथमप्युन्नमितं न चुम्बितं तु। Śāk. III, 23. The word पक्ष्मल (*adj.* is formed by adding the affix ल (लच्) to पक्ष्मन्; which is one of the words of the सिध्मादि class, by 'सिध्मादिभ्यश्च Pān. V. 2. 97. साचीकरोति—turns aside; न साचि (an indec; according to some *f.*; see Mukuṭa on Ak.) असाचि; असाचि साचि संपद्यमानं करोति साचीकरोति; *cf.* साचीकृतचारुवक्त्रः। Ragh. VI. 14. व्याजेनापि—even by the show (of refusing to grant my request). He means that she does it in such a charming way that I feel as good as I had obtained my desire, निर्वर्तयति—accomplishes, brings about; *cf.* चरणालंकारं निर्वर्तयति। *supra* P. 88.

P. 146. चन्द्रिकया—See p. 132. Chandrikā it seems lingered there collecting flowers long enough to see the Vid. sleeping on the stone-slab while returning, and reported the matter to Nipunikā, who in her turn reported it to Irāvatī. अलिन्द *m.* a raised seat or dais (Mar. ओटा) in front of a house. With the speech compare that of the Queen in the Vikr.—हञ्जे निपुणिके सत्यं त्वया भणितमिदं लतागृहं प्रविशन्नार्यमाणवकसहाय आर्यपुत्रो दृष्ट इति। Act. II. p. 56. संशयान्मुक्त—referring to the dangerous snake-bite. प्रष्टुं च—the च shows that she was going to say something in addition. Probably it was—"and to find out what the fellow is doing there at this time." Irāvatī was somewhat surprised to hear that the Vidūṣaka was asleep in such an unusual place all alone. She suspects that some intrigue must have been afoot and wishes to go there. But she stops in the middle of her speech as she probably does not wish to state her suspicions so early, before she got some more light on the affair. सावशेषमिव etc.—Nipuṇikā finding that her mistress paused after च, remarks to her that the sentence appeared to be incomplete. Irāvatī proceeds to complete it not exactly as she had intended, but with a sarcastic joke. चित्रगतं &c.—"and to propitiate the *picture* of the King." (It is the same picture which was seen by Mālavikā and Bakulāv. on the wall of the pleasure-house). Nipuṇikā is surprised to hear that the *picture* of the King, and not the King himself, is to be approached, and Irāvatī gives her the reason, to complete the sarcasm, thus: "Now there is no difference, to my mind, between the King in person and his picture; for, as he has transferred his affections from me to another, he has no heart so far as I am concerned, and the inanimate picture can well take his place. It thus does not matter whom I go to propitiate,—since neither will listen to me. I shall do it just to quiet my conscience." It seems that Nipuṇikā did not fully understand her mistress, otherwise she would have said something more than a mere इत इतो भट्टिनी. The reading adopted by Mr. Raddiśāstri is यादृशश्चित्रगतो भर्ता न तादृशः एव। अन्यसंक्रान्तहृदय आर्यपुत्रः। But in this एव has no force. Again, what is the meaning of तादृशः? The Śāstrī says, न तादृशः वस्तुतस्तु तथा न। This will mean 'Although the King is depicted in the picture as loving me, really he is not such; *i. e.* he only pretends to love me'. Probably the Śāstrī means न तादृशः अधुना मयि वर्तमानः। But then the clause अन्यसं॰ would hang loose. So to avoid this difficulty it will be better to read the two parts together as one sentence, omitting एव; यादृश...अन्यसंक्रान्त॰; but in this case either भर्ता or आर्यपुत्रः becomes redundant and must be dropped; then Irāvatī may be taken to mean—I like the picture better than the King in person; for there he is depicted as devoted to me; and so I shall propitiate him as drawn in the picture. But then the word केवलं in the next sentence goes against this. Again our reading is more sarcastic and better suited to the resentful character of Irāvatī. उपचारातिक्रमं—This refers to the treatment of the King (at the end of Act III) by Irāvatī.

P. 148. चेटी—A message comes to Irāvatī from Dhāriṇī. Dhāriṇī, it will be remembered, had imprisoned Mālavikā and Bākulā. at the special request of Irāvatī and not because she herself had any grudge against them. After a suitable interval, she now wishes to set them free, saying that at that stage of her life (that is how we must interpret it, otherwise एष काल: becomes meaningless) it is hardly proper for her to be jealous. This is borne out by the events in the fifth Act; see where the Queen asks the Parivrājikā to decorate Mālavikā in the best possible way. It was merely out of deference to Irāvatī that the imprisonment was ordered. If now Irāvatī would have no objection (यद्यनुमन्यसे), then only Dhārinī would like to set the two girls at liberty, and so please the King (आर्यपुत्रस्य प्रियं कर्तुं) of whose partiality for the girls she was already aware. She thus flatters Irāvatī. The other reading *viz* आर्यपुत्रमपि तव कृते विज्ञापयामि। is not satisfactory. It means—'I will request the king for your sake', *i. e.* to favour you. But this is meaningless; for the King was ready (though ostensibly) for reconciliation with Irāvatī and the latter did not stand in need of any intercession by Dhāriṇī on her behalf. It was Irāvatī who had refused to be reconciled.

नागरिके etc.—But Irāvatī is a young lady whose anger has not yet cooled down and this message does not improve her temper. But of course Dhāriṇī had the power and Irāvatī could do nothing if Dhāriṇī wished to do as intimated. The latter, therefore, sends a courteous reply apparently giving her consent, but in a tone which is full of latent resentment. का वयं—How can we, I or any one else, command the all-powerful Queen to do this or that? कस्य वान्यस्य—She means—We all live by your grace. You can, therefore, do what you like. विपणिगत इव बली०—the point of comparison is that both are corpulent, being well fed, and can enjoy sleep even in an open place without the least concern. विपणि *f.* a market place; *cf.* पूराबमासे विपणीस्थपण्या। Ragh. XVI. 41; विपणन्ते अत्रेति विपणिः (where people buy, sell, and exchange), from वि+पण 1st conj. Ātm. to transact business; affix इ (इन्). निद्रायते—see p. 142 above.

"The bull here referred to is a Vasu or पोळ who is sacred, being let loose as a part of funeral obsequies. Such a bull has the fullest liberty to go anywhere he pleases, and being sacred no one will tie him. He lives on grain which all consider it good charity to supply to him, and he also helps himself to the grain etc. exposed for sale in shops, and no one considers it fit to take any serious notice of the matter. He is usually extremely well-fed and becomes very fat, and squats quietly near some shop *and dozes away without any fear of being disturbed.* ....The people willingly put up with him. It does not seem that much change has come over the institution of these Vasus since the days of Kālidāsa"—S. P. Paṇḍit.

अत्याहितं—Something that greatly alarms; a great evil; as an exclamation we may translate it as 'Oh! alas! न खलु—can it be that part of the poison still remained (and that he may be dead, or is about to die)?

P. 150. प्रसन्न॰—his complexion is bright, *i. e.* not haggard like that of a corpse. अपि च—And, the additional reason why we need not suspect anything untoward is that, &c. उत्स्वप्नायते—talks in his sleep. उत्स्वप्नाय् (Ātm.) is a denominative from उत्स्वप्न (adj.) meaning 'talking in one's sleep' (उत्पन्नः स्वप्नः स्वप्नप्रलापः यस्य स उत्स्वप्नः । स इवाचरति उत्स्वप्नायते।) कास्य आत्मनीनः—whose devoted partisan can he be called? *i. e.* no one's (न कस्यापि). आत्मनीन *adj.* devoted to one's self; (आत्मने हितः) from आत्मन्+affix ख, by "आत्माध्वानौ खे' Pāṇ. VI. 4. 169. हताशः—wretched; see note at p. 94. कितव —a rogue, a rascal; *cf.* कथमनेन कितवेन विप्रलब्धास्मि। Śāk. V. The reading कस्यैष आत्मनियोगसंपादने विश्वसनीयो हताशः means—Who can regard this wretch as a confidential friend for the execution of the business entrusted to him? But this remark will be in favour of the King whose secret he was betraying by his talking in the dream and so is not fit in the mouth of Nipuṇikā. सर्वकालं—always. इत एव—from us, *i. e.* Irāvatī and the other queens. We give him sweetmeats and still he proves ungrateful (कृतघ्नः *infra*) to us. स्वस्तिवाचनमोदकैः:—sweetmeats given away as presents on the occasion of *svastivācana* ceremonies; (sometimes the gifts themselves are called स्वस्तिवाचनस, as in Vikr. II. p. 80—ईदृशः स्वस्तिवाचनवानुपरोधो बहुशो भवतु।) स्वस्ति वाच्यते अनेन that by which one (*i. e.* a Brāhmaṇa) is made to utter a blessing, अन (ल्युट्) being added करणे; or स्वस्ति इत्यस्य वाचनं यस्मिन्. The Svastivācana is a particular religious rite preparatory to any solemn observance, performed by sprinkling water on the heads of the Yajamāna and other persons and invoking blessings (स्वस्ति) on them with the repetition of certain *Mantras* &c. कुक्षि—belly. इरावतीमति॰—The Vid. pauses a little in his sleep after uttering the words भवति मालविके and then complete his sentence by adding these words.

एतदत्याहितम्—'This is the अत्याहित you were afraid of', referring to Irāvatī's remark just before (p. 148). Said by Nipuṇikā sarcastically. भुजङ्गभीरुक—The Vidūṣaka's fear of snakes is so deep-rooted that his comparisons also have reference to them; *cf.* किं न्वेतद्भुजंगनिर्मोकमिव संमुखेऽस्माकं निपतितम्। Vik. II. ब्रह्मबन्धु—See note on this word at p. 102. भाययिष्यामि—I will frighten. The *causal* of भी 3rd conj. has three forms भाययति, भाययते and भीषयते. The Ātm. forms are used only when the agent of the causal verb is the cause of fear (मुण्डो भाययते, भीषयते; but कुञ्चिकया भाययति); hence the reading भीषयिष्यामि found in some editions is gramatically faulty.

अर्हति उपद्रवस्य—deserves to be troubled; Irāvatī says this in a revengeful spirit. The use of the genitive with अर्ह् should be noted as being unusual. The reading एषोऽर्हति कि॰ सर्पदंशस्य though better according with the revengeful spirit of women is not justified by the context. Besides Irā. would not go the length of wishing that even when incensed. She merely wanted to see him frightened and to enjoy the fun. कृतघ्नः—because, while he feeds on *my* food, he wishes that my rival should eclipse me. अविधा—*Cf.* p. 60 above where the exclamation has occurred. सर्पः—दर्वीकर. *v. l.* also means a snake (दर्वीं फणं करोतीति) भर्तः—shows the loving anxiety of Mālavikā for her now accepted lover.

P. 152. हा धिक्—she says this in anger and sorrow as she sees the King followed by Mālavikā, and, her worst suspicions are realized. सप्रहासम्—laughing loudly (when he discovers that he was frightened for nothing). फलितम्—I thought that I got the (*viz.* being *really* bitten). He is referring to the notion universally believed in by the Hindus, that if a person falsely pretends some evil as having befallen him, the gods visit him with its reality in retribution.

पटाक्षेपेण—पटस्य आक्षेपेण 'tossing the curtain aside', showing the mode of entrance when a person is in great hurry or confusion. Sir Monier-Williams who takes पट + अ (not) क्षेप, thus obtains the strange meaning of *not* tossing etc., and then suggests that it may be the incorrect form for पटीक्षेपेण ; but all this is quite unnecessary. कुटिलगतिः—having the zig-zag motion of a snake ; *cf.* जिह्मग and भुजङ्ग.

निर्विघ्नमनोरथः—(Bahu. comp.) wherein all your desires have been fulfilled without any obstacle or interruption. दिवासंकेतः—An appointment to meet in a certain place by day. मिथुनस्य—referring to Malavikā and the King. From her original vague suspicions and the ravings of the Vidūṣaka about Mālavikā excelling Irāvatī, followed by the presence of the King with Mālavikā in such a place as the Samudragṛha, Irāvatī concludes that the two lovers had met there by special previous appointment. दूत्याधिकारविषया—With regard to the duties of your ambassadorship (or your office as a go-between). दूत्य is not different in meaning from दौत्य which occurs on p. 92. Irāvatī taunts Bakulā, also, because from what was heard in Act III., she thinks that the present meeting must have been planned and brought about by Bakulāvalikā.

किं न खलु etc.—"Does Indra forget (to rain on) the earth because the frogs (दर्दुर *m.*) may be croaking ?" देवः—Indra, the rain-god. Indra stands for the King, the Earth for Irāvatī, and the frogs for such comparatively insignificant creatures as Māla. and Bakulā. Bakulā. wishes to please Irāvatī by comparing her to the Earth; she means, that whatever they two might have said to the King, that could not have influenced him any more than the croaking of the frogs could influence the rain-god, and the King's love for Irāvatī was bound to continue unabated as before. The frogs croak before and during the monsoons, but the cloud does not therefore the less pour down rain on the Earth. This passage has suffered much in the matter of reading; we have adopted Mr. Paṇdit's as yielding the most natural sense. *V.l.* वर्षितुं विरमति would mean the same, but विरम् used with the infinitive is a strange idiom. *V. l.* पृथिवीं वर्षितुं स्मरति has to be explained by taking दर्दुराः to refer to Bakulāv. and पृथिवीं to Mālavikā. "Does Indra remember to send showers to the earth because the frogs croak? no; he does it of his own accord; so will the king love Māla., because I speak in her favour? no; he loves her of his own accord". But it is certain that Bakulāv. would not dare to call Mālavikā पृथिवी and talk of the King's love for her in the presence of Irāvatī, and hence this reading has to be rejected.

मा तावत्—don't say so (addressing Irāvatī and referring to her speech अपि निर्विघ्न॰ etc.) दर्शनमात्रेण—by your mere sight प्रणिपातलङ्घनं विस्मृतः—has forgotten (and forgiven) the fact that you did not accept his homage (see III. 23) at that time and he continues to love you. भवती पुनः etc.— But you are the irreconcilable lady that you were: *you* don't forget, as you ought, whatever fault the King might have committed. अद्यापि—even now. प्रसादं ग्रह् *lit.* 'to become clear'; hence, 'to be reconciled'. *Cf* गङ्गा रोधःपतनकलुषा गृह्णतीव प्रसादम्। Vikr. I 7; the phrase originally refers to *physical* clearness (*e. g.* प्रससादोदयादम्भः कुम्भयोनेर्महौजसः। Ragh. IV. 21); it has then been metaphorically used of *mental* clearness, as freedom from anger, passions, etc.

P. 154. अनुपपन्नं—Lit. what cannot be properly explained; improper. "You are angry when there is no occasion for it; this is inexplicable in your case; for कदा etc."

Verse 16. Construe :—

(हे) वरतनु, तव मुखं कारणात् ऋते कदा क्षणम् अपि कोपपात्रताम् आगतम् ? विभावरी अपर्वणि ग्रहकलुषेन्दुमण्डला कथं भविष्यति, कथय।

कदा आगतं is a question of appeal, meaning that it had never been the seat of anger (was never clouded by anger). कोपपात्रतां—कोपस्य पात्रं भाजनं, तस्य भावः ॰ता ताम्. As ordinarily used, the word कोपपात्र means some one against whom the anger is directed; but here it is in the sense of something in which the anger exists. अपर्वणि—on a day which is not a पर्व-day; the Parva-days are those of the new and full-moon; here the full-moon day, on which alone a lunar eclipse can occur. ग्रहक॰—This refers to the popular notion that eclipses are caused by the planet Rāhu swallowing (obscuring) the sun and the moon. विभावरी *f.*—the night. Der. विभाति नक्षत्रादिभिः (*lit.* brilliant,' 'bright' —with stars etc.). कथय कथं भविष्यति—Just as there cannot be a lunar eclipse unless it is the full-moon day, so Irāvatī would not be angry unless there was sufficient provocation. Compare प्रभवन्त्योऽपि हि भर्तृषु कारणकोपाः कुटुम्बिन्यः। *supra* I. 18. The King means—As you have never been angry without cause, so you should not be on this occasion also.

सुष्ठु व्याहृतं—'well spoken'—said in irony; she means that it is really ill spoken, since there was ample cause for her anger. अन्यसंक्रान्तेषु—transferred to another, *viz.* Mālavikā. अस्माकं भागधेयेषु—our good luck, *viz.* our being loved by you. ततो हास्या भवेयम्—she misinterprets the King's speech and says—You are right in saying that I am angry out of place; for my anger will be futile when you no longer love me. I shall only make myself ridiculous if I get angry knowing this.

Verse 17. Construe :—

उत्सवदिवसेषु कृतापराधः अपि परिजनः बन्धं न अर्हति इति मया एते मोचिते मां प्रणिपतितुम् उपगते च।

उत्सवदिवसेषु—This probably refers to the excuse planned above (p. 130).—दैवचिन्तकैर्विज्ञापितो राजा सर्वबन्धनमोक्षः क्रियतामिति। At a time when all people are rejoicing.

दृष्टो भवत्याः etc.—This again is ironical. 'Truly, I see to-day how you are my partisan'—meaning really that Dhāriṇī is now seen to have no special partiality for her (Irāvatī). Irāvatī is referring to the message which she received from the Queen (p. 148); it is unnatural to understand पक्षपातः as meaning 'partiality towards the King,' as is done by Mr. Ayyar.

बन्धनभ्रष्टः etc.—The Vidūṣaka has liberated Mālavikā only to see her again fall into the hands of Irāvatī, as he apprehends will happen. As a domestic pigeon might escape from its cage only to be seized by a kite, so Mālavikā has escaped from her confinement only to be recaptured. Here कपोत corresponds to Mālavikā and चिल्ला to Irāvatī. Mr. Paṇdit understands Dhāriṇī by चिल्ला, which is inappropriate, as Māla. had just escaped from Dhāriṇī's hands. कपोत *m.* a pigeon (*cf.* the Marathi कबडा) ; चिल्ला *f.* a kite. Or this may simply mean—Māla. will fare a worse fate; a severe punishment will be meted out to her now. Here we cannot understand by गृहकपोत the King as suggested by some; for the King has not yet escaped from the trouble caused by Irāvatī, as he himself further says--कथं नु खल्वस्मात्संकटात् &c.

P. 156. यदृच्छा—Accident, chance. एतत्—*i.e.* how Mālavikā and Bakulā. came to be liberated. ब्रह्मबन्धुना—See p. 102. कृतः प्रयोगः—The scheme was concocted and put in operation. अस्य कामतन्त्रसचिवस्य नितिः—A stroke of policy on the part of this (Vidūṣaka), the King's minister in Cupid's department. The King has different ministers for different branches of administration; the Vidūṣaka manages that of love matters. Compare how the King himself calls the Vidūṣaka his कार्यान्तरसचिव (p. 20).

यदि नीते etc.—This passage presents a variety of readings, of which the one adopted in the text is the most natural. The Vidūṣaka takes up the word नीति from Irāvatī's previous speech and humorously says this. "Oh, you talk of my Policy ! I should forget even the Gāyatrī, if I were to learn a syllable of Policy." It is a form of oath natural in the mouth of a Brāhmaṇa, and it gathers strength from the fact that forgetting the Gāyatrī is sinful for a Brāhmaṇa, who must remember *that* at least. By नीतेरक्षरं पठेयं he is denying even the slightest acquaintance with works on Polity (नीतिशास्त्र). The गायत्री is the well-known Vedic prayer to the Sun which every Brāhmaṇa has to repeat in his *Saṃdhyā*. Some think that this may also mean—if I were to read and remember one syllable of Nīti I should forget the Gāyatrī—being a blockhead. But if the Vid. were such a block-head as not to remember the two at one and the same time, he would not be able to remember any other thing as well, which is absurd.

वसुलक्ष्मी—is mentioned once before (p. 10). पिङ्गल—seems to have been the name of a pet monkey kept in the palace. बलवत्— *adv.* 'exceedingly;' *cf.* बलवदपि शिक्षितानां Śāk. I. त्रासिका—frightened (*p. p. p.* of the causal of त्रस् 4 P. to fear), प्रवात॰—may also mean 'in a place exposed to strong gusts of wind;' see note on p. 16.

न किमपि—not in the least. प्रकृतिं प्रतिपद्—regain her natural state, of mind (being free from the fright). प्रकृति—the natural state, as opposed to विकृति.

P. 158. संज्ञापयामि—is equivalent to संज्ञां प्रापयामि, being the causal of सम्+ज्ञा. साधु रे पिङ्गलवानर-the monkey's act comes as a god-send at a time when the royal party was having the worst of it at the hands of Irāvatī; this makes the Vidūṣaka hail it with delight. स्वपक्षः can be interpreted in two ways:—(1) 'your side'; the King being his master, the monkey belonged to his side, which he thus saves from a fix; (2) or by स्वपक्ष the Vidūṣaka may be jocularly referring to himself; he describes himself as the monkey's caste-fellow, since he resembles him in strange gestures, curious dress, etc. Compare how the Vidūṣaka uses the same image in Vikr. V. p. 125 (आश्रमवासपरिचित एव शाखामृगः।); in the same play a maid-servant also describes him as: आलिखितो वानर इव (Act II. p. 28). अतः परं-She is afraid that the Queen, on coming to know what has taken place, might punish them more severely. (अपूर्णे एव) पञ्चरात्रे—this was the period fixed by the Queen; see p. 76. दोहदस्य is to be connected with पञ्चरात्रे—"the five nights of (*i. e.* connected with the order concerning the fulfilment of) the *dohada* of the Aśoka tree". संनद्ध—endowed with; *cf.* लतेव संनद्धमनोज्ञपल्लवा। Ragh. III. 7. आश्वसितु सखी—Baku. assures Mālavikā that she may now entertain no fears since the Queen has promised to reward her in the event of the Aśoka flowering within five nights. Any punishment that she would have meted out would now, therefore, be cancelled, as Dhāriṇī would remain true to her word. प्रमदवनपालिका—the female gardener in charge of the Pramadavana, who makes the announcement from behind the curtains. पृष्ठतो भवावः—we shall follow her; see the Queen after her.

Critical Appreciation of the Act IV

The ingenious trick of the Vidūṣaka, the surprised visit of Irāvatī and the gladdening news of the blossoming Aśoka tree captivates our attention and enlivens the whole play. The trick of the Vidūṣaka relieves us from the tension of the suspense and gives an optimistic colour to the main theme. The meeting of the lovers in the Samudragṛha prepares us for the realisation of the theme, but the arrival of Irāvatī gives an unexpected turn to the events in the play. The blossoming of the Aśoka tree, however, makes us eager to see the further development of the theme. Thus, the audience osicillates between hope and despair, joy and sorrow.

Agnimitra, though intensely loving Mālavikā, is courteous enough to pay a visit to the queen and to inquire about her health. His show of courtsey to Irāvatī is ridiculous. Surprisingly we find him, in this act, somewhat active. Unaccompanied by the Vidūṣaka, he putting forth a pretext, goes to the Samudragṛha. Mālavikā's jealousy for Irāvatī is well revealed in her talks with Bakulāvalikā. Her smartness and boldness are displayed in her pleasing taunt to the king viz. यो न बिभति...भर्ता. The calculated planning and execution of the snake-bite plot indicate the resourcefulness of the Vidūṣaka. Though recokned as a conventional fool, he proves himself to be an able Kāryāntara (or Kāmatantra) Saciva. His practical wisdom is seen in his taking into confidence Jayasenā for the implimentation of the plan. His reply to Mādhavikā speaks for his ready-wittedness. However, his ravings in sleep creates complications for the lovers. Irāvatī feels sincere repentance for her disregard for the king's prostration. Hence, like a true Āryan wife, she decides to propitiate her lord drawn in a picture in the Samudragṛha. Though jealous and naughty, she has affection for the daughter of her co-wife. On learning the fright of Vasulakṣmī, Irāvatī forgets the fault of her lord & requests him to run to the rescue of the child. Bakulāvalikā's playful nature is revealed when she teases Mālavikā in the Samudragṛha (*cf.* सखि, भर्तुर्वल्लभैषा।). Her encouraging words to disheartened Mālavikā prove her merits as a true friend. The Pingala-vānara-episode is saved the lovers from the awkward and unpleasant situation.

This act, with its enlivening incidents and the elements of surprise and suspense, is perhaps the most interesting one in the whole drama.

Act V

P. 160. **उपक्षिप्त**— 'thrown up' *i. e.* erected. **कृतसत्कारविधेः**—The comp. सत्कारविधि is Madhyamapadalopī. विधि means such act as decorating the place near Aśoka with coloured powders, after cleaning it, hanging up garlands of flowers &c. meant for its reception by the Queen and King shortly to follow. Some understand by सत्कारविधि the Aśoka's दोहदपूरण; but that cannot be meant now, as it has put forth flowers. **वेदिकाबन्धः**—the building of a *Vedikā* (a small raised seat covered with a roof supported on pillars). "The reading **भित्तिबन्धो** is very inferior,', remarks Mr. Paṇdit, "and must have been suggested by an imperfect understanding of the word घरअ (in the Queen's specch on p. 174 संकेतघरअं कप्पिदो) As a घरअ was spoken of it must needs have walls". **अनुष्ठितनियोगं**—When the Udyānapālikā (at the end of Act IV) went to the Queen to report the Aśoka's having blossomed, we must suppose that she received orders to build the *Vedikā*, which is the नियोग here referred to. Having done that, she is now proceeding to report the execution of the work to the Queen.

दैवस्य—good fortune. Since the Aśoka has flowered, luck is in her favour. **तथा चण्डी**—(excessively) angry like that, to that extent. तथा must refer to the Queen's action in imprisoning Mālav. and Bakulāv. in an underground cellar. **प्रसादसुमुखी**—inclined to do her favour; *cf.* त्वं मे प्रसादसुमुखी भव देवि नित्यं। *infra* V. 20. **अभ्यन्तरः**—'one of'. **किमपि**—*adv.* 'for some purpose, or other' (I do not know what it may be). Mr. Ayyar has unnecessarily corrected this into कामपि, so as to make it agree with मञ्जूषां. **चतुःशालं**—a quadrangle enclosed by halls on the four sides. (Read in the text चतुःशालतः for चतुःशालातः। चतसृणां शालानां समाहारः चतुःशालं or शाली). Such buildings seem to have been the fashion in those days; *cf.* आर्ये द्रौपद्याश्चतुःशालकमिदं। Veṇī. I.; अलं चतुःशालमिदं प्रवेश्य। &c. Mṛich. III. 8. **कुब्ज** *m.*—a hump-backed male (*cf.* the Marāthi word कुबडा).

विद्यापारगामिनां—Those who have 'gone to the end of the lores', *i. e.* have studied completely the fourteen kinds of lores; *cf.* षडङ्गमिश्रिता वेदा धर्मशास्त्रं पुराणकम्। मीमांसा तर्कमपि च ह्येता विद्याश्चतुर्दश ॥ Or विद्या may mean *V*edic lore—the Veda and its six *aṅgas viz.* शिक्षा कल्प, व्याकरण, निरुक्त, ज्योतिःशास्त्र, and छन्दोविचिति or छन्दः-शास्त्र. नित्यदक्षिणा—a gift of money given every day as a pious act, without any motive, or sometimes with the object of securing some special blessing (as here). The Brāhmaṇas were, of course, engaged to perform an अनुष्ठान (the performance of some holy rite, the muttering of Vedic *mantras* &c.) that would ensure long life to the prince and prevent any mishap to his life, and were paid for this labour. The practice of giving नित्यदक्षिणा or नित्यभोजन to Brāhmaṇas continues to this day in many Indian households.

P. 162. सेनापतिना—by Puṣpamitra ; he is called सेनापति not because he was Agnimitra's general (as some have wrongly supposed), but because he retained his title of Senāpati of the Maurya kings even after he became King. See Introduction. यज्ञतुरंग० नियुक्तः—*i. e.* on the occasion of the *Aśvamedha* sacrifice performed by Puṣpamitra. The Aśvamedha was a sacrifice of great importance and significance; it was performed only by a king (and hence it is called राजयज्ञ later on, p. 190), who claimed for himself the little and' position of a supreme or universal sovereign.

"A horse of a particular colour was consecrated by the performance of certain ceremonies, and was then turned loose to wander at will for a year. The king, or his representative, followed the horse with an army, and when the animal entered a foreign country, the ruler of that country was forced either to fight or to submit. If the liberator of the house succeeded in obtaining or enforcing the submission of all the countries over which it passed, he returned in triumph with the vanquished Rājās in his train ; but if he failed, he was disgraced and his pretensions ridiculed. After the successful return a great festival was held, at which *the horse was sacrificed*" —Dowson's Classical Dictionary.

भर्तृदारक—*m.*, 'the king's son', the Crown Prince. आयुर्निमित्तं—for the preservation and prolongation of his life. The piousness of the act would constitute a charm by which evil was supposed to be averted. सुवर्ण—*m.* a particular coin of gold, 16 *māṣas* in weight; *cf.* दशसुवर्णस्य रुद्धो द्यूतकारः प्रपलायितः। Mṛich. II. दक्षिणीय *adj.* worthy of receiving the Dakṣiṇā, from दक्षिणा + ईय (छ) added by Pāṇ. V. I. 69. मङ्गलगृहे—in the 'auspicious house'; this must be some sort of a temple or worshipping-hall in the place. लेखकर *m.* a writer, a reader. विजयदण्डैः—'the conquering armies' (दण्ड *m. n.* an army); *cf.* दण्डचक्र p. 18, and विजयदण्डैः again on p. 178. महासार—*adj.* 'of great value'; *cf.* महासारप्रसवयोः *supra* I. 15. रत्नवाहनानि-Mr. Ayyar's translation of this as 'vessels of gems' is not very clear. Some interpret it as 'the carriages that brought the gems', but then the word रत्न, to which the *adj.* महासार should principally refer, becomes subordinated. It seems better to understand it as रत्नानि च वाहनानि च as the Calcutta commentators have done, the वाहनs including elephants, palanquins, chariots, etc. शिल्पकारिका—a maid-servant versed in one or more of the practical arts (*śilpa*; see p. 14 for the word). °भूयिष्ठ परिजनं—'servants mostly consisting of'; भूयिष्ठ at the end of a comp. has this sense; *cf.* अभिरूपभूयिष्ठा परिषद्। Śāk. I. उपायनीकृत्य—sending as presents. ०नीकृत्य is a च्वि-formation and is explained as न उपायनं अनुपायनं, अनुपायनं उपायनं संपद्यमानं कृत्वा उपायनीकृत्य श्वः—In its Prakṛt form सुवो may be seen the origin of the Gujarāti word सवारे. पश्यतीति—इति 'so it is reported'.

P. 164. प्रसूनलक्ष्मी—'the beauty or splendour of flowers'. धर्मासन—'the seat of justice', the throne, seated on which the king administers justice. प्रतिपालय—to wait upon.

वैतालिक—See page 58, note on the word; from वैताल + ठक् Pāṇ. IV. 4. 8; or by 'प्रयोजनम्' (ठञ्) Pāṇ. V. 1. 109; *lit.* 'one singing in different तालs'. He was a kind of poetical panegyrist or bard attached to the Court, whose duty it was to announce (in songs) fixed periods of the day, to awaken princes at dawn with music and song, to celebrate the master's victories etc. These bards are generally introduced in dramas in pairs (*e. g.* in Śāk. V.) and sometimes alone (*e. g.* Vikr. II). दण्डेन—by means of the punishment (defeat) meted out to them (enemies). दण्ड may also mean 'the army.'

Verse 1. Construe :—

परभृतकलव्याहारेषु आत्तरतिः त्वं विदिशातीरोद्यानेषु अङ्गवान् अनङ्गः इव मधुं नयसि, (हे) वरद, प्रबलस्य ते रिपुः विजयकरिणाम् आलानत्वं गतैः वरदारोधोवृक्षैः सह अवनतः।

परभृत etc.—परभृतकलव्याहारेषु आत्तरतिः—'taking delight in, enjoying, the indistinct but sweet cooings of the cuckoos. This explains why he passes the spring in the gardens. For परभृत see note on परभृता IV. 2. The cuckoo, particularly the male bird, coos sweetly in the spring; *cf.* पुंस्कोकिलो यन्मधुरं चुकूज। Kum. III. 32. **मधुं नयसि**—You pass the spring. **विदिशा**—here means the river of that name; the word is also applied to a town (Agnimitra's capital) situated on it, which is the modern Bhilsā in Scindia's dominion. **अङ्गवान् अनङ्ग इव**—As though you were Cupid incarnate. The word रति, in आत्तरति, is well-chosen. आत्तरति suggests the sense of 'who is accompanied by रति, his wife,' and it makes the comparison of the king with Cupid more appropriate.

आलान—*n.* the post to which an elephant is tied; *cf.* चकम्पे तीर्णलौहित्ये तस्मिन्प्राग्ज्योतिषेश्वरः। तद्गजालानतां प्राप्तैः सह कालागुरुद्रुमैः॥ Ragh. IV. 81. **आलानाङ्करुपोढ बलस्य**—*v. l.* Here आलान means the chains (or rope) with which the elephants were tied down; ०कैः—'bearing the marks of the chains or ropes.' **उपोढबलस्य** may mean—whose army is powerful, or whose power is increased. **वरद**—a complimentary epithet of address to the king expressing his generosity, introduced probably for the purpose of alliteration with वरदा. The वरदा is the modern river Wardha, which is a tributary of the Godāvarī.

वृक्षैः सहावनतो रिपुः—This is a poetical way of saying that the invasion was successful. The elephants of the victorious hosts of the King were tied to the trees on the banks of the Varadā, a river which lay in the territory invaded. The trees bent under the strain of the elephants tugging at their ropes, and the vanquished foe at the same time bent his head in reverential obedience to Agnimitra's supreme prowess. For various other ways of construing परभृतकलव्याहारेषु, see com. **परभृत व्याहार** in the case of the King may mean the songs of bards &c. We have here followed the most natural way of connecting this with आत्तरतिः which follows immediately.

Verse 2. Construe :—

(हे) सुरोपम, दण्डानीकैः विदर्भपतेः श्रियं हृतवतः तव परिघगुरुभिः दोर्भिः प्रसह्य रुक्मिणीं (हृतवतः) शौरेः च उभयोः चरितं वीरप्रीत्या सूरिभिः विरचितपदं क्रथकैशिकान् मध्येकृत्य स्थितम्।

विरचितपदं—etc.—The construction is—(हे) सुरोपम, क्रथकैशिकान् मध्येकृत्य स्थितं उभयोः चरितं सुरिभिः वीरप्रीत्या विरचितपदं (वर्तते); उभयोः being explained by दण्डानीकैः विदर्भपतेः श्रियं हृतवतः तव, and परिघगुरुभिः दोर्भिः प्रसह्य रुक्मिणीं (हृतवतः) शौरेः च। Here विरचितपदं is taken as the predicate. Another construction, though not a better one, is that followed by the com., which see. सूरिभिः विरचितपदं—'having the words of it arranged in a verse by learned men (poets); *i. e.* celebrated in song by learned men. वीरप्रीत्या—they did it because they loved to hear of and recite noble and heroic deeds. सुरोपम—*voc. sing.*, addressed to the king—'O you who are like a god in beauty and prowess;' introduced here merely for the sake of alliteration, like वरद in the preceeding śloka. Kāli. is fond of this comparison; *cf.* देवसरूपमेत्य। Ragh. VI. 59; शमरतेऽमरतेजसि पार्थिवे। Ragh. IX. 4. सूरि—*m.* a learned man (धीमान्सूरिः। Amara). *Cf.* वंशे स्मन्पूर्वसूरिभिः। Ragh. I. 4. When taken with the exploits of Krisna this refers to Vyāsa and other sages who (as in the *Bhāgvata*) had sung his exploits. चरितं—the deeds, exploits of. क्रथकैशिकान् मध्येकृत्य स्थितम्—'which remains, having placed the Krathakaiśikas in the middle'; *i. e.* performed with reference to the क्रथ॰ मध्येकृत्य has here the force of an adverb, being used in the sense of 'with regard to.' The use of स्थितं is analogous to that in व्याप्य स्थितं रोदसी। Vikr. I. 1. क्रथकैशिक is another name for the विदर्भ country; *cf.* Ragh. V. 39 where Mall. explains क्रथकैशिकानां as विदर्भदेशानाम्; see also our note *ad loc.* Krathakaiśika is a class of Kṣatriyas, said to be descended originally from Kratha end Kaiśika, who were the sons of one Vidarbha; so the word Kra° has come to be used synonymously with Vidarbha.

दण्डानीक—is the same as दण्डचक्र (p. 18); अनीक *n.* army, forces. परिघगुरुभिः—as large and strong as परिघ (iron bars). दोर्भिः—the plural is used because Krisna (as Viśnu) had *four* arms. The comparison of arms to iron bars is common in Kālidāsa; *cf.* नगरपरिघप्रांशुबाहुः। Sāk. II. 15; also

Ragh. XVI. 84. शौरि was one of Krişṇa's many names; lit. 'the descendant of Śūra, '—Śūra was his grandfather. प्रसह्य च रुक्मिणीम्-The forcible carrying off of Rukmiṇī by Krişṇa is one of the many familiar incidents of Krişṇāvatāra. Rukmiṇi was a daughter of Bhīmaka, King of the Vidarbhas. She was betrothed to Śiśupāla, but she had fallen in love with Krişṇa, to whom she sent a letter begging him to come to her rescue. Her brother Rukmin was one of Krişṇa's enemies, and tried his best to get her married to Śiśupāla; but on the very wedding-day Krişṇa came and snatched her off with force, having defeated both Śiśupāla and Rukmin. Mr. Pandit infers from this śloka that there must have been extant in Kālidāsa's time compositions (like the *Harṣacarita* and the *Vikramāṇkadevcarita*) in which this victory of Agnimitra over the Vidarbha King was celebrated. There do not seem to exist, however, sufficient grounds for entertaining such a theory. See Introduction.

P. 166. जयशब्द—Words expressive of victory. The जयशब्दs here are the two ślokas of the bards. Usually this refers to the words जय, जयतु जयतु भर्ता &c. with which the king is greeted by servants, bards &c. मुखालिन्दतोरणं—मुखे स्थितस्य अलिन्दस्य तोरणम् ; the arch (तोरण) of the terrace (अलिन्द) at the front entrance to the palace (मुखे). समाश्रिता—*fem.*, because the door-keeper is a female.

Verse 3. Construe :—

कान्तां सुलभेतरसंप्रयोगां विचिन्त्य विदर्भपतिं बलैः आनमितं श्रुत्वा च आतपे धाराभिः अभिहतं सरोजम् इव हृदयं दुःखायते च सुखम् अश्नुते च ।

सुलभेतरसंप्रयोगां—union (संप्रयोग) with whom is not easy. सुलभेतर—Other than easy,' *i. e.* असुलभ or दुर्लभ. आनमित—causal; 'made to bend low'; *cf.* अवनतो रिपु: *supra* śl. 1. धाराभिः etc.—like a lotus, parched by the sun's heat and having a shower of rain. Grief and joy are to the heart respectively what आतप and धाराs are to the सरोज. दुःखायते—feels pain; denom. from दुःख. There is a slight technical fault in the syntax here; विचिन्त्य and श्रुत्वा go with दुःखायते, although the agents of these actions are different; it is rather the King, and not his हृदय, that considers and hears. This is known as समानकर्तृकत्वव्याघात, and it is usual to explain such grammatical lapses by understanding some such words as स्थितस्य मम after विचिन्त्य and श्रुत्वा.

P. 168. **एकान्तसुखितः**—completely happy (एकान्तं यथा तथा सुखितः). **प्रसाधनगर्वं वहसि**—(Since) you are proud of (your skill in) decoration. **वैदर्भं**—Special to the Vidarbha country, according to the local custom prevalent there. **विवाहनेपथ्य**—the dress, ornaments etc. specially to be worn on the wedding-day. The student may read Kum. VII. 7–26 for a detailed description of marriage-costume. **मदपेक्षानुवृत्त्या**—मदपेक्षाया अनुवृत्त्या (acting in accordance with); or मदनपेक्षया out of regard for me *i. e.* my feelings, अनुवृत्तिः agreeable conduct यस्याः; *cf.* for this sense नानुवृत्तिर्न संततिः। Uttar. VII. 5. कान्तानुवृत्तिचातुर्यं *ibid.* III. **पूर्वचरितैः**—she has behaved similarly before.

कुसुमसौभाग्य—the beauty of its flowers; *cf.* प्रसूनलक्ष्मी above p. 164. **ममारम्भः**—my effort, *viz.* ordering Mālavikā to fulfil its *dohada*, so that it might blossom without further delay. **यथार्हसंमानसुखितं**—As it was held to be an occasion for general rejoicing, she had given gifts and presents to the inmates of the seraglio, and made them happy. **यथार्ह**—according to the position and dignity of each. **पुरोग**—*lit.* going at the head; the principal person deserving of mention.

P. 170. **राजा सहर्षं**; the stage-direction सहर्षं shows that the King was glad at the chance, now offered, of once again meeting Mālavikā. **किंचित्परिवृत्तयौवनः**—*i.e.* the season is now advanced.

Verse 4. Construe :—

अग्रे विकीर्णकुरबकफलजालविभिद्यमानसहकारं परिणामाभिमुखम् ऋतोः यौवनं चेतः उत्सुकयति।

अग्रे—in our front. **विकिर्ण** etc.—विकीर्णकुरबकं च तत्फलजालकभिद्यमानसहकारं च "in which the Kurabaka flowers are scattered (on the ground) and the mango-trees (सहकार) are bursting with a load of fruit"; for कुरबक see note on p. 74 (कुरबकं श्यामावदातारुणम्). The other way of taking the compound, pointed out in the com., is not so good. The mango-tree begins to bear fruit generally at the beginning, and is at its height towards the end, of spring. **परिणामाभिमुखं**—'about to ripen,' *i. e.* about to end. **उत्सुकयति चेतः**—makes the observer's heart anxious; for it reminds him that the days of enjoyment will soon pass away. उत्सुकयति is denom. from उत्सुक.

दत्तनेपथ्य इव—as if it has been specially adorned. The flowers appear like so many ornaments put on it. **स्थाने**–By this the King means to say that its being late in blossoming was justifiable, inasmuch as now its spelendour is unparalleled. There was sufficient excuse for its slowness since it wanted to surpass others in its flower-beauty.

Verse 5. Construe :—

प्रथमं सूचितवसन्तविभवानां सर्वाशोकतरूणां कुसुमानि निवृत्तदोहदे अस्मिन् संक्रान्तानि इव।

संक्रान्तानीव—For, there was such a wealth of flowers on the Aśoka **विस्रब्धो भव**—take courage ; here is something reassuring. The Queen used hitherto always to prevent Mālavikā being seen by the King. But now she has permitted her to stand by, from which the Vidūṣaka infers that Dhārinī no longer minds the results following their meeting, that probably she intends to consent to their union even.

Verse 6. Construe :—

प्रियया उपस्थिता इयं देवी विनयात् विस्मृतहस्तकमलया नरेन्द्रलक्ष्म्या (उपस्थिता) वसुमती इव माम् अभ्युत्तिष्ठति।

P. 172. **उपस्थिता प्रियया**–*sc.* मालविकया. अनुत्थिता प्रि० *v. l.* is not good; for Māla, as a servant could not have risen up after Dhāriṇī. The King compares Dhāriṇī to the Earth, and Mālavikā to Lakṣmī. **नरेन्द्रलक्ष्मी**—the regal glory (personified). **विस्मृतहस्त०**—without the (usual) lotus in her hand. Lakṣmi is associated with lotuses in literature; not only that she resides in a lotus (*cf.* the epithet पद्मालया) but she generally carries one in her hand; *cf.* स्फुरदरविन्दचारुहस्तां श्रियं। Śiś. VIII. 64; and Ragh. IV. 5. The King means that nothing was wanting, in the way of beauty or splendour of appearance, to make the comparison complete, except that Mālavikā had no lotus in her hand.

कौतुकालंकारस्य—Madhyam. comp.; see com. **कौतुक** *n.* the marriage-ceremony; *cf.* कन्यकातनयकौतुकक्रियां स्वप्रभावसदृशीं वितेनतुः। Ragh. XI. 53. It may also mean festal dress; but that is not the meaning here. °गतमिव सलिलं—*Cf.* नलिनीदलगतजलमतितरलं &c. (द्वादशपञ्जरिकास्तोत्र). दक्षिणेतरत् (neuter)—'other than right,' *i. e.* 'left'; *cf.* भुजभेतर p. 166. The throbbing of the left eye is a good omen in the case of women; *cf.* अहो अपाङ्गको मे प्रस्फुरति किमपि वामः। *supra* p. 48.

What Mālavikā says is this –"I know why this marriage-dress is put on me. It is because Dhāriṇī wanted to test the skill of Kauśikī in the art of dressing (*cf supra* p. 168, भगवति यत्त्वं प्रसाधनगर्वं वहसि etc.), and therefore it could not mean anything more than that. Still (तथापि)—*i. e.* although there is thus occasion for nervousness or expectation, my heart beats tumultuously and my eye is exhibiting good omens (thus, inspite of myself, I cannot help thinking that the dress *may* mean that the Queen has some intention of uniting me with the King". This explanation alone brings out the force of तथापि. Some understand by जानामि निमित्तं that Mālavikā had already come to know directly or indirecty of the Queen's intention (to allow her marriage with the King); but the Queen had not as yet directly given any indication either to Māla. or to any one else. She did not tell it even to the Parivrājikā when she asked her to dress Māla. (See Vidū.'s speech on p. 168 for the plausible pretext given out for it). Again the हृदयकम्प and नयनस्फुरण are suggestive of some great auspicious event to come, and it would, therefore, be absurd to introduce them by तथापि. Māla. means that as her heart is throbbing and her left eye yielding a good omen she may expect the Queen to grant her her desired object.

Verse 7. Construe :—

अनतिलम्बिदुकूलनिवासिनी लघुभिः आभरणैः (उपलक्षिता एषा) उदयोन्मुखचन्द्रिका गतहिमैः उडुगणैः (उपलक्षिता) चैत्रविभावरी इव मे प्रतिभाति।

उदयोन्मुखचन्द्रिका—*adj.* to चैत्रविभावरी 'in which moonlight is about to appear' *i. e.* when the moon is about to rise. गतहिमैः- 'without mist', in a sky free from mist; *cf.* हिमनिर्मुक्तयोर्योगे चित्राचन्द्रमसोरिव Ragh. I. 46. For विभावरी see IV. 16. The Chaitra night is chosen specially because it is proverbially fine. The reading लघुभिः does not harmonize with the number implied in उडुगणैः; the Chaitra-night has not few stars, but a host of them. The epithet गतहिमैः is introduced to emphasize their brilliance; while अनतिलम्बितदुकूलनिवासिनी corresponds to उदयोन्मुखचन्द्रिका, because when the moon is not yet risen, only a portion of its light is visible above the horizon, which can then be compared to a short white garment of silk.

P. 174. **तरुणीसजनसहायस्य** &c.—संकेतगृहं a rendezous, a place where lovers meet by appointment. There is a hidden reference here to his coming union with Mālavikā, as is shown by the stage-direction सस्मितम्, although ostensibly तरुणीजन refers to his other wives (*e. g.* Irāvatī) in the palace. The Aśoka has been transformed into a संकेतगृह by the erection of the *Vedikā* (p.160).

Verse 8. Construe :—

अयम् अशोकः देव्याः ईदृशानां सत्काराणां भाजनत्वं न नेयः (इति) न, यः माधवश्रीनियोगे सावज्ञः त्वत्प्रयत्ने पुष्पैः आदरं शंसति।

नायं न नेयः—The two negatives yield the sense of one emphatic affirmative; *cf.* न च न परिचितः I. 11 न खलु गोप्तरि नाग्निमित्रे V. 20. "The Aśoka ought necessarily to be made the receptacle of such honours as the Vedikā-bandha, since it (in its turn, has shown its high respect for you; because it defied the command of the spring, and blossomed only when *you* endeavoured for the same." **माधवश्रीनियोगे**—because its usual flowering season is the beginning of the spring; for माधवश्री *cf.* मधुलक्ष्मी on p. 24.

यौवनवतीं इमां—The Vidūṣaka of course means Mālavikā, but he deliberately words it in such a way that it can be taken otherwise also; and when the Queen actually inquires whom that इमां referred to (for as yet her intention of giving Mālavikā to the King is not made known), he promptly answers by shifting it to the beauty of the Aśoka's blossoms.

संनिधिवियोग—a Locative Tatp. (संनिधौ वियोगः) separation, although there is proximity (of the lovers). A happy phrase with which may be compared Eng. 'living death'.

Verse 9. Construe :—

अहं रथाङ्गनामा इव, मे प्रिया सहचरी इव, नौ अननुज्ञातसंपर्का धारिणी रजनी इव

P. 176. अहं **रथाङ्ग** &c.—He compares himself and Māla. now in the presence of Dhāriṇī to a pair of *Chakravāka* birds who also suffer संनिधिवियोग at night. **रथाङ्गनामन्**—रथाङ्ग नाम यस्य 'whose name is रथाङ्ग *i. e.* चक्रं,—is the bird called चक्र, or more commonly चक्रवाक. The Chakravāka bird and his mate are always seen together during day-time, and in Sanskrit literature they are described as the highest type of conjugal affection; but it is believed that at night they are separated owing to an inevitable decree of fate. Compare रथाङ्गनाम्नोरिव भावबन्धनं बभूव यत्प्रेम् परस्पराश्रयम्। Ragh. III. 24; and एषापि (चक्रवाकी) प्रियेण विना गमयति रजनीं विषाददीर्घतराम्। Śak. IV. 16. **नौ**—An instance of a *Sāpekṣa* comp., नौ being connected with संपर्क.

तस्मिन् विदर्भविषयोपायने—See Sārasaka's speech (p. 162). Almost all of these presents were immediately submitted to the King, except two artist girls, who are now introduced. **अलघु**—'not light or quick, slow, dull, heavy.' उपस्थान—waiting upon. The reason given by the Kanchukī for not including them when the rest of the presents were sent is plausible but the poet has skilfully enough invented it, since he could not introduce them early, they being necessary characters in the unfolding of that part of that plot which is to follow.

अपूर्वं—*i. e.* which now we are entering for the first time. **राजकुलं०**—the palace (*lit.* a royal residence). **प्रसीदति मे हृदयम्**—'While I ought to be afraid and nervous on this occasion, I am on the contrary feeling cheerful.' The other maid, who also feels similarly, explains this by applying the popular saying· आगामि सुखं &c; she means—since we feel cheerful, something good and welcome is in store for us. For समवस्था see notes, IV. 7.

परस्परमवलोकयतः—because they recognized the two maids as soon as they entered.

P. 178. **अभिविनीते**—instructed or trainrd in. **अभियोगः**- *V. l.* deep or special study. **अभ्यन्तरे**—acquainted, familiar wife; proficient in; *cf.* अहो प्रयोगाभ्यंन्तरः प्राश्निकः *supra* p. 54, and our note thereon. **अनयोरन्यतरा**—It is not stated what he was going to do with the other.

मालविके कतरा ते etc.—The Queen wants to give the maid to Mālavikā, but she does not say that at once; she merely asks whom she will like to have as a companion in music, because Mālavikā is still in the service of the Queen, and the new servant would be Mālavikā's companion.

भर्तृदारिका—Princess. बाष्पं विसृजतः—owing to the sudden recognition they are overwhelmed with emotion. का वा इयम्—*i. e.* this Mālavikā, whom you seem to have known before and whom you are addressing as 'Princess' now.

चन्दनं खलु–etc.—'I have used sandal-wood for slippers'; *i. e.* put a noble thing to an ignoble use, by employing a Princess (Mālavikā) as a servant. The student should note that the Eng. word 'sandal' is quite distinct from 'sandal' meaning चन्दन, and there is no relation between the two.

P. 180. अत्रभवती—*sc.* Mālavikā. इत्थंभूता—*i. e.* become a servant, although she was a Princess. गूढं—*adv*,. 'Secretly'.

श्रुतपूर्व—this refers to सोदर्या पुनरस्य &c. (Act I. p. II). स्वरसंयोग—'voice' (*lit.* a combination of sounds); *Cf.* वीणायाः स्वरसंयोगः। Śāk. V. दुःखेन विभाव्यते—'is clearly perceived (*i. e.* recognized), with difficulty'. Owing to her being disguised as an ascetic, the maids could not recognize her till they heard her voice. आप्तवर्गः—a collection or circle of friends. वैक्लव्यम्—low spirits, dejection; *abs. n.* fr. विक्लव.

P. 182. उपलब्धम्—it is understood (now that you have explained it). तथागतभ्रातृकां—*i. e.* in the custody of Jayasena, being captured by his अन्तपाल. भवत्संबन्धापेक्षया—with a view to form a connexion, or regardful of the connexion to be formed, with you. *Cf.* प्रतिश्रुतसंबन्धः p. 18. निविष्टः—encamped. गताध्वा—having travelled (a part of) their way, *i. e.* the distance to be gone over in a day.

Verse 10. Construe :—

तूणीरपट्टपरिणद्धभुजान्तरालम् आकर्णलम्बिशिखिपिच्छकलापधारि कोदण्डपाणि निनदत् आपातदुष्प्रसहं प्रतिरोधकानाम् अनीकम् आविरभूत्।

तूणीर etc.—The principal sentence is प्रतिरोधकानां अनीकं आविरभूत्, the remaining five words being descriptive epithets of अनीकं (a collection, a band of). प्रतिरोधक—*m.* a waylayer, a highwayman. Der. प्रतिरुणद्धि पथिकान्वर्त्मनीति। तूणीर॰—across their breasts were tied the straps (पट्ट) attached to the quivers (तूणीर) आकर्ण—कलाप means here a sort of head dress or conical cap made of peacock's feathers (such as is still seen worn by some mendicants). *V. l.* आपार्ष्णि०—means 'hanging as far as the heels.' But there is no reason why the robbers should have carried bundles of feathers reaching to their heels, which would have hindered their free motion. **आपातदुष्प्रसहम्**—आसमन्तात्पातः आपातः—a falling or bearing down upon from all sides; hence a sudden or fierce attack. *Cf.* आपातदुः सहः स्नेहसंवेगः। Uttar. VII.

भयं रूपयति—She remembers the scene which she had witnessed, and having the timidity of a young girl, shudders with fear at its very recital. **सार्थवाह०**—warriors in service of the merchants (सार्थवाहानां योद्धारः).

P. 184. **कष्टं**—painful, being tragic. The King easily guessed that her brother Sumati must have perished while defending the ladies. **सोदर्यः**—brother. See our note on (p. 18)

Verse 11. Construe :—

दुर्जातेः इमां पराभिभवकातरां परिप्सुः भर्तृप्रियः प्रियैः असुभिः भर्तुः आनृण्यं गतः।

परीप्सुः—noun from the *desider.* of आप् 5th conj. with परि meaning 'to protect, to defend'; wishing to protect. *Cf.* ये न परीप्सन्ति भार्यां बध्यमानां। Mahābhārata; व्यायामेन परीप्सस्व जीवितं। *ibid.* **दुर्जात**—See *supra* p. 96. **दुर्जातेः**—*V. l.* दुष्टा जातिस्तस्याः, from the men of the wicked tribe (the savages). **असुभिः भर्तुः आनृण्यं गतः**–dying in the master's service is the highest form of making a return for the favours received. **आनृण्यं**—*abs. n.* from **अनृण**—'free from debt' (न विद्यते ऋणं यस्य).

ईदृशी लोकयात्रा—*i. e.* death awaits all; *cf.* जातस्य हि ध्रुवो मृत्युः। Bg. II. 27. **सफलीकृतभर्तृपिण्डः**—who showed that his master's food (पिण्ड) was not (eaten by him) in vain, *i. e.* who did the best possible service in his power and thus discharged his duty prefectly. **अग्निसात्कृ**—to consign to the flames; *cf.* स चकार शरीरमग्निसात् Ragh. VIII. 72. The taddhita affix सात् is added by 'तदधीनवचने' Pān V. 4. 54, to show that a thing is completely under the subjugation of another. **पुनर्नवीभूत०**—For when she lost her brother who was her support after her husband, she felt as much grief again as she did when she became a widow.

इमे काषाये—Wearing such garments was a principal item in the uniform of the Buddhistic sect in those days. Such garments are worn by Sanyāsins also in these days. **आटविक** *m.* a forester. Der. अटवि + ठक् (अटव्यां भवः) **सज्जनस्य एष पन्थाः**—Mr. Pandit remarks on this—"This approval of taking the Buddhistic yellow-brown uniform shows that the drama belongs to an age when Buddhism was yet honoured." But this much cannot be inferred from this sentence alone. For the King is speaking here courteously. The only legitimate inference that can be drawn from this that is Agnimitra did not look upon Buddhism with hatred. **अवसानं**—end, termination.

P. 186. **किं नु खलु** "What will he say now ?" This mental remark is the outcome of her anxiety as to the decision of the King about the marriage, a reference to which was made by the Parivrājikā in the words **भवत्संबन्धापेक्षया** (P. 182). Compare in a similar context the words of Śakuntalā—किं नु खलु आर्यपुत्रो भणति। Śāk. V.

परिभवोपहारिणः—bringing on humiliation or degradation. **परिभवप्रहा०रिणः**—*v. l.* परिभवेन प्रहा०—striking with degradation or insult. **०पनिपातिनः**—*v. l.* following close upon a misfortune; he means 'misfortunes never come alone'; *cf.* रन्ध्रोपनिपातिनोऽनर्थाः। Śāk. VI

Verse 12. Construe :—

देवीशब्दक्षमा सती इयं प्रेष्यभावेन नाम स्नानीयवस्त्रक्रियया पत्रोर्णम् वा उपयुज्यते

प्रेष्यभावेन—&c.—**नाम** implies a mild censure (कुत्सा as given in the Com.). **देवीशब्दक्षमा सती**—although she fully deserved the title "Queen' by reason of her birth in a royal family. The word देवी contains the King's view about the turn the events should take, anxiety for which was displayed in Mālavikā's preceeding remark किं नु खलु सांप्रतं भर्ता भणति। **स्नानीयवस्त्रक्रियया**—by being used as a bathing garment or a garment for wiping off the body after the bath. **पत्रोर्ण**—a washed and glossy silken garment. **वा**—is used in the sense of इव. The King means—As it would be an indignity to a silk-garment to be used as a bathing cloth. so was this position of a servant (highly improper) in the case of Mālavikā.

अभिजनवती—अभिजन-noble birth; *cf.* अभिजनवतो भर्तुः श्लाघ्ये etc. Śāk. IV. 18. **अनाचक्षणयां**—आचक्षाणा is the pres. part.

fem. of चक्ष् Atm. 2nd conj. with आ. असांप्रतं कृतं—she means—Since you know that Mālavikā was a Princess, you ought to have told it and not kept it secret. The Queen makes this remark to show her innocence in the matter. शान्तं पापं *lit.* 'may evil be quelled, an expression used in the sense of 'God forbid,' to show one's disapproval of or disagreement with what another has said. नैभृत्य *n.* silence (abst. noun from निभृत 'silent' ; *cf.* निभृतद्विरेफं Kum. III. 42) ; or it may mean 'concealment.'

लोकयात्रागतने—Mr. Pandit and other editors interpret this as 'while living in this mortal world', 'who had assumed the human form.' It seemed better and more natural, however, to understand लोकयात्रा as जीवनार्थं भ्रमणं (see com.), wandering for livelihood from place to place as all Sādhus do in India even to this day. The other reading देवयात्रा—'holy pilgrimage.' also supports our interpretation. सिद्धादेशेन—whose words were infallible (सिद्ध *lit.* already fulfilled as it were), bound to come true. त्वत्पादशुश्रुषया—She means—As she was destined to serve some one it was most desirable that she should serve *you*, and so I allowed her to continue in your service.

P. 188. कथान्तरेण—On account of another story (*viz.* the one related just now by the Parivrājikā). अन्तरितम्—separated, temporarily shelved aside. He was going to give the minister's message when the turn of events led the Parivrājikā to tell the story and he had to hold it up ; as it now ended, he would proceed to communicate it. Here we are to remember that Kanch. was on the stage all the while the Pari. was relating the story after his entrance to introduce the two maids. See p. 176. अवधारितमस्माभिः—we have considered and settled.

द्वैराज्यं—*n.* a dominion divided between two rulers (द्वौ राजानौ यत्र द्विराजा देशः। तस्य भावः द्वैराज्यम्।) अवस्थापयितुकामः—See note on विलोभयितुकामया p. 74.

Verse 13. Construe :—

शीतोष्णकिरणौ नक्तंदिवम् इव तौ उभौ उत्तरदक्षिणे वरदाकूले विभज्य पृथक् शिष्टाम्।

शिष्टां—Imperat. third person dual of शास् 2nd conj. 'to rule'. नक्तंदिवं—नक्त च, दिवा च, a Dvandva of the two indeclinables नक्तं and दिवा, here used as a noun being the object of विभज्य. According to Pān. (see com.) the comp. नक्तंदिवं is always used as an adv. (अव्ययीभाव) in the sense of the Loc. But there are instances like व्यस्तरात्रिंदिवस्य (Kum. II. 8; see Malli's remarks on it), दिवामन्या रात्रिः (used by Patanjali) &c; on the strength of these, it can be held that नक्तं and दिवा may also be used as Nom. or Acc., and so the poet might have used नक्तंदिवं as Acc. to विभज्य here. *Cf.* विभज्य नक्तंदिवमस्ततन्द्रिणा । Kir. I. 9, and our note *ad. loc.*

शीतोष्णकिरणौ—शीतकिरणश्च उष्णकिरणश्च; *cf.* **शीतांशु** and **धर्मांशु**; **शीतकर** and **चण्डकर** which are more usual.

जीवितसंशयः—referring to the mishaps that might have occurred while he was in the enemy's power, being a captive. For जीवितसंशय *cf. supra* p. 120, अहमेव ब्राह्मणस्य &c. **कल्याणी**—excellent.

Verse 14. Construe :—

द्विधा विभक्तां श्रियम् उद्वहन्तौ तौ नृपती (द्विधा विभक्तां) धुरम् (उद्वहन्तौ) रथाश्वौ इव परस्परावग्रहनिर्विकारौ संग्रहीतुः ते निदेशे स्थास्यतः ।

संग्रहीतृ—*m.* a charioteer; may also be taken with ते, you keeping them in check, *i. e.* their sovereign-lord. **परस्परावग्रहनिर्विकारौ**—causing no disturbance to you, being mutually restrained, *i. e.* each not allowing the other to grow aggressive. **अवग्रह**—*m.* restraint (निग्रह); *cf.* स्वयं विधाता सुरदैत्यरक्षसां अनुग्रहावग्रहयोर्यदच्छया । Śiś. I. 71. Or this may mean—not inclined to trouble each other, each governing his kingdom in peace (being checked by you.)

P. 190. **प्राभृतक**—*n.* प्राभ्रियते इति प्राभृतं, प्राभृतमेव प्राभृतकं; an offering (to gods); or a gift (given as a token of friendship). **सोपचारं**—with due formality, proper respect; for other senses, see p. 146. **ततोमुखं**—*lit.* 'with the face towards that'; 'that' refers to the पुष्पमित्रसाकाश्यं, whence the Queen was expecting news of her son Vasumitra. **हृदयं**—*i. e.* our thoughts. **अतिघोरे**—*v. l.* to a very dangerous post: °**भारे**—*v. l.* to a very arduous task.

स्वस्ति etc.–This is one of the few letters that have surrvived in recorded Sanskrit literature; the student should carefully note the style in which a letter ought to be written. The स्वस्ति at the beginning is merely a fromal expression of auspiciousness. **यज्ञशरणात्**—the place from which the letter is sent is put in the abl. case. यज्ञशरण (*lit.* 'sacrifice—house'. शरण meaning गृह) is the enclosure, or camp where the sacrifice was performed. **वैदिशस्थं**—विदिशा एव वैदिशं (नगरं) स्वार्थे अण्। तत्र तिष्ठतीति तं 'being at Vaidiṣa' *i. e.* Vḍiśā. It is also possible to explain वैदिश as विदिशानगरेण उपलक्षितो देशः वैदिशः। **आयुष्मन्तं**—'the long-lived one,' corresponding to the Marāthi चिरंजीव. **अनुदर्शयति**—'informs', 'writes as follows.'

राजयज्ञ—the *As'vamedha* sacrifice; यज्ञानां राजा राजयज्ञः, like राजदन्तः, *Cf.* यथाश्वमेधः क्रतुराट् सर्वपापापनोदनः। Ms. XI. 26. It is wrong to identify this with the Rājasūya sacrifice, because the latter has nothing to do with *a horse let loose for a year*, which is done only in the Aśvamedha. From the com. strike off fhe line from राजयज्ञो राज° to त्रिकाण्डशेषः। **राजपुत्रशतपरिवृतं** – see the Śruti quoted by Kāt., from which it would appear that only a hundred princes were to accompany the horse as its guards. **निरर्गलः**—unchecked, allowed to wander at will.

P. 192. **सिन्धोः**—of the river Sindhu. This is not to be confounded with the Indus, but it is a small river in Mālvā, mentioned by Kālidāsa in the Meghadūta I. (वेणीभूतप्रतनुसलिला तामतीतस्य सिन्धुः। s'l. 29). See Introduction. **अश्वानीक**—a cavalry regiment. **यवनानां**—the Greeks are meant here. See Introduction. **प्रार्थितः**—Lit. sought to be seized: attacked; *cf.* तत्प्रार्थितं जवनवाजिगेतनराज्ञा। Ragh. IX. 56. **संमर्दः**—*m.* a tumultuous battle, a hand-to-hand fight.

Verse 15. Construe :—

ततः धन्विना वसुमित्रेण परान् पराजित्य प्रसह्य ह्रियमाण मे वाजिराजः निवर्तितः

धन्विना—*lit.* 'By him who wields a bow eminently,' 'by that mighty warrior'; प्रशस्तं धन्व अस्यास्तीति धन्वी fr. धन्वन् *n.* (a bow) + affix इन् (इनि) added to words of the व्रीह्यादि class by Pāṇ. V. 2. 11. Here इन् shows प्राशस्त्य. **प्रसह्य**—orginally gerund from सह् with प्र (having borne grest stress), treated as an indec,; forcibly.

अंशुमतेव सगरः—As in the case of Sagara, whose hoase was similarly brought back (प्रत्याहृत) by his grandson Ams'umat.

Allusion–Sagara was a king of Ayodhyā and was born in the Solar race. He had two wives, Kes'inī and Sumatī. Kes'inī had only one son, Asamañjas, through whom the royal line was continued, Ams'umat being the son of Asamañjas. Sumati had 60,000 sons. Sagara, engaged in the performance of an *as'vamedha* sacrifice, the last of a series of 100, appointed these the guards of his horse. The horse, however, was stolen by Indra and taken to Pātāla. Sagara's 60,000 sons searching for it dug their way to the lower regions; they found the horse grazing near the hermitage of the sage Kapila, whom they charged with its theft. Kapila, thereupon, in wrath burnt them to ashes. Their remains were discovered by Amśumat who succeeded in propitiating Kapila and brought back the horse to his grandfather who then completed the secrifice. Dilīpa was the son of this Amsumat.

विगतरोषचेतसा—'With your mind free from anger (or dissatisfaction).' It is nowhere mentioned in the text why Agnimitra should have been angry with his father. Mr. Pandit conjectures that he disapproved of the young boy's being sent on a dangerous mission, but that is hardly likely; no true Kṣatriya would shrink from, but on the contrary would exult at, such a mission. For a more probable explanation given by Prof. Tawney, see Intro. p. 30; he conjectures that the रोष was due to Puṣpamitra's persecution of the Buddhists, with whom Agnimitra was in sympathy. **वधूजन**—Agnimitra's Queen.

Verse 16. Censtrue :—

भर्त्रा वीरपत्नीनां श्लाघ्यायां धुरि स्थापिता असि। वीरसूः इति अयं शब्दः तनयात् त्वाम् उपस्थितः।

भर्त्रासि etc.—As you have a heroic husband, you are a वीरपत्नी, and since the husband is himself the best of heroes, you are the chief of वीरपत्नीs. That position you have been already holding. But now you get the further distinction of being a वीरसू (*lit.* 'giver of birth to a hero', a hero's mother). inasmuch as your son has proved himself to be a real hero. To be a Vīrasū was the highest ambition of the Kṣatriya ladies; *cf.* अपीप्सितं क्षत्रकुलाङ्गनानां न वीरसुशब्दमकामयेताम्। Ragh. XIV.

4. धुरि—at the head of; *cf.* धुरि प्रतिष्ठापयितव्य एव p. 32. शब्द—title; *cf.* यस्मिन्नीश्वर इत्यनन्यविषयः शब्दो यथार्थाक्षराः। Vik. I. I; द्वितीयगामी न हि शब्द एष नः। Ragh. III. 49.

Verse 17. Construe :—

(स) एतावता वीरविजृम्भितेन नः चित्तस्य विस्मयं न आदधाति अपां दग्धुः अग्नेः ऊरुजन्मा इव यस्य त्वम् अप्रधृष्यः उच्चैः प्रभवः।

P. 134. एतावता वीरविजृम्भितेन-एतत्परिमाणमस्य एतावान् by such display of heroic deeds; by वीर we are to understand वीर्य; विजृम्भित—*lit.* 'the unfolding of; *i. e.* display, mainifestation of; hence 'exploit.' विस्मयं न आदधाति—He means--we are not surprised at this his exploit, because it was quite expected of him; nay, we expect yet more brilliant deeds of valour from him (this brings out the force of एतावत्) as he is the heroic son of a heroic father. यस्य त्वं उच्चैः अप्रधृष्यः प्रभवः—whose origin (*i. e.* father) you are, great and irresistible. उच्चैः *adv.* has here an adjectival force. अप्रधृष्यः—not to be braved or resisted irresistible; *cf.* अधृष्यः Ragh. I. 16, उरुजन्मा —the sage Aurva. अपां दुग्धुः अग्नेः—*i. e.* the वडवानल.

The allusion here is to the story of the sage Aurva and the Vādava fire. The sons of king Kṛitavīrya destroyed the descendants of their family-priest Bhṛgu down to the children in womb in order to recover the riches which Kṛitavīrya had given them. One woman concealed her unborn child in her thigh, which issued forth from that place glowing with lustre and blinding its persecutors. This boy was called Aurva, as he was produced from the thigh (ऊरु). From his anger proceeded a flame of fire that threatened to destroy the world, but at the persuasion of his Pitṛs he cast it into the sea where it assumed the form of a being with the face of a horse and where it is supposed to feed upon waters. His son was Ṛchīka, father of Jamadagni.

यज्ञसेनश्याल—See *supra* I. 7. ऊरीकृत्य—or *v. l.* उररीकृत्य—'having accepted', *i. e.* 'including'. अत्या अभिजनं—her noble birth (which has now been dicovered). त्याब्य &c.—I must keep my promise (to give her in marriage to the King) which can only be done if I get your consent; so you should not object to it, and thus help me in keeping my word.

P. 196. आभरणानां मञ्जूषास्मि संवृत्ता—She means that she has been loaded with the ornaments which the ladies give away to her as marks of their joy on that occasion. साधारण: अभ्युदय:—this glory is common (as there is no envy between them and me).

सदृशं खलु etc.—It is quite proper that you, who are all-potent, say so. There is a slight sarcasm lurking in this message. प्रभवन्त्या: is a veiled way of saying 'You have the power to do as you like; what is the use of consulting me?' प्रथमकल्पितं न युज्यते अन्यथा कर्तुम्। Certainly you should not alter what you originally proposed to yourself. The इति is to be understood to govern both the preceding clauses, so that सदृशं...अन्यथा कर्तुं becomes the object of विज्ञापयति. Prof. Parānjape is wrong in taking इति which the latter sentence only (प्रथमसंकल्पित न युज्यते अन्यथा कर्तु), which he puts in apposition to वचनं—"The Queen's words (in her message) that she ought not to break her original promise". With this construction we want another इति to complete the Pratīhārī's report of Irāvatī's speech, but there is only one इति available in the text.

प्रथमसंकल्पितां—*Cf.* संकल्पितं प्रथममेव मया तवार्थे भर्तारमात्मसदृशं सुकृतैर्गता त्वम्। Śāk. IV. 13. त्वया अनुज्ञाता—Because she was Sumati's sister. इदानीमपि-now (*i. e.* when Māla. is discovered to be a Princess) as before (when she was your servant). प्रियनिवेदनानुरूपं—The प्रिय (welcome news) is about the victory of Vasumitra. प्रतीच्छतु—receive, accept. जोषं—*ind.* 'silently'; *i. e.* shows no readiness to accept Mālavikā.

P. 198. विदुषकमवेक्षते—in order that the Vidūṣaka might suggest to the Queen that Mālavikā should be presented to him with the dignity and pomp of a Queen which he does in his next speech.

अथ वा—The Vidūṣaka had already given one explanation *viz.* सर्वोऽपि नववर: etc.) of the King's silence. Now he suggests an alternative one, being directed by the King's look. The first was in jest, in keeping with his character; the second is in earnest. प्रणयविशेषं—lovingly. दत्तदेवीशब्दां—You should properly accord her the title of 'Queen', by observing the ceremonial custom (of dressing her properly &c., as is done afterwards). **अभिजनेनैव** etc.—Her very birth in a royal family is as good as the title Devī. She means that what was suggested as necessary was a mere formality and was therefore in a way superfluous. The Parivrājikā points out in the next Śloka that it is not a mere matter of form.

Verse 18, Construe:—

(हे) कल्याणि, आकरसमुत्पन्ना अपि मणिजातिः असंस्कृता जातरूपेण संयोगं न हि अर्हति।

अपि—to be construed with मणिजातिः. **मणिजातिः**—the 'jewel-species,' *i. e.* any gem. **आकरसमुत्पन्ना**—coming from a mine (and not artificial). **असंस्कृता**—not well cut and polished.

जातरूपं—gold; जातं रूपं यस्य; or प्रशस्तं जातं an excellent production; रूप indicating प्राशस्त्य (प्रशंसायां रूपम्). Here Māla. is compared to मणिजाती and the King to जातरूप; *cf.* रत्नं समागच्छतु काञ्चनेन। Ragh. VI. 79.

मर्षयतु—please pardon me (*lit.* bear with the fault I committed), Dhāriṇī now remembers that in the hurry and joy of the occasion the fact that Mālavikā was not in a dress fit for a princess had been overlooked. A Princess ought to be dressed in a *mahāvastra* (valuable silk garment). **कौशयपेत्रोर्ण**—both कौशेय and पत्रोर्ण (See V. 12) mean 'a silk garment'; but कौशेय is a generic and पत्रोर्ण a specific term, and hence their use together in a compound is allowable.

अवगुण्ठनवतीं कृत्वा—*i. e.* she covered her whole body with the garment. *Cf.* कास्विदवगुण्ठनवती नातिपरिस्फूटशरीरलावण्या। Śāk. V. 13.

P. 200. **त्वच्छासनात् अप्र०**—"I cannot make any reply (indicative of refusal or hesitation), because it is your order and I must accept her". This is one of his many gallant speeches. Tārānātha reads त्वच्छासनं प्रत्यनुरक्ता वयं। I take delight in obeying *i. e.* I am ready to obey your order; (**अपवार्य**) हन्त प्रतिगृहीतम् (Aside) Oh, I (accept the reward). This reading is to be rejected because it shows the King's impartinence to accept Māla. as his wife which he has taken care to avoid throughout this scene. It is difficult to see how Tārānātha paraphrases this as त्वद्दानात्प्रागेव स्वीकृतं which Prof. Tawney translates as (Aside) I consented to take her before you gave her. हन्त प्रतिगृहीता—the Parivrājikā breathes a sigh of relief and joy at finding that in the end the marriage *has* come about. अनुकूलता—favour, indulgence (towards the King). परिजनमवलोकयति—she merely glances at the servants, meaning that they should salute Mālavikā as the Queen ; the servants take the hint and receive and salute Mālavikā with the title भट्टिनी.

परिव्राजिकामवेक्षते—as much as to say, "How do you think of all this ?" चित्रं—strange. She says she expected as much from Dhāriṇī.

Verse 19. Construe:—

भर्तृवत्सला: साध्व्य: प्रतिपक्षेण अपि पतिं सेवन्ते, समुद्रगाः अन्यसरितां शतानि हि अब्धि प्रापयन्ति ।

अब्धि—the sea is poetically described as the husband of rivers and they as his wives; *cf.* Ragh. XIII. 9. The reader should remember that this is the sentiment of an age when polygamy prevailed especially in royal households.

उपचारातिक्रमेण—when she disregarded the King's prostration (at the end of Act III.). तदा अपराद्ध &c.—that was a fault on my part; but in doing that as it has now turned out I acted in a way favourable to you, since it enabled you to further your suit, which now has had a happy termination. The tone of this message, too, indicates her petulance and concealed dissatisfaction.

संदेशमनुज्ञास्यति—will do as she says. Insert in the text the stage-direction इति निष्क्रान्ता। after अनुगृहीतास्मि which has been omitted through oversight.

P. 202. चरितार्थ—who has obtained what he would. समाजयितुं—to honour; to offer congratulations or greetings; fr. सभाज् 10 conj.; to express one's joy at &c., *cf.* स्नेहात्सभाजयितुमेत्य दिनान्यमूनि। &c. Uttar. I. 7; ऋषयो देवं सभाजयितुमागताः। Śāk. V.

सभाजनाक्षराणि—words conveying your congratulations ; words of greeting (from you). पातयिष्यामि—Read—ष्यामि.

परवानयं जनः—I am entirely in your power on account of the love you show me; I have no independence of action; I must do as you desire.

Verse 20. Construe:—

(हे) देवि, त्वं मे प्रसादसुमुखी नित्यं भव एतावत् एव हृदये प्रतिपालनीयम् प्रजानाम् ईतिविगमप्रभृतिः आशास्यं अग्निमित्रे गोप्तरि न खलु संपद्यते (इति) न।

देवि—चण्डि *v. l.* 'O passionate one'; this may be explained as—As you are prone to be angry you should give up your anger and be favourable to me; but still the reading is bad as the King is not expected to refer to her irascibilty with any propriety here. प्रसादसुखी—*Cf.* देवी प्रसादसुमुखी भविष्यति। *supra* p. 160. प्रतिपालनीयम्—to be borne in mind. The reading मृगये प्रतिपक्षहेतोः '(this much) I seek (desire) for the sake of your rival (*i. e.* Māla.)' is rejected, because in the first place it will mean that the King wants her प्रसाद for the sake of her rival and not on account of any genuine desire on his part for it; secondly, it will be improper to call Māla. the Queen's प्रतिपक्ष, since she had given her away to the King affectionately; he should rather call her प्रियसखी.

भरतवाक्य—(so called after भरत the founder of the Dramatic science) is the technical name given to the stanza at the end of a play which contains an expression of general peace and goodwill and is sung by the actor in his capacity as an actor. आशास्यं etc.—"while Agnimitra is the ruler the wishes of his subjects are bound to be fulfilled." Construe—अग्निमित्रे गोप्तरि (सति) (तस्य) प्रजानां (यत्) ईतिविगमप्रभृति आशास्यां, (तत्) न संपद्येत (इति) न खलु। आशास्य *n.* a desired thing. See Ragh. V. 34. ईतिविगमप्रभृति—containing in it such things as the disappearance of all ईति &c. ईति *f.* 'a public calamity' of which six are mentioned in the śl. quoted in the com. They are, (1) excessive rain; (2) droughts (no rain); (3) locusts; (4) rats (in fields); (5) parrots (eating and destroying ears of corn); and (6) foreign invasions. Some add स्वचक्रं (danger from one's own army &c.) to the number, reading the second half as परचक्रं च सप्तैता ईतयः स्मृताः। *cf.* निरातङ्का निरीतयः। यन्मदीया प्रजा &c. Ragh. I. 63. अभ्यधिगमात्-*v. l.* means 'acquiring of property', mercantile return (निध्यादेः प्राप्तिः).

न संपद्यते इति न—The two negatives give the sense of one emphatic affirmative; *cf.* नायं देव्या भाजनत्वं न नेयः। *supra* V. s. According to Kāṭayavema the reference in this verse to Agnimitra signifies that the play was written and staged during the reign of King Agnimitra, thus making Kālidāsa a poet at his court. This view, however, stands by itself and lacks confirmation from other sources.

The भरतवाक्य here seems to be said by the actor as King अग्निमित्र against the general rule; *cf.* Rāghavabhaṭṭa's remark on this in his com. on the Śāk.—भरतवाक्यं नटवाक्यम्। नाटकाभिनयसमाप्तौ सामाजिकेभ्यो नटेनाशीर्दीयते इत्यर्थः। प्रस्तावनानन्तरं नटवाक्याभावादत्र भरतवाक्यमित्युक्तिः। This shows that the rules about the Nāndī and भरतवाक्य were not so binding in Kālidāsa's days.

Critical Appreciation of the Act V

The Praveśaka, at the beginning of this act, informs us about the political development in the play. Vasumitra, the eldest son of Dhāriṇī, has been appointed by Puṣpamitra to protect the sacrificial horse. Dhāriṇī is anxious about the safety of her son and is giving liberal gifts to worthy Brahmins to ensure his safety. Vīrasena has defeated the king of Vidarbha, and has set free Mādhavasena, who has sent accomplished maidens and other gifts to Agnimitra. The queen Dhāriṇī has ordered the celebrations in honour of blossoming of the Aśoka tree. Thus the political background is unfolded through the conversation between Madhukarikā, उद्यानपालिका and सारसक. The happy news of the victory of Vīrasena prepares us for the happy ending of the play.

The main act is full of narration which clearly shows that the author is in a hurry to wind up the various threads of the play. Agnimitra reveals his statemanship when he decides to divide the Vidarbha kingdom between the two cousins. The blossoming of the Aśoka tree has almost drivan away the feeling of jealousy from the queen's mind. The revealation that Mālavikā is a princess and the victory of Vasumitra makes Dhāriṇī completely reconciled to her lot. She is now so jubilent that of her own accord she offers Mālavikā to the king. Irāvatī is very cleverly kept away at the time of the union of the lovers. She is not at all reconciled till the end. She is almost forced to give her consent to the union of the lovers and her unwillingness is revealed in her remark : सदृशं खलु देव्याः प्रभवन्त्या वचनं प्रथमसंकल्पितं न युज्यतेऽन्यथा कर्तुमिति। Her hesitation to give consent stands in sharp contrast to the voluntary consent given by Dhāriṇī. The hurried narration of the events leads to the union of the lovers and with the Bharatavākya, the play ends.

An Alphabetical Index of Verses

Occurring in this Drama

The Subhāṣitas occurring in the play

(The figures refer to the pages of this Edition.)

I. Sentences.

अतिमात्रभासुरत्वं पुष्यति भानोः परिग्रहादनलः।
अधिगच्छति महिमानं चन्द्रोऽपि निशापरिगृहीतः॥ p. 28

अनातुरोत्कण्ठितयोः प्रसिध्यता समागमेनापि रतिर्न मां प्रति।
परस्परप्राप्तिनिराशयोर्वरं शरीरनाशोऽपि समानुरागयोः॥ p. 98

अप्याकरसमुत्पन्ना मणिजातिरसंस्कृता।
जातरूपेण कल्याणि न हि संयोगमर्हति॥ p. 198

अर्थं सप्रतिबन्धं प्रभुरधिगन्तुं सहायवानेव।
दृश्यं तमसि न पश्यति दीपेन विना सचक्षुरपि॥ p. 22

उपदेशं विदुः शुद्धं सन्तस्तमुपदेशिनः।
श्यामायते न विद्वत्सु यः काञ्चनमिवाग्निषु॥ p. 54

छेदो दंशस्य दाहो वा क्षतेर्वा रक्तमोक्षणम्।
एतानि दष्टमात्राणामायुष्याः प्रतिपत्तयः॥ p. 122

न हि बुद्धिगुणेनैव सुहृदामर्थदर्शनम्।
कार्यसिद्धिपथः सूक्ष्मः स्नेहेनाप्युपलभ्यते॥ p. 130

पात्रविशेषे न्यस्तं गुणान्तरं व्रजति शिल्पमाधातुः।
जलमिव समुद्रशुक्तौ मुक्ताफलतां पयोदस्य॥ p. 14

पुराणमित्येव न साधु सर्वं न चापि काव्यं नवमित्यवद्यम्।
सन्तः परीक्ष्यान्यतरद्भजन्ते मूढः परप्रत्ययनेयबुद्धिः॥ p. 4

प्रतिपक्षेणापि पतिं सेवन्ते भर्तृवत्सलाः साध्व्यः।
अन्यसरितां शतानि हि समुद्रगाः प्रापयन्त्यब्धिम्॥ p. 200

मन्दोऽप्यमन्दतामेति संसर्गेण विपश्चितः।
पङ्कच्छिदः फलस्येव निकषेणाविलं पयः॥ p. 52

लब्धास्पदोऽस्मीति विवादभीरोस्तितिक्षमाणस्य परेण निन्दाम्।
यस्यागमः केवलजीविकायै तं ज्ञानपण्यं वणिजं वदन्ति॥ p. 36

शिष्टा क्रिया कस्यचिदात्मसंस्था संक्रान्तिरन्यस्य विशेषयुक्ता।
यस्योभयं साधु स शिक्षकाणां धुरि प्रतिष्ठापयितव्य एव॥ p. 32

The Metres used in the Play, their Definitions and Schemes

1. Sanskrit Verse is regulated by quantity, and not by accent, as in English. A पद्य or stanza consists of four पादs or quarters. A पाद is regulated by the number of syllables (अक्षरs) or syllabic instants (मात्राs). When the पादs are all in one metre, it is called a समवृत्त, to which type most of the metres conform; those are अर्धसमवृत्तs wherein the first पाद corresponds with the third and the second wtih the fourth, called respectively *odd* and *even* pādas. A third class is विषमवृत्तs which are very rare.

2. The vowels अ, इ, उ, ऋ and ऌ are short, and the rest long. The quantity of a syllable is determined by its vowel. A syllable with a short vowel is called लघु (light) and one with a long vowel is called गुरु (heavy).

3. But a लघु syllable becomes गुरु if it is followed by an Anusvāra, or a Visarga, or a conjunct consonant, or when it occurs at the end of a पाद*.

4. Three successive syllables form a गण (foot); marking a short syllable as ⏑ and a long one as —, the different गणs, which are eight in number may be exhibited as follows †:
य ⏑ — —; र — ⏑ —; त — — ⏑; भ — ⏑ ⏑;
ज ⏑ — ⏑; स ⏑ ⏑ —; म — — —; and न ⏑ ⏑ ⏑.
A short syllable is sometimes indicated in the definition by the letter ल, and a long one by ग.

5. Excepting four lines (II. 4.) of Prakrit verse, the Mālavikā. has 95 stanzas, distributed in 21 different metres, which we give below in the alphabetical order of their titles. The metre in each case is also named in the com. in this Edition.

---

* सानुस्वारश्च द घश्च विसर्गी च गुरुर्भवत् ।
वर्णः संयोगपूर्वश्च तथा पादान्तगोऽपि वा ॥

† आदिमध्यावसानेषु यरता यान्ति लाघवम् ।
भजसा गौरवं यान्ति मनौ तु गुरुलाघवम् ॥

अनुष्टुभ्—(also called श्लोक). Def. श्लोके षष्ठं गुरु ज्ञेयं सर्वत्र लघु पञ्चमम्। द्विचतुःपादयोर्ह्रस्वं सप्तमं दीर्घमन्ययोः ॥ There are many varieties of this metre, but the one defined is the commonest. Each pāda of it consists of 8 syllables of which the sixth is long and the fifth short, and the seventh in the second and fourth pādas is short and in the first and third pādas long. The rest of the syllables may be either short or long.

Examples—I. 10, 14, 15, 19; II. 7. 9; IV. 4, 6, 12, 14; V. 9, 11, 12, 13, 15, 16, 18.

अपरवक्त्र—Def. अयुजि ननरला गुरुः समे तदपरवक्त्रमिदं नजौ जरौ। The odd quarter, which has 11 syllables, is scanned as न, न, र, ल, ग; and the even quarter, which has 12 syllables, as न, ज, ज, र. This is an अर्धसम वृत्त. *Ex.*—III. 20.

आर्या—Def. यस्याः प्रथमे पादे द्वादश मात्रास्तथा तृतीयेऽपि। अष्टादश द्वितीये चतुर्थके पञ्चदश सार्या ॥ This belongs to the class of metres regulated by the number of मात्राऽ or syllabic instants. The four पादऽ contain respectively 12, 18, 12 and 15 Mātrās. This is a very common metre in the dramas of Kālidāsa.

Examples—I. 3, 5, 6, 7, 8, 9, 13, 18, 20, 22; II. 1, 2, 10, 11, 13, 14; III. 7, 8, 9, 13, 16, 18, 19, 22, 23; IV.—2, 3, 5, 7, 10, 17; V. 4, 5, 6, 19.

इन्द्रवज्रा—Def. स्यादिन्द्रवज्रा यदि तौ जगौ गः। Each quartar has 11 syllables. Sch.—त, त, ज, ग, ग. *Ex.* V. 17.

उपजाति—Def. [स्यादिन्द्रवज्रा यदि तौ जगौ गः। उपेन्द्रवज्रा जतजास्ततो गौ ॥] अनन्तरोदीरितलक्ष्मभाजौ पादौ यदीयावुपजातयस्ताः ॥ [इत्थं किलान्यास्वपि मिश्रितासु वदन्ति जातिष्विदमेव नाम ॥] An उपजाति is a mixture of one or more pādas of इन्द्रवज्रा (see above) with one or more of उपेन्द्रवज्रा, (11 syll.,sch. ज, त, ज, ग, ग,), so as to form one stanza. A mixture of other metres also in this manner is called an Upajāti. The student is recommended in each case to scan and find out whether a pāda, is in Indra. or Upendra. *Ex.* I. 2, 16, 17; III. 10; IV. 8; V. 14.

[उपेन्द्रवज्रा—See उपजाति above]

[औपच्छन्दसिक—See मालभारिणी below]

द्रुतविलम्बित—Def. द्रुतविलम्बितमाह नभौ भरौ। 12 syllables. Scheme—न, भ, भ, र. *Ex.*—III. 6; IV. 13; V. 7.

पुष्पिताग्रा—Def. अयुजि नयुगरेफतो यकारो युजि च नजौ जरगाश्च पुष्पिताग्रा। Odd pāda—12 syllables; scheme न, न, र, य. Even pādas—13 syllables.—Sch. न, ज, ज, र, ग. This is an अर्धसम वृत्त. *Ex.*—I. 11.

पृथ्वी—Def. जसौ जसयला वसुग्रहयतिश्च पृथ्वी गुरुः। 17 syllables. Sch. ज, स, ज, स, य, ल, ग. The pause occurs after the eighth syllable. *Ex.*—III. 17.

प्रहर्षिणी—Def. त्र्याशाभिर्मनजरगाः प्रहर्षिणीयम्। 13 syllables; Sch. म, न, ज, र, ग. The pause occurs after the third syllable. *Ex.*—I. 21.

मन्दाक्रान्ता—Def. मन्दाक्रान्ता जलधिषडगैर्म्भौ नतौ ताद्गुरू चेत्। 17 syllables. Sch. म, भ, न, त, त, ग, ग. The pauses occur after the fourth and the tenth syllables. This is the metre exclusively used by Kālidāsa in his *Meghadūta*. *Ex.*—II. 6, 8; III. 4; IV. I.

मालभारिणी—(also called औपच्छन्दसिक, of which it forms a special variety) विषमे ससजा गुरू समे चेत्सभरा येन तु मालभारिणीयम्। Odd pāda, 11 syllables; Sch. स, स, ज, ग, ग. Even pāda, 12 syllables; Sch. स, भ, र, म. This is an अर्धसम, वृत्त. *Ex.*—III. 3, 11.

मालिनी—Def. ननमयययुतेयं मालिनी भोगिलोकैः। 15 syllables. Sch, न, न, म, य, य. The pause occurs after the eighth syllable. *Ex.*—II. 5; III. 12.

रुचिरा—Def. जभौ सजौ गिति रुचिरा चतुर्ग्रहैः। 13 syllables. Sch. ज, भ, स, ज, ग. The pause occurs after the fourth syllable. *Ex.*—IV. 16.

वंशस्थ—Def. जतौ तु वंशस्थमुदीरितं जरौ। 12 syllables. Sch. ज, त, ज, र. *Ex.*—III. 15.

वसन्ततिलका—Def. उक्ता वसन्ततिलका तभजा जगौ गः। 14 syllables. Sch. त, भ, ज, ग, ग. *Ex.*—I. 12; IV. 9; V. 3, 10, 20.

वियोगिनी—Def. विषमे ससजा गुरुः समे सभरालोऽथ गुरुर्वियोगिनी Odd quarter—10 syllables. Sch. स, भ, ज, ग. Even quarter—11 syllables; sch. स, भ, र, ल, ग. This is an अर्धसम वृत्त. *Ex.*—III. 2.

शार्दूलविक्रीडित—Def. सूर्याश्वैर्यदि नः सजौ सततगाः शार्दूलविक्रीडितम्। 19 syllables; sch. म, स, ज, स, त, त, ग. The pause occurs after the twelth syllable. *Ex.*—I. 4; II, 3; III. 5; IV. 15.

शालिनी—Def. मात्तौ गौ चेच्छालिनी वेदलोकैः। 11 syllables. Sch. म, त, त, ग, ग. The pause occurs at the fourth syllable. *Ex.*—III. 14, 21; V. 8.

शिखरिणी—Def. रसै रुद्रैश्छिन्ना यमनसभलागः शिखरिणी। 17 syllables. Sch. य, म, न, स, भ, ल, ग. The pause occurs after the sixth syllable. *Ex.*—III. 1.

स्रग्धरा—Def. म्रभ्नैर्यानां त्रयेण त्रिमुनियतियुता स्रग्धरा कीर्तितेयम्। 21 syllables. Sch म, र, भ, न, य, य, य. The pauses occur after the seventh and the fourteenth syllables. This is the longest metre in ordinary use. *Ex.*—I. 1; II. 12.

हरिणी—Def. नसमरसला गः षड्वेदैर्हयैर्हरिणी मता। 17 syllables. Sch. न, स, म, र, स, ल, ग. The pauses occur after the sixth and the tenth syllables. *Ex.*—IV. 11; V. 1, 2.
